# PRINCIPLES OF INTERNATIONAL POLITICS

## PEOPLE'S POWER, PREFERENCES, AND PERCEPTIONS

### SECOND EDITION

Bruce Bueno de Mesquita

New York University

and

Hoover Institution at Stanford University

CQ PRESS

A Division of Congressional Quarterly Inc.
Washington, D.C.

JZ
1242
.B84
2003

*To the memory of my teachers. They showed me what life lived with dignity is, and they taught me to reflect on how our world works. Though I can no longer turn to them for counsel, still I listen for their whispers on the wind.*

*Abraham Bueno de Mesquita, 1910–1982*
*Clara Bueno de Mesquita, 1916–1997*
*Abramo Fimo Kenneth Organski, 1923–1998*
*William Harrison Riker, 1920–1993*

CQ Press
1255 22nd St., N.W., Suite 400
Washington, D.C. 20037

Phone, 202-729-1900
Toll-free, 1-866-4CQ-PRESS (1-866-427-7737)

www.cqpress.com

⊗ The paper used in this publication meets the minimum requirements of the American National Standard for Information Sciences—Permanence of Paper for Printed Library Materials, ANSI Z39.48-1992.

Book design, cover, charts, maps: Gerry Quinn
Maps on pages 25 and 39: Karen E. Rasmussen/Archeographics

Printed and bound in the United States of America

06  05  04  03  02      5  4  3  2  1

**Library of Congress Cataloging-in-Publication Data**

Bueno de Mesquita, Bruce, 1946–
    Principles of international politics : people's power, preferences,
and perceptions / Bruce Bueno de Mesquita.—2nd ed.
        p. cm.
    Includes bibliographical references and index.
    ISBN 1-56802-771-0 (pbk. : alk. paper)
    1. International relations—Philosophy.    I. Title.
JZ1242.B84 2003
327.1′01—dc21                                               2002153279

# BRIEF CONTENTS

# CONTENTS

# TABLES, FIGURES, AND MAPS

## FIGURES

## MAPS

# PREFACE

A textbook is the first exposure most students have to the study of international affairs. It is an opportunity to shape how students think about international events for the rest of their lives and a chance to organize the thinking of those who will go on to business, government, or academic careers that involve intimate concern with foreign policy and international politics. Today's students are our future and so must be well-informed, not only about the facts of history but also about ideas that will guide their thinking. I have tried here to present students with a view of international relations grounded in the scientific method, anchored in history and current events, and focused on a unified theoretical theme.

Often international relations is studied as a subject divorced from daily politics or as a scattershot sampling of competing ideas and conjectures. Often it is presented as a mysterious subject that depends on wisdom without the assistance of science, rather than as a subject amenable to the scientific method. And all too often it is treated as if events were unique and unpredictable when they can be predicted and explained through the judicious application of analytic tools, logic, and empirical rigor. This book gives students those tools.

## THE APPROACH

*Principles of International Politics* is unique in its theoretical focus; its attention to logical, empirical, and analytic rigor; and its historical sweep. Central among my convictions is that international politics is a product of the normal pulls and tugs of domestic affairs, that leaders (not nations) make policy decisions and do so to maximize their prospects of staying in office, and that decisions, therefore, are strategic, taking into account expected responses by adversaries and supporters and designed to maximize the leader's (not the state's) welfare. I call this view the strategic perspective. The quest for personal political power guides policy choices, and the cumulative effect of policy choices gives rise to what we call the international system. Therefore, domestic politics, foreign policy, and international politics are inextricably linked. We cannot make sense of international relations without considering all three.

As the theoretical backbone, the strategic perspective is always at the core of each explanation and comparison within the book, whether I discuss the end of the cold war in 1990 or the emergence of the modern sovereign state during the High Middle Ages. I explain why terrible leaders who bankrupt their countries and oppress their citizens persist in office for a long time, while leaders who provide peace and prosperity are frequently ousted. Democratic peace is explained, as is the role of power in the initiation and escalation of disputes. The book explores at length trade sanctions, pressures for trade protectionism, and their links to domestic political considerations, as well as issues of international law, international organizations, and alliance formation and reliability. I suggest why Saddam Hussein could sensibly believe that the United States would back down during the Persian Gulf War and why his conclusion proved wrong. Students learn why and how unwanted trade wars can occur and the conditions in which economic sanctions are likely to be effective or ineffective. I take them through a careful examination of globalization, with clear arguments about who the winners and losers are likely to be from free trade. I explore paths to war and peace, as well as questions about the functions of international organizations and international law. Innumerable other topics are also addressed and are always related to the volume's theoretical framework.

The book lays out competing arguments and evaluates both their logical coherence and empirical reliability, frequently combining historical examples with nontechnical summaries of statistical evidence. It sets out a detailed investigation of realist and liberal theories and bureaucratic and interest group approaches, all the while employing the strategic perspective to compare and contrast, lending coherence to a topic that is often overwhelming. In this new edition I have tried to make even the most demanding concepts readily accessible and interesting to beginning students by offering many illustrative applications in each chapter and by writing in a more easily understood style. At the same time, I have attempted to make the book meaty enough so that students will want to return to it long after they have completed the introductory course..

Theoretical ideas are unlikely to help students or keep their interest without historical and current examples. This volume is full of such examples, from the opening paragraph to the very end. I intentionally chose examples from across thousands of years of human history, though naturally with an emphasis on current events. The broad historical sweep is designed to serve two purposes. First, it is a way to introduce students to important events that have shaped the modern world, from the Battle of Marathon two thousand and five hundred years ago to the Treaty of Westphalia in 1648 to the terrorist attacks on the United States on September 11, 2001, and the ongoing war against terrorism. Second, it is a way to demonstrate the universal applicability of the strategic perspective and the analytic tools that accompany the scientific investigation of competing hypotheses.

## METHODOLOGY

The book introduces methods for investigating foreign policy decisions from the strategic perspective, beginning with concepts in their simplest forms and gradually building on that knowledge, keeping undergraduates' capabilities foremost in mind. Although the ideas are sophisticated, they require only skills possessed by beginning college students to be understood. I have worked from the assumption that readers have had no prior exposure to international relations, statistics, or model building. Additionally, to ensure that the methods are easy to understand and apply, the book has been classroom tested in a host of different institutions, from large state schools to small private colleges. I have incorporated feedback from students into every aspect of the presentation.

Students are exposed to tools that include decision theory, social choice theory, and game theory. The book teaches them how to calculate expected utilities, solve complete information games and simple incomplete information games, and evaluate one-dimensional and two-dimensional spatial models. They learn the median voter theorem and the manipulability that arises when foreign policy issues are linked together. They gain exposure to problems of collective action and the difficulties of monitoring and sanctioning international misconduct, as well as to the problems that arise in trying to coordinate international interactions and deal with the distribution of valuable, scarce resources.

## ORGANIZATION AND PEDAGOGY

The book is organized so that ideas and techniques are cumulative. The Introduction and eighteen subsequent chapters follow a natural sequence for use in either a semester or a quarter system. The second edition builds on the objectives of the first edition while adding substantial new and expanded material. The first chapter is entirely new, giving students an overview of more six hundred years of world history. This chapter helps build a common base of knowledge among readers. The discussion of the scientific method moves to Chapter 2 so that the Introduction and first two chapters provide both the historical and the philosophical foundations of the book. The book also offers, in Chapter 6, an expanded discussion of the origins of the modern state system while introducing two entirely new chapters on the subject of international political economy. Chapter 13 explores globalization and its relationship to trade and currency policy. Chapter 14 delves into international law, international organizations, and international norms of conduct. These two chapters also provide students with a basic introduction to important ideas in economics, especially supply and demand and comparative versus absolute advantage. The discussion of terrorism has expanded, and many chapters touch on the role of terrorism in international affairs. All other chapters have grown to include insights from the most recent research and to incorporate important developments in the world so that examples are fresh and up to date.

Because historical examples, concepts, and techniques are interspersed throughout, always in mutual support of each other, the book can readily be taught from a variety of perspectives. The instructor can emphasize events, ideas, hypotheses, historical analysis, formal analysis, or statistical analysis as suits his or her style, needs, and preferences. To facilitate learning, each chapter begins with an outline listing major topics and ends with a summary that highlights the major points made in the chapter. The theoretical arguments and the historical and contemporary examples are accompanied by an impressive array of maps, figures, charts, tables, and images. Each of these includes a substantial, contextual caption that allows the illustration or figure to stand alone as a summary statement of an important idea. In addition, many critical thinking boxes pose puzzles that students can solve by applying concepts that have been introduced in the book. (Many of these are picked up in the student workbook as problem sets.) Because there are many new concepts, there is also a glossary of key terms and ideas so that students can spend their time learning ideas rather than memorizing terms. The book also has an extensive bibliography and two indexes (subject and author), as well as in-text citations and footnotes. These all serve as valuable guides for students who want to explore the field further or to begin to do bibliographic or original research. Everything has been designed to stimulate students' interest and understanding and to encourage students to continue their investigation of international relations.

## A Unique Teaching and Learning Package

There is ample additional support for these diverse approaches in the ancillary materials that accompany the text, such as the student workbook and online instructor's manual. These materials, thoroughly revamped for the second edition, include contributions both from D. Scott Bennett, their author, and from me. Bennett's superb student workbook—*Applying the Strategic Perspective*—and instructor's manual—*The Strategic Perspective in the Classroom*—are extraordinarily rich and valuable accompaniments to the text. They have been thoroughly redone for the second edition, with my active participation, to provide considerably expanded coverage and more extensive problem sets. Each of these supplements includes nearly one hundred original figures and tables that have been specially created to help instructors teach the technical material and to help students master it.

The instructor's manual—now online at http://bdm.cqpress.com—provides "at a glance" lists of topics and methods, explores key topics and arguments in depth, identifies important points to raise in class, and suggests discussion questions and links to relevant topics in the book. As versatile as the textbook itself, the instructor's manual provides users with materials that both complement and help flesh out core ideas. The reasonably priced student workbook is a wonderful supplement that students can use to hone their technical and conceptual skills. In the workbook, students are able to walk through the technical material one step at a time, starting with simple problems and graduating to more difficult ones. Now instructors can easily find answers to these technical problems in a solutions manual on CD–ROM, conveniently packaged together with a user-friendly test bank designed by Stephen Quackenbush (SUNY, Buffalo) and Will Moore (Florida State University) and with PowerPoint lecture slides created and class tested by Erik Gartzke (Columbia University) and Andy Enterline (University of North Texas).

*Principles of International Politics* is unique in other ways as well. The book introduces theoretical material introduced to illuminate some of the most difficult questions about contemporary international relations. I identify essential links between theory and real-world decision making. The Web site that accompanies the volume—http://bdm.cqpress.com—includes a software package similar to that used by the U.S. government in making major foreign policy decisions and by large corporations in dealing with significant policy choices. Students can now use the Policy Forecaster software, simplified for easy use and interpretation, to explain and predict current international problems, whether the problems involve issues of international political economy, security studies, or anything else.

The Policy Forecaster is referred to frequently throughout the text. It is more readily integrated into teaching the course than was true in the first edition, because I have linked key lessons in many chapters to applications in the Policy Forecaster. Students can use it early on to calculate the location of the median voter or the center of power on any issue. They can compare predicted outcomes on issues with the predictions one might make by just examining the distribution of power without regard to policy preferences. Here students will see dramatic differences between structural viewpoints and the strategic perspective. Students can "replay" the diplomacy leading up to World War I, look for alternative solutions to the Kosovo War, or pursue ways in which President Bill Clinton might have put together a legislative victory on NAFTA other than the way he did. Other new data sets cover policy questions in Afghanistan and the Middle East, as well as the dispute between India and Pakistan over Kashmir. Students can build their own data sets concerning the war on terrorism or other current topics and follow their chosen issues throughout the course. Students can also modify data sets (following the instructions laid out in Chapter 18) that are provided with the Policy Forecaster to see how changes in position or in level of effort (salience) might have altered one or another decision maker's influence over foreign policy choices. Different students can assume the roles of different decision makers and use their strategic insights to compete with one another as participants in the Cuban Missile Crisis, World War II, or some other event for which the class or instructor constructs a simple data set. The applications are endless. Learning is always reinforced by doing. With the Policy Forecaster, "doing" has never been made easier or more realistic for students. They can play out the roles taken by real decision makers, using a tool that decision makers use in making foreign policy choices.

Moreover, all of the tables and figures from the second edition textbook and workbook are available on the Web site in .pdf format and PowerPoint slides, thereby minimizing the amount of fuss instructors go through in putting classroom presentations together. Each is designed to convey important ideas and to make clear the logic behind fundamental conclusions. This rich package of additional materials will facilitate teaching the ideas in *Principles of International Politics*.

## ACKNOWLEDGMENTS

*Principles of International Politics* is my effort to explain a way of looking at international relations and to reshape how the subject is taught. If it succeeds in doing so, the credit belongs to those who have helped me along the way. A textbook provides a unique opportunity to express thanks, not only to those who helped with the book at hand but also to those whose teaching, inspiration, and guidance have shaped the way I think. It is my pleasure to take this opportunity to thank them here.

This book was inspired by Kenneth Organski, my teacher, mentor, and friend. Without his urging, it surely would not have been written. To be fair, Ken tricked me into writing the book, but that is another story. This was to have been a joint effort by Ken and me, but the tragic terminal illness of his daughter and then his own untimely death precluded that collaboration. He had begun to work on the discussion of power, and I have borrowed liberally from the draft text he left behind. How I wish I had his wisdom, insight, and elegant turn of phrase to share with you throughout this book. He is missed by all who loved him and all who knew him.

William Riker's shadow will be found on every page of this book. The principles of international politics are every bit as much an expression of his understanding of politics as they are of mine. Never have I known a more profound thinker. His was truly the intellect of a once-in-a-century man. I hope my effort does some small justice to his memory.

My parents, Abraham and Clara Bueno de Mesquita, survived Hitler, fled their homelands, and spent fruitful and rewarding lives in demanding times. They ensured that my sisters, Mireille Bany and Judy Berton, and I had every opportunity for fulfillment. Their lessons and their aspirations inspire me still.

Teachers leave indelible marks on our lives. I wish to express my gratitude to my most important classroom teachers, too many of whom are no longer with us: Henry Morton (Queens College), Richard Park (University of Michigan), Solomon Resnik (Queens College), Donald Stokes (University of Michigan), Phyllis Taylor (third grade), Lionel M. Yard (Stuyvesant High School), and many others inspired me to want to teach. To touch the lives of students as they have done is one of life's remarkable accomplishments.

I have benefited from the counsel of many colleagues who, of course, cannot be held accountable for my failure to heed all of their advice. Certainly the advice I did take has greatly improved my effort. D. Scott Bennett, Larry Cohen, Daniel Faiver, Andrew Farkas, Robert E. Harkavy, David Hayes, Jacek Kugler, Alan Lamborn, Joseph Lepgold, James Morrow, Kenneth Rodman, Alexander Rosenberg, Randolph Siverson, Kiron Skinner, Alastair Smith, Allan Stam, Herbert Tillema, Douglas Van Belle, and Suzanne Werner provided me with much valued guidance.

I also am indebted to the many reviewers of various parts of the manuscript, including Mark Crescenzi (University of North Carolina, Chapel Hill), Jeffery Dixon (Wright State University), Andrew Enterline (University of Texas), Erik Gartzke (Columbia

University), Alan Kessler (University of Texas, Austin), David Leblang (University of Colorado, Boulder), Douglas Lemke (University of Michigan), Rose McDermott (University of California, Santa Barbara), Jeffrey Ritter (Rutgers University), Andrew Sobel (Washington University), Christopher Sprecher (Texas A&M University), and Richard Stoll (Rice University). Additionally I owe an enormous debt of gratitude to Kenneth Schultz (University of California, Los Angeles), who undertook a careful technical review of the manuscript. Some of these reviewers have been students of mine; I have been the student of all of them. Although they are too numerous to name, I thank all of my students, who, over the years, have suffered through my efforts to identify and explain the principles of international politics as I see them.

CQ Press has been an author's dream publisher. Randolph Siverson first suggested this project to Brenda Carter, director of CQ's college group. I thank him for doing so. Brenda persuaded me that CQ was the right way to go, and I have never regretted the decision. I told her at the outset that I hoped to write a text with a point of view and that I was more interested in making my viewpoint clear than in writing a "garden variety" text to maximize sales. She and the rest of the CQ team never wavered from their commitment to that vision. My editors for the first and second editions, Charisse Kiino and Elise Frasier, respectively, did everything right to provide me with the support I needed to make this book turn out as well as possible. They gave me unflinching support and brought great good humor to the whole project. Lorna Notsch provided invaluable assistance in the selection of maps and photographs that enhance and complement the text. Lisa Sanchez made certain all cover and printing issues went smoothly. Paul Pressau shepherded the manuscript through to completed pages. Joanne Ainsworth copyedited the manuscript and significantly improved its clarity and accuracy. Steph Selice proofread the text, and Pat Ruggiero created the new index. Gerry Quinn designed the first edition, including the cover, figures, and maps. Early in the production process I received drafts of figures much altered from the copy I provided the press. With trepidation I was asked whether Gerry should go ahead and alter my original designs. The answer was an unequivocal "yes." Gerry has a masterful sense of how to convey information through figures; the book is vastly better because of his efforts. I have continued with his design in the second edition and am ever grateful to him for his keen eye. Wow, what a team. Thank you all.

The Department of Politics at New York University (NYU) and the Hoover Institution at Stanford University provide me with all the support one could hope for when researching and writing a book. I thank both NYU and the Hoover Institution for their continued support (and for fine and civilized, not to mention tasty, coffee hour).

My final and greatest debt belongs to my family, who has been a constant source of support and patience. My wife, Arlene, helped with proofreading, making it possible to complete this project on schedule and still make it to the opera on time. I cannot sing her praises sufficiently. I am most grateful not only to Arlene but also to Erin, Jason, Ethan, Rebecca, and Gwen for making life fulfilling.

# FOUNDATIONS OF INTERNATIONAL POLITICS

On the fifth of June in 1465, just outside the city of Avila, Spain, a group of nobles, discontented with the domestic and foreign policies of Enrique IV, king of Castile, assembled to express their displeasure:

> They caused a platform to be erected in a great plain outside the city and placed on top of it an effigy seated in a chair, which they said represented the person of the king. . . . They accused the king specifically of four things: that he deserved to lose the royal dignity, and therefore Alonso Carrillo, archbishop of Toledo, removed the crown from the effigy's head . . . that he deserved to lose the administration of justice, and . . . the count of Plasencia removed the sword that it held aloft . . . that he deserved to lose the government of the kingdom, and . . . the count of Benavente removed the scepter that it held in its hand . . . that he deserved to lose the throne and seat of kingship, and Diego López de Zúñiga with harsh and brutal words, knocked the effigy out of the chair. (Quoted in O'Callaghan 1975, 573)

The events of that spring day in Spain more than five hundred years ago encapsulate the ultimate fear of every political leader: the fear of being ousted from office. That distant protest in Avila is not so different from the decision of the U.S. Congress on December 19, 1998, to impeach President William Jefferson Clinton even while he, as commander in chief of the armed forces of the United States, directed an American military campaign against Iraq. Enrique IV, as Spain's commander in chief, also led his country into war when faced with the threat of ouster from office. The experiences of Clinton and Enrique point to a common thread that runs timelessly through all of international relations. Leaders seek the means to stay in office, and foreign policy actions influence those prospects.

International relations is the product of the cumulative impact of the foreign policies of the nations of the world. Foreign policies are always linked to and partially shaped by internal politics, especially domestic political concerns that influence a leader's prospects of retaining his or her job. Leaders in every nation and at all times live in dread of being kicked out of government. This is *the* essential fact of politics that we must comprehend if we are to understand international relations. All leaders—whether of nations, international organizations, multinational corporations, or anything else—promote the welfare of those they lead not out of altruism but out of a desire to stay in power. Such motivation can certainly be consonant with good and wise leadership. The wish to gain and retain power ensures that leaders take actions that are neither random nor irrelevant to the welfare of their subjects. The desire to hold power encourages leaders to refrain from doing excessively foolish things. Injudicious risks heighten the likelihood of being overthrown. It is for these reasons that any study of international affairs should begin with an understanding of how leaders translate their personal interests and ambitions into actions of the state. This is the underlying viewpoint that guides this book. Let us take a moment to discuss the central philosophy of this volume and elaborate on the governing principles of our approach.

## GOVERNING PRINCIPLES

This book is designed to convey a point of view; it is not intended as a general review of research on the subject of international relations. In setting out a particular way of thinking about international relations, we will have the opportunity to explore alternative outlooks on it that are currently dominant. Although I will not be shy about disagreeing with much of this received wisdom, I am committed to presenting a fair view of the logic and evidence undergirding these varied approaches.

The point of view expressed in this book consists of the following three principles:

1.  The actions leaders take to influence events in the international arena are motivated by personal welfare and, especially, by a desire to stay in office. Leaders' concerns for the national interest are subordinate to personal interests. If the two coincide, then so much the better; if they do not, then leaders will choose what they believe to be best for themselves.
2.  International relations cannot be separated from domestic politics. Every foreign policy action is undertaken in the shadow of the domestic political consequences the action is expected to produce. Therefore, if a foreign policy is expected to achieve beneficial consequences for a nation in the long term but in the short term will result in the ouster of the leader, then that policy will not be pursued.
3.  Relations between nations and between leaders are driven by strategic considerations. As such, foreign policy decisions are designed to influence international affairs. To be effective in this they must be taken with an eye toward the reaction they will create. The reaction expected from a policy choice is compared with the reaction

anticipated from other policy options. Leaders pick the policy they believe will produce the best outcome for themselves, knowing that at the same time rivals are choosing policies to enhance their own well-being.

Most studies of international relations do not distinguish between the interests of individual leaders and the interests of the states they lead. Instead, whether they focus on conflict resolution or economic interactions such as trade, most studies assume that leaders are benign in the sense that they are trying to do what is best for their nation. The first principle of this book draws attention away from a focus on nations and puts it more squarely on leaders and leadership. This perspective compels us to explore questions about the extent to which we can speak meaningfully about any nation having a collective interest. It forces us to think about why seemingly successful and effective leaders get turned out of office whereas some manifestly terrible leaders persist in office for a very long time. Take, for example, Winston Churchill. As Britain's prime minister during World War II he established his country as one of the last bastions of democracy in Europe during the darkest days of the war before ultimately guiding it to a valiant victory against Nazi Germany. Yet, in the final days of the war, the British electorate voted

*President George W. Bush speaks in South Bend, Indiana, seeking popular support for military action against Iraq's Saddam Hussein. The president's conviction was that a preemptive strike against Iraq was necessary and that the United States "must deal with threats today before they become incredibly serious tomorrow." Some have speculated that the administration's heightened campaign against Iraq was intended to draw attention away from Bush's domestic problems. Others considered the president's proposed actions against Iraq a justifiable foreign policy unrelated to other issues.*

Churchill out of office. In contrast, such dictators as Saddam Hussein in Iraq, Mobutu Sese Seko in Zaire (now the Democratic Republic of the Congo), Mao Zedong in the People's Republic of China, Josef Stalin in the Soviet Union, and Ferdinand Marcos in the Philippines managed to remain in office for decades even as they impoverished their citizens. Even defeat in war, it seems, is not sufficient reason to overthrow some dictators. This certainly is a puzzle that raises questions about leadership, morality, and the motives behind and the consequences of foreign policy.

The second principle also deviates from current thinking about international affairs. The dominant view today tends to see international politics as a function of factors outside the control of any one nation or leader. It says that how nations interact with one another is often predicated on external, uncontrollable factors. Thus, interactions between nations are often considered to be knee-jerk reactions rather than motivated by strategic considerations. One such external factor commonly thought to shape international political interactions is the distribution of power. Those nations endowed with great wealth and weaponry are thought to shape international affairs by influencing who does what to whom and when. This is why people speak of superpowers and major powers, such as the United States and the Soviet Union after World War II or the United States today, as imposing their will on weak allies. Those less well endowed must simply go along.

Until now, concern about how international affairs is linked to domestic politics has played second fiddle to the study of how structural factors such as the distribution of power shape international politics. In this book I make clear that the links between domestic politics and international affairs lead to a full-blown theory of international relations capable of explaining many of the prominent puzzles about international cooperation and international competition. Furthermore, I show that if we ignore the interdependencies between domestic politics and international relations, we are dooming ourselves to gross misunderstandings of how the world actually works. If political leaders act as if foreign policy is "high" politics not subject to the "low" politics of domestic maneuvering and horse trading, then they are likely to make serious errors that could endanger us all.

The third governing principle views the unfolding of international relations as a function of reasoned decision making. The structural perspectives that have dominated thinking since the end of World War II (and are discussed more fully in Chapter 4) give little attention to individual choices. They see international affairs as dominated by factors outside the control of decision makers. Nations react to changes in the international environment like pinballs responding to the tilt of the machine and the obstructions they happen to encounter as they bounce their way through the pinball maze. Consequently, these structural perspectives provide little room for strategic maneuvering. Even many foreign policy perspectives that give relatively less weight to external factors are still insufficiently attentive to strategic decision making.

## Organizational Features of This Book

In this book I will guide you as you form your own opinion on how best to make sense of international relations. I provide the tools needed to evaluate the merits of the principles set out in the previous section as well as those that guide alternative perspectives. Each chapter builds on discussions in previous chapters to develop increasingly complex levels of analysis. In this introduction I set out general ideas in broad terms. Chapter 1 provides an overview of political and economic history from the fifteenth century to the present to establish a common factual background as we progress through the remainder of the text. Chapter 2 offers a perspective on how the scientific method can be applied to international relations. In that chapter, we examine standards with which to evaluate competing explanations of important features of international relations. Although the chapter deals with abstract ideas about logic and evidence, it is important in guiding our assessment of the material in succeeding chapters.

The third chapter provides a detailed discussion of a single decision, the decision in 1492 by Ferdinand and Isabella of Spain to support Christopher Columbus's search for a route to Asia. That decision illustrates many of the most important principles examined in this book. I also introduce important analytic concepts, such as expected utility theory and game theory, that I apply throughout the book. These concepts have motivated the design of a specific model of decision making available on the World Wide Web at http://bdm.cqpress.com for students working with this book. Throughout these pages I raise questions surrounding foreign policy problems that can be addressed using the Web-based model. This model also allows you to investigate and predict outcomes of current events in foreign policy.

In the fourth and fifth chapters I lay out several approaches to understanding international affairs. Discussion of these competing views recurs throughout the book, with particular emphasis on the strategic perspective (introduced in Chapter 5). That perspective draws attention to the interplay among domestic politics, international affairs, and the interests of the decision maker (as opposed to the nation). In Chapter 6 we learn more about the strategic perspective and the origins of national sovereignty as well as current threats to the role of the state as the dominant international organization. In Chapters 7 and 8 we look at the meaning of power and its limitations. We will see that power by itself—the ability to make others do what they otherwise would not want to do—is insufficient to explain the outcomes of many major international events. In Chapter 9 we examine the role of preferences—that is, an assessment of the order in which decision makers favor alternative outcomes—in international affairs, and we learn the median voter theorem, a crucial tool for predicting decisions in international affairs. Chapters 10 and 11 introduce ideas about perceptions. Perceptions encompass what people believe about their situation and the choices confronting them. These beliefs can, of course, be dramatically different from reality.

The topics that form the core of the remaining chapters build on our emphasis on foreign policy decision making as a function of domestic politics. In Chapter 12 we look at how domestic political institutions and regime types (for example, democracies, monarchies, dictatorships) influence foreign policy choices. We will see how regime types push leaders to favor or oppose certain types of conflict or certain types of trade policies. We will see that the pursuit of bad policies that impoverish citizens and lead to defeat in war can, under some institutional circumstances, be good politics. We will also see when good policy is good politics. This provides one of many opportunities to think about how self-interested foreign policy decision making and morality can be both mutually reinforcing and at odds with one another.

Following our examination of domestic influences on foreign policy in Chapter 12 we will move on to examine features of international affairs that involve pairs or multiples of states, carefully attending to how domestic considerations influence these interstate interactions. Here we will examine topics such as trade, alliances, arms races, war and lesser conflicts, and economic sanctions.

In Chapters 13 through 18 we build logically on earlier material, using many of the tools that have been introduced to evaluate decision making. In these chapters we see how domestic politics interacts with external concerns to shape international politics. Chapter 13 expands on the importance of domestic politics in foreign affairs by looking both at internal interest groups and at the linkages between states over questions of trade and globalization more generally. Here we take a close look at who the winners and losers are likely to be as a consequence of efforts toward globalization, and we assess important aspects of the international political economy, with emphasis on the logic and evidence regarding the impact of free trade and currency policies on social welfare. In Chapter 14 we investigate the role of international law, rules, regulations, and organizations on how states and leaders interact. This chapter focuses on the difficulties in discerning whether international law and international organizations alter behavior or merely reflect and codify national interests. Chapter 15 examines the role of alliances in international politics and helps provide an understanding of when and why some alliances are reliable and others are not. Chapters 16 and 17 expand on earlier themes to show that the distribution of power, the structure of international interactions, and arms races do not arise in a political vacuum but reflect domestic as well as international political power, preferences, and perceptions. These chapters provide alternative explanations of the causes of war. Throughout the first seventeen chapters you will be introduced to ideas about decision making, uncertainty, and problems of collective action and how they relate to international cooperation and conflict. We will investigate how international politics can run aground because of the difficulties decision makers face in coordinating actions with others. We will see how these coordination problems are linked to environmental issues and to other issues about the distribution of assets, such as territory, trade privileges, and natural resources. We will consider the problems leaders confront in trying to monitor and punish deviant behavior.

In the final chapter, I provide a detailed explanation of the hands-on Web-based tools I have developed for predicting and influencing foreign policy. The model detailed in the last chapter is a product of the many concepts introduced throughout this book. The set of tools it offers has helped the U.S. government formulate foreign policy since 1981 and, according to government statistics, has generated accurate predictions over 90 percent of the time. In somewhat simplified form, it is available to you to do your own policy assessments. You will have practical means to translate theory into action, and you will be asked to do so throughout this book as part of the integrated perspective. Before you get to Chapter 18, you will already have been introduced to many of the core ideas contained in that chapter and you will already have done exercises using the forecasting model. Indeed, you will find applications of aspects of that model introduced and integrated throughout the text.

This is a book about ideas. The facts of history help illustrate and support or refute the contending ideas about foreign policy and international relations. Those facts are intentionally chosen from many different periods of history to highlight the generality and universality of the principles of international politics. By learning how to marry ideas to facts, we can all become experts at evaluating the foreign policies that shape the international relations of our time.

## THE CORE CONCERNS OF INTERNATIONAL RELATIONS

Almost everything that leaders of nations do can have a bearing on international relations and on their own welfare. States come into contact with one another on so many different levels and in such diverse circumstances that it is tempting to think that each and every interaction is unique and special. If this were so, there would be no point in writing about international affairs. After all, if every relationship between nations is unique in its fundamentals, then there really is nothing to be learned either from the past or from general principles. Such a view would be very depressing, indeed. Fortunately, there is overwhelming evidence that each event or contact between nations is not unique; that useful lessons can be learned from history.

Whether the domain of concern is international trade, cultural exchange, coordination of national military policies, agreement on the use or protection of worldwide resources, protection or exploitation of the global environment, territorial competition or war, a few concepts can go a long way in helping us understand the decisions of national leaders and their representatives and anticipate national actions or behavior. A one-sentence summary of what international relations is all about might read something like this:

> International relations is the process by which foreign policy leaders balance their ambition to pursue particular policy objectives against their need to avoid internal and external threats to their political survival.

This sentence cannot be left to stand alone. It represents too drastic a departure from more conventional views to be accepted at face value. The currently most influential approaches to international relations—known as realism, neorealism, and liberalism—ignore leaders. Instead, these approaches treat states—rather than people—as actors and assume that domestic factors make little difference when it comes to major developments in international politics. Because conventional views see states as the relevant actors, they assume that the objectives in international affairs have to do with improving the welfare of states. The approach taken in this book—I call it the strategic perspective—rejects these ideas, assuming instead that individuals make choices, not states, and they do so to enhance their own personal welfare and not necessarily the state's. The rest of this book is an effort to elaborate and clarify and thus demonstrate that this one sentence captures the essence of international relations.

## THE LINK BETWEEN DOMESTIC POLITICS AND INTERNATIONAL POLITICS

International relations is viewed typically as a subject that is radically different from any other aspect of politics, especially domestic politics. Yet it is the contention of many who study foreign policy, myself included, that domestic and international politics have much in common. There is, however, at least one essential difference between the two. In the arena of purely domestic affairs, political leaders need not worry that their actions will prompt a foreign country to jeopardize their hold on power.[1] Domestic politics involves the selection by leaders of policies and actions designed to keep them in office. In international affairs, leaders must worry that their foreign policies not only may mobilize domestic opposition capable of overthrowing them but also may irritate a foreign rival, sparking attack and possible defeat. This difficult choice between domestic and foreign opponents is especially pronounced among leaders of weak countries with few friends and is less of a problem for heads of powerful states or for heads of states with strong, reliable allies.

A foreign policy that is popular at home may prove to be a great irritant abroad. Conversely, a foreign policy designed to deter a foreign adversary or intended to satisfy the demands of a foreign foe may irritate domestic opponents or lose the support of domestic backers. This difficulty can arise whether the government in question is autocratic or democratic, although who and how powerful the domestic constituents are will surely vary depending on the nature of the regime. I offer two examples, one from autocratic Afghanistan and the other from democratic Israel.

The former leaders of the Taliban government in Afghanistan saw the tension between domestic pressures and foreign opposition in action following the terrorist

---

[1] Indeed, even this claim may exaggerate the difference between domestic politics and international relations. There are probably few, if any, purely domestic issues. Even the most seemingly mundane domestic political question may have international ramifications. Corporate tax breaks in Arizona, for example, may be sufficient to persuade companies to locate factories there instead of in Mexico or South Africa or Sri Lanka.

attacks against the United States on September 11, 2001. The core supporters of the Taliban leadership included Osama bin Laden and others in al-Qaeda's terrorist network. These backers provided significant funding and security for the Taliban leaders. To break with them would surely have aroused an active effort by al-Qaeda and its allies to depose the Afghan rulers and replace them with others more likely to cooperate with al-Qaeda. Yet the United States and its key allies were visibly banding together after September 11, 2001, ostensibly to overthrow the

> What policies might some other country follow that would be popular there but would make the United States likely to attack it and overthrow its leaders? Can you offer a concrete example of such an action?

Taliban government unless it broke with Osama bin Laden. The Taliban chose to gamble on the American response rather than break with al-Qaeda. Apparently, Afghanistan's leaders did not believe that the United States and its allies would take decisive action to overthrow them if they failed to turn over Osama bin Laden and other terrorist figures. They were wrong in their belief. Sometimes, however, the belief that a rival will not take decisive action proves correct. The United States did not take such steps after the

*The post–Taliban government of Afghanistan is building a close friendship with the United States. Hamid Karzai, Afghanistan's interim prime minister, traveled to Bagram Air Base on March 30, 2002, to thank coalition forces for helping Afghanistan liberate itself from the Taliban government and from the influence of al-Qaeda's terrorist organization. General F. L. "Buster" Hagenbeck, commander of U.S. ground forces in Afghanistan, joined Mr. Karzai as he spoke to the crowd.*

bombing by terrorists of the World Trade Center in February 1993 or following the Iraqi-sponsored attempt on George Bush's life during a trip to Kuwait in April 1993. The U.S. government took only modest steps following the destruction of the American embassies in Kenya and Tanzania in 1998 and after the attack on the U.S. Navy ship, the USS *Cole,* in Aden, Yemen, in October 2000.

Consider, now, the problems every Israeli prime minister from Yitzhak Rabin to Ariel Sharon has faced when contemplating building new Israeli settlements on land claimed by the Palestinians. If he draws significant electoral support from religious groups, he knows that he must advance that constituency's interest in building settlements if he is to stay in office. This electoral support was especially important for Prime Ministers Benjamin Netanyahu and Sharon, both of the Likud Party. But by permitting construction of settlements in certain areas, he raises the risk of war with the Palestinians and their allies in the region. Although Israel has been successful in its military campaigns to date, one can never be certain of war's outcome. Even victory may be, to borrow a phrase from President John F. Kennedy, "ashes in the mouth of the victor." Israel is a small country that has lost thousands of its young men and women to war. This is a high price indeed, one that will cause a democratically elected prime minister to think twice before pursuing policies that risk such losses in the future. Certainly the balancing act that foreign policy leaders like Israel's prime minister or Afghanistan's rulers must perform to achieve their goals while holding on to power is more difficult than the comparable act of a purely domestic politics counterpart (a city mayor, for example).

Still, whether we are dealing with domestic politics or international affairs, there are important common components. All of politics is concerned with making choices about the acquisition and allocation of scarce resources. This is true of economics as well, which is concerned primarily with exchanges in a marketplace, usually involving a buyer and a seller. In a marketplace, scarcity of goods and competition for them determine prices, as explained in Chapter 13. This is rarely true in politics. Politics is more often concerned with collective decision making rather than individual choices. Of course, there are gray areas between economics and politics.[2] Politics generally is about the authoritative allocation of resources. This means that political decisions about who gets what are not motivated by supply and demand as they might be in a marketplace. Instead, political influence and political consequences play important roles in determining who gets what when politicians make the choices. Examples of such authoritative allocations of valuable resources that affect international relations include defense budget decisions in legislatures, military coordination among allies, or tariff policies influencing international trade.

---

[2] Important branches of economics are concerned with group decisions, but in market contexts. This is true, for example, of the theory of the firm or of macroeconomics.

Politics generally focuses on decisions that affect groups of people. These groups might be organized around political parties, labor unions, ethnic identities, special interests (the Sierra Club, the National Rifle Association, the Flat Earth Society, the World Federalists), or any number of other orientations. The groups may not even be formally organized at all. People may come together simply out of a common motivation to act in special circumstances. When they do, their collective efforts can profoundly change the political map and its impact on future international relations.

Consider, for example, what happened in August 1991 when hundreds of thousands of ordinary Russian citizens converged on Moscow's Red Square to express support for the existing Russian government. They helped overturn a coup initiated by opponents of political and economic reform in the Soviet Union. The coup failed largely because of the outpouring of political support for the existing government from ordinary people. In its wake, however, politics did not continue as usual for the political leadership. Mikhail Gorbachev, the leader of the Soviet Union, was unable to adjust to the newfound strength of the backers of political and economic reform. By the year's end, he was out of power and the Soviet Union no longer existed.

*On Monday, August 19, 1991, Soviet president Mikhail Gorbachev was overthrown in a coup d'état. Armored personnel carriers, tanks, and other military vehicles were deployed to secure Moscow. Here we see a crowd of Russian citizens resisting the coup—eventually with success— by preventing an armored personnel carrier from making its way toward Red Square, the seat of the Soviet government. Days later Gorbachev returned to power, only to step down shortly after and be replaced by Boris Yeltsin. The power, preferences, and perceptions of the people were mustered to defeat efforts by Soviet hardliners to consolidate control of the government. The central conflict of the post–World War II world came to a peaceful end in part because enough people stood up and said they would not tolerate the Soviet system any longer.*

Politics is the domain of competition among groups and individuals for special advantages, particularly over control of power and wealth. Such political competition involves the risk of punishment as well as the opportunity for rewards for one's actions. In international politics, leaders continually risk being punished by foreign adversaries and domestic foes. And in international affairs, there are few institutions comparable to domestic police forces and courts by which to regulate effectively how nations relate to one another. Unlike domestic affairs, international relations involves only a few commonly accepted means of regulating and enforcing rules of behavior—these means are reflected in international law and in international organizations—when the stakes are high and national leaders are disinclined to abide by common norms of action. This is one important reason why most studies of international relations draw attention to the state as the fundamental actor on the international stage. In this examination of international politics, however, while we pay attention to states, we also are attentive to domestic interest groups, individuals, and, when appropriate, nonstate actors such as multinational corporations, environmental groups, and the like. All these participants in international politics are capable of shaping the policies followed by states and of altering the course of international affairs.

## IS THE STATE THE CENTRAL ACTOR?

Nation-states are places with defined territorial boundaries over which their leaders exercise sovereignty, or self-rule. They are sometimes thought of as the ultimate arbiter of international relations. All the political parties, special interest groups, ethnic groups, and so forth within territorial boundaries are generally presumed by international relations scholars and by political leaders to have some special attachment to their country. That special attachment—called patriotism or loyalty—is believed to encourage groups to put aside "petty" differences when some foreign adversary challenges the nation's welfare. Indeed, it is commonplace to argue that domestic, "partisan" politics should end at water's edge. Many, although certainly not all, maintain that it is harmful to permit domestic concerns to influence international affairs. For example, Democratic members of the House of Representatives voiced this argument during the 1998 debate on the impeachment of Bill Clinton while the U.S. military was simultaneously bombing Iraq. Republican members of Congress rejected this contention and voted to impeach the president rather than wait until the hostilities with Iraq were over. Whether international politics benefits from or is harmed by partisanship is a subject taken up much later in this book.

If patriotism is a strong force that leads people to set aside their partisan differences when it comes to foreign policy, then it makes sense when studying international politics to treat domestic matters as at most a sideshow. For those who hold this view, the nation-state is the principal entity or political unit studied in international politics. Even the name of the subject, inter*national* relations, presumes that the topic of study concerns how nations rather than individual leaders relate to each other.

Conventional views of international politics speak little of the ambitions and interests of individual decision makers or specific groups. Rather, such specifics are conveniently set aside in favor of the national interest to maximize the security and perhaps the wealth of all citizens. It is this judgment about the importance of the national interest that originally prompted special attention to the subject of international relations, resulting in its divorce from the study of routine domestic affairs. Such a view is at odds with how real international relations takes place, however. It is too likely to lead to wrong answers about the most fundamental puzzles of international affairs. The very notion of a national interest is deeply problematic, and few interesting problems in international affairs can realistically and effectively be separated from their domestic political backdrop. This means that much of the time leaders, rather than states, are the fundamental actors on the international stage. Generally, when I refer to actions by a nation I am using the term as shorthand for "leaders of the state."

## Solving International Relations Puzzles

What are the fundamental puzzles in international relations and how might the principles that guide this book help us better understand their solutions? These puzzles involve everything that influences how states and national leaders interact. We are concerned, for example, with the horrors of war and with the costs and benefits of trade. We are interested in how and why nations sometimes manage to cooperate with each other, yet sometimes compete even at the level of deadly conflict. We are curious about the formation of bilateral alliances and multilateral negotiations. We wish to understand international organizations that exist to regulate international commerce and international peace, such as the United Nations, the World Trade Organization, and the International Court of Justice.

We are interested in international law, such as the law of the sea or the international copyright conventions. These bodies of law regulate use of natural resources found under the world's oceans and protect intellectual property rights, respectively. We are intrigued by uncodified norms and customs of behavior between states that facilitate cooperation and dampen conflict. Some such norms of conduct occasionally get written down as laws of behavior—agreements on the treatment of prisoners of war, for example—but oftentimes rely instead on mutual understandings rather than signed agreements. For many centuries people could move freely across national borders without passports. Indeed, before World War I passports were not widely required for international travel. Custom, rather than law, guided decisions on whether to permit or block people from crossing national frontiers. We want to know how resources influence actions, but we also want to know whether resources shape choices more or less than do individual wishes and desires.

Each of these subjects, and many others, are explored in the chapters that follow. These various issues are generally discussed in terms of four broad categories of problems: coordination, distribution, monitoring, and sanctioning. Coordination, as explained in detail especially in Chapters 8, 14, and 15, entails finding ways for states or leaders to act together in pursuit of common objectives. Distribution concerns the allocation of scarce goods among citizens, leaders, and states. Monitoring involves detecting situations in which one or another leader or state has cheated on an agreement. Sanctioning concerns punishing cases of cheating. These four generic issues are at the core of cooperation and competition. Much of what is challenging about international affairs revolves around how to cope with various combinations of these four issues.

The traditional issues in international relations can be understood as various combinations of coordination, distribution, monitoring, and sanctioning. For example, why do nations go to war? Some argue that wars are fought to gain territory, to acquire wealth, to impose policies, or to spread values. Each of these is an argument involving distributional issues between rivals. Whether allies can be counted on to help out in time of war is a question of both coordination and monitoring. Sanctions encourage compliance, as do rewards (distribution): sanctions function as the "stick" and rewards are the "carrot." The production of parts, such as automobile components, electronics, or textiles, in one place and their assembly in another generally involve difficulties in coordinating decisions across multiple governments. How this coordination is achieved is an important problem in international trade relations. Protecting endangered whales or dolphins as they swim from the territorial waters of one state to the territorial waters of another, or even as they swim in the open ocean, involves problems of both coordination and distribution. What is more, it can be very difficult to monitor the exploitation of resources (dolphins, hydroelectric power) that can move from jurisdiction to jurisdiction. Knowing whether one country's fishermen have overfished in international waters can be difficult to detect. International treaties provide a common means of addressing these problems and represent an important feature of international efforts at cooperation. Trade disputes and even wars are sometimes the product of failed efforts to reach cooperative understandings. A common source of dispute between neighboring states involves disagreements over the benefits derived from river systems that flow across national borders. If the upstream country dams a river, for example, the downstream country (or countries) may be deprived of vital energy, drinking water, food from fish and fowl, recreation areas, and so forth, all of which can precipitate conflict.

Through the remainder of this introduction we will look at how power, preferences, and perceptions combine with leaders' self-interest to shape international questions of coordination, distribution, monitoring, and sanctioning. In so doing we will clarify how states relate to each other and establish how we might better predict and influence the course of international relations.

## Power, Preferences, and Perceptions:
## The Three Pillars of International Relations

International relations as a subject is primarily about the choices and actions that political leaders take in the name of their nation to influence how their state relates to other states. Interstate relations are motivated by leaders' preferences for certain goals over other goals. These preferences are tempered by the power to pursue those goals and by perceptions or beliefs about the costs and benefits associated with seeking out one goal over another. The preferences, power, and perceptions of leaders are not the only factors in play. Ultimately, foreign leaders, like all political leaders, must judge the preferences, power, and perceptions of the people whose support they need or whose opposition they must avoid to retain office. This is true whether support or opposition comes from domestic or foreign interests.

Usually threats to power and authority arise from among competing elites who desire to hold office. Such competition is at the heart of succession crises in hereditary monarchies, in authoritarian dictatorships, and in political democracies. But threats to a leader's authority can also come from ordinary people. Mass riots and grassroots revolutions sometimes lead to the overthrow of governments. Mass support may also play a role in preserving a particular regime. Earlier I discussed the August 1991 gathering in Moscow's Red Square of hundreds of thousands of Russian citizens intent on deflating a coup in progress. Those who gathered believed that they could help shape the course of events. They acted on this *perception* by mobilizing the *power* they had in numbers to display their *preference* for continuing with the reforms of the existing government and to prevent going back to the days of dictatorial rule. Although such events are probably less common than elite infighting, they can be at least as devastating to a leader's prospects of political or even physical survival. Thus international relations is about how the power, preferences, and perceptions of different people—leaders, their rivals, and ordinary citizens—shape the actions of states toward one another.

**Power.**   Success in influencing relations between states depends on the ability of a particular state to muster the relevant political, economic, and military resources that persuade or coerce another state into actions it would rather not take. Ultimately, power is about mobilizing resources to alter the behavior of others.

Simply put, power is an instrument for promoting and achieving goals. As such, it is a mistake to think of the quest for power as the ultimate goal of foreign policy leaders or of the nation they represent. Rather, power is the servant of ambitious leaders prepared to take risks to advance the objectives they hold dear. Thus, although power provides the wherewithal to take action, the preferences of political leaders, as well as those of their opponents and their backers, are what motivate action.

**Preferences.**   Foreign policy goals and the ways nations interact with each other are reflections of the preferences, or desires, of key foreign policy leaders and those constituents whose support they require to stay in office. The preferences of constituents are important because if a leader's preferences are sufficiently inconsistent with the wants and desires of those interests, then, like Enrique IV, he or she runs the risk of being overthrown. Such a risk emanates from two sources. Opponents capable of jeopardizing a leader's authority may arise from within the state, as was true of the count of Plasencia, the count of Benavente, and Diego López de Zúñiga in the case of Enrique IV. Additionally, opponents may arise from outside the state. Enrique IV, for example, had to worry about Alonso Carrillo, archbishop of Toledo, who represented the authority of the greatest foreign power of Enrique's day, the Catholic Church. Being overthrown, of course, means that a leader loses control over the selection of national goals and over the mobilization of the resources needed to enforce national actions. This is an outcome every decision maker wants to avoid because it contradicts his or her own self-interest.

> Give a few examples of internal challengers who want to replace the president of the United States or the prime minister in China. What foreign threats do these leaders face? How about the leader of Iraq? Israel? India? What foreign threats challenge their ability to lead effectively? Can you name a political leader who was overthrown or politically defeated by domestic opponents of his or her foreign policy? Draw up a list of leaders who were ousted by foreign adversaries.

**PERCEPTIONS.** Leaders' perceptions about reality also affect foreign policy decision making. Leaders may misjudge the amount of resources or degree of power they can mobilize on behalf of their nation or miscalculate the level of political support that will follow from their pursuit of articulated preferences. They may hold a world view or ideology that limits how they perceive the actions and intentions of rivals. They may frame problems to emphasize possible gains (as any individual does when buying a lottery ticket) or they may emphasize possible losses (as when citizens insist that a government remove all risks associated with nuclear energy, driving cars, flying on airplanes). Perceptions may lead policymakers to take greater risks than they had intended or to forgo opportunities they did not realize they had. Rivals know this and so have incentives to mislead their adversaries and, sometimes, even their friends. Thus national leaders must be ever vigilant, sifting through all available information in order to judge best which of the threats, offers of assistance, or other actions by friend and foe alike are mere bluffs and which are credible dangers (or benefits) to the society they lead and to their own interest in promoting their ambitions.

## SELF-INTEREST: THE DECISIVE MOTIVATION FOR ACTION

Power, preferences, and perceptions are the tools used by leaders to develop political and policy ambitions and assess risks associated with their pursuit. These notions of ambition and risk emerge through the decisive filter of self-interest. National leaders' self-interest typically includes both the desire to hold on to the reins of power and the desire to act on personally held beliefs.

A fundamental problem in international relations is that the actions that help leaders keep their jobs sometimes are at odds with the substantive goals or beliefs those leaders hold. Consequently, foreign policy decision makers are frequently trapped between taking action in accord with sincerely held beliefs at the risk of losing their jobs to foreign or domestic opponents or forgoing personal policy preferences in order to hold on to power. Leaders' own interests may pull them in contrary directions, greatly complicating decision making.

British prime minister Winston Churchill's declaration that he would not preside over the dissolution of the British colonial empire is a case in point. As World War II drew to a close and Britain again turned to electing a government (having maintained a coalition government of all parties during the war years), Churchill declared that "without freedom there is no foundation for our Empire; without Empire there is no safeguard for our freedom" (James 1974). The British people apparently disagreed. At the very first opportunity the British electorate turned Churchill, the heroic prime minister of the war, out of office. They did so in 1945 at the very time of the Potsdam summit, attended by Britain, Russia, and the United States, where the postwar world order was defined. The empire was dismantled by Churchill's successors. Churchill lost his job, but he did stick to his position. He did not preside over the dissolution of the British Empire.

International politics is framed by the principle that self-interest motivates those in power to do the best they can for the people who keep them in office. In democracies, this is a substantial proportion of the people; in dictatorships, "the people" may in fact be a very small group of generals, bureaucrats, or other key supporters. This means that leaders in democracies are more likely to do what they believe is good for most of their citizens; autocrats are more likely to worry about the welfare of their cronies. In each case, to do otherwise is to risk political failure, loss of office, and, most critically, loss of power. This is a risk worth taking only if one believes that the value of other goals, such as specific policy objectives, outweighs the benefits of office. This principle of self-interest is a guidepost for those who want to understand history as well as current affairs. Here we want to understand both.

The most important aspect of international affairs is the way in which national leaders translate their self-interest into foreign policy decisions and actions. The reason I focus on decision makers and their choices is quite simple. Nations do not make decisions. Nations do not feel secure and wealthy, threatened and poor. Nations do not make agreements or wage war; they do not obey laws or break them. People do these things. They may do them in the name of the nation they lead or represent, but it is individuals who choose goals, actions, and strategies. It is individual citizens and leaders who bear the costs of failure and enjoy the benefits of success for the actions taken in the name of their state.[3]

---

[3] A policy fails from a given individual's perspective when the policy yields results that are worse for that individual than the results expected had the policy not been pursued. Likewise, we may think of success as a policy outcome that improves upon what was expected had the policy not been pursued.

The state is merely a metaphor for the collection of groups and individuals living within a sovereign territory. In a sense, states become nations because the people living within a sovereign territory share more in common with each other than they do with those living outside that territory. Sometimes the bundle of shared values that define a nation is referred to as the national culture or national character. The presumption that there are such shared values within a state may be true much of the time, but surely it is not true all of the time. Not every state is a nation and not every nation is a state. For example, the Kurds, an ethnic group with their own language, history, and culture, are dispersed throughout the Middle East, with large minority populations in Iraq and Turkey. They are not a majority in any country. Kurds often think of themselves as a nation, but they do not exercise sovereign rights over any territory. They are not a state. The rapid dissolution of Yugoslavia at the end of the cold war and the subsequent fighting among many of its regions and ethnic groups suggests that Yugoslavia was a state but not a nation.

Among those residing within a state, it generally falls to relatively few leaders to formulate foreign policy and conduct international affairs. These leaders are central to

*Kurds demonstrate in Germany in their frustrated quest to turn the Kurdish nation into a sovereign state. The demonstrators hold up pictures of nationalist leader Abdullah Ocalan, who was arrested and brought to trial in Turkey for plotting the overthrow of the Turkish government. On June 29, 1999, Ocalan was sentenced to death by a Turkish court. Kurds in Iraq and Turkey continue their struggle to achieve independence and sovereignty.*

international relations because they link external actions taken in the name of the state to the internal political consequences of those actions. It is in this linkage capacity that they combine their own self-interests with the welfare of those at whose pleasure they hold power.

Leaders differ from ordinary citizens in at least two respects. First, by virtue of their position as leader they can muster more resources than ordinary citizens to promote particular policies or goals. Second, leaders are more likely than ordinary citizens to be held accountable for policy failures and to be rewarded for policy successes. Leaders' ambitions for the state and for themselves are fairly evident from the actions they take. As such, leaders are held personally responsible for any negative consequences arising from the use of national resources in pursuit of their goals. Leaders who use resources unsuccessfully are likely to lose the authority to use them in the future. The risks associated with failure create in leaders a powerful self-interest to do a good job, where a "good job" is defined as one that satisfies the wishes of those whose support leaders need to hold on to power. When those whose support is needed are not representative of the population in general, then a "good job" may entail actions that are contrary to the general welfare.

Leaders must be ambitious people. Otherwise they would not subject themselves to the risks of office. Failure carries with it a real risk of banishment, or even execution. For leaders, the potential rewards of being in power must outweigh the accompanying risks. Because positions of national leadership seem always and everywhere to be highly competitive (there has never been a shortage of candidates to be king, president, prime minister, or dictator), prospective leaders must single themselves out so that they can convert their ambition into reality. The ambition to lead encourages bold actions. A successful leader is one who walks a fine line by displaying enough ambition and risk taking to attract the support needed to gain office while not being so bold as to inflict costs on followers, who might then be led to seek a new leader. Even after they attain high office, leaders must continue to distinguish themselves. In the process of setting themselves apart they may attract strong domestic or foreign opposition, as happened to Enrique IV in 1465 and Adolf Hitler in 1939 after Germany invaded Poland. At the same time, of course, leaders can attract wealth, power, and adulation.

Most people desire a sense of personal security and well-being. Political leaders—whether the local city mayor or the president of the United States—seek policies that will enhance the security and well-being of their essential supporters. This leads to a view of nations as decision makers, interested only in maximizing national security and enhancing national wealth. Such a viewpoint necessarily overlooks variations within a nation in the degree of ambition, level of competence, and propensity for boldness of different internal candidates for national leadership, as well as variations in citizen and elite notions of what is good for the nation. It is a viewpoint that assumes that all leaders can be treated as if they were the same: nations maximizing wealth or security.

In fact, leaders differ markedly in the degrees of ambition, boldness, and competence they display. Likewise, political supporters differ in the goals they seek to achieve. For example, the politically powerful may be more interested in imposing a particular religious order or developing a hefty Swiss bank account than in boosting security and national wealth. Even when leaders seek to maximize security or wealth, they may go about it very differently. For example, Hitler took risks that were so great they ultimately led to his destruction and the destruction of Nazi Germany. Conversely, Neville Chamberlain, prime minister of Britain in the late 1930s, was so fearful of taking risks that he ended by placing his nation in jeopardy. Chamberlain granted territorial concessions to Hitler to achieve "peace in our time." Instead, Hitler invaded Poland. Chamberlain's timidity contributed directly to the onset of World War II and his own political downfall.

> Name some leaders whose actions seem contrary to their citizens' interests. Why do you think some leaders who steal fortunes from their nations manage to survive in office for a long time?

To understand how nations and their leaders behave toward one another, we must examine how decision makers face variations in circumstances, political ambition, and risk. In doing so, we will see how decision makers, guided by self-interest, take risks that lead nations to choose differently from one another under like circumstances.

## SUMMARY

International relations is concerned with any aspect of politics that influences how nations relate to one another. Because it shapes the choices of foreign policy leaders, domestic politics strongly influences relations between states. Policymakers must strike a balance between the needs of vital domestic interests and the external pressures imposed by foreign interests. How leaders determine the appropriate trade-off between domestic and foreign concerns depends on their degree of ambition, the risks they are willing to take, and their perceptions of how choices influence their own self-interest.

In this book I stress that to speak of a nation's policies or a nation's interests in any other than metaphoric terms is problematic. Instead, I focus on the decision-making elements that shape foreign policy choices and their link to the international system. In doing so I highlight the importance of calculating the costs and benefits of alternative courses of action and estimating the likelihood that one or another approach to a problem will succeed or fail. This approach differs markedly from other approaches to studying international affairs.

The problems of international politics fall into four broad categories or various combinations thereof. These include problems of distribution, coordination, monitoring, and sanctioning. The application of power in pursuit of preferred outcomes, colored by perceptions about how others will react to alternative courses of action, serves to both generate and resolve these problems. Because actions are tempered by expectations about the reactions they will elicit, foreign policy decision making is inherently strategic. As we proceed in our study of international relations we will develop the skills to effectively evaluate policy choices within an environment where no one is always able to get whatever he or she wants. As the Rolling Stones aptly taught us, "You can't always get what you want—but if you try sometimes, you just might find, you get what you need."

## SUGGESTED READING

Most chapters provide citations to relevant literature in the text. Here, however, I offer a few suggested readings now, having avoided citations that might break the flow of the introductory material. Those who want to delve more deeply into any subject touched on in the chapters that follow would do well to use the cited works listed in the bibliography.

On linkages between domestic politics and international relations: James Rosenau (1963, 1969); Robert Putnam (1988); Bruce Bueno de Mesquita and David Lalman (1992); Alex Mintz (1993); James Fearon (1994); and Kenneth Schultz (1998).

Early works on strategic interaction in international affairs: Thomas Schelling (1960); Graham Allison (1972); and Steven Brams (1985).

On foreign policy and leadership survival: Bruce Bueno de Mesquita and Randolph M. Siverson (1995); Suzanne Werner (1996); Hein Goemans (2000); and Bruce Bueno de Mesquita, Alastair Smith, Randolph M. Siverson, and James D. Morrow (2003).

# MODERN POLITICAL ECONOMIC HISTORY AND INTERNATIONAL POLITICS

THE FOURTEEN HUNDREDS

THE FIFTEEN HUNDREDS

THE SIXTEEN HUNDREDS

THE SEVENTEEN HUNDREDS

THE EIGHTEEN HUNDREDS

THE TWENTIETH CENTURY

Today, as throughout human history, heads of state and policymakers must choose their course of action in international politics. Whether they seek the best outcomes for their country or their own personal aggrandizement, they must weigh the facts and the logic of their circumstances in deciding what to do. Decision makers need knowledge and skill in making their choices, and we need them to have that knowledge and skill because what they do may have great consequences for the future of their state and the world as a whole. In this chapter we focus on developing a common historical background that touches upon the most important events of the past several centuries and their place in contemporary international relations. This gives us a common set of factual referents to draw upon as we develop the tools for analyzing international affairs.

The events of history are sometimes described as a sequence of chance—path dependent—developments. Such a view leads to the memorization of key dates and names rather than an appreciation of how intertwined the events of history really are. If we think of historical developments and change as arising by chance, then we have no reason to believe that lessons for the future can be taken from a study of the past. This book rejects that viewpoint and maintains that lessons can be learned from history. To learn those lessons we must understand what has transpired and why. This chapter gives a necessarily too-brief answer to the question, What has happened? The next chapter introduces ideas and tools for answering the question, Why did and do things happen as they do?

Although we can readily imagine alternative courses history might have taken, still we should not infer that the actual flow of events was due to happenstance in the past or that it is likely to be due to happenstance in the future. What happened in history is largely dependent on the anticipated consequences of alternative courses of action that were not chosen. These alternative courses—sometimes called counterfactual histories—are what did not happen. An assumption held throughout this book is that history can teach us lessons for the future, both by understanding why particular choices were made and by understanding why other choices, leading to alternative histories, were not made. To examine decisions in an informed way, we need to know something about what decision makers knew or believed at the time they made their choices.

The distinction between what is known when a decision is made and what is known later is an important element in judging the past and in the evaluation of arguments about the future. Decisions can only be made before the fact, so knowing the prior flow of events and its causes often is instrumental in shaping the views of decision makers about what to do next. Of course, using information that is known afterward when evaluating the decisions leaders make is both unfair and misleading when developing explanations or causal arguments. Historians and political scientists studying international relations commonly confuse what was known before the fact with what is known after the fact. For example, many scholars who are interested in determining the causes of large-scale, destructive wars such as World War I focus their research only on big wars (Organski and Kugler 1980; Gilpin 1981; Kennedy 1987). Yet, the decision makers of the time did not know they were entering into an extraordinarily long, widespread, and costly war. Probably, had they known how devastating these wars would be, at least some of them would have been more inclined to settle their differences without resorting to violence and its attendant costs. For example, we know now that the German invasion of Poland on September 1, 1939, led to World War II. But the leaders of the time did not know that. In fact, contemporary newspaper accounts referred to it as the "German-Polish War."[1]

The making of foreign policy decisions, the shaping of international politics, and our understanding of arguments and evidence depends on two basic but fundamentally different components: facts and theoretical perspective. This chapter looks at important facts of history to establish some basic shared knowledge. In Chapter 2 we examine the tools for evaluating facts in light of logic and evidence.

I begin with essential facts about the political and economic history of the past 550 years. Of course, I can only offer a rudimentary review of history. Those who want a more in-depth treatment should consult any of the numerous excellent book-length accounts of world history. A suggested list of such readings can be found at the Web site for this book, http://bdm.cqpress.com.

---

[1] My mother, who fled Belgium when it was bombed by the Nazis on May 10, 1940, always said that World War II started on May 10, 1940. When I pressed her about the German invasion of Poland eight months earlier, she responded, "Oh, that was the German-Polish War."

## THE FOURTEEN HUNDREDS

The year 1453 produced a host of important developments. It marked the collapse of the Byzantine Empire. This empire, the successor to the ancient Roman Empire, fell with the success of Islamic Ottoman Turkey in taking control of Constantinople. For many historians, the end of the Byzantine Empire also marks the end of the Middle Ages and the beginning of the modern era. The argument that 1453 ends the Middle Ages is closely tied to the economic consequences of the fall of Constantinople and, incidentally, the implications of those economic consequences for Columbus's later voyages of discovery.

> What are some of the similarities and differences between monarchies and modern democracies? In what ways is monarchy closer to democracy than to autocracy? In what other ways is monarchy closer to autocracy than to democracy? When did monarchy change from being elective to being hereditary?

The victory by the Turks meant that they were able to cut European traders off from directly exploiting land routes to the spice trade with India and beyond. As we will see when I introduce the concept of expected utility maximization in Chapter 3, the increased costs and risks of the overland routes to Asia contributed to the search by European powers for a sea route to India, China, and Japan. Thus, Spain's decision to back Columbus in his quest for such a path to Asian trade followed directly from the heightened costs of overland trade brought about by the defeat of the Byzantine Empire by the Ottoman Turks. Spain was motivated by Ferdinand and Isabella's interest in securing their personal hold on power and by their desire to enrich and strengthen themselves by enriching and strengthening their kingdom. Indeed, as we will see later, one of the characteristics of monarchy that sets it apart from modern autocracy is the closer link between the monarch's personal welfare and the welfare of "the state," a link that is largely absent in rigged-election autocracies.

Other events in Europe at the time set the stage for future developments and conflicts over the next several centuries and even into our own time. Germany—then a loose confederation of princely states—had been ruled by the Habsburg dynasty since 1273. Habsburg rule, however, took a great leap forward in power when Frederick III became the Holy Roman Emperor in 1452. The Holy Roman Empire was probably the most powerful secular authority in Europe at the time, with only the Catholic Church being at least as powerful. The Habsburgs maintained their control over the Holy Roman Empire until 1806, when it ceased to exist. Still, in the intervening centuries, German political, cultural, and military influence waned and waxed, helping to set the stage for German ambitions in the First and Second World Wars and perhaps even contemporary Germany's great influence within the European Union.

The years 1452–1453, then, witnessed the emergence of critical new powers in northern Europe and the development of southeastern Europe's ties to Asia through Turkey. Still other events were unfolding that helped redefine the political map and interests of Europe's leading powers. In the west, England and France finally resolved the Hundred Years' War (1337–1453). At the war's outset, England held vast territories in what today is called France. English kings claimed the French throne just as French kings made claims on the English crown. The French emerged victorious from the Hundred Years' War, expelling England from almost all of its continental territories and helping to solidify France's borders along lines close to those of modern France. The French victory also helped define the French nationality and nationalism, a process already under way by 1302, when the French king, Philip the Fair, launched a war against Pope Boniface VIII and called upon the people of France to die for their country (*pro patria mori*). Similar consequences for England emerged from the Hundred Years' War. In the process of losing the war, modern England began to take form.

MAP 1-1
**Holy Roman, Ottoman, and Russian Empires, 1400s–1500s**

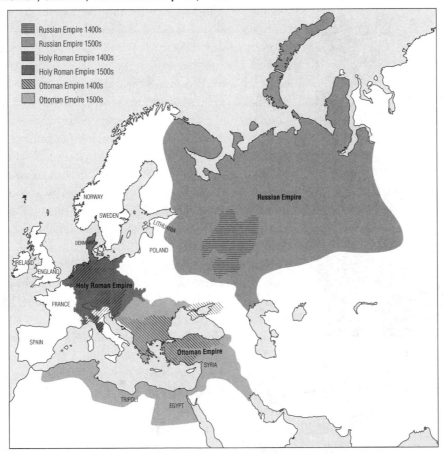

*Competition for control of Europe is evident in the expansion of the Holy Roman, Ottoman, and Russian Empires during the 1400s and 1500s.*

None expressed better the profound change in national self-awareness in England than did William Shakespeare in writing two centuries later about Henry V and the English success in the Battle of Agincourt (1415):

> This day is called the feast of Crispian:
> He that outlives this day, and comes safe home,
> Will stand a-tiptoe when this day is named,
> And rouse him at the name of Crispian. . . .
> And gentlemen in England now a-bed
> Shall think themselves accursed they were not here,
> And hold their manhoods cheap whiles any speaks
> That fought with us upon Saint Crispin's day.

The Hundred Years' War secured English national consciousness and the gradual development of an English "culture" that is distinctly different from that of France. Although England was already well on the way to establishing its common law and parliamentary government, 1453 and its aftermath mark a crucial turning point in English and French history. The emerging political institutions in England served to strengthen the Crown both at the expense of external interests—especially the Catholic Church—and internal rivals, most notably the wealthiest earls and dukes. These institutional developments were, in other words, the product not of chance ideas but of strategic maneuvers by England's king (and France's as well) to make secure his own political position. The strategic linkage between domestic political considerations and foreign affairs is laid out in detail throughout the remainder of this book.

In the northeastern part of Europe equally momentous events unfolded only a quarter of a century later. Modern Russia was born in 1480, when Ivan III, having defeated Asia's Mongols—the heirs of Genghis Khan—created an independent Russian state. His successor, Ivan the Terrible, then set about building a Russian empire that would make Russia a major competitor for political influence throughout Europe, a position Russia maintains to this day.

Halfway across the world other pivotal events were taking place. Developments in modern-day Mexico in 1430 helped set the stage for some of the most significant developments in the sixteenth century. During the

*Ivan the Terrible (1530–1584) became Russia's first tsar in 1547. He introduced a code of law in 1550, restructured government, and greatly extended the Russian dominion, including expansion into Siberia. Ivan also stretched Russian commercial ties as far as England. Despite these achievements, his enslavement of Russian peasants and repressive rule earned him the title "Terrible."*

eleventh and twelfth centuries, the then nomadic Aztecs encountered and eventually overtook the Toltec civilization in the Valley of Mexico. The Aztecs elected their first king, Tenoch, in 1349. He ruled for more than forty years. During this time, control of Mexico was divided among numerous competing tribes, but in 1430 a league of three Aztec cities formed (Tenochtitlan, Texcuco, and Tlacopén) to build an empire. The three-city league fought wars with its political rivals, fairly quickly establishing Aztec control over an empire that ranged from the Pacific Ocean to the Gulf of Mexico. In less than a century, this empire and the imperial pursuits of Spain would clash, leading to the conquest of Mexico by Hernán Cortés in 1518 and, together with the destruction of Peru's Inca Empire, the beginning of the European colonization of the Western Hemisphere.

## THE FIFTEEN HUNDREDS

As the fifteenth century drew to a close, Spain was united, schisms that had divided the papacy appeared to be resolved, England and France were emerging from decades of

*Tenoch, a tribal leader of the early four-teenth century, founded Tenochtitlan, one of the most important Aztec cities during the subsequent two centuries. The city played a central role in the creation of the Aztec empire. Tenoch is seen here wearing a white robe and sitting on a reed mat. The white robe symbolizes authority, and the reed mat indicates that he is a ruler.*

war, and European monarchs seemed poised to expand their influence throughout the New World. Yet other events were taking place that challenged the fundamental world order inherited at the turn of the century.

The fifteen hundreds witnessed the flowering of the Protestant Reformation with its attendant implications for the secularization of Europe. Habsburg control over the Holy Roman Empire provided a crucial backdrop for the success of the Protestant Reformation. Martin Luther posted his ninety-five theses in 1517, challenging the legitimacy of the Catholic Church's religious and political hegemony in Europe. The monarchs of northern Europe saw this and a slew of other anti-Church protests and declarations as a political opportunity to undermine the pope's authority and to weaken the influence of the Catholic Church as a competitor for political influence. Protests against the Church leadership's apparent venality and corruption served the political interests of monarchs. The Reformation gave them an opportunity to foster loyalty both by promoting nationalism and by encouraging new, Protestant religions as an alternative to Roman Catholicism. By fostering the legitimacy of Protestant religious principles, monarchs could deprive the Church of the power inherent in its ability to excommunicate individuals or to deprive whole communities of the sacraments (through interdiction). Prior to the Protestant Reformation, western Europeans who failed to subscribe to the teachings of Roman Catholicism exposed themselves to severe prejudice and extreme risks. Earlier efforts to reform the Catholic hierarchy's power met with disaster as experienced, for instance, by the monk Girolamo Savonarola, who was burned at the stake on May 23, 1498, for condemning Church practices and the lavish lifestyle of the Church's leaders. What Savonarola could not do successfully from his base in Florence—right in the backyard of the papacy—Martin Luther and others could do from their more remote outposts in northern Europe. With the advent of the Reformation, those who no longer subscribed to Catholicism did not need the Church hierarchy to serve as intermediaries between them and God. People could practice new forms of Christianity, knowing that their leaders supported these practices, and in this way the Church was weakened. The changing perception of the Catholic Church played an important part in increasing the apparent power and influence of secular political institutions throughout Europe. Because many people no longer believed that their salvation depended on the Church's approval or on confession to a Catholic priest, local rulers were strengthened in their ability to assert sovereign authority. Thus, changes in beliefs resulted in fundamental changes in the real power of states as opposed to the supernational church.

The Catholic leadership, of course, did not stand by idly while its power was eroded. A counterreformation was launched that was part reform and part oppression of Protestant dissenters. By the seventeenth century the political-religious disputes in Europe came to a head, culminating in the Thirty Years' War (1618–1648) and the decline of the papacy and Catholic Church as a great power in Europe.

While the struggle for national emergence and sovereignty continued in sixteenth-century Europe, Suleiman the Magnificent (1520–1566) built on the successes of the Ottomans in the previous century. He turned Ottoman Turkey into the Ottoman Empire, exercising significant political and economic control from Asia Minor to North Africa and spreading into Europe. In the last great battle in Europe between Islamic and Christian beliefs until our own time, Suleiman laid siege to Vienna in 1529. Islam's influence in Europe was largely defeated as the Ottoman Empire was forced to gradually retreat from its European holdings. A similar clash in Europe between Christians and Muslims would not arise again until the end of the cold war, when the collapse of the Soviet Union led Yugoslavia to unravel into its constituent parts, producing wars in Bosnia and Kosovo, wars involving disputes between European Christians and Muslims. And, although not strictly a war between Christian and Islamic values, our own time has now also produced the antiterrorism war begun in 2001 between the United States, its allies, and the Muslim extremists in Afghanistan known as the Taliban and their partner, al Qaeda.

The search for a sea route from Europe to Asia in the fifteenth century, as discussed at length later, failed, but in the process of searching, Columbus and others after him made European leaders aware of the vast resources of the Americas. Hernán Cortés fought and defeated the Aztecs in his quest for wealth for himself and his sovereign. Francisco Pizarro had much the same motivations when he overthrew the Inca Empire in what today is Peru. By the last two decades of the sixteenth century, tremendous amounts of wealth were being extracted from the Americas and shipped to Europe. Piracy became a critical source of private and national wealth. Indeed, the English were such effective privateers that Spain was losing a substantial portion of the wealth it took from the Americas because of theft on the high seas by English pirates, many of whom were handsomely rewarded by the English Crown. This led in 1588 to the Spanish monarch's decision to mount a fierce naval armada designed to destroy England's threat at sea. The Spanish Armada, however, was soundly defeated by a combination of bad weather and the more mobile, faster ships of England, marking the decline of Spain and the ascent of England as a great naval power.

By the close of the fifteen hundreds, Spain and Portugal, the two great naval powers of that century, were in decline. Islam was turned back from Europe, although it had secured its hold in North Africa and Asia Minor. The exploitation of America's wealth stimulated colonization, leading to the establishment of permanent European settlements and holdings in North and South America. The world of international competition and commerce had become much larger than it was one hundred years earlier. The greatest power in Europe—the Catholic Church—faced its last battle for domination, a battle it would lose as the Protestant Reformation spread across northern Europe.

## THE SIXTEEN HUNDREDS

Much of Europe was enveloped in war from 1618 to 1648. The Thirty Years' War was partially a religious conflict and partially about competing ambitions to establish national empires. It ended with the Treaty of Westphalia, marking for many the defining moment of transition to the modern state-dominated international system. The new international order following the Thirty Years' War consisted of a system in which territorial, sovereign governments lived securely within usually well defined borders and exercised control over political, military, economic, and social life within those borders. Today we give little thought to a world without states. Yet the state as we understand it has not always existed and may not always exist in the future.

The Treaty of Westphalia contains more than one hundred specific articles laying out the terms and conditions of the war's end. Most of these articles deal with the allocation or restoration of valuable resources among the participants. A few articles, however, pertain directly to the establishment of territorial sovereignty and to the specific rights and privileges of states. Article 64 establishes territoriality and the right of the state to choose its own religion, as well as the right to noninterference by other states in any of these matters. This article codifies the end of Roman Catholicism's hegemony in Europe. Article 65 spells out the rights of sovereign authority with regard to foreign policy. For example, it establishes that no supernational authority (that is, the Catholic Church or the Holy Roman Empire) can make or negate alliances made between sovereigns for the purpose of protecting each nation's security. Similarly, Article 67 establishes that sovereign states can determine their own domestic policies, free from external pressures and "with full Jurisdiction within the inclosure of their Walls and their Territorys" (Croxton and Tischer 2002; www.tufts.edu/departments/fletcher/multi/texts/historical/westphalia.txt).

MAP 1-2
**Europe in 1648**

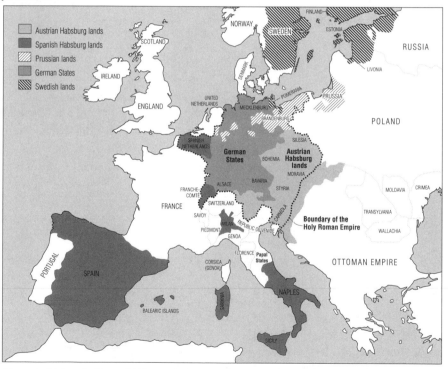

*The Treaty of Westphalia, which marked the end of the Thirty Years' War and an important step in the evolution of sovereignty, redrew the map of Europe and redefined the norms and rules of international law that states were expected to obey. The influence of the Catholic Church in political affairs was greatly diminished, and new alignments emerged. It is interesting to note that no defeated monarch was overthrown by the victors in the Thirty Years' War.*

The Westphalian System unquestionably marks a crucial point in international affairs, but it would be a mistake to think that the modern state sprang up suddenly and completely as a result of the Thirty Years' War. Competition between church and monarchy had already put changes into motion, with the Treaty of Westphalia punctuating the changes that were taking place.

By the end of the Thirty Years' War, Europe's "balance of power" had fundamentally changed. Not only had the Catholic Church declined markedly in influence, but also political power had shifted to France. The war killed about half of all Germans, and France's monarch emerged as the new dominant power in Europe. The ascent of France marked the pinnacle of absolute monarchy as captured by the French king Louis XIV's famous phrase, "L'état c'est moi" ("I am the state"). Louis innovated in government and in national security. He was one of the first sovereigns to maintain a permanent standing army rather than rely on hiring mercenary soldiers to fight when needed. The adoption of a permanent standing army was accompanied by great technological improvements in drill, fighting skill, and weaponry, all of which contributed to strengthening the central authority of the state ruled by an absolute, hereditary monarch.

See if you can find three or four examples of individuals who were elected king over someone else with at least as good a claim to be heir to the throne. Look up the institution in England called the witenagemot. How did it work to select the king? Compare it with the volk moot, used in England in about the ninth century. How do these two institutions compare with modern-day democracy?

The Thirty Years' War punctuated a change in monarchy that had been gradually emerging for some time. Throughout much of the Middle Ages and even before the Norman Conquest of Britain in 1066, monarchy was elective rather than strictly hereditary. Noble birth was a requirement for kingship, and being the child and heir to the previous monarch was a great advantage in gaining the crown, but still, election was required. Election of monarchs sometimes led to the selection of someone other than the immediate heir apparent to the throne. The change to heredity as the fundamental means of choosing kings carried important implications for foreign policy. Kings never have to answer to many people, but hereditary kings usually have to answer to even fewer than elected kings. As we see later, when leaders require the support of very few people, they have incentives to promote their own wealth and that of the few at whose pleasure they serve rather than promote the welfare of the many who live in their society. So it was for monarchs who were less beholden than they had been. Their relative independence from the well-being of their subjects unleashed foreign policy adventures oriented toward securing wealth and power—wealth and power that did not devolve to the people. This meant that war changed in its intensity. The pressure to fight in unpopular wars and the burden of paying for such adventures through heavy taxation eventually destroyed the political advantages of the new monarchism over its older feudal form. By the eighteenth century the failings of absolute, hereditary monarchy gave rise to revolution and to dramatic changes in political institutions, leading to the emergence of the two dominant forms of modern government: rigged-election autocracy and liberal democracy. The first stirrings of threats to monarchy, however, arose even before the Thirty Years' War ended.

The English Civil War (1642–1648) saw Oliver Cromwell temporarily overthrow the British monarchy. The English king, Charles I, was beheaded, suggesting a move away from monarchy either to dictatorship or possibly even a nascent democracy. But Cromwell's efforts failed and the monarchy was restored. Still, the power of the Parliament increased as the monarchy became more and more dependent on financial backing from Parliament to pursue its policies.

Experiments with republican government had occurred over many centuries. The Italian republics had flourished during the Renaissance, only to decline as they lost their quasi-republican forms of governance to be taken over by oligarchs. In the Netherlands, great wealth accompanied the move to a semi-republican form of government among city magistrates. As in England, the shift toward a partially representative government in the Netherlands was accompanied by a tremendous outpouring of entrepreneurial activity and great economic prosperity.

The new ideas and debates about government, including the earlier ideas of Thomas Hobbes in *The Leviathan* (1651) and John Locke's ideas in his *Two Treatises of Government* (1690), unleashed a wealth of views about government as a social contract between the ruler and the ruled. These and other ideas, coupled with the religious consequences of the Thirty Years' War, helped contribute to a wave of new settlers in the New World, settlers who seemed committed to experimenting with innovative forms of government designed to escape the oppressive burdens of monarchy. Whereas the early forays into the Americas by Europeans seemed to focus on limited stays designed to extract tradable goods (for example, furs, lumber, new foodstuffs, and other crops) and mineral wealth, the new European arrivals seemed more interested in permanent settlements. The Dutch occupied Nieuw Amsterdam, later New York, as a very active seat of commerce. The Pilgrims and other dissenting groups settled up and down the North American East Coast in search of religious freedom and economic opportunity. It should be understood that their quest for religious freedom often meant freedom to practice their religious views and not freedom for others to practice dissenting views. The Mayflower Compact, an agreement on governance signed by the Pilgrims aboard the *Mayflower*, served as an early model for a self-governing community and helped pave the way for reforms in governing institutions that pervade American history and that represented a departure from the confiscatory economic policies monarchs often pursued toward their subjects.

The latter half of the seventeenth century presaged other dramatic changes in international politics. By the end of the century, William and Mary sat on the throne in England, but political parties had emerged as a critical source of political influence in Parliament. The English prime minister became a figure of considerable political consequence rather than merely a spokesman for the Crown. In science, the discoveries of Isaac Newton and others began to change how educated people understood the world. Laws of nature were discovered and the scientific method of experimentation and empirical evaluation began to supplant religious conviction as the basis for reasoned arguments. This, too, weakened the claim of monarchs to rule by divine right; that is, by the will of God. The world again was on the verge of tremendous changes in attitudes and on the edge of significant shifts in political and economic factors governing international relations.

## THE SEVENTEEN HUNDREDS

Spain had entered a long period of decline by the end of the sixteenth century. The opening of the eighteenth century turned Spain into a crucial source of political struggle in Europe. The War of the Spanish Succession (1701–1714) might reasonably be called a world war. It not only involved many European powers, including Spain, Italy, Germany, Holland, France, England, and others, fighting in military theaters throughout Europe, but also involved extensive naval engagements at sea. The immediate cause of the war was the death of Spain's Charles II without an heir. Charles willed the crown to Philip of Anjou, the grandson of France's Louis XIV. The French and the Spaniards agreed to make Philip king and to unite France and Spain. Such a union represented a threat to the security of virtually all other European monarchs.

The intention of making Philip of Anjou king of a united Spain and France prompted an alliance between England, Holland, Prussia, and Austria. The alliance backed the Archduke Charles of Austria for the Spanish crown. War followed and with it numerous French defeats. However, in 1711, the Austrian emperor Joseph I died and Archduke Charles of Austria succeeded him as the new Holy Roman Emperor. With Charles now Holy Roman Emperor, the alliance became concerned lest Austria hold too much power if Charles also secured the throne in Spain. With Charles in his new position, the threat that the Habsburgs would once again secure their domination over European politics led the other alliance partners to reach a compromise with the French.

The Treaty of Utrecht (1713) ended the war. Philip became king of Spain; the French and Spaniards agreed never to unite; Great Britain secured control over Gibraltar, Newfoundland, Nova Scotia, the Hudson Bay Territories, and a monopoly over the slave trade in Latin America. The Treaty of Utrecht imposed limitations on France's designs for greater power in Europe, prevented further expansion of Habsburg influence, and greatly improved Britain's prospects for political ascendancy.

Almost inevitably, the aftermath of the War of the Spanish Succession saw an increase in tensions between France and the Great Britain. These two powers fought each other in the Seven Years' War in Europe and in the associated British-French War

(1754–1763) in the Americas. The British-French War culminated in England taking control over the Ohio Valley and forging close ties with American Indian tribes. Recognition by Britain of Native American tribes threatened the interests in land speculation in the Ohio Valley by American colonists, including many of American's founders. The aftermath of the war helped contribute to tensions between the American colonists and England while also promoting closer ties between the colonists and France. It was, as well, in this war that George Washington first attracted attention as a military leader.

Although the war in the Americas later turned out to have profound consequences for world history, the main action in the Seven Years' War at the time was perceived to be in Europe. That is, the decision makers of the day did not foresee—how could they?—that the "side-show" in the Americas would eventually become fundamental to world events. This is a good reminder that decisions can only be judged based on what decision makers know and believe at the time they choose, and not based on what we come to know later. In Europe, France, Austria, and Russia fought against Britain and Prussia. Among its many consequences, the Seven Years' War led to the emergence of Prussia under Frederick the Great as a major European power. It also was instrumental in the establishment of the Great Britain (created out of England, Wales, and Scotland by an act of Parliament in 1707) as the leader in global colonization. Prussia, of course, remained a major force in European affairs, eventually defeating Austria in the Seven Weeks' War (1866) that gave rise to the modern conception of Germany.

The Seven Years' War and its accompanying battles in North America cost the British government dearly. In an effort to recoup its costs, the English Crown launched new, aggressive tax policies, including the infamous stamp tax in the American colonies. Once again, monarchy led to an effort to make people pay for policies they had not endorsed. Harking back to a principle established by England's Edward I in 1297 when he signed *Confirmatio Cartarum* to gain economic support for a war he wanted to fight in Gascony (France), the colonists cried out against taxation without representation, a refrain then also in common use among anti-English factions in Ireland. All English subjects in principle had the right to refuse a tax levied by the Crown. Gradually, colonial resentment and British ineptitude escalated into an urge for independence, leading to the Declaration of Independence in 1776. War followed with the colonists performing poorly against the better trained and better equipped British troops. However, the war took a favorable turn for the would-be Americans when a large French fleet aided in defeating the British. The British unequivocally accepted American independence when they signed the Treaty of Paris in 1783.

The early American government floundered as it struggled to formulate a workable government among the original colonies while also finding a way to capitalize on international trade in a world in which the British kept American ships out of British-controlled ports. From this early stage of development, when America still was a poor, dependent, "third-world" backwater, its potential as a seafaring power and the opportunities for trade encouraged a strong free-trade, antiprotectionism attitude among its early leaders. Building on the writings of Locke, Hume, and others, this country's founders crafted the American Constitution and with it a dramatic new experiment in democratic, republican rule in which merit rather than aristocracy was to be the cornerstone of a person's progress through life. To be sure, reality was much more checkered than the rhetoric of the day, but still, the American experiment in governance reflected a dramatic departure from absolute, hereditary monarchy and its confiscatory tax policies. Slavery remained an issue of contention, being one of the important factors that led to the creation of a federal structure of government. Eventually the federal bargain would unravel, leading to the American Civil War (1861–1865) nearly a century later.

Not long after the success of the American revolutionaries, Europe itself experienced a major assault on the dominance of monarchy as the primary means of government. England was already well on the way to a form of constitutional monarchy when the French Revolution shook the world. The French Revolution overthrew the monarchy and proclaimed a republic based on the ideas of liberty, fraternity, and equality; that is, just the opposite orientation of monarchic institutions. The Reign of Terror followed

*This cartoon illustrates the changes in the French social order prior to the French Revolution. The first panel shows the improved condition of the peasants and their hopes for a better way of life. In the second panel, the aristocracy, clergy, and peasantry unite in supposed equality. The actual dismal situation of the peasantry is shown in the last panel. By the end of the French Revolution, tens of thousands from all social levels had been executed. The government was in disarray, which led to the rise of a new emperor, Napoleon Bonaparte.*

in which thousands of French aristocrats and ordinary French citizens were beheaded as the new leadership sought to remove the vestiges of nobility and inequality from French rule. The French revolutionaries fought one another from within, failed to put together a well-structured government, and led the country into chaos. In 1795, Napoleon succeeded in seizing political control, and France drifted from republic to imperial power.

## THE EIGHTEEN HUNDREDS

Europe was embroiled in the Napoleonic Wars from 1795 to 1815, with Napoleon having himself declared emperor in 1804. Napoleon's army—using the first universal military training system—swept across Europe and North Africa. In 1802 he agreed to the Peace of Amiens, in which Great Britain surrendered many of its colonial holdings to France in exchange for the French agreeing to withdraw from Egypt. By 1805 Napoleon suffered a serious setback when his navy was defeated at the Battle of Trafalgar, marking the end of France's threat to invade England. A year later, in 1806, the Prussians were defeated at the Battle of Jena, resulting in Prussia's loss of its Polish territories, a matter that became a fundamental issue for Hitler's Germany at the outset of World War II. Napoleon himself was finally defeated at the Battle of Waterloo in 1815 and sent into exile, where he died or, more likely, was murdered by poisoning.

Napoleon's conquests left an indelible mark on Europe. He helped rationalize governance in much of Europe while imposing the Napoleonic code of law. Even today one can find the influence of French law in significant parts of Europe and in Louisiana in the United States because of Napoleon's conquests. Following his defeat, the victors, including Austria, Great Britain, Prussia, and Russia, created the Concert of Europe to coordinate foreign policy among the great powers in the hopes of preventing a future Napoleon from jeopardizing sovereign control in Europe's states. Among the more dramatic actions taken by the Concert of Europe, forged at the Congress of Vienna, the victors agreed to restore the French monarchy and bring France back in as one of the great powers. Meanwhile, the revolutionary storm unleashed at the end of the seventeen hundreds continued largely unabated.

Efforts to topple monarchy and establish more popular government arose in 1830 and again in 1848 as dissident youths and others took to the barricades. Although these movements failed, they planted the seeds for sharp changes in the years to come. In England, the monarch was increasingly a constitutional figurehead, and the prime minister and Parliament were the growing seats of power. By 1835 Britain adopted a voting rights act that made it clearly into a constitutional monarchy—a new form of government—in which the House of Commons was the source of political power. During this same period, English domination of the seas was unquestioned and British banking was fundamental to the colonial and other ambitions of much of Europe. The nineteenth century marked the peak of British colonial power, especially in India, elsewhere in Asia, and in Africa.

England surged far ahead of its competitors for several reasons. Britain, as an island-nation, developed superior naval capabilities to foster and support its colonial holdings and to secure its borders against foreign threats. Additionally, the industrial revolution took place in Britain earlier than on the European continent, in large measure because of the greater responsiveness to entrepreneurial ideas and land enclosures that rationalized agriculture in England. Also, England had a stronger orientation toward relatively free trade than did France and others. This orientation promoted greater competitiveness in English industry, promoting more efficiency and more rapid economic growth.

The English quest for new goods and new markets helped fuel its imperial ambitions. Between 1839 and 1842, for instance, Britain fought China in the Opium War that arose out of China's efforts to prevent Britain from importing opium into China from Britain's colony in India. The British won the war, ended by the unequal Treaty of Nanking. Under the terms of this treaty, Britain obtained control over several Chinese ports, including Hong Kong, which it returned to China on July 1, 1997, upon the expiration of its lease over that territory. The English also gained special privileges and legal protections in China. The Chinese received little in return, hence the term "unequal treaty." Unequal French and American treaties with China followed soon thereafter, solidifying the era of imperial expansion.

As part of its expansionist designs, the United States fought Mexico in the Mexican-American War (1846–1848). The United States established the Rio Grande as its border with Mexico and secured ownership over vast territories through purchase (the Louisiana Purchase) and through conquest, including Texas, California, and the present-day plains states. These states were taken from the sovereign Native American tribes of those areas. American expansionism was not wholly confined, however, to the North American continent. In 1854, American naval ships forced the shogun-led Japanese military government to open Japan's ports to American trade. By 1867, internal dissent within Japan led to the resignation of the shogun, the end of the shogunate's over 250-year rule, and the reassertion of the emperor's role as the primary leader of Japan. The Meiji Restoration of 1868 allowed Emperor Mutsuhito to reassert the emperor's traditional powers that had lapsed during the shogun period. This led for a time to a more pro-Western orientation and an effort in Japan to adapt to Western ideas and business practices. However, the military party gained substantial influence in Japan's newly created parliament in 1878. The military opposed European ideas, favoring instead Japan's own role as an expansionist, imperial power. The party encouraged Japan to pursue expansion onto the Asian continent. This led, in turn, to the Sino-Japanese War of 1894 and the Russo-Japanese War a decade later. With these two wars, Japan established itself as a significant political power in Asia, taking control of substantial portions of China and Korea. Japanese expansionist ambitions in Asia continued until its defeat in World War II.

Meanwhile, on the European continent, the struggle to control Europe's destiny continued. Otto von Bismarck first succeeded in unifying Prussia with several smaller German princely states during the Seven Weeks' War (1866), in which, to the surprise of most European leaders, he quickly, easily, and successfully defeated Austria. This war marked the end of the Concert of Europe system that had been forged half a century earlier in the wake of Napoleon's defeat. Austria, at risk of losing its status as a major power, was forced to accept an arrangement with Hungary that resulted in the creation of the Austro-Hungarian Empire to try to shore up its declining political position relative to Prussia. Just four years later, Bismarck went to war against France, defeating Napoleon III in the Franco-Prussian War of 1870–1871. With France's defeat, Bismarck succeeded in unifying the remaining German princely states, creating modern-day Germany. He also established Prussia/Germany as the rising power of Europe and France as a state in decline. This set the stage for the two world wars of the twentieth century.

*The Sino-Japanese War (1894–1895) represented Japan's first effort to become an imperial power and demonstrated the extent to which control over government had fallen into the hands of the military following Japan's "opening" to the West three decades earlier. During the war, artists prepared drawings of great battles for use in newspaper and magazine stories. This image of a Chinese battleship being sunk in the Yellow Sea was possibly drawn—as was common at the time—even before the relevant naval battle took place. These pictures were designed to inspire national fervor for the heroic exploits of the Japanese navy.*

The nineteenth century was not only a time of continental expansion for America and a time when it began to spread its influence abroad, but it was also a period of rapid economic growth and the establishment of the United States as a transcontinental power. Following the American Civil War, the United States incorporated vast territories as new states. With the building of the transcontinental railroad, the U.S. government made it possible to control its continental territory and provided a cheap and fast means to transport people and goods across the continent. Likewise, the construction of the Panama Canal greatly stimulated commerce between the East Coast of the United States and the West Coast and beyond, shortening the time and cost of shipping goods between ports on the Atlantic and Pacific Oceans. By the end of the nineteenth century, the United States was actively engaged as a colonial power, gaining influence in the Philippines and Cuba as a result of America's defeat of Spain in the Spanish-American War. The United States was well on the way to supplanting Britain as the richest country in the world.

MAP 1-3

**U.S., British, and Japanese Colonialism, circa 1900**

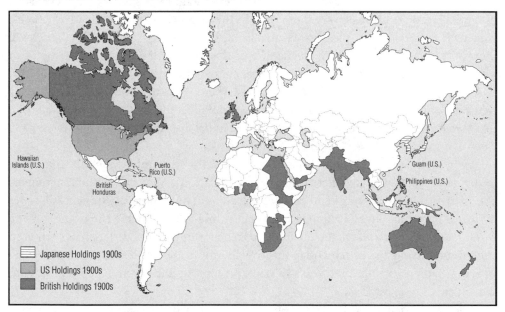

*The impulse for colonial expansion was especially strong in the eighteenth and nineteenth centuries. By the beginning of the twentieth century, colonialism was starting to wane, with the Americas almost completely liberated from their eighteenth-century rulers. Nevertheless, colonialism remained an important feature of foreign policy and economic expansion until the end of World War II. Although old colonial ties remain strong indicators of current economic relations among European and non-European states, little of the world remains under the control of foreign "hosts" today.*

## THE TWENTIETH CENTURY

The centuries between the fifteenth and the seventeenth witnessed the consolidation and gradual decline of monarchy. The eighteenth and nineteenth centuries were, broadly speaking, a period in which those who adopted more democratic forms of government and more capitalist modes of economics enjoyed burgeoning wealth and influence in the world. Some changes were to the good—as in the expansion of rule of law and improvement in living conditions—and some involved the imposition of colonial rule on people who fought for and preferred to pursue their own destinies. Many of these centuries-old patterns culminated in dramatic global changes during the twentieth century.

Revolutions against monarchy and oligarchy arose in Russia in 1905 and China in 1911. Mexico likewise gave birth to a popular revolution seeking to overthrow oligarchy. By 1914, tensions between the expansionist designs of the Austro-Hungarian Empire in Europe and Serbian nationalism led to a seemingly minor tragic event, the assassination of the prospective heir to the Austro-Hungarian throne, Archduke Franz Ferdinand in Sarajevo, Serbia. Following the assassination, Austria issued an ultimatum to the Serbian government that essentially called for the Serbs to give up their sovereignty. As tensions mounted, Europe's great powers chose sides in the dispute. Russia sided with the Serbs. Under the terms of the Triple Entente, an alliance between Russia, France, and England, those states also took sides with Russia. Under the terms of the Dual Alliance between Germany and Austria, those two great powers backed one another, with additional support coming from Romania, Turkey, and elsewhere. Fearing an aggressive move by Germany, the Russians mobilized, prompting a mobilization by Germany as well. In a short time, the conflict over Serbia had escalated to involve all of the great powers on the Continent, and World War I had begun.

Fought between 1914 and 1918, the war greatly accelerated political change in Europe and fundamentally altered international relations. About nine million combatants died during World War I and perhaps at least as many civilians (although still fewer than died in the Taiping Rebellion in China in the mid-1860s). By the end of the war, the world had experienced its first truly modern trench warfare. Gas warfare had been used effectively, raising the specter that future war would be nonconventional. Modern weapons had greatly increased war's carnage, prompting intense efforts to find ways to avert such a future cataclysm.

The war ended with the Treaty of Versailles imposing harsh terms on Germany, including a tremendous economic burden by way of reparation payments to help France and others recuperate from the costs of the war. One consequence of the war's end was that the map of Europe was redrawn. The Austro-Hungarian Empire ceased to exist, being replaced by independent countries carved out of its territory. Germany was greatly weakened, but so too were the victors, especially England, France, and Russia. The United States, under President Woodrow Wilson, emerged as the most powerful nation in the world. Wilson's Fourteen Points called for a major transformation in international politics. In an effort to prevent a future Great War, as World War I was then called, the victors created the League of Nations to maintain peace through collective security. The United States, however, seeking to return to a role of isolation, did not join the League, ensuring that it would lack the teeth necessary to play a major role as a peacekeeper.

One of the tenets promoted by Woodrow Wilson in his Fourteen Points was the idea that people should be free to choose their own government, thereby helping seal the terminal fate of monarchy and advancing Wilson's objective of making the world safe for democracy. Unfortunately, Wilson did not endorse the idea that self-determination should necessarily carry over right away into colonial areas. One of those dejected by that failure of the Treaty of Versailles at the time was a young man named Ho Chi Minh, who later emerged as the leader of North Vietnam. He led the Vietnamese wars against the French and then the Americans in Indochina and Vietnam throughout the 1950s, 1960s, and into the 1970s, in part for that right of self-determination. Regrettably, in the process he imposed communist rule in Vietnam with its attendant dictatorship and oppression of the very principle of self-determination that he at one time advocated. To this day, the Vietnamese people do not have the right to freely elect their own government.

World War I imposed extreme costs on the tsarist regime in Russia. By 1917 the tsar's government faced revolution. The Russian Revolution succeeded in overthrowing the monarchy and led briefly to a liberal, democratic government. That government, however, was weak and unable to consolidate its power when faced with a challenge by Lenin's Bolsheviks. Between 1917 and 1922 Lenin converted Russia into a Soviet Republic with a socialist government led by the Communist Party as the vanguard of the proletariat. This meant that ordinary people would have little if any say in government because (according to the communist regime) they were susceptible to bourgeois influence and suffered from a trade-union mentality that did not allow them to see the big picture of the hypothesized shared self-interest of working people everywhere. Therefore, decisions would be centered in the hands of the elite in the Communist Party, they being the vanguard of the proletariat who understood the proper path to socialism.

The Russian Revolution launched a bold experiment in the application of Karl Marx's and Friedrich Engel's ideas of communism as an alternative to capitalism. The communist economic ideal was that each would contribute to society according to his or her ability and each would receive whatever was needed from society in return. Many people saw the ideas of communism as the likely long-term successor to monarchy—then in its final death throes—and to liberal democracy. Communism seemed to combine an integrated view of economics and politics that promoted equality on both fronts. As appealing as the ideal may have seemed, it was an utter failure in practice as a basis for economics or politics. Faced with few incentives to be productive—since what people received from the state was not supposed to depend on what they produced—people shirked, trying to benefit from the labor of others (called free riding) while doing little themselves. Like monarchy before it, communism/socialism unintentionally discouraged people from hard, productive labor because they were not rewarded in proportion to their effort. Those who did work hard were, in essence, subjected to the confiscation of their earnings to support others who did not work hard. Thus, communism, like monarchy, hampered economic growth and prosperity for the common people.

Because the communist political system was grounded in such beliefs as the existence of common interests among all working people, dissent among workers could not be tolerated. Thus, Lenin established the Communist Party as the vanguard of the proletariat to protect against the risk that ignorant and impressionable workers—the proletariat—would undermine his revolutionary objectives. The difficulty was that communism assumed that an entire class of people—workers—necessarily shared the same preferences about domestic and foreign policies. When Lenin observed that the proletariat did not act as if all of its members shared a common core set of preferences, it became necessary to stifle their opportunity to express dissent. The result was that the political system naturally lapsed into dictatorship as the economy languished in the absence of individual incentives to produce. These problems, already manifest by the early 1920s, became much worse following Lenin's death. Josef Stalin replaced Lenin and gradually converted the Soviet system into a personal dictatorship. He did so by purging anyone and everyone he even suspected of disagreeing with him. Almost all of the top political leaders were branded as enemies of the people and executed during the latter part of the 1930s. Stalin likewise created a man-made famine in the Ukraine, leading to the deaths of millions of people he feared were disloyal to him. Stalin, like absolute monarchs before him, became answerable to only a handful of people whose support was needed to maintain him in power.

While the communist movement took hold in Russia after World War I, fascism rose as another alternative to monarchy in Italy under Mussolini starting in 1922 and in Germany under Hitler from 1933 onward. Fascism, like communism, gave rise to harsh dictatorships with no respect for rule of law or for individual rights. The extreme economic circumstances in Germany after World War I provided the impetus for dictatorship to replace Germany's democratic Weimar Republic. With the onset of the Great Depression in America and across Europe in 1929, the global economy went into a tailspin. Germany was unable to make war reparation payments, millions were out of work, global trade collapsed, and the German currency was all but worthless. In this atmosphere, Adolf Hitler and his followers gained popularity, winning seats in the Reichstag, the German parliament. Hitler quickly converted early electoral success into burgeoning political influence and, through shrewd maneuvering, saw himself elevated to the post of chancellor of Germany. Once he reached this position, Hitler suspended democratic elections and never again allowed himself or his National Socialist Workers Party (the Nazi Party) to face the will of the people. He might well have done so, however, because by all appearances he was incredibly popular as he rebuilt Germany's military might and standing in Europe.

Germany had been banned from rebuilding its military after World War I under the terms of the Treaty of Versailles. Nevertheless, Hitler went ahead and did so in the 1930s and then used the German military to reoccupy land given up at the end of the war. Seeing that he could get away with his actions, he became emboldened. At Munich in 1938 Hitler struck a deal with Britain's prime minister, Neville Chamberlain, by which Hitler could take over parts of Czechoslovakia. Chamberlain's appeasement of Hitler was warmly welcomed in Britain at the time. However, when Hitler then attacked Poland in September 1939, the British realized that Hitler's declaration that he had "no more territorial claims in Europe" was a lie. Winston Churchill emerged as the new prime minister, and England declared war on Germany immediately following the September 1, 1939, German invasion of Poland. The French and others also quickly joined in the war against Germany.

Russia, however, was not among the Allied powers declaring war on Germany. Under the terms of the Molotov-Ribbentrop Pact, signed in the summer of 1939, Stalin's Soviet Union and Hitler's Germany were allies. They had agreed to the partition of Poland, with some of Poland going to Germany and other parts to Russia. Remarkably, anticommunist Germany and ostensibly antifascist Russia joined in a common cause. That common interest, however, was broken when Hitler later invaded the Soviet Union, pushing Stalin into a wartime alliance with the British, French, and Americans.

Although there is speculation that President Franklin D. Roosevelt wanted to enter the war on Britain's side almost from the outset, the United States remained militarily aloof from the war in Europe, working on its own domestic economic problems until Japan bombed Hawaii's naval base at Pearl Harbor on December 7, 1941. Before that moment, American war policy largely consisted of providing substantial economic assistance to England (called lend-lease) but no military contingents or commitment. The British prime minister, Winston Churchill, in one eloquent speech after another during those dark days of 1940 and 1941, following the defeat of France, Belgium, and the Netherlands by Germany, reiterated at every opportunity that England stood alone in defense of freedom and democracy. By the beginning of 1942, however, the United States was fully committed to the war effort in Europe and Asia.

Prior to the attack on Pearl Harbor, Japan's expansionist ambitions in Asia were being thwarted by an American trade embargo imposed by President Roosevelt. In a daring decision, the Japanese leaders concluded that their best chance of prevailing in Asia depended on removing the latent threat that the United States would enter the war to stop them. They concluded that if they could cripple the American navy, then they could take control of essential areas in Asia before the United States could rebuild and mount a counterattack. The Japanese hope was that if they realized their ambitions, the United States would see it as a fait accompli and live with the consequences rather than fight a costly, protracted war. By bombing Pearl Harbor, the Japanese hoped to wipe out the American Pacific Fleet and achieve their objectives. They failed and, as they themselves anticipated, the consequence of that failure was a high probability of subsequent defeat in the war.

With the United States fully committed to the war effort, its economy began to expand rapidly and the Great Depression began to fade into the past. America's industrial capacity was unmatched by Japan or by Germany and its ally Italy, even after taking into account the capabilities of the huge areas conquered by the German army or the millions of slave workers and prisoners who were forced to labor on behalf of Germany's war effort. With intense military pressure from Russia in the east and from the Americans, British, Free French, Polish expatriates, and others in the West, the tide of battle turned against Germany. Likewise, in the Pacific, America's naval victory at Midway destroyed so much of the Japanese fleet that the war in Asia also turned in favor of American interests. In June 1945, Hitler's Germany lay in ruins and accepted an unconditional surrender. Mussolini's Italy had been beaten earlier as the Italian people themselves overthrew their dictator and joined the Allied side. In August 1945, Japan, having continued to fight, was compelled to surrender following the American atomic bombings of Hiroshima and Nagasaki, announcing the arrival of the nuclear age. Japan's surrender, unlike Germany's, was not completely unconditional. Japan was allowed to retain its emperor.

World War II was the deadliest conflict in all of history. Tens of millions died, including twenty million Russians. Approximately six million Jews were murdered in Germany's concentration camps, eliminating almost all of Europe's Jewry. Additionally, the Nazis singled out gypsies, homosexuals, communists, Slavs, and other groups for extermination. Despite overwhelming evidence that such exterminations were taking place, few countries willingly provided homes for those seeking refuge from Nazi-dominated Europe. Only Mexico and the Dominican Republic, for instance, unconditionally opened their doors to Jews fleeing Europe. The United States maintained strict immigration quotas, even turning ships of refugees back to Europe and to certain death. The Swiss government, ostensibly neutral throughout the war, likewise refused to provide a safe haven for those fleeing the murderous policies of the Nazi regime.

By 1945 it was evident that the Nazis would lose and so planning for the postwar world began. The negotiations among the British, Americans, and Russians at Yalta and then Potsdam as the European war drew to a close established some principles that were intended to guide the postwar world. Most of Eastern Europe, having been liberated from the Nazis by the Soviet army, fell under Soviet control. Stalin's government quickly imposed communist dictatorships. Germany was partitioned, with portions controlled by the United States, France, England, and the Soviet Union. Sovereignty was restored in Western Europe to all of the countries that had previously been subjugated by Germany during the war, and these states went about the business of holding competitive elections to choose their own leaders. In the parts of Germany not controlled by the Soviet Union; that is, in what came to be called West Germany, a new constitution was written creating a democratic government with competitive elections, civil liberties, rule of law, and the like. The United States similarly helped write a democratic constitution for Japan and helped put that country on the way to a liberal, democratic society.

At the end of World War II, the United States was by far the most powerful and richest country in the world. While much of the rest of the world's economy lay in the ruins of war the American economy was thriving. In an effort to resuscitate the global economy, the United States launched the Marshall Plan that helped rebuild Europe. Although such assistance was also offered to the Soviet Union, it refused. Through the establishment of the Bretton Woods monetary system, discussed later, and the creation of the United Nations, the United States and its allies attempted to erect a sound economic and security framework for the postwar world. The United Nations was designed around two main bodies for dealing with fundamental matters, the General Assembly and the Security Council. The former contains representation from every member country. The latter is a smaller body that is the key United Nations instrument for addressing threats to peace. The Security Council is made up of rotating seats and five permanent seats. The permanent members—the United States, Russia, France, England, and China—each has a veto. This means that the United Nations cannot intervene in a security matter if intervention is opposed by any of these five states.

Severe cracks in cooperation among the war's victors emerged within two years of the end of the war. By 1947 it was evident that the Soviet Union would not continue as a cooperative ally working with the United States, Britain, France, and others. In 1946, Soviet tanks gathered on Iran's border, threatening to overrun that country. A quick response by the United States prevented the spread of Soviet influence to that oil-rich and strategically located country. Two years later, in 1948, Stalin stopped allowing Allied trucks to enter the western sector of Berlin, thereby cutting the city off from supplies. The city of Berlin, like all of Germany, had been partitioned at the war's end. Berlin, however, was an enclave surrounded by East Germany. President Harry S. Truman stood up to the Soviet threat by creating an airlift that supplied the people of Berlin with their needs. The Soviets backed down and once again allowed truck traffic from the West into Berlin. By now it was clear that a cold war (approximately from 1947 to 1989) had emerged between the United States and its Western European allies on the one hand and the Soviet Union and its allies on the other.

The rift between communism and capitalism, between dictatorship and democracy, grew worse with the victory of China's communists under Mao Zedong over the autocratic Kuomintang government. The latter retreated from China's mainland to Taiwan, where it created the Republic of China and where, after decades of autocratic rule, it has now created a democracy with a thriving economy. The People's Republic of China, for its part, continues to claim Taiwan as a rebellious province and does not recognize the government on Taiwan as a sovereign state. The mainland of China fell far behind Taiwan in economic performance, although the economy of China proper has grown at an impressive annual rate since about 1979, when Deng Xiaoping, then China's leader, introduced economic reforms. China, however, persists as one of the world's more autocratic regimes, remaining far behind Taiwan in the development of democratic government. The cold war turned hot between 1950 and 1953 following North Korea's invasion of South Korea. Korea had been divided between communist North Korea and autocratic, anticommunist South Korea following World War II. China pitched in to help the North Koreans. The United States and others, under the auspices of the United Nations, intervened to push the North Koreans and China back above the 38th parallel, the previously established line of partition. The Korean War ended in 1953 with the reestablishment of the prewar line of partition, but American troops have remained stationed in South Korea since then to help ensure that the North does not again attempt to invade the South. In the meantime, North Korea grew into one of the most reclusive, secretive, and heavily militarized regimes in the world. South Korea has moved from autocracy to democracy and it has experienced extraordinary economic growth. While the North and South Korean people had comparable per capita incomes in the 1950s, today the people of the South enjoy a per capita income that may be as much as ten times larger than that in the North.

Partially in response to pressures unleashed by World War II and partially because of political pressure brought to bear by the anticolonial rhetoric of the Soviet Union, the years following the war experienced a tremendous proliferation in national liberation and decolonization. Britain agreed to quit India and create independent Indian and Pakistani states at the end of the 1940s. Likewise, under extreme pressure from fighters within Palestine, Britain gave up its control in that part of the world, leading to the creation of the state of Israel. The bloody war that followed between Israelis and Palestinians persists as one of the most dangerous conflicts in the world.

The 1950s and early 1960s saw much of Africa freed of its colonial "masters." Tragically, few of the liberated colonies of Africa, following their struggles against colonialism, emerged as successful states that promote the welfare of their own citizens. Instead, most

*Two Congolese tribal chiefs come to the capital city of Leopoldville on June 8, 1960, to elect nine chiefs to the Leopoldville provincial council for terms beginning after independence from Belgium takes effect on June 30. Despite a promising beginning, the Congo, like most other former colonies in Africa, soon abandoned democracy for a despotic and kleptocratic government in which the rulers stole the wealth of the state and left the people in misery and oppression.*

have become petty dictatorships dominated by corrupt bureaucrats and "kleptocratic" leaders who seem more inclined to take national wealth and foreign aid and channel it into personal bank accounts than to spend it on national programs to stimulate economic and social well-being.

By the 1960s the United States and the Soviet Union seemed to be making progress toward a long-term means of living with each other. The development of nuclear weapons and intercontinental missiles had created an environment of mutual assured destruction (MAD) in which each side feared that a conflict with the other could expand into a war that would leave the earth in ruins. Probably the major turning point toward a modus vivendi followed the Cuban Missile Crisis in October 1962. With Soviet influence having spread to Cuba through Fidel Castro's successful communist revolution, the United States under President John F. Kennedy made an effort to topple the Cuban regime. The American-planned and American-sponsored Bay of Pigs invasion was intended as a Cuban expatriate invasion of Cuba that would foment a popular uprising. It failed to do so, but it did prompt the government of Nikita Khrushchev in the Soviet Union to further strengthen its ties to Castro. One manifestation of those strengthened ties was that the Soviet Union sought to use Cuba as a place in which it could put missiles to threaten the United States (and other countries in Latin America). Once the effort to put Soviet missiles in Cuba was uncovered by reconnaissance photographs, Kennedy called for their removal and emphasized that there was a grave danger of nuclear war if the missiles were not removed. After two weeks of severe tension, including an American naval blockade of Cuba, the Soviet Union agreed to remove the missiles, and Kennedy promised not to invade Cuba and secretly agreed to remove American missiles from Turkey. After the crisis was resolved it became apparent that the two nuclear superpowers needed to find a way to coexist.

The prospects of peaceful coexistence improved during Richard M. Nixon's presidency when the United States and the Soviet Union adopted a policy of détente toward one another. Arms control agreements were negotiated. The Vietnam War (1965–1973) between the United States and North Vietnam ended in an American withdrawal and subsequent defeat of the South by America's adversaries in North Vietnam, but at least this irritant to Soviet-American relations was removed. Meanwhile, President Nixon and his secretary of state Henry Kissinger began a dialog with China that eventually led to renewed contacts and diplomatic relations after decades of estrangement following the post–World War II Chinese Revolution. Likewise, after the 1967 and 1973 Arab-Israeli wars, Nixon and Kissinger helped encourage Egypt's President Anwar Sadat to make a significant peace overture to Israel.

Sadat offered to visit Jerusalem and make peace with Israel. Menachem Begin, then the Israeli prime minister, and Sadat took courageous steps that culminated in the Camp David Accord brokered with the help of President Jimmy Carter in 1979. Since then, the Israelis and Egyptians have maintained diplomatic relations, and Egypt, along with Israel, receives substantial American foreign aid. Despite the peace agreement between the two, however, relations between Israel and Egypt are cool because the successor to the assassinated Anwar Sadat, Hosni Mubarak, has done little to promote improved relations between his country and Israel.

At roughly the same time that the United States was helping build a peace settlement between Israel and Egypt, the Soviet Union broke with détente by invading Afghanistan in 1979. President Carter, declaring himself surprised by the Soviet move, reduced trade with the Soviet Union and cooled relations. The year 1979 saw other momentous events, including the overthrow of the shah of Iran by a fundamentalist Muslim movement led by Ayatollah Khomeini. Near the end of 1979, the American embassy staff in Tehran, Iran, was taken hostage in a gross breach of international law and diplomatic conduct. The Americans were held hostage for more than a year, being released at the time of Ronald Reagan's inauguration as president of the United States. Relations between the United States and Iran have remained strained since. The Iranian revolution marked the

*The boundaries that define the beginning and end of international events can be hard to discern. For many, when the Berlin Wall was torn down it was evident that the cold war was over. Some saw this event as the natural conse-quence of Gorbachev's reform program. Others viewed Reagan's huge defense expenditures in the 1980s as the fac-tor that precipitated the end of the cold war by forcing the Soviets to choose between reform or eventual bankrupt-cy. A case can also be made that the 1975 Helsinki Accords hastened the end of the cold war. Pictured above are Soviet premier Leonid Brezhnev and U.S. president Gerald Ford after signing the Helsinki Accords. In exchange for Western recognition of the sovereignty of East Germany, the Soviets agreed to allow the international community to monitor human rights in the Soviet Union and Eastern Europe. This right legitimized the Solidarity movement in Poland and external pressure for reform on the Soviets and their allies. Perhaps Helsinki provided just enough of an opportunity to force the hands of the Soviets and to end the cold war fifteen years later.*

beginning of the current era of fundamentalist Islamic contention throughout the Muslim world. This continues to be one of the central sources of international dispute and friction in the Middle East, Asia Minor, western China, and in Indonesia, Malaysia, and elsewhere in Asia.

When Ronald Reagan became president in 1981 he implemented a massive military spending program that was, at least in part, designed to force the Soviet government to choose between continued competition and potential economic collapse or fundamental policy change. The Strategic Defense Initiative (Star Wars as it came to be called) was also intended to put the Soviet Union on notice that the United States would no longer live within the confines of the old policy of mutual assured destruction. Rather, the United States under Reagan sought the means to keep the American people secure by neutralizing the threat of a ballistic missile attack. While these pressures mounted so too did internal pressure for change throughout Eastern Europe. The Soviets agreed to the Helsinki Final Act in 1975 by which the United States recognized the sovereignty of East Germany and acknowledged as permanent the partition of Germany that ended World War II. In exchange, the Soviets recognized West Germany and agreed to planks regarding human rights and the authority of watchdog groups to report on human rights violations throughout the Soviet Union and Eastern Europe. These groups and the legitimacy of such reportage fostered by Helsinki paved the way for antigovernment uprisings in Eastern Europe. The Solidarity trade union movement in Poland, for instance, was emboldened by the publicity ensured through Helsinki as well as by the positive attitude toward change supported by the Polish pope John Paul II.

As Leonid Brezhnev and his short-lived Soviet successors passed from the scene, the Soviet Union underwent dramatic internal changes. Mikhail Gorbachev took over the government and soon thereafter launched a program of economic reform and liberalization of the Soviet hold over its East European empire. By 1988 British prime minister Margaret Thatcher, reacting to the dramatic changes taking place in the Soviet bloc, declared that the cold war was over. In 1989 the Berlin Wall, the prime symbol of Soviet oppression in Europe, was torn down and within two years after that the Soviet Union no longer existed. The American-Soviet rivalry that had defined the years between 1945 and 1990 was replaced by resurgent American influence around the world, a surge in democratization all over the globe, and a rapid shift to market-based economies and away from state-planned socialism.

The last decade of the twentieth century saw efforts to define a new world order. The end of the cold war removed many of the restraints that had held smaller prospective conflicts in check out of fear of exacerbating U.S.-Soviet relations. With the Soviet Union out of the picture, war erupted in the Persian Gulf and in numerous pockets of ethnic rivalry throughout Eastern Europe, but most notably in Chechnya, Bosnia, Kosovo, and other parts of the former Yugoslavia. At this writing, these and other rivalries—most notably the War on Terrorism—persist as indicators that the tectonic plates of international affairs are still shifting and feeling the aftershocks of the end of the cold war. In counterpoint to these conflicts, the cold war's end has also fostered new arenas of cooperation. Russia, the successor state to the Soviet Union, for example, is now a partner of the North Atlantic Treaty Organization (NATO). NATO was originally formed to help contain the Soviet Union, yet today, close ties of cooperation appear to be emerging between the United States, western Europe, and Russia.

This brief overview of history provides a useful backdrop against which to think about international politics. International politics is not the product of randomly emerging events. As I have tried to make clear, events are the product of patterns of choices made by decision makers responding to and creating new circumstances in the international arena. The next chapter provides some ground rules to help guide our thinking about facts and events.

CHAPTER 2

# EVALUATING ARGUMENTS ABOUT INTERNATIONAL POLITICS

## THEORIES AS SIMPLIFICATIONS OF REALITY

History provides a description of reality, whereas theories provide prospective explanations of reality. All theories offer simplified representations of the facts that collectively make up what we think of as reality. Each theory simplifies in its own way what we know and believe. Theorizing about international politics is important in part because reality is much too complex to be made comprehensible without some form of simplification. Neither history nor current events can be understood as the totality of all the factors that go into defining a past or current circumstance.

This chapter develops rules for selecting among competing explanations and evidence so that we form a shared basis for judging facts as evidence. By using the scientific guidelines set out in this chapter, you will be able to evaluate the logic and evidence for alternative explanations of international relations. We will draw distinctions between assumptions and hypotheses. We will distinguish between the empirical accuracy of hypotheses and assumptions and become familiar with the "first principle of wing-walking" as a guideline for choosing among competing theories. The distinctions made here are fairly abstract, but they nevertheless constitute the basis for applying the scientific method to international affairs.

Policymakers cannot make decisions and implement policies with hindsight, although they can draw on lessons from the past. When they act, they must do so on the basis of the information at hand at the time they choose a course of action. This means that they—and we, as students of politics—need to understand how to make choices while still in the dark about how things will turn out. And that means having some way to evaluate arguments and evidence before results can be known.

As noted in Chapter 1, our understanding of arguments and evidence about international relations depends both on facts and theoretical perspective. Some people seem to think that knowing the facts is all that is necessary to explain adequately what has happened in history or what will happen in the future (Skocpol 1984; Ragin and Becker 1992). Such a viewpoint discourages interest in perspective or theory. An outlook that focuses on facts alone inescapably leads to an inaccurate view of international relations. This is true because an approach based strictly on facts is impossible: everyone brings to the table some theoretical perspective on every question of international cooperation or competition. Indeed, the very selection of facts to look at is shaped by theories that we carry around with us, just as how we interpret those facts is shaped by that theoretical point of view. Employing a useful set of tools—that is, an effective theoretical perspective—for making sense of facts may allow us to predict the range of actions available to a policymaker or policymakers in international affairs and may even help us predict how things will turn out. In doing so we will perhaps be able to engineer better decisions in the future than have sometimes been made in the past.

Before beginning to assess international politics thoughtfully, we need to examine how theoretical arguments and factual evidence are used to understand international relations. These ideas about how to argue, combined with some core perspectives, will form the basic tools of our examination of international affairs. The available tools will not prove to be equally useful, nor will any one tool always prove to be the best way to think about every aspect of international politics. But some tools will have decided advantages over others in particular situations, perhaps even in most situations.

We need to pick and choose what we think is important. If you were asked to list the causes of World War I, it is unlikely that you would include the discovery of gunpowder in China hundreds of years ago as a contributing factor, yet it would have been exceedingly difficult for those nations involved in the conflict to have wreaked so much destruction and fomented a world war without gunpowder. But who would consider such a remote development central to an explanation of the origins of World War I?

If you were asked to explain the collapse of the Soviet Union and the peaceful end of the cold war, it is unlikely that you would discuss the Helsinki Final Act, which in the mid-1970s led the United States and its European allies to recognize the borders of East Germany in exchange for the Soviet government's conceptual acceptance—although certainly not the practice—of principles of human rights. Yet, without the Helsinki Final Act it is likely that political dissent in the Soviet Union, and especially in Eastern Europe, would have been more harshly suppressed. The accords in effect gave the international community a license to protest what previously had been treated diplomatically as an internal affair of the Soviet Union. Still, in the greater scheme of things, the Helsinki agreement might not be given more than a footnote in the explanation of the end of the cold war (see, for example, Gaddis 1997). From these examples you can see that the explanation of any event depends significantly on which facts we choose to focus on and which facts we choose to ignore.

Do we explain the demise of the cold war by attending to the internal political and economic problems of the Soviet Union, or by emphasizing the impact of the U.S.-Soviet arms race rivalry? Perhaps European efforts at détente or the threat from China encouraged the Soviets to redefine their attitude toward the United States. Each of these explanations is plausible. Some are complementary, whereas others are contradictory. Making choices about matters such as these constitutes the first step in theory building.

## WHAT IS A THEORY?

Theories are statements about the expected relationships between variables. Expectations are formed by linking some variables as causes or probabilistic contributors to other variables as consequences in a series of logically connected arguments. The logical connections stipulate the relationship between the variables. A variable is a characteristic, event, idea, and so forth that can take on more than one value. Constants—that is, characteristics, events, ideas, and so forth that have only one value—are not variables. Consequently, theories are not primarily about constants, although constants can play a contributory role. All theories include dependent and independent variables. A dependent variable is something that we hope to explain; an independent variable is something that we think will provide us with all or part of the explanation of the different values taken on by the dependent variable. Of course, one theory's dependent variable may be another theory's independent variable.

In the theory of arms races, for example, the dependent variables generally include such concepts as the arms expenditures of a country and the likelihood that a country will find itself at war. These are the phenomena that theories of arms races are designed to explain. Notice that the dependent variables are not individual events like "World War I" or the "1995 U.S. defense budget." Rather, World War I might be an event that constitutes one of many events captured by a dependent variable, such as the "likelihood of war." The 1995 U.S. defense budget, likewise, is an example of a defense expenditure decision; it is not itself a variable but rather a single value or single observation that is one part of a variable list of values or observations.

Some common independent variables in theories of arms races include the magnitude of the perceived threat coming from an adversary (often measured as that country's level of arms expenditure) and the domestic demand for consumer goods, public services, and so forth rather than defense (that is, guns vs. butter). Changes in the values of the independent variables (for example, increases or decreases in the level of perceived threat; changes in public demands for consumer goods and social services) are expected to lead to changes in arms expenditures or in the likelihood that the country will fight a war. For example, an increase in the perceived magnitude of a foreign threat is hypothesized to lead to an increase in arms expenditures. Thus, the theory of arms races states relationships between its independent variables and its dependent variables. It does not state a detailed explanation of a single event; rather, it tries to provide an explanation for at least one class of events.

The relationships between independent and dependent variables implied by any theory (including, of course, arms race theories) constitute its predictions. These predictions are often referred to as hypotheses. They are the empirical implications drawn from the theory's logical connections between variables. The reasons the variables are expected to be related to one another in the way claimed in a theory constitutes the theory's explanation of the phenomena or generalizations with which it is concerned.

Predictions serve as a way of testing a theory's explanation (Friedman 1953). Reliable explanations almost certainly suggest that at least some reliable prediction is possible, provided the necessary tools of measurement and observation are available. Accurate predictions, however, can be achieved even without a meaningful explanation, and a meaningful explanation may lead only to limited predictive accuracy. Consider an example of accurate prediction without an attendant explanation. Cricket chirps are highly correlated with the temperature of the air. If we know the number of cricket chirps per minute, we can predict the temperature outside quite accurately even though we may not have a clue about why crickets chirp as often as they do. It is certainly more likely that the temperature influences the chirping of crickets than that cricket chirps influence the temperature.

## CONSTRUCTING THEORIES

How is a theory constructed? In some ways there are as many answers to this question as there are theories—or theorists. But every theory has some core features in common. For example, every theory contains a set of assumptions. The assumptions of a theory are its crucial building blocks. Assumptions specify the group of simplifying conditions under which the theory is expected to be a helpful tool for explaining and predicting the phenomena with which it is concerned. In the study of international politics, a researcher selects assumptions that reflect his or her views and understanding of international affairs. Consequently, different researchers adopt different assumptions as they try to explain a broad range of international events.

For instance, one well-regarded theory of international politics is called neorealism. Neorealist theorists are interested in explaining when the set of states in the world and the relations between them are stable and when they are not. To do so, they assume that states are unitary actors without any internal domestic divisions or factions even though they know that in every state many individuals, often with different opinions, are involved in decisions that influence international politics. Neorealists make the implicit judgment that the variation in opinions across decision makers is not sufficient to distort the predictions made by a theory that assumes states are unitary actors. Conversely, those who theorize based on the notion that bureaucracies shape foreign policy reject the idea that states are unitary actors, preferring instead to focus on the organizational mission of specific bureaucracies and their leaders. Naturally, these researchers know that on some issues, like the American declaration of war against Japan on December 8, 1941, there was virtual unanimity among responsible decision makers in the United States. They know that the unitary actor assumption can be a helpful convenience in some cases, but they believe it oversimplifies reality in too many cases to be of real help in structuring a reliable account of international affairs.

Assumptions are the principle means by which theorists simplify reality. Assumptions describe the set of conditions under which the theory's predictions are expected to hold. That means that one of the most important questions to ask about any theory is whether its assumptions limit the domain of circumstances that the theory is capable of addressing to such an extent that the theory seems trivial. If a theory's assumptions prevent it from addressing the events or phenomena in the real world that motivated its construction in the first place, then the theory's value is certainly going to be quite limited.

If, for instance, we are interested in explaining why small wars occur, then a theory that *only* addresses the causes of global war is not very helpful. Such a theory does not provide an answer to the question that motivated the construction of the theory in the first place. Of course, this does not mean that a theory of global war would not be useful for a theorist concerned about small wars. But, it does mean that theories are judged and compared in the context of what they are intended to explain and predict. In general, the more events or facts a theory can explain with a limited set of assumptions, the more useful the theory will be. This is the principle of parsimony. Thus, a theory of war that does not require you to distinguish between big wars and little wars has greater potential value for the study of war than does a theory of nuclear war or a theory of short, low-cost, bilateral wars or a theory of trade wars. A theory of politics that also explains war is more useful still, even though it was not constructed to explain war alone.

## Judging Theories

Judgment of any theory revolves around its logical truth or falsity and whether its predictions are trivial or useful. The logical truthfulness of a theory is a question of consistency, meaning that no assumptions can contradict others contained within the same theory. The accuracy of empirical predictions about what happens in the world is the primary means we have to judge the usefulness of a theory as an explanation for the real-world events that concern us. As human beings we often make value judgments, but we should not confuse these with dispassionate evaluation of the logic and evidence for and against a theory. We do not have to like a theory's implications for those implications to be true. And we certainly cannot make the world a better place by ignoring unpleasant or inconvenient realities. In fact, we must confront those realities through logic and evidence so that we can think about how to improve the world without violating the laws of nature.

## THE IMPORTANCE OF LOGICAL CONSISTENCY

A good starting place to judge a theory's value is to evaluate whether its assumptions contradict each other. If they do, there will be considerable confusion about exactly what the theory predicts or what its explanation is. And this confusion will be irreconcilable. The presence of internal inconsistencies means that at least part of the theory is false on logical grounds. We will not even need to look at reality to judge its usefulness. Predictions that depend on logical contradictions cannot be useful because, whatever is observed, the opposite might just as easily be a prediction that can be defended using the same theory. These predictions will be of the type "if A then B, but also if A then not B, and, maybe, if not A then B," and so forth. In fact, such a theory has nothing valuable to say about the relationship between A and B.

Contradictions are sometimes unintentionally overlooked or sidestepped when scholars construct theories or arguments about international affairs. We can guard against such oversights by insisting that assumptions be stated clearly and explicitly. Only when we know all of a theory's assumptions can we figure out the logical connections that link independent and dependent variables in that theory. There is no room for careless reasoning because such reasoning can get us—and the world—into too much trouble. To see how much trouble imprecision can cause, consider the following assumptions from a prominent theory of international politics:

> Since the desire to attain a maximum of power is universal, all nations must always be afraid that their own miscalculations and the power increases of other nations might add up to an inferiority for themselves which they must at all costs try to avoid. Hence all nations who have gained an apparent edge over their competitors tend to consolidate that advantage and use it for changing the distribution of power permanently in their favor. . . . The status quo nations, which by definition are dedicated to peaceful pursuits and want only to hold what they have, will hardly be able to keep pace with the dynamic and rapid increase in power characteristic of a nation bent upon imperialistic expansion. (Morgenthau 1978, 215–217)

The above statement is drawn from perhaps the most influential international relations theorist of the past several decades, Hans Morgenthau. His theory of realism (discussed in greater detail in Chapter 4) focused on power as the essential determinant of how nations relate to one another. His was a brilliantly parsimonious effort at developing a comprehensive set of generalizations, or laws, about politics among nations. Much of his theory offered keen insight and wisdom, which is why his writings are still influential today. Yet his theory housed fundamental contradictions, as reflected in the above quotation. And these contradictions make it difficult to figure out exactly what Morgenthau is arguing.

On the one hand, Morgenthau's theory of realism is about a world in which each and every nation (assumed to be a rational, unitary actor) wants to get as much power as possible. In fact, each nation wants power so badly that it pursues the acquisition of more and more power at any cost. On the other hand, we are told that there are at least two kinds of nations in the world: status quo powers, which are content with what they have and so do not pursue increases in their power, and imperialist powers, which are dissatisfied with the amount of power they have and so try to gain more. What, then, does the theory predict about the relationship between a nation's power and its actions? One part of the argument stipulates that a nation faced with the opportunity to gain power will pursue that opportunity no matter what (that is, at any cost). The other part says a nation might or might not pursue the opportunity to gain power, depending on whether it is a status quo type or an imperialist expansionist type. How do we recognize whether a nation is imperialistic or status quo oriented? The answer apparently is based on hindsight: What did the nation do when faced with the opportunity?

No matter what a nation does when faced with the chance to gain power, its actions must have contradicted some condition of the theory and must be consistent with some other condition of the theory. Its behavior is not, in fact, predicted by the theory at all. Or—and this is much worse—it behaved in a manner that is apparently consistent with the theory because it behaved in accord with one of the two contradictory conditions. The theory cannot be proven to be wrong, even in principle.

Morgenthau's theory of realism provides no guidance as to who is and who is not a status quo power or an imperialist power, except after the fact. If a nation does not reach out for more power, then we can say it must be a status quo nation satisfied with what it has. If it does reach out for power, then it might be an imperialist power, in accordance with the second condition of the argument, or it may simply be any type of state (including a status quo state), in accordance with the first condition of the argument (recall that the first assumption states that all states seek power whenever the opportunity presents itself). Thus, the theory fails to provide guidance about one of the very phenomena it was designed to address. Inconsistencies in its assumptions rule out the possibility of reliable predictions.

The logical dilemma Morgenthau created is readily corrected. Let's assume that the world is made up of two types of states, imperialist states and status quo states. Suppose, contrary to Morgenthau, we assume that the difference between these two types of states is that imperialist states seek power regardless of the costs, whereas status quo states seek power only if there is no attendant cost but will pay a cost to maintain their current power. Assume further (as Morgenthau does elsewhere) that seeking or preserving power always involves potential costs. Such a theory has surprising implications.

If two imperialist states confront each other, each will seek to take power from the other regardless of the cost. This suggests that they will fight until one of them no longer has any power—that is, until one of them no longer exists as a sovereign state. If two status quo states confront each other they will not fight, regardless of the difference in their power, because any fight involves potential costs. If an imperialist state and a status quo state confront each other, the imperialist state will be prepared to fight, whereas the status quo state faces a quandary. Either it must voluntarily give up power to the imperialist state—clearly a costly action—or it must fight to protect what it has—also a costly action. Presumably, the status quo state will pursue whichever option has the lower expected cost. Following this through to its logical conclusion, our theory predicts that the world eventually will consist either of many status quo states and no imperialist states or of a single imperialist state. No other combination of states can persist once each state has had an opportunity to confront each other state.

Solving Morgenthau's logical inconsistency reveals a theory that does not at all resemble reality. Conflicts between nations reveal that not all nations can be status quo powers. Likewise, that some countries live in peace with others indicates that not all states are imperialistically inclined. It is difficult indeed to find evidence that suggests that the world is being reduced to a single monolithic imperial power or to a global collection of peace-loving status quo powers. The revised theory is logically sound, but empirically of no interest. Morgenthau's theory required inconsistency to adequately account for the variety of actions we can readily observe in international relations. Without that inconsistency, his theory cannot explain reality. Yet with it, we cannot say *what* the theory explains. This is why logical consistency is so important.

> How would the implications of Morgenthau's revised theory change if status quo states did not avoid all costs but instead were willing to tolerate lower costs than imperial states? Could imperialist and status quo states coexist?

## TRUTH AND FALSITY IN ASSUMPTIONS

Assumptions are not casual statements to be taken seriously when convenient and ignored otherwise. An assumption is a defining characteristic of a theory. A theory cannot exist outside of its assumptions because it is the logical connections among the assumptions that imply the theory's predicted relationships among variables. I emphasize the importance of consistency because it is virtually impossible to know what is being argued when theorists (or policymakers) contradict themselves. And we cannot evaluate arguments if we do not know what they are.

Because assumptions are so important, it may seem appropriate, even important, to establish whether a stated assumption is true or not. However, in my opinion this is not a fruitful basis for evaluating a theory. As I explain my view on this issue, keep in mind that my viewpoint, although quite common in the physical sciences and in much of economics, is controversial among some social scientists.

To begin with, what exactly is meant by "true" or "false" when it comes to assumptions? We can distinguish between the two on purely logical grounds. A true theory is one in which the predictions follow logically from the assumptions. This is a somewhat narrow use of the term, and you may prefer to substitute the phrase "logically true" in its place in the discussion that follows. If the predictions do not follow from the assumptions, then we can say the theory is false. A theory with contradictions in it, then, is false (at least with regard to the parts influenced by the contradictory assumptions). Morgenthau's theory, or at least part of it, is, in these terms, false. Note that I have not arrived at this judgment because I disagree with any one of his assumptions. My disagreement with any of his assumptions would be a matter of taste or personal judgment. Whether two (or more) assumptions are mutually contradictory is not a matter of taste, it is a matter of logic.

We can distinguish true and false from the notions of useful or trivial. The usefulness of a theory is an empirical question. If the theory makes predictions that reliably help us understand the phenomena that motivated the theory's construction, then the theory is useful. If the predictions are irrelevant or excessively inaccurate with regard to the phenomena of interest, then the theory is trivial when applied to the phenomena that motivated its development. So while true or false refers to the internal logic of the theory, useful or trivial refers to its empirical value. False theories are inevitably trivial.[1] Some true theories are also trivial because they fail to account for the facts we hoped to explain. What we all seek to discover are theories that are both true and useful.

Because "true" and "false" refer to internal consistency, I do not attempt to establish whether this or that individual assumption is true or false. What I do address is whether the set of assumptions behind a theory is both true and useful. The set is true if the assumptions do not contradict one another and the predictions derived from the theory follow logically from the assumptions. The set is useful if the assumptions lead to explanations and predictions that are consistent with reality according to some stated criteria for evaluating the theory's empirical performance. Although individual assumptions may describe a world we do not care about (and so may be trivial), a single assumption cannot contradict itself (and so is neither true nor false).

---

[1] Even if some of the predictions of a logically inconsistent theory are supported by the empirical record, the theory must be false. Although the empirical record suggests that it is worthwhile to construct a theory that in fact truly leads to predictions about the events supposedly "predicted" by the false theory, the falseness of the theory still cannot be in doubt. Logical inconsistency can allow one to make almost any claim or statement. Any part of a theory that is logically inconsistent is of no empirical interest per se. So too is any part that fails to pass the stated criteria in empirical tests of the theory's usefulness.

No set of assumptions can be true in the sense that it represents an exhaustive cata-log of the factors that influence the phenomena the theory is expected to explain and, perhaps, predict. All theories are necessarily simplifications of reality. The only alterna-tive to a simplification of reality is reality itself, in all of its infinite complexity. Therefore, assumptions always leave something out.

Even recognizing this, we still may object that some assumptions are not true in the sense that they misrepresent an important part of reality. Yet when people say such assumptions are not true, they really mean that they are not useful. For example, it is common among many international relations researchers to talk about the national interest (Krasner 1978) or the nation's foreign policy. The nation is treated as if it were a unitary, singular actor, almost as if it were a human being. Such a description of a nation is obviously not true in some empirical sense. No nation consists of a single person or of a large number of people who unanimously hold the same opinion about every foreign policy matter.

The unitary actor assumption seems to be at odds with reality much of the time. But does that necessarily mean that we should toss it out? Although it *may* not be a useful assumption, I am confident that such a judgment cannot be made at the time the assumption is stated. We must always keep in mind that theories inevitably simplify real-ity in order to make explanation and prediction feasible and practical. Assumptions are the vehicle through which theorists simplify. Perhaps the unitary actor assumption sim-plifies too much, and perhaps it does not. We can judge the value of assumptions (apart from their internal logical consistency) only in terms of their output. What does this or that assumption contribute to the theory's explanation and prediction of events? This is the relevant question for judging its value. Tossing out the unitary actor assumption means that we must dispose of our inclination to talk about the *nation's* policy, the *state's* interests, and so forth. So embedded is the notion of the state as a meaningful concept that we should be cautious about throwing out the unitary actor assumption before demonstrating that there is a more useful simplification of reality.

If an assumption provides many accurate predictions, then it does not simplify real-ity too much. If it does not provide many helpful and accurate predictions, then it does simplify too much. We can make these sorts of judgments only after we have evaluated the whole of any theory and have seen what happens as we drop each of its assumptions, one at a time. We cannot tell how valuable an assumption is going to be on philosophical grounds. The value of one or another assumption is a practical matter. If an assumption adds to the theory's predictive ability more than it takes away, then it is useful. Because the addition of assumptions increasingly restricts a theory's domain, it is important that we have only enough assumptions to deal with the circumstances of interest. The more assumptions we add, the fewer are the circumstances to which it can be applied. Therefore, it is useful to know exactly which assumptions from a theory are required to produce each of its hypotheses. Some hypotheses may need only a few assumptions, whereas others require the whole set. If any assumption is not required for the predictions that follow from a theory, then that assumption need not be included in the theory.

The most common objection to one or another assumption is that it is not true in the sense that it is not realistic. This is the most common reservation about the unitary actor assumption. It is also a common objection to theories in which decision makers are assumed to calculate costs and benefits and compare alternative strategies on the basis of their expected returns. The trouble with this point of view is that it implies that the person making the claim or standing in judgment of some theory already knows what the true (or at least a truer) theory of international politics is. But if we knew what the right assumptions were, then we would have no need to theorize further. Our only remaining task would be to construct the instruments needed to implement the actions and strategies implied by the true theory (if, indeed, it is action oriented). Thus, when critics argue that an individual assumption is false, they are really saying that either they have evidence that the implications or predictions that depend on the assumption are false or they are making an argument based on taste, their personal likes and dislikes.

Arguments based on differences in taste generally are not productive. Just as different people find different forms of music or painting or literature or movies or foods or clothing appealing, so too do different people find different theoretical perspectives more or less appealing. The best way to deal with such differences in opinion about what are potentially fruitful assumptions is to put alternative views of the world to the test of history and to the test of the future. In this regard it is wise to be pragmatic. None of us truly knows exactly how international relations works, just as no one truly knows how the physical world works. If we knew completely how any physical or human sphere of study really worked, then that subject would be a dead subject. No new research would be needed no matter how many new facts were accumulated or how much time had passed. If the phenomena are fully explained there is nothing new to say. No one is still studying the causes and cure of smallpox, for example. A full explanation has been achieved. Perhaps a new variety of smallpox will emerge in the future (as has happened with tuberculosis), thereby creating a need for new theorizing or new empirical research, but for now the subject has nothing left for study. This is not the case with international politics. In international politics, we must judge whether one theory or another explains more of the facts of interest without creating more confusion than clarity.

## THE FIRST PRINCIPLE OF WING-WALKING

Explanations are always tentative. Theories are expected to prevail only as long as they outperform rival explanations of the same phenomena. If a more accurate, more predictive explanation comes along it is likely to supplant less successful theories. This may happen quickly or it may take many generations, but eventually better ideas come to prevail over inferior ones.

Sometimes theories, although capable of being proved false, can accommodate the discovery of *some* contradictory evidence. They are judged to be false only if the body of contradictory evidence grows large enough. Consider, for instance, Ptolemy's theory of mechanics, which predated Newton's theory. No one today relies on Ptolemaic theories of motion to explain the movement of planets and stars even though for most everyday purposes the Ptolemaic view does as well as Newtonian mechanics and Einstein's theory of relativity. Ptolemaic theory persisted for a long time, but the ideas of Copernicus, Kepler, and others eventually shook confidence in it. Ptolemaic astronomy predicts fewer events correctly than does Newtonian theory. For instance, although Ptolemy's theory did rather well in predicting the motion of heavenly bodies, it did not do well in predicting the trajectory of falling objects on earth.

Ptolemaic theory contends that planets do not follow elliptical orbits around the sun but, rather, follow epicycles (roughly, loop-the-loops) around the earth. Such a pattern of

*Theoretical assumptions shape how we view the world, whether that world is the physical universe or the domain of politics. The Ptolemaic perspective (left) dominated thinking for two millennia, while the Copernican system (right) has been dominant for about five hundred years. Some keystones of the Ptolemaic view include the assumption that Earth was at the center of the universe and that objects were naturally at rest unless put into motion. God was seen as the prime mover required to put the planets, sun, and other heavenly bodies into motion. The Copernican system placed the sun at the center of our solar system, with the planets revolving around it. Later, scholars like Kepler, Galileo, Newton, and others elaborated on Copernicus's insight, introducing the ideas that orbits are elliptical, objects are naturally in motion unless brought to rest, and gravity is a force that brings objects to rest, perhaps obviating the need for God as a prime mover. Changes in scientific assumptions can fundamentally alter how we understand even the most commonplace experiences, thereby giving us new insights into how our physical or social world works.*

movement is consistent with observations taken from the night sky. If you plot the location of a distant planet from night to night over the course of the year, you will not observe an orderly path of motion. The path can be made predictable, however, if you assume that the planet loops back from time to time. These epicycles generally provide accurate predictions. But once we accept Copernicus's theory that the sun, not the earth, is at the center of the solar system, Ptolemaic astronomy no longer makes sense. Eventually, the evidence against the Ptolemaic view became too great for the theory to be sustained. Rival arguments did a better job of explaining "the facts," including those the Ptolemaic perspective simply could not accommodate.

Clearly, we need some guidelines to help us judge when the evidence or the flaws in an argument are sufficient to conclude that the theory or argument in question is inadequate. In our everyday lives we make such judgments all the time. Few of us rely on our daily horoscope to plan our activities. Reading horoscopes may be fun, but there just does not seem to be a reliable relationship between prediction and reality. We have concluded that it is not an adequate tool. It is the accumulation of evidence and counterarguments about what happens in reality that is at the heart of choosing among competing theories. We would be rather alarmed to discover that our foreign policy leaders choose their actions according to horoscope readings. In fact, false rumors that Ronald Reagan relied on astrological readings during negotiations with Mikhail Gorbachev created quite a stir and not a few jokes at Reagan's expense.

Sometimes we cling to a theory even when we know it is not reliable. Usually we do so in observation of the first principle of wing-walking.[2] If you are out on the wing of an airplane in flight (and I *really* recommend against finding yourself in such a situation), don't let go of what you are holding on to unless you have something better to hold on to. Even then, you may have to think twice about letting go. Knowing that something better is available does not mean that the alternative is sufficiently attractive that you will immediately want to make the switch, especially if there are associated risks or costs. This is one reason why Ptolemaic mechanics held sway for so long. However hard it was to believe that planets loop back on themselves, there was no point in giving up that theory until something better (such as Newtonian mechanics) came along. Even then, switching was costly, and so people clung to the old ideas for a long time. Newtonian mechanics were not regularly taught in British schools for one hundred years after their development.

The first principle of wing-walking is particularly relevant when dealing with beliefs about how things work in the world. Giving up beliefs is costly. The benefits of a new set of beliefs had better be large enough to compensate for the costs of abandoning old ones. If the benefits are not expected to exceed the costs, then it seems unlikely that any of us would give up our beliefs. One reason that international politics may be predictable is that beliefs are not easily abandoned. Because leaders stick to their beliefs until it

---

[2] I thank Kenneth Shepsle, who first introduced me to this principle.

becomes too costly to continue to do so, behavior is likely to run a predictable course. If we can assess people's beliefs, we can begin to understand how they perceive the world and we can use that knowledge to predict their decisions and actions.

Consider this simple example of the costs of switching from an inferior tool to a superior one. Suppose you are doing a fix-up job at home. Maybe you are assembling a new television stand or wiring a stereo. In either case you probably will need a screwdriver. Now maybe you do not have the best-fitting screwdriver for the job, but you do have a screwdriver that will work, even if it will wiggle around in the screw a bit too much. Most of us would know that a better screwdriver exists, but most of us would not spend the time and money involved in getting the better tool. After all, we probably won't be needing the new tool very often and the screwdriver we have is adequate—not ideal, but adequate. Maybe it will do some damage to the head of a screw, but then we do not anticipate having to fiddle with the screw again in the foreseeable future.

So it is with the selection and the use of theories. We do not always strive to use the best tool because identifying the best tool may be too costly, or even if we know what tool to use, it may be too costly to learn how to use it. The more convinced we are that we have an adequate alternative, the lower the costs have to be to justify a switch in tools. If the stakes are large enough, and errors are expected to be sufficiently costly, then we probably will spend the time and money to learn about a better tool. If, for instance, we need to repair a fighter aircraft with a screwdriver, then we will probably get the best screwdriver available for the task. The cost of an error is too great to risk using the wrong tool. Crossed stereo wires are one thing, a malfunction at 40,000 feet at twice the speed of sound is quite another.

The first principle of wing-walking was an essential (although unspoken) feature of the national security debate in the United States during the presidency of Ronald Reagan. At that time, the noted physicist (and father of the hydrogen bomb) Edward Teller proposed a defensive response to the threat of nuclear holocaust. The policy Teller proposed was to develop a defense against incoming missiles. This was known officially as the Strategic Defense Initiative (SDI), introduced in the previous chapter. Its critics dubbed it "Star Wars." Teller's proposal represented a sharp departure from existing American policy and a return to a military approach more commonly seen before World War II.

Before World War II an important feature of any nation's military policy was to maintain a strong defense against foreign aggression. The emergence of a nuclear threat, however, changed this thinking in the United States. Americans introduced the idea of mutual assured destruction (MAD), in which it was thought that the best defense against nuclear war was an offense so powerful that it could ensure its possessor's ability to wreak unacceptable destruction even after an opponent had launched a successful first-strike attack. Under MAD, cities and civilian populations were the priority targets of attack rather than weapons and military installations precisely because it was thought that the fear of such devastating and demoralizing losses would curb anyone's appetite for war. SDI would have changed that by providing a protective shield against the destruction of cities. Among the many arguments made against SDI, one focused on the technical feasibility of the program. Another relied on the first principle of wing-walking. Many observed that nuclear deterrence through MAD had successfully protected peace and stability for decades. They believed that there was no good reason to switch to a different approach that might or might not prove to be a significant improvement over existing policy. They chose to live with the existing theory of nuclear security (nuclear deterrence) rather than switch to a new theory based on defense (SDI). Debate over SDI persists, with the administration of George W. Bush committed to pushing forward on the development and deployment of an antimissile defense system while opponents decry the effort as a risk to international stability.

The first principle of wing-walking forces us to pay attention to the costs as well as to the benefits of alternative ways of thinking about a problem. This principle of costs and benefits is one of the reasons that some rather disappointing theories of international politics remain prominent long after they have been shown to be lacking in explanatory or predictive capabilities. The first principle of wing-walking is the reason that Morgenthau's flawed theory continues to be taught and believed in by researchers and policymakers alike. Whatever its weaknesses, for these scholars either realism seems sufficiently adequate (as Ptolemaic mechanics seemed adequate for so long) or the costs of switching to an alternative theory seem too high to merit its abandonment.

The first principle of wing-walking encourages caution in rejecting theories. It reminds us to be skeptical of new ideas while also encouraging us to be open to persuasive evidence against old ideas. One threat to such openness arises because we have certain "habits of mind" that help us in thinking about things (Margolis 1993). Consider a simple example. Look around you and make a list of some of the objects that you see that are moving and some that are not. Perhaps you have noticed that the chair you are sitting on is quite still (or are you rocking back on its legs?) but that people around you are moving about. Surely you can draw up a long list of things that are moving and things that are still. In fact, *no* object is still. After all, you, your chair, this book, and everything else around you is hurtling through space at tremendous speed.

One of Galileo's great intellectual triumphs was to begin his theorizing by assuming that objects can naturally be in motion unless they are brought to rest. He assumed that this was true of objects like himself, the planet Earth, the stars and everything else. Galileo's assumption contradicted a well-established "habit of mind" of his day, and, perhaps, even of ours. People usually follow their senses. In Galileo's day they were used to thinking that stones and trees and especially the earth did not move. It seemed to Galileo's contemporaries that some objects moved—like the sun or the moon—and other objects stood still. To them, Galileo's assumption seemed absurd, and so, therefore, did the implications or predictions of his theory.

Galileo assumed that objects were in motion until a strong enough force (such as gravity) brought them to rest. Conversely, the standard assumption about motion (or rest) required that some force be exerted to set an object in motion and that, once that force was dissipated, the object would come back to rest. This, of course, created the problem of what first impelled the object to move, leading (quite pleasingly from the point of view of the Catholic Church) to an argument in support of God as the prime mover. Such arguments are less persuasive to many of us today. Still, we rely heavily on our senses to make judgments about physical things—judgments that often turn out to be wrong. The senses suggest that the sun moves around the earth. We see it rise in the East every morning and set in the West. Even today the language we use to describe dawn and dusk depends on the notion that the sun is moving around the earth, rising and falling, rather than that the earth is moving around the sun and around its own axis.

The notion that objects are naturally in motion represented a radical departure from conventional thinking in Galileo's day. It not only violated people's sense of what was true, but it also contradicted the teachings of the Catholic Church. That, of course, got Galileo into a great deal of very serious trouble. Rather than face the consequences of his heresy, he reluctantly agreed to stop teaching that the earth moved, but neither his recanting nor commonsense observations could change reality or the evidence that would gradually be amassed to show that Galileo was right. It took the Catholic Church about 350 years to agree that Galileo was right, which it finally conceded in 1992. It took most of the world much less time than that. But however long it took, the resolution of the issue did not depend on whether we liked the assumption or not, nor on whether Galileo recanted his politically incorrect view or not; it depended on the predictions that followed from the assumption (in conjunction with his other, less controversial assumptions, such as a friction-free surface) and the consistency between the evidence in the world and the expectations from theories that assume objects move until stopped rather than stand still until moved. Galileo's experience teaches us to be humble about assumptions and encourages us not to be overly resistant to new ideas. We should not be too quick to dismiss a theory because we doubt its assumptions. Rather, we should wait for the evidence about the theory's predictions. The proof of the theory is in the testing; not in our judgment of the quality of its assumptions.

One final comment about assumptions and the first principle of wing-walking is in order before we move on. Sometimes people are tempted to dismiss a theory because they believe the assumptions reflect some bias. In fact, they may be right. Capitalists tend to dismiss Marxist arguments on these grounds, much as Marxists often dismiss free market–oriented theories based on ideological bias. This is just another guise by which people object to assumptions on the basis of differences in taste. Whether assumptions are selected because of a bias or not does not matter as long as the standard for evaluating the usefulness of assumptions is how well the theory performs in predicting and explaining events. If tests are biased, then there will be a problem. However, despite the motivation behind its construction, the theory itself is best judged on the basis of whether it accounts for the facts it was constructed to explain and predict. Biased assumptions have no advantage over unbiased assumptions (whatever those may be) in regard to empirical performance.

## THE CASE STUDY METHOD AND TESTING THEORIES

In international relations research, it is common to evaluate the empirical usefulness of theories by presenting one or several case histories that are consistent with a theory's predictions. The evaluation of a theory through the close scrutiny of a single event and the associated details is often referred to as a case study. Case studies can be helpful tools for developing ideas about a phenomenon or for shedding light on a specific event, but when cases are selected because they are consistent with a particular claim, they are not a test of the accuracy of the claim.

Selecting cases because they are consistent with a theory is not a fair test of the theory. For example, consider the following test of the claim that arms races cause war. We look at the circumstances of relevant nations just before the Napoleonic wars, World War I, and World War II, and we see that in each case an arms race was in progress. We infer, therefore, that the claim that arms races cause war is true. This inference is not warranted by the evidence because there are many other examples in which arms races were not succeeded by war. Picking cases because they are consistent with theory leads us to miss all those cases that could refute the theory.

Sometimes people try to justify selecting cases that are consistent with the theory under study by noting that they are picking a "difficult" case. Usually this just compounds the problem because the case is "difficult" in the sense that it is not representative of the class of events that the theory seeks to explain. That is, the case is difficult because it has some features that make it extremely unusual. Cases for investigation should be selected because they represent a wide array of variation on the independent *and* dependent variables, not because they represent a particular value on the dependent variable or because they seem difficult because confounding factors are in operation. The principle of random case selection has been well established among statisticians for about a century.

Remember that theories are about relationships among variables, not about constants. Yet many, many investigations of the causes of very large wars examine only the constants. There are literally thousands of studies on the causes of World War I. Many of these evaluate a theory, or at least some hypothesis, about the causes of deadly, long, multilateral wars. But these studies select facts based on a particular value of the dependent variable. In fact, the dependent variable turns out not to be a variable at all. It is a constant within the case, which leaves nothing to be explained. For instance, understanding the causes of large wars requires that we understand how those causes differ from the causes of small wars or other types of conflicts. Looking at only large wars leaves no variation in the thing to be explained—namely, the causes of large wars. If we want to know what makes them large, we must also know what factors prevent other conflicts from turning into large wars. We need cases with different scales of war that can be compared with one another.

A similar problem in selection bias is common among studies of international political economy because such studies focus on regimes and cooperation. Many researchers are interested in evaluating what impact regimes have in encouraging cooperation. Regimes in this context are organizations, institutions, or norms that regulate a pattern of behavior (Ruggie 1975; Krasner 1983; Keohane 1984; Morrow 1994b). Usually the interest in regime studies is in explaining cooperation between states. Commonly, the researcher selects a case with a known cooperative outcome and then looks for the existence of an international regime or organization that can be said to have fostered the cooperative outcome. Perhaps the author is correct in the assessment of the role of the regime, but this does not at all tell us whether similar regimes also operated in settings that did not lead to cooperation between states. The question of whether certain regimes promote cooperation (a relationship between variables, including the presence or absence of a regime and the presence or absence of cooperation) simply cannot be evaluated without knowing more about the tendency of the regime context to produce cooperative outcomes compared with circumstances not imbedded in a regime context. Are there regimes designed to foster cooperation that end up yielding conflict? Of course there are, but studies typically do not pay attention to these failures and so produce biased inferences. The Organization of Petroleum Exporting Countries (OPEC), designed to foster cooperation among oil-producing and -exporting countries, is frequently home to conflict among its members over what their oil production quota ought to be. Although widely studied by economists and others interested in cartels, there are few studies of OPEC among regime theorists interested in international cooperation.

Are there instances of cooperation without a regime? Again the answer is yes. For decades, the U.S. government and the Israeli government have demonstrated a high degree of cooperation without relying on a formal alliance agreement. Although substantial research has been done on U.S.-Israeli relations, little of it has been conducted by international relations specialists interested in the role of regimes in fostering cooperation.

The cases of OPEC and U.S.-Israeli relations help sort out how important regimes are in fostering, or not fostering, cooperation (Downs and Rocke 1990, 1995). Selecting on the dependent variable by only picking cases of cooperation in regimes introduces an analytic bias and makes use of knowledge about what ultimately happened, knowledge that the decision makers could not possibly have before the fact. Analytic bias and hindsight are two elements that we should avoid in designing ways to assess how well alternative theories perform empirically.[3]

---

[3] Selecting on the dependent variable is a problem for any argument concerned with identifying factors sufficient to cause a result, but it is not a problem when the concern is only to identify factors that are necessary for a result (see Most and Starr 1989).

Before leaving our discussion of case studies, I will add one more set of thoughts to the discussion. It is possible to establish or refute certain claims of a theory unambiguously through the use of even a single case study. Consider the difference between necessary conditions, sufficient conditions, and necessary and sufficient conditions. Necessary conditions refer to circumstances or factors that must be present in order for the consequence to happen. If they are absent, the consequence cannot occur. For example, exposure to smallpox bacteria is necessary to contract smallpox. If smallpox bacteria are not present it is not possible to contract the disease. Exposure to the smallpox bacteria, however, is not sufficient to contract smallpox. For example, one might be immune and still be exposed to the bacteria. The immunity ensures that the disease will not develop. Sufficient conditions refer to circumstances that, if they arise, ensure that the consequence will happen. For example, being the sole winner of the big prize in a state lottery is sufficient to guarantee that a person receives great wealth, but it is not a necessary condition. Great wealth can be achieved through many other means, including inheritance, great success in business, writing many best sellers, and so forth. None of those conditions is necessary for great wealth, but each is sufficient. Necessary and sufficient conditions satisfy both necessity and sufficiency. That is, the condition must obtain for the consequence to happen, and the consequence is guaranteed to happen if the condition is met.

> Can you think of examples of international organizations in which the member states commonly fight (verbally or even violently) with each other? Can you think of examples of states that generally cooperate despite having no formal agreement between them about the conditions for cooperation?

Now let us think about case studies, necessity, sufficiency, and interstate cooperation. Tables 2-1, 2-2, and 2-3 look at whether or not a regime is present (the independent variable) in a set of circumstances and relate this to whether or not that set of circumstances culminates in cooperation or conflict (the dependent variable). The regimes literature suggests a hypothesis that says that regimes foster cooperation, a topic I explore in much greater depth in Chapter 14. Table 2-1 shows an example of thirty hypothetical observations that support the inference that the presence of a regime appears necessary but not sufficient for cooperation. Table 2-2 illustrates hypothetical evidence for thirty observations that support the claim that regimes are sufficient but not necessary for

TABLE 2-1

### Regimes and Cooperation: Necessary Conditions

| Regime | Cooperation | Conflict |
|--------|-------------|----------|
| Yes | 10 | 10 |
| No | 0 | 10 |

cooperation. Table 2-3 depicts a pattern in which regimes are both necessary and sufficient for cooperation. Keep in mind as you read these or any other "data tables" that the numbers in the cells of the table represent how many cases fit the value of the row and column variables.

In Table 2-1 we can see that whenever cooperation is observed (the dependent variable), we also observe that a regime is present. At the same time it is evident that regimes do not guarantee cooperation; half of the time when a regime is present there is still conflict, but there is never cooperation without a regime. This is what is meant when we say it is a necessary condition. If there are no problems with assigning cases to each category in the table, then a single instance of cooperation without a regime, such as the U.S.-Israeli case, refutes the hypothesis that a regime is necessary for cooperation.

Table 2-2 shows that whenever a regime is present there is cooperation, although cooperation can also occur without a regime. Thus, Table 2-2 illustrates the case in which the presence of a regime is sufficient to produce cooperation but not necessary. This is evident from the fact that there are cases of cooperation without regimes. Table 2-3 shows that cooperation occurs only if a regime is present and that conflict arises only if a regime is absent. Table 2-3 illustrates both necessary and sufficient conditions. It is evident that if there is one instance of a regime that does not lead to cooperation, as in the case of OPEC, then regimes are not sufficient to guarantee cooperation. Either the U.S.-Israeli case or the OPEC case refutes the argument that regimes are necessary and sufficient to ensure cooperation.

TABLE 2-2

**Regimes and Cooperation: Sufficient Conditions**

| Regime | Cooperation | Conflict |
|--------|-------------|----------|
| Yes | 10 | 0 |
| No | 10 | 10 |

TABLE 2-3

**Regimes and Cooperation: Necessary and Sufficient Conditions**

| Regime | Cooperation | Conflict |
|--------|-------------|----------|
| Yes | 15 | 0 |
| No | 0 | 15 |

Suppose a theory makes a weaker prediction than that implied by necessity, sufficiency, or both. If a theory predicts that something is possible under certain conditions—not necessary or sufficient, nor even probable—then we can prove the claim with just one case. A single demonstration that the specified conditions have occurred and the possible outcome has arisen is adequate to prove such a weak claim. These claims are known as existence claims. Let's look at an example.

Two similar and widely held theories suggest that wars that fundamentally alter the structure of international relations, especially relations between the most powerful states, must be large, costly wars.[4] An alternative view, the theory of strategic competition between states, suggests that it is possible for a system-transforming war to occur even if the war is short, and costs relatively few lives. The Seven Weeks' War, fought in

---

[4] These theories are discussed in Chapter 16. They are known as the theory of the power transition and the theory of hegemonic war.

1866 between Prussia and Austria with participation by Italy and several small German principalities, is an example of just such a war (Bueno de Mesquita 1990a). The existence claim of the strategic perspective that is set out in Chapter 5 is proved because this small, relatively low-cost war transformed how the states of Europe related to each other as suggested by the strategic perspective but in contradiction to other theories. This one case does not prove that the theory from which the claim is derived is true, just that the specified phenomenon can exist in contradiction to some other theory.

Most theories about international relations or, for that matter, any other social phenomena make predictions that are probabilistic. Such hypotheses typically say something like, "the more the independent variables increase in value, the more likely it is that the dependent variable will increase." For instance, a typical hypothesis might say "the more balanced power is between rival states, the more likely they are to live peacefully with each other." A single case study cannot provide any information about the credibility of such a hypothesis. The hypothesis claims that there will be a mix of outcomes (that is what it means to be probabilistic) associated with changes in the values of the independent variables but that the mix of values will tend toward peaceful relations as power becomes more equal between rivals. Even two or three cases are insufficient to evaluate the accuracy of the hypothesis in a convincing way. When hypotheses are probabilistic, confidence either in a claim or its refutation improves as we observe larger and larger numbers of relevant cases. That is, probabilistic hypotheses are better tested with statistical methods than with a small number of individual case histories.

## A Standard for Comparing Theories

How can we choose among competing theories? We can use the first principle of wing-walking. This means that we choose one theory over another if it outperforms the competing theory (Popper 1963; Laudan 1977; Lakatos 1978). The criteria applied here are straightforward. When two theories make predictions about the same phenomena or set of events, one is judged to be better than the other if it explains those facts accounted for by the rival theory plus some additional facts not explained by the competing theory. Furthermore, the allegedly better theory must explain these additional facts without adding a net surplus of newly unexplained circumstances. Thus, our standard of judgment is quite pragmatic. The more things a theory can explain, and the fewer the errors it makes compared with alternative theories, the better it is. A theory will be abandoned only after the evidence shows that a competing theory does a superior job of accounting for the facts. It is not enough to get more things right; the theory must also not get more things wrong that were previously accounted for. There must be a net improvement in prediction. There are, of course, practical difficulties in the implementation of this, or any, standard. But at least this is removed from arguments about personal tastes and imbedded in criteria on which people can agree.

I use seven criteria to turn the theoretical discussion into practical rules for assessing arguments. The criteria adopted here have been suggested by Kenneth Waltz (1979, 13), one of the most prominent students of international affairs. These criteria are as follows:

1. State the theory being tested.
2. Infer hypotheses from it.
3. Subject the hypotheses to experimental or observational tests.
4. In taking steps two and three, use the definitions of terms found in the theory being tested.
5. Eliminate or control perturbing variables not included in the theory under examination.
6. Devise several distinct and demanding tests.
7. If a test fails, ask whether the theory flunks completely, needs repair and restatement, or requires a narrowing of scope of its explanatory claims.

These seven criteria capture at minimum what is needed for a theory to remain a contender in the struggle to discover how international politics works. By carefully applying these criteria to the tools of analysis available to us, it should be possible for us to come to a better understanding of international affairs.

## WHY DO WE NEED THEORIES?

You may well wonder what need there is to worry at all about abstract theoretical perspectives on how international politics works. Why, for instance, don't we just get on with the business of describing and explaining international affairs as they are? Do national leaders *really* care about theories or scientific standards in devising their policies, or is it enough to have good judgment, wisdom, some knowledge of history, and maybe a little luck? These are good questions that deserve serious consideration and serious responses.

The business of describing, explaining, predicting, and perhaps engineering international affairs is not as simple as it may seem. Knowledge of the facts, for example, is a far cry from understanding those facts or comprehending why circumstances evolved in the way they did (Farkas 1999). It seems almost impossible to talk about the facts of international politics without worrying about standards for judging evidence and the means of evaluating competing theories about what is happening before our eyes (Popper 1963; Lakatos 1976, 1978; Laudan 1977; Rosenberg 1988; Margolis 1993). How else are we to know which facts are relevant and which can safely be ignored?

Just consider today's headlines. Someplace in today's newspaper there is a story about an international dispute, possibly over trade barriers, ethnic rivalries, border clashes, or religious differences. Perhaps Turkey and Greece are arguing over the possibility of admitting Turkey into the European Union. Maybe India and Pakistan are engaged in a dispute over their claims to Kashmir. Possibly the United States and Canada disagree about the interpretation of NAFTA. Maybe Mexico is threatening to seal its border, cutting off Central Americans trying to pass through Mexico to enter the United States as undocumented aliens. China, Vietnam, Malaysia, Taiwan, and others may each be claiming the rights to oil deposits near the Spratly Islands in the South China Sea. Iran and Iraq may be quarreling over the treatment of Shia Muslims, or Israel and Syria over the Golan Heights. Romanians and Moldavians may be disputing the location of boundaries between their territories.

Whatever the headlines, it will be evident that there are lots of different ways to explain each of these conflicts of interest. News accounts of ethnic rivalry, the balance of power, economic dependency, or imperialism reflect ideas about theories or organizing principles that explain international affairs. Such common ideas as "do unto others as you would have them do unto you," "an eye for an eye, a tooth for a tooth," or "turn the other cheek" are just a few ways people think about what encourages countries to resolve their differences or discourages them from doing so. Each is part of some theory of international relations developed as a tool that might help us understand how nations relate to each other. Each tool directs us to focus our attention on different facts and offers a different explanation of events.

Theories about norms may turn our attention toward the history of past interactions between particular states. If we focus on norms, then we are likely to be concerned about the domestic social and cultural constraints leaders face. Perhaps the cultural or social values in some countries make using violent strategies especially costly for political leaders. In that case, norms could be a pacifying influence in foreign policy. Balance-of-power theory, by contrast, encourages us to seek out facts about the power resources of states and to assume that nations are inherently hostile toward one another. We would be more concerned with the wealth and military might of states if we took a balance-of-power perspective than if we approached a rivalry from the perspective of cooperative norms. From the point of view of a theory of cooperative norms, such as the theory of liberalism discussed in Chapter 4, power would be thought less consequential than, for example, the history of shared interests and cultural values.

The choice among alternative theories, or tools, and the standards for evaluating them are not only important for us as students and citizens but are important as well for those individuals entrusted with the responsibility for making the myriad decisions that describe the relations between nations. Decision makers probably do not choose their courses of action by throwing darts at a list of options. Surely if we believed that our leaders make life and death decisions in such an irresponsible way we would throw them out of office. And that, remember, is a risk that people who are ambitious to lead do not engage in lightly. All leaders around the world rely, knowingly or unconsciously, on some tools or theories of international affairs to help guide their decisions. Leaders often quote the principles or hypotheses derived from such tools as the justification for their decisions. Consider two examples of principles used by leaders in critical foreign policy settings.

Admiral Isoroku Yamamoto, the architect of Japan's attack against Pearl Harbor, was fond of saying, "an efficient hawk hides his claws" (Prange 1981, 13). Here is a generalization about international affairs that helped guide the secretiveness behind Japan's planning and execution of its attack. It may or may not be a useful or helpful principle, but it certainly was an important one. After all, it was not inevitable that the Japanese would choose the secret and aggressive course of action that they did choose on December 7, 1941.

The Japanese might just as readily have taken a different point of view. They might have subscribed to a hypothesis commonly argued by those who believe in the theory of deterrence. Had they accepted a deterrence point of view, the Japanese might have openly declared in 1941 that they would launch a severely punishing attack against American interests unless the United States lifted its trade embargo against Japan and stopped threatening its activities in the Pacific. Probably Japan's leaders would not have wanted to say exactly what the threatened punishment would be or exactly when it would take place. That would have put their fleet of aircraft carriers at unnecessary risk. Still, they might have chosen an open threat intended to alter America's behavior. Such an approach would have relied on an utterly different assessment of the appropriate tools for accomplishing their objectives than the tools implied by their secret, clandestine attack. Had they believed they could deter the United States by persuading Franklin Roosevelt that the costs of his policies toward Japan outweighed the benefits, then the threat of punishment alone might have been sufficient to achieve their goals. They might never have attacked any American facilities at all. Indeed, later we will see how Japan came to choose the stealth approach, in which their intentions and actions were kept secret as long as possible, over the deterrent alternative, in which their alleged intentions, if not their actions, would have been common knowledge to all concerned parties. Had Japan's intentions been common knowledge,

*Admiral Isoroku Yamamoto was the architect of Japan's attack on Pearl Harbor on December 7, 1941. Several days later, he received congratulations from Japan's emperor for the navy's successful sinking of the British ships* Prince of Wales *and* Repulse. *Admiral Yamamoto correctly anticipated that if the U.S. fleet was not crippled at Pearl Harbor and if the war was not won by 1943, then Japan would most likely lose.*

the United States would have known of them; the Japanese government, in turn, would have known that the American government knew Japan's intentions; the American government, for its part, would then have known that the Japanese government knew that the Americans knew Japanese intentions; and so forth. We will learn when the threat of punishment can be sufficient to induce the desired behavior and when a threatened punishment must actually be carried out.

Leaders often talk about "maintaining the balance of power" or "promoting a favorable balance of power" (which usually means having a great imbalance in their favor) as guidelines to conducting their nations' foreign policies. Indeed, a few illustrations may help suggest that a concern with the theory of the balance of power is as old as history and as fresh as today's headlines. Consider the following three quotations. Each reveals a concern about the balance of power between rivals. The first comes from the Gospel according to Luke, the second from a memorandum by Sir Eyre Crowe to the British government shortly before the outbreak of World War I, and the third from the memoirs of Henry Kissinger, Richard Nixon's notable national security adviser and later secretary of state.

> What king, going to make war against another king, sitteth not down first and consulteth whether he be able with ten thousand to meet him that cometh against him with twenty thousand.
>
> Or else, while the other is still far away he sends a delegation and asks terms of peace. (Luke 14:31)

> History shows that the danger threatening the independence of this or that nation has generally arisen, at least in part, out of the momentary predominance of a neighboring State at once militarily powerful, economically efficient, and ambitious to extend its frontiers or spread its influence. . . . The only check on the abuse of political predominance derived from such a position has always consisted in the opposition of an equally formidable rival, or of a combination of several countries forming leagues of defence. The equilibrium established by such a grouping of forces is technically known as the balance of power. (Quoted in Hartmann 1978, 316)

Throughout history the political influence of nations has been roughly correlative to their military power. While states might differ in their moral worth and prestige of their institutions, diplomatic skill could

*Henry Kissinger, U.S. secretary of state from 1973 to 1977, meets with the president of Kenya, Jomo Kenyatta, in Nairobi. The United States sought improved relations with many African nations in an effort to prevent the spread of Soviet influence in that part of the world. Many African leaders appear to have been willing to take an anti-Soviet stance in exchange for foreign assistance from the U.S., assistance that did more to keep these leaders in office than to better the living situations of their citizens.*

augment but never substitute for military strength. In the final reckoning weakness has invariably tempted aggression and impotence brings abdication of policy in its train. . . . The balance of power . . . has in fact been the precondition of peace. (Kissinger 1979, 195)

Such examples suggest that leaders, at least some of the time, take very seriously the theories that have been used to try to make sense of history. Theories probably do not determine choices in a mechanistic way so much as they serve as signposts for leaders who must map out a foreign policy course. That is one reason why it is important to understand the tools that shape their judgments, even if those tools prove to be faulty or just plain wrong. Even if a theory is woefully inaccurate, if leaders rely on it we should strive to understand it and to understand why it goes wrong and with what consequences. Later, I believe you will be convinced that the balance-of-power theory is incorrect in many of its most important predictions. Yet it strongly influences how leaders make decisions. Surely it is as important for us to understand what consequences follow from reliance on incorrect arguments as it is to understand what consequences emerge from reliance on correct arguments. By comprehending the faults with a theory we may help prevent foreign policy errors in the future.

> Can you think of a current foreign policy dispute in which one state is threatening another with dire consequences if the latter does not change its behavior? Has the exact nature of those consequences been made clear (for example, economic sanctions, military action, severing of diplomatic relations, or the like)? Can you think of a dispute in which a state seems to be hiding its true intentions, saying one thing but seemingly doing another? What is more reliable information, what a state's leaders say they are doing or what they are observed to be doing?

## GUIDELINES FOR EVALUATING ARGUMENTS AND EVIDENCE: THE SCIENTIFIC METHOD

With so many alternative ways to think about what is going on in international affairs, amassing facts and making decisions can be a daunting task. Fortunately, there are sensible guidelines to help us and our leaders evaluate the effectiveness of these alternative ways of thinking about international problems and to decide when a perspective is probably wrong. By using these guidelines, we can expect to make reasonable and helpful judgments about the quality of different arguments and the credibility of the evidence for or against those arguments.

What I am referring to here is use of the scientific method. The scientific method imposes only a few basic conditions. In doing so, it guides our application of the first principle of wing-walking by helping us to see when to hold on to an old theory and when to let go and embrace a new one. As I emphasized earlier, scientific analysis requires logical consistency. This means that we must state clearly how one set of factors implies or causes another set of factors. Competing arguments must be evaluated through experiments that control for confounding, alternative explanations. In the physical sciences this is a much easier requirement to satisfy than in the social sciences. Within the field of international politics, "controlled experiments" usually means that theoretical expectations are evaluated against historical data. The cases selected for evaluation must be representative of the class of events in which we are interested. Since no one case study can be representative, case studies alone are not adequate as scientific tests of an argument. The representativeness of cases also means that we choose randomly with regard to factors that are not part of the argument. Randomness ensures that the tests control for the possible effects of other factors. Tests must also be replicable. That is, different researchers examining the same body of evidence should reach the same conclusions even if they are unfamiliar with each other's investigations. The conclusions are not based on personal judgments or on personal values. Theories lead to empirical predictions. This is why both the logic and the evidence for or against a theory is so important.

Predictions are always contingent. They differ from prophecies in that scientific predictions state that if certain conditions are met, then certain results are expected to follow (Gaddis 1992; Ray and Russett 1996; Bueno de Mesquita 1998). When other conditions are met, then the theory may predict other outcomes. Prophecies are not concerned with the conditions from which consequences follow; they are concerned only with the consequences. Scientific predictions can be about things that have already happened or about things that have not yet happened. For example, using Newtonian mechanics we can predict the location of Mars in the night sky on any day of any year, past, present, or future. If Mars were observed to be somewhere other than the predicted location, then the theory on which the prediction was based would be called into question. This would be just as true if Mars proved to have been somewhere else on a past date or a future date. Tests of theories about international affairs also rely on predictions. Sometimes the evidence is based on how closely past events fit the expectations of a given theory. In the most demanding cases, the evidence for a theory pertains to predictions about events that have not yet happened. Both types of predictions are emphasized throughout this book, and you will learn how to make reliable predictions about events that have not yet happened.

The scientific method focuses our attention on the internal, logical consistency of alternative explanations of "the facts" and compels us to look for critical, replicable tests and evidence that allow any of us to reach theoretically and empirically defensible conclusions about competing arguments. We may disagree about the interpretation of the evidence or the weight to be given to it in assessing the strengths and weaknesses of a theory, but at least we will be able to discuss these matters based on the same criteria, even if we do not share common judgments or expectations. Of course, you may disagree about the appropriateness of the scientific method, and I may be wrong about its value. There certainly is no shortage of sensible, knowledgeable people who have concluded that the standard methods of science are not applicable to politics. But whether these standards can be applied to international politics is not a matter to be resolved by assertion; the proof of this pudding really is in the testing.

Many prefer to speak of the art of politics rather than the science. I respectfully disagree, but, of course, it is not enough to assert a point of view. I must demonstrate the applicability of the scientific method or acknowledge failure. This is why it is important to discuss the criteria to be employed when judging arguments and evidence and to consider alternatives that others might prefer to use. Judgments about alternative theories are important because the costs of wrong decisions in international affairs can be devastating. We certainly want to avoid using wrong ideas or ideas that are inappropriate for the problem at hand.

## WHEN A THEORY IS WRONG

The notion that a theory can "go wrong" does not seem terribly complicated. Most of us probably understand this phrase in pretty much the same way. For one thing, we probably would have no problem agreeing that if a theory regularly leads to predictions that are inconsistent with reality, then the theory, rather than reality, is wrong. After all, reality is what it is. Reality may be "wrong" in a moral sense. We may not like what happens, but it still incontrovertibly happens.

Some theorists argue that reality is wrong when what actually happens does not conform to the theorist's expectations of what should have happened. Marxist theory sometimes exhibits this characteristic because it gets interpreted along Marxist ideological lines. Marxism as a theory is intended to explain changes in economic and social relations over time. It is an effort to explain history and to predict the future course of events. Class conflict is presumed to be inevitable in Marxist theory. If class conflict does not arise, then Marxist theorists usually presume that something is wrong with people's class consciousness. The theory is presumed to be correct and people are presumed to be mistaken.

Soviet founder Vladimir Ilyich Lenin, a theorist as well as a revolutionary leader, devised such concepts as a "trade union mentality" and the "vanguard of the proletariat" to deal with the problem of inconsistencies between predicted behavior and observed behavior. A trade union mentality is, in more modern parlance, equivalent to false consciousness. Because some members of the working class might, according to this notion, misunderstand their true interests, Lenin constructed the idea that a group such as Communist Party elites was needed to lead the way for the proletariat. According to Lenin, party elites, the vanguard of the proletariat, could be better trusted than workers to know what was in the true interest of the working class. Indeed, many argue that Lenin's concept of the vanguard of the proletariat ensured that Marxist theory would, if put into practice along Leninist lines, evolve into a dictatorial ideology. Lenin, in fact, argued in his essay "What Is to Be Done?" against any debate regarding socialist ideology. His logic inevitably led to the conclusion that if the observed facts contradicted socialist or Marxist predictions, then the facts were in error because they reflected a bourgeois ideology.

Marxist predictions and reality were not consistent with one another in 1914. Marxist theorists predicted that a world war could not happen because the workers of the world would recognize their common class interests and the divergence between their interests and those of the aristocratic and capitalist classes who were making war. The workers simply were not expected to agree to serve in the armies of their countries, fighting against their class fellows from other lands. Marxist theorists greatly underestimated the power of nationalist feelings to join people together, even against members of their own "class." Indeed, Marxism had no room for nationalism, because nationalism competes with class as an organizing principle. Marxist predictions about World War I proved wrong, but Marxist theorists dismissed the problem as being an error of the workers, who were fooled

by false consciousness (that is, nationalism, trade union mentality, and the like), rather than an error of the theory. They invented auxiliary arguments to cope with the failed predictions of their theory. It took repeated failures, culminating in the early 1990s, before most Marxist theorists accepted the overwhelming evidence that their theoretical perspective was wrong. As suggested by the first principle of wing-walking, Marxists were conservative in their willingness to surrender their preferred theory. They needed to be convinced by a great preponderance of evidence. They had to reach the point at which they recognized that their auxiliary arguments had become unsustainable.

The addition of auxiliary arguments to a theory is not inherently problematic. If the new arguments explain previously unexplained events without becoming wrong when applied to previously explained events, then the gains in explanation can exceed the costs in lost parsimony. A theory is more or less parsimonious depending on how many facts it explains compared with the number of assumptions it requires to make predictions. In general, the more events or facts a theory can explain with a limited set of assumptions, the greater the potential usefulness of the theory and the greater its parsimony. So, if auxiliary arguments (like nationalism, trade union mentality, encirclement by the bourgeois states) are added and explain only one event each, then there is no improvement in parsimony. In fact, such additions are

*Marxist theory not only fails the tests of logical consistency and empirical reliability; it also failed in practice. Here we see two Lithuanian girls playing on a fallen statue of Lenin in August 1991. Marxist theory seems to have gone the way of Lenin's statue.*

evidence that the theory in question is degenerate. That is, the theory needs to make up a special explanation for each new circumstance and so really is no explanation at all (Lakatos 1976, 1978; Christensen and Snyder 1997; Elman and Elman 1997; Schweller 1997; Vasquez 1997; Walt 1997; Waltz 1997).

The principle of parsimony is important because it provides one benchmark by which we can choose among competing theories. When a theory or its auxiliary statements need to be changed to suit many—sometimes even each—new observation, then we should suspect that the theory is just plain wrong.

## SCIENTIFIC THEORIES MUST BE FALSIFIABLE

How we judge predictions is certainly open to some dispute. Some theories do not allow any possibility that evidence can show them to be wrong. Such theories are not *falsifiable*. They may be true (or not), but we have no way to be confident they are true or useful, short of faith. Indeed, religious beliefs can be thought of as a set of theories or tools devised to explain human behavior and phenomena in nature. They may be true (or not), but we cannot judge their veracity by normal scientific standards; we must rely on faith. Core religious beliefs, such as a belief in the existence of God, cannot be falsified, although lesser religious arguments, such as when the world is expected to come to an end, clearly can be shown to be false (although maybe not convincingly to a believer). It is essential that a theory seeking the imprimatur of science be susceptible to possible falsification. A theory that has scientific standing is one for which it is possible to imagine a test or set of tests whose results would lead us to conclude that the theory, or at least its central predictions, are just plain wrong. If no such test can be imagined, then the theory really is an article of faith rather than an article of science.

Can you think of an explanation of foreign policy that is falsifiable? Can you think of an explanation that is not falsifiable? When journalists explain clashes between ethnic groups by saying that the fighting stems from cultural differences or from the fact that the groups have hated each other for hundreds of years, are the journalists making a falsifiable claim? Is the claim false? How can you account for the periods of peaceful coexistence between such ethnic groups in light of the journalistic explanation of their clashes?

Sometimes people are confused by this idea of falsifiability. They think, "Well, if a theory is true, it cannot be falsified, so how can falsifiability be helpful with true theories?" I want to be very clear. Falsifiability does not have to do with whether an argument is true or false, but rather with whether conditions exist in principle under which one would conclude that the argument was false. In short, true claims cannot be falsified, but they can be falsifiable. For example, every object near the earth's surface falls at thirty-two feet per second if we assume that there is no air friction. Apparently this is true despite the fact that the simplifying assumption that there is no air friction is never precisely met. It is also a falsifiable claim. If, for instance, you let go of a rock near the earth's surface, there is no air friction, and there is nothing holding the rock back or otherwise interfering with it and it rises rather that falls, then the hypothesis would be disproved. Thus, we can state the conditions for falsification. Whether they are satisfied or not is related to falsification; whether they can be stated or not is sufficient to establish falsifiability. One objective throughout this volume is to sort out which theories of international relations are falsifiable and which are not. We can do this by examining the logic of each theory and the evidence for and against it relative to alternative theories. We saw earlier that an important part of Morgenthau's theory of realism is not falsifiable according to the standards of science. Those who subscribe to it may be right about how the world works, but we have no way to tell. Falsifiability and the examination of logic and evidence are ways we can assess the relative merits of competing explanations while upholding the first principle of wing-walking.

## SUMMARY

The first principle of wing-walking establishes that we should not abandon one theory for another until the new theory proves to be a better tool for explaining the events of interest. The reliability of predictions is the primary standard for judging the relative merits of competing explanations of events. Theories provide the linkage between assumptions and empirical generalizations. They stipulate how variables relate to each other. In doing so, theories identify the causal or probabilistic association between independent and dependent variables. They provide a simplified view of reality that is believed to reduce the complexity of the real world to its essential components.

Assumptions describe the set of conditions under which a theory is expected to apply to the phenomena of interest. Hence, assumptions define a theory's relevant world of applicability. If the assumed world is too far removed from the world in which we live, then the theory's predictions will prove unreliable and we will conclude that the theory is useless or trivial. If the assumptions contradict each other on logical grounds, then the theory is logically false and so cannot provide a coherent explanation of the world in which we live. Consequently, theories will be judged based on their logical consistency and empirical usefulness. Taste or aesthetic appeal are not critical in evaluating alternative explanations of international affairs; adherence to the requirements of the scientific method is critical.

CHAPTER 3

# CHRISTOPHER COLUMBUS AND INTERNATIONAL RELATIONS

COLUMBUS'S PROPOSAL, OR FERDINAND AND ISABELLA'S AMBITION

FACTORS THAT SHAPE FOREIGN POLICY CHOICES

DISCOVERING AMERICA: AN EVALUATION OF POLITICAL ECONOMY AND NATIONAL SECURITY

LESSONS SUGGESTED BY COLUMBUS'S EXPERIENCE

TOOLS AND SOLUTIONS: AN ILLUSTRATION OF THE USE OF DECISION THEORY IN THE STUDY OF INTERNATIONAL RELATIONS

GAME THEORY, OR WHY PEOPLE SOMETIMES CHOOSE WHAT THEY DO NOT LIKE BEST

SUMMARY

In this chapter we will focus on the decision of the fifteenth-century Spanish monarchs Ferdinand and Isabella to back the voyages of Christopher Columbus in his search for a water route to Asia. The story of Columbus is known to almost everyone, yet few have considered its implications for international politics. An examination of Columbus's odyssey—how it was initiated, by whom, and why—provides an opportunity to introduce strategic thinking about foreign policy in a familiar setting. At the same time it serves to emphasize the point that the ideas explored in this book are timeless. The logic used to account for events that took place five hundred years ago and the logic used to account for events happening today are the same. In the course of our study I will introduce some of the tools of decision theory and those of its subbranch, game theory. Decision theory concerns how an individual weighs alternatives; it offers a powerful means by which to assess individual decision making. Game theory provides a means to evaluate how two or more people, interacting with each other though not necessarily sharing the same objectives, make choices while mindful of one another's maneuverings.

In Chapters 1 and 2 I laid out a set of core principles. Here I will illustrate how these principles influenced the Spanish decision to finance Columbus's proposed journey to Asia across the Atlantic Ocean even as they led the Portuguese, French, English, and others to reject it. The story of Columbus is enduring. It presents many features of international politics that are relevant today.

## COLUMBUS'S PROPOSAL, OR FERDINAND AND ISABELLA'S AMBITION

In fourteen hundred and ninety-two Columbus sailed the ocean blue. We all know that. It is curious, though, that most of us know very little about why Columbus, an *Italian* navigator recently employed by the *Portuguese* court, sailed under the *Spanish* flag. The story behind Ferdinand and Isabella's decision to back Columbus's journey contains almost every important element of international relations. It is a tale about the pursuit of self-interest, shaped by people's power to influence decisions, by their preferences for some policies over others, and by their perceptions about whether those policies can succeed in meeting the two fundamental challenges facing all governments: the quest for security and the pursuit of wealth or satisfaction. By "security" I mean the ability to fend off external challenges to the sovereign authority of the state and its leaders in order to maintain the international status quo (Morrow 1991a). By "wealth or satisfaction" I mean the ability to bestow benefits on those citizens whose support is needed to fend off internal challenges to the authority of the political leadership. Security is sought to minimize risks, whereas satisfaction is pursued to fulfill ambition.

Ferdinand and Isabella were not the first monarchs to be offered the opportunity to back Columbus's expedition. The monarchs of Portugal, France, and Britain were also given the chance. Yet, only Spain agreed. The others showed little or no interest. With hindsight we know that Columbus's discoveries eventually brought great wealth and power to Spain. During the century before his voyage, the Catholic Spanish kingdoms of Aragon, Castile, and Navarre and the Islamic kingdom of Granada were wracked by civil unrest, costly foreign wars, unstable alliances, and frequent conflict with the powerful Catholic Church. In the century that followed Columbus's discoveries, a unified Spain (incorporating Aragon, Castile, Navarre, and Granada) became one of the greatest powers of the world. The once-divided Spanish kingdom established a

*The policy of exploration and expansion proposed by Columbus (right) made it possible for King Ferdinand and Queen Isabella to turn Spain into a global economic and military power.*

83

worldwide empire, largely funded by the tremendous wealth extracted from the New World.

The structure of the international system—that is, the complex web of interdependencies between sovereign states reflected in the array of conflictual and cooperative interactions between nations—and the specific relations among particular members of this system were transformed in ways that greatly favored Spain for a long time thereafter. The distribution of power shifted in Spain's favor in ways that were almost unimaginable before Columbus's voyages. Spain became more influential and more valuable as an ally than it had ever been before. The interests and ambitions of the Spanish leaders had to be considered by all of the world's important nations before they chose their own courses of action. Judged from today's perspective, the decision of Ferdinand and Isabella to support Columbus's plan was surely a resounding foreign policy triumph. Columbus offered an opportunity simply too good to be missed. At the same time, it seems that the decisions of Portugal, France, and England to reject Columbus's proposal were foolhardy. Apparently they turned down an opportunity to "get rich quick" at a rather low cost and on easy terms. Such an outlook betrays a common error in thinking that we must be careful to avoid. Although we know how Columbus's adventure turned out, no one during the years between 1485 and 1492, when he tried to sell his idea to sail westward to the Orient, could have known of the great rewards to follow. Given what it knew at the time its decision had to be made, Portugal's choice to reject Columbus's proposal was every bit as good and sensible as Spain's decision to accept it. The same can be said of the other European states of the day. Hindsight must not provide the basis for judging the merits of decisions made with only the benefit of foresight.

## FACTORS THAT SHAPE FOREIGN POLICY CHOICES

What are some of the key factors that enter into foreign policy decisions like the ones made by Spain and Portugal? How does self-interest get translated into concrete decisions about actions to take or actions to avoid? When making foreign policy decisions policymakers must assess the probability of the success or failure of their policy choice, calculate its expected costs, and determine the expected utility of that policy compared with alternatives.

### PROBABILITY OF SUCCESS OR FAILURE

Each decision maker has to determine the probability of the success of a given policy choice. In the case of Columbus's proposed expedition to Asia, Spain and Portugal had to form a judgment about the probability that the voyagers would succeed, first, in reaching their destination and, second, in returning to their home port. Essentially, they had to act on their perceptions about whether the voyage was destined to fail or actually had a chance of succeeding. This involved knowledge about the technical difficulties or risks of the venture as well as information about the possible political or military reactions of adversaries who might fear Columbus's success. The fact that other sailors with ideas similar to Columbus's had set forth across the Atlantic never to be heard from again was strong evidence that the probability of success was low.

## POLICY COSTS AND POLITICAL COSTS

Decision makers have to consider the costs of backing a particular policy choice. Ferdinand and Isabella had to think about how much money, time, and personnel to commit to Columbus's venture. At the same time they had to consider how else that time, money, and personnel might be utilized. The first type of costs—the actual expenditures—are transaction costs. Some of these are borne before a transaction takes place. For example, the terms of the agreement between the Spanish government and Columbus had to be negotiated. After agreeing on a particular transaction, costs can arise in enforcing the terms of the agreement. For Ferdinand and Isabella, all of these costs—negotiating, enforcing, and implementing the voyage of discovery—constituted transaction costs (Williamson 1985; Kreps 1990). The second type of costs—the alternative uses of resources—are opportunity costs. Opportunity costs are not out-of-pocket expenses. Rather, they are the forgone alternative uses of valuable resources.

Transaction costs and opportunity costs are important components of foreign policy decision making, whether the policy problem at hand is military, economic, social, religious, or what have you. Policy costs must be borne by someone, and those costs act as a drag on the self-interest and ambition of political leaders. When followers bear costs that are not accompanied by worthwhile rewards, they are likely to become dissatisfied. Such dissatisfaction raises the risk that they will seek means to overthrow their leaders (Lamborn 1991; Bueno de Mesquita, Smith, Siverson, and Morrow 2003). Thus, a too-costly policy choice can lead to the ultimate in political costs—loss of power.

Within the framework of political costs and policy costs, several distinctions are worth noting. Self-interested actors are necessarily concerned with both the benefits that they gain from their actions and the costs they must shoulder. When costs are expected to exceed benefits from a particular action, that action becomes unattractive. It is important to recognize that costs and benefits can take several forms. The most obvious form is pecuniary. Pecuniary benefits include the monetary and political gains from holding office. Pecuniary costs include the price paid in time and effort to hold on to political office. There can also be nonpecuniary costs and benefits. These include the psychological gains from gambling on high stakes; the satisfaction of outmaneuvering an opponent; or the psychic price paid in shame, guilt, or grief for engaging in ruthless behavior. Upholding one's ethical standards or acting in a moral way provides nonpecuniary benefits. If it happens that pecuniary and nonpecuniary considerations pull a decision maker in opposite directions, then the ultimate choice he or she makes will depend on the relative magnitude of all costs and all benefits, both pecuniary and nonpecuniary.

## EXPECTED UTILITY OF A POLICY COMPARED WITH ALTERNATIVE POLICIES

Finally, policymakers have to calculate the expected utility, or the anticipated costs and benefits, of the returns if a policy choice proves successful. The monarchs to whom Columbus made his proposal had to more than simply calculate the power, wealth, and prestige to be derived from finding a westerly route to the Indies. Rather, each decision maker had to contemplate the marginal gain in power, wealth, and prestige over and above what they could have expected to get by doing something else. It is here that the notion of opportunity enters into the picture. It is the calculation of net gains and losses that lies at the heart of our concern with self-interest. Leaders who ignore the costs and benefits of their actions—leaders, for instance, who are blindly compelled by circumstance or context—cannot survive for long except through plain luck. And luck is hardly a solid foundation on which to risk one's future in pursuit of one's ambitions.

Instead of luck, leaders are more likely to rely on calculated risks. For example, Saddam Hussein took a calculated risk in ordering Iraq's army to invade Kuwait in 1990. He calculated that there was only a small chance that the United States would take military action to expel the Iraqis from Kuwait. His personal estimate of the risk of U.S. intervention proved wrong, but he could not have known it would be wrong beforehand. Calculated risks sometimes lead to failure, as in the case of Saddam Hussein's invasion of Kuwait or the Taliban's decision to back Osama bin Laden after the September 11, 2001, attack against the United States, but sometimes they succeed. President John F. Kennedy took a calculated risk when he declared that the United States would put a man on the moon before 1970. America's prestige was put on the line when the Soviet Union's space program ran far ahead of the U.S. program. The successful American moon landing in 1969 ended the space race and gave the United States a great boost in international prestige.

Expected utility estimates allow leaders to make calculated risks. By assessing the alternative consequences that might arise from a course of action, decision makers can compare the costs and benefits of those consequences with the costs and benefits associated with alternative courses of action. For each consequence there must be some estimate of the probability that it will arise. The costs and benefits of that consequence are multiplied by the probability that it will actually happen. The expected utility estimate approximates the value of costs and benefits that will be experienced given the different actions that could be taken and the different risks, rewards, and punishments associated with each action. Because costs and benefits are multiplied by their probability of occurring, the resulting value equals a person's best guess as to what he or she will end up with by pursuing this or that course of action. In fact, you can think of people being just as happy taking compensation now that equals their expected utility as going ahead and taking the calculated risk whose end result will be more—or less—than their expected utility.

Let us consider, then, the perceived prospects of success and the associated costs and benefits that each decision maker believed would follow from Columbus's journey. We will see how political power, preferences, and perceptions shaped the Spanish and Portuguese interests in pursuing a westward passage to the Indies. We will then consider the alternatives to Columbus's proposal (sailing east around Africa, going overland via caravan routes, doing nothing) and their expected costs and benefits to see why Spain chose to back Columbus while others chose not to. In doing so, we will be careful to base our assessments only on what was known or believed at the time. In this way we can begin to think carefully about constructing rules for explaining and predicting foreign policy choices and understanding the consequences of these choices for international relations.

## DISCOVERING AMERICA: AN EVALUATION OF POLITICAL ECONOMY AND NATIONAL SECURITY

Wealth grew substantially in Europe in the centuries just before the Black Death (the epidemic probably of bubonic plague) of the mid-thirteen hundreds. By the end of the fifteenth century Europe had largely recovered from the economic slowdown that followed the plague. As wealth once again expanded, a taste for the spices, silks, and other luxuries of Asia emerged among the swelling pool of consumers with the means to purchase them. The demand for these goods rose more rapidly than the supply, pushing prices up and providing opportunities for merchants to make vast fortunes, much as trade today is stimulated by rising demand that increases prices and encourages the discovery or creation of new sources of supply. The trade also provided monarchs with the opportunity to secure great wealth not only through the imposition of taxes but through direct investment as well, provided they could gain an advantage over their rivals in the trade with the Indies. These exchanges with Asia also offered diplomatic opportunities to establish colonies (which functioned more as trading posts at that time), build alliances, enhance national security, and proselytize for the Catholic Church, then the dominant religious force in Europe. In addition, these exchanges yielded opportunities to learn about technologies unknown in Europe. The Chinese, for example, developed gun powder, movable type for printing, paper production methods, and improved wind and water mills long before these technologies were developed in or found their way to Europe.

The overland routes via caravan were slow and costly. There was a high risk of theft and spoilage, and for European traders there was the added uncertainty of Muslim control of the routes after 1453. Because the prospective benefits in wealth and power were so large, and the existing caravan routes so risky and costly, many European leaders preferred to search for alternative routes to Asia. Indeed, so valuable was the opportunity for improved trade that governments were prompted to impose extreme secrecy on their navigational discoveries or technological innovations, which might enhance their chances of gaining an advantage. The discoveries of sea routes and new territories were treated as state secrets roughly equivalent in importance to the modern-day treatment of nuclear weapons technology. It was against this backdrop of opportunity that Christopher Columbus came forward with his bold plan.

## THE OFFER TO PORTUGAL

Columbus first put forth his proposal to Portugal. He would sail for Japan by going west from the Canary Islands. According to his reckoning, the distance to Asia was about 2,400 nautical miles. He did not think that a significant land mass was in the way of the passage, although he did expect to encounter some unknown islands. Columbus understood that there was a real risk that there would be no opportunity to reprovision his ships once he departed from the Canary Islands, but he did not view this as a severe problem. He believed his ships could carry enough food and fresh water for such a journey. He felt that he would have no trouble reaching his destination (or returning safely). Columbus asked Prince Juan II of Portugal to fund his project—and was turned down flat. Why?

Portugal was arguably the world's greatest sea power in the fifteenth century. Thanks to the vision of Prince Henry the Navigator, Portuguese sailors had developed lucrative trade routes and colonial expansion along the North African coast and as far away as the Azores, about 900 miles out in the deep water of the Atlantic Ocean. The Portuguese Crown had managed many of these explorations without paying for them directly. Explorers and adventurers had been happy to sail at their own expense, provided they received adequate rewards and recognition if they succeeded. Columbus initially sought direct payment for his adventure rather than a contingency fee, but this was only a small impediment. Of much greater consequence was the judgment of Portuguese scientists that the distance between Portugal and Japan going west was not much different from the distance between these two countries going east around the tip of Africa. They did not agree with Columbus's guess that the journey would be just 2,400 miles. Instead, they thought the distance from the Canary Islands to Japan was about 10,000 miles (it is actually about 10,600 miles), plus an additional 900 or so miles from Lisbon to the Canaries.

The difference in estimates was crucial. From the Portuguese perspective, the probability that ships could reach Asia by sailing west was almost zero. No ship of the day was capable of a 10,000-mile-long journey without stopping in ports along the way for food and water. Quite simply, the Portuguese government believed that such a journey was doomed.

What's more, at about the same time that Columbus made his offer, Bartholomew Dias discovered the Cape of Good Hope at the tip of Africa and, therefore, implicitly the passage up the eastern side of Africa and on to Asia. Dias was already under commission by the Portuguese government and had, by the late 1480s, discovered critical features of an eastward journey to the Indies. The sea route he found offered ample opportunities for resupplying ships at coastal stations along the eastern shores of Africa. The Portuguese did not see any added marginal value in pursuing Columbus's adventure. Dias's discovery could serve the ambitions of Juan II at quite acceptable costs and with quite tolerable risks.[1]

Portugal expected no marginal gain from sailing west rather than east. The distance to Japan going around Africa is about 12,000 miles, a distance almost equivalent to the Portuguese estimate of the distance of the westward route. The eastward approach had a much higher probability of succeeding because there were known places to obtain food and water. The proposed westward passage, in contrast, offered no apparent opportunities to restock along the way. As such, the Portuguese felt that any westward expedition was sure to fail. Thus, from the Portuguese perspective, Columbus's proposal offered a low probability of success, moderate costs, and a marginal expected gain of zero. Portugal, already in possession of a prospective trading advantage stemming from Dias's discoveries, wisely turned Columbus down. And given what was known at the time, Portugal was right. It was better for the Portuguese to focus their energies on securing their trade opportunity via the eastern passage. Indeed, Portuguese power reached its peak in the sixteenth century largely because of the great wealth derived from Portugal's advantageous trading position in Asia.

## THE OFFER TO SPAIN

Disappointed, Columbus sought support elsewhere. His brother, Bartholomew, tried to entice the kings of France and England, but they, embroiled in domestic political problems, showed no interest. Columbus approached the Spanish government in 1486, but received scant encouragement. He stayed on for much of the next six years, repeatedly being put off, awaiting the findings of governmental commissions studying his proposal. He was told that a firm decision could not be made until after Spain resolved some of its internal problems, most notably its war with the Muslim-dominated Spanish state of Granada.

The year 1492 marked a period of transition for Spain. The defeat of Granada in January meant that all of the important kingdoms of Spain were now united under the control of the Trastámaras family. Within six months Ferdinand and Isabella (both of the Trastámaras family by birth) drove the Muslims and the Jews out, thereby securing Catholicism's control over all of Spain. The Catholic Church's Inquisition ordered all unconverted Jews to leave Spain by August 2, 1492 (the very day, incidentally, that

---

[1] Portugal was slow to exploit the benefits implied by Dias's discovery. It did not actually take advantage of the eastern route until 1495, when Vasco da Gama established Portugal's foothold in Asia. Dias accompanied da Gama on his first voyage around Africa. The prospect of gaining a trade advantage by making use of the route around the Cape of Good Hope seems to have been understood by the Portuguese right away. Their delays were partially a result of a false sense of security: they did not view Spain as a serious competitor.

Columbus began his first voyage of discovery). Through these acts, the Spanish monarchs helped mend broken fences with the Church (which had a new pope at the beginning of 1492) and also helped reduce the domestic political strife that had tormented much of Spain for the preceding one hundred years. Now they were ready to turn to the proposal made by Columbus.

The Talavera Commission had reported to Isabella in 1490 that Columbus's plan "rested on weak foundations" (Morison 1955, 27) and advised against backing him. Members of the commission felt that Columbus greatly underestimated the distance across the ocean between Spain and Japan. In short, they shared the Portuguese assessment that the probability of successful completion of the voyage was very low. Columbus countered with evidence of his own, but it was not persuasive.

Ultimately, as we all know, Ferdinand and Isabella changed their minds. Why did they conclude that his proposal was worth the risk when no other monarch had made the same decision? Certainly it was not that Columbus was prepared to bear the costs. He began by insisting that the Spanish monarchs pay the costs of the expedition in advance. He also sought a 10 percent share for himself and his heirs of any wealth generated by his discoveries. Later, Luís de Santangel, responsible for the privy purse under Ferdinand (making him roughly equivalent to the secretary of the treasury), noted that the initial costs for Columbus's expedition were small. Santangel offered to take responsibility for raising the funds and he noted that the additional costs (Columbus's 10 percent share) only mattered if the venture succeeded. Apparently, Columbus had softened his original position and was now ready to accept a contingency fee. Of course, if Columbus succeeded, the value to Spain would be enormous: Spain would dominate a lucrative trade route. Under existing circumstances Spain had no access to the Indies at all.

The Spaniards did not know of the eastward route around the tip of Africa because the Portuguese kept the navigational charts secret. The Italians, Arabs, and others garnered the benefits from the overland trade. Under these circumstances, Spain's calculations were necessarily quite different from those of the Portuguese. Although both agreed that the probability of success was low and the initial costs small, Portugal, in possession of the trade advantage yielded by Dias's discoveries, placed no extra value on success by Columbus. Spain, with no alternative means of accessing the wealth of Asia, attached very high utility (or value) to success by Columbus. For Ferdinand and Isabella, Columbus's proposed journey represented the only real opportunity they had to gain the wealth, power, and prestige that was associated with being a significant participant in the Asian trade. Their self-interest dictated giving Columbus a chance just as surely as Juan II's self-interest dictated Portugal's refusal.

Despite the low chance of success, the expected utility of backing Columbus—that is, the value of finding a westward passage multiplied by the probability of completing a journey using that passage—was larger for Spain than were the expected utilities of any of its alternatives. The only other option for Ferdinand and Isabella was to accept a dis-

MAP 3-1

# The World in 1493: What *Is* Reality?

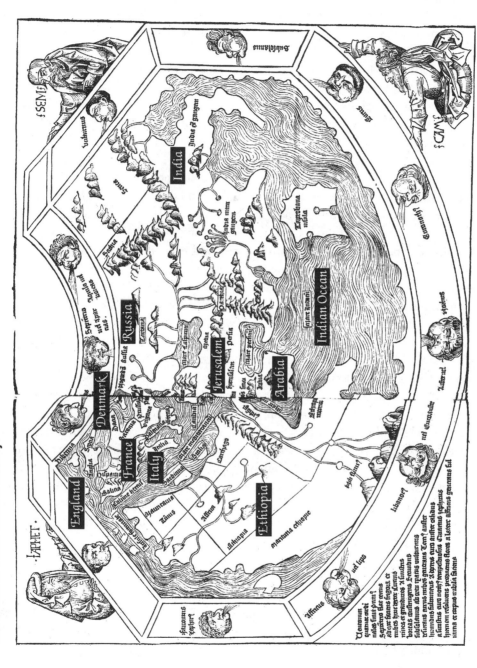

*Here we see the world as it was perceived in Columbus's day. Compare the view of India in 1493 to a modern map. Are there actual rivers that correspond to the rivers shown in 1493? What is the large island that is shown in the Indian Ocean? Is it Sri Lanka, Madagascar, or something entirely fanciful? Can you locate Italy, France, Egypt, Ethiopia, Russia, China, Australia, Japan, or the Western Hemisphere? Can you label the mountain ranges shown on the map? Notice the land bridge that joins Africa to the Far East. Does this exist? This view of the world gives us one reason to be awed by Columbus's navigational skills. To say that he sailed in the dark is an understatement.*

advantageous situation—one that saw their Arab and European rivals dominate the Asian trade routes while they themselves remained relegated to weakness and dependence. For them the prospective reward made the risk of failure worthwhile. Success by Columbus was their best opportunity to satisfy their own political and economic ambitions. This was not true for the leaders of any other European state. A reasoned calculation of costs and benefits led Ferdinand and Isabella to accept the risky proposition that had been rejected straightaway by the monarchs of Portugal, England, and France.

The mythology of Columbus's voyage suggests that he set out on his adventure through uncharted waters in a quest for the riches of the Indies and the salvation of souls by spreading Catholicism throughout the kingdoms of Asia. Although there is some truth to these myths, they are not adequate to explain his journey. The elements behind the myth should have had equal appeal to any European state, but only one chose to endorse his plan. It makes more sense to understand the voyage in its foreign policy context. It was part of Ferdinand and Isabella's aspirations to make Spain the strongest power of their day. Although Columbus was wrong in his estimation of the distance to the Indies, and in fact he never found a westward route that could rival Portugal's eastward passage, Spain did become a first-rate power.

As right as the Portuguese were about the inadvisability of Columbus's plan, they did not anticipate (how could they?) that a vast continent lay just 3,000 miles to their west, ready to yield enormous wealth and bestow immense power on those who succeeded in colonizing it. At first, Spain grew rich by extracting vast quantities of silver and gold from the New World. Later, a more enduring source of wealth helped fill its coffers: trade. Indeed, even Spain's decline can be traced to the discovery of the Americas. The Spanish Armada sailed for England in 1588 to put an end to the English-backed piracy of Spanish ships carrying precious cargoes from the Americas. Its defeat marked a turning point in the fortunes of both Spain and England. The former entered a period of decline while the latter gradually became master of the seas and the dominant power in European affairs. Spain's gamble paid off, but only for a time. Columbus's discoveries fostered intense rivalries between the European nations competing for a share of the wealth of the Western Hemisphere. Ultimately, with the emergence of the United States as a great power in the twentieth century, Spain's achievement culminated in the loss of European domination over international affairs.

## LESSONS SUGGESTED BY COLUMBUS'S EXPERIENCE

The benefits that flowed from the Americas to Spain did not result from Columbus's being right about a westward passage to Asia, but rather were the consequence of Columbus's being lucky. Chance or serendipity should never be overlooked as an element in international affairs. Still, the ability to recognize and capitalize on opportunities, even chance opportunities, is a crucial factor in successful leadership. This was true in the fifteenth century, and it remains true today. The ability to recognize an opportunity when it presents itself depends on making careful decisions that rely on the estimation of probabilities and the assessment of costs and benefits attached to alternative outcomes and alternative strategies. No one can foresee every contingency, but prudent foreign policy leaders attend to the probable development of events that can hinder or advance their interests.

## THE RIGHT POLICY FOR ONE LEADER MAY BE WRONG FOR ANOTHER

Ferdinand and Isabella understood that their power was not likely to grow significantly without risk taking. They realized that by taking risks, such as funding Columbus, they

MAP 3-2
### The Three Routes to "the Indies"

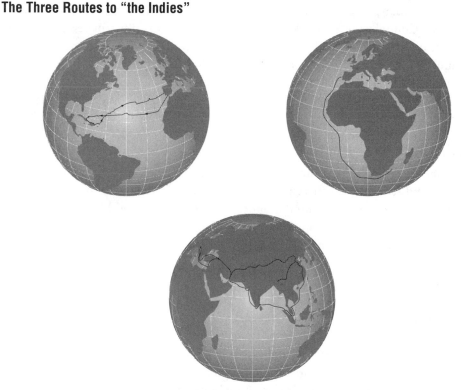

*These three globes show the western route that took Columbus to the Americas but was intended to take him to the Indies (top left); the overland caravan route that had been known for centuries (bottom); and the sea route around Africa that was discovered by Bartholomew Dias just as Columbus was trying to sell his plan to Portugal (top right). Gambling on the western route was Spain's best chance for access to the riches of the Indies, but it was not the best option for Portugal, Italy, the papacy, the Arabs, or any of the other actors on the international scene.*

were opening up an opportunity to gain great benefits for their nation and for themselves. They also recognized that the potential losses associated with the risks were not very large. At worst, they would lose three ships and their crews—this at a cost roughly equal to less than one week of entertainment for royal visitors. The prospective losses undoubtedly were of greater concern to the sailors and their families than they were to the Spanish monarchs. However small the perceived probability of success, the benefits of gaining a foothold in the Asian trade were worth the effort. In short, Spain's opportunity costs were small. The Spanish monarchs preferred a small chance of success to no chance at all.

Portugal, however, had other uses for the money and sailors that would have been needed to support Columbus's journey. Portugal was a great sea power. It knew how to capitalize on the eastward passage to the Indies and already controlled important trade routes to and around the African coast. It had a record of successful and profitable exploration. Columbus's proposal offered Portugal no improvement over the opportunities it already had. Columbus offered risks without the prospect of sufficient rewards to feed the ambition of Portugal's leaders. Naturally, the Portuguese could not anticipate that Columbus would stumble upon an unknown world of vast resources and even vaster potential.

The difference between the Portuguese and the Spanish decisions illustrates the important fact that two leaders, faced with the same choice, may make utterly different decisions, with neither one making the "wrong" choice. Indeed, the story of Spain and Portugal's response to Columbus's proposal highlights the observation that both the Spanish and Portuguese leaders made carefully reasoned decisions designed to maximize the wealth and security of their respective nations and, through these means, to maximize their own chances of retaining political power. In one case this meant ignoring Columbus; in the other, it meant supporting him. Each leader seized hold of better opportunities and passed up inferior choices.

## THE IMPORTANCE OF CONTEXT

The decision to support (or dismiss) Columbus was not made in a vacuum. Ferdinand and Isabella had to consider the implications of his success or failure in the context of their domestic and international political welfare. How would friends, enemies, and neutral parties react to this endeavor? Would they gain favor with important foreign dignitaries (like the pope or rival monarchs) or with prospective backers at home? How would the Cortes, the parliaments in the Spanish kingdoms, respond to the expenditure of tax revenues on such a risky venture? Would the wealthy nobles and Church leaders be emboldened to object to the king and queen's reckless use of funds, as had happened to Enrique IV little more than two decades before, or would they be supportive of this bold gamble on which the fate of Spanish influence might turn? Ferdinand and Isabella's calculations were made in the context of the international and domestic environments that influenced and were influenced by Spanish policy. The international system reflected the great power of the pope, France, England, Portugal, and others relative to Spain. In particular, the Spanish monarchs were concerned with ongoing competition for power between Spain (sometimes aligned with France) and Portugal (frequently aligned with England) and with recurring fears of a renewed Muslim invasion of Spanish lands. At the same time, the domestic environment was characterized by intense competition for control of revenues and government policy.

**INTERNATIONAL ENVIRONMENT.** The structure of the international political environment exerted great influence on the calculations of all the players involved in Columbus's story. The Portuguese, the Spanish, the British, the French—all were interested in attaining wealth and security. Spain possessed less wealth and probably less security from foreign invasion than any key nation in fifteenth-century Europe. Consequently, the Spanish had to take bigger chances if they were to get ahead.

Powerful states were aligned against Spain. England and Portugal had coordinated their foreign policies since the late fourteenth century, frequently at Spain's expense. France and the papacy were sometimes friendly to the Spanish throne and sometimes not. The papacy had been particularly irritated with Spanish support of the "false" pope during the Avignon schism that threatened the Church's influence in the late fourteenth and early fifteenth centuries. Even after the French had abandoned the schismatic pope, Spain stuck with him. Additionally, Spanish claims on Sicily and other Italian territory created the threat of war with several Italian city-states. Spain could not rely on any European power to help protect its interests in the event of a conflict with its neighbors. Ferdinand and Isabella had to find a way to ensure their country's welfare—and, thereby, their own. In a hostile environment, Spain could not rely on fickle allies or good fortune to keep it safe from aggressive rivals. The acquisition of external wealth, however, could give Spain the power and security it sought. As it turned out, Columbus's projected 2,400 miles to Japan was almost the right distance to the fortune that awaited Spain in the New World.

**DOMESTIC ENVIRONMENT.** Domestic political and economic conditions also played a crucial role in leading the Spanish to back Columbus and the others to dismiss him. England and France were both too unsettled internally to attend to Columbus's proposal. The leaders of these countries were too busy trying to hold together their respective governments to give adequate attention to Columbus's plan.

In England, the Wars of the Roses were just drawing to a close when Columbus began trying to attract support for his plan. In 1485, at the beginning of Columbus's quest, the Battle of Bosworth Field brought the Tudor family to the English throne. But the fighting for control of the monarchy did not end there. In June 1487, as Dias was finding his way around the southern tip of Africa, Richard III's army mounted a significant attack on Henry Tudor. At the Battle of Stoke, the Yorkist rebels were finally dealt a decisive defeat by the supporters of Henry VII, ensuring victory for the Tudors. The English Crown would remain too preoccupied with internal strife, however, to pursue external wealth and aggrandizement for several more years. By the late 1490s, however, after Columbus had made his first voyage to the West, England was able to turn its attention outward, backing Sebastian Cabot in his journey of exploration and discovery of North America. From that moment, England became Spain's political and economic rival not only in the context of its Eurocentric alliance with Portugal, but also in its competition with Spain for control over the Americas.

Initially, Columbus was unable to attract serious attention to his cause in Spain, itself faced with demanding internal and international strife. Ferdinand and Isabella could hardly worry about Spain's greater glory when they had yet to consolidate their hold on its various feuding territories. They were busy dealing with internal rivalries and external enemies. The former included resolution of tax disputes, infighting among Spain's influential families, and the crucial succession crisis that followed their marriage in 1469.

The succession crisis was triggered when Enrique IV, then king of Castile, objected to his daughter Isabella's intention to marry Ferdinand of Aragon. Enrique declared Juana (who was suspected to be an illegitimate daughter of Enrique's wife) to be his true daughter and heir, thereby attempting to disinherit Isabella. The internal contest for political control of Castile triggered by Enrique's recognition of Juana was not without significant international overtones. Enrique IV arranged for Juana to marry a younger brother of King Louis XI of France, thereby forging an alliance between Castile and France designed to weaken the influence of the kingdom of Aragon in Spain. Columbus, in fact, is reported to have served the French in a naval engagement against Aragon during the revolt that followed. The internal disagreements among competing Spanish families drew Castile, Aragon, and France into an international dispute that persisted for several years. It was not until Ferdinand and Isabella had defeated Juana and her backers and had driven the Muslims out of Granada that it became possible for them to give serious attention to Columbus's scheme.

The intertwining of domestic politics and foreign policy was shaped by, and in turn helped shape, the structure of relations among Europe's key states. Foreign policy leaders then as now looked over their shoulders at crucial domestic constituencies. Spain's leaders knew that the international arena of exploration and trade provided opportunities to satisfy domestic wants; they also knew that the domestic arena, with its concerns over taxation and internal power struggles, provided checks against their own ambition. As I noted in the Introduction, this linkage between domestic affairs and international relations is an abiding theme of international politics. It remains at least as important today as it was five hundred years (and more) ago. So too are the principles of decision making, the competition for allies, and the quest for economic and political security.

## TOOLS AND SOLUTIONS: AN ILLUSTRATION OF THE USE OF DECISION THEORY IN THE STUDY OF INTERNATIONAL RELATIONS

The problem faced by the Spanish monarchs was to find a way to participate in the trade with the Indies. The Asian trade was important because it could bring wealth and greater power to Spain, thereby advancing Ferdinand and Isabella's ambitions. The difficulty was in figuring out *how* to be players in that trade.

Several solutions to this problem were possible. Ferdinand and Isabella might simply have given up their ambition to be competitors for the Indies trade and lived with the benefits and the costs connected to whatever other pursuits they might have followed. Such a solution would not have entailed losing anything that they already had, but it would have involved sacrificing a significant opportunity.

Alternatively, Ferdinand and Isabella might have sought control of existing overland caravan routes or attempted to establish new ones. But in this they had no geographic advantage. The Italian and Arab traders in control of the already well established routes possessed ample experience and recognized authority in controlling the flow of traffic over those paths. Spain would have been undertaking a highly risky endeavor if it had attempted to take control of these routes or even if it had attempted to establish new, competitive roads to the East. A costly war could have been the result.

The Spanish might have tried to go east around Africa. Doing so would have risked war with Portugal. The Portuguese were not likely to look the other way while Spanish ships tried to break the Portuguese monopoly on the eastern route. In fact, the Spaniards did not yet know the way east around the tip of Africa. And even if they did find the way, they would have had to compete with a Portugal already ahead in developing ports where their ships could stop for supplies. Consequently, an eastern approach to the Indies carried with it not only the costs associated with discovery of the eastward route, but the prospective costs of war as well.

A solution, and the one Ferdinand and Isabella ultimately undertook, was to find a westward route to the Indies. With its low costs—and in spite of its equally low probability of success—it presented Spain its best option to become a competitor in the Asian trade.

All of these possibilities and many others can be represented more precisely using the tools of decision theory. The essential tools in this case include estimations of the probability of success or failure associated with each of the possible solutions and estimations of the utility, or individual subjective value, connected to the prospective (that is, expected) costs and benefits of the competing solutions. By linking the probabilities to the utilities we can estimate the expected, or anticipated, costs and benefits associated with alternative strategies. Such expectations can form the basis of decision making without being biased by hindsight.

So far I have discussed in words the reasoning that went into the decisions of Spain and Portugal. Now I offer a more precise, algebraic representation of the connection between the tools, the problem, and the possible solutions. The algebra will help ensure precision in our reasoning, but otherwise it will not really change anything said thus far. Later, however, as I introduce more tools of reasoning, we will see that simple algebraic representations can help us avoid logical errors and reveal new insights that might otherwise have escaped our attention. After all, mathematical sentences contain much less ambiguity than do ordinary sentences. That, in fact, is the primary virtue of using algebraic expressions to talk about politics. It is why Galileo said that the laws of nature are written in mathematical characters. Indeed, we will see that some seemingly compelling reasoning about international relations falls apart when scrutinized using algebraic expression. The occasional math that I employ is not difficult and will help to clarify thinking about international affairs.

## SPAIN'S EXPECTED UTILITY

Let's designate $p_{west}$ as a shorthand way of saying "the probability of success in achieving Spain's objectives (that is, reaching the Indies and becoming rich and powerful) by going west." Probability is expressed as a number between 0 and 1, where 0 means the condition never occurs and 1 means it occurs for certain. Therefore, $1 - p_{west}$ stands for "the probability of failure to achieve the objectives by going west." This second value is equal to $1 - p_{west}$ because in this case only two outcomes are possible for Spain: success or failure in achieving its objectives by going west. Since one of these two outcomes must occur, we are certain that the sum of their probabilities equals 1. Anytime I specify a problem with probabilistic outcomes, I will make sure that the sum of the probabilities equals 1. Of course, for many problems there can be more than two possible outcomes; still, the sum must equal 1.

Let's define $p_{east}$ similarly. This probability evaluates Spain's chance of achieving success by going east. Similarly, I use $p_{overland}$ for its chance of achieving success via the overland route, and $p_{nothing}$ for its chance of achieving success through its decision to give up and do nothing about gaining a foothold in the Asian trade. Each of these terms stands for a number that falls somewhere between 0 and 1 and reflects the judgment at the time of the chance of succeeding if, for instance, Ferdinand authorizes taking the specified action (that is, going west, east, overland, or doing nothing).

Let's assume that Isabella and Ferdinand believe that the probabilities of achieving success by going east, west, or overland are about equal. We can then say that $p_{east} = p_{west} = p_{overland} =$ a number larger than, but close to, 0.[2] It is evident that the Spanish

---

[2] It is likely that $p_{west}$ was not in fact equal to $p_{east}$. Going east involved fewer technical difficulties than going west because it was known that there were places along the eastward passage where ships could stop to obtain supplies. It was thought that there would be no such places via the western route across the Atlantic. This must have increased Ferdinand and Isabella's subjective (that is, personal) estimates of the probability of success associated with going east. But going east also involved the risk of war with Portugal and the attendant impediments to success. Ships would have been sunk, supply stations destroyed, and so forth, all of which would have reduced the probability of success in going east while also raising the costs.

monarchs believe Spain has no chance of succeeding in gaining the great wealth and power associated with the Asian trade if they choose to give up and do nothing to enhance Spain's economic and political circumstances. Therefore, we can assume that $p_{nothing} = 0$. Regardless of the specific value attached to the other probabilities, we can now say in general that

$$p_{east} = p_{west} = p_{overland} > p_{nothing} = 0. \tag{3.1}$$

Equation 3.1 indicates that the probabilities of success going east, west, or overland are equal, and all of these probabilities of success are greater than the probability of success in doing nothing, which equals 0.

Now let's denote the benefits of an action with the letter $b$. For Ferdinand and Isabella we can accurately characterize the utility they attached to the benefits of the alternative solutions to their problem as follows:

$$b_{east} = b_{west} = b_{overland} > b_{nothing}. \tag{3.2}$$

That is, the benefits from going east, west, or overland are equal, and all of these approaches will bring greater benefits than doing nothing. By any of these means, Spain can gain access to the wealth, power, and prestige attached to the Asian trade, provided, of course, that they are successful in their attempt. Giving up has less value because obviously there is nothing to be gained by not trying, and there is no apparent alternative means available to Spain of gaining equivalent power, wealth, and prestige. We can treat $b_{nothing}$ as equivalent to failure in any of the strategies under the simplifying assumption that failure means that the status quo will prevail.[3]

Now let's denote the costs of an action with the letter $c$. We can depict the costs of doing nothing, pursuing the westerly route, pursuing the easterly route, or going overland as follows:

$$c_{nothing} < c_{west} < c_{east} \text{ and } c_{overland}. \tag{3.3}$$

In this expression the respective costs appear in order from lowest to highest. Notice that the cost of doing nothing is expected to be lower than the cost of pursuing the westward route. After all, doing nothing involves no transaction cost at all. No ships have to be built and no crews have to be outfitted and paid; nothing has to be done. For the sake of simplicity, then, let's set $c_{nothing} = 0$.

---

[3] Of course, it is likely that failure following a war with Portugal, Italy, or the Arab traders would have meant the imposition of penalties that would have made the utility of failure worse than the status quo.

Going west is less costly than going east or seeking an overland approach to the Indies. The latter two prospective solutions involve a significant risk of war with Spain's neighbors, as well as costs in time, money, and personnel necessary to establishing routes. These same three costs also figure in Columbus's plan, but there was no real chance of war over an attempt to discover a westerly approach to the Indies. We do not know whether $c_{east}$ is larger, smaller, or about the same as $c_{overland}$ but, as we will see shortly, it does not matter for determining the policy preference of the Spanish monarchs.

If Spain succeeds in any of these endeavors to reach Asia, then it will realize the utility or value attached to the net benefits, $b - c$ (that is, benefits minus costs) of the chosen strategy. If Spain tries and fails, then it can expect to gain whatever benefits are associated with the status quo (the benefits of doing nothing); however, the monarchy will still have to endure the costs attached to that particular approach. How are Ferdinand and Isabella to choose what to do?

One sensible approach is to pick the solution that was *expected* to yield the greatest net gain (that is, the benefits minus the costs).[4] In doing so, it makes sense for Ferdinand and Isabella to pay attention not only to the costs and benefits, but also to the chances that the benefits will actually be gained. The way to do this is to calculate the expected utility associated with each solution and then select the solution that yields the largest expected quantity. Such a calculation requires that for each solution under consideration we take the relevant costs and benefits of each possible outcome and multiply them by the probability that those particular costs and benefits will be experienced. This can be expressed mathematically as $p(b - c)$. In this way we are able to take into account how much risk is attached to alternative strategies, as well as the possible costs and benefits of those strategies. By doing this multiplication we weight, or average, the costs and benefits by the chance that the action will lead to the proposed outcome. If we then add together these calculated values for each possible outcome, we get the measure of the total predicted value of a particular solution (the expected utility). The general formula for expected utility ($EU$) is

$$EU = p_1(b_1 - c_1) + p_2(b_2 - c_2) + \ldots + p_x(b_x - c_x), \tag{3.4}$$

where each term refers to the expected value of a particular outcome from the set of all possible outcomes $(1, 2, \ldots, x)$.

We can now compare the expected utility of the alternative solutions and pick the one that seems best. Of course, Ferdinand and Isabella did not actually sit down with

---

[4] I emphasize the word "expected" because, of course, Ferdinand or Isabella or any other decision maker can choose based only on what he or she knows or believes at the time the decision is made. Choices may turn out to be wrong. Costs may be higher than expected and benefits may be lower than expected. Still, it is sensible to choose what seems best at the time of the decision.

quill and parchment in hand and do this kind of calculation before making their foreign policy choice. Rather, I *hypothesize* that such a calculation reliably represents how people intuitively approach problems and make decisions. This is a way of generalizing about the foundation of people's choices; it assumes people are logical and systematic about things that matter to them so that they think about the potential costs and benefits associated with the choices they make.

Using the general formula for expected utility we can express the expected utilities of Spain's alternative solutions in the following equations:

$$EU_{east} = p_{east}(b_{east} - c_{east}) + (1 - p_{east})(b_{nothing} - c_{east}) \tag{3.5}$$

$$EU_{west} = p_{west}(b_{west} - c_{west}) + (1 - p_{west})(b_{nothing} - c_{west}) \tag{3.6}$$

$$EU_{overland} = p_{overland}(b_{overland} - c_{overland}) + (1 - p_{overland})(b_{nothing} - c_{overland}) \tag{3.7}$$

$$EU_{nothing} = p_{nothing}(b_{nothing} - c_{nothing}) + (1 - p_{nothing})(b_{nothing} - c_{nothing}) = b_{nothing}. \tag{3.8}$$

Equation 3.5 reads "the expected utility of going east equals the probability of succeeding via the eastward route multiplied by the benefits of succeeding minus the costs associated with going east plus the probability of failing via the eastward route multiplied by the utility of failing minus the costs of the effort." Equations 3.6 through 3.8 can be read similarly, only substituting the appropriate action for "east." Notice that doing nothing is equivalent to obtaining for certain the benefits from pursuing no solution to Spain's problem and bearing no costs. Given the assumptions we have made about the relative values of the probabilities, benefits, and costs, we can see that $EU_{west} > EU_{east}$ and $EU_{west} > EU_{overland}$. Equations 3.1 and 3.2 indicate that the probabilities and benefits of Spain's proactive solutions are equal, whereas equation 3.3 indicates that the costs of going west are smaller than the costs of going overland or east as there is no risk of war. According to our hypothesis, then, going west should be preferred over pursuing overland routes or sailing east.

It is less clear what the preferred choice should be between going west or doing nothing. We can start by comparing the relevant expected utilities. If $EU_{west} < EU_{nothing}$, then we predict that the Spanish monarchs would do nothing because the net expected gain from doing nothing is larger. If $EU_{west} = EU_{nothing}$, then we predict that Ferdinand and Isabella would be as likely to back Columbus as they would be to do nothing. Finally, if $EU_{west} > EU_{nothing}$, then we predict that Spain's leaders would support Columbus's venture. Notice that the theory of expected utility decision making gives firm predictions about policy choices based on expected gains and losses.

In order to determine what conditions must be met for the last of these three comparisons to be true, we would start by restating the relationship using the relevant formulas for expected utility—in this case, equations 3.6 and 3.8, respectively:

$$p_{west}(b_{west} - c_{west}) + (1 - p_{west})(b_{nothing} - c_{west}) > b_{nothing}.$$

We can expand this using algebra, multiplying the terms through and dropping the terms that cancel out to get

$$p_{west}b_{west} - c_{west} - p_{west}b_{nothing} > 0.$$

Solving for $c_{west}$ by rearranging the terms, we find that

$$c_{west} < p_{west}(b_{west} - b_{nothing}). \tag{3.9}$$

Thus, if

$$c_{west} < p_{west}(b_{west} - b_{nothing}),$$

then

$$EU_{west} > EU_{nothing}.$$

We can restate this in words as follows: "The marginal gain in benefits from sailing west rather than doing nothing ($b_{west} - b_{nothing}$) discounted by the probability that the Indies would successfully be reached by sailing west ($p_{west}$) has to exceed the expected cost from taking the westward route in order for Ferdinand and Isabella to favor supporting Columbus over doing nothing." In fact, this is pretty obvious. So obvious that you may wonder why it is worth going through all of this algebraic rigamarole. The answer to that question will become clear as we go along.

It is evident that the potential marginal gain, if the voyage is successful, is very large. Although the chance of success is small, so too are the anticipated costs. The choice for Ferdinand and Isabella seems to have come down to doing nothing or taking the risk involved in Columbus's plan. Apparently the anticipated costs were small enough to make it worth their while to gamble on Columbus. In fact, a critical feature of the actual decision appears to have been that the keeper of the privy purse, Luís de Santangel, reduced the cost to zero for the Spanish monarchs. Samuel Eliot Morison reports that Columbus made a take-it-or-leave-it offer to the Spanish Crown in 1492, which in fact Ferdinand and Isabella did refuse. However,

> just as, in bargaining in a bazaar, a storekeeper will often run after a departing customer to accept his last offer, so it happened here. Luís de Santangel, keeper of

Ferdinand's privy purse, called on the Queen the very day that Columbus left Santa Fe and urged her to meet Columbus's terms. The expedition, he pointed out, would not cost as much as a week's entertainment of a fellow sovereign, and *he would undertake to raise the money himself*. . . . Isabella . . . jumped at this, her really last chance. She even proposed to pledge her crown jewels for the expenses, but Santangel said that would not be necessary. (Morison 1955, 30, emphasis added)

By his actions, Santangel made the cost of the westward route equal to zero ($c_{west} = 0$) for Ferdinand and Isabella, although not for himself. Since the probability of achieving success by going west was greater than zero ($p_{west} > 0$), although not by much, Santangel guaranteed that the requirement represented by equation 3.9 would be met. Therefore he guaranteed that the Spanish monarchs would choose to back Columbus rather than do nothing even though they understood that there was only a tiny chance of success. This simple mathematical representation helps account for the choice made by the Spanish monarchs and provides a guide to the critical final element in their decision.

## PORTUGAL'S EXPECTED UTILITY

For Portugal, the expected probabilities of success were quite different from those for Spain. The Portuguese had overcome a critical obstacle to developing a viable eastern approach: they had found the way around the Cape of Good Hope. Having done so they could begin to develop supply stations along the eastern shores of Africa. Consequently, if they sailed east the probability of success was high, whereas if they sailed west, went overland, or did nothing, it remained low. For Portugal,

$$p_{east} > p_{west} = p_{overland} > p_{nothing}.^{5} \tag{3.10}$$

The prospective benefits were probably ordered by the Portuguese in the same way they had been ordered by the Spaniards:

$$b_{east} = b_{west} = b_{overland} > b_{nothing}. \tag{3.11}$$

The costs of going east for the Portuguese were small, perhaps even smaller than the costs of going west. After all, by going west they risked losing ships and sailors to the unknowns of the Atlantic crossing. Going east did not hold the same hazards, at least not to the same extent. Resupply stations could be established, and that, of course, would be costly. But, then, so too would be designing new ships capable of holding sufficient provisions for the length of time the Portuguese thought it would take to reach Japan by

---

[5] Alternatively, the Portuguese might have thought that the chance of success going overland was greater than the chance of success going west. The distance going west was believed to be larger, and arguably the Portuguese thought that the westward route was associated with greater obstacles to success. For our purposes, it does not matter which of these two beliefs they held.

crossing the Atlantic. Once the supply stations were established for the easterly approach, the marginal costs of making the voyage around Africa would be quite small:

$$c_{nothing}, c_{east} < c_{west} < c_{overland} \tag{3.12}$$

Given these assumptions, we can express the expected utilities for each available strategy in the following equations:

$$EU_{east} = p_{east}(b_{east} - c_{east}) + (1 - p_{east})(b_{nothing} - c_{east}) \tag{3.13}$$

$$EU_{west} = p_{west}(b_{west} - c_{west}) + (1 - p_{west})(b_{nothing} - c_{west}) \tag{3.14}$$

$$EU_{overland} = p_{overland}(b_{overland} - c_{overland}) + (1 - p_{overland})(b_{nothing} - c_{overland}) \tag{3.15}$$

$$EU_{nothing} = p_{nothing}(b_{nothing} - c_{nothing}) + (1 - p_{nothing})(b_{nothing} - c_{nothing})$$
$$= b_{nothing}. \tag{3.16}$$

Under the assumed probabilities, benefits, and costs for Portugal, sailing east yields greater expected gains than sailing west or attempting to secure an overland route. This is so because the costs of going east are smaller for Portugal than the costs of going overland, and the costs of sailing east are at least not larger than the costs associated with sailing west. At the same time, the probability of being successful by going east is larger than the probability of being successful by going west or overland. Therefore, $EU_{east} > EU_{west}$, and $EU_{east} > EU_{overland}$. Choosing between doing nothing or sailing east, then, was the only real decision the Portuguese had to make. According to the logic of pursuing the greatest expected gain, the Portuguese Crown should choose the eastern route to the Indies over living with Portugal's (rather attractive) status quo, provided that $EU_{east} > EU_{nothing}$, or, equivalently,

$$p_{east}(b_{east} - b_{nothing}) > c_{east}. \tag{3.17}$$

Given how small the cost of going east probably was, and how large the probability of achieving success by going east had become after Dias's discovery of the Cape of Good Hope, we can see that the requirement represented by equation 3.17 has certainly been met. It is little wonder that the Portuguese pursued their explorations around Africa as a means to build trade routes to Asia.

## GAME THEORY, OR WHY PEOPLE SOMETIMES CHOOSE WHAT THEY DO NOT LIKE BEST

Picking a sensible solution to the problem faced by Spain or Portugal turns out to be fairly straightforward with the tools offered thus far. But understanding these tools and other tools that might help foreign policy leaders in their decision making requires more knowledge about the fundamental building blocks that support probabilities, benefits, and costs.

In this chapter we have considered the relative advantages of seeking Asia's wealth by going overland, sailing around the tip of Africa, or sailing across the Atlantic Ocean. The simple decision theory formulation has provided us with a basis for predicting what choice each national leader would make. We have not yet considered why Columbus decided to undertake his journey without payment and gamble on a contingency fee that might never be collected, either because he might fail or because the Spanish monarchs might renege on their promise to pay him a share of what he brought back. (Indeed, the Crown did renege on its promise, which led to a long court battle that Columbus's son finally won.) Let's consider the way in which Columbus's decision to work on a contingency-fee basis was shaped by his expectations about what the Spanish Crown would do. In doing so, I will introduce one of the most important conceptual tools used in this book: game theory. Game theory is the fundamental tool for analyzing strategic decisions.

The problem facing Columbus and Ferdinand was complicated.[6] They both had many choices. Columbus could have held out for a high price, thinking that he could try again to get support from France or England. He might have agreed to reduce his price, taking only out-of-pocket expenses up front and receiving a contingency fee if he were successful. He might have given up his plan altogether. He also might have contemplated any payment scheme in between, so that something was paid right away and his "performance bonus" would have been suitably reduced upon evidence of success. For his part, Ferdinand could have said yes to any pricing arrangement, preferring cheaper deals to costlier ones. And he could have said no under any or all circumstances.

For the purposes of illustration, I am going to pare down the number of choices available to Columbus and Ferdinand. Let's suppose that Columbus has just two choices. He could offer to sail west looking for Japan only if he is paid his fee up front, or he could sail west on a contingency-fee basis (as he did), taking his chances that the Spanish monarch will honor the promise to pay Columbus a percentage of what he finds. Now let's suppose that Ferdinand's only choices are to say yes or no to whichever of these proposals Columbus proffers. What is important to realize here is that even though Columbus makes his proposal first, before Ferdinand chooses any action, the choice Columbus is expected to make differs from what he really wants because it is determined by the fact that Ferdinand does not have to make his choice until after Columbus has made an offer. The decision making here can be likened to a game, one involving just two players (Columbus and Ferdinand). However, unlike in many board games, the player who goes last in this game has the advantage.

---

[6] For simplicity, we will reduce our discussion to just two actors, Columbus and Ferdinand.

In analyzing the decisions made by Columbus and Ferdinand, we will examine only one stage of choices, the final stage. Earlier, as I have noted, Columbus had asked for a high price. Ferdinand had rejected Columbus's proposal. We pick up the problem just when Columbus can either continue to insist on a high price, testing whether Ferdinand will yield in the face of a take-it-or-leave-it offer, or make a more modest proposal to see if the king will say yes to a reduced price.

We can think of the decisions to be made as making up a game between Columbus and Ferdinand. In any game, each player chooses at least one move, where a move is an action like "charge a high initial fee for looking for a route to Asia" or "charge a low initial fee for looking for a route to Asia but be paid extra on a contingency fee basis if success-ful." Ferdinand's choices might be portrayed simply as "approve the voyage" or "reject the voyage." A *strategy* is a complete plan of action in a given game. This means that a strategy includes a contingency plan for every action that the other player or players could possibly select. A player's strategy states what he or she will do under every possible circumstance.

To solve a game we need to identify the strategies that each rational, self-interested decision maker trying to do as well as possible would employ. By "rational" I mean only that the players do what they believe is in their own best interest given what they know at the time of choosing. In Chapter 9 I will provide a more detailed definition of rationality.

The main solution concept for games is called a Nash equilibrium. A Nash equilibrium is a set of strategies in a game such that no player has a unilateral incentive to switch to another strategy. That is, given the expectation about what the other player will do in each contingency, a player's plan of action is part of an equilibrium if that player has no reason to change his or her mind and do something differently. John Nash, the subject of the book *A Beautiful Mind* and a movie of the same name, won the 1994 Nobel Prize in economics in part for proving that for every possible finite game there exists at least one circumstance in which no player has a unilateral incentive to change his or her moves; that is, a Nash equilibrium exists.

Games have rules about how decisions are made. The basic rule is that the participants try to anticipate the consequences of alternative actions and choose the actions

---

Identify a current foreign policy problem. List all of the players—sometimes I will refer to them as stake-holders—who have an interest in trying to influence the resolution of the issue you have chosen. As you work through this book, you will encounter more information about these stakeholders, including the outcome they currently say they support, how influential they could be in deliberations on the question at hand, and how salient the issue is for them.

As you progress through the chapters of the book, you will acquire skills with which to develop reliable predictions about what is likely to happen on this issue and even skills in figuring out alternative courses of action to influence the outcome. You will also be introduced to software called the Forecaster that can be found at http://bdm.cqpress.com. You will learn how to use this software to make predictions about the issue you have chosen so be sure to pick one that is interesting. Plenty of possible issues can be "ripped from the headlines" of the newspaper.

they believe are in their best interest given what other players are expected to do in their own interest. The interests of the players are reflected by the payoffs, or expected utilities, associated with each possible outcome of the game. A game can be represented by a tree of choices (called the extensive form) or by a matrix of payoffs (called the strategic, or normal, form). Here we will use the extensive form to examine the Columbus-Ferdinand game. We will discuss strategic form games in Chapter 5.

An extensive form game consists of choice nodes, which are points in the game at which a player must choose an action. The choice nodes are linked to other choices (or to outcomes) via branches. Any number of branches (including an infinite number) can emerge from a choice node, but only one branch can lead to a choice node. Thus, each of the branches extending out from a choice node leads to a different place in the game. That place is either another choice node or a terminal node—that is, a place where the game ends. This means that each specific path or sequence of possible actions in a game is unique. In this way game theory reflects some of the ideas of path dependence. Path dependence is an argument sometimes made by historians or historically oriented students of international politics that suggests that the sequence of history is unique. Game theory provides one useful way to address this assumed uniqueness while preserving the idea that there are logical and predictable bases for how international affairs unfold.

Figure 3-1 illustrates the game between Columbus and Ferdinand in extensive form. Columbus must choose between demanding a high price and demanding a low price for his services. Ferdinand must decide whether to approve or reject Columbus's proposed voyage. Let's assume that Columbus will be most satisfied if Ferdinand approves the voyage at a high price. We will assign this outcome a payoff, or value, of 4 for Columbus. Columbus's second-best outcome would be to have Ferdinand approve the voyage at a low price. Let's say that this has a value of 1 for Columbus. Let's assume further that it does not matter to Columbus whether he asks for a high price or a low price if Ferdinand is going to say no anyway. In this case, Columbus will be dissatisfied. We can represent his dissatisfaction by assigning it a payoff of 0.

Ferdinand, presumably, will be best satisfied by agreeing to support Columbus's

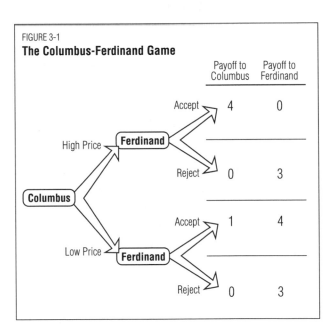

FIGURE 3-1
**The Columbus-Ferdinand Game**

*Decisions are strategic. Columbus could not just set a price on his services and then expect that the Spanish king would pay it. Before deciding on what price to charge, he had to think carefully about how Ferdinand would respond to alternative proposals.*

voyage at a low price. We can attach a value of 4 to this outcome. Ferdinand's next-best outcome can be reached if he rejects the proposal outright. We will assign a value of 3 to this outcome. Finally, Ferdinand's least-desired outcome would be to support Columbus's journey at a high price. This has a value of 0 for Ferdinand.

In Figure 3-1 the choice nodes are identified with the name of the player making a choice, and the terminal nodes are identified by sets of payoffs. Branches are shown as arrows linking any type of node to any other type of node. The payoffs to each player are listed in the order in which the players move. Thus, in Figure 3-1 Columbus's payoffs are always listed first (as he is the first player to make a choice) and Ferdinand's payoffs are listed second. Columbus, seeking to enhance his own well-being, desires as large a payoff as he can expect to get. This might lead you to expect that he will ask for a high price, yet this is not correct. To see why it is not correct, we must solve the game. The game is easily solved by using a method called backward induction. This is a fancy way of describing a simple process.

The players in a game care about the consequences of their actions. Hence, they plan ahead. Like chess players, they think about how their opponent will respond to the different decisions they could make. The easiest way to do this sort of thinking ahead is to write down the game tree, as we have done. Then, by starting at the end of the tree (that is, at a terminal node) and working back to the beginning (that is, to the first choice node), the player can decide which choices are best, given the other player's anticipated moves, in order to reap the best possible payoff. In doing this the player must exhaust the moves at all terminal nodes first, then at all the nodes that come just before the terminal nodes, and then at all the nodes just prior to those, and so forth all the way to the beginning of the tree. Because all the players want to do their best, they will make a choice at each stage in the game that will maximize their own welfare. Thus, if one action is expected to result in a worse payoff farther down the tree than some other action, then the one with the better expected payoff in the end will be chosen. In other words, a player will always pick the highest payoff he or she can get at each choice node, based on expectations of how the other player will respond farther down the tree. This pattern of always choosing the action that is expected to produce the best feasible outcome for a player in subsequent moves in the game is called subgame perfection. Subgame perfection is a way of playing a game by looking ahead to contemplate what others will do in reply to the player's choice. Each choice is expected to be a best reply to the actions of the other players at each stage in the game.

Figure 3-2 shows the solution to the Columbus-Ferdinand game. The figure here is the same as Figure 3-1 except that some branches of the game tree are represented as shaded arrows and others as unshaded arrows. The shaded arrows show the actions that each player will choose at each decision node if the rules for playing the game are followed—that is, if the players are doing what they believe is in their own best interest. An equilibrium outcome represents the solution to the game. An outcome occurs when the path of shaded arrows is uninterrupted from the beginning of the game to its end. If Columbus decides to insist on a high price, for example, then Ferdinand will choose to reject the proposed journey. He would make this choice because the value he places on rejecting a high-priced voyage (3) is greater than the value he places on accepting a high-priced voyage (0). If, however, Columbus asks only for a low price (in this case, a contingency fee), then Ferdinand will accept Columbus's proposal because he would net a higher payoff (4) than if he rejected the proposal outright (3). Since Columbus is interested in his own welfare, and because he is in a strategic situation in which he knows that Ferdinand's preferences (that is, payoffs) must ultimately shape his own, Columbus elects to offer to seek a westward passage to Asia on a contingency-fee basis. Although he would most prefer to ask for a high price, by thinking ahead Columbus realizes that Ferdinand will most likely reject a high-priced offer, leaving him (that is, Columbus) empty-handed. However, he knows that by scaling back and offering to undertake the journey at a lower price (that is, on a contingency-fee basis), Ferdinand is much more likely to accept his offer, thereby affording him (that is, Columbus) the opportunity to reap a large reward down the road.

The simple strategic situation depicted in Figure 3-2 points to several important strategic lessons. Decision makers do not always pursue the course of action they like best. Instead, as the Columbus-Ferdinand game illustrates, they often compromise on their objectives to maximize their expected gain. They do this in recognition of the fact that their decisions are constrained by expectations about how others will react to their choices. Historians looking back on Columbus's decision to journey so far and at such great risk for no better than a contingency-fee reward might conclude that Columbus was foolish or (as is more often thought to be the case) simply uninterested in wealth. Indeed, history portrays Columbus as a great navigator, adventurer, and discoverer. It pays scant attention to his motivation for personal gain. Yet we know that he pressed his claims for his contingency fee after his final voyage. The game implies that his decision was shaped by a concern for

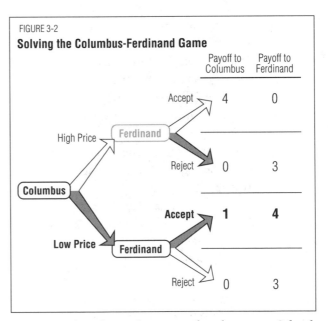

FIGURE 3-2

**Solving the Columbus-Ferdinand Game**

Decision makers do not always get what they want. Columbus had to settle for little money and a weak commitment from Ferdinand to pay him later in order to gain the opportunity to look for a westerly route to the Indies. If Columbus had held out for a higher price, chances are Ferdinand would have dismissed him.

an event that did not happen: his actions seem to have been motivated by the fear that Ferdinand would deny him any opportunity to seek his fortune by searching for a westward route to Asia. Ferdinand's threat to reject an expensive journey was credible. Since Columbus in the end did not ask for a high price, Ferdinand did not need to reject the proposed journey. But it is nevertheless crucial to understand that *the threat of that rejection* was part of Ferdinand's complete plan of action; it was part of his equilibrium strategy and it was the part that got Columbus to agree to sail "on the cheap." Often, strategic situations draw attention to the impact on foreign policy of decisions *not taken* in anticipation of their grave consequences.

Throughout the cold war, for example, both the United States and the Soviet Union threatened to adopt foreign policies that the other abhorred. Each built up its military arsenal, apparently in preparation for use against the other, or at least against the other's allies. Yet Soviet and American troops never faced off against each other in sustained combat at any time between 1945 and the collapse of the Soviet Union in 1991. One possible explanation is that each anticipated dire consequences, including possible nuclear war, if it engaged the other in combat. As the costs of such a confrontation would have outweighed the benefits, each looked for ways to control their rivalry and to gain advantage without war. Thus here, as in the Columbus example, the expectation of events that did not happen was important in shaping the foreign policy decisions of the cold war era. Reasoning about events that did not happen—that is, about counterfactual events—is rarely found in purely historical, statistical, or case history analyses. Yet it is fundamental to game theoretic analysis.

The Columbus-Ferdinand game points to other issues as well. One such issue concerns a fundamental problem in politics: the inequitable distribution of valuables. Columbus was unsuccessful in trying to collect his contingency fee. In fact, he was imprisoned for his efforts. Ferdinand's promise to pay Columbus a share of whatever of value he acquired was not backed up by any credible means of enforcement. Ferdinand was the law in Spain. Even today countries governed by monarchs or dictators do not have reliable legal systems that people can appeal to if an agreement or contract is violated. The power of individuals, rather than the power of the law, determines who gets what. In democracies this is less true because the rule of law is usually an important feature of democratic institutions.

The unreliability of legal enforcement is one reason that foreign investment flows more often to democratic countries than to autocratic countries. The legal framework common to democratic governments provides a credible commitment that commercial contracts will be enforced (Moore 1966; Przeworski 1991; Haggard and Kaufman 1995; Weingast 1997; Bueno de Mesquita, Smith, Siverson and Morrow 2003). When governments can confiscate other people's property or wealth without legal recourse, investors are reluctant to risk their money. This problem of credible commitment accounts for much of Russia's failure in attracting foreign money after the collapse of the Soviet

Union (Bueno de Mesquita 2002). The Russian government's policies have been too fickle for many foreign investors. This problem also explains why the vast majority of foreign investment in China that has helped to fuel its rapid economic expansion has come from Hong Kong and Taiwan and not from Europe or America. Hong Kong, formerly a British colony, strove to gain favor with Chinese authorities before the British handed it over to China in 1997. Economic investment in China aided the Hong Kong elite in currying favor with China's central authority. Taiwanese leaders, for their part, view foreign investment in China as a lever with which to influence the Chinese government's policies toward Taiwan. Hence, the economic risks of such investments are secondary to their potential political gains.

The Columbus-Ferdinand game also points up the problem of anarchy. Columbus entered an agreement that he could not be sure would be enforced. Ferdinand reneged because it did not turn out to be in his interest to pay Columbus his share of the profits. In the arena of foreign policy, no legal authority can credibly punish nations or leaders who violate agreements. Economic sanctions might be imposed, as was done against Iraq during the 1990s and against Cuba (by the United States) beginning in 1960. But sanctions are effective only if no influential countries break ranks and deal openly or in secret with the punished party. International organizations such as the United Nations can impose punishment, but these organizations have few means to enforce their decisions. International politics is often said to be anarchic because there is no binding legal system with real enforcement power that can be brought to bear on strong states that violate the "law." In Chapters 11 and 14 we will see that there are ways for foreign policy leaders to make credible or enforceable agreements. Finding ways to do so is fundamental to producing cooperation in international affairs. When commitments or promises lack credibility, international interactions are inefficient because resources must be dissipated in monitoring and possibly sanctioning violations. The United States spent billions of dollars erecting a system of spy satellites to monitor Soviet arms agreements, but spent virtually nothing to monitor military agreements with Britain.

Part of Ferdinand's power derives from the fact that Columbus made the first move. Ferdinand was not so eager for Columbus's

> Try your hand at constructing a simple game in which moving first provides an advantage. How does this game differ from the Columbus-Ferdinand game? What is the equilibrium outcome of the Columbus-Ferdinand game (no voyage, a high-priced voyage, a low-priced voyage) if Ferdinand moves first so that the sequence of play is reversed?

voyage that he made an offer to pay for it before Columbus put terms on the table. Had he done so, Columbus might have inferred that Ferdinand really wanted to see a voyage undertaken and might therefore have raised his price.

The sequence of moves in foreign policy decision making often shapes the final outcome. It is very common for international negotiations to stall over seemingly minor factors because neither side wishes to signal eagerness for agreement, lest its bargaining position be weakened. When the United States and North Vietnam launched negotiations to resolve the war they fought from 1965 to 1973, their efforts bogged down over the shape of the negotiating table in Paris. In truth, no one cared that much about the table's shape, but neither side wanted to make the first concession. Neither side wanted to end up, like Columbus, agreeing to a deal largely dictated by the other side. This is a recurring problem in the conflict between Israel and the Palestinian Authority. One reason mediators are sometimes used in international disputes—like the United States in negotiations between Israel and the Palestinian Authority—is that a mediator can act as an honest broker. If that role is compromised by the appearance of favoritism, then mediation breaks down. If a mediator is trusted by both sides, each side tells the mediator what concessions it is willing to consider and the mediator can then choose when and what information to convey from one side to the other and back to produce an agreement that both sides will accept. International trade, law, and security organizations such as the World Trade Organization, the International Court of Justice, and the UN Security Council are designed to serve as mediators. These organizations can be helpful in resolving differences by allowing the disputants to avoid the "you first—no, you first" syndrome common in bilateral negotiations.

*Foreign Minister Shimon Peres of Israel (center) clasps the hands of Greece's foreign minister Georgios Papandreou (right), and Turkey's foreign minister, Ismail Cem (left), in Tel Aviv on April 25, 2002. Greece and Turkey, both allies in NATO, have fought several wars and came close to fighting another in 1996. This meeting with Peres immediately followed a meeting with the besieged Yasser Arafat, president of the Palestinian Authority, who was unable to leave his headquarters in the West Bank city of Ramallah because of Israeli military action following terrorist strikes against Israeli civilians. Papandreou and Cem hoped that their own success at restoring peaceful relations between their countries would serve as a role model for the Israelis and Palestinians. Such negotiations make clear that mediators, as honest brokers, often help adversaries find common ground to resolve international disputes.*

## SUMMARY

The story of Christopher Columbus illustrates how national leaders jockey for political advantage through foreign policy. The Spanish Crown sought to improve its financial situation and its influence among European heads of state by seeking an alternative route to the Indies. When Ferdinand balked at putting his money into what looked like an extremely risky venture, his "budget director" privately raised the necessary outfitting funds and Columbus agreed to sail on a contingency-fee basis. This set Columbus on his way in the name of the Spanish Crown. The Portuguese, English, and French monarchs were each made the same offer, but each declined to take it up. Portugal declined because it had a superior alternative (a known—and known only to Portugal—route), and the English and French refused because they were distracted by major domestic problems that precluded any thought of Columbus's risky scheme. By using expected utility calculations, we saw that it was sensible for Ferdinand to accept Columbus's proposal, and it was equally sensible for the other European leaders to reject his proposal. The logic of expected utility calculations forms an essential part of how we will view foreign policy and international relations decision making throughout this book. These calculations provide an important foundation from which to predict and explain foreign policy choices.

Columbus's decision to accept a contract based on a contingency fee evolved from consideration of the strategic circumstances (albeit simplified here) driving his actions. We used the concepts of game theory and Nash equilibria to examine why Columbus gave up his most desired outcome—a high fee in advance—in exchange for a lower-priced contingency fee. We found that, for Columbus, pursuit of his most desired outcome would have netted him only rejection. Ferdinand appears to have been motivated by a desire to improve his foreign policy position cheaply. Because he held a strong position relative to Columbus, Ferdinand was able to dictate the terms that he found favorable. Had Ferdinand exhibited a real desire to back the westward voyage, Columbus could then have accepted or rejected Ferdinand's proposed fee and thereby possibly have extracted better terms.

We have also learned several additional points from our game theoretic investigation. For example, the sequences of moves in negotiations can be critical. Sometimes moving first allows a decision maker to control what is considered (that is, the agenda), providing an advantage. At other times, depending on the structure of the strategic situation, moving first reveals a player's hand and forces that player to succumb to a strategic advantage possessed by decision makers who move later. In strategic situations, the motivation to do as well as can be expected can result in decisions, like Columbus's, to compromise rather than pursue the most desired outcome. Therefore, it is risky to infer what leaders or nations want just from their actions alone. We must also take into consideration the constraints they face, including the likely actions of their rivals. Often, foreign policy decisions are motivated by a desire to avoid a worse outcome. Although a worse outcome is a real danger, we should realize that, since it does not often occur, it is usually ignored by conventional, nonstrategic studies of international politics. Yet focusing investigations only on what actually happens can lead to erroneous explanations of important international events.

# CHAPTER 4

# INTERNATIONAL POLITICS FROM A STRUCTURAL PERSPECTIVE

<a>EVALUATING ALTERNATIVE PRINCIPLES</a>

DEFINING THE PUZZLES OF COOPERATION AND CONFLICT

STRUCTURAL PERSPECTIVES

SUMMARY

International relations is filled with difficult questions that intrigue and beguile us. Chief among these is why nations sometimes cooperate with each other and other times engage in bloody, violent conflicts. That nations do both is not in dispute. Why and when nations cooperate or compete, however, is a puzzle hotly debated by policymakers and theorists alike. The solution to this puzzle is of great intellectual interest; more important, it is the best hope we have for building a more humane world.

In this chapter and the next, I introduce three ways of thinking about international relations that will help us better understand why nations sometimes cooperate with one another and at other times engage in competition and conflict. In this chapter we will focus on the structural perspective. In Chapter 5 we will examine the interest group, or bureaucratic, perspective and the strategic perspective. Each of these core perspectives is designed to help us sift through the infinitely vast pool of facts available to us by drawing our attention to a few key concepts that are essential to an understanding of international relations. Although these core perspectives share a common goal, they disagree on which facts to examine and on what those facts should reveal.

## EVALUATING ALTERNATIVE PRINCIPLES

The central task before us is to evaluate alternative perspectives in regard to how reliable they are in helping us organize facts and expectations in a way that allows us to accurately predict future developments. In this chapter we will examine theories that focus on structural aspects of the international system to explain outcomes and make predictions. These theories are concerned with such factors as the distribution of power and whether or not states are organized hierarchically. They do not include the belief that national concerns, such as the individual characteristics of a nation's decision makers or the organization of its government, have a consequential impact on the course of international relations. In this chapter I introduce you to three especially influential bodies of structural theory: neorealism, liberalism, and Marxism. Each provides a different way of thinking about how to promote international cooperation and prevent conflict, and each offers a different view on what roles can be played by international law and international organizations.

Accuracy of prediction is the primary means by which to choose among alternative theoretical perspectives. A theory has failed (or is at risk of failing) if it makes more wrong predictions than some alternative theory designed to explain the same phenomena. In such a case, the alternative theory is preferable because its account of events has proved to be more reliable. The concern for predictive accuracy will direct our attention to situations of conflict or cooperation in which competing theories, based on alternative assumptions about how the world works, offer different expectations about how events unfold in international affairs.

As we investigate the facts relevant to understanding international relations and the theories or perspectives used to explain those facts, we need to be mindful of several considerations. First, we need to know what a theory assumes about international relations. For instance, does it assume that each nation can be thought of as a single, unified entity, as in structural perspectives that focus on how all states interact, or does it assume that each nation is made up of many competing constituencies with different goals and different attitudes toward how to achieve those goals, as in the interest group or bureaucratic perspective? Does a theory assume that international relations depends on fundamental, common human characteristics like self-interest, as in the strategic perspective, or does the theory assume that international politics depends on culturally or historically determined values that vary from place to place and from time to time, as in theories based on what is called constructivism?

Second, we must be concerned with logical consistency. Once assumptions are stated they lay down a framework within which to evaluate how variables (that is, changing factors) influence one another. The predictions derived from any theory should follow as logical implications from the set of assumptions that have been stated. Inconsistencies among the assumptions or between the assumptions and proposed predictions make it impossible to say exactly what a theory leads us to expect. Consequently, logical inconsistencies jeopardize our ability to evaluate competing theoretical perspectives. They represent a significant threat to the scientific potential of a theory by making the application of the scientific method all but impossible. Therefore, it is crucial that we identify any logical inconsistency in a theory's arguments.

Third, personal taste has no place in judging facts or theoretical perspectives. We cannot dismiss a point of view simply because we think its assumptions are unrealistic or because we object to a theory's conclusions. Our objective is to understand how international relations works. And no one yet fully understands how nations relate to one another. Consequently, no one has stated a completely realistic and accurate theory. This is true in every field of human inquiry, whether we are speaking of the physical sciences, the humanities, or the social sciences. This realization should humble us and make us reluctant to dismiss a point of view simply because we do not like it.

## DEFINING THE PUZZLES OF COOPERATION AND CONFLICT

Before turning to our discussion of the structural perspectives on international relations that form the heart of this chapter, we should come to a better understanding of the core facts that motivate our subject. These facts, you recall, concern international cooperation and conflict or competition. What exactly is meant when we speak of cooperation or competition? What are some examples of each and why is it surprising (at least from some perspectives) that national governments cooperate with one another or compete with one another? Those theorists who focus on cooperation, especially as it relates to trade and investment, generally study the international political economy; those more concerned with sources of potential conflict and hostility tend to focus on security studies. In either case, the objective is the same: to understand how relations of cooperation and competition take shape across national boundaries.

### EXAMPLES OF INTERNATIONAL COOPERATION

It is my contention that leaders and, indeed, all people are motivated primarily by concerns for their own well-being. Even when we observe altruism at work, as when one government contributes vast sums of money, food, or medicine to another, it is not hard to imagine that self-interest lies behind this generosity. This is not to say that the world is driven by selfishness, just that self-interest is a guiding force in international relations. Many who hold this view find it strange when nations cooperate with one another. Each nation, they contend, must surely fear that other nations will take advantage of it if it lets its guard down. In domestic affairs, the weak have recourse to enforceable laws to protect them from bullies and scoundrels. In international politics they do not. Yet, cooperative arrangements are commonplace in international politics. These cooperative arrangements generally involve the development of international organizations and laws or norms of international behavior, collectively sometimes referred to as regimes, that help leaders in different countries coordinate their actions with the intention of providing mutual benefits to the participating parties (Taylor 1976, 1987; Keohane and Nye 1977; Axelrod 1984; Axelrod and Keohane 1986; Stein 1990; Krasner 1991; Sebenius 1992; Morrow 1994b).

National governments have forged numerous such global unions of international cooperation. The Universal Postal Union, founded in 1874 and now administered through the United Nations; the International Atomic Energy Agency, formed in 1957 and now boasting more than 120 members; United Nations peacekeeping forces; and the International Court of Justice are but a handful of the many examples of international agreements with global reach. Sometimes economic interests bring groups of nations together in efforts to control or influence the price of such commodities as oil or coffee or cocoa. These groups are known as cartels. Best known among these producer cartels is the Organization of Petroleum Exporting Countries, or OPEC for short. The oil ministers in the countries that belong to OPEC usually meet every three months to set oil production quotas for the membership. Through their cooperative efforts they hope to influence the price of crude oil. In the 1970s, for example, OPEC's coordination of oil exports by its members produced an "oil shock" that sent gasoline and heating oil prices much higher than ever before. In recent years, however, OPEC has not been very successful. Some countries that produce significant amounts of oil do not belong to the organization, and some countries that do belong cheat on their quotas. Russia, the world's largest oil producer, as well as the United States, Norway, Britain, and Mexico are all examples of crude oil–producing states that do not belong to OPEC. In fact, the real price of products derived from crude oil is no higher today than it was before the oil shocks of 1973 or 1979.[1]

The General Agreement on Tariffs and Trade (GATT), first established in 1947, is another example of an international organization that coordinates and promotes business. The GATT and its successor institution, the World Trade Organization (WTO), were designed in part to foster free trade by eliminating tariffs and quotas among the industrialized economies of the world. The GATT and the WTO have established rules that limit protectionist trade policies by its member states. Since this free trade regime includes just about all of the major industrial economies, the GATT and the WTO seem to have had a profound influence in liberalizing trade policies and, thereby, stimulating trade. Naturally, the degree of cohesion among the member states of the GATT and the WTO has fluctuated notably over the years as have the interests of individual members. Whether the GATT, the WTO, OPEC, or other cartels are successful or not, they represent important efforts to foster international cooperation among states.

Organizations such as the World Bank, the International Monetary Fund (IMF), and the Asian Development Bank were created to coordinate gift giving in the form of foreign aid from rich countries to poor countries. These international organizations influence economic policy choices by making the availability of loans contingent on the willingness of recipient countries to follow prescribed economic programs such as those that promote low inflation and foster growth. In recent years, for instance, the IMF has

---

[1] Real prices are distinguished from nominal prices. For example, suppose a gallon of gasoline cost $0.38 in 1970 and $1.30 in 1999. These are nominal prices. Now suppose that because of inflation, $1.00 in 1970 is the equivalent of $3.50 in 1999. In this case, the nominal $0.38 price of a gallon of gasoline in 1970 is equivalent to $1.33 in 1999, so that the real price has barely changed. In fact, to the extent it has changed at all, it has gone down.

tied its assistance to Russia to the Russian government's willingness to hold down inflation. The World Bank often supports economic programs designed to stimulate spending by governments, often on large construction projects like dams, airports, and highways. These projects are intended to help the economy grow while expanding employment. Unfortunately, such projects sometimes provide an easy venue for unscrupulous politicians to hide millions of dollars in graft and corruption. This is what happened in the Philippines and in Indonesia when the World Bank extended assistance to those countries. International economic organizations such as the World Bank and the IMF rarely intervene in local politics to influence the design of political institutions or the conduct of leaders; instead, they confine their activities to encouraging policy choices that they hope will be for the better.

Little of the foreign aid that is given by one government to another can easily be traced to consciously selfish motives on the part of the donor. Rather, such aid seems to be given with a genuine humanitarian desire to assist the neediest of our fellow human beings (Lumsdaine 1993). The Scandinavian countries, for example, were among the first to pledge financial aid to the Palestinians to help them build a viable society out of the Gaza Strip and Jericho following the agreement signed in 1993 that briefly ended years of warfare between Israel and the Palestine Liberation Organization. How can such an action be explained in an arena of politics so often thought to be defined by considerations of power and distrust? Certainly the Scandinavians, with virtually no Palestinian or Jewish populations and no obvious security concerns in the Middle East, will not be the prime beneficiaries of the aid they have given. Rather, they seem to be motivated by a desire to encourage cooperation with others and thereby share in the intangible benefits of peace that follow. It is easier to tie the actions of donors whose contributions are larger in absolute terms to self-interest because they tend to extract policy or economic concessions from recipients.

The examples we have discussed here create a puzzle for those seeking to understand the principles of international politics: why do nations with divergent, selfish interests sometimes cooperate with one another, even doing so when there is no apparent tangible benefit to be gained? This is one of the most enduring questions in the study of international affairs.

## EXAMPLES OF CONFLICT AND COMPETITION

Although cooperation seems to be the hallmark of some relationships, others are characterized by enduring conflict and competition. Rivalry and bickering were constants in the relationship between Syria and Israel for decades, even as tacit agreements kept their antagonism within carefully controlled bounds. The relationships between other states may experience flashes of hot rivalry, followed by years of subdued antagonism. In these cases disputes remain dormant for years, even decades, only to erupt suddenly and violently like a powerful volcano. The relationship between Bosnia and Serbia is an example.

Their enduring rivalry, shackled by the constraints of the cold war, resurfaced with great violence and destruction once the Soviet Union ceased to exist. Conditions in the Balkans today are so reminiscent of those existing in the years just before World War I that one is tempted to say that in the Balkans history has repeated itself (see Maps 4-1 and 4-2).

The relationship between Argentina and Britain constitutes another example of a rivalry that continued for years without any outward signs of hostility until, after sporadic efforts at negotiations, it erupted briefly into violence. After decades of mutual indifference or low-level antagonism, Britain and Argentina engaged one another in a spasm of warfare over the Malvinas/Falkland Islands (whose name is even in dispute) in 1981. The relationship between Greece and Turkey is yet another example of hot and cold rivalry. Intermittent fighting has been a characteristic of this relationship for the past two centuries, a characteristic that continues today despite their respective memberships in the North Atlantic Treaty Organization (NATO—another example of international cooperation). As recently as 1996 they appeared to be on the verge of war with each other, although last-minute concessions by Greece averted open fighting. Enduring

MAP 4-1
## Yugoslavia's Cold War Stability, 1945–1990

MAP 4-2
## Yugoslavia's Disintegration, 1991 to the Present

*Yugoslavia's six federated republics coexisted peacefully for forty-five years after the end of World War II, but with the secessions of Slovenia and Croatia in June of 1991, Yugoslavia began to distintegrate. War erupted in Bosnia in April 1992 after Muslims and Croats there voted for independence. That same month, Serbia and Montenegro proclaimed a new Federal Republic of Yugoslavia. The Dayton Peace Accord brought the bloody Bosnian war to an end in November 1995, but by March 1998 fighting had broken out once again. Ethnic Albanians in Kosovo, a province of Serbia, were agitating for autonomy. After Serbian forces began a brutal campaign of "ethnic cleansing" (a tactic they had also applied in Bosnia), NATO stepped in in April 1999 and launched an air war that established peace to the region in less than three months. Why was there so much stability during the cold war years and so little after 1991?*

rivalries such as these pose a puzzle for those who seek to understand why some states coexist successfully whereas others do not (Goertz and Diehl 1995; Bennett 1996, 1997a, 1997b; Maoz and Mor 1996).

The relationship between the United States and the Soviet Union during the cold war was one of mutual fear and deep distrust, although the two superpowers did avoid any overt episodes of sustained violence. Their rivalry was so profound that it influenced the content of most international relations for decades. The attitudes, policies, friendships, and enmities of many nations were judged by whether they were in the Soviet sphere of influence or in the American sphere of influence. A sphere of influence is a circle of countries dependent on or particularly supportive of a more powerful and influential country's policies and activities. Following the Machiavellian principle that my enemy's enemy is my friend, nations assumed friendly or hostile relations based on which of the two superpowers other nations associated with. Those who had frequent friendly exchanges with the Soviets were more or less assumed to be the enemies of the United States, whereas those friendly toward the United States were treated with suspicion by the Soviet government.

> Make up a list of countries that were in the Soviet sphere of influence. Make another list of those in the American sphere of influence. Have any members of the Soviet sphere become members of the American sphere of influence? Did any countries move from one sphere to the other before the collapse of the Soviet Union? Can you identify countries that were in neither sphere of influence? What factors do you think explain why some countries were in one sphere or the other or in neither?

Other nations emerge from long years of hostility to become close friends and allies. The relationships between the United States and Britain after the American Civil War and Germany and France after World War II are examples of this. Probably the most consequential example of such a turnaround is the changed relationship between the United States and Russia following Mikhail Gorbachev's decision to allow the East European countries within the Soviet sphere of influence to drift away and pursue their own destinies. Cautiously at first, and then more and more eagerly, the United States and Russia have tried to forge a genuine friendship. Soviet/Russian cooperation with the United States during the 1991 Gulf War would surely have seemed an impossibility to most political leaders just a scant one or two years earlier. Whether relations will continue to improve between these two nuclear powers is of major concern to contemporary foreign policy leaders.

Just as hostility sometimes melts away into friendship, so too can hostility emerge out of nowhere. Hostility and warfare are not restricted to states with histories of mutual antagonism or broad disagreement. It is not at all uncommon for closely allied states to suddenly be at odds with one another, perhaps even fighting wars against one another. Examples of such unanticipated hostility abound: Prussia and Austria in 1866, the Soviet Union and Hungary in 1956, Honduras and El Salvador in 1969, the United States and Panama in 1989, Iraq and Saudi Arabia in 1991, and Russia and the Republic of Georgia in 1993. This too is a mystery. It is important to understand why and how this happens if we are to promote peace and prevent war.

## STRUCTURAL PERSPECTIVES

By far the most prominent perspective for studying international politics centers on structural features that make nations interdependent and create what we call the international system. Structural features are the characteristics of the set of nations that make up the international system, rather than the characteristics of any one particular state. These include the distribution and fungibility of power, the concentration of national interests on security, and the predictability or uncertainty surrounding relations between states.[2] From a structural point of view these factors are the central determinants of international politics. Although limited in its potential to explain differences in foreign policies from leader to leader, or even from country to country, and despite an inability to address how the structure of the international system changes, structuralist approaches are efficient ways to address the enduring questions of international politics.

Figure 4-1 depicts in simplified form the essential features of two prominent structural theories: neorealism and liberalism. We will discuss the variations between these two theories in detail in the next two sections. What these two theories share, however, like all structural theories, is a belief that characteristics such as the configuration of poles (blocs of nations centered on great powers) essentially shape, if not determine, the course of international affairs. Variations in individual national or subnational group interests, or even individual national control over power, are much less important than the distribution of these factors across all nations.

The flow of causality in structural theories states that structure dictates goals, and goals in conjunction with structure lead to certain outcomes. Essentially, nations are

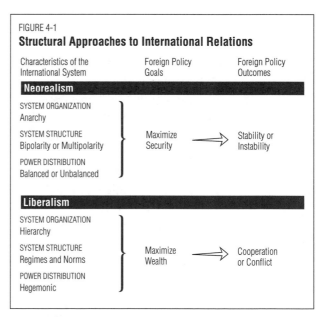

FIGURE 4-1

**Structural Approaches to International Relations**

| Characteristics of the International System | Foreign Policy Goals | Foreign Policy Outcomes |
|---|---|---|
| **Neorealism** | | |
| SYSTEM ORGANIZATION Anarchy | | |
| SYSTEM STRUCTURE Bipolarity or Multipolarity | Maximize Security | Stability or Instability |
| POWER DISTRIBUTION Balanced or Unbalanced | | |
| **Liberalism** | | |
| SYSTEM ORGANIZATION Hierarchy | | |
| SYSTEM STRUCTURE Regimes and Norms | Maximize Wealth | Cooperation or Conflict |
| POWER DISTRIBUTION Hegemonic | | |

*Structural theorists maintain that international relations is shaped largely by factors beyond the control of decision makers. Factors internal to the state, such as domestic politics and national institutions, exert little or no influence on the structure of international affairs.*

---

[2] "Fungibility" means the ease with which resources or capabilities can be transferred from one dimension of international relations (say trade policy) to another dimension (say alliance security) to make a nation more influential in the latter.

role players. And the role played by each nation is determined by its place in the international system. Great powers engage in competition to control the international system, whereas smaller states seek benefits through association with great powers or by remaining outside the sphere of great power competition. All nations, whether large or small, want to maximize the same goal, although what that goal is differs from theory to theory. Neorealists, for example, assume that security is the most important goal. Liberal theorists, in contrast, assume that accumulation of wealth is the most important national goal. Whatever internal differences exist in the political institutions of different states, and whatever variations exist in the interests of different leaders, they are irrelevant from the structural point of view. All leaders have the same goal, although they follow different policies to achieve that goal. The individual actions of nations differ only because of the place or role those nations occupy in the international system. The objectives are universal. Individual perceptions matter only insofar as they lead decision makers to believe mistakenly that they occupy a different position in the international structure than they actually do.

## NEOREALISM

The most prominent of the structural theories is neorealism. It was developed by Kenneth Waltz (1979) as a significant modification of its precursor, realism. Hans Morgenthau's theory of realism first appeared in the late 1940s and was expanded throughout the 1950s and 1960s. It posits that nations are always interested in gaining power. Factors such as domestic political interests or ideological orientations lie outside the domain of international relations. Nations are continually engaged in competition and conflict in their efforts to acquire power. They cooperate with one another by joining alliances and coordinating military preparations only on temporary, short-term bases and only when it serves their interests in gaining power at someone else's expense.

The power to influence events is conceived in relative terms, with factors such as national wealth, population, military preparedness, and territorial assets being crucial elements. No matter how much the total pie of resources might grow, a nation's position in the international system can be evaluated only by comparing its total resources against those of every other state. The greater a nation's share of important resources, the more powerful it will be.

The realist viewpoint had a fundamental problem that came to be known as the security dilemma (Jervis 1976, 1978). Nations are successful if they increase their power to influence events. But as a nation becomes more and more powerful, other nations become more and more inclined to join together in opposition to its rising influence. This creates a paradox: the more powerful a nation becomes, the more likely it is to find itself the victim of a power-grab by a stronger countercoalition or alliance of adversaries, suggesting that it really is not more powerful at all.

**NEOREALISM'S BASIC ARGUMENT.**    Neorealism was developed by Waltz and refined by others (Christensen and Snyder 1990; Mearsheimer 1990; Glaser 1992; Schweller 1994) in an effort to correct the deficiencies in Morgenthau's realist theory. Neorealism starts with five core assumptions:

1. States are unitary actors.
2. States are rational.
3. The international system is anarchic.
4. States want to maximize their security.
5. States seek gains in power so long as those gains do not place their security at risk.

It then offers three key hypotheses:

1. Relative gains in power are more important to states than absolute gains in power (Grieco 1988a, 1988b; Powell 1991; Snidal 1991; Mercer 1995).
2. The distribution of power tends to be balanced.
3. Systems with just two dominant states (bipolar systems) are more stable than those with more than two dominant states (multipolar systems).

There are, additionally, several auxiliary hypotheses. These concern bandwagoning (joining the threatening and usually stronger side in a dispute to gang up on a weaker adversary) or balancing (joining the threatened and usually weaker side in a dispute to bring power into balance and gain greater leverage) and offense dominance and defense dominance (Christensen and Snyder 1990; Morrow 1993; Schweller 1994). Offense dominance refers to situations or eras in which use of offensive weaponry and offensive maneuvers in disputes provides larger advantages than use of defensive weapons and defensive postures. Defense dominance is just the reverse. A shorthand way to think about this distinction is to consider when, in a military confrontation, there may be advantages to moving first or to moving second. This is a special case of the issue raised concerning game theory and Columbus and Ferdinand's expectations. Because actions and reactions are partially shaped by expectations of what the other side will do next, deciding when to go first and when to go second is of particular strategic importance.

Waltz's most important innovation was to suggest that nations are not interested in maximizing their power but instead are interested in maximizing their security. By this he and other neorealist thinkers (Grieco 1988a, 1988b; Niou, Ordeshook, and Rose 1989; Gowa 1994) meant that a nation would no longer seek additional power if doing so jeopardized its sovereignty by prompting others to gang up and take some of its power away. In this view nations are concerned with relative gains in their competition with other states (Grieco 1988a, 1988b; Powell 1991; Snidal 1991). It does a nation no good to gain new resources if, in the process, others gain even more resources, leaving the first party relatively worse off. Waltz explains his emphasis on relative gains as follows:

> When faced with the possibility of cooperating for mutual gain, states that feel inse-cure must ask how the gain will be divided. They are compelled to ask not "Will both of us gain?" but "Who will gain more?" If an expected gain is to be divided, say, in the ratio of two to one, one state may use its disproportionate gain to implement a policy intended to damage or destroy the other. Even the prospect of large absolute gains for both parties does not elicit their cooperation so long as each fears how the other will use its increased capabilities. (1979, 105)

By focusing on security rather than on the resources that confer power, Waltz shifted dis-cussion away from the idea that states want to gain as much power as possible to the notion that states want to optimize their power so as to make themselves secure. Neorealists view power purely as a means to achieve national ends, not as the end itself. Because they are rational, states want to maximize their expected utility based on secu-rity. This is accomplished by avoiding a power increase today that makes the state worse off tomorrow. For Morgenthau and other early realists, power was the goal of states. For Waltz and other neorealists, security is the goal. For both, however, if nations achieve their goal a stable international system will be the result.

**STABILITY.**    Stability in the Waltzian theory turns out to be an interesting and complex concept. Emerson Niou, Peter Ordeshook, and Gregory Rose (1989) have turned Waltz's verbal argument into mathematically precise statements offering logical connections that can be readily evaluated. They have shown that stability can be divided into two component parts. They call one part system stability. This refers to the survival of all states from one period of time to the next. The international system is not system stable if one or more states is eliminated (see also Gulick 1955). For example, the international system was not stable immediately after World War I, when Austria-Hungary ceased to exist. The system was also unstable in 1991, when the Soviet Union ceased to exist as a single independent state.

The second component of stability is what Niou, Ordeshook, and Rose call resource stability. Waltz focuses much attention on the efforts of states to balance power, which he sees as a crucial component of stability. Resource stability addresses this notion of bal-ancing. A system is resource stable if the relative power of each state remains the same from one period of time to the next. Niou, Ordeshook, and Rose have shown that almost any distribution of power is compatible with system stability. If the world operates according to the assumptions of neorealist theory, the international system will rarely be resource stable because there is a constant give and take of power between nations seek-ing to maximize security; the world will, however, typically remain system stable. If system stability is compatible with a range of power distributions, however, there is no logical reason to expect the distribution of power to move toward an equal or balanced distribution. This contradicts a central hypothesis of neorealism. If stability does not depend on power being more or less equally balanced between rivals, then foreign policy decisions that depend on balance-of-power arguments are inherently flawed. Simply put, if we accept the assumptions of neorealism, then its claim that a balance of power promotes stability is wrong. We return to this issue to see evidence about power distributions and instability in Chapter 16.

Nations in a neorealist world choose what is in their best interest (that is, security) most effectively if they are not hampered by uncertainty. Thus, uncertainty about how power is distributed within a system is of particular concern to neorealists. They argue that uncertainty about the distribution of power will be greatly diminished when the system is structured into two central power blocs—that is, into a bipolar system. Bipolar systems relieve uncertainty because the presence of just two great powers leaves those powers in a better position to control most of the action in international politics and because it is clear with which of these two great powers less powerful nations are aligned. In essence, neorealists contend that bipolarity eliminates uncertainty, and uncertainty increases the risks of the kinds of misjudgments, misperceptions, and miscalculations that can lead to instability. Conversely, a multipolar system (those having more than two blocs or poles) is conducive to uncertainty and therefore fosters the kinds of miscalculations, misperceptions, and misjudgments that promote instability.

Karl Deutsch and J. David Singer (1964) have made the exact opposite argument. Although they agree with Waltz that multipolarity produces more uncertainty than does bipolarity, Deutsch and Singer contend that multipolar systems are more stable than bipolar systems. States in a multipolar world, they reason, know that they must make risky decisions while confronting uncertainty. The riskiness of the situation makes them particularly cautious and conservative. One manifestation of this caution is that states are less likely to undertake new strategic initiatives that might upset the status quo. Therefore, multipolar systems are more stable than bipolar systems.

Of course, it is entirely possible that some decision makers react to uncertainty by being cautious, whereas others react by making bold choices fraught with misperceptions, miscalculations, and misjudgments. If some leaders react to uncertainty one way and about as many others react the other way, then neither bipolarity nor multipolarity, nor any other source of uncertainty, would have a uniform impact on stability (Bueno de Mesquita 1975, 1978, 1981b). This possibility, however, cannot be entertained in system-level theories because those theories treat states rather than individual leaders as the primary role players. Variations in the personal characteristics or proclivities of individual leaders are assumed to be of

> Think about the argument that bipolarity enhances stability while multipolarity encourages instability. Can you identify an unstated assumption that allows us to reach this conclusion? How do the assumptions of neorealism listed above logically lead to the conclusion that bipolar systems are more stable than multipolar systems?

minor consequence when compared with the role-setting considerations of the whole structure of the international system.

**ANARCHY AND THE INTERNATIONAL SYSTEM.**    Neorealists worry about balancing, bipolarity, and relative gains because they start from the assumption that the "state of nature" is a state of war; that is, the international system is assumed to be anarchic. This means that there is no central authority that can enforce agreements between states. International politics in this view is a self-help system. States must seek security exactly because they cannot count on any larger authority to protect them; they must protect themselves. This is why relative gains are important from the neorealist perspective.

By assuming anarchy, neorealism implies that organizations such as the United Nations, the International Court of Justice, and the World Trade Organization cannot do much more than provide a means by which individual states can coordinate their activities and help each other on a case-by-case basis. Might, not law, makes right in the anarchic world in which states pursue their own national interest and not the objectives that international law and international organizations set as priorities. In consequence, international law is fluid and weak. In fact, a glance at the workings and setup of the United Nations suggests that there is merit to this notion.

The United Nations membership has two primary bodies for dealing with the major foreign policy problems of the day: the General Assembly and the Security Council. The former includes all member states, with each state having one vote. The General Assembly does not make distinctions between states based on size, wealth, or influence. The Security Council, in contrast, consists of just five permanent members and a rotating membership of an additional ten states. The five permanent members are the United States, Russia, China, the United Kingdom, and France. These nations, the victors of World War II, each have the power to veto any proposal that comes before the Security Council. All other member states, with the exception of Israel, have the opportunity to rotate onto the Security Council from time to time.[3] However, they do not possess veto power. Thus, as suggested by the self-help view of anarchy, member states cannot count on having their individual points of view prevail on a national security matter, even if the vast majority of the General Assembly shares their view. National security matters are routinely referred to the Security Council. If a permanent member of the Security Council decides to vote against the majority in the General Assembly, then the view of that permanent member prevails. This is a clear case of an organization that is ostensibly responsible for promoting equitable enforcement of international law operating on the basis that might makes right.

---

[3] Israel does not rotate onto the Security Council because UN rules stipulate that Security Council members must represent a regional bloc. Israel, a Middle Eastern state, is not considered a representative of its regional bloc by the other members of that bloc. There are efforts afoot to redress Israel's unique status by making it a member of the European bloc, but so far this has not happened.

The notion that international politics is organized around anarchy is equivalent to assuming that international politics is a noncooperative game. In noncooperative games, promises between players (states in this case) are not binding. Promises are enforced by self-interest and not by external authority. As a rational, unitary actor, each state chooses its own best reply to the actions of other states.

From the neorealist's viewpoint, foreign policy is not a particularly compelling subject. Because "the necessities of policy arise from the unregulated competition of states" (Waltz 1979), each country's foreign policy is chosen exclusively in response to its place in the international system's structure, not in relation to general principles of international law or custom. The structure of the system (anarchic, balanced or unbalanced power, bipolar or multipolar) is a given; it is not a product of national foreign policy

*These images show two perspectives of the same event. The upper image shows U.S. secretary of state Colin Powell giving a speech to the World Summit on Sustainable Development in Johannesburg, South Africa, on September 4, 2002. Despite being repeatedly interrupted by protestors opposed to American environmental policy, he defended that policy and America's efforts to improve conditions for the world's poor. Powell's vantage point might be characterized as one of authority derived from the great power of the United States. In the lower photo, we see protestors actively demonstrating against Powell's speech amidst efforts to remove them from the hall. Whether the power of nations or the power of impassioned people will prevail is a central concern. Structural theories support the idea that national power matters far more than does citizen protest.*

maneuvers. Foreign policy decisions do not create anarchy, a balance of power, or bipolarity. Rather, anarchy, the distribution of power, and polarity create foreign policy decisions. The structure of a system is outside the control of decision makers, and it is the structure alone that determines policy choices. Consequently, if you know a system's structure, and you know a given state's position in that structure, then you know precisely what that state's foreign policy will be, regardless of its internal politics.

Neorealists recognize that individual national foreign policies may sometimes tilt toward pursuing economic goals or other objectives besides security. But when push comes to shove, these pursuits will be put aside to protect and enhance the nation's security. Structural features such as distribution of power and polarity are the truly fundamental characteristics of international relations according to neorealism. Only they can reveal when security and sovereignty are at risk. Consequently, neorealists assume that with few exceptions no amount of trade or religious satisfaction or cultural affinity or anything else can substitute for one iota of national security. The desire to preserve sovereignty dominates all other possible interests. This means that neorealism assumes that nothing of genuine importance to international relations takes place within a state. Rather, everything that is important to international politics takes place between and among nations. For neorealists, differences in the personalities, preferences, and power bases of domestic political leaders are basically irrelevant, as are cultural, religious, or social differences.

## SOME LIMITATIONS OF NEOREALISM

Although neorealism's switch from a focus on power to a focus on security seemed to clear up problems with the realist approach, closer examination reveals that the neorealist approach suffers from at least as important a limitation as did its precursor. Neorealists conclude that a world with only two great powers is necessarily more stable and secure than a world with many great powers. Yet this does not follow logically from neorealists' arguments concerning security.

Consider the following hypothetical situation. Suppose there is an international system dominated by two very powerful states called A and B. If A's share of power is 51 percent and B's share of power is 49 percent, then A can ensure its security for all time by invading B and taking away all of its resources. According to the neorealists, because A truly is more powerful than B, A can defeat B for certain, or at least A has a very high probability of success (Morgenthau 1978; Waltz 1979; Niou, Ordeshook, and Rose 1989). If this can occur, however, then the international system cannot be stable. Instead, it will undergo a momentous change: it will go from being a system with two dominant states (bipolarity) to being a system with only one dominant state. In fact, the A, B international system can be stable, and its members secure, only if the distribution of power is *exactly* equal between A and B. Indeed, in seeming recognition of this implication, Waltz and other neorealists contend that the international system naturally gravitates toward a balance of power (although what exactly is meant by a balance of power, as we will see, is not that clear).

Compare the bipolar structure of an A and B system to one with three states. Suppose nation (or alliance) A controls 45 percent of the power in the international system, nation (or alliance) B controls 40 percent of that power, and nation (or alliance) C controls only 15 percent of that power. This is a multipolar system, and, according to neorealists, it should be less stable than a bipolar system. Yet, if each of these three nations wants to maximize its security this multipolar system will be more stable than any bipolar system except the one in which A and B each control exactly half of all power. Let's see why.

If A were to attack C, B would defend C. If B did not defend C, then A would gain control over C's power, giving A 60 percent of all available power.[4] If that happens, B would surely be swallowed up by A in A's efforts to eliminate any future threat to its security. Since B, like all nations, is motivated to maximize its security, it must defend C from A to prevent its own demise. Alternatively, if A attacks B directly, then C would come to B's defense. C's reasoning is exactly the same as B's. To do otherwise would seal C's fate, along with B's. By the same logic, B cannot attack C. If it did, A would defend C against B to prevent B from gaining enough power to defeat A later. After all, if B conquers C, then B's share of power would exceed A's. Finally, B and C might contemplate attacking A, but if at war's end A were destroyed and B and C did not share exactly the same amount of power, then whichever nation was in command of the most power at war's end would destroy the other. Neither would want to participate in a policy that ensured its subsequent destruction. Remember, although they might promise to share the victors' spoils equally, under anarchy there is no reason to believe that the other will honor that promise later.[5]

Indeed, if we accept the neorealist imperative of security over power, then the multipolar example above has a straightforward resolution. If nation C gives A five of its fifteen units of power, then A will have 50 percent of the total power and the system will be perfectly stable. Neither B nor C will ally with A because to do so risks leaving A with more than 50 percent of the power. Instead, B and C will be linked in a permanent arrangement of mutual protection. Provided war is not cost free, B will not threaten C because any net loss in existing resources leaves B vulnerable to A. By shifting power to A, C ensures that A has 50 percent of the power and C and B in combination have 50 percent of the power. Such a system is multipolar and perfectly stable.

---

[4] I assume for simplicity's sake that the war is costless. If the war is costly, but still leaves A with over 50 percent of all remaining power after the fighting stops, then the end result is the same. If the end of the war leaves A with less power than B (and C no longer exists), then the war has jeopardized A's security and so, according to the neorealist principle of security maximization, should not have been fought in the first place.

[5] For more detailed development of the ideas contained in these examples, see Niou, Ordeshook, and Rose (1989) in which the logic of neorealism is carefully examined. I thank James Morrow for suggesting parts of this discussion in conversation.

The logic behind neorealism's focus on security maximization leaves very few circumstances in which a major war or other substantial destabilizing event could occur in a multipolar world and numerous circumstances in which a major war or other destabilizing event could occur in a bipolar world. Nevertheless, Waltz (1979) and fellow neorealist John Mearsheimer (1990) insist that bipolarity enhances stability and multipolarity promotes instability. Yet, this claim is contradicted by the *logic* of their theory, thereby casting doubt on the validity of the entire proposition. I will have more to say about the empirical record (that is, historical evidence) for the central hypotheses of neorealism as we go along.

For neorealist theorists, the balance of power acts as a stabilizer, protecting the system against the natural inclination of each nation to maximize its security. Over time, neorealists contend, the distribution of power among states will become more and more equal. And equality, as we have seen, is essential for stability in a bipolar system. But an equal distribution of power does not seem to be essential for stability in a multipolar system. In fact, it appears that a balance of power in a multipolar system can be achieved with almost any distribution of power, provided that no one has more than half of all the power in the system. The hypothetical situation that we put forth supports the realists' attachment to balance of power as a stabilizing element in a bipolar world, but it contradicts its destabilizing claim for multipolar structures.[6] This implies that the theory's logic problems in this area may be corrected by some adjustment in the initial assumptions and that a more sophisticated specification of the theory might resolve this particular difficulty.[7]

Volgy and Bailin (2003) propose one such modification. They divide power into three constituent parts: relative, structural, and domestic. In this way they hope to bring greater "realism" to structural theories like neorealism. Relative power is akin to what neorealists have in mind when they speak about power; that is, the potential military advantage each state has relative to each other state. By "structural power" Volgy and Bailin mean possession of the ability to shape the rules or architecture of the international system. This form of power is more like that discussed in theories of the power transition or hegemonic war (Organski 1958; Keohane and Nye 1977; Organski and Kugler 1980; Gilpin 1981; Tammen et al. 2000). In these theories, states try to control the organization of international intercourse rather than seek to maximize their security. I discuss these "liberal" or hierarchical theories a bit later. Finally, by "domestic power" Volgy and Bailin have in mind a reflection of the internal capacity of the state to mobilize

---

[6] I urge you to examine the careful arguments in Niou, Ordeshook, and Rose (1989) on the question of what constitutes a balance of power. We will return to this topic in Chapter 6 when we examine factors that increase or decrease the risk of war.

[7] Of course, once new assumptions are introduced to alleviate the problem we have identified, we must see what impact those new assumptions will have on other aspects of the theory. Introducing new assumptions is unlikely to leave other claims of the theory unaltered.

resources for its own purposes in contention with the demands and pressures of other internal interests (Organski and Kugler 1980; Tammen et al. 2000). This viewpoint is more akin to the perspectives taken up in the next chapter. Volgy and Bailin have attempted to integrate the main competing views of international politics while trying simultaneously to reconcile logical or empirical limitations in each. Theirs is a bold effort. Whether it is successful it is too early to say because their integrative approach has not yet been subjected to close scrutiny.

## LIBERAL THEORIES

Liberal theories emerged as a counterweight to the neorealist perspective. Unlike realist approaches, these theories acknowledge the frequent occurrence of international cooperation. Indeed, a desire to explain such cooperation is their first point of departure from neorealism. Furthermore, for liberal theories, structural hierarchy—which implies the presence of an actor that can authoritatively enforce agreements between states—rather than anarchy is the central organizing principle of international politics. The presence of a hegemonic state—that is, an overwhelmingly dominant power—helps enforce norms of conduct and maintain regimes. Norms are generally observed patterns of conduct. For example, most nations most of the time respect the territorial boundaries of their neighbors. They do so because this is an accepted norm of conduct. Although the United Nations exists, in part, to enforce this norm, it can do so only with the consent of its members. Thus, territorial integrity cannot be enforced easily as a matter of law but is generally enforced as a matter of shared values, or norms. Regimes are sets of international laws, rules, and organizations designed to promote coordination among nations with shared interests (Krasner 1983). Norms and regimes combine to provide the behavioral basis by which the international system's hierarchical structure promotes cooperation and supports the assumed natural inclination of nations to maximize their wealth.

**LIBERALISM.** Robert Keohane and Joseph Nye's theory of interdependence (1977), or liberalism, is the most prominent systemic, structural theory concerned more with the international political economy than with problems related to security. Liberalism and neorealism quite naturally focus on different variables. For the structural theory of liberalism, power distributions are not as important as distributions of shared interests produced, for instance, by trade regimes or cultural norms. Trade regimes are agreements and relevant enforcing institutions or organizations designed to regulate and enforce specific trade policies. Their function is to promote cooperation among participants and, in fact, they are often successful in doing so. Cultural norms, or shared values, promote cooperation by making clear what sorts of behavior are unacceptable and open to punishment. Of course, the feasibility of punishment for violating norms or regime expectations depends to a large degree on the assumption that the international system is hierarchical rather than anarchic. Theories that share the liberal perspective are more likely to treat international law as a serious constraint on national action, even when the law is contrary to a nation's self-interest, than are theories, such as neorealism, that subscribe to anarchy.

Adherents of liberalism believe that pursuit of cooperative mechanisms to generate wealth is a principal objective of nations in addition to, or even instead of, national security. According to liberal theorists, power and security vary from issue to issue; they are not unidimensional features of the nation and the system. Thus, liberal theory considers power to be less fungible than does neorealism. Because a nation's power is assumed by liberal theorists to vary from one issue area to another, nations cannot easily capitalize on their influence over one set of problems to exert influence on a different set of problems.

Japan is a case in point. Japanese views on trade must be taken very seriously by the world community. Yet Japan cannot, or at least thus far has not, translated its great influence over trade decisions into great influence over military decisions. For liberal theory, this difficulty in transferring influence from one domain to another—this lack of fungibility—is a central aspect of international affairs. For neorealists, the opposite is true. Power in one domain is power in all domains because the resources that can be used to influence decisions in one area can serve as the basis for tacit or explicit threats in other areas. For neorealists, Japanese economic might translates into political and military influence because Japan can threaten to withhold access to its markets and products if other nations pursue noneconomic policies the Japanese do not like.

The differences in emphasis on fungibility and hierarchy lead neorealists and liberals to focus on quite different aspects of international politics. For example, if power is fungible, as suggested by realists, then it makes sense to think of trade policy as serving the state's broader concerns with security. If, however, power is issue specific, as suggested by liberal theory, then it makes more sense to think of trade policy as driven by economic concerns rather than security issues. After all, if the benefits from trade cannot readily be converted into military might, then trade policy really cannot be a significant instrument of national security policy.

There are interesting arguments and evidence in support of both views. Joanne Gowa (1994), Edward Mansfield (1994), and Gowa and Mansfield (1993) contend that free trade has direct, negative effects on security that make some governments reluctant to support free trade regimes and prefer protectionist trade barriers such as tariffs and quotas. Their argument parallels Waltz's contention that states focus on relative gains rather than absolute gains. If two countries engage in trade, and one gains more than the other, the "winner" can put those extra gains into military spending and ultimately threaten the security of the less successful trading partner. Gowa calls this a security externality that results from trade, meaning that trade has this unintended security effect.

Brian Pollins (1989a, 1989b), M. J. Gasiorowski and Solomon W. Polachek (1982), and Polachek (1980) offer evidence in support of liberal theory. Yi Feng (1991) and

James Morrow, Randolph Siverson, and Tressa Tabares (1998), however, provide a theoretical argument buttressed by substantial evidence that delineates conditions under which Gowa's security externality claim holds true and other conditions under which the claims of liberal theory hold. Their argument provides a basis for distinguishing between neorealist conditions and liberal conditions in the international system that allows us a view of international affairs that is not dominated by one set of conditions but that accommodates both.

Structural liberals focus on international regimes as possible explanations of cooperation among states (Keohane and Nye, 1977; Keohane 1984). Cooperation is not viewed as a general systemic characteristic. Rather, cooperation is viewed as a characteristic of international politics that is compartmentalized according to particular issues or dimensions of international intercourse. Thus, nations might cooperate and fight simultaneously. For example, in 1990 Iraq and Kuwait cooperated as OPEC members to promote higher crude oil prices and fought with each other over border disputes. Consequently, when liberal theorists talk about regimes they mean the rules, norms, and institutions that help coordinate international behavior in specific domains.

**THE PROBLEM OF COLLECTIVE ACTION.**   According to the liberal perspective, the thread that binds nations into a system is the need to overcome problems of collective action—that is, situations in which individual incentives lead to inefficient collective outcomes. This is also known as market failure. These problems arise under two types of circumstances. One type, sometimes known as the tragedy of the commons, involves situations in which a group of people have access to a common pool of resources that may be depleted by any one member or combination of members of the group (Ostrom 1990; Hollick 1991; Ostrom, Gardner, and Walker 1994; Keohane and Ostrom 1995). This type of resource is divisible but not excludable. That is, all can gain access to the good (nonexcludable), but having gained access, anyone can use up the good (that is, it is divisible and can be depleted). The second type of collective action problem arises when an international organization or regime provides public, or collective, goods (the terms are interchangeable), which are indivisible and nonexcludable (Olson 1965).

A good is indivisible when one person's consumption of that good does not affect the amount of the good that another person or group can consume. Nonexcludability means that anyone belonging to a relevant group can consume the collective good. Fire protection is an example of such a good. If you and I live in different apartments in the same building and you pay taxes toward fire protection and I do not, I will still derive the same benefits from the fire department that you derive. If an apartment in the building is on fire, I cannot be excluded from having my apartment protected by the fire department even though I have not paid the taxes. And the fact that you and other residents have paid the taxes does not diminish the amount of protection I receive. The good is nonexcludable and indivisible. Free trade and defense are two important examples of public goods in international relations.

In contrast to public goods, private goods are not subject to problems of collective action. With private goods, the person or group who produces or receives the good gets to consume it and can prevent others from doing so. Personal income is an example of a private good. Private goods are both divisible and excludable.[8]

The significance of the tragedy of the commons is well illustrated by the efforts of the environmental movement to create new international regimes and norms of conduct designed to prevent depletion of common-pool resources. Consider, for example, the commercial harvesting of fish and hunting of whales in international waters. Fish and whales swim freely in the world's oceans. Fishing fleets from many countries earn their living harvesting tuna, abalone, or lobster. If any of these species is harvested at a rate that exceeds its natural ability to replace itself, then it will become extinct and no one will be able to fish for it again. The commercial hunting of whales during the past one hundred years brought some of those species to the brink of extinction.

Provide additional examples of public goods in international relations. Give examples of ways in which the United Nations provides public goods to its members. Give examples of private goods that the United Nations provides to members. Why can some members of a public goods–providing group get away with paying less than what seems to be their fair share of the cost of providing the good? Give some examples of common-pool resources. How has the environmental movement influenced how nations deal with common-pool resources to prevent the tragedy of the commons? Research the law of the sea on the Internet. How does it reduce the threat of the tragedy of the commons?

Why does overfishing (or overhunting) occur if, as is surely the case, those who fish commercially understand the consequences of harvesting too many of any variety of fish? Individually they are motivated to earn as much as possible, which generally means catching as much as possible. They are worried about personal income (a private good) more than the long-term consequences of overfishing. It is in just such situations that the tragedy of the commons arises. Everyone benefits from protecting common-pool resources, but each individual wants others to bear the costs of restraint.

A primary objective of the environmental movement is to promote legislation, regulation, and norms of conduct designed to avoid the tragedy of the commons. Some of these efforts have proved to be successful over a relatively short period of time in altering norms of conduct, at least in some parts of the world. The United States, for example, prohibits the importation of tuna caught by fishing fleets that do not use dolphin-friendly fishing nets. Environmentalists have succeeded in making the American tuna

---

[8] In reality, goods are generally partially public and partially private. Very few goods are purely collective goods. Still, some (like fire protection, defense, antipollution regulations, and free trade) come close.

market responsive to avoiding tuna products that endanger dolphins. Because the United States is a large marketplace, many other countries have adopted regulations to ensure that their fleets use dolphin-friendly nets.

Since dolphin security, not national security, is protected by these regulations, neorealism provides a scant basis for explaining the success of these efforts. Liberal theory, however, offers a perfectly straightforward explanation. An international norm of conduct has been established because removing or reducing common-pool resource problems enhances national wealth. It also explains why some countries ignore these norms. For them, the benefits of exploiting common-pool resources exceed those of adhering to international norms of conduct. If all nations conformed to established norms, then there would be no tragedy of the commons and no need for environmental watchdog groups.

International organizations that provide public goods often face the problem of collective action. Individual members of a relevant organization may be motivated to "cheat" for a variety of reasons. If everyone recognizes that some decision makers will take advantage of common interests, then all decision makers have some incentive to do so. To avoid being exploited by others, a nation may be exploitative itself. Or a member may take advantage of others within the organization—particularly if everyone else is thought to be abiding by some norm, principle, or agreement about behavior that ensures the provision of the public good—in the hope of gaining benefits for itself without bearing the costs of producing those benefits. The nation hopes to "free ride" on the actions of other nations in bearing the burden of promoting cooperation and protecting the regimes that facilitate that cooperation (Olson 1965; Olson and Zeckhauser 1966; Palmer 1990; Sandler 1992). In essence, they want to derive the benefits from public goods without contributing to the cost of producing those goods.

Support for NATO is an example of the free rider problem. The United States has historically paid more than its fair or proportional share of the costs of maintaining Europe's defense through its support of NATO. Other member states, believing that their defense is not as costly as the United States believes, simply accept the level of defense that those U.S. expenditures provide without contributing more themselves. Of course, they pay something toward the costs of NATO, but then they also receive private benefits beyond the collective good of defense. For example, NATO employs some of their citizens. UN peacekeeping operations are another instance in which free riders abound. Although not all members contribute equally (or proportionally) to these endeavors, all nations gain benefits from the peace the action is charged with maintaining. Free rides (or at least pretty cheap rides) are common features of the international organization landscape. The free riders get the benefits of the public good without paying the cost. But if some free ride, then the amount of the public good that is provided is less than what it would have been if all riders bore their fair share of the burden.

In an interdependent world it is necessary for nations collectively to set up mechanisms (that is, regimes) for identifying cheating and punishing it when it is observed.

This is a complicated problem because sometimes cheating is hard to detect and sometimes evidence mounts that cheating has taken place when in fact it has not. The available information is sometimes misleading. The problem is further complicated because even if cheating is detected and there is agreement that the culprit should be punished, nations still have to coordinate with each other to establish what the punishment should be and how it should be administered. At this juncture, the risk of problems of collective action arises again as some nations may try to free ride on the benefits of punishing a wayward state. The case of UN peacekeeping operations is an example. Although free riders benefit from the punishment's imposition, they do not share in the possible political or economic costs of the punishment. In fact, payments to the United Nations for peacekeeping efforts are almost always in arrears as members seek the benefits while trying to avoid the costs. In recent years, the United States, particularly, has been notable for its failure to pay its dues and honor other obligations to the United Nations.

## Liberal Theories and the Promotion of Cooperation

In building up a system of cooperation, it is certainly undesirable to punish a nation mistakenly; at the same time, true cheaters must not go unpunished. The mechanisms or political institutions that are developed to monitor adherence to international norms

*Leading military and political officials in Pakistan stand with their heads bowed as a Muslim cleric recites prayers for twenty-three Pakistani soldiers killed in Somalia on June 5, 1993, while serving there as part of the United Nations peacekeeping force. The long line of coffins emphasizes the fact that the collective benefits of peace entail high costs, reminding us why so many states prefer to gain a free ride at the expense of others.*

must not be so overbearing or cumbersome that they drive nations out. Figuring out how the international system can reward cooperation and how it can punish cheaters through well-structured rules and regimes is central to understanding how liberal theory approaches international affairs.

Liberal theory focuses on two main solutions to the problem of promoting cooperation: hegemony and repeated interaction. Each solution can play a prominent role in promoting cooperation, but each also suffers from important deficiencies.

**AMERICAN HEGEMONY AND BRETTON WOODS.**   Under hegemony, a hegemonic, or dominant, state is willing to bear the extra burden of providing public goods, such as enforcing a free trade regime, in order that all may benefit. It is in exactly this sense that liberal theories assume that international politics is hierarchical rather than anarchic. The hegemon is a central authority that is able and willing to enforce agreements and punish cheaters.

At the end of World War II, the United States assumed responsibility for providing public goods to the international community—that is, it became a hegemon. It did so by signing the Bretton Woods Agreement. Under the terms of this agreement, the United States took on significant responsibility for helping to stabilize world currencies and control global inflation. By guaranteeing that the dollar could be converted to gold on demand by central banks in other countries, the United States created what was known as a dollar–gold equivalence standard. It provided a means to control inflation and stabilize the world money supply by making the U.S. dollar the world's reserve currency. Thus, currencies acquired fixed exchange rates pegged to the value of the dollar. The cost of one ounce of gold was set at $35, so that anyone could trade an ounce of gold to the U.S. government for $35. Through this exchange rate mechanism the United States guaranteed the stability of currencies by absorbing the costs of inflation itself. At the same time, the United States joined and strengthened the International Monetary Fund and the International Bank for Reconstruction and Development, now known as the World Bank. These two institutions were designed at Bretton Woods, the former to stabilize currencies and economies and the latter to foster economic recovery and development. Each has evolved since then into a quite different organization with changed functions.

By August 1971 the global economic situation had changed dramatically from the days of American dominance in 1945. With deficits growing in the United States and with pressure from the British and French to convert dollars they held to gold, President Richard Nixon reneged on the agreement reached at Bretton Woods (Gowa 1983). This put an end to the fixed exchange rate system that had been created at Bretton Woods and moved much of the global economy to a system of floating exchange rates. Whereas under Bretton Woods the fixed exchange rate mechanism dampened global inflation by shifting the burden to the United States, under the floating exchange rate system currencies respond to market forces. One consequence of this shift was a rapid devaluation of the dollar against gold and a sustained outbreak of global inflation. Before President

Nixon put an end to the Bretton Woods arrangement, for example, gold sold for $35 per ounce. Afterward, it soared to as high as $400 an ounce. Indeed, so dramatic were these changes that the discarding of the Bretton Woods Agreement and its aftermath sparked debate over whether an end to American hegemony had been reached (Gowa 1983; Keohane 1984; Russett 1985; Strange 1987; Nye 1988; Kugler and Organski 1989). Today, however, it seems clear that American hegemony, if anything, has increased.

A significant problem with hegemony as a solution to collective action problems is that, as liberal theorists acknowledge, the international system only rarely sees the emergence of a real hegemon. Furthermore, it can be quite costly for a hegemon to assume the burden of providing public goods, as Nixon's 1971 decision to renege to avoid inflation so dramatically demonstrates. Consequently, a hegemon cannot be counted on to provide public goods, especially when doing so is contrary to its interests. In fact, it is at least as easy to point to historic examples of dominant states using their position to extract tribute from dependent states as it is to find examples of them providing public goods.

The unpredictability of hegemons is one reason that liberal theorists began to investigate regimes and norms as alternative mechanisms that nations use to resolve collective action problems. Little evidence has emerged, however, to demonstrate that behavior is actually altered in response to regimes or norms. Having said this, we will see how international law, international organizations, and domestic political institutions might induce states to behave differently from the way they would if such laws and organizations did not

> Give some examples of a hegemon providing public goods. What are some examples from history of hegemonic states extracting tribute or wealth from weaker states without in turn providing a public good to resolve a collective action problem?

exist. We will see how, out of self-interest, leaders form and join organizations and agree on rules designed to tie their own hands by limiting their future choices. The earlier discussion of self-regulation of tuna fishing through changing norms already pointed to one way that leaders accept rules that restrict freedom of action for the benefit of long-term interests.

**COOPERATION THROUGH REPEATED INTERACTION.**    The second solution to fostering cooperation depends on the idea that self-interest can promote cooperation in the long run, even when short-term interests favor conflict, or at least the absence of cooperation. Liberal theory relies here on a concept called the shadow of the future. This concept states that under certain circumstances decision makers who benefit in the short run from noncooperation can be persuaded to engage in cooperative relationships if they are shown that to do so would garner them a long-term stream of benefits (Taylor 1976; Axelrod 1984).

The logic for promoting cooperation when short-term interests encourage noncooperative behavior is best depicted by a game called the prisoners' dilemma. The story behind the prisoners' dilemma—which you can see played out almost any night of the week on just about any television police show—is that two confederates in crime have been arrested. Each is held in a separate cell, with no communication between them. The police do not have enough evidence to convict both of them of the serious crime they allegedly committed. But they do have enough evidence to convict them of a lesser offense. If the prisoners cooperate with each other and both remain silent, they will be charged and convicted of the lesser crime. If they both confess, they will each receive a stiff sentence. However, if one confesses and the other does not, then the former will get off with only a light sentence (as part of a plea bargain) whereas the latter will be put away for a very long time.

Let's call the payoff that each prisoner receives when neither confesses (that is, when they cooperate with each other) the reward ($R$) and the payoff each receives if they both confess the punishment ($P$). If one prisoner cooperates by remaining silent while the other defects by confessing, then we will say that the cooperator gets the sucker's payoff ($S$) and the defector gets a payoff we'll call the temptation ($T$).

In the game of the prisoners' dilemma, $T$ is worth more than $R$, which is worth more than $P$, which is worth more than $S$ ($T > R > P > S$). For repeated versions of the game (that is, when people play it over and over again), we will assume that $R$ is more than twice as large as the combined value of $T$ and $S$ ($R > [T + S]/2$), implying that it is better for the players to cooperate than it is for them to alternate between confessing and cooperating over time. If, for example, $R$ is worth 3 points, $T$ is worth 6 points, and $S$ is worth 1 point, then over time the two players could learn through experience to alternate the $T$ and $S$ payoffs between them. This could be achieved simply by one player choosing to defect when the other chooses to cooperate and then the first player choosing to cooperate when the second defects. This leaves them each with an average benefit of $(6 + 1)/2$, or 3.50 points, which is larger than $R$ at 3 points. If, however, $T$ is worth less than 5 points—say it's worth 4.50 points—then alternating between cooperation and defection is not as good a strategy as trying to find a way for both to cooperate: $(4.50 + 1)/2 = 2.75$ points versus $R$ at 3 points.

Table 4-1 displays the possible outcomes of the prisoners' dilemma. Notice it does not specify the order of play. This is because under the rules of the game, the players each must make their choices without knowing what the other player's choice will be. (Remember, they are being held in separate cells with no communication possible.)

The game can be solved by finding the Nash equilibrium. (Recall that a Nash equilibrium is the set of strategies from which no player has a unilateral incentive to switch.) Player A (or Player B) can start by asking himself or herself what the best move to make is if B chooses to cooperate and what the best move is if B chooses to defect. By

TABLE 4-1

**The Prisoners' Dilemma**

|  | Player B's Choice | |
|---|---|---|
| **Player A's Choice** | Cooperate | Defect |
| Cooperate | R, R | S, T |
| Defect | T, S | P, P |

examining the implications for him or her of B's potential choices, A can determine which move will be most advantageous (though A cannot know what B will ultimately choose to do). Of course, A can also calculate from B's viewpoint, seeing what would be best for B if A cooperates or defects. In this way, both players can formulate their complete plan of action—their strategy—for the game.

The prisoners' dilemma is an interesting way to look at problems of cooperation and conflict because it has a surprising implication. Notice that whatever choice A assumes B will make, A is better off defecting than cooperating. If B cooperates, A will earn $T$ by defecting and only $R$ by cooperating. Because $T$ is more valuable than $R$, it is in A's self-interest to defect. If A assumes that B will defect, then A earns $P$ by defecting, which is not very good but still better than choosing to cooperate and thereby only earning $S$ (the worst result). Thus, by defecting A can guarantee herself or himself a stiff prison sentence or a chance to get off with only a light sentence but avoid altogether the possibility of receiving a very long prison sentence.

The same logic holds for B. Whatever A decides to do, B is better off defecting. Defection is each player's dominant strategy. In consequence, they each will end up with the second-worst outcome and be handed a stiff prison term. Had they been able to coordinate their choices and cooperate with each other, they could have guaranteed themselves a light sentence, the second-best outcome. Thus, by choosing rationally they each suffered an outcome that was worse than what they would have gotten if they had cooperated. This type of outcome is said to be *pareto inferior*. In contrast, a *pareto optimal* outcome is one in which no player is made worse off and at least one is made better off. Joint cooperation is *pareto optimal*, but the players do not seem to have a rational path to get there because no matter what the other player is expected to do, each finds that defecting dominates cooperating because it earns a bigger reward. This is the dilemma. If international politics frequently involves situations like this, then it seems that conflict rather than cooperation would prevail, as suggested by neorealism's focus on anarchy.

Many situations in international relations mimic the conditions of the prisoners' dilemma. Consider the example of telecommunications in the United States and Mexico. The Mexican government wants to sell its telephone services to Spanish speakers in the United States while still protecting its fledgling telephone industry against American competition. When Mexico privatized its telephone company (Telefonos de Mexico), it guaranteed the company a continuing monopoly for about a decade so that it could get on its feet, forge strategic alliances (which it did with Sprint), upgrade its equipment, and thereby compete in the marketplace. Although American telephone service providers such as MCI, Sprint, and AT&T would prefer to avoid negotiations with Telefonos de Mexico and enjoy open access to the Mexican telephone market, they also want to prevent the Mexican company from enjoying equal access to the large Spanish-speaking telephone marketplace in the United States. The Mexican government, being sensitive to its domestic political situation, is protecting its industry even as it seeks to gain free access for its phone company to the U.S. market. The United States, for its part, has also imposed restrictions on behalf of its home industry in an effort to reduce competition from Telefonos de Mexico for the U.S. Latino market. In effect, both "players" (Mexico and the United States) have sought $T$, leaving their opponents with $S$. Had each government opened its telephone market fully at the outset, each country's industry would have concentrated on the market niches in which it could be most competitive and productive. American and Mexican consumers would have enjoyed the greatest benefits. By working cooperatively and promoting free trade in telecommunications, then, each would have achieved the best outcome for both, $R$. Instead, because $P$ (both governments impose restrictions on access by the other country's telephone services) is better than $S$, and $T$ is better than $R$, each has followed a protectionist, regulatory policy that prevents achieving the best outcome for both governments through cooperation. Resistance to free trade globally arises from trade involving the prisoners' dilemma, where each state wants to protect its own industry but enjoy unfettered access to the markets in other countries.

International players may find themselves involved in this type of troubling situation over and over across an indefinite period of time. For example, during the cold war years the United States and the Soviet Union faced off repeatedly in situations where mutual cooperation would have benefitted both but mutual distrust prevented (potentially costly) attempts at cooperation. Distrust, in fact, is at the heart of the prisoners' dilemma *and* at the heart of arms races. Because the prisoners' dilemma is a noncooperative game, promises made by either player or both players to cooperate with the other mean nothing. Whatever agreement might have been reached previously, each should recognize that the other player could exploit the situation by defecting. So neither can count on any promise given by the other. This is a perennial problem when rival states unilaterally agree to reduce arms. The promise is not binding, nor is it credible, and if one state disarms and the other does not, the one that cheats gains a significant advantage. This is also a problem in trade relations where promises to open markets are made but no means of enforcing those promises are adopted.

How can one escape the prisoners' dilemma? Suppose that the sucker's payoff is bad, but not fatal. That is, suppose it is something from which one can recover over time. If the game is played an indefinite number of times, then it makes sense to experiment by starting out by cooperating. If the other player also cooperates, both are better off. If the other player does not cooperate, he or she can be punished if the first player then chooses not to cooperate again. Over an indefinite period of repetition, the small, one-time loss from that initial sucker's payoff becomes trivial against the possible benefit if the other player subsequently cooperates, provided enough value is attached to future payoffs. If this is the case, then each player can credibly declare that his or her strategy will be to make the move the other player made in the previous round of interaction. If a player defects, then both players will get caught up in a cycle of repeated defection; if a player cooperates, however, a cycle of cooperation can continue indefinitely.

Axelrod (1984) has shown that if the shadow of the future is large enough to allow a player to recover from a temporary setback, then possible equilibria of the game include cooperation. The key is that each player must believe that there is sufficient time to recover from a setback and that the risk of setback is amply rewarded by the prospects of a stream of high payoffs later resulting from cooperation. Defecting now and exploiting the cooperation of the other player provides a short-term benefit, but one that is more than offset by the indefinite stream of punishment that follows when the other player stops cooperating too.

How can players credibly promise to cooperate with one another when they are involved in an indefinitely repeating prisoners' dilemma? It turns out that the solution depends on being able to communicate to the other player how you plan to play the game and establish a credible scheme for punishing cheaters. The North American Free Trade Agreement (NAFTA) between the United States, Canada, and Mexico is, in essence, a declaration of what each country's strategy is for dealing with trade relations in the future. Each promises to keep its market open to the others largely unfettered by tariffs and nontariff barriers. Although there are areas where nontariff barriers exist within NAFTA (for example, U.S. environmental requirements imposed on Mexico), these are part of the agreement and so do not represent cheating. NAFTA has rules and procedures for mediating disputes over alleged cheating. But even without an international regime like NAFTA, it is possible for mutual self-interest to be effective in designing a strategy that leads to cooperation between states engaged in an indefinitely repeated prisoners' dilemma.

A strategy called tit-for-tat, or "do-unto-others-what-they-just-did-to-you," is an effective way to play the prisoners' dilemma game when it is repeated indefinitely (or infinitely) and when the shadow of the future is sufficiently large.[9] Tit-for-tat simply involves doing on each move what the other player did to you on the previous move. If Player A defects in any round of play, then Player B will defect in the next round. In this way Player B punishes Player A for cheating. If A cooperates in any round, then B will cooperate in the next round. This is B's way of rewarding A rather than exploiting A's cooperation. The same, of course, holds for Player A. Such a cooperative move by B (or A) would not be rational if the game were played a known number of times, but it is rational when the game is played indefinitely with a large shadow of the future so that there is a big cumulative impact on each decision maker's welfare from cooperating. Tit-for-tat is what Axelrod terms a "nice" strategy. It is quick to forgive and quick to punish; it is also easy for each decision maker to observe the emerging pattern of play.

---

[9] If $\delta$ is the shadow of the future, then it is sufficiently large when $\delta > (T - R)/(T - P)$ and $\delta > (T - R)/(R - S)$. If these inequalities are satisfied, then cooperation can be a subgame perfect strategy.

Tit-for-tat cannot succeed in making cooperation an equilibrium strategy if the repetitions of the prisoners' dilemma are for a known number of times. In fact, in such a situation, the dilemma cannot be escaped. The reason is simple. Suppose you and I were to play this game five times. We might each promise to cooperate at the outset. We might even play a nastier strategy than tit-for-tat that increases the cost of punishment. We might follow a punishment strategy called a grim trigger. Under this punishment strategy, I declare that if you defect even once—even by accident—I will never cooperate again. It is easy to see that tit-for-tat becomes indistinguishable from the grim trigger once someone has defected. Now, it is straightforward for me to calculate that I cannot punish you if you defect the fifth time we play the game because there will not be a sixth repetition. Of course, you realize that the same holds for me. So, we each have an incentive to defect in the fifth round because at this point the game is not going to be repeated and there can be no punishment for defecting. That means that the fourth round of play really seems like the last part of the repeated game. However, I already know that you have a dominant strategy in the fifth round and that that strategy is to defect. As such, the fourth round really is now like the last repetition because I will have no subsequent opportunity to punish you for defecting. Therefore, because each of us will defect in the fourth round, round three will become like the last repetition, and so on down to round one. When the number of repetitions are known, the chance to cooperate unravels, pushing us to defect even in round one because there will be no opportunity to recover from the sucker's payoff in the future by avoiding the punishment payoff and obtaining the reward payoff.

How large must the shadow of the future be to induce players to play tit-for-tat and cooperate? To see the answer let us be more precise about the idea of a shadow of the future. The idea is that people attach more value to something that they receive today than they do to the same thing received tomorrow or the day after or the day after that. That is, they discount the value of something to be received in the future as compared with something they get now. Let us define the shadow of the future as $\delta$ such that $0 < \delta < 1$. The larger $\delta$ is, the larger is the shadow of the future. Suppose $R = 3$ and $T = 4$, $P = 2$, and $S = 1$. If players cooperate, then they each receive 3 the first time they interact and place a value of $3\delta$ on cooperating a second time and $3\delta^2$ for the third cooperative interaction and $3\delta^3$ for the next cooperative interaction and so on. If they cooperate repeatedly over an infinite time horizon, the sum of their expected payoff equals $3/(1 - \delta)$. That is, the sum of the infinite series $R\delta^0 + R\delta^1 + R\delta^2 + R\delta^3 + \ldots + R\delta^\infty$ is known to converge on the value $R/(1 - \delta)$ provided $0 < \delta < 1$. Now suppose one player defects and the other cooperates. The defector gains the big payoff of $T$ for that round but then faces a payoff of $P$ for all subsequent rounds because the other player switches to defection as a punishment. Then the original defector's payoff is $4 + 2\delta + 2\delta^2 + \ldots$, which can be summarized as $4 + 2\delta/(1 - \delta^2)$. Suppose $\delta = 0.90$ for each player, then if both players always cooperate, each receives a utility of 3 for each round across an infinite horizon of rounds. The current value a player attaches to 3 each round over that horizon, discounted by

$\delta = 0.90$, is equivalent to a payoff of 30—that is, $3/(1 - 0.90)$. If one player defects in the first round and then faces the punishment payoff for the rest of the game, the current discounted value of the payoff is $4 + 2\delta/(1 - \delta^2)$ in this case; that is, $4 + (2 \times 0.90)/(1 - 0.81)$, or 13.47. In fact, gaining the temptation payoff $T$ and then facing punishment yields a higher payoff than cooperating for only two rounds given a discount factor or shadow of the future as high as 0.90 and given the payoffs as currently valued. By the third round of interaction, the cooperators have earned 8.13 and the cheater has earned only 7.42. What about the victim of cheating? In the first round, this player gets the sucker's payoff of 1 and then, having chosen the grim trigger punishment strategy, receives $2\delta/(1 - \delta^2)$ for the remaining period of play. For the assumed payoff values, never cooperating if someone once cheats you leads to a cumulative payoff equivalent to 10.47 over an infinite horizon. That is, $1 + [(2 \times .09)/0.19] = 10.47$. Clearly not only is the cheater better off if the players can get back on the path to cooperation, but so is the one doing the punishing. This makes the threat of permanent punishment incredible because the two players have an incentive to renegotiate after a period of punishment so that they can switch to cooperation and improve their lot. Still, there is no guarantee that they will cooperate forever.

It is important to recognize that with a large enough shadow of the future, and with indefinite repetition, cooperation *can* be an equilibrium strategy, and therefore the prisoners' dilemma can be escaped. But we must also realize that cooperation is not the only equilibrium strategy, even with indefinite or infinite repetition. Defection and just about every mix of moves in between always defecting and always cooperating are other possible equilibrium strategies. In fact, a well-known result in game theory, called a Folk Theorem, is that almost any combination of moves can be an equilibrium if a game is repeated an infinite or indefinite number of times. It is also important to note that tit-for-tat is an effective, but not foolproof, way to encourage cooperation in the indefinitely repeated prisoners' dilemma. As the examples above show, there can be incentives to cheat from time to time provided a switch back to temporary cooperation can be negotiated quickly enough. What is more, valuing the future a lot does not always guarantee an increased incentive to cooperate. That depends on the structure of the situation.

Robert Powell (1999) has shown that in situations in which players can punish short-term exploitation in the long term, as in the prisoners' dilemma, a large shadow of the future encourages cooperation. In those cases, benefits are netted immediately through exploitation; in consequence, future costs are high. The desire to avoid those high costs encourages cooperation. The trade-off between current and future costs and benefits in a "guns versus butter" setting looks quite different, however. In some situations states that spend money on arms ("guns") now rather than on current consumption ("butter") acquire long-term rewards for short-term defection. The more a state values future consumption, the more attractive it is to that state to spend on the military now so that the state is in a stronger position to attack a rival and secure additional consumption opportunities by extracting resources from the vanquished state in the future. In this case, a large shadow of the future makes cooperation *less* likely because costs are borne now (some current consumption is forgone to build up military capabilities for the future), but there are future rewards from defecting. Depending on the temporal sequence of costs and benefits, a large shadow of the future can make cooperation more likely or less likely.

Liberal theory is not as parsimonious as neorealism, but it does provide an improved basis for understanding cooperation. In doing so, it also provides a basis for understanding conflict precipitated by collective action problems. It is less successful in explaining how cooperation may be achieved in situations where conflict and competition are brought about by fundamental disagreements rather than by internecine arguments over the division of a commonly shared pie (Brams and Taylor 1996). Neither is it effective in handling distributive problems, especially those not combined with commitment or coordination problems. Regimes and norms are useful ways of thinking about coordination or commitments, but they are not well suited to handling genuine conflicts of interest such as those that arise with distribution problems. In situations where one side's gains come directly at the expense of the other side, with no offsetting compensation for the loser, then liberal theory has little to offer. Wars are sometimes thought of as zero-sum games, in which the winner wins exactly what the loser loses. Two-player zero-sum games do not have cooperative solutions precisely because the two parties have opposing interests. However, even zero-sum situations can offer incentives for some participants to cooperate if there are three or more players.

CONFLICT AND UNCERTAINTY.    Liberal theorists view conflict as a product of uncertainty or misinformation about the intentions of other states. If violations of norms of behavior could always be detected and punished sufficiently to make cheating unacceptably costly, then collective action problems would be resolved. Everyone would have a strong incentive to cooperate. Cheating and free riding on the efforts of others would be eliminated (Palmer 1990; Sandler 1992). If the coordinating mechanisms of regimes, norms, and the like are working effectively, then they are disseminating information to the states that make up the international system. Information is presumed to help states avoid conflict because they know that others will know if they misbehave (Axelrod and Keohane 1986; Haas 1992). Keohane, for example, maintains that

> international systems containing institutions that generate a great deal of high-quality information and make it available on a reasonably even basis to the major actors are likely to experience more cooperation than systems that do not contain such institutions, even if fundamental state interests and the distribution of power are the same in each system. (1984, 245)

The view that information improves cooperation is somewhat problematic, however. Even when states have complementary interests—which is always the case when there is a coordination problem between them—they may also have distributional issues that create a conflict of interest. If this is true, then from a logical standpoint information will not always improve cooperation. As we will see in Chapter 17, when we zoom in on arguments about norms that enhance cooperation, it is entirely feasible for decision makers to choose a violent, conflictual course of action because they are well informed and to eschew such behavior when they are suffering from uncertainty or incomplete information about the capabilities or intentions of others. A brief example may help illustrate the point.

Rivals in war often have common interests that can be realized only through mutual agreement, as required in liberal theory. The treatment of prisoners and the regulation of certain weapons are just two examples (Morrow 1998). Germany and the Allied powers (Britain, France, Russia, and the United States) had a common interest in ending World War II on a mutually acceptable basis. The problem was how to achieve such an agreement. One way would have been to weaken one side's position so severely that it was prepared to accept an unconditional surrender. In fact, this is what happened. Such a solution is costly, and states generally look for other ways to resolve disputes. Indeed, unconditional surrender is rare. Even Japan was allowed to impose one condition (preservation of its emperor) on its surrender in 1945 despite the devastation of Hiroshima and Nagasaki. A more recent example would be Saddam Hussein's avoidance of an unconditional surrender at the end of the Gulf War, despite the fact that his armed forces were completely routed (Haselkorn 1999).

Let's consider how high-quality information might have influenced the eventual resolution of World War II. German chemists had developed nerve gas to which there was no known antidote well before the war was over. Such a highly lethal weapon can quickly kill or incapacitate large numbers of people. The German government, as we know, was not reluctant to use toxic gases against civilian populations, as long as there was no credible threat of retaliation in kind by the Allies. Millions of innocent people were murdered in German concentration camps, many by lethal doses of cyanide.

Hitler and others in Germany believed, erroneously, that the United States had developed nerve gas. The primary basis for their belief was recognition that many of Germany's best chemists were living in exile in the United States. Hitler apparently believed that because they were the best, they too had developed nerve gas (Brown 1968). Had he known the truth—had he possessed high-quality information on this matter—he may very well have ordered the use of nerve gas in combat, knowing that the Allies could not retaliate in kind. It is conceivable that use of nerve gas over cities would have had an effect on the Allies comparable to the effect that use of the atom bomb had on Japan. It is plausible that the use of nerve gas would have prompted a conditional surrender at war's end rather than the unconditional surrender ultimately imposed. A conditional peace would have been potentially disastrous, perhaps leaving the Nazi regime in power in Germany. Secrecy, then, led to a better result than one that might have been obtained with high-quality information. Better information is not a guarantor of cooperation, and poorer information does not necessarily make conflict more likely.

## MARXISM

Marxism is yet another systemic, structural theory, although again it focuses on different characteristics of a system from those emphasized by realism and liberalism. Marxism employs class structure and economic forces to explain why some nations play the role of imperialist or colonial powers while others are relegated to the role of exploited, dependent, or colonized territory. Whereas neorealism views the distribution of power as the defining element of the international system, Marxist theory posits that the distribution of class interests is the primary dictator of international relations. As such, Marxism recognizes variations in interests, but only across large classes of citizens and not within socioeconomic classes.

According to Marxist theory, workers are on the periphery of political influence and capitalist employers are at its core. States dominated by capitalist interests need to expand their markets. This is done by colonization or imperial domination of weaker, poorer, peripheral areas. The core, imperialist powers are compelled to practice expansionism because their avarice, combined with the presumption that they have depleted the resources of their own domestic environments, forces them to seek additional wealth

*View of the destruction of Nagasaki following the American atomic bomb attack in August 1945. In the foreground a gateway (torii) that once led to a Shinto shrine still stands. The shrine and surrounding buildings were destroyed by the blast. The gateway remains because the power of the blast went through and around the structure.*

outside of their borders. Eventually, competition for domination of peripheral areas brings the capitalist states into conflict with one another for control over ever-scarcer new markets. This, ultimately, leads to war.

Marxism enjoys some political appeal, especially among the disadvantaged. Yet its demanding assumptions about the relationship between class role, history, and individual interests lead to hypotheses that are inconsistent with the historical record. For example, Marxist theorists assume that there can be a dictatorship of the proletariat. By this they mean that the government can reflect the interests of all workers through the auspices of a dictator who shares those same interests and represents all workers equally well. Of course, this is possible only where all workers share a common view of what is desirable and a common view of how best to achieve desirable goals. As we will see in Chapters 6 and 9, however, assumptions about unanimously held interests or preferences among large groups are problematic. It should be apparent that when a group is large, as is the group of all workers, then it is unlikely that all members will agree on every foreign (or domestic) policy question. If they do not agree, then the dictator cannot represent all interests equally well. In fact, it is possible for many different majority coalitions to form, each supporting a different, perhaps even contradictory, set of solutions to policy problems.

James Madison, writing in the *Federalist* No. 10 nearly a century before Karl Marx, offered a powerful critique of the expectation of unanimously held preferences:

> As long as the reason of man continues fallible, and he is at liberty to exercise it, different opinions will be formed. . . . The diversity in the faculties of men, from which the rights or property originate, is not less an insuperable obstacle to a uniformity of interests. The protection of these faculties is the first object of government. . . . A zeal for different opinions concerning religion, concerning government, and many other points, as well of speculation as of practice; an attachment to different leaders ambitiously contending for preeminence and power; or to other persons of other descriptions whose fortunes have been interesting to the human passions, have, in turn, divided mankind into parties, inflamed them with mutual animosities, and rendered them much more disposed to vex and oppress each other than to cooperate for their common good.

Madison goes on to suggest a solution to the fact that people are likely to hold different opinions on important policy questions:

> The smaller the society, the fewer probably will be the distinct parties and interests composing it; the fewer the distinct parties and interests, the more frequently will a majority be found of the same party; and the smaller the number of individuals composing a majority, and the smaller the compass within which they are placed, the more easily will they concert and execute their plans of oppression. Extend the sphere and you take in a greater variety of parties and interests; you make it less probable that a majority of the whole will have a common motive to invade the rights of other citizens; or if such a common motive exists, it will be more difficult for all who feel it to discover their own strength, and to act in unison with each

other. Besides other impediments, it may be remarked that, where there is a consciousness of unjust or dishonorable purposes, communication is always checked by distrust in proportion to the number whose concurrence is necessary. Hence, it clearly appears, that the same advantage which a republic has over a democracy, in controlling the effects of faction, is enjoyed by a large over a small republic.

Those who purported to put Marxist theory into practice, like Lenin or Mao, recognized the veracity of Madison's critique. The imposition of one-party rule and dictatorship would have been superfluous if workers' preferences were unanimous (even if no other class's preferences mattered). Lenin, in essence, made this clear in his essay "What Is to Be Done?" in which he argued that there could be no disagreement or open debate and discussion on socialist ideology because there were only two ideological choices: bourgeois or socialist. Any belittlement of or disagreement with socialist ideology necessarily strengthens bourgeois ideology. If unanimity of preference were a reality, real elections would represent no risk to the leadership. If workers disagree on important policy matters, then Marxist theory, when put into practice, must inevitably lead to dictatorship because Marxist expectations cannot be sustained if the working class does not speak with just one voice on political, social, and economic matters. The notion that different people have different interests, even if they are members of the same class, contradicts Marxist theory. Lenin endorsed the idea that the Communist Party was the "vanguard of the proletariat" precisely to suppress the variation in preferences that actually existed within socioeconomic classes as well as between them. Marxism shares with neorealism and perhaps with liberalism the idea that what people want is dictated by the structure of the environment in which they exist and not by their individual values and interests.

In its favor, we can say that Marxism, as a theory, is a comprehensive effort to explain a wide variety of phenomena, from individual behavior to the actions of nation-states. But, it is also a theory lacking in empirical support for its major claims and burdened by an unenviable record in its application to real-world situations.

## SUMMARY

All structural theories focus attention on cross-national, global characteristics that define the international environment. They are not concerned with national attributes such as the kind of government a country has or the way its bureaucracies are organized and operate or with specific international interactions such as the relations between specific pairs of states (for example, between the United States and Britain, Nepal and India, or Nigeria and Mexico). Neorealism assumes that the desire of all states is to gain security; Liberalism, that the objective is to gain wealth; and Marxism, that all people within a given socioeconomic class share common values that transcend national boundaries.

It is important to realize that in their various guises structural theories have had a profound influence on the course of history, especially during the twentieth century.

Marxism became a guiding principle for policymakers in the Soviet bloc and in many developing countries for many decades after World War I. Its main rival in international affairs has been one or another form of realism, with its emphasis on the national interest and an abhorrence of arguments based on values or ideology. Indeed, the renaissance of realism after World War II was prompted by a sharp reaction against what was thought to be the idealism of people like Woodrow Wilson, who wanted to link international politics to principles of self-determination and due process for all peoples. Idealism, sometimes considered a forerunner of liberalism, supports the belief that cooperation flows from democratic institutions and economic interdependence. Besides realism, the other counter to idealism was Lenin's Marxist revolution in Russia in 1917. It is not much of an exaggeration to say that modern international history has been a playing-out of the differences in assumptions and beliefs held by Marxists and realists, in part as a reaction to Wilsonian idealism. Clearly, these are theories with practical importance as well as theoretical or abstract interest. Lately, both realism and Marxism have been under intellectual and political assault, so we will have to be careful to weigh the strengths and merits of these theories before embracing either of them or before casting them out.

Table 4-2 offers a brief summary of the structural theories we have discussed.

TABLE 4-2
## Structural Theories of International Relations

| Characteristic | Neorealism | Liberalism | Marxism |
|---|---|---|---|
| Brief Summary | International system is naturally conflictual | International system is naturally cooperative | Conflict is natural between economic classes; cooperation is natural within classes |
| Nature of System | Anarchy reigns at the international level, forcing nations to fend for themselves and leading to a balance of power; system is either bipolar (two main powers in a state of balance with one another, with lesser nations clustered around one or the other of these) or multipolar (more than two powers); bipolarity characteristic of international system between 1945 and 1991 while multipolarity characteristic of international system at all other times (unipolar nature of contemporary system is not accommodated by this perspective) | Power is structured hierarchically; a hegemon, or dominant power, enforces the norms and maintains the regimes that have been perpetuated and shaped by many nations; in the absence of a hegemon, cooperation promoted through regimes or institutions that foster the exchange of information | Class structure and economic forces cause some nations to be imperialist and dominant and others to be exploited and dependent; nations with strong capitalist interests (a hunger for wealth) must constantly look for ways to expand their markets, which leads to colonization and imperial domination of poorer nations |

*(Table continues on next page)*

TABLE 4-2   *(Continued)*

## Structural Theories of International Relations

| Characteristic | Neorealism | Liberalism | Marxism |
|---|---|---|---|
| Role of Nations | Nations' roles are determined by overall system structure, not by free will | Nations' roles are determined by overall system structure, not by free will | Nations' roles are determined by distribution of class interests, with workers at the periphery and employers at the core |
| Assumed Universal Goals | Security is each nation's primary goal; because of anarchy, nations must protect their sovereignty; the most powerful nations have large internal markets and so need not cooperate with other nations in order to ensure their wealth | Wealth is each nation's primary goal; nations are interdependent, making the distribution of shared interests (as produced by trade regimes or cultural norms) a significant concern; cooperation leads to wealth | All people within a given socio-economic class share common values, which transcend national boundaries |
| Outcomes | Stability in the form of bipolarity is a general systemic characteristic created when nations try to maximize their security; multipolarity is unstable | Cooperation is possible because of the regimes and norms that regulate behavior; cooperation is rewarded and cheating is punished; cheating arises because of collective action problems and the desire to free ride; a hegemonic power provides public goods, thereby resolving collective action problems; a large shadow of the future helps foster cooperation and resolve collective action problems | Core imperial powers are expansionist due to their hunger for wealth; competition among capitalists for domination of territory leads to war |
| Fungibility of Power | Power is fungible—that is, power in one domain (trade, military, etc.) is power in all domains | Power is not fungible—that is, power in one domain is power in that domain alone; within each state, degree of power and level of security vary from one issue to the next | Power resides in measures of production (i.e., land, labor, capital) and can be applied to any problem |
| Effectiveness | Provides an explanation of conflict but does not really explain cooperation; its few specific predictions seem to be contradicted by the record of history: for example, no great power war occurred during the period of bipolarity, but since this period coincided with the development of nuclear weapons and the introduction of instant mass communications, among other technological advancements, it is not evident that the absence of a great power war can be attributed to bipolarity | Provides effective explanation of cooperation but performs less well in explaining conflict; as hegemony is not clearly defined, except by historical example—and there are few such examples—it is not clear that this theory predicts very much at all about actual international relations; although international regimes and norms clearly do exist, it is not evident what impact they have on how nations relate to one another | Represents a parsimonious effort to explain international relations, but the assumptions lead to faulty predictions about behavior and action in the international arena: for example, the outbreak of World War I defies theory because workers in different countries will not put patriotism or nationalism ahead of class consciousness and fight one another; in practice, Marxist theory generally leads to political oppression, deprivation of human rights, and diminished national and individual wealth |

# CHAPTER 5

# INTERNATIONAL POLITICS FROM
# GROUP AND DECISION-MAKING PERSPECTIVES

In Chapter 4 we looked at theories of international relations that are based on a structural perspective. In this chapter we discuss theories that are based on group and decision-making perspectives. Whereas the structural perspective maintains that factors external to individual nations give shape to foreign policy decision making, the group and decision-making perspectives assume that factors internal to individual states are the keys to understanding international relations. According to these theories, individual and group interests within each nation shape the foreign policy choices that, in aggregate, create the structure of the international system. Individual decision makers, interest groups, bureaucracies, and government institutions set policies for dealing with classes of international events while seeking to avoid personal political risks. These individuals and groups all influence the foreign policy decision making of their nations' leaders. All of the perspectives addressed here, then, are, to a greater or lesser extent, concerned with how individuals make choices.

## THE BUREAUCRATIC, OR INTEREST GROUP, PERSPECTIVE

The bureaucratic, or interest group, perspective highlights the importance of bureaucracy and local interests in shaping international affairs. This perspective, characterized by the study of public opinion, interest groups, and bureaucratic organization and politics within each nation, is oriented more toward explaining specific foreign policies than it is toward accounting for global, macro-level, systemwide phenomena (Art 1973; Posen 1984; Risse-Kappen 1991). Most notable among the theories attached to this perspective are those concerned with organizational roles, principal-agent problems, and standard operating procedures (Cyert and March 1963; Allison 1972; March 1976, 1993; Sagan, 1993; Gartner 1997).

Interest group approaches focus on power and interests within individual states rather than on the aggregate characteristics of the attributes of all states. Organizational confusion or bureaucratic infighting are core ideas in understanding decision making. The narrow, selfish interests of competing, influential groups shape policy choices. In consequence, idiosyncratic foreign policies emerge from an environment characterized by bureaucratic and organizational inertia or competition and petty interests. An emphasis on minimizing costs and maximizing individual objectives leads to decision making devoid of concern for the national welfare. Because internal politics rather than external constraints take center stage in interest group approaches, notions about international regimes or norms of conduct are not given serious attention. International relations is simply a muddling-through process in which narrow, local interests dominate thinking and motivate actions. Indeed, the very concept of a "national interest" is hotly contested by adherents of the interest group perspective.

Figure 5-1 sketches the fundamental characteristics of theories of international relations oriented toward organizational, bureaucratic, interest group politics. It highlights activities *within* states, the very features given short shrift in structuralist theories of the sort depicted in Figure 4-1. At the same time, Figure 5-1 makes clear that these approaches greatly discount the importance of conditions outside a nation's boundaries, treating these as lesser elements in the formation of international affairs. Such theories are concerned more with predicting and explaining national foreign policy actions than with understanding the international consequences of those actions. Bureaucrats and interest groups look for ways to maximize their own expected welfare with scant regard to the larger international consequences of the choices they advocate. Their personal well-being (that is, their expected utility) does not depend on the success or failure of foreign policies, except, perhaps, in extreme cases where their state (and, therefore, their employer) ceases to exist. Thus, international affairs are simply the unintended consequence of national actions, as depicted in Figure 5-1.

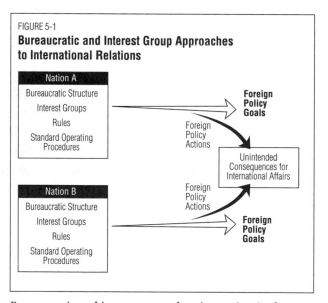

FIGURE 5-1

**Bureaucratic and Interest Group Approaches to International Relations**

*Bureaucratic and interest group theorists maintain that international relations is a muddling-through process that reflects the narrow self-interest of domestic groups. Selfish agents and bureaucratic standard operating procedures dominate foreign policy decision making, rather than strategic calculations about the success or failure of the state.*

While structural theories are primarily concerned with the abiding elements of the international system (that is, the domain of international politics), bureaucratic, interest group theories are concerned with national choices and national actions that vary from country to country (that is, the domain of foreign policy). Structural theories and interest group theories, then, are separate, independent, complementary perspectives designed to explain the two major elements of international affairs. In fact, this is precisely how most students of international relations think of the two. Foreign policy and international politics are studied as two separate domains, each important, but each largely independent of the other.

## ORGANIZATIONAL ROLES IN FOREIGN POLICY

For those who believe that international affairs is the consequence of organizational influences within each state, government organizations such as the Department of State, the Department of the Navy, the Office of Management and Budget, and the House of Representatives are central players in the formation of foreign policy. Each of these domestic organizations or institutions has a particular set of objectives to fulfill. None is primarily concerned with the national interest as that term is understood by structuralists. That is, none is charged with the responsibility of making the nation *as a whole* better off. Instead, the secretary of the navy, for example, is interested in enhancing the visibility and importance of the navy and in promoting national well-being through the activities of the navy. Perhaps the secretary's main objective is to expand the size of the department's budget (Niskanen 1973; Straussman 1978; Wildavsky 1979). The secretary of state and the minions attached to the Department of State are interested in keeping the navy and other offices in the Department of Defense out of foreign policy decisions as much as possible. The State Department wants to monopolize foreign policy decision making and maximize its share of the federal budget. Indeed, the leader of any government office has an interest in maximizing his or her role in government affairs even if that means making inefficient decisions from the national perspective.

Examples of such organizational or bureaucratic competition are extraordinarily commonplace in government, even when the decisions that have to be made involve fundamental aspects of the national welfare. After fifty-two American diplomats and government employees working in the U.S. embassy in Teheran, Iran, were taken hostage in 1979, President Jimmy Carter decided to launch a rescue effort. The mission involved a mixed bag of soldiers from different branches of the U.S. armed forces operating under a chain of command that included army, navy, and air force officers. The effort was scrubbed after two of the American helicopters involved suffered mechanical failure and another collided with a C-130 transport plane that was also part of the mission. In fact, the navy helicopters involved were being flown under army command and were not properly equipped for the mission at hand. Designed for operation over water, the navy helicopters lacked adequate air filters for effective operation across the sand-filled expanse of their flight path over Iran.

There has been speculation that Carter launched the rescue mission in an effort to buoy his falling popularity and save himself politically (Gartner 1997). However, his inexpert handling of the competing branches of the armed forces left him with a compromise solution that involved many factions and no one in charge. As a result, the effort failed and Carter's popularity plummeted further. The Americans remained prisoners of the Iranian government until Ronald Reagan took office on January 20, 1981. The United States was made to look inept, causing its military reputation to suffer in the international community.

Although it is unfortunate that narrow organizational interests prevail over broader concerns with the national welfare, we must recognize that such interests often do take precedence. No matter how idealistic we would like our leaders to be, the fact is they are motivated by their own self-interest. Sometimes they can better serve that interest by promoting the importance of the agency or department they head up than by taking a back seat to some other government bureaucracy. How, after all, can leaders of an organization fulfill their ambition to rise to greater prominence or influence without drawing attention to their unique leadership qualities? Such qualities are not well displayed by staying in the background, sublimating one's own interests to some broader conception of the national good. And to sacrifice one's organization for the greater good probably means losing the support of those key decision makers who are needed to advance one's career. As a result, the self-interest and ambition of bureaucrats and others who are not directly accountable for the success or failure of foreign policies can place the nation at risk.

This type of pressure—choosing between the welfare of the nation as a whole and the welfare of individual political interests—was apparent during the 1993 debate in the United States over the North American Free Trade Agreement (NAFTA) between Canada, Mexico, and the United States (Kugler 1994; Conybeare, McCarthy, and Zinkula 1995). Many members of Congress who opposed NAFTA admitted to journalists off the record that they thought a free trade arrangement with Mexico and Canada would be good for the American economy. As a report in the *New York Times* explained, "Most opponents profess anxiety about NAFTA's impact on the local economy. But in private, some admit that their opposition owes more to calculations of political survival than to judgments of economic merit" (November 16, 1993, A26). Their votes against the agreement are readily explained: constituencies they relied on for reelection included concentrations of workers in industries that were expected to be harmed by competition with cheap (though less productive) Mexican labor. Although these members of Congress realized that growth of the Mexican market would in fact benefit millions of workers across the country, they feared the adverse consequences of NAFTA on their own electorally

> Locate a military installation near where you live. In what way does its location reflect national security concerns, and in what way does it reflect the clout of local politicians? Could the military installation do its job as well, or better, if it were located elsewhere?

powerful constituents. In effect, they voted to keep their jobs rather than to improve the national welfare.

Congress passed NAFTA by a narrow margin. A structuralist might say that bureaucratic and individual considerations were supplanted by the national interest. But adherents of the interest group point of view would disagree. NAFTA passed, they would argue, because President Bill Clinton staked his reputation on its success. In fact, Clinton made numerous side deals with members of Congress to insulate them from NAFTA's adverse consequences. For example, he imposed environmental restrictions that ensured protection of some workers from Mexican competition because Mexican businesses could not meet those environmental requirements and still remain cost effective. After the president promised to protect citrus growers in Florida, they switched their position on NAFTA just one day before the vote. The president made similar promises to wheat farmers. Clinton gradually forged a coalition that was just big enough to win (Riker 1962). He gave away only as much as he needed to in order to prevail. Once he had enough votes, he stopped making side deals. NAFTA did not pass because of the national interest alone but because lots of individual political payoffs were made to protect specific members of Congress. In effect, Clinton gave up bits of the national interest to gain approval of a modified, watered-down NAFTA.

In a similar vein, it appears that President George W. Bush's decision in 2002 to support a 30 percent tariff on imported steel was designed to enhance his and Republican reelection prospects. Steel workers and other union members strongly supported Bush's opponent, Al Gore, in the 2000 presidential election. That election was basically a tie. Bush appears mindful that both Nixon and Reagan pursued trade protectionism in their campaigns for second terms and successfully weakened the hold of the Democrats on labor votes and improved their prospects of reelection. If that is the motivation for Bush's steel tariff, then he, like Democratic members of Congress from auto-manufacturing districts, is allowing foreign policy to be shaped by domestic considerations rather than his own expressed view of the national interest in free trade.

Nongovernment interest groups share many of the features of government bureaucracies and organizations. They too act in their own self-interest when lobbying, coercing, or otherwise influencing foreign policy decision making. Interest group leaders, like their government counterparts, want to keep their jobs and advance their ambitions. As such, they do not exhibit any overarching concern for the national welfare. This, presumably, is why leaders of the United Automobile Workers union opposed NAFTA and pressured members of Congress with automotive industry–dependent constituencies to oppose the agreement. Automobile workers feared that NAFTA would encourage American automakers to move their assembly operations to Mexico, where cheap labor was available. For them, NAFTA represented a real threat to their job security. Opposing it, then, was entirely consistent with their self-interest. Rust-belt steelworkers, likewise, face job losses because the steel they produce is more expensive to buy than is some specialized steel made in Europe and in Japan. Steelworkers, like autoworkers, support trade protection not because of its demonstrable beneficial effects for the nation (see Chapter 13), but because tariffs are good for them. Tariffs almost certainly are not good for most of the rest of us.

## PRINCIPAL-AGENT PROBLEMS

One of the central aspects of bureaucratic organizations is what we call the principal-agent problem. A principal is a person in charge who must delegate some tasks to underlings. An agent is the person who acts on the principal's behalf, collecting information, implementing policies, and evaluating performance. Of course, one person's agent may be another person's principal. For instance, the president of the United States is an agent of the American electorate. The electorate is the principal. The president's performance on the job is evaluated by the principal—the electorate—who decides whether to reelect the president or to choose a different person to hold that office. The president's cabinet members, however, are agents of the president. An easy way to think about the distinction is to identify who is the boss and who is the subordinate in a given relationship. The

*Condoleezza Rice, President George W. Bush's national security adviser, talks with her Russian counterpart, Vladimir Rushailo, in Moscow on July 25, 2001. The United States and Russia were embroiled in an intense dispute over the American intention to scrap the Anti-Ballistic Missile Treaty (ABM) and build a national missile defense. The U.S. administration, asserting its power, repeatedly indicated its intention to abandon the ABM treaty unilaterally if necessary.*

subordinates are generally agents and the boss is generally the principal (Brehm and Gates 1997).

Principals seek agents who will faithfully execute the principal's wishes. There are several problems with this, however. First, the reason a principal needs an agent usually is that the principal does not have the time and expert knowledge to deal with every issue that comes up. For example, it is unlikely that the president or members of the cabinet, or even their immediate subordinates, know enough to coordinate successfully the details of a humanitarian relief effort in places like Rwanda or Somalia. Consequently, high-level government officials must rely on the specialized knowledge of lower-level agents to formulate the specifics of a policy. This means that the agent has considerable influence over the process. If the agent's objectives or beliefs about what action is best are not exactly the same as the principal's, then the agent is in a strong position to tilt choices away from the principal's precise goals, shaping policy to fit more closely with the agent's objectives rather than with the principal's.

Second, agents are selected to do many tasks. Naturally, they will not share exactly the same preferences and goals as their principals across the full range of those tasks. Although a principal can punish an agent for failing to follow instructions (for example, by reducing an agent's pay or even firing an agent) a potent problem remains. How does a principal know that an agent has shifted implementation of a policy away from the principal's true interests and toward the agent's? Because the agent has private knowledge in the form of expertise that the principal does not have, the principal cannot easily identify which outcomes are most likely on a given issue. As such, it is difficult to evaluate an agent's performance. Monitoring what an agent does is itself a difficult task that must rely on yet more agents or redundant bureaucracies. The principal often just does not have enough specialized knowledge to reach a reliable conclusion about how well the agent is performing (Weingast 1984).

The president, for instance, relies on the Office of Management and Budget (OMB) to assess the economic consequences of alternative policies. The economists and other officials within OMB have their own beliefs about what constitutes good economic policy. Their beliefs, including their judgments about how best to frame the economic questions they are asked to address, can shape the answers they provide to the president. The Congress of the United States has become sufficiently distrustful of OMB's assessments that it has set up its own agency to evaluate the budgetary consequences of alternative policies. The Congressional Budget Office (CBO) is designed to provide independent economic assessments. And yet the members of the CBO, no less than the bureaucrats in OMB, are agents with their own agendas and interests. Neither the members of Congress nor the president and his staff have enough personal expertise about economics to judge the accuracy of OMB or CBO claims. The picture is further clouded by the fact that many private interest groups and individual economists frequently provide the government with their own, often contradictory claims about the social, political, and economic consequences of alternative policies. Not surprisingly, the principals have a hard time sifting through the information and determining whether their agents are truly pursuing the principals' goals or altering them to stay in line with the agents' goals.

The problem is all the greater when the president relies on information provided by international bureaucrats such as officials of the United Nations or World Bank. These individuals are not directly beholden to the U.S. president for their jobs. International matters requiring reliance on the bureaucrats of international bodies leave foreign policy decision makers even more vulnerable to being misled into pursuing policies that are not really in line with their views. Should the president trust the advice of international environmental watchdog groups or multinational corporate executives about how best to negotiate clean air legislation across the U.S.-Canadian frontier? The United States exports pollution in the form of acid rain to Canada. Environmental interest groups, presenting themselves as agents of U.S. well-being, have urged the U.S. government to impose stiff fines on industrial polluters, especially southern utility companies, as a way to reduce the flow of acid rain to Canada. At the same time, corporate executives contend that little harm is done in Canada by the highly dissipated effluents of U.S. factories and power plants. Each interest group purports to speak on behalf of the interests of the American public on a consequential international economic issue. Each provides persuasive evidence for its perspective, and each is an interested party that stands to benefit from having its point of view integrated into foreign and domestic policy. Naturally, the president, lacking independent information on this complex subject, finds it difficult to formulate an economically (if not politically) wise policy.

On national defense issues the problems are at least as complex and vulnerable to influence by self-interested bureaucrats as are economic issues. Imagine how difficult it is to evaluate the cost of a new submarine or bomber. Congress and the president lack the expertise to evaluate alternative submarine or bomber designs, or even to assess what the exact capabilities of such weapons should be. Although companies such as General Dynamics and Tenneco possess expertise when it comes to designing submarines, they also cultivate a strong self-interest. Each wants to get the contract, and each wants the contract to be large. Meanwhile, the navy has its own opinion of what a submarine should be capable of and how much it should cost. But the navy also takes the view that a new submarine is more important for the national defense than is, say, an air force bomber. Not surprisingly, the air force and companies that might make a bomber, such as Lockheed Martin, also have a viewpoint, and it is one that favors bombers over submarines. And the complexity goes on. Whose advice should Congress or the president rely on? Filled with uncertainty, these principals must make choices based on potentially biased information from self-interested agents.

Finally, the principal's problem is made still more complicated by the fact that many foreign policies have, at best, uncertain consequences. During the 1990s, for example, the governments of western Europe and the United States were repeatedly confronted with the need to determine a policy to deal with conflict in the former Yugoslavia. No one could be sure whether military intervention would resolve the situation, stabilize the situation, or lead to a quagmire that would bog down American and European troops indefinitely. Under such circumstances, it is especially difficult for the principal to separate out legitimate advice from the agent's private interests. In such an environment, even principals dedicated to the national interest cannot be sure that what they do will enhance that interest. They are to some degree at the mercy of agents who may be hard to control and whose interests may diverge from those of the principal.

Despite these problems, a principal can still partially discipline the behavior of agents so that they do not wander too far from the interests of the principal. This is done by taking advantage of institutional constraints and information about policy preferences (Morrow 1991b). Consider the simple principal-agent problem depicted in Figure 5-2. The figure shows a line, or continuum, that defines the range of policy options available to a decision maker who is contemplating an arms control arrangement with a foreign government. The principal might support full bilateral disarmament, no arms control agreement at all, or any degree of arms control in between. Points along the line show the most desired policy from the perspectives of the principal, the principal's agents, and the foreign leader. These most desired policies are called ideal points. We will assume that each actor likes the policies closest to his or her own ideal point best.

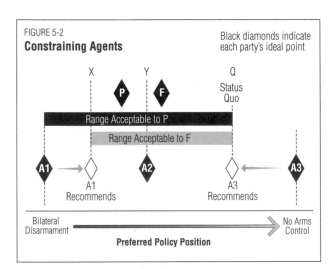

FIGURE 5-2
**Constraining Agents**

Black diamonds indicate each party's ideal point

Selfish agents who are supposed to represent the interests of leaders or the public have some latitude to distort policy choices, although they do not have an entirely free hand. Leaders can infer information from their agents' biased recommendations and punish those agents who are caught distorting information.

Let's denote the foreign leader and her ideal point as point F. The principal and his preferred treaty terms can be designated point P. Point Q is the current arms control policy between the two countries (that is, the status quo relationship). The black bar in the figure depicts the range of treaty terms that P likes better than Q. Since P already has Q as a policy for certain, he is interested only in changes that will improve the policy from his point of view. Thus, P prefers all treaty terms to the left of Q and opposes all of those to the right of Q. The other party to the treaty, F, is not as willing as P to accept bilateral disarmament, but she is willing to reduce arms below their current level. F will not accept any terms outside the light gray bar.

Now let us think about three possible agents, called A1, A2, and A3. We will label the preferred treaty terms of each agent with these names on the policy continuum. As we can see, A1 favors bilateral disarmament, A2 supports some reductions beneath current levels, and A3 wishes to remove all arms control restraints.

We will assume in this example that P does not know the preferred arms control arrangements of A1, A2, and A3; nor does he know F's ideal point. By implication, then, P does not know the range of treaty terms between points P and F that F will accept in replacement of Q. This is information known only to F and, through their foreign policy expertise, to A1, A2, and A3. Because they have each made a careful study of F's policies (something that P has not had the time or inclination to do), A1, A2, and A3 are called upon by P to help determine an appropriate proposal to offer to F. What happens?

If A1 makes a recommendation on treaty terms, we can be certain that she will not recommend her ideal point. Although P would be willing to accept and propose A1's ideal point (it is inside the black bar, meaning it is at least as good for P as the status quo), A1 knows that F will reject the proposal (it is outside the gray bar and thus not as good for F as the status quo). Since any further mutual arms reduction agreement with F is better from A1's point of view than no deal at all (the continuation of the status quo), A1 would be worse off by recommending her most preferred treaty terms. The situation has disciplined her to make a more modest proposal: X is a more sensible recommendation for A1 to make. It is the treaty term closest to A1's ideal point that both P and F prefer to the status quo. However, P is unlikely to accept A1's recommendation. P knows that if F's ideal point is to the left of P's, then F would certainly accept either X or P in a take-it-or-leave-it deal, as both points would be an improvement for F over the status quo. If F's ideal point is to the right of P's and to the left of the status quo, then P knows from A1's recommendation that F's preference must be close enough to P's ideal point that X is acceptable to F. Otherwise, A1 would not have proposed X. If F's ideal point is to the right of Q, then no change in the status quo will be acceptable to both P and F. So, P knows that if any of his agents proposes treaty terms to the left of P's ideal point, then P can propose his own preferred treaty terms. In this instance, A1 has no ability to fool P into accepting more extreme terms than P wants, even though P knows neither A1's true preference nor F's.

Agent A2's ideal point lies to the right of P's and to the left of F's. A2 is best off suggesting treaty terms Y, exactly at A2's ideal point. P does not know F's true arms control preference nor, therefore, the range of choices that F prefers to the status quo. Neither does P know A2's true ideal point. So when A2 suggests an arms control treaty with terms Y, P accepts the recommendation and proposes Y to F. Anything farther to the left runs the risk of being rejected by F. Of course, we know that P's preferred treaty would be accepted by F—that is clear from Figure 5-2—but P does not have this information. Thus, A2 is able to steer P toward a more moderate treaty than P prefers. Notice that A2 can get what he most wants. P cannot tell that A2 has deviated from P's best interest.

A3 wants to terminate the current arms control arrangements with F. To achieve this, he must choose the best of his several options. He could suggest treaty terms that P would recommend but that F would reject, such as point X. However, if he did this, P would then know that either A3 is not really an expert about F or A3 misled P. In either case, A3's future effectiveness would be diminished. Thus, in this case, A3 does not really have this option. If A3 proposes anything to the left of P's ideal point in an effort to promote a failed negotiation in which F rejects the proposed new agreement, scuttling arms control, thereby advancing A3's policy agenda, P will opt for his most preferred treaty terms, as we saw in our analysis of P's response to A1's recommendation. A3's best option, then, is to propose keeping the status quo. P does not know if F is to the left or to the right of the status quo, nor does P know that A3 is to the right of the status quo. What P can infer from A3's recommendation is that either A3 prefers no deal to a treaty or F does not want a new treaty at all. If the cost of proposing a treaty and having it rejected is high, then P will probably follow A3's advice. If the cost is low, however, then P does not lose in proposing his ideal point.

Our analysis demonstrates that the agents are limited in what they can get away with, even when the principal has no information other than what he is told by the agents. A1 cannot generate a treaty proposal that is farther to the left than P's ideal point. A3 cannot generate one that is farther to the right than the status quo. Only A2 is able to generate a proposal that is not the status quo and that is at neither F nor P's ideal point. It turns out that the agent in the best position to advance his own self-interest is the one whose preference overlaps that which the principal is willing to accept.

If A1, A2, and A3 were all agents of P simultaneously, P would gain additional leverage even though the information conditions remain the same. No agent will propose a solution to the treaty problem that results in an outcome that is contrary to his own interests. That is, an agent who wants to see a deal reached between F and P will not propose maintaining the status quo and no agent who desires the status quo over any treaty will propose treaty terms. Therefore, if A1 proposes anything left of P, A2 proposes Y, and A3 proposes Z, it is a good bet that P will offer his own ideal point as the terms of the arms control treaty. By having redundant agents spread all over the map, P has increased the odds of receiving reliable information that allows him to maximize his own interests. Even if A1, A2, and A3 each held preferences between P and Q, P would benefit from redundancy. Although he might not realize that he could propose his own ideal point and succeed, he would still pick the recommendation from those made by A1, A2, and A3 that was closest to his own ideal point. That would be the recommendation of A2. Indeed, one subtle implication of this analysis is that the most effective advisers are those who generally agree with the principal (Calvert 1985).

Of the three agents in the example, the one whose advice is most likely to shape P's decision is the one whose ideal point happens to be closest to P's. It is commonly observed that leaders surround themselves with so-called yes-men. These are people who rarely disagree with the principal. Alexander George (1980) has argued that leaders should avoid a circle of yes-men and avail themselves of diverse sources of information. He contends that doing so would improve decision making. Randall Calvert (1985), however, has shown that this is not logically correct. Andrew Farkas (1999) has shown that George's contention is inconsistent with foreign policy outcomes, whereas Calvert's argument is consistent with foreign policy choices. The reasoning behind Calvert's argument is worth examining because it contradicts intuition and yet is quite straightforward.

To see how Calvert's argument works, let's look at the example of Lyndon Johnson during the Vietnam War. As president he received contradictory advice on how to handle the war. As early as 1964 George Ball, the deputy secretary of state but not a Johnson confidant, had urged Johnson to get out of Vietnam. He reiterated this point of view over the succeeding years. In 1968 Clark Clifford replaced Robert McNamara as secretary of defense. Clifford and Johnson shared a long political history, and Clifford was a trusted adviser. But although Clifford had supported the policy in Vietnam in its early years, he ultimately concluded that the policy was a failure and that the United States had to find a way out. Whereas Johnson had largely dismissed the same argument when it came from Ball, he endorsed it when it came from Clifford. Why? The crucial difference was that when Clifford said it was time to get out, he was making what to Johnson was an unexpected and therefore notable statement; coming from Ball, the same statement was not unexpected and therefore not notable. Ball almost always disagreed with Johnson whereas Clifford almost always agreed with him. That Ball turned out to be right is known only through hindsight. But that Clifford was a trustworthy adviser with interests in line with Johnson's was knowable to Johnson during his presidency. Therefore, it is quite logical that Johnson would feel more informed by and responsive to disagreement coming from Clifford than disagreement coming from Ball.

When advisers who generally disagree with a principal offer advice that deviates from the beliefs of that principal, no one is at all surprised. The principal will likely simply discount or even ignore the advice. The principal does not learn anything new from the disagreement of someone who typically disagrees anyhow and so will not be responsive. Such an adviser is believed to have a different understanding of the world at the outset, and the adviser's advice does not contradict that prior belief. If advisers who normally disagree with the principal happen to agree on some occasions, the principal's behavior is not necessarily altered either, although the principal might need to adjust his or her view of the adviser. The principal, in such a situation, does what he or she wants anyway. And what the principal wants is supported by his or her own expectations and reinforced, in this instance, by the advice received.

If, however, an adviser who usually agrees with the principal surprises the principal by disagreeing, then that disagreement cannot easily be chalked up to the fact that the adviser holds significantly different interests. All prior experience supports the view that this yes-man adviser and the principal have the same or similar interests. The disagreement represents consequential new information that requires the principal's careful reflection about the choice to be made.

## STANDARD OPERATING PROCEDURES

Governments must find ways of dealing with the sort of competition that characterized the debate over NAFTA or the planning of the Iran rescue mission. As we saw, problems posed by NAFTA were reconciled through the use of side deals or the threat of political punishment. Problems surrounding the Iran rescue mission, however, were never adequately addressed. One way that governments can deal with organizational competition of the sort that affected the Iran rescue mission is to establish standard operating procedures, or SOPs. SOPs are an important aspect of the foreign policy perspective on international affairs. They are designed to help decision makers choose courses of action on both an everyday basis and under the pressures and stresses of crises. Because decision makers and bureaucrats charged with implementing policies cannot take the time to calculate the best response to every situation that arises, SOPs are valuable "off-the-shelf" reactions developed from earlier, careful evaluations of classes of events. By setting out preordained procedures for responding to certain classes of events, SOPs enhance the efficiency of foreign policy decision making.

At the time of the Iran hostage crisis, the United States did not have SOPs in place for rescuing embassy personnel who were taken prisoner. There had been no reason to develop a set at any earlier time. Prior to the events at the American embassy in Teheran, such a violation of international law and international norms of conduct was virtually unprecedented. Thus, the inadequate response of the United States to Teheran's actions is not all that surprising. The failure of the rescue mission is less easily explained. Still, the interest group perspective provides some insight into certain aspects of the failed mission.

There is evidence that planning for the April 24, 1980, mission began as early as the previous November, just days after the hostages were seized. This suggests that ignorance about the configuration of helicopters and the like, though contributory, cannot tell the whole story of the botched effort. The competing bureaucracies—in this case the various branches of the armed

*President Lyndon Johnson listens intently to his trusted friend and adviser, Clark Clifford. Clifford rarely disagreed with the president, and both men strongly supported U.S. intervention in Vietnam at the outset of the Johnson administration. When Clifford's views on U.S. policy in Vietnam changed, however, Johnson was compelled to reexamine his own views.*

forces—surely could anticipate many of the stumbling blocks associated with alternative rescue strategies. However, knowing that one or another plan would ultimately be enacted, each bureaucracy had an incentive to manipulate the details of that plan to enhance its own interests at the expense of the other branches. Thus, the organizations involved had at least some incompatible incentives. By allowing these incentives to dominate their shared interest in seeing the rescue mission succeed, the competing bureaucracies ended by contributing to that effort's failure and thereby confounded the presumptive national interest in seeing the mission succeed.

Standard operating procedures are typically designed to deal with recurrent problems for which a fairly standardized response can be expected to enhance efficiency. A problem with SOPs is that they can also lead to inefficient responses to complicated situations. This happens because SOPs are not sufficiently flexible to take into account the nuances of unique situations. SOPs suffer from the problem of what is sometimes called bounded rationality (Simon 1957; Binmore 1990; Sargent 1993).

Bounded rationality refers to choosing a course of action without fully taking into account all of the possible alternative responses, their probability of occurring, their costs, and their benefits. Instead, an off-the-shelf SOP is used to facilitate a quick, but possibly flawed, choice about how to respond to a particular situation. Bounded rationality is efficient and fully rational in that it recognizes that searching out information and examining all possible responses can be costly in time and effort. In fact, an exhaustive search of alternatives becomes irrational when decision makers find that the costs of continuing their search have outstripped the expected benefits of finding a better response.

Let us consider a common SOP and how it can benefit or harm foreign policy decision making. The United States military, and indeed just about everybody else's military, has rules of engagement. These SOPs provide guidelines for officers in combat zones. Rules of engagement cover such decisions as when it is appropriate or inappropriate to fire weapons, when it is appropriate or inappropriate for a pilot to back off from a confrontation with enemy aircraft, and when it is appropriate or inappropriate to launch an air-to-air missile at a real or supposed adversary. Of course, the rules of engagement are continually updated and adjusted to specific local circumstances, but their broad brushstrokes are well established to reduce the need to make brand new decisions in every circumstance that might arise. This gives some aspects of decision making a rather bureaucratic, routinized cast, but it also diminishes the risk of bad judgments under stressful conditions. SOPs are a way of giving added control to high-level leaders who are far from the scene of the action. At the same time, they take control away from lower-level functionaries, even though these are the individuals actually on the scene. In this way, SOPs reduce confusion about how to respond to a newly arisen circumstance at the expense of flexibility.

In Germany in 1914 the plan for mobilizing troops in response to a potential Russian threat revolved around SOPs that specified calling up troops and deploying them by railroad. Unfortunately, these procedures were locked into the railroad schedules in such a way that once the German kaiser had decided to mobilize troops and send them toward Russia, he was unable to call them back. So, even if he had changed his mind, Kaiser Wilhelm would have been unable to avoid a clash between his army and the Russian army once he had put the mobilization procedures into play. Some believe that World War I might have been averted had the kaiser not been locked into this set of mobilization SOPs. Although we will never know for sure what the effect of increased flexibility might have been, certainly the conjecture that World War I might have been avoided gives us pause in thinking about the costs, as well as the benefits, that can be associated with SOPs.

Examples of failed SOPs are easy to find. For instance, the U.S. navy ship USS *Vincennes* mistakenly shot down an Iranian commercial airliner because the airliner's crew did not respond according to expectations when ordered to do so by American naval officers patrolling in the Persian Gulf. The airplane was over the gulf during a tense time. It had wandered off course and was perceived as a threat to American ships in the area. The rules of engagement having been satisfied, the relevant SOP was put into action and a missile was fired at the aircraft, destroying it and killing all of the civilians on board. It was learned only later that the airliner was simply off course, carried no weapons, was unfamiliar with American rules of engagement, and was a commercial flight representing no threat whatsoever. Despite such depressing examples of failed SOPs, we should realize that most of the time SOPs perform well in aiding decision making during tense or pressured times. If they did not work well, they would be abandoned, because their failures would serve no one's interests.

## STRATEGIC PERSPECTIVE

The strategic perspective on international affairs combines aspects of structural theories with those of bureaucratic theories while taking into account how expectations and perceptions, as well as reality, influence actions. In theories that examine international affairs from this point of view attention is paid to constraints on decision makers that arise from internal, domestic sources and from external, international pressures. Thus, these theories presume that international politics is dependent both on internal, domestic political calculations and external, structural factors. The strategic perspective emphasizes rational, self-interested calculations about the costs and benefits of alternative courses of action. Policymakers possess strategic sophistication that helps them maximize their chances of being reselected as leaders by internal constituencies that may choose to support or abandon them and by external actors who may try to impose their will on the state. To keep their jobs, leaders must attend to external and internal restraints and inducements. Although their ambition to remain in power encourages them to be attentive to policies that enhance national wealth and security, it is important to recognize that these goals are in fact only a means to an end, not the ends themselves. One of the most important features of international relations from the strategic perspective involves the tension between international and domestic pressures. Leaders sometimes must choose between actions that will satisfy domestic constituents but irritate foreign adversaries or actions that will appease foreign opponents but displease domestic constituents.

The strategic perspective is the most recently developed of the three core perspectives on international relations that we have examined. Although researchers have touched on aspects of the strategic perspective for many decades, the necessary tools for its systematic development have been available only since about the mid-1970s. Most notable among those tools is the application of game theory, particularly the use of sequential games with limited information of the sort we examined in Chapter 3. Game theory, as we have already seen, is a tool for identifying equilibrium behavior under the assumption that what each person chooses to do is influenced by her or his expectations about how others will respond and how those responses will influence the individual's welfare at the end of the process. By "equilibrium behavior" I mean behavior stemming from actions that are chosen in such a way that no participant in the "game" has an incentive to switch to a different action unless others switch as well. That is, no one has an incentive to switch unilaterally to a different set of actions. The incentive to switch is determined by self-interest. Numerous studies now apply the strategic perspective to explain just about every facet of international politics and economics.

Strategic approaches often assume that foreign policy choices are designed to advance the agenda of the leaders responsible for implementing those policies. As such, these choices must represent some balance between possibly unrealistic domestic political demands and the limited possibilities of action given the external interests and resources arrayed against the nation. The national interest is a problematic concept from this perspective, although sometimes useful generalizations can be made by assuming that foreign policy follows the interests of the median chooser. The median chooser, or median voter, is the person whose support tips a majority toward a policy coalition. In this sense the strategic perspective is somewhat more sympathetic to the option of treating the state as a unitary actor than are interest group theories.

In interest group models, the national interest is a meaningless idea: interest groups, government bureaucrats, and organizational leaders pursue the maximization of their own welfare, not the nation's. In the structural approach discussed in the previous chapter, the interests of domestic constituencies are irrelevant when it comes to making policies that influence national security. In models of strategic politics, however, leaders take domestic interests as well as foreign realities carefully into account because they want to survive to enjoy the benefits of office. They cannot afford to ignore risks associated with external or internal threats to their control over the benefits of being in power. Alan Lamborn (1991) distinguishes between political risk and policy risk. By "political risk" he means the danger that one's choices will backfire at home. By "policy risk" he means the danger that one's actions will produce bad policy consequences. The distinction between political risk and policy risk neatly captures the idea that both domestic and foreign constraints influence all decisions that shape international politics. It is the calculation of the anticipated behavior of domestic and foreign actors that is, from this perspective, the key to understanding foreign policy and international politics (Baldwin 1995; Bolks 1998).

Figure 5-3 displays a generic representation of the strategic point of view. It emphasizes that foreign policy goals are molded both by domestic considerations and by responses to external pressures. The viewpoint displayed in Figure 5-3 assumes that actions in international affairs are the product of strategic maneuvering as the foreign policy interests of different states come together. These maneuvers have domestic and international consequences that affect the welfare of the state as well as that of individual leaders. Finally, the theory predicts that the conjunction of domestic and foreign pressures, goals, and strategies explains the fundamental characteristics of the international system. This perspective is somewhat more complex than our other two perspectives. As such, it is less succinct than either. At the same time, it remains a fairly straightforward approach that possesses the potential for explaining important events in international affairs that neither the structural perspective nor the interest group perspective can explain.

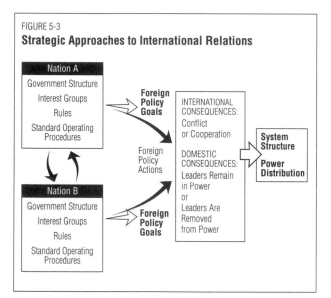

FIGURE 5-3
**Strategic Approaches to International Relations**

*Strategic theorists maintain that international relations is the product of strategic calculations concerning the domestic and international consequences of alternative choices. Leaders seek to maximize their own welfare within the constraints of external and internal pressures. They must be able to keep key domestic constituents satisfied and foreign adversaries at bay. Therefore, successful leaders pursue policies that enhance the welfare of core constituents without provoking the ire of foreign rivals.*

An important difference between the strategic approach, the interest group perspective, and the structuralist orientation involves the relationship between foreign policy and systemic, or international, politics. Structuralists view foreign policy as a separate domain from international politics. The interest group approach is interested in foreign policy only; it does not consider international politics at all. Both of these approaches see the two areas as distinct. The strategic viewpoint is different. It states that international politics and its chief characteristics are the consequence of foreign policy choices. Foreign policy decisions, in turn, are constrained or limited by the structural conditions that prevail at the time choices have to be made. Thus, foreign policy and international politics are not separate domains; in fact, they are entwined and interdependent features of international affairs. One cannot be understood absent the other.

An example will help clarify the usefulness of the strategic point of view. It is impossible to understand the disintegration of the Soviet Union and the end of the cold war without taking into account Mikhail Gorbachev's calculations in the late 1980s about the policies that would best secure his hold on office in competition with conservative Russian leaders like Yigor Ligachev and more liberal leaders like Boris Yeltsin. In other words, we must know what domestic realities led Gorbachev to make the foreign policy choices he made. At the same time we cannot understand the end of the cold war and the disintegration of the Soviet Union without looking as well at the external pressures brought to bear on the Soviet government by the actions of the United States and the other members of NATO, not to mention the actions of the East European states. Hence, pressures emanating from the international arena are as important to understanding Gorbachev's actions as are pressures derived from internal sources. The strategic perspective, as we will see, will best help us to combine these various aspects to explain how the cold war came to an end with the breakup of the Soviet Union.

Before continuing our discussion of the core perspectives of international relations, it may be helpful to review Table 5-1, which offers a comparative review of the interest group and strategic approaches to international relations. These, together with the structural approaches introduced in Chapter 4 (and summarized in Table 4-2), will serve as points of departure for many of the discussions presented in the remainder of this book.

## COMPARING THE CORE PERSPECTIVES

Theories based on structural, interest group, and strategic perspectives recur throughout the remainder of this book. Each of these perspectives encompasses an analytic outlook thought to be important for comprehending national security policy, international relations, and problems of international economic exchange. Sometimes they compete as prospective explanations of international affairs. At other times they complement one another, each explaining one part of the whole puzzle of international relations. It will be evident as we go on that I believe the strategic perspective offers the best framework for explaining fundamental issues in security studies and in international political economy. However, I encourage you to draw your own conclusions about which perspective is most effective in explaining international relations. These conclusions should be based not on my preference but rather on evidence and logic. One of my primary objectives in writing this book is to help you evaluate which of the "tools"—or combination of tools—in each of these "tool boxes" is best for interpreting and then dealing with problems in the world around us. To begin to help you build a perspective on international affairs, it is essential that we confront the differences across the core approaches.

TABLE 5-1

## Leadership Theories of International Relations

| Characteristic | Interest Group Perspective | Strategic Perspective |
|---|---|---|
| Brief Summary | Domestic politics is naturally conflictual; private interests and organizational missions dominate concerns over national welfare | Domestic politics produces opportunities for conflict and for cooperation; politicians choose policies thought to give them the best chance of remaining in power |
| Nature of System | Organization of domestic politics is hierarchical; organization of external politics is irrelevant; hierarchy can be overcome through agents' expertise, which allows them to steer their principals in foreign policy decision making | Organization of domestic politics is hierarchical while organization of international politics is anarchic; international affairs is best understood through the lens of noncooperative game theory |
| Role of Leaders | Decision makers implement policy formulated by their agents; policies often involve standard operating procedures and so appear to be boundedly rational; bureaucrats and interest groups try to steer decision makers to make their preferred policy choices; national interest, if it exists at all, is subservient to the personal interests of bureaucrats, interest groups, and individual decision makers | Decision makers select policies strategically to manage the domestic and foreign political consequences of their actions; the foreign policy choices of individual leaders give shape to the international environment; decision makers are rational in that they seek out policies that they think will maximize their personal welfare; the national interest, if it exists at all, is pursued when it happens to coincide with the interests of the individual leader |
| Assumed Universal Goals | Primary goal is political advancement of group interests, whether they be those of a bureaucracy or a nongovernmental interest group; national policy priorities are defined by groups in terms of their mission and interests rather than in terms of some sense of national well-being | National leaders establish goals designed to promote their personal political survival and retention of power; when necessary, personal goals that are in competition with domestic interests will be traded off to satisfy domestic supporters; likewise, policy goals that are in competition with the goals of foreign rivals will be traded off to ensure personal political survival |
| Outcomes | Foreign policy is the idiosyncratic consequence of domestic political interests; there is no clear correspondence between foreign policy choices and international outcomes; bureaucratic politics leads to muddling through | Foreign policy shapes and is shaped by domestic and foreign considerations; policy decisions are made strategically to enhance the welfare of the political leadership; effective leaders succeed in keeping key domestic backers happy and key foreign rivals at bay, thereby producing political stability |
| Fungibility of Power | Power is not fungible—that is, power in one domain (trade, military, etc.) does not carry over to other domains | Power is somewhat fungible because leaders maneuver strategically to ensure that they can use their power on issues that influence their prospects of staying in power |
| Effectiveness | Provides an explanation of domestic muddling through in politics and a boundedly rational explanation of seemingly irrational (from a national perspective) policy actions in states; suggests a highly path-dependent view of foreign policymaking | Provides a rational explanation of international politics based on domestic and foreign policy considerations; offers a strategic account that seems to fit well with the evolution of cooperative and conflictual relations between nations |

## HIERARCHY VERSUS ANARCHY

One major difference across the core approaches concerns whether international politics is anarchic or hierarchic. In an anarchic system, nations cannot appeal to any reliable source of support outside themselves. Consequently, anarchy means that nations must be guided by the principles of self-help. In an international system that is hierarchic, however, most nations can turn for help to states or international bodies above them in the hierarchy. In a hierarchic system, only a hegemonic state is forced to rely on itself and, of course, hegemonic states rarely face serious threats to their well-being. Thus, we can say that hierarchy does not require self-reliance whereas anarchy does.

First, what exactly is hierarchy? To answer this question, I will briefly consider how politics is usually organized within a country. In a federal system, such as that existing in the United States, Canada, and India, the national government takes precedence over local political units on some issues, and local units take precedence over other issues. In the United States, for example, the federal government is solely responsible for the delivery of first-class mail, its judiciary's decisions are empowered to override state-level judicial rulings, and only the central government has the authority to enter into treaties with foreign powers. The federal government has the right to raise an army, with the president as its commander in chief, but states have the right to raise state militias and individuals have the right to bear arms. This means that the legitimate authority to use force is somewhat dispersed, although ultimately it resides with the federal government. Within a federal structure each agency empowered to use force has a monopoly in its own jurisdiction. For example, the U.S. army is prohibited from deploying domestically, except to respond to an external threat such as arose on September 11, 2001. Local and state police and federal agencies like the FBI, tasked with managing interstate crime, deploy force at home. For our purposes it is important to understand that only the federal government has the right to use force against, or sign treaties with, foreign governments. Only the central governmental authority is empowered to make decisive cooperative or conflictual agreements with jurisdictions beyond its national boundaries. Of course, this is also true for centrally organized nations that do not have constituent provinces or states.

From the interest group perspective, the hierarchical or anarchic organization of international politics is not a very important matter. Since international politics is the product of foreign policy decisions, the critical organizing principle is the way in which decisions are made within and by each state. The external environment is simply a backdrop to those decisions.

In the interest group perspective, the decision to order the use of force, for example, is made primarily in response to local domestic political pressures. Thus, although the executive, as the designated leader, has the legitimate right to commit the state to a violent or peaceful course, that leader is in fact acting as an agent of the many local, influential interests. The decision-making process may be hierarchically organized, but there is still considerable upward pressure to constrain or limit what leaders can do.

There is little argument with the notion that the internal affairs of nations are organized hierarchically, but there is substantial disagreement about the organizing principle behind international politics. Neorealists, for example, assume that international politics is organized anarchically so that there are no governing rules or norms of action that bind states to behave in certain ways. Rather, states behave according to their national interest, not according to principles of enforceable law. In fact, the assumption of anarchy is at the root of the saying "might makes right." However, not all structuralists consider the international system to be anarchic. Realists and neorealists do, but those who believe in liberal theory or interdependence theory assume that the system is organized hierarchically. From an interest group perspective, international politics is largely irrelevant. Domestic politics, of course, is assumed to be organized hierarchically. The strategic point of view generally assumes that international affairs are anarchically organized.

From the strategic perspective, it is not very important to establish whether foreign policy or international politics is organized hierarchically or anarchically. Because both domestic and international factors shape choices, decision making is more important and more complex in the strategic perspective than in either of the other two perspectives. If leaders or states can enter into binding agreements and enforceable contracts, then a set of tools known as cooperative game theory is especially appropriate for investigating politics. If, however, principles of anarchy dominate, then a different set of tools, known as noncooperative game theory, is appropriate. Noncooperative game theory does not preclude cooperation as its name implies. Rather, it is concerned with identifying how decision makers can cooperate with one another when their promises are not enforced by anything except their own self-interest. This is exactly the circumstance in an anarchic international system. Leaders make calculations about costs and benefits and choose what they believe is in their best interest. In a hierarchical international system—or in cooperative game theory—leaders can make binding promises that can be appealed to a higher authority if broken.

In the remainder of this book I will assume that international politics today is anarchic. Using the tools of noncooperative game theory, some of which I have already introduced, we will attempt to account for cooperation and conflict between states without having to resort to notions of hierarchy or supernational authority.

## CORE ASSUMPTIONS ABOUT POLICY AND SECURITY RISKS

The structural, interest group, and strategic perspectives take entirely different views of how foreign policy decision makers make trade-offs between personal and national policy and security concerns. These differences can be understood by making use of indifference curve analysis. An indifference curve represents policy mixes of equal value to the relevant decision maker. As the name implies, any mix of two (or more) policies that falls on a particular indifference curve is as good as any other mix that falls on that curve. Thus, any combination of policies, such as defense spending and free trade, or national security and domestic welfare spending, on the curve is equally acceptable to the decision maker. Any combination that includes more utility for the decision maker on at least one of the two linked policies and no less on the other is more desirable and falls on a higher indifference curve. Any combination that includes less utility on at least one of the policy questions and no more on the other is less desirable and falls on a lower indifference curve. To draw an indifference curve linking policies to one another we must assume that choices regarding each policy can be represented on a line or continuum. The two policy dimensions are linked by placing the issues at ninety degrees so that one forms a horizontal axis and the other a vertical axis. Points in the resulting coordinate space reflect mixes of policy choices arranged so that the decision maker's utility for the choices increases as we move to the right and up in the space.

In keeping with our previous discussion, let's consider three policy dimensions on which decision makers must always choose: personal political security, personal policy desires, and national security. The personal political security of leaders increases if they back policies that succeed at home and abroad. National security increases if leaders pursue policies that win over rival perspectives in the international arena. Personal political security and national security may come at a price. That price is the cost leaders pay in giving up their true policy beliefs or preferences in exchange for political success. How big a political risk leaders are willing to take depends in part on how much they value particular policy choices relative to controlling threats to their leadership position. Leaders must contemplate their policy gains or losses in relation to their own desires. They must calculate the domestic personal political security gains or losses they can expect to experience as a result of their policy choices. And they must calculate the external national security gains or losses associated with their policy pursuits. Our three core perspectives differ in how these calculations are made.

**INDIFFERENCE CURVE ANALYSIS.** Leaders want to make choices that give them the most benefits at the lowest cost. Certainly they do not want to make choices that leave them worse off than the status quo. In evaluating an alternative, a leader might consider how much policy satisfaction and how much personal security satisfaction the alternative provides. Ideally, any decision maker would like to have infinite policy satisfaction and infinite personal (or national) security satisfaction, but realistically it is likely that some trade-off will have to be made between the two. Figure 5-4 depicts this possible trade-off. Here, the x-axis represents how much personal security satisfaction a choice would provide and the y-axis represents how much policy satisfaction it would provide. Imagine that point X represents a choice that is expected to give a certain amount of policy satisfaction and a certain amount of personal security satisfaction. Now imagine that another choice provides less policy satisfaction than that offered by point X but gives just enough extra personal security satisfaction to make the second choice equally appealing to the decision maker. This second choice is at a point of indifference relative to the first choice.

It is a point that represents an alternative with a different mix of conditions from those represented by X but that is still an acceptable alternative for that decision maker; it is neither better nor worse than X.

If we were to plot all the points of indifference to point X, we would get an indifference curve like the one in Figure 5-5. The decision maker will prefer strategies that yield benefits above the curve to strategies that yield benefits on the curve; likewise, the leader will prefer strategies that yield benefits on the curve to those that yield benefits below it. This is true because all points above the curve give as much satisfaction on one dimension (the x-axis or the y-axis) as a point on the curve and give more satisfaction on the other dimension. Points below the curve have the opposite characteristic. They can give equal satisfaction on one dimension but give less satisfaction on the other.

Every point in the issue space lies on some indifference curve, so that one can imagine an infinite number of indifference curves in any space. The utility from the mix of choices on the x-axis and the y-axis is always greater for a point on a higher indifference curve than for any point on a lower indifference curve. Thus, in Figure 5-6 points on curve C are preferred to points on curve B, and those on curve B are preferred to those on curve A.

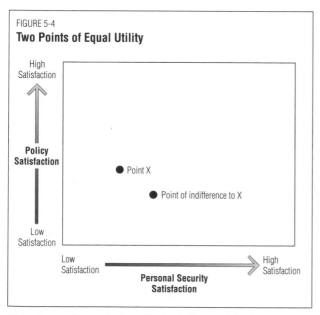

FIGURE 5-4
**Two Points of Equal Utility**

*Decision makers gain benefits both from achieving pre-ferred policy outcomes and from being seen as personally important to the resolution of differences in negotiations. Leaders can be equally happy with different mixes of policy outcomes and personal gains derived from their role in the negotiations.*

The amount that a decision maker is willing to trade off between policy satisfaction and personal security satisfaction is not the same everywhere on an indifference curve, as shown in Figure 5-7. In the middle of the curve, policy and security are valued about equally. At the top or bottom, one of the two sources of satisfaction becomes more valuable to the decision maker. This makes sense because a leader wants to maintain at least some personal security and at least some policy satisfaction. As the amount of security approaches zero, the amount of policy satisfaction that the leader would trade away for personal security increases dramatically. In this way, indifference curves reflect the notion of decreasing marginal utility for more and more of a given benefit.

Different decision makers often have indifference curves with different shapes. Depending on the slope of the curve, the decision maker may care more about one dimension (or axis of benefits) than another.

We can readily think of examples of decision makers who emphasize policy satisfaction, regardless of the personal political risks they run, and we can just as readily think of examples of politicians who will accept any policy as long as the policy enhances the personal well-being of the politician.

When we speak of ideologues we usually mean leaders who are unwilling to compromise their policy principles to avoid political costs. Inevitably, such leaders face severe political challenges precisely because they are not attentive to the political price of contradicting the wishes of core constituents. Similarly, when we speak of political opportunists we have in mind leaders so concerned with "winning" that they will give up every policy they favor in order to stay in power. Consider a dramatic illustration of an ideologue, taken from an interview in an underground bunker in West Beirut in the early 1980s when the Israelis crushed the Palestine Liberation Organization (PLO) in Lebanon. George Habash, the subject of the interview, was a Marxist adherent of the PLO and a terrorist:

> The air in the bunker was stale and musty and "Dr. George" sat erect at a small table.... To him the fact that the battle in south Lebanon had been lost seemed totally insignificant.... "I thank God," ... he shouted bringing his fist down on the table, "that I lived to see the day that a Palestinian army fought an Israeli army. Now I can die. I don't need to see any more." (Friedman 1995, 150–151)

Obviously, the reality of defeat scarcely mattered to Dr. Habash. What mattered was the symbolic victory of having fought. He stood up for the policy he believed in, perfectly content to have done so despite its having led to defeat. Osama bin Laden, al-Qaeda terrorist leader, appears to be similar in his gratification at having fought America even if in doing so he ensured the devastation of his organization, the death of many of his adherents, and the defeat of his allies in the Afghan Taliban government.

On the other side of the ledger, consider the image former British prime minister Margaret Thatcher drew of the opportunistic Italian prime minister Giulio Andreotti:

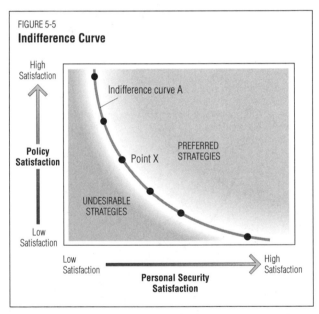

FIGURE 5-5
**Indifference Curve**

*There are infinitely many combinations of policy satisfaction and personal security satisfaction that give a decision maker equal utility. These combinations define the shape of an indifference curve. Combinations of policy satisfaction and personal security satisfaction that fall below an indifference curve provide less utility than do combinations that lie on the indifference curve. Combinations of policy satisfaction and personal security satisfaction situated above an indifference curve provide more utility than do those that lie on the indifference curve.*

Prime Minister Andreotti . . . apparently an indispensable participant in Italian governments represented an approach to politics I could not share. He seemed to have a positive aversion to principle, even a conviction that a man of principle was doomed to be a figure of fun. He saw politics as an eighteenth-century general saw war: a vast and elaborate set of parade ground maneuvers by armies that would never actually engage in conflict but instead declare victory, surrender or compromise as their apparent strength dictated in order to collaborate on the real business of sharing the spoils. [He demonstrated a] talent for striking political deals rather than a conviction of political truths. (Thatcher 1993, 70)

Few leaders are as extreme as Habash or Andreotti. The general characteristics of leaders, however, can be readily depicted by examining how they make concessions between political satisfaction and policy satisfaction.

Consider the generic characteristics depicted in Figure 5-8. The figure displays indifference curves for two decision makers, A and B. A is willing to trade away larger amounts of y-axis benefits (policy satisfaction) for smaller amounts of x-axis benefits (personal security satisfaction) than is B. A would be just as happy to have policy satisfaction at level P1 (which is quite high) as to have policy satisfaction at the much lower level P2, provided that personal security satisfaction rose from S1 (which is rather low) to S2. Notice that the drop from P1 to P2 is larger than the increase from S1 to S2. This indicates that personal security is more important to this decision maker, given current circumstances, than is policy satisfaction. This leader is willing to make a large policy concession in order to gain a relatively small increase in personal security.

Decision-maker B's indifference curve is shaped quite differently from decision-maker A's, suggesting different rates at which security and policy satisfaction can be exchanged. Clearly, B cares more than A about policy satisfaction. B would not accept the mix of personal security and policy satisfaction represented by point X. In contrast, A would be very pleased to receive the benefits represented by point X. Point X is below B's indifference curve, but above A's.

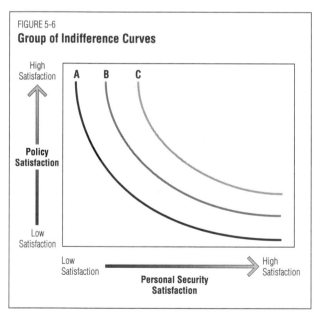

FIGURE 5-6
**Group of Indifference Curves**

*A decision maker gains more utility from any combination of policy satisfaction and personal security satisfaction on indifference curve C than from any combination of policy satisfaction and personal security satisfaction on indifference curve B. Any combination of satisfaction on indifference curve B gives the decision maker more utility than does any combination of satisfaction on indifference curve A.*

Notice that for leader A, point X provides just as much policy satisfaction as does the policy mix represented by the intersection of points S2 and P2. At point X, however, A gains additional personal security satisfaction (S3 > S2). Consequently, A is better off choosing the policy mix at point X than choosing the mix represented by the intersection of S2 and P2. The same cannot be said for leader B.

The shape of an indifference curve tells us the range in which a large concession in policy satisfaction is worth a small improvement in personal security for each decision maker. This relative rate of exchange is called the marginal rate of substitution. The rate at which trade-offs are assumed to be made or to vary is one of the areas in which the interest group, structural, and strategic perspectives differ.

**TRADE-OFFS BETWEEN POLICY SATISFACTION, PERSONAL SECURITY, AND NATIONAL SECURITY.** From the interest group point of view, foreign policy decision making is driven solely by domestic political considerations. Thus, any choice that maximizes the personal security of the regime leadership will be chosen, regardless of its implications for external national security (except to the extent that threats to national security also jeopardize the personal interests of particular bureaucrats, interest groups, or individuals). Figure 5-9 denotes this condition by presenting security interests as a set of dashed horizontal lines. Higher personal security is preferred to lower personal security—that is, higher personal security is of greater utility than lower personal security, or U1 > U2 > U3 > U4— for bureaucratic decision makers or politicians driven by the exigencies of domestic political considerations. These leaders do not care to sacrifice any amount of personal political security for improved *national* security. Before taking national welfare factors into account, these leaders will first try to acquire as much personal political security satisfaction as possible. They are not prepared to trade away any amount of personal political security for some promise of greater national satisfaction through reduced foreign threats.

Figure 5-9 can help explain the attraction of standard operating procedures. Recall that SOPs are off-the-shelf responses to critical

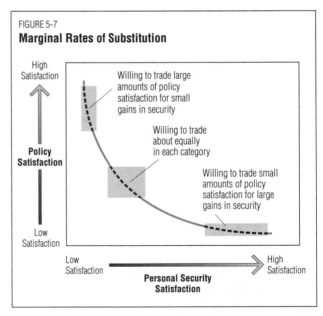

FIGURE 5-7
**Marginal Rates of Substitution**

High Satisfaction

Policy Satisfaction

Low Satisfaction

Willing to trade large amounts of policy satisfaction for small gains in security

Willing to trade about equally in each category

Willing to trade small amounts of policy satisfaction for large gains in security

Low Satisfaction

High Satisfaction

**Personal Security Satisfaction**

*The rate at which a decision maker will give up some policy satisfaction to gain more personal security satisfaction or vice versa depends on how much utility the decision maker gains from each dimension. Sometimes leaders will make large concessions on policy matters to gain a small increase in their personal security satisfaction.*

situations. By selecting predetermined responses to crises, bureaucratic leaders and politicians are able to escape some amount of responsibility for unsuccessful international endeavors. When SOPs fail, they can blame the architects of the SOPs—perhaps their predecessors or faceless organizations—rather than take the blame themselves. In this way, bureaucratic leaders may actually enhance their internal political viability in the face of failure.[1]

As is evident from Figure 5-10, the structural (realist/neorealist) point of view is very different from the interest group outlook. (Figure 5-10 is a relatively accurate depiction of the liberal/interdependence outlook as well, although this theory tends to place less emphasis on national security than does the realist/neorealist theory.) For structural theories like realism and neorealism, national security is fundamental. States are unitary actors precisely because no internal considerations can ever be as important as the attainment of security against external threats to national sovereignty. Structural realists assume that leaders (or, really, nations) prefer national security above all else. This means that they would not give up any amount of national security satisfaction for improved personal political security.

The implicit assumption in the interest group and structuralist models that leaders do not trade off across sources of utility is a strong restriction on how these approaches allow us to think about foreign policy and international affairs. In the interest group context, this assumption indicates that no magnitude of external crisis would capture the attention of political leaders if attending to the crisis jeopardized at all their hold on political power at home. Even an infinitesimal increase in personal risk would not be worth significant enhancement of the national welfare. Although major military crises might not be overlooked in this context, trade crises brought on by retaliatory tariffs or economic sanctions imposed by foreign adversaries would likely be ignored if the leaders' key constituents were not affected. Of course, whether such externally

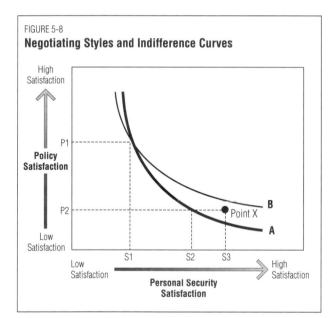

FIGURE 5-8
**Negotiating Styles and Indifference Curves**

High Satisfaction

P1

**Policy Satisfaction**

P2
Point X

B

A

Low Satisfaction

S1    S2    S3

Low Satisfaction    High Satisfaction

**Personal Security Satisfaction**

*Decision makers A and B would look alike to a negotiator if both were at position P1,S1. Yet A would accept proposal X while B would reject it. In fact, decision maker A is overpaid at point X. A would shift on policy satisfaction from P1 to P2 for as little difference in personal satisfaction as is represented in the shift from S1 to S2. The difference between S2 and S3 is overcompensation. Decision maker B would reject proposal X because he or she would have to shift to a lower indifference curve.*

---

[1]Of course, there are other reasons for the popularity of SOPs. Without them, it is difficult for large organizations to function efficiently, because they do not have the time, personnel, or money to address each issue that arises as a unique problem.

motivated economic crises are neglected, as suggested by the interest group point of view, is a question that can be resolved only by looking at the empirical evidence.

The realist notion that states have a preference for national security over all other considerations is similarly quite restrictive. Indeed, from the structural perspective, internal domestic politics are essentially irrelevant. They simply do not exist when it comes to questions of national security. Whatever variations there may be in the political outlook of different leaders of the same state, those differences become trivial, or disappear altogether, in the face of any level of external threat to the nation's security. More national security is preferred to less no matter how much personal security can be gained by sacrificing a little national security.

The key here is to understand that domestic politics concerns disappear in the face of *any level* of external threat, including minor threats. Nations pursue interests other than national security only after national security is assured. But since national security is never fully assured, the realist/neorealist point of view can never attend to questions of trade, environmental agreements, or any other issues of international cooperation, other than to ask how they influence security against foreign threats. Because security must be assured, structural realist theories cannot entertain the possibility that decision makers trade away any prospect of enhanced security, even an infinitesimal amount, in exchange for great wealth or the advancement of political, social, or ideological goals.

Given the structuralist approach's preference for national security, we might well wonder how such an approach can explain the reluctance of the United States to enter World War II when America's most important trading partner at the time (Britain) was facing the risk of extinction, or why Mikhail Gorbachev sacrificed the viability of the Soviet Union's East European empire in pursuit of internal personal security gains. In both cases a genuine threat to the national security as it is conceived by structural realists existed. Later we will examine how the structural realist perspective, with its assumption of such a strong preference for external security, measures up to the empirical evidence.

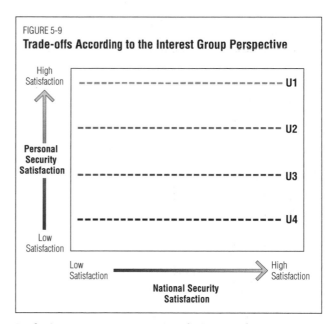

FIGURE 5-9
**Trade-offs According to the Interest Group Perspective**

*In the interest group perspective, decision makers care about their personal security so much that they would not sacrifice any personal welfare to improve national security. The curve labeled U1 is preferred to U2, U2 is preferred to U3, and U3 is preferred to U4. Maintaining U1 personal security with low national security is better from this point of view than achieving the highest level of national security, even if doing so means giving up just a little personal security satisfaction.*

179

The strategic perspective of international relations does not assume that leaders (or nations) have such strong preferences for either personal or national security. Instead, as is evident in Figure 5-11, the indifference curves between personal and national security satisfaction indicate a willingness to trade off gains on one dimension of security for gains on the other.

If leaders treat all comparably sized threats to their political survival equally, whether those threats arise from domestic discontent or from external dissatisfaction, then the indifference curves will be straight lines. If, however, leaders are more concerned with one kind of threat than another, then the indifference curves will bend upward or downward, depending on the interests of the decision maker. In the range of curve AB in Figure 5-11, for example, we see the interests of a leader who is willing to sacrifice relatively large amounts of personal security for small gains in national well-being. By contrast, in the range AC we see a leader who is willing to sacrifice large amounts of national security for small gains in personal welfare security.

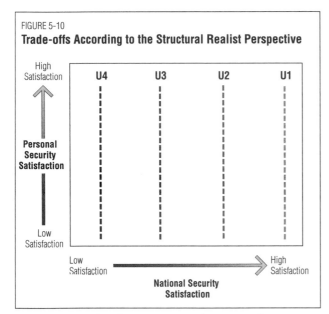

FIGURE 5-10
**Trade-offs According to the Structural Realist Perspective**

High Satisfaction

Personal Security Satisfaction

Low Satisfaction

U4    U3    U2    U1

Low Satisfaction → High Satisfaction

**National Security Satisfaction**

*In the structural realist perspective, decision makers care about national security so much that they would not sacrifice any national security to improve personal security satisfaction. The curve labeled U1 is preferred to U2, U2 is preferred to U3, and U3 is preferred to U4. Maintaining U1 national security with low personal security is better from this point of view than achieving the highest level of personal security, even if doing so means giving up just a little national security.*

Unlike the other two perspectives, the strategic approach takes into consideration both domestic and external threats to security in the formulation of policy. Leaders are willing to shoulder a higher risk to their security on one dimension in exchange for a diminution of threats on the other dimension. Attention to domestic politics or international security will vary from time to time as one or the other dimension rises in salience. When domestic conditions jeopardize a leader's hold on power, he or she will pay more attention to acquiring internal personal security satisfaction. When external threats loom large, however, and become a potential source of threat to the leader's self-interest, he or she will seek ways to bolster national security satisfaction.

In its presumption that foreign policy leaders shift attention back and forth between external national security and internal personal well-being, the strategic point of view differs fundamentally from the other two perspectives. Of course, whether the assumptions of this view make sense can be determined only by examining the evidence.

We will do just that when we examine the ability of each of these theories to predict changes in foreign policy and in international politics.

**NON-TRADE-OFF PREFERENCES REVISITED.**     Before we proceed, let me reemphasize the risks and importance of assuming preferences that preclude trade-offs. We have already noted that national security interests manifest the qualities of such preferences in realist/neorealist structural theories. No amount of policy satisfaction can substitute for any loss in national security. This is true, of course, because the approach assumes that there must be satisfaction with the attained level of external security before any consideration can be given to policy goals that do not improve security.[2] In contrast, in the interest group perspective leaders have a nontradeable preference for personal internal security over external national security. They need not have such a strong preference, however, when comparing policy goals with their personal security satisfaction. Instead, it is possible that such decision makers do care about policy goals and are willing to risk their jobs to promote particular policy objectives, as suggested by the principal-agent problem. Indeed, it is well known that bureaucrats sometimes pursue their own policy agenda, even at the expense of the executive or legislature at whose pleasure they serve. This is the essence of the principal-agent problem. Bureaucrats or special interest groups with specialized knowledge and personal objectives can mislead the very people for whom they work in order to promote their private policy goals. Naturally, if their deception is detected they may lose their jobs. This is the personal security risk they take. Just as naturally, if they go undetected,

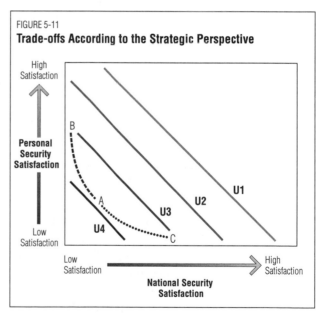

FIGURE 5-11
**Trade-offs According to the Strategic Perspective**

In the strategic perspective, decision makers care about both personal security and national security. The curve labeled U1 is preferred to U2, U2 is preferred to U3, and U3 is preferred to U4. The rate at which decision makers will trade away one form of security for the other depends on the shape of their indifference curve and on where they are located along that curve.

---

[2] It is not as clear from the structural liberalist view whether leaders can be presumed to be uninterested in policy preferences. It is likely that in this set of theories trade-offs are possible between security and policy. In particular, leaders (or the national interest they represent) pursue wealth maximization, which requires wealth-producing policies. Thus, there may be a trade-off between policy and security, although not between personal security and national security. Wealth policies are presumably preferred to national security, and national security is always preferred to personal security. If these suppositions are accurate, then they represent a central difference between liberalism and realism. Unfortunately, neither theory is clearly enough defined to establish if this is true.

they can gain policy benefits that satisfy their policy concerns. Depending on how willing they are to place their jobs at risk, they may be more or less likely to trade away some personal security for policy goals.

The assumption of preferences without trade-offs is not evident in the strategic approach. From the strategic point of view, the principal-agent problem and related issues can arise in internal competition over policy (as in the interest group perspective), but they can also arise in external dealings with leaders of other states. The strategic view differs, then, from the interest group approach in this additional way. Not only are leaders willing to trade off one type of security for another, recognizing that each affects their ability to hold on to power, but they are also willing to trade policy interests against security interests with both insiders and outsiders (Putnam 1988; Tsebelis 1990b; Bueno de Mesquita and Siverson 1995; Bueno de Mesquita, Smith, Siverson, and Morrow 2003).

An understanding of international affairs requires that we devise methods for estimating how, if at all, people make trade-offs among personal security risks, national security risks, and policy goals. Surprisingly, these issues have only just begun to capture the attention of students of politics (Bueno de Mesquita, Newman, and Rabushka 1985, 1996; Putnam 1988; Rogowski 1989; Tsebelis 1990b; Lamborn 1991; Bueno de Mesquita and Stokman 1994; Bueno de Mesquita, Smith, Siverson, and Morrow 2003).

## THE THREE PERSPECTIVES ILLUSTRATIVELY APPLIED TO COLUMBUS

We will now return to the historical case of Christopher Columbus's journey of discovery. Why did Ferdinand and Isabella decide to back Columbus's very risky plan to seek a westward route to the Indies when so many other European powers declined the opportunity? It is possible to think of this "Columbus question" in systemic, structural terms; in bureaucratic, interest group terms; and in terms of the strategic interactions between the Spanish Crown and its domestic and foreign competitors.

### THE COLUMBIAN VOYAGES OF DISCOVERY:
### A NEOREALIST EXPLANATION

How might structural realists describe the resolution of the "Columbus question"? Spain's position in 1492, they would say, was one of weakness and relative political isolation from the power centers of Europe. This weakness and isolation compelled Ferdinand and Isabella to seek ways of improving Spain's power and security through internal growth and development. Spain's relative weakness made it a peripheral player in Europe's multipolar system in which Portugal, the papacy, the Holy Roman Empire, France, Britain, and a few Italian city-states represented the great powers of the day. To gain security, Spain had to find some way to alter the distribution of power so that it could compete more effectively against its powerful neighbors. Columbus offered such a way, and so it was taken.

The realist perspective does not leave much room for individual variations in preferences or perceptions to shape policy. Probably, from a realist perspective, Portugal should have accepted Columbus's proposal in order to prevent Spain or any other rival state from gaining the chance to increase power or security that might arise from a successful westward voyage to Asia. The Portuguese should have hedged their bets by co-opting Columbus to ensure that their advantaged position in the international system would be preserved and protected. For a structural realist or neorealist, then, the decisive factor was the competition between Portugal and Spain to prevent (on Portugal's part) or to attain (on Spain's part) growth in power and security. Spain's rise in power, they would say, was evidence of realist principles at work. The Spanish Crown sought to enhance Spain's security, and it did so. Portugal's eventual decline was inevitable, given the Portuguese government's failure to act according to essential realist principles. But if structural realism represents an accurate description of behavior rather than a normative prescription of what nations ought to do, how can it explain Portugal's failure to take the appropriate steps to secure its power? In fact, one strength of the neorealist perspective is that it suggests testable propositions about national actions that we can investigate and support or disprove in our efforts to evaluate the theory from which they are derived.

## THE COLUMBIAN VOYAGES OF DISCOVERY: AN INTEREST GROUP EXPLANATION

The interest group approach comes at the "Columbus question" from a quite different perspective. According to this view, the Spanish were slow to agree to Columbus's proposal because the king and queen had first to satisfy the wishes of internal constituencies eager to wrest control of Granada from its Muslim rulers; manage political conflicts between the aristocratic interests of Aragon and those of Castile, neither of which wanted to see a united Spain succeed under the domination of the other; and deal with tax controversies that embroiled the estates (approximate equivalents of the modern notion of socioeconomic classes) and the regional Cortes (the parliaments of the Spanish provinces) in bitter battles and occasional bloodshed. In other words, Columbus's proposal was a decidedly low-priority concern.

The Columbian adventure took place only because of the fortuitous, last-minute intervention of Luís de Santangel, who promised to take responsibility for raising privately the funds needed for Columbus's voyage. Santangel's success in overcoming the negative assessment of the Talaveras Commission and the opposition of the king reflected Santangel's skill. He proved adept at mobilizing resources and shaping the king's agenda. Perhaps Santangel, acting as Ferdinand's agent, manipulated the king into doing something Santangel favored but that Ferdinand would not have chosen to do if he had been better informed. (The king, after all, had given Columbus a final negative just before Santangel's intervention.) But because of his minister's personal interest in Columbus, Ferdinand ultimately decided to go along with the venture. Apparently, some grander sense of the national interest or global ambition was not important to either Santangel or Ferdinand.

According to this perspective interest group politics led Spain to decline Columbus's offer for many years. But convergent interests—coupled with Santangel's influence as keeper of the privy purse—led to a reversal in Columbus's fortunes in Spain in 1492. The interest group approach, with its emphasis on local pressures as determinants of foreign policy, would point to internal balancing, rather than external ambition, as the most important factor in the resolution of the Columbus question.

Bureaucratic inertia kept Spain from seizing the initiative early, and serendipity in the form of Santangel's intervention saved Spain from casting Columbus out to seek a patron elsewhere. These factors are the sorts of evidence that an interest group theorist would offer in support of that view. Of course, we would need answers to additional questions. How, for example, had Santangel risen to such a powerful position? What factors contributed to the trust and confidence that Ferdinand placed in him? Might Santangel have displayed unusual skill and dedication to advancing Spain's—or at least the Spanish monarch's—welfare on previous occasions? If so, this suggests a tie between Santangel's success and Spain's national interest. Or, was Santangel's own political success just luck? Was Santangel a yes-man who almost always agreed with Ferdinand? If so, was the fact that he disagreed on this occasion sufficiently notable that it led Ferdinand to change his mind about the potential merits of Columbus's proposal? Answers to these questions would help further clarify the usefulness of the interest group perspective in answering the "Columbus question."

## THE COLUMBIAN VOYAGES OF DISCOVERY:
## A STRATEGIC EXPLANATION

From the strategic perspective, Ferdinand and Isabella were attentive to both internal pressures and external structural limitations. Once they had established their policy objectives, they were able to concentrate on the implications of alternative strategies for their relations with friendly and hostile constituents both at home and abroad. Spain's position in the international power pecking order did not dictate their actions (as in structural realism), nor did the lucky interest of Santangel and his exertions on behalf of Columbus. Rather, Ferdinand and Isabella took action based on their perceptions of how other states would react to Spain's decision to pursue or forgo Columbus's proposal. At the same time, their perceptions of how domestic interests (like Santangel and the aristocracy) would react to their choices also shaped their decision. Ultimately, Ferdinand and Isabella made the choice that they felt would produce the greatest benefits for themselves and, indirectly, for Spain while all the time conscious of the internal and external risks and rewards associated with the alternatives before them.

Game theory suggests that Ferdinand and Isabella would have contemplated the risk of war with the Arabs or Italy that might result from their pursuit of an overland caravan route to Asia. They also would have worried about the consequences of competing with Portugal for supremacy over the eastward route to Asia. Ferdinand and Isabella would have asked: How will this venture alter our relationships with our sometime ally France and our frequent foe Britain? How will it affect our relationship with the pope? The Holy Roman Emperor? The leaders of Sicily and Naples? The Spanish monarchs, in this viewpoint, would have assumed that each nation's leaders would have their own unique perspective, formed by calculations of internal political, social, and economic costs and benefits; personal predilections for taking risks, behaving aggressively, or acting cooperatively; and personal views of their own place in the international arena. Spain's power relative to that of its rivals would have been important, but so too would have been the interests of rival elites within Spain. Ferdinand and Isabella would certainly have remembered the unhappy experience of Isabella's father, Enrique IV, who became embroiled in civil war to retain his crown. With that experience in mind, the Spanish monarchs would have been careful to secure support from key aristocrats inside Spain. They might have argued that Columbus, if successful, could help ease the tax burden borne by the Crown's supporters.

The policy that Ferdinand and Isabella ultimately chose to pursue took into account the strategic implications of both Spain's external welfare and the monarchs' internal hold on power. They formed a view of how to balance external and internal interests, with neither universally taking precedence over the other. Their desire to maximize their own welfare was constrained by the competition for welfare maximization manifested by competing internal and external interests. They had to choose between emphasizing efforts at controlling the risks of external defeat, even if it heightened domestic dissatisfaction, and efforts at controlling domestic unrest, even if it meant increasing the dangers from external adversaries. In essence, Ferdinand and Isabella had to find a way to protect domestic interests under external constraints and external interests under domestic constraints. Neither consideration would inherently or always dominate the other.

Strategic calculations concerning the domestic and international consequences of a westward expedition account for the years of delay between Columbus's initial presentation of his plan to the Spanish monarchs and the actual implementation of that plan. These years were filled with calculated actions. For example, Columbus maneuvered to reduce the costs that kept the Spaniards from agreeing to his plan, and he tried to anticipate their countermoves in attempting to select advantageous responses. Recall that he eventually agreed to sail on a contingency-fee basis. Evidently, he recognized that to overcome the opposition of the Spanish Crown to the costs of his plan, he would have to make some accommodations—that is, he made a strategic alteration to his plan. As Columbus made his adjustments, Ferdinand and Isabella maneuvered to consolidate their control over disparate internal competitors and to shore up relations with external opponents before seeking some larger means of expanding Spain's place in the international system. Improved relations with the pope, for example, was certainly part of a strategic plan. Of course, the strategic approach must also be able to explain how

Portugal, externally, and Juana (Isabella's competitor as heir to the throne of Castile), internally, allowed themselves to be outmaneuvered. Whether it can do so in a manner consistent with the facts will be one way of testing its usefulness as a theory of international relations.

## SUMMARY

It should be clear that the reasoning behind the three core perspectives on international politics differs considerably from one approach to the next. Structuralism emphasizes the distribution of power or the constraints of international regimes on international politics. Competition and interdependence are central features of relations between states. Actions are inspired by motivations common to all nations. These motivations involve seeking national security or national wealth to promote the national interest. Local concerns are submerged in the face of external threats.

Interest group theories emphasize competing bureaucracies and interests within states. They give scant attention to external conditions that might influence foreign policy decisions. The national interest is almost a meaningless abstraction. Decision makers compete for control over national resources, and in doing so they may make decisions that are contrary to the overall welfare of the state. Decisions are structured around the promotion of narrow interests and are simplified through the use of organizational concepts such as standard operating procedures. Leaders hope to advance their interests ahead of their domestic rivals by exerting control over political agendas, the organizations that implement policies, and the formation of SOPs.

Theories embedded in the strategic viewpoint emphasize the interplay between domestic interests and external constraints. Leaders try to maximize their chances of holding on to the benefits they gain from political power, including the opportunity to implement policy goals. To do so, they must worry about internal challenges to their authority and external reactions to their policies. They must find a way to balance domestic demands against foreign realities without tilting so much in one or the other direction that they stimulate a domestic usurpation of their power or a foreign intervention in their affairs. Political leaders must find an appropriate mix in emphasizing the protection of national security, the advancement of the welfare of their key domestic constituents (whether the country is democratic or authoritarian), and the promotion of their own political interests. Decisions involve continuous and possibly quite complex strategic calculations about how local and foreign decision makers will respond to their actions.

Sometimes these three core perspectives lead to complementary expectations about behavior; more often they lead to contradictory expectations. Much of the remainder of this book will be used to evaluate explanations of specific international issues from these alternative points of view. Each will be given a fair shake, and each will be subjected to the quite rigorous standards of argument and evidence required by the scientific method.

CHAPTER 6

# DOMESTIC POLITICS AND INTERNATIONAL INTERACTIONS: THE CENTRAL UNITS OF ANALYSIS

Any perspective on international affairs begins with assumptions about the way in which international relations is organized. These include specification of the relevant units, identification of the mechanisms or factors governing the relationships between these units, and recognition of the implications of these relationships for action. As we saw in Chapters 4 and 5, the state is most commonly identified as the relevant unit of analysis in the study of international relations. To avoid deflecting attention from the fundamental arguments made by each of the perspectives introduced in the last two chapters, I postponed a discussion of exactly what is meant by "the state" until now. An explanation of what states are and how they evolved is necessary at this juncture, however, because the strategic perspective that dominates this book argues that individual leaders and their constituents, not the state, are the optimal units for investigating international affairs. A state-centric perspective ignores what goes on within the state. It discounts the importance of variations in the personalities, abilities, and interests of different leaders and treats the state as if it, and not people within it, makes decisions. Although such a view is parsimonious in that it allows us to ignore the institutional, social, cultural, historical, and political variations within nations, whether it is effective in explaining foreign policy and international politics is an empirical question that we now evaluate.

In this chapter I first provide a definition of the state and review briefly the history of states as organizations, elaborating on the historical overview offered in Chapter 1. I also offer a review of other institutional or organizational arrangements that have been common throughout the history of international affairs. Then I examine the logical implications of the assumption that the state is a unitary actor, comparing those with the implications of treating the state as made up of many individuals, each with his or her own power, preferences, and perceptions (defined more thoroughly in the next several chapters). These individuals are viewed as acting under the constraints of national and international institutional rules and norms. We will see that breaking states down into constituent individual decision makers provides a view of international affairs radically different from that shown if we see the state as a unitary actor.

## THE ORIGINS OF THE STATE

The modern sovereign state can be defined as a territorial entity within which a single government has the legitimate right to use force against those inhabiting the territory. The existence of states implies the existence of several institutions that are important for understanding international relations.

First, according to our definition, states are territorial. This means that they have defined borders that delineate the domain within which it is legitimate for governing authorities to use force and the domain within which it is not legitimate for them to use force. Thus, the general understanding of what constitutes a state implies a core principle of international law. States do not have the right to use force outside their borders in an effort to interfere in the affairs of other states. Borders, then, are a critical institutional feature of international relations. All states are territorial and so all states have borders. As obvious as this may seem, we will see later that intergovernmental relations have been organized in the past without reliance on borders.

Second, those who control the borders—that is, those who rule the state—have the exclusive right to enforce rules within the territory defined by the borders. This is an essential feature of sovereignty. A sovereign is the sole legitimate arbiter of the rules within a given state. Because the sovereign has the sole authority to enforce these rules, the state has policing powers. Thus, the internal institutional arrangements established by the sovereign profoundly influence the rules and mechanisms for choosing public policy, including foreign policy. They do so, in part, by determining where sovereign authority resides. There is, indeed, an important difference between a leader like Louis XIV, France's sovereign monarch in the seventeenth century, and Abraham Lincoln, the American president from 1861 to 1865. Louis XIV declared, "L'état c'est moi" (I am the state. Or, more emphatically: The state, it is me!), meaning that he had exclusive sovereign authority. In contrast, Lincoln declared that the government was "of the people, by the people and for the people," indicating that sovereign authority resided in the citizenry. Where sovereign authority resides is critical in shaping internal and external policies. For example, the empirical observation that democratic states do not fight wars against one another may well be explained by the fact that sovereign authority in democracies tends to reside in the hands of the population at large, which is not true in authoritarian states. In Chapter 12 we will see why this is so and how such issues might influence fundamental aspects of international affairs. Today, wherever sovereign authority resides, that authority conveys the unique right to use force. This has not always been the case. In earlier times, the authority to use force in a given locale was not the exclusive right of the sovereign but, rather, reflected complex feudal ties of homage and fealty.

Third, borders are a natural source of conflict in international relations (Vasquez 1993, 1995, 2000; Senese 1995, 1997; Huth 1996; Siverson and Starr 1991) because shifts in their location expand or contract sovereign authority. Border disputes are common because borders are a significant constraint on the authority of rulers. One way rulers can expand their authority is to usurp the sovereign claims of another ruler by snatching some territory and redefining the location of the state's perimeter. Indeed, the word "international" implies the importance of borders in establishing sovereign domains.

Fourth, because each state defines a domain within which its rulers have sovereign authority over the use of force, international law views all states as legally equivalent entities. This is one reason that international relations is primarily about how states as disparate as the United States and Botswana interact, rather than about how corporations such as AT&T, Microsoft, or General Motors interact with states such as Japan, Belgium, or Luxembourg. Although AT&T may be more powerful, richer, and more populous (in regard to employees and stockholders) than Luxembourg, it has none of the sovereign rights that Luxembourg, as a state, enjoys. Luxembourg, for example, is a member of the United Nations. No corporation can hold this status, no matter how large or wealthy it is. AT&T cannot vote in the UN General Assembly or sit on the Security Council. Luxembourg can. Neither Nestlé nor British Petroleum, two giant European firms, can have membership in the European Parliament or be on the Council of Ministers of the European Union. Luxembourg can (and does).

The Treaty of Westphalia, as mentioned in Chapter 1, marked the end of the Thirty Years' War (1620–1648) and generally is used to demarcate the beginning of the modern state system. But it would be a mistake to think that the modern state sprang up suddenly, fully conceived and matured, with the signing of the Treaty of Westphalia. In fact, the modern state was a work in progress in 1648 and, of course, still is. It is my contention that the modern state is best understood as a set of evolving institutions, with the evolutionary process having been set in motion as early as 1122 by the Concordat of Worms.

During the papacy of Gregory VII (1073–1085), the Catholic Church challenged the authority of the Holy Roman Emperor, as well as the kings of England and France. At that time, the pope was only somewhat more consequential than other bishops. He was elected by the electors of the Holy Roman Empire and not, as today, by the College of Cardinals. Indeed, the College of Cardinals was then a newly created institution with little authority.

Gregory VII was a reformer who sought the right to select the bishops of the Church, a privilege controlled at that time by kings. Pope Gregory argued that the Catholic Church needed to control the appointment of bishops because secular authorities were selling the positions to the highest bidder. Whether this was his true concern, or whether Gregory was attempting to assert papal authority, the consequences of the investiture struggle that followed planted the seeds for the modern state.

After a series of short-lived papal schisms, in which the Holy Roman Emperor denied the authenticity of the pope in Rome and designated pretenders in his place, a deal was struck. That deal, known as the Concordat of Worms, stipulated that the pope would select or nominate bishops, who would then be elected with the consent of the king. Furthermore, the king would control the regalia—that is, the rights and privileges, including the income—of a bishopric between the death of a bishop and the investiture of his successor, whereas the Church would control the regalia once a bishop was in office. Although to the modern eye this seems like a small matter, in fact the agreement at Worms accelerated the decay of the feudal system and stimulated the birth of the modern state.

The regalian rights granted to the king by the Concordat of Worms created an early property right, or source of sovereignty, that adhered to the king as the agent of the territory (the bishopric) under his control. The king could pass this right only to his successor. He could not sell the right, nor could his heirs retain it if they were not made the monarch. Thus, it was not the king's personal property to do with as he pleased. He held it on behalf of his subjects in the regalian see, acting in the role of their fiduciary. This gave birth to a concept known as the king's two bodies (Kantorowicz 1957). The king, as an individual, had rights and privileges that were distinct from his rights and privileges as the agent of the people within the sovereign territory of the state. He held the rights to the income from regalian bishoprics as a custodian for the state and not as his personal property. In this sense, the king as sovereign could not be distinguished from the state (hence, the unitary actor assumption), but the king as an individual could be readily distinguished from the king as sovereign. This distinction took on such importance that by the time King Charles II was beheaded in England in 1632, we find that the act of Parliament condemning Charles the man was written on behalf of and in the name of Charles the king. Technically, King Charles—through the mechanism of Parliament—condemned the man Charles.

Further, the Concordat of Worms established the lines along which the Church and kings competed for authority and, in doing so, created an incentive structure that led to the development of the institutions of modern states. Specifically, as the value of the income from vacant regalian sees grew, so too did the king's incentives to acquire that income by refusing to accept the pope's nominee for bishop. Bishops were crucial agents. Who they saw as their principal, the person to whom they owed loyalty—the king or the pope—was a fundamental political matter. If the value of the income from a bishopric was greater than the political value the king derived from avoiding disagreement with the pope, then the king stood to gain great influence at the expense of the hegemonic Catholic Church. In such cases, the king could refuse the pope's nominee unless the nominee was someone from whom the king expected loyalty. This meant that as wealth grew, kings could wrest more and more control from the Church because the pope could get bishops elected only by nominating those candidates hand-picked by the king. This left the pope motivated to do what he could to slow economic growth, reduce the value of vacant regalian sees, and secure his own political control over secular authorities. Finally, the property right established by the Concordat of Worms meant that, as the king's wealth expanded, the Church would increasingly lose out in its competition for power with kings who enjoyed broad-based territorial sovereignty. This sovereignty was ultimately codified in the Treaty of Westphalia, which marked the demise of Church domination in Europe (Bueno de Mesquita 2000).

The competition over political control set in motion in 1122 spawned a variety of new political institutions that precipitated the development of common law and the jury system in England during the twelfth century and inspired numerous administrative innovations in France, England, and elsewhere during the twelfth and thirteenth centuries. Although the Concordat at Worms bought the Church domination in Europe for some five centuries, at the same time it sent kings down the path toward sovereignty that culminated in their emergence as the sole authorities inside their borders on matters of religious belief, taxation, police power, and national security. Because the Church was eliminated as a supernational authority with the ability to enforce agreements (by threatening excommunication or interdiction), international relations as we know it emerged under anarchy—that is, under a system without a supernational authority—where each state was left responsible for protecting its own borders.

## INTERNATIONAL RELATIONS WITHOUT THE STATE

Structural theories are particularly dependent on the assumption that states are the defining units of international politics. This dependence limits the relevance of these theories throughout history, since states have not always existed as we know them. Structural realists are content to note that the state is the central unit today; they see no reason to doubt that this will continue to be so. Still, if the state's existence and domination of international politics is an accident of history, rather than an inevitable development, then perhaps, so critics argue, it will cease to be the key actor in the near future (Ruggie 1986, 1998). Some argue that the state has already ceased to be the key actor, pointing to the important role of multinational corporations, transnational regimes, nongovernmental organizations (NGOs), and the Internet. Marxist theory assumes that the state will gradually wither away to be replaced by an anarchic, classless, but cooperative society.

Critics of realism who argue against placing so much emphasis on the state note, as suggested earlier, that the state has not always been the organizing unit behind international politics. They point out that in medieval times the concept of territorial boundaries—a critical, defining feature of any state—was not well understood (Krasner 1984; Ruggie 1986). King John of England, for example, was simultaneously king and lord. As king he was the political equal of his contemporary, King Philip Augustus of France; but in his role as lord of Brittany he owed homage and fealty to Philip. Thus, a king could be equal to and subservient to another king at one and the same time, depending on the issue in dispute. With territorial claims properly configured, indeed, a king could be superior, equal, and inferior to another individual all at the same time. This is certainly confusing to our way of thinking; we see territorial boundaries and state sovereignty much more clearly than did those living in the twelfth or thirteenth centuries. Yet the medieval idea of fealty may not be so different from modern relations between national governments and large corporations. American firms that assemble electronic appliances in El Salvador certainly exert great influence over that country's tax policies and perhaps over other policy areas as well. Because such corporations provide so much employment, and such a lift to the national economy, they have an influence that is perhaps equal to that of a sovereign. Yet they are not sovereign, and they are not equal when it comes to law enforcement or to being, at least in principal, subject to local administrative, judicial, and daily customs. The interplay between corporations and governments, especially of smaller states, is not so different from the interplay of kings who owed each other fealty under the feudal circumstances of the Middle Ages.

Nomadic peoples like the Mongols under Genghis Khan managed to conquer much of the world between Africa and Korea during the twelfth and thirteenth centuries while having only a scant sense of territorial property rights as we understand them today. They had little notion of themselves as a state and much more notion of themselves as a set of interlocking clans. Nevertheless, they clearly engaged in intergovernmental, international politics. The Mongols sought and formed alliances with others, including the king of Cathay (China). Some European rulers, like Pope Innocent IV, unsuccessfully pursued alliances with the Mongols to balance their power against a common adversary, the Muslim rulers of the Holy Land (Morgan 1986).

Nomadic people—including Bedouins in the Middle East, some Native Americans, and the Mongols of Asia—typically did not view territorial rights as adhering to specific land at all times. Rather, they saw these rights as rights to travel with their herds from grazing area to grazing area as the cycle of seasons unfolded. They laid no apparent claim to the land in any other context than their right to graze their animals at the appropriate time of year. Certainly, they were not organized as territorial states. Still other societies organized themselves around principles of family ties and kinship rather than any clear sense of aggregate territorial claims. For these groups, families, clans, and tribes defined political boundaries rather than did borders and property rights.

Thus, structural theories, although properly viewed as especially relevant to the modern state system, are less helpful in explaining international relations across the long span of history between the collapse of Greece and the events of 1648.

## DOMESTIC POLITICS AS AN ALTERNATIVE TO THE STATE

Theories that are based on strategic interaction embrace the notion that national foreign policies are dependent on both domestic and international political circumstances. According to these theories, domestic and international political considerations shape the attitudes of leaders with respect to the goals they pursue and help define the strategies they adopt to achieve foreign policy objectives.

The strategic perspective is at home with or without the unitary actor assumption. Recall that for structural realists the state is a unitary actor in that it chooses policy objectives and strategies to maximize its security in the international context. For strategic theories, international policy objectives need not be determined just by a state's position in the international structure; nor are they dictated by the pursuit of national security maximization. Rather, political leaders choose international policies with an eye toward maximizing their own individual welfare. These theories recognize that the welfare of political leaders is intimately tied to their performance on the job, even if they are absolute monarchs or dictators. Every leader is accountable to some set of domestic political interests, whether it is the inner circle in the court, the military elite that controls the guns, or the mass public that controls the ballot box. Leaders choose policies and actions that they believe will make their critical constituents better off so that their constituents will want to maintain them in office. In doing so, leaders take into account the reactions of foreign powers to their choices. It does little good to satisfy domestic constituencies only to be overthrown by disgruntled neighbors.

According to the strategic viewpoint, foreign policy leaders have one eye firmly fixed on what will "sell" at home and the other focused on the international context within which they must implement their objectives. Decision makers try to influence domestic constituencies so that they have reasonable, attainable goals. Leaders are charged with choosing the strategies that will give them the greatest chance of achieving those goals and thus securing their own hold on power. Key foreign policy leaders do not pick goals themselves; rather, they reflect the interests of those whose support they need to stay in power. Emphasis is placed on the likely reaction of domestic rivals, constituents, and other states to the chosen actions. In this sense, theories of strategic interaction are, at a minimum, concerned with relations between pairs of states, putting each state in a context of relations with specific other states and with specific domestic political interests.

The strategic point of view disagrees with the purely domestic politics perspective embodied in the interest group approach. The point of disagreement centers on the importance of international conditions in determining the choices that foreign policy leaders make. Interest group theories largely dismiss what goes on outside the state; in contrast, the strategic approach takes these into consideration. Theories rooted in the strategic perspective also disagree with structural theories in that the latter dismiss the importance of domestic considerations. Structural approaches view domestic politics as inconsequential when it comes to important international choices. The strategic perspective, as we have seen, finds domestic politics to be integral to understanding international decision making. Policies are pursued in light of domestic pressures (tempered by internal arguments about what can be accomplished internationally) and internal and international structural constraints on strategic options.

Some approaches to our subject—bureaucratic theories, for example—are rooted in the view that foreign policy is just another form of domestic politics. Such approaches treat individuals or interest groups as the basic unit of analysis. From the perspective of these theories, the notion that the nation can be treated as if it were a cohesive, coherent decision-making unit seems naive and even foolish. Instead, the nation is viewed as no more than a metaphor for a plethora of competitive, vexatious individuals and their bureaucracies bent on promoting their own interests. This stands in sharp contrast to the notion that the nation is a unitary whole, pursuing the national welfare unfettered by concern for any narrower, constituent interest. In fact, the rejection of the unitary actor assumption is one of the most fundamental distinguishing characteristics of both the interest group and strategic perspectives. The structural outlook, of course, depends on the unitary actor assumption. This assumption, relatively innocuous in a world of absolute monarchs, such as that existing in 1648 (although even then court factions and other interest groups certainly existed), is today more problematic, given the layers of competing interests within and across state boundaries.

For theories concerned with individual decision makers, a critical question is how the individual's decisions are constrained by the domestic political environment. Typically, individuals or groups of individuals are assumed to be limited in their choices of action by the existence of national government rules and institutions. For example, the method by which elections are conducted in a democracy can have a profound influence on foreign policy decisions. In democratic political systems in which candidates with a plurality of votes win, the views of voters with extreme foreign policy preferences are blunted; candidates who openly support such extreme views are highly unlikely to succeed in winning under such a system (Duverger 1955; Downs 1957; Cox 1997). Therefore, more extreme views are frozen out of foreign policy decision making. In the case of systems employing proportional representation, however, extreme preferences are rewarded at the ballot box and typically do play a role in foreign policy decision making.

In proportional representation systems parties win legislative seats in approximate proportion to the percentage of popular votes that they receive. Consequently, even parties that garner only a small share of voter support may enjoy legislative representation.

Such systems often produce multiparty, coalition governments. In multiparty governments, the support of small parties is crucial to forming an effective coalition government. This allows small parties (with potentially extreme views) to exert influence on foreign policy well beyond their size. This has often been true of small religious parties in Israel and is sometimes true for the environmentally focused Green Party in Germany. Both of these countries have proportional representation electoral rules.

If important aspects of international politics are affected by the internal affairs of a state, then structural theories are certainly limited in their ability to effectively explain international outcomes. They simply do not leave room for variations in international politics in response to domestic rules and interests. In contrast, theories focused on domestic politics have much greater merit in explaining the mechanisms of international relations. But for interest group or bureaucratic theories to be credible, we need to understand how domestic institutions and domestic interests shape foreign policy and international politics. If a review of domestic considerations provides alternative definitions of the national interest, or even denies its existence, then an approach that involves strategic interaction across levels of analysis must be a better explanation of state behavior in international affairs. In the following section, we will address this matter and find that the very idea of a national interest is at the least deeply problematic and at the most meaningless.

## CAN DOMESTIC POLITICS AFFECT THE DEFINITION OF THE NATIONAL INTEREST?

Because structural theories place no great importance on domestic political affairs, whereas other approaches do, examining the impact of domestic institutions and rules on international affairs provides us with a critical test of the effectiveness of structuralism in explaining international relations. Of course, such an examination will simultaneously illuminate for us how foreign policy and international politics depend on domestic political considerations.

Critical tests allow us to separate the predictions of competing theories so that we can decide whether one theory works better than another. In this way, we can form a general understanding of how to think about international relations. We now can use some tools introduced earlier and introduce other tools that can help us start to choose among theories. To begin, I construct an example of how domestic political competition in the Soviet Union—an authoritarian state—influenced the end of the cold war. I further elaborate on that example by then exploring how the international community responded to the policy changes brought about as a consequence of internal Soviet domestic political competition. The analysis of the end of the cold war is important both substantively and analytically. Substantively it points out the importance of domestic politics in influencing the foreign policies even of authoritarian states while helping us understand a major international event. Analytically, it provides an opportunity to introduce the idea of "win sets," a tool that will be used on several other occasions throughout this book to illustrate how linking issues together can reshape negotiations and policy outcomes.

I wrap up this discussion by providing an example from American presidential elections. This example illustrates how something as seemingly minor as voting rules in democracies can sharply influence national security policies and points out the implications of this observation for the definition of the national interest. These examples should be read as posing broad questions about the structuralists' contention that the national interest is a central concept governing international behavior. At the same time, they demonstrate the potential explanatory power of those viewpoints that stress domestic political constraints and competition.

## END OF THE COLD WAR: WIN SETS AS A TOOL FOR UNDERSTANDING POLICY

A central goal of Soviet foreign policy from 1945 until about 1989 was to maintain control over its East European empire. The members of the Warsaw Pact, which included Bulgaria, Czechoslovakia, East Germany, Hungary, Poland, and Romania, were not free to pursue foreign policies that the Soviet government opposed. When Warsaw Pact states tried to move away from the Soviet sphere of influence and pursue independent policies, the Kremlin reigned them in and forced them to toe the line. The Hungarians learned this lesson quite painfully in 1956 when Soviet tanks put down their efforts to develop their own, independent policies. The Czechs had much the same experience in 1968. In 1979 the Afghans, who were not members of the Warsaw Pact but who were nevertheless within the Soviet sphere of influence, also learned this lesson. When Polish workers led by Lech Walesa began to threaten the stability of Poland's government in the 1980s, there was widespread fear that once again Soviet troops and tanks would enforce the USSR's will on its captive allies.

The relationship between the United States and the Soviet Union improved or worsened during the cold war years in part in response to variations in Soviet aggression and expansion in Eastern Europe and in other parts of the world. Consequently, the essential features of the international system during this time depended on Soviet (and American) actions toward third parties. For many observers this meant that international politics was dictated by the maneuvering of the two superpowers for political advantage. Under these circumstances the Soviets could not afford to give up their control over Eastern Europe because to do so would jeopardize their position as a superpower. Improving relations with the United States could never be as important as preserving their standing in the international system. In fact, the loss of Eastern Europe and the collapse of the Warsaw Pact did contribute to the end of the Soviet Union as a superpower and, ultimately, its end as a state. This leaves observers who focus on balance-of-power politics, such as realists and neorealists, baffled as to why the Soviet Union took the actions it did. From the perspective of those who consider foreign policy a part of domestic politics, however, the actions of the Soviet Union are less puzzling.

## DOMESTIC SOVIET PREFERENCES AND THE END OF THE COLD WAR

The collapse of Soviet domination of Eastern Europe can be explained, at least in part, by the location of internal policy preferences and the ambition to retain or gain political power at home. This explanation requires some assumptions and analytic tools that can help us understand at least one way to look at the link between domestic political ambitions and international politics.

Soviet politics in 1987 or 1988 might conveniently be simplified by describing two prominent issues that dominated internal political debate and maneuvering. These

MAP 6-1
### Europe at the End of the Cold War

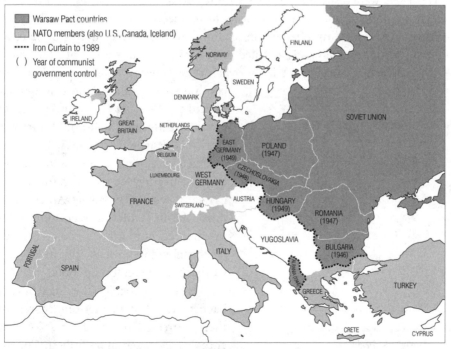

*The cold war divided Europe into three camps: NATO members; those behind the "Iron Curtain" who were the members of the Warsaw Pact; and those who were neutral, such as Austria and Switzerland. Since the cold war ended, the influence of the Western powers has spread eastward. Today, four former members of the Warsaw Pact belong to NATO. These include the former German Democratic Republic (East Germany), which is now part of unified Germany; Hungary; Poland; and the Czech Republic.*

issues were how to relate to the United States in foreign policy and how to get the domestic Soviet economy moving. During the Brezhnev years the Soviet economy stagnated, falling further and further behind the industrial democracies of NATO. As had happened before when the Soviet economy was in trouble, there was some debate among the leaders of the Soviet Union as to whether more centralized planning or more liberalization of market forces would help generate the wealth needed to maintain military competitiveness with the West while still fostering political tranquility at home. Vladimir Lenin in the early days of the Soviet Union and Nikita Khrushchev in the early 1960s had both grappled with this problem. When Mikhail Gorbachev came to power in the mid-1980s, he too had to confront this question. There was also debate over whether economic and military security would be enhanced or diminished by improving foreign relations with the West, and with the United States in particular.

During the period under discussion, internal Soviet political interests were divided into three main camps: the Gorbachev faction, the Ligachev faction, and the Yeltsin faction. At the time, Mikhail Gorbachev was the head of the Soviet government. Gorbachev and his backers were relative moderates with regard to both economic reform and foreign relations. They favored small reforms in the economy and some consequential, although not dramatic, improvement in relations with the United States, perhaps along the lines of the détente that had prevailed prior to the Soviet invasion of Afghanistan in 1979. Yigor Ligachev, Gorbachev's main rival for power, was a relative hard-liner, firmly committed to maintaining a tough stance toward the West and a controlled, centrally planned economy at home. Shortly after Gorbachev's ascent to power, Boris Yeltsin emerged as a spokesman for more radical change, urging economic reform and an easing of tension in Soviet-American relations. Yeltsin favored a freer, more market-oriented economy than either Ligachev or Gorbachev but essentially followed the Gorbachev line on foreign policy.

Figure 6-1 locates the Ligachev, Gorbachev, and Yeltsin factions in regard to their expressed policy desires (or preferences, as discussed more fully in Chapter 9) on these two policy issues in the late 1980s. The figure shows the two issues as linked together. Point Q shows the approximate location of the status quo in U.S.-Soviet relations and Soviet domestic economic policy.

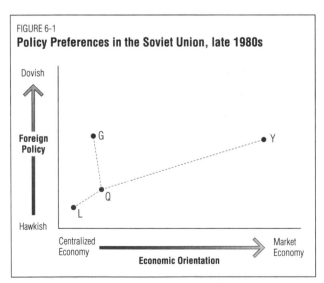

FIGURE 6-1
**Policy Preferences in the Soviet Union, late 1980s**

*Preferences concerning foreign policy and the economy were quite varied in the Soviet Union in the late 1980s. The dispersion of interests provided an opportunity to form different winning coalitions involving quite dramatic changes in policy.*

The status quo policy strongly supported a controlled, centrally planned economy and a relatively tough and hostile attitude toward the West. Of course, this was a time when Soviet troops were still fighting in Afghanistan; when Soviet policy was considered a menace to the pro-labor, anticommunist Solidarity movement in Poland; and when the Soviets and the United States seemed to disagree on just about every important policy issue of the day. Gorbachev inherited this status quo posture from his predecessors at the Kremlin.

To understand the evolution of Soviet policy, we need to start with a few simplifying assumptions. First, we need to assume that to defeat the status quo policy any proposal in the Soviet Union requires the support of the Ligachev-Gorbachev factions, the Ligachev-Yeltsin factions, or the Gorbachev-Yeltsin factions. This is about equivalent to assuming that a majority of power or clout was needed to win, with clout coming from a mix of influence over the military and over bureaucrats (or, the *nomenklatura*, as the key figures were known in the Soviet Union). Power is discussed and defined more carefully in Chapters 7 and 8. For now, it is used simply to mean the ability of some to make others do that which they otherwise would not want to do. In the examples here, power or collective influence is used to alter policy over the objections of those with insufficient clout to prevent the policy change. Second, I assume that any combination of foreign and domestic economic policies closer to Ligachev's ideal point—the policy he most wants—and denoted by the letter L in Figure 6-1, is preferred by the Ligachev faction to any policy combination farther away from L. Similarly, policies closer to G (Gorbachev's ideal point) are preferred by the Gorbachev faction to policies farther away from G. Finally, policies closer to Y (Yeltsin's ideal point) are preferred by the Yeltsin faction to policies farther away from Y. This assumption that the desirability of policy choices decreases as they move farther from a decision maker's most preferred policy is called single-peakedness. The phrase "single peaked" is used to remind us that such preferences create a peak like the summit of a mountain at the most preferred outcome, with preferences sloping down, forming the sides of the mountain, the farther away a choice is from the most preferred option, that is, from the peak. I address the details of this assumption in depth in Chapter 9.

Given these assumptions, we can see that Yeltsin dislikes the status quo more than Gorbachev, and Gorbachev dislikes the status quo more than Ligachev. Lines GQ, YQ, and LQ show the distance between the points that are preferred by each faction to the status quo. These lines can be viewed as prospective radii of indifference curves such as those introduced in Chapter 5. As with those, the indifference curves here reflect policy mixes of equal value to a decision maker. However, unlike the indifference curves in Chapter 5, these indifference curves reflect preferences for two issues rather than preferences for two dimensions on a single issue. As such, and because we are assuming that the preferences are single peaked and that the decision makers attach equal importance or salience to each issue, these indifference curves form circles. Any point equidistant from a decision maker's ideal point on the two linked issues is liked or disliked equally. Points closer to a decision maker's ideal point are preferred to points farther away. Thus, the circular indifference curve at any distance from a decision maker's ideal point can be thought of as a ring around the mountain slope whose summit—the single peak—is the ideal point. In this way, the indifference curves might be thought of as creating a topological map of the mountain slope representing preferences farther and farther from the summit that is the decision maker's ideal point or most desired outcome.

Figure 6-2 reproduces the information depicted in Figure 6-1, but with some added information. In Figure 6-2 concentric circles center on points Y, L, and G. The outer perimeter of each of these circles represents points of indifference among mixes of economic and foreign policies for the Yeltsin, Ligachev, and Gorbachev factions. Any point on the perimeter of one of these circles is just as well liked as any other point on the circle by the faction located at the circle's center. Any point inside a circle is preferred by the relevant faction to any point on the circle's perimeter, which is that actor's indifference curve. This is true simply because any point inside the circle is closer to the most desired policy of the relevant decision maker than is any point on the perimeter of the circle or, in fact, of any other circle that could be drawn that is still farther away from that faction's ideal point.

Lines LG, YG, and LY in Figure 6-2 represent the contract curves between Ligachev and Gorbachev, Yeltsin and Gorbachev, and Ligachev and Yeltsin, respectively. A contract curve denotes all the efficient solutions to a bargain or trade between two decision makers. In Figure 6-2, the contract curves consist of all the points at which Gorbachev's indifference curves are tangent to Yeltsin's indifference curves, Gorbachev's indifference curves are tangent to Ligachev's indifference curves, and Yeltsin's indifference curves are tangent to Ligachev's indifference curves. To avoid clutter in the figure, I have not drawn an indifference curve for Yeltsin that is just touching one for Ligachev, but remember, the space is full of indifference curves. For any curve drawn for Ligachev, for example, you can draw an indifference curve for Yeltsin that is tangent to it. That is, the point at which the two decision makers' indifference curves just touch—the points of tangency—are the points of likely agreement between the relevant decision makers because their marginal rates of substitution—the amount of one good that each would trade away to gain more of another good—are the same on the contract curve. Although typically we draw only a few indifference curves, in reality we could draw infinitely many so that all the points of tangency together form a line (or a curve). Those points of tangency among two decision makers' indifference curves are called the contract curve and are special because they maximize the joint satisfaction of the decision makers relative to all other policies equidistant from the ideal point of any one of them. Let me explain this more fully.

I have drawn only a few indifference curves on Figure 6-2, but in principle it is possible to draw infinitely many, making the figure a solid mass of such curves. At any fixed distance from Gorbachev's ideal point, for example, there is a set of policies with which he would be equally happy (or unhappy). These are the points on the perimeter of a given indifference curve. If he insists on no less than the amount of satisfaction offered by that particular policy, then Yeltsin can maximize his own satisfaction only if that policy is located on Gorbachev's indifference curve at exactly the point at which it touches Yeltsin's indifference curve. If we hold Gorbachev's satisfaction with the policy constant, it is evident that any other point on Gorbachev's indifference curve necessarily falls on an indifference curve for Yeltsin that is farther from his ideal point than the policy represented by the point of tangency between Gorbachev's curve and Yeltsin's. Thus, Yeltsin likes the policy denoted by the point of tangency more than any other policy, given Gorbachev's indifference and given that the two of them can form a coalition. The same would be true for Gorbachev if we hold Yeltsin's satisfaction constant. This concept can be extended, of course, to the points of tangency between Yeltsin and Ligachev or Gorbachev and Ligachev. Thus, for each pair of decision makers, the contract curve denotes all their possible agreements on how much policy satisfaction to trade for personal satisfaction. Any deviation from the trades on the contract curve is inefficient. Trades off the contract curve necessarily make one decision maker worse off than he would be on the contract curve while not necessarily making the other decision maker better off. Therefore, the points on the contract curve meet the conditions known as Pareto optimality: at least one person is made better off and no one is worse off than at any other point in the array of possible outcomes.

In Figure 6-2 the contract curves are drawn as straight lines because I have made the simplifying assumption that each faction views the two policy dimensions as equally important. If economic reform were more important to any of them than foreign policy choices, then the contract curve for that faction would form an arc rather than a straight line. Whether the arc would have bent upward (favoring an increase in foreign policy liberalization, as happened) or not depends on the specific shape of the indifference curves for the relevant faction. Although it should be clear that the exact shape of the contract curve (the likely points of agreement) depends on the relative salience of the policy dimensions being compared, that facet of the analysis is too technical an issue to explore further at this

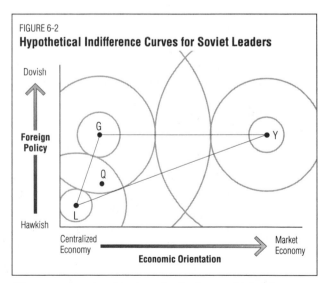

FIGURE 6-2
**Hypothetical Indifference Curves for Soviet Leaders**

*The contract curves between Gorbachev and Ligachev, Gorbachev and Yeltsin, and Ligachev and Yeltsin provided opportunities to make the Soviet economy both more and less market oriented and more and less friendly toward the West in the late 1980s.*

juncture. The essential point here is to see how we can predict the range of possible policy changes from a minimal amount of information about the desires (preferences) and relative clout (power) of the key Soviet factions.

## WINNING PREFERENCES INSIDE THE SOVIET UNION

Line YQ in Figure 6-1 denotes the distance from the status quo to Yeltsin's most preferred mix of policies, just as lines GQ and LQ denote the same information for Gorbachev and Ligachev, respectively. Recall that any policy that is as far away from G as Q is as distasteful to Gorbachev as is the status quo, located at Q, and that any policy that is as far away from L as Q is just as distasteful to Ligachev as the status quo. Finally, any mix of policies that is as far away from Y as Q is as undesirable to Yeltsin as the status quo. Given these assumptions, we can draw a circle centered on G, tangent to Q, and with radius GQ such that any point inside the circle represents a set of policies more desirable to Gorbachev than is the status quo whereas any point on the perimeter of that circle represents a policy mix that Gorbachev finds no more and no less desirable than the status quo. Similar circles with the radii LQ and YQ and each tangent to Q could be drawn centered on L and Y, respectively, to portray the same relationships for Ligachev and Yeltsin. The circles with radius LQ, YQ, and GQ are of special interest among all of the indifference curves that can be drawn because they provide a way of comparing all policy alternatives specifically with the policy in force at the time (that is, the status quo). If any two factions were to agree on a change in policy, it would be because the two each believed that the new policy was better for them than was the status quo. Otherwise, they would stick with the status quo.

Recall that we assumed that a winning coalition of political interests in the Soviet Union required support from any two of the three factions. Then we can say that the intersection of policies preferred to the status quo for any two factions represents the set of possible policies around which a coalition could be formed to overturn the status quo. These intersections consist of all of the win sets—that is, all of the politically viable new policies on economic reform and foreign policy—that emerged during the period under examination. Win sets represent the policies supported by one or more coalitions that are powerful enough to defeat the existing policy, thereby representing outcomes that are better for all members of a winning coalition than is the status quo policy.

Figure 6-3 shows the policies preferred by Gorbachev, Ligachev, and Yeltsin when compared with the status quo. It is apparent that Gorbachev and Yeltsin differed quite dramatically in their attitude toward economic reform. It is also apparent that they hold essentially the same preference with regard to foreign policy. Although both are more moderate on this question than Ligachev, neither favors major reforms on the foreign policy dimension. Yet, it was just these types of reform that actually occurred. Gorbachev gradually loosened Soviet control over Eastern Europe, just as the United States had been urging the Soviets to do since the end of World War II. Ultimately, he loosened control so much that all of the East European states left the Soviet sphere of influence. The Warsaw

Pact collapsed, and each member went off in its own direction, pursuing closer ties to the West, building democratic governments, and constructing more market-oriented economies. In effect, Gorbachev gave up peacefully virtually everything in Europe that had created and sustained the cold war to begin with. How can this be explained given the interests or desires displayed in Figures 6-1 through 6-3?

Figure 6-3 also shows the possible winning coalitions. If you look closely you will see that there is a tiny area of overlap between Ligachev and Yeltsin's policies that are preferred to the status quo. This means that it is possible for these two factions to form a coalition that could overturn the status quo and replace it with a policy involving a slight economic liberalization and a slight increase in hostility toward the United States and its allies. But if we assume that the likelihood of a bargain being struck between two parties decreases as the size of the area of overlap between their interests decreases, then, clearly, finding the right combination of policies that is likely to lead to a Ligachev-Yeltsin coalition is extremely difficult. As the win set gets smaller, proposed bargains have to be more and more precise to wind up inside both fac-

tions' "preferred-to" sets. This is no problem if each person's ideal point and degree of salience for the issues in question are common knowledge. But in reality decision makers can only guess at what others really want and how badly they want it. Preferences and salience are not generally known to everyone. A bargain between Yeltsin and Ligachev would have to be very precise indeed, because only a very slight variation could push the policy combination outside the win set and therefore make it incapable of overturning the status quo.

By far the largest opportunity for forming a coalition links the Gorbachev and Yeltsin factions. This win set has several interesting and important features. Points E1 and E2 in Figure 6-3 denote the feasible range of bargains on economic reform, and points F1 and F2 display the possible range of movement on the foreign policy dimension. Obviously, there is much more room for maneuvering on the foreign policy dimension than there is on the economic dimension. The basic spatial orientation of

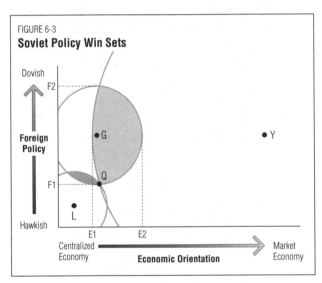

FIGURE 6-3
**Soviet Policy Win Sets**

*The alignment of interests among key Soviet political factions in the late 1980s created opportunities for winning coalitions involving the Gorbachev and Yeltsin factions, the Gorbachev and Ligachev factions, or the Yeltsin and Ligachev factions. The winning coalition that included Gorbachev and Yeltsin provided support for a substantial improvement in Soviet foreign relations with the West and smaller changes in the market orientation of the Soviet economy. This is precisely what happened. Soviet economic reforms stalled while Gorbachev allowed the Soviet East European "empire" to dissolve.*

the Yeltsin-Gorbachev win set is vertical, not horizontal, meaning that there are many foreign policy changes, including quite radical foreign policy reform, that both prefer to the foreign policy status quo.

In fact, even though neither Gorbachev nor Yeltsin was primarily a foreign policy reformer, foreign policy reform, as noted, is exactly what did occur. There was little that Yeltsin could do to persuade Gorbachev to tolerate significant economic change, and, in fact, Gorbachev barely tolerated any. Just how much economic and foreign policy change the two factions could actually agree on depended, of course, on the information available to each about what the other factions wanted; on their skillfulness as negotiators; and on the actual shape of their indifference curves. That is, did their indifference curves favor the economic reform axis or the foreign policy axis? If there was no uncertainty, we would expect the agreement to fall somewhere on the contract curve between Y and G. The contract curve would be the straight line, GY, between each faction's ideal point if each cared equally about both issues. The contract curve would be shaped in an arc if this were not the case.

Select a pair of current, linked foreign policy issues from a newspaper or magazine article. Be sure the issues involve the same three or more decision makers or groups of decision makers who are competing to influence the resolution of the issues. From what you have read about their points of view, estimate each actor's most preferred resolution of each issue using a ranking scale that runs from 0 to 100. Explain what each value means. Pick the scale so that preferences are single-peaked. Draw a graph indicating the ideal point of each decision maker and the status quo. Identify the combinations (or coalitions) of decision makers that are powerful enough to alter the status quo. Draw the win sets for these decision makers and write up your prediction of how they will settle these issues. Check back when the issues are resolved and see how well you have done at predicting the outcome.

The new policy also depended on the give and take of influences outside the Soviet Union, including the actions of the United States and the other members of the NATO alliance, France, and Eastern Europe (the erstwhile members of the Warsaw Pact). Even without external pressures, it is clear that Yeltsin and Gorbachev had substantial domestic political incentives to moderate Soviet policy toward the United States relative to the status quo. And as we will see in the next section, the external influences on Soviet policymaking were likely to push Soviet policy toward even greater accommodation to Western interests. We should pause to take note that domestic factors had a dramatic effect on Soviet policy and on the subsequent structure of international politics; an effect that is ignored by structural theories. Once we recognize the important part played by domestic affairs within the Soviet Union we realize why structural theorists were baffled by the collapse of the cold war status quo. This point is further elaborated in the discussion to follow.

## EXTERNAL PRESSURES TO THE END OF THE COLD WAR

Figure 6-4 depicts the change in the Soviet Union's policy stance before 1989 to its new, 1989, policy stance in regard to its relations with the West and its internal economic structure. But Figure 6-4 does more. It places the new Soviet position in its broader, international context. In the European context (as distinguished from the exclusively domestic Soviet context examined in Figure 6-3), the status quo among all of the relevant actors was more pro-Western than even the new (1989) Soviet stance and considerably more market oriented in economic terms than the Soviet Union found desirable. This is evident in Figure 6-4 if we observe the location of the status quo point on the two fundamental dimensions of foreign policy and economic policy and compare it with the position of the Soviet Union after Gorbachev took domestic factors into account and altered policy in 1989.

Despite the marked foreign policy reforms instituted by Gorbachev by early 1989, the world seemed little prepared for the collapse of the Berlin Wall, which signified the end of Soviet domination of Eastern Europe when it occurred later that year. Yet dramatic change in foreign policy should have been the expected order of the day. Figure 6-4 reveals why significant additional Soviet concessions to the West should have been expected by the relevant policymakers if they had paid attention to power and preferences.

Recall that the dominant win set in Figure 6-3—the purely domestic assessment—includes a large area of possible foreign policy concessions. In fact, if the need for politi-

cal support had been even greater than that depicted in the domestic example, both Yeltsin and Gorbachev would have been prepared to undertake even more foreign policy reform than is suggested by the location of the contract curve between them. After all, their win set extends well above the contract curve. What led Gorbachev to accept these larger foreign policy concessions?

In Figure 6-4 the European setting consists of five crucial actors: the Soviet Union, which is situated at a point on the Gorbachev-Yeltsin contract curve (see Figure 6-3); the United States, which favors policies that are much more pro-Western and pro-market than those favored by the Soviets or exhibited by the prevailing status quo; NATO (excluding the United States); France; and Eastern Europe, which represents the elements in the Soviet sphere of influence that might have been "up for grabs."

The United States, NATO, and France together constituted a coalition strong enough to block Soviet expansion in Europe

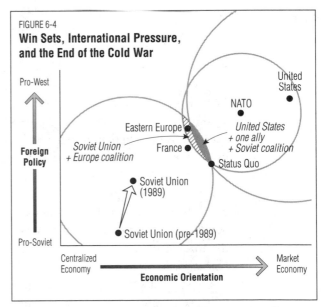

FIGURE 6-4

**Win Sets, International Pressure, and the End of the Cold War**

*Internal domestic pressures produced important policy changes in the Soviet Union in 1989. Further change was motivated by international Soviet interactions with members of NATO and with the erstwhile members of the East European Soviet bloc. The winning coalitions pushed for further foreign policy reform but not for substantial additional economic reforms.*

during the cold war, but it was not a strong enough coalition to defeat the Soviet Union or to pry from its grasp the East European states within its sphere of influence. The inability of the U.S-NATO-French coalition to do more than block Soviet expansion is evident from its failure to intervene when the Soviets invaded Hungary and Czechoslovakia in 1956 and 1968, respectively. Likewise, the Soviet Union and its East European Warsaw Pact allies could not defeat the pro-Western alliance in Europe during the cold war. However, it was able to block the European coalition's expansionist designs. For example, the United States and its European allies were restrained from absorbing Yugoslavia into their sphere of influence after Yugoslav leader Tito broke from the Soviet sphere in 1948. The United States could not force the Soviets to tear down the Berlin Wall after it was constructed in 1961. At the same time, the Soviets could not force the United States and its allies to withdraw from the sectors of Berlin—a city situated in the heart of East Germany—ceded to them at the close of World War II. In short, Europe was at a standoff. This means that during the period examined in Figure 6-4, a winning coalition required more members than just the Soviet Union and Eastern Europe or just the United States, NATO, and France. I suggest that a winning coalition required support from the United States and the Soviet Union or from the Soviet Union and all of Europe. Either of these combinations would have been sufficient to break the deadlock between the United States and the Soviet Union that was the central feature of the cold war. In other words, the international status quo could have been changed through external pressure if enough power could have been mustered for the task

With these specifications in mind, I have drawn in Figure 6-4 the possible win sets in Europe for 1989. I have left out the circular indifference curves (that is, the preferred-to sets) of some of the actors except the Soviet Union to avoid crowding the figure. In this way it is easily seen that the win sets include the Soviets. Clearly, in 1989 the Soviets faced external pressure to liberalize their foreign policy further. They did not face comparable pressures to liberalize their economic arrangements. Indeed, the win sets anticipate a small shift toward greater welfare economics or greater protectionism in trade. In any event, the fundamental movement suggested by the win sets in Figure 6-4 is for greater Soviet acceptance of a more pro-Western foreign policy. And in fact, major reforms on the foreign policy dimension did take place. External pressures pushed Gorbachev to accept greater foreign policy reform than the Yeltsin/Gorbachev internal coalition alone would suggest. On the economic dimension, to be sure, reforms were undertaken relative to the economy under communist control, but those reforms were—and remain—much less dramatic than the foreign policy reforms. Russia in 2002 just began to liberalize sufficiently on property rights so that real property could be bought or sold without government approval, a restriction that greatly limited any real sense of property rights. Property rights are essential for a market economy.

This example reveals rather starkly why it should not be surprising that the Soviet Union chose to pursue a policy of dramatic foreign policy change while instituting only modest economic reform. The interests of the relevant internal and external actors provided a natural environment for the Soviet leadership under Gorbachev to agree to the large-scale foreign policy reform that ultimately rang the death knell of the Soviet Union and of the cold war. Yet these sweeping changes certainly were not motivated by any self-destructive desire to topple the supremacy of communism in the Soviet sphere. Rather, they seem to have been the product of efforts to hold on to political power and to forge the internal agreements necessary to gain support from a key rival faction while still responding to external pressures for change. By this reckoning, the emergence of the Yeltsin faction was crucial both to Gorbachev's success as a reformer and, finally, to his political defeat.

In the end, Gorbachev did try to pull back a little from his reforms. He used troops to quell uprisings in the Baltic republics and even turned toward hard-line communists to reconstruct his own government after extremists in the Soviet military, the KGB (the Soviet Secret Police), and the Communist Party tried to overthrow him in a coup in August 1991. But by then it was too late. Gorbachev was unable to salvage his leadership or to save the Soviet Union. His foreign policy reforms were of such breathtaking magnitude that he

*The August 1991 coup exposed Soviet Premier Gorbachev's political weaknesses. After the coup was defeated, he returned to office, but made the mistake of appointing hard-liners from the communist party and the KGB (the Soviet secret police) to his new cabinet. This was not what the people or many politicians wanted. Gorbachev was unable to hold on to power. He was replaced in a peaceful power transfer by Boris Yeltsin, his one-time protégé. Within the year the Soviet Union ceased to exist and Yeltsin emerged as the president of the newly constituted Russian Republic.*

inevitably lost political power to Yeltsin. Ironically, all that he did he did in the name of pre-serving his own hold on power (which he succeeded in doing for nearly two years after the fall of the Berlin Wall). Although these changes affected the international system most dra-matically, they are best explained first by the internal competition over policy preferences and then by linking that competition to external, international constraints.

The explanation of the end of the cold war developed here represents a fundamental challenge to structural theories and a significant challenge to interest group theories. Structural theories, as you know, assume that each nation is a unitary actor. Consequently, when it comes to fundamental policies that influence the survival of the state, internal differences of opinion are considered inconsequential. Yet, domestic dif-ferences in policy objectives within the Soviet leadership played a crucial role in toppling the Soviet Union from its position as one of the world's two superpowers. Simply put, the structural view as an explanation of the end of the cold war is wrong.

Interest group theories pay scant attention to what happens beyond a nation's bor-ders. For these theories, infighting of the sort depicted in Figure 6-3 is precisely what gives shape to foreign policy. Localized competition for power, for control over national treasure, or for control over policy decisions determines policy shifts, not any considera-tion of the overarching national interest. Personal political security far outweighs national issues. Figure 6-3 provides support for the interest group perspective. But Figure 6-4 suggests that the ultimate demise of the Soviet Union and the end of the cold war did not happen purely in response to pressures within the Soviet Union. External responses to Soviet needs helped to cajole the Kremlin into granting larger and larger foreign policy concessions in its quest for economic aid. The United States, NATO, and even Eastern Europe all exerted pressure that helped to convince the Soviet leadership that it needed to continue down the path initiated by their own domestic competition. Contrary to the interest group or bureaucratic perspective, internal factors alone do not explain what happened to the Soviet Union.

## THE 1992 PRESIDENTIAL ELECTION

We have now seen the important role played by domestic politics in an authoritarian state. The means for domestic factors to influence international politics is even greater in democracies, where factors as seemingly innocuous as voting rules can reshape politics. Consider the American presidential election in 1992.

In November 1992, Bill Clinton was elected president of the United States. He defeated George H. W. Bush, the incumbent, and H. Ross Perot, a maverick, independent challenger. Although it is undoubtedly true that Bush, Clinton, and Perot are immensely complicated people, we might summarize who they are (in regard to politics) by describ-ing each of them as a bundle of policy goals on the central questions of the day. In doing this I am making the simplifying assumption that to know Bush, Clinton, or Perot's chance of success in the electoral contest of 1992, you need only understand what their policy stances were in relation to the desires of the American electorate. I further assume that each of them had sincerely held policy goals in mind but that each also wanted to win the election. Each had to make some trade-off between policies he really wanted and what he believed the electorate wanted. I do not assume, as does structuralism, that a quest for national security is of paramount importance, nor do I assume, as do interest group and bureaucratic theories, that each politician is willing to do anything to get elected. What I do assume is that each cares about public policy, about the welfare of the nation, and about personal political well-being. Each is willing to trade benefits on one of these three dimensions for benefits on any other of these dimensions.

In the 1992 presidential election, Clinton received about 43 percent of the popular vote, Bush received 38 percent of the popular vote, and Perot received 19 percent of the popular vote. Clinton, of course, was inaugurated president on January 20, 1993. In the discussion that follows, I am interested only in the foreign policy stances of Clinton and the other candidates before the election. What Clinton or any of the other candidates did after the November election could not have any bearing on his electoral chances in 1992. What we are seeking to find out is whether variations in domestic political conditions could have profoundly altered who got elected and thus altered U.S. foreign policy after inauguration. If domestic conditions influenced who got elected, then American foreign policy and, therefore, international politics on the whole were altered by factors judged to be unimportant by structural theories. Alternatively, we might find that American policy was shaped by external considerations and reflected an agreed-upon best way of enhancing the nation's welfare, as suggested by structural theories. This example will shed light on an important substantive matter—the unfolding of American foreign policy in the early 1990s as a function of electoral rules—and on an important theoretical concern.

*During the 1992 campaign H. Ross Perot, seen on the left, George Bush, in the middle, and Bill Clinton, on the right, greet one another as they prepare to debate the domestic and foreign policy issues of the day. American foreign policy would have looked very different if Perot or Bush had won. Who wins an election depends, in part, on the particular way votes are translated into an outcome. Under the plurality system, in which the winner takes all, Clinton was the clear victor. In a runoff system, it is likely that Bush would have been elected. Other common voting methods would have propelled Perot, with just 19 percent of the first-place votes, to victory. It is important not to ignore variations in domestic political institutions and preferences when analyzing foreign policy and international politics.*

The election of Bush or Perot instead of Clinton probably would have meant significant differences in the foreign policies adopted by the United States. Perot, who staked out a fair trade policy stance during the campaign, probably would have tried to promote greater economic protection for American industry than Clinton. Clinton, for his part, favored more trade protection than did Bush, although not to the extent that Perot favored it. This is why, for example, Clinton was willing to support NAFTA only after additional side agreements were accepted by Mexico to protect American jobs and the environment. In contrast, Bush was prepared to accept NAFTA as it had already been negotiated, and Perot was unwilling to accept NAFTA at all.

The three candidates also differed markedly in their approach to national security policy. One indication of their differences can be found by examining their attitudes about the size of the defense budget. Perot indicated that he would not cut the defense budget to the extent that Clinton wanted to cut it but would cut it more than Bush. Of course, these were not the central issues over which most of the electorate made their choices. As Clinton argued throughout the campaign, it was, in fact, "the economy, stupid." But this fact serves only to highlight how dependent foreign affairs can be on domestic factors. After all, if the president is elected on domestic issues and if one presidential candidate differs from another markedly on foreign policy, then the implied foreign policy differences are simply swept into office and implemented on the coattails of domestic policies. And if the structure of the international system—the configuration of alliances, the distribution of power, and sources of instability—is a product of the myriad foreign policy choices made by world leaders, especially the leaders of superpower states like the United States, then domestic choices are at the very heart of international relations.

## POLICY OBJECTIVES IN THE 1992 PRESIDENTIAL ELECTION

The policy goals of Clinton, Bush, and Perot can be displayed along two lines, or continua. One line represents the candidates' trade policy goals and the other represents the candidates' desires with respect to defense expenditures. Figure 6-5 shows the policy position most desired by each of the three candidates on each of these policy dimensions. The figure contains the same assumption as the Soviet cold war example; namely, that the farther away an alternative is from the outcome most desired by the

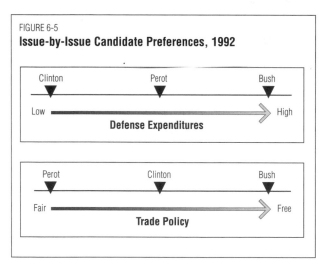

FIGURE 6-5
**Issue-by-Issue Candidate Preferences, 1992**

*In the 1992 presidential election race H. Ross Perot probably had the support of the median voter on issues related to defense expenditures, whereas Bill Clinton probably had the support of the median voter on issues related to trade policy.*

candidate in question, the less support that candidate is willing to give to that alternative. In other words, the attractiveness of a possible foreign trade policy and a possible defense expenditure policy falls off for each candidate in direct relation to that policy's distance from the candidate's most preferred policy, as it is identified on the figure. This is the notion of single-peaked preferences mentioned earlier and elaborated on later in Chapter 9. I will maintain this assumption throughout the remainder of this discussion. Voters whose most preferred policy on trade and on defense expenditures can be located anywhere along the two issue continua also desire alternatives close to their most preferred policy more than alternatives farther away.

Although the voters, for the most part, did not make their choices based specifically on these issues, the candidates' preferences will nevertheless presumably translate into action if they are elected. Knowing the policy preferences of each candidate, then, should inform us about what type of foreign policy will be pursued under a Clinton, Bush, or Perot administration or even under a coalition agreement between any two of these candidates.

Those who voted for Clinton, by the assumption of single-peaked preferences, preferred his policies to those of Bush or Perot. Similarly, Bush voters preferred Bush's policies and Perot voters preferred Perot's policies. This means that if Clinton had gone head to head against Perot on trade policy, he would have won by a large majority. Not only would Clinton have received 43 percent of the vote from those who liked his trade policy best, he would have received an additional 38 percent of the vote from those who preferred Bush's trade policy but who, given a choice only between Clinton or Perot, found Clinton's policy the better alternative (that is, the alternative closer to their preferred outcome—Bush's policy—on the continua). In the same way, Clinton would have easily defeated Bush if the election were only about trade policy. Clinton would have received 43 percent of the vote from Clinton backers plus an additional 19 percent of the vote from Perot backers who liked Clinton's outlook on trade better than they liked Bush's. On defense policy, however, in one-on-one competition, both Clinton and Bush would have lost to Perot. In the election it was not possible to vote for Clinton on trade policy and Perot on defense policy. The electorate had to choose one of the three candidates. This means that we must put these two issues together to understand how the election results will influence defense expenditures and trade policy.

Figure 6-6 shows the location of Bush, Clinton, and Perot in regard to trade policy

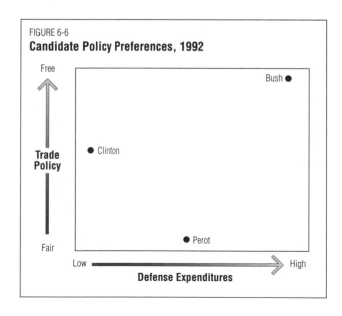

FIGURE 6-6
**Candidate Policy Preferences, 1992**

and defense expenditures when their attitude toward each are linked together. In the figure I use Cartesian coordinates (an x-axis and a y-axis) just as in the cold war example to represent the political interests of Bush, Clinton, and Perot as they are derived from the two continua in Figure 6-5. The horizontal axis shows the objectives of the three candidates with regard to defense expenditures. The vertical axis shows their objectives with regard to trade policy. The points associated with Clinton, Bush, and Perot depict each candidate's most preferred policy on the linked issues of defense expenditures and trade liberalization.

Although Figure 6-6 tells us what policy combinations were favored by Clinton, Bush, and Perot, it does not inform us about how the electorate viewed each candidate's pair of policy positions. Figure 6-7 makes use of the assumption that each voter's preference for alternative policies decreases as the alternative gets farther away from the voter's most preferred position. It also makes use of the assumption that the voters for each candidate shared their candidate's policy preferences on trade and on defense expenditures. I infer the distribution of voter policy interests from the actual vote distribution in the presidential election. By doing so, I ignore the possibility of strategic voting.[1]

Figure 6-7 contains a set of dividing lines that separates the figure into three distinct voting blocs: a pro-Clinton area, a pro-Bush area, and a pro-Perot area. In each voting bloc in the figure a pie chart indicates the actual percentage of votes that each candidate received (Clinton, 43 percent; Bush, 38 percent; Perot, 19 percent). By making the simplifying assumption that trade policy and defense expenditures were the only aspects of the candidates that mattered to voters, we get a sense of which trade and defense preferences were most popular. The pie charts in Figure 6-7 indicate that the voters were not evenly distributed among all of the possible policy stances on trade policy and defense expenditures.

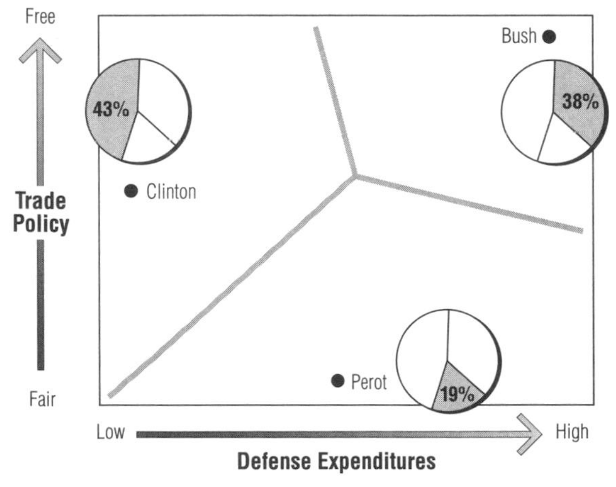

Figure 6-7 contains enough information to tell us still more about the voters. We can infer second-place preferences as well as first-place preferences from its spatial display. Combining the information in Figure 6-7 with information gleaned from surveys of prospective voters before the election, I

FIGURE 6-7
**Voters' First Place Choices, 1992**

---

[1] Strategic voters might not vote for the candidate they most prefer. Fearing that the candidate they least prefer will be elected, voters who believe their second-choice candidate has a better chance than their most preferred candidate might cast their vote for their second choice to prevent their third choice from winning.

show in Figure 6-8 what the voters' first-, second-, and third-place preferences were for the candidates.

Figure 6-8 shows six possible voting blocs as they relate to trade and defense expenditure policy. The lines divide the distance between candidate positions equally.[2] They form regions, or voting blocs, that show the range of policy positions that would prompt a vote to select that particular combination of first-, second-, and third-choice candidates. For example, the region labeled P,B,C refers to the bloc of voters who preferred Perot first, Bush second, and Clinton third. It will be evident as we develop this example that second-place preferences carry considerably more weight under some rules for counting votes than they do under others. How much weight a voting procedure gives to second- or third-place preferences in some cases plays an important role in determining the winners and losers in an election. Consequently, the weighting of second- and third-place preferences can profoundly influence foreign policy in ways unforeseen by structuralist theorists.

## VOTER INTEREST, VOTING BLOCS, AND ELECTORAL RULE

Continuing with our example of the 1992 U.S. presidential election, let's assume that we know the first-choice candidates for each voting bloc by looking at the election results. Based on surveys, the overwhelming second-choice candidate for Bush supporters was Perot. The second-choice candidate for Clinton backers was Perot. Let's assume for this example that Perot backers preferred Bush over Clinton by a margin of 2 to 1.[3] Thus, we find that there were four main voting blocs for this election, and two additional blocs that contained essentially no voters (see Figure 6-8). In effect, it appears that hardly anyone liked Bush best and Clinton second or Clinton best and Bush second.

Those voters oriented toward free trade and a large defense establishment wanted to see Bush reelected president first and, barring this, would have accepted Perot in office next. Voters who most preferred Bush, then, represented one key voting bloc. Voters who were security minded, but who thought there should be a peace dividend following the collapse of the Soviet Union, probably

FIGURE 6-8
**Voter Factions and Complete Preferences, 1992**

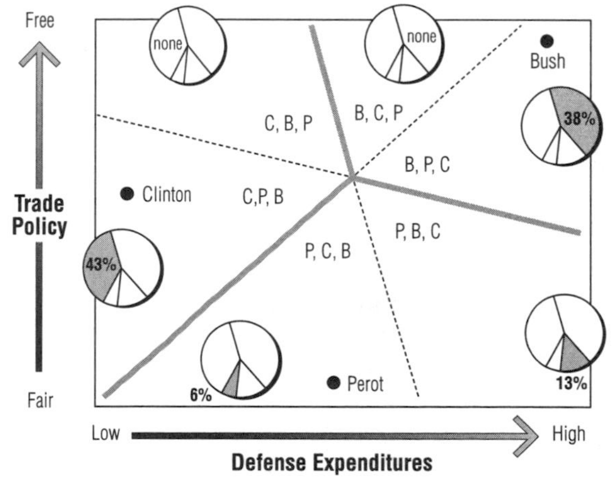

---

[2] More precisely, these lines are the perpendicular bisectors of undrawn lines—the contract curves that link the policy preferences of each pair of candidates.

[3] This is a bit of an exaggeration but one that helps to illustrate the argument about domestic conditions and international politics. In actuality, although more Perot voters did prefer Bush to Clinton, it was probably not by as large a margin as we are assuming here.

liked the idea of a somewhat reduced, but still large, defense budget. Among voters with this point of view, those who believed in free trade policies liked Perot best and Bush second best, whereas those who wanted to see a reduction in defense spending but favored protectionist trade policies liked Perot best and Clinton second best. These factions made up two additional voting blocs, one with Bush in second place and the other with Clinton in second place. In both cases, Perot was these voters' first choice. Those inclined to reduce defense spending and to support moderately protectionist trade policies liked Clinton best and Perot second best. These voters represented the final voting bloc of interest. The preferences of the four key voting blocs are summarized in Table 6-1.

In Table 6-1 we assume that the second-place split among Perot backers was roughly two-thirds pro-Bush and one-third pro-Clinton. Using the information in this table, we can ascertain whether key elements in American foreign policy could have been determined solely by the rules used to add up votes.[4] If this is the case, then interest group or bureaucratic competition over which electoral method is employed in fact determines important aspects of international politics. This flies in the face of structural views, which emphasize the role of the national interest in determining international politics. To emphasize the impact that electoral methods can have, I hold the interests of the voters

TABLE 6-1
## Voter Preferences, 1992

| Voter Bloc | Size (percent) | First Choice | Second Choice | Third Choice |
|------------|----------------|--------------|---------------|--------------|
| Bush Backers | 38 | Bush | Perot | Clinton |
| Clinton Backers | 43 | Clinton | Perot | Bush |
| Perot Backers (1) | 13 | Perot | Bush | Clinton |
| Perot Backers (2) | 6 | Perot | Clinton | Bush |

constant throughout this example. In other words, although the vote preferences depicted in Table 6-1 will remain constant, the outcome of the election will vary based on the use of differing (but fair) rules for counting votes. By holding the policy goals constant, I ensure that if there is a national interest embodied in the wishes of the people, it remains unaltered throughout the analysis. This example, then, represents one fundamental way to explore a central difference in expectations between structural theories on the one hand and the strategic politics or interest group perspectives on the other.

Of course, the voting rules for picking the U.S. president do not change (or rarely change) from election to election. But different countries employ different rules. This means that the example helps us see both how U.S. policy is shaped by the particular rules used in the United States, as well as how other democratic societies—even those with the same mix of preferences—might end up with radically different foreign policy results in consequence of their use of a different electoral method.

---

[4] The Constitution of the United States does not stipulate how votes should be counted or what voting rule or procedure should be used in any detail. The Constitution just assumes that the voting procedure will be fair. The most precise stipulation is with regard to the use of the electoral college in electing the president. The electoral college is a most unusual procedure. The voting procedure, or method for counting votes across all electoral offices except president, varies from state to state within the United States.

Under the plurality voting rule in which the candidate with the largest share of the vote is the winner, Clinton clearly was the winner of the 1992 U.S. presidential election.[5] With the preferences assumed in Table 6-1, we can see what might have happened had the election been held under different democratic rules. Let's assume that 13 percent of the 19 percent of voters who supported Perot liked Bush better than they liked Clinton. The remaining 6 percent, then, preferred Clinton. If Perot's backers were strategic, they would have thrown their support to the candidate they liked second best. In that case, Bush would have won 51 percent of the vote and Clinton would have garnered only 49 percent of the vote, thereby making Bush president. However, Perot's supporters preferred to back a losing candidate and thereby express their displeasure rather than cast a vote for someone who they considered the lesser of two evils.

Suppose, however, that the United States used the runoff election system that is widely used elsewhere in the world. In runoff elections, a second round of voting is held if no candidate wins a majority (more than 50 percent) in the first round. In the second round, one candidate must win a majority of the votes cast (barring an exact tie) because only the two top contenders from the first round are allowed to compete in the second round. France used this system for many years. Russia uses it today, as do the city of Berkeley, California, and the state of Georgia, to name but a few other examples.

In the second round, Perot would be eliminated as a contender for the presidency because Bush and Clinton each received more votes than Perot. Under this system, of course, Perot's backers are not deprived of their right to vote in the second round just because they backed the weakest candidate in the first round. Indeed, since the ballot is secret, they cannot be disenfranchised. The runoff system would have given Perot's supporters the opportunity to express their displeasure by voting for Perot in the first round and then a second opportunity to make a choice in the final round between the remaining candidates without detracting from their support for Perot. In the runoff, Clinton would receive his original 43 percent, plus 6 percent from the Perot backers who like Clinton better than Bush. Clearly, Clinton does better in round two than in round one (49 percent versus 43 percent). Despite this improvement, however, Clinton would lose the runoff election because Bush would now receive 51 percent of the vote: his original 38 percent plus 13 percent from the Perot backers who like Bush better than Clinton. Had the United States been using the runoff system so common in other democracies, Bush apparently would have been reelected to a second term in 1992.[6]

---

[5] Presidential voting in the United States is a bit more complicated because of the electoral college. The votes in the electoral college nowadays, however, are basically determined by plurality voting within each state.

[6] The 1993 vote by the Olympic Committee to choose a site for the Olympics in 2000 perfectly reflects the effects that a runoff system can have. Olympic Committee rules called for the city with the fewest votes to be eliminated after each round until one city received a majority of the vote. Although no city mustered a majority until only Beijing and Sydney were left in the running, Beijing did dominate the earlier voting. In fact, Beijing won every vote except the last, and decisive, one. In the last round, the supporters of eliminated contenders voted for Sydney over Beijing. As such, Sydney became the host city for the 2000 Olympics.

Is there any sensible, commonly used voting rule that would render Perot victorious, in spite of his meager 19 percent showing? The answer is an emphatic yes. A common voting rule used in many committees and in some international sporting events allows voters to rank candidates from most preferred to least preferred. Votes are weighted by the rank position of the candidate. For example, in our case candidates might receive 2 points for each first-place vote they received, 1 point for each second-place vote they received, and 0 points for each third-place vote they received. This system is called the Borda count.

In our electoral example, we know that each candidate's only first-place votes are from their own backers. If we give 2 points to each first-place vote, then Clinton would receive 86 points, Bush would receive 76 points, and Perot would receive 38 points. With second-place votes worth 1 point each, Clinton supporters would provide Perot an additional 43 points and Bush supporters would provide him an additional 38 points. Perot's backers, divided in their second-place choices, would provide Bush and Clinton 13 and 6 additional points, respectively. The total points for each candidate, then, would be as follows: Clinton, 92 points; Bush, 89 points; and Perot, 119 points. In this case, Perot would be the clear winner. Second-place preferences would propel him to victory.

This same result can also be achieved by calculating the votes using the Condorcet method. In this method—which many consider to be the fairest—candidates are pitted against each other in a one-on-one competition. The Condorcet winner, if there is one, is the alternative that wins in all one-on-one competitions. When a Condorcet winner does not exist, then there is a social cycle, a concept I discuss in Chapter 9. In our example, if Perot went head to head against Clinton, Perot would receive 57 percent of the vote (19 + 38) to Clinton's 43 percent of the vote; if Perot went head to head against Bush, he would receive 62 percent of the vote (19 + 43) to Bush's 38 percent of the vote. Again, Perot would win.

The above example highlights how important internal political procedures, and the internal political power to control the selection of those procedures, can be in shaping a country's foreign policy. With plurality voting, the international community could expect the United States—the greatest military and economic power the world has ever known—to adopt large defense cuts and more protectionist trade policies. Had the United States used a runoff system, however, the international community would have been justified in planning for a free trade economic policy and only small defense cuts. Finally, if the United States had used a more intricate system such as the Borda count, then the international community would have expected to see intermediate defense cuts and greater economic protectionism. Clearly, internal rules—that is, the bureaucratic or organizational procedures in the United States—rather than external structure or strategic calculation, alone have the potential to fundamentally alter American foreign policy even though the internal preferences of the electorate are constant. This is just one critical feature of internal decision making that rivets the attention of those who focus on the individual rather than the state as the central unit of analysis in international affairs. Our example has shown rather starkly how the role played by the world's greatest power is susceptible to change without any apparent regard for external, systemic considerations.

Electoral rules, rather than international roles, have been key determinants of essential features of American foreign policy and its place in the international system.

A significant number of U.S. presidents have been elected without securing the support of a majority of voters. Even when a majority has been achieved, there are numerous examples of margins so small that even minor changes in turnout could have altered the outcome. John Kennedy defeated Richard Nixon in 1960 by just such a margin; eight

Change the vote totals in our example without giving any candidate a majority and see how small a percentage you can assign to the candidate with the fewest first-place votes and still have that candidate win under the Condorcet method. Does this help explain why candidates in plurality voting systems take very similar policy positions and gravitate to the political center? Construct another example in which the Condorcet winner is not the winner using the Borda count.

years later Nixon beat Hubert Humphrey for the presidency, again by a thin margin. Had Nixon lost in 1968, would Humphrey then have traveled to China and paved the way for reestablishing diplomatic relations with that country as Nixon did? It is generally agreed that only a president with strong conservative, anticommunist credentials could have opened relations with China. Similarly, would Humphrey have ended the Bretton Woods agreement, an act that greatly devalued the dollar and sent world currencies into an inflationary spiral? This too is unlikely. In the 2000 presidential election the vote was so close between George W. Bush and Al Gore (who won the popular vote but not the electoral college vote) that it ended up being determined by a Supreme Court ruling over how to count "dimpled chads" on some Florida ballots. How American foreign policy would have looked under Gore no one can know for sure. Numerous other examples could be put forward to show how razor thin electoral margins in the United States produced substantial foreign policy shifts of just the sort that structural theories ignore. Many of these changes, including the recognition of China and the abandonment of the Bretton Woods regime, altered the structure of international interactions. The point should be clear: domestic politics matters.

To nail down the importance of electoral rules, let's look at one additional example that raises questions about the meaningfulness of the notion of a national interest. There is an important, commonly used procedure in voting that we did not examine in the above example. Suppose that the United States, like many parliamentary democracies around the world, used a proportional representation system. Congress, then, would reflect the distribution of voter preferences exhibited by the three candidates in our previous example. Using win sets we can see that a majority coalition could be erected in favor of higher defense spending or in favor of lower defense spending, in favor of more free trade or in favor of less free trade. Indeed, a majority coalition could be constructed for any mix of defense spending and trade policy imaginable, making the notion of the national interest difficult to interpret (McKelvey 1976, 1979; Schofield 1978).

Figure 6-9 shows three win sets capable of effecting change from the preelection status quo on the two policy issues in our example. These majority legislative coalitions, arising from a proportional representation system, show that a Clinton-Bush coalition (the area labeled "C-B") would favor increased free trade and reduced defense spending, a Perot-Clinton coalition (the area labeled "P-C") would favor reduced defense spending and reduced free trade, and a Bush-Perot coalition (the area labeled "B-P") would favor increased defense spending and reduced free trade. Thus, depending on how votes are counted and who cooperates with whom, pretty much any policy outcome would be possible. A majority could be constructed to favor a policy and, with the same voters a different majority coalition could also be constructed to oppose the very same policy. In such a circumstance, how can we speak of a national interest? The concept of a national interest becomes little more than a statement of the normative preference for foreign policy of a particular observer. If the national interest is supposed to reflect the best choice for a country, then "best" is either a question of an individual's personal taste or a question of what most people desire. In the latter case, Figure 6-9 makes it abundantly clear that majorities can both want and not want a policy X. In either case, there are potentially as many definitions of the national interest as there are commentators to say what it is.

*Richard Nixon traveled to China in 1972, thereby ending China's long isolation from contact with the United States. It is likely that only a president with impeccable conservative, anticommunist credentials could have undertaken this foreign policy initiative. With one bold action, Nixon showed that the great wall that had grown between the U.S. and China could be overcome. Here he and his wife, Pat Nixon, are seen with the Great Wall of China behind them, perhaps signifying that the U.S. and China had crossed over a huge barrier.*

## ALTERNATIVE INTERPRETATIONS OF THE DOMESTIC POLITICS EXAMPLE

We know that structuralists maintain that the fundamental unit of analysis in international affairs is not the individual, or even the influential individuals, within each state. Rather, they say, it is the nation itself. For structuralists, the variations in foreign policy goals suggested by our electoral methods example would not influence the actual choices made by the United States in the international political arena. The structure of the system would see to that. This is why the unitary actor assumption is so much more important to structural theories than to interest group or strategic perspectives.

Remember, every theory requires simplifying assumptions. From the structuralists' point of view, the variations in policy that result from the kinds of factors focused on in the discussion in the previous sections really are not crucial to international politics. The range of choice, they argue, is highly restricted by the distribution of power and the organization of politics at the international level. Thus, a neorealist might argue that the differences in foreign policy choices between Clinton, Bush, or Perot are trivial by comparison with the range of choices available to states with a less central role in international politics. Neither Bush nor Clinton nor Perot could choose a truly radical course of action because their prospective responsibilities as the leader of the greatest power in the international system preclude them from doing so. They could not, for example, choose to withdraw from international trade, as have Albania or Myanmar (Burma) on occasion. They could not choose to reduce the U.S. defense budget to a level comparable to that of Costa Rica because to do so would jeopardize American and, perhaps, global security. Thus, neorealists feel justified in making predictions that depend on the assumption that internal variations in rules, leaders, or what have you are just not significant enough to alter the fundamentals of international politics.

An examination of the empirical record refutes the structuralists' assertions by providing innumerable examples of the relevance of domestic influences on choices made by individual leaders concerned with international affairs. Nixon went to China, whereas Humphrey almost certainly would not have. Jimmy Carter made human rights an important litmus test in U.S. relations with other countries, whereas Nixon and Gerald Ford did not. Ronald Reagan

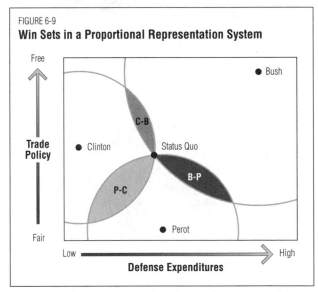

FIGURE 6-9

**Win Sets in a Proportional Representation System**

*By linking decisions on trade policy to decisions on defense expenditures, it would have been possible in a proportional representation voting system to assemble a majority in favor of greater defense spending (B-P) or less defense spending (P-C or C-B) and in favor of freer trade (C-B) or fairer trade (P-C or B-P). When majorities can be assembled in favor of almost any policy position, it is difficult to know what is meant when people speak of the national interest.*

challenged the notion that the cold war could not be won. Although his predecessors saw the cold war as a regrettable stalemate, Reagan increased pressure on the Soviet Union and helped to precipitate its demise. Mikhail Gorbachev gave up the Soviet East European empire peacefully, an action his predecessors certainly would not have ever contemplated. In fact, so contrary was this to the international status quo, few observers were able to anticipate it even mere weeks before it happened. In direct contradiction to structuralist claims, Gorbachev jeopardized Soviet national security for the (unfulfilled) hope of economic assistance. All of these cases serve to falsify a central tenet of structural realism— namely, that the international structure alone informs the relationships between states.

## SUMMARY

The three core perspectives on international affairs focus on different levels of analysis. Structural theories are centered on the characteristics of the international system. These theories assume that the state is the central actor in international politics, that domestic politics are mostly inconsequential in international relations, and that the state can be thought of as a unitary actor. According to this approach, states try to maximize the national interest, defined in terms of either security or wealth. Relations between states are anarchic (for realists) or hierarchic (for interdependence theorists).

The interest group, or bureaucratic, approach views domestic factors as key to understanding foreign policy. The central domestic considerations include the internal political structure, the distribution of internal political influence among interest groups, and the dependence of leaders on bureaucrats for information and for implementing policies. International politics has no place independent of individual foreign policies. Far from pursuing the national interest, decision making is characterized by inefficiency and narrow, selfish individual or organizational interests. External structural factors have little or no place in these theories, making the anarchy or hierarchy of the international system virtually irrelevant. The state is not a unitary actor and is not the central unit of analysis. States are made up of often competing interests; it is the bargains these interests strike that determine foreign policy goals

*On November 15, 2001, Russian president Vladimir Putin joined President George W. Bush at Crawford High School in Crawford, Texas, to answer questions from students. President Bush made the point that when he was growing up, Russia (then part of the Soviet Union) was America's main enemy but today Russia and the United States are friends, "working together to break the old ties, to establish a new spirit of cooperation and trust so that we can work together to make the world more peaceful."*

and actions. Foreign policy is potentially chaotic and certainly not consciously geared toward maximizing national security or any other national objective. From this viewpoint, the notion of a single national interest is nonsensical.

Strategic politics theories, grounded in the notions of strategic interaction, generally assume that pairs of actors, including but not limited to pairs of states, are the central unit for purposes of evaluating strategies and actions taken in international relations. The strategies and goals that motivate the selection of actions are shaped by the domestic give-and-take of interest group and organizational or bureaucratic politics as well as by the external constraints of the international environment.

Strategic theorists view international politics as the playing out of the multitude of foreign policies created by the domestic political considerations of each state. As such, it is the global manifestation of innumerable foreign policy choices. These choices are reached in a contemplative, reasoned manner. The inefficient politics of "muddling through" common in the interest group perspective represents an incomplete, partial description of international relations or of foreign policy from the strategic perspective. International politics can be viewed as both hierarchic or anarchic, with little advantage to be gained by imposing the demanding assumptions of a hierarchical viewpoint. The national interest is not a particularly meaningful concept. Instead, the political interests of leaders are at the core of what they choose to do. Of course, to keep themselves in power they try to make choices that benefit key constituents without provoking costly exchanges with foreign adversaries. International politics and foreign policy are, therefore, inextricably intertwined. Viewpoints that ignore this interdependence have a serious handicap that probably cannot be overcome.

# What Is Power?

Power is a concept of unending interest to the human psyche. Popular literature is rife with stories of conflict between the powers of good and the powers of evil. Science fiction movies routinely depict the human struggle for survival against powerful alien enemies, resistant to bullets and bombs but vulnerable to the superior power of the unique human spirit. Television documentaries regularly reassure us with tales of great national sea or air power. In international politics, world leaders speak of the need for a favorable military balance to justify large expenditures on weapons. But they also speak of the power of the pen as mightier than that of the sword, suggesting that power resides most strongly in the persuasiveness of ideas rather than in coercive force.

Power is the most frequently invoked concept in international relations. But what does "power" mean, and what do different meanings imply about international affairs? In this chapter I introduce the many facets of the concept of power. I begin by offering a definition of power. I then separate it into its constituent parts: persuasion, rewards, punishment, and force. We will proceed by examining the fungibility of power to evaluate how easily power in one domain, such as trade, can be converted into power in another domain, such as military might. I end the chapter with an examination of the history of the relative power of the most influential nations of the past two hundred years.

In addressing what power is and what it is not, we must address five issues. First, we need to know whether power is determined by calculation of a nation's quantity of resources or by relational characteristics; second, we need to know whether power is fungible or domain specific; third, we need to know which aspects of power are tangible and which are intangible; fourth, we need to establish how power changes; and fifth, we need to know what factors can enhance a state's power when its resource base is small.

## DEFINING POWER

Power is most commonly defined as the ability of one actor, A, to get another actor, B, to do something B would not otherwise do. An actor can be either an individual or a group. An exercise of power by actor A over actor B takes place only if actor B alters its actions in response to actor A's wishes when B would not have done so on its own. We presume that the reason A wants to change B's actions or expectations is so that B will do what A desires.

This common definition of power has many subtle variations, and more will be suggested later in this chapter. For now, let me briefly offer two similar views of power found in the international relations literature. Hans Morgenthau, the dean of the realist school of international politics, defined power as the quality that permits "man's control over the heart and actions of other men" (1978, 30). Clearly, control over the hearts of men is a poetic way of saying that one actor controls or constrains the desires of another in an effort to control the latter's actions. Fredrick Frey, another distinguished scholar of international affairs, formulated the definition more precisely. He defined power as the "relations between actors such that the behavior of one actor at least partly causes the behavior of another" (quoted in Cohen 1989, 15). These two illustrations suggest the degree of commonality in definitions of power.

Our definition of power requires that for power to be exercised there must be at least two actors who disagree over what should be done at the time power is exerted. Further, the exercise of power implies that the actor whose behavior changes alters its actions to fit more closely with the preferences or objectives of the other actor because the other actor has applied some form of tangible or intangible pressure. If actor B changes its behavior entirely on its own, rather than in response to or in anticipation of pressure from A, then A cannot be said to have exercised power over B.

Knowledge of the relative power of the actors involved in a disagreement over an appropriate course of action is necessary (though not sufficient) to predict what each party will end up doing. Knowledge of power relationships is an essential element in the explanation and prediction of much international behavior. By itself, though, knowledge of relative power is insufficient to predict outcomes. Asymmetries in motivation to achieve a given objective, unwillingness to bear costs associated with using power, difficulties in coordinating the exercise of power, and an inability to tolerate the domestic fallout from foreign adventures—even successful ones—can all adversely affect an accurate prediction. Many of these elements contributed to the failure of the United States to prevail in Vietnam, despite the widely held belief at the time that the United States possessed the resources to make North Vietnam accept the U.S. goal of preserving South Vietnamese independence. In Chapter 8 we examine in depth the limitations of the concept of power as an explanation of international affairs. In this chapter we explore a more general concept of power and examine its common usage in international relations.

Power as a concept is difficult in part because our commonsense notion of who is or is not powerful is so often violated by experience. Consider, for example, the meaning of power when applied to war. In 1965 President Lyndon Johnson acquired almost open-ended authority to conduct a war against North Vietnam. The Gulf of Tonkin Resolution marked a turning point in the war in that the armed forces of the United States shifted from a purely advisory role in Vietnam to one of active combat. The Soviet Union never made a comparable commitment to its ally, the government of North Vietnam. By war's end in 1973 several million American soldiers had seen service in Vietnam. The United States had spent tens of billions of dollars and dropped more bomb tonnage over North Vietnam than had been dropped over Germany in all of World War II. America's air force completely dominated the skies over North and South Vietnam. Although American military pilots faced serious antiaircraft barrages, the North Vietnamese had no air combat capability with which to challenge American bombing sorties. American soldiers were better equipped, better trained, better defended, and vastly more effective in combat than were the North Vietnamese and their southern Vietcong allies. For every American life lost in Vietnam, it is estimated that about twenty North Vietnamese lost theirs (Mueller 1980). By any conventional senses of the term, the United States was vastly more powerful than North Vietnam. Only one stark fact stands in relief to this conclusion: North Vietnam won the war.

The defeat of the United States in Vietnam is a puzzle for those who equate power with the quantity of resources a country can bring to bear in war. Apparently, counting soldiers, guns, airplanes, warships, money, and so forth did not provide a proper reckoning of the power of the United States compared with that of North Vietnam. An alternative view of power says that we know the Vietnamese were more powerful because they won (Blainey 1973). In fact, such a definition reduces the term to meaninglessness by reducing the concept to something that we can evaluate only after the fact and based only on how things turned out. In this chapter we are concerned with translating our understanding of power into predictions about outcomes.

Power is fundamentally relational. It is not simply equivalent to possession of resources. If a potentially powerful party does not care about an issue over which there is disagreement and is therefore unwilling to use its resources to gain an advantage, then a successful exercise of power will never occur. Great wealth on a desert island does not give one monetary power. Neither does the biggest gun convey military power if there is no one to threaten, or if one is afraid to make a threat.

That power is relational is evident from the numerous historical examples in which an apparently weak state prevailed over an apparently strong state. The relational quality of power, however, is not merely a curiosity to be displayed when discussing America's defeat in Vietnam or tiny Israel's repeated military victories over its more populous, richer, larger, seemingly better-endowed Arab neighbors. The relational quality of power points up some fundamental features and limitations of power as we have defined it. For example, its relational nature implies that power can be cyclical. Thus, A may exert power over B, which may exert power over C, which in turn may exert power over A. The children's game of rock, paper, scissors deftly conveys how the definition of power can form a cycle: a rock can break scissors, scissors can destroy a piece of paper, and a piece of paper can contain a rock. Thus, power relationships can be inherently ambiguous; in one domain one actor's power may be vulnerable to another's, and in a different domain the latter may succumb to the former.

The relational quality of power suggests that power is not particularly fungible. That is, power in one context cannot easily be carried over into another context. The dalai lama and the pope may both have the power that comes from moral suasion, but neither can translate that power into military might. In an age of greater religiosity, such as Europe experienced during the Middle Ages, the pope's power derived from his ability to threaten a person's soul through excommunication. Under these conditions the pope was able to raise great armies, such as those mustered to fight in the Crusades. But today the pope's authority is much more limited. He cannot translate religious threats into a military advantage as he could centuries ago, even though his religious authority is the same to devout Catholics today as it was centuries ago.

## METHODS OF EXERCISING POWER

Four fundamental methods are open to nation A to exercise power over nation B:

1. A can use *persuasion* to convince B that B really should do, out of its own free will and interest, what A wants it to do.
2. A can offer B rewards for changing its actions in accordance with what A wants.
3. A can threaten B with punishment if B does not do what A wants.
4. A can take direct action and *force* B to do what A wants against B's will.

There is a profound qualitative difference between the first three methods of exercising power and the last. Methods 1, 2, and 3 allow nation B to *choose* to act as A desires. The means A uses to achieve its goal differ, but the outcome is the same. Whether persuaded by argument, moved by rewards, or frightened by the threat of punishment, B chooses to do what A wants done. When A uses force, however, it eliminates B's ability to choose. It is precisely for this reason that the use of force is always the most costly way of exercising power, at least in the short run.

### PERSUASION
Exercising persuasion means that nation A seeks to redefine the situation for nation B so as to induce B to change its mind. Persuasion is the art of campaigning on behalf of one's cause (Riker 1996). Nation A may appeal to sentiments, values, ethics, morals, and principles in its effort to persuade B. Or it may bring out facts that B has overlooked, for

example, highlighting undesirable consequences to B's policy position. Nation A may point out rewards and punishments that will accrue to nation B if it pursues one course over another. As long as nation A sticks to persuasion, all it will do is talk.

Much of diplomacy consists of this kind of talk. The bulk of international business is carried out through judicious use of the art of persuasion, and talk is all that is needed. Most actors exercise persuasion continuously in international relations. Persuasion is typically a first step in trying to control the behavior of others because it is clearly the least expensive of all ways of exercising power. Because its costs are low and it is universally available it is clearly the method of choice of those who lack the resources to do much else. For A to convince B means that B would adopt the desired new behavior of its own free will. The benefits for A would be cheap and lasting. From time to time, A might need to provide new information or otherwise offer encouragement to B so that B does not revert to its previous views. But where interests are aligned, persuasion can be an effective and efficient tool. Where there are no genuine common interests, however, persuasion is limited in its effectiveness. Although persuasion is the cheapest method of exercising power, it is not cost free. Appropriate resources are necessary. The leaders of a nation wishing to persuade another nation to undertake a particular course of action must have credible arguments. It helps if the two nations share common values and the nation wishing to convince the other is admired and seen as having a credible concern for shared values and interests. This is one way that a common ideology can provide useful information to encourage one leader to listen to the rhetorical arguments of another (Goldstein and Keohane 1993). Having a point of view in alignment with the values and goals of the elites in those nations one wants to influence can be a great asset.

The United States attempted to punish India and Pakistan for testing nuclear weapons. The U.S. imposed ineffective sanctions. The sanctions against India were cheap talk. The United States sanctioned trade on items that represented a miniscule part of the American economy (and, indeed, even of the Indian economy). Some, especially in India and Pakistan, viewed America's stance as hypocritical and paternalistic. The United States had helped in the development of Britain's nuclear arsenal and looked the other way while Israel became a nuclear power. Also the United States and the Soviet Union relied on nuclear deterrence to keep the peace during the cold war but apparently doubted that the same deterrent logic would work in India or Pakistan.

Liberal theory, with its emphasis on shared norms, places great stock in persuasion as a means of exercising power. Neorealist arguments, by contrast, put little emphasis on persuasion. For neorealists, international politics is about self-help. Persuasion is meaningful only as a way to inform someone of what is in his or her own interest. Shared norms of conduct do not enhance persuasion from the neorealist or realist viewpoint. Bureaucratic theories and interest group outlooks put considerable emphasis on persuasion. From these perspectives, knowledge is an important source of power. The principal-agent problem introduced in Chapter 5 stems precisely from the ability of advisers or experts to persuade their bosses to undertake a particular course of action.

The strategic perspective embraces persuasion as a form of power. It recognizes that rhetorical arguments can be persuasive either because genuinely shared interests are being addressed or because a bluff can sometimes be effective. The strategic perspective distinguishes between cheap talk and costly signals. Cheap talk involves statements or arguments (like persuasion) that cost nothing to make. Costly signals, in contrast, involve statements that cost something to make. For example, when President Jimmy Carter blocked the sale of American grain to Russia in 1979 and tied its resumption to Russian withdrawal of its invading army from Afghanistan, he sent a costly signal. American grain farmers had to be compensated by the government for their lost revenue. Failing to do so would have cost President Carter votes in the 1980 presidential election. By contrast, the American sanctions against India in 1998 following India's test of nuclear weapons was cheap talk. The congressionally mandated sanctions barely affected either Indian or American business interests because India purchased very few of the contraband items from the United States to begin with. No significant voting bloc in the United States was affected by the sanctions, so the president and members of Congress could be confident that there would be no domestic political fallout from imposition of sanctions. The Indian government, likewise, had no significant way to impose costs on the United States in retaliation for those sanctions. Thus, the American sanctions against India amounted to cheap talk.

Cheap talk is effective as persuasion when the parties involved share common interests. In such cases, cheap talk between them helps clarify mutual interests and may point the way toward effective collaboration on achieving shared interests. Efforts at bluffing—that is, pretending to be different (say, stronger or weaker) than one really is—are doomed to failure according to the strategic perspective if the bluff does not entail a cost. Bluffing works in poker precisely because the declaration that one holds good cards is backed up by a costly wager. No opponents will fold just because a player says he or she has a good hand, but they might fold if he or she bets enough to persuade the other players that it is in their interest to lose the hand rather than risk more money. Everyone understands that a big bet may be an honest signal of a strong hand, or it may be a bluff. Sometimes bluffs get called, and the bluffer, having failed to persuade the opposition, loses a lot of money. The costly signal, the big bet, is indeed truly costly.

## REWARDS

The second method of exercising power is through the offer or provision of rewards. The issue of rewards may have already surfaced as part of persuasion. Nation A may have dangled rewards in front of nation B in its efforts to persuade B to reconsider its position.

Although here I deal with rewards separately from persuasion, it should be clear that in reality persuasion and rewards are frequently combined. The proffering of rewards makes A's efforts at persuasion more effective. Rewards are costly to A and so signal A's greater commitment to the point of view it is promoting than is true when A relies only on persuasion.

The rewards offered by nation A to nation B are obviously designed to tip B's choice toward the alternative preferred by A. Presumably, in the absence of sufficiently valuable rewards, nation B would select a course of action different from that preferred by A. The rewards, then, must be designed to compensate B sufficiently so that it is prepared to change its action. Depending on the amount and kind of rewards A can offer, B may now find that it is genuinely in its best interest to do as A wishes. Thus, whereas persuasion relies on new information to change B's point of view, rewards rely on an alteration of B's cost-benefit calculus, even when new information about the merits of the competing choices would otherwise not alter B's behavior.

On the international level there is a wide range of rewards, both tangible and intangible, that one nation can extend to another and a wide range of initiatives open to a

*Efforts to build a cooperative environment between North and South Korea have proven to be extremely difficult. Shown here is a modest, but moving, effort at such cooperation. Following an agreement to allow a few dozen South Koreans to visit relatives in North Korea, Yoon Kum-chol (center) traveled to North Korea to meet his two sisters on April 8, 2002. Kum-chol and the other South Koreans permitted to enter North Korea had neither seen nor spoken with their families in the North since the 1950–1953 Korean War.*

nation with the will and the wherewithal to reward another. International dealings among nations frequently involve negotiations between donors and recipients. The negotiations specify what rewards are required, how the resources are to be mobilized in the donor's system, and how the beneficiaries of the reward in the recipient country will try to induce the desired change in behavior.

A political reward by nation A to nation B may take almost any form. Consultation with a country's political leadership over an important issue could be an important reward. This is what the United States did for Boris Yeltsin in Russia after the latter complained in 1994 of being left out of NATO's decision to use force against Serbia. The U.S. secretary of state met with the Russian foreign minister for an extensive briefing session. This consultation carried with it a signal of special regard that Yeltsin was able to transform into a political

> Under what conditions might consultation by the U.S. secretary of state with the Russian foreign minister or prime minister be cheap talk and under what conditions might it involve a costly signal? Did American efforts to bolster Boris Yeltsin at home in 1994 cost the United States anything with its allies or with domestic political constituencies? Did the United States have a common interest with the Russians over how best to resolve concerns over the use of NATO force in Serbia in 1994? In 1999?

asset at home. Rewards might take the form of a grant of increased self-government to a dependent area, or support for another nation's position at an international conference, or even a promise not to embarrass another nation by calling to public attention facts that the latter would prefer remain hidden.

Rewards may be economic, designed to benefit a sector of the recipient's economic elite and the slice of the economy they represent. Examples include expanded markets for industrial or agricultural products, financial help, advantageous rules for trade, and access to raw materials or technical assistance. The American decision to provide Mexico with $40 billion of assistance to help resolve the Mexican financial problem caused by its devaluation of the peso in January 1995 provides a clear instance of economic rewards. Under the terms of NAFTA, the Mexican government had agreed to open its markets to American goods after almost three-quarters of a century of protectionist trade policies. The U.S. government, eager to see Mexico retain its open trade policy, offered the economic bailout as a reward to Mexico for not closing its markets again in the face of financial trauma. The policy proved a great success. Mexico paid back the low-interest loan early and in full while continuing to maintain an open market in accordance with NAFTA. Indeed, it proved so successful that by 2002 trade between Mexico and the United States had approximately tripled over what it was in 1995. Mexico became the second-largest trading partner of the United States and with a good prospect of passing Canada to become the largest trading partner.

Consider another example of the use of rewards to change behavior. The United States, disappointed that the king of Jordan supported Iraq's president Saddam Hussein during the Persian Gulf War in 1991, wanted him to join in the Arab peace negotiations with Israel after the war's end. This provided the king with an opportunity to undo the damage to his international reputation that had resulted from his support of Saddam Hussein. But Jordan's King Hussein held back from entering into peace negotiations, apparently fearing Syria's reaction. Jordan was in deep debt, with almost $7 billion of international obligations, and begging for financial relief. President Bill Clinton dangled the possibility of a cancellation of Jordan's $700 million debt to the United States and offered help with other creditors. He also offered to provide Jordan with arms if the king would move on negotiations with Israel. Jordan, presented with these substantial incentives, entered into negotiations in high gear.

## PUNISHMENTS

The divide between persuasion and rewards on the one hand and punishment on the other represents an important distinction among the four methods for exercising power. Punishment represents a clear escalation in tension between the party exercising power and the recipient of that exercise of power. Punishments are actions that have unpleasant consequences for the punished party. Any action can be used as punishment by nation A provided that the action has a consequence that nation B would prefer to avoid. Just as the line dividing persuasion and rewards is mostly a heuristic device, the line dividing rewards and punishments is as well. Withholding a reward or threatening to do so is an obvious way to punish. And abstaining from some punitive action that would otherwise be taken is clearly a reward. In all cases, nation A intervenes to alter the balance of relative gains and liabilities that will accrue to nation B in its choice of alternative courses of action so that it is advantageous for B to do what A wants.

There is a difference in the consequences engendered by rewards and those engendered by punishment. Granting a reward sometimes occasions gratitude, and if the strings attached are not too obvious or too onerous, it may increase the good feeling between people. The threat of punishment, however, is likely to arouse ill feeling, the more so if it is effective. The range of actions that may constitute effective punishments is clearly wide. The use of information may constitute an effective punishment. For example, the leader of nation A might impart to the people of nation B information that the leaders of nation B wish them not to know. During the cold war the United States did this continuously to the Soviet Union through Radio Free Europe and numerous other means. American broadcasts aimed at Cuba are designed to achieve this goal as well. Tokyo Rose's radio broadcasts to American GIs during World War II were intended to weaken their resolve against Japan and, thereby, punish the United States for its war effort.

Going a step further, nation A could help the domestic opposition in nation B, perhaps even trying to overthrow the government in question. The U.S. government did just this in, among other places, Guatemala in 1951, Cuba in 1961, and Iraq in 1992–1994. In 1998 Congress agreed to budget $100 million as assistance (or as bounty) for an Iraqi opposition group if it succeeded in overthrowing Saddam Hussein. Clearly, the offer is a reward for Iraqi dissidents and is aimed at creating a punishment for the Iraqi regime. Thus far, this exercise of power has failed, reminding us that power alone does not decide how international events turn out.

International punishments might take the form of economic maneuvers rather than overt threats to a government's survival. For example, states might withdraw economic assistance or disrupt trade. Sometimes these measures are limited and selective; other times they are total. The 1990s appear as vintage years for the use of embargoes to punish international miscreants in an effort to make them abandon objectionable policies (Hufbauer, Schott, and Elliott 1990; Tsebelis 1990a; Martin 1992; Morgan and Schwebach 1995; Doxey 1996; Smith 1996). An embargo against Iraq begun in 1991 has dragged on for years

> How can we evaluate the effectiveness of sanctions or punishments mandated by law as a response to certain actions? Is it best to examine instances in which the punishment is invoked, or do we need to find a way to assess the likelihood that the threat of punishment or the anticipation of punishment deterred prospective offenders from the undesired action? How might we evaluate successful deterrence when no response is observed?

with little effect on the stability of the Saddam Hussein regime. By contrast, an embargo against Haiti was effective in 1993–1994, as was the threat of embargo against North Korea in 1994.

As noted earlier, the United States automatically imposed economic sanctions on India in May 1998 following India's five nuclear tests. In this case, the punishment strategy took effect after the fact on a nondiscretionary basis: Congress had earlier passed a law requiring economic sanctions in the form of reduced aid and the elimination of sales of certain defense-related products in the event a country tests a nuclear device. This means that a country violating American expectations, such as India, knows that there will be punishment. Of course, this also suggests that the sanctions can be effective only with those who derive significant rewards in the form of aid and trade with the United States. Those who do not will not greatly fear the punishment. Thus, most of the time when punishment is invoked, it is a safe bet that it will be ineffective. Otherwise, the offending action would not have been undertaken in the first place. A potential recipient can anticipate the costs of punishment. So-called anticipatory punishment is a form of power worthy of more careful examination.

**ANTICIPATORY PUNISHMENT.**     Punishments can be carried out, or they can just be threatened. The effectiveness of punishments can be purely anticipatory. Anticipatory punishments offer many advantages over those that must be implemented. Successful threats of punishment may be an inexpensive way of exercising power. To be effective, a threat must be credible, and that in itself involves some costs. For example, Congress has limited the president's power by passing a law obliging the imposition of sanctions under certain contingencies. But costs associated with credible threats are generally smaller than those that accrue when a punishment is actually meted out. Creating the anticipation of punishment may avoid significant costs while still being effective. Let us consider some examples that illustrate how anticipation of punishment can be sufficient to exercise power.

High-ranking emissaries of the Israeli government came to Washington just before the Six-Day War between Israel and several Arab states in 1967. They came to inform the American government of their plans and to establish whether or not the Americans would support their aims and their intended means of achieving those aims. A similar mission to Washington was repeated when Israel launched its 1982 attack on Lebanon. It is a mistake to think that the Israeli government sent representatives out of politeness or out of consideration for the feelings of their American allies. In 1956, when the Israelis together with Britain and France sought to overthrow Egyptian president Gamal Abdul Nasser and wrest control of the Suez Canal away from Egypt, they had not sent a comparable mission—and they paid a significant price for this oversight.

The Eisenhower administration's response to being kept in the dark before the attack on Egypt was to oppose the attack and make the aggressors—each of whom was an American friend—retreat and return their gains. The Israelis were made to give the Sinai back to Egypt. They learned a powerful lesson: In any war the United States had better be informed and had better not explicitly oppose Israeli plans. Otherwise, a short-lived victory will be followed by a humiliating defeat. This is why in 1967 and 1982 the Israelis "voluntarily" informed the American government of their decision to fight.[1] Implicitly, they were testing the American reaction to their proposed course of action and the likelihood of any anticipated punishment. Similarly, no one today believes that the foreign policies of East European leaders during the cold war reflected anything other than a continuous exercise of power on the part of the Soviet Union. The leaders of Eastern Europe had learned to anticipate how costly it would be for them to deviate from the Soviet line. In fact, during the last years of the cold war the Soviet menace loomed so large that no overt threat was needed to obtain compliance with Soviet desires.

The Soviet Union established the credibility of its threat to punish wayward allies during the early years of the cold war, and they reinforced that threat whenever it was challenged. The Soviets put down movements for greater independence in Poland in the 1950s and invaded Hungary in 1956 to defeat a movement that threatened to take Hungary out of the Soviet-backed Warsaw Pact. The Russians erected the Berlin Wall in the early 1960s to keep East Germans from fleeing to the West and invaded Czechoslovakia in 1968 when it appeared that the Czech government would liberalize policies and move Czechoslovakia away from Soviet influence. The Soviet invasion of Afghanistan in 1979 was also motivated by a concern to suppress the emergence of a government that might accept reforms.

---

[1] The Israelis did not give the American government advance warning of the 1973 Yom Kippur War because the Egyptian and Syrian governments succeeded in fooling both Israeli and American intelligence and caught Israel by surprise.

In the absence of prior credible exercises of power, it is difficult to assess how important anticipation actually is in specific cases. When two parties profess agreement, there is no ready empirical way to tell whether one party would dominate the other if agreement broke down. The Suez Canal crisis is again a good illustration.

Before the Suez War, Britain had been the closest ally of the United States, clearly sharing a common world view on most issues. Britain's association with the United States protected its global image as a major power. Britain, together with the United States and the Soviet Union, was still considered one of "the Big Three" that had prosecuted World War II, won it, and decided upon the division of the spoils. At the time, it was hard to separate the extent to which Britain's status as a great power was the result of its friendship with the United States and the extent to which Britain held its exalted international standing on its own. Uncertainty about Britain's global authority masked American power to shape British (and French) behavior. Just how able the United States was to exert power over Britain was revealed in the Suez crisis when the United States threatened to sell large quantities of the British pound sterling on the open market. Fear of the economic consequences of such an action pushed Britain and its war partners to retreat, leaving Nasser in control of the field. British submission to American demands shattered any remnants of the illusion that England was "independent" of the United States in vital international security matters.

The United States later had cause to regret what it had done during the Suez War. Both President Dwight Eisenhower and Vice President Richard Nixon were to express regret at American interference with British, French, and Israeli aims. Nasser showed little gratitude toward the United States, and his hostility toward the West in general continued unabated. The U.S. action was a factor in French president Charles De Gaulle's chafing under American control and the French decision to reduce its role in NATO. It also played a role in forming Nixon's view that radical Arab leaders would respond only to pressure, not to rewards. Nixon put this view

*The Soviet invasions of Hungary in 1956 and Czechoslovakia in 1968 (pictured here) certainly established the credibility of Russian threats to punish wayward allies. The picture also shows how motivated even ordinary citizens can be to protect their homeland. Czech citizens can be seen tossing stones and whatever is at hand at a Soviet tank. On this occasion their daring failed, but just such defiance helped bring down unpopular communist governments throughout Eastern Europe between 1989 and 1992.*

into policy during his presidency in the form of American support for Israeli military action. Certainly the complexity of these power relationships led to some ambiguity on the effectiveness of anticipatory punishment during the Suez Canal crisis.

**BLUFFED THREATS OF PUNISHMENT.**    Anticipatory threats of punishment can be an effective and inexpensive means of exercising power. Because of this, national leaders have incentives to bluff from time to time. They do so by making threats they have no intention of carrying out. Such bluffs are well and good when they succeed, but, of course, adversaries know that their rivals have incentives to bluff. This means that sincere threats will sometimes be challenged, with the challenger coming to regret its decision when the threat is implemented (Kim and Bueno de Mesquita 1995). But it also means that a nation will sometimes bluff, only to have its bluff challenged. Then the bluffer will be the one to suffer the consequences of its insincere threat.

If a threat fails to extract the desired behavior, and the country issuing the threat does not follow through on the punishment it promised to deliver, then the leaders of that country are revealed as bluffers. They are likely to face significant domestic and international consequences. Whether the damage is greater domestically or internationally is a function of the distribution of power in the domestic and international political environments. This often depends on domestic political institutions in ways that make regime types critical to understanding how power can be used. Let me explain.

When an international threat is unmasked as a bluff, leaders are exposed to political attacks and criticisms by domestic opponents. These domestic opponents will probably argue that the bluff exposed the nation to international humiliation; that the leaders cannot be relied upon to handle foreign affairs; that the international credibility of the nation is being squandered; and that foreign opponents will now know that they can take advantage of the nation with impunity. The success of these charges will depend in some measure on the leaders' power position within the domestic political environments—that is, it depends on what regime type the leaders operate within. In general, leaders of democratic states are most vulnerable to domestic fallout from failed foreign policies, and autocrats are least vulnerable. This is true because democratic leaders are more likely to be thrown out of office when their policies fail than are autocrats or dictators. One implication of this generalization is that democratic leaders are more careful in choosing foreign policies than are their autocratic counterparts. Indeed, because the domestic costs of failed policies are so much greater for democratic leaders than for monarchs or authoritarian leaders, democratic leaders are more likely to be credible and less likely to be bluffing when they make international threats. In addition, their threats are more likely to be effective against democratic rivals than against autocratic opponents. The latter can more easily weather the domestic political consequences of bluffing and can more readily withstand foreign policy defeats than the former. Thus, the ability to credibly threaten punishment for misdeeds is concentrated in the hands of democracies, giving them a form of power less often possessed by autocracies. Conversely, the ability to overcome the costs of bluffs or to withstand foreign threats is concentrated in the hands of autocrats (Bueno de Mesquita and Lalman 1992; Fearon 1994; Schultz 2001; Bueno de Mesquita, Smith, Siverson, and Morrow 2003). This gives them, in turn, a form of power less often possessed by democrats. Simply put, democrats can more credibly threaten punishment, whereas autocrats can more readily tolerate threatened punishment.

## FORCE

Force, our final method of exercising power, occurs when one nation seeks to control the behavior of another by coercing it through the use of superior military might. Force is most frequently used when elites believe there is no other way to change the other party's calculation of costs and benefits to produce the desired change of behavior. The behavior desired by nation A is not acceptable to nation B under any circumstances if B has anything to say about the matter; therefore, choice must be taken out of B's hands, and B must be compelled to do what A wants.

The primary use of force or compulsion in international relations is war, the subject of Chapters 16 and 17. Through warfare, nations act to seize territory or riches that they cannot gain in any other way, or they set out to topple governments with which they cannot deal. Force is used only reluctantly. As a means of influencing others, warfare is a last resort. It is used only when a nation cannot persuade, buy, bribe, or threaten its way to a desired goal. The desired goal must be worth more than the costs expected to be incurred in achieving it. And because compelling another nation to do what it does not wish to do is always costly, the use of force is rare. In major wars, the secondary costs that result from dislocations in the life of the civil society can be as big as the primary costs that derive directly from the fighting. The decision to wage war may also be costly to the leader who makes it, for wars affect large numbers of people, and when they are not successful the backlash is both powerful and wide. Leaders who lose wars are often replaced (Bueno de Mesquita, Smith, Siverson, and Morrow 2003).

Compulsion is possible short of all-out war. War requires that both sides use force against one another. Sometimes, however, only one side uses force and the other side capitulates in recognition of its inevitable defeat. This generally happens when the preponderance of force is so great on one side that the other side yields in advance rather than face annihilation, waiting only to be certain that the threatener really intends to use force and is not bluffing. The Czechs, for example, gave in to German demands after the Munich Pact of 1938. The Czechs agreed to what Adolf Hitler and the Western powers demanded because resistance was clearly hopeless. More recently, the government of Haiti gave in to American demands that its military leaders resign and exile themselves and permit President Jean-Bertrand Aristide, whom they had expelled from power, to return. They capitulated to American demands when they knew that contingents of U.S. paratroopers were already in the air on their way to Haiti.

In sum, it is important to distinguish between the use of force and all other forms of exercising power. When nation A uses force to compel nation B, A is not trying to change B's mind, which is the case when persuasion, rewards, and punishments are used. In seeking to coerce B to do what A wishes, A attempts to render B's desires irrelevant—that is, to take away B's choices. This is the critical difference between force as punishment and force as compulsion. The concrete action may be the same, but in the former instance force is used to change the calculus of costs and benefits of the punished party and in the latter force is used to take away the ability to choose. Moreover, punishment is designed to change future behavior; force as compulsion is directed at controlling present action.

The successful use of force depends on a complex web of conditions. These conditions include factors such as motivation (or lack thereof) and a willingness to endure costs. Limitations to power will occupy our attention in Chapter 8, but here we will explore how well power can predict outcomes when force is used.

## MEASURING POWER

Power is most frequently estimated by counting both tangible and intangible assets, such as guns, gross national product (GNP), industrial output, and the like. In fact, there is quite an active industry dedicated to the estimation of power. The best-known academic effort to measure the power of states has been undertaken by the Correlates of War (COW) project at the University of Michigan. Researchers there have amassed data on many different variables used to estimate national capabilities. These include a state's military expenditures, military manpower, iron and steel production, commercial fuel consumption, urban population, and total population. By constructing a measure known as the composite capabilities index, these researchers have allowed us to assess each nation's share of these six resources as a proportion of the world total (with the world defined in rather narrow terms before 1920). The composite capabilities index produces results that are closely associated with power estimates based on GNP. GNP data, however, are not available for many countries before World War II and for almost none before 1920. The composite

In Chapter 3 I asked you to identify a foreign policy issue and to list the stakeholders who have an interest in trying to influence the issue's outcome. Now I would like you to estimate the potential power or influence each stakeholder has relative to each other. To do so, I suggest you identify the one stakeholder (or more) with the greatest potential power. Assign that stakeholder a score of 100. Rate everybody else relative to that 100 so that two players, one with 60 and one with 40, could just offset the influence of the one with 100 if each tried as hard as could be.

Now that you have estimated the power of each player can you predict how the issue you chose is likely to be resolved using just the power information? How would you make such a prediction? This is a good time to think about the difference between structural theories and theories of strategic interaction. Theorists of strategic interaction do not think power alone is sufficient to predict policy decisions accurately. Structural theorists think that knowing how power is distributed is central to explaining what happens in international politics.

capabilities index, in contrast, has been estimated for many countries as far back as 1816. This measure has shed much light on the relationship between national capabilities and conflict initiation and outcomes.

Using the composite capabilities measure, we can review briefly the history of major power capabilities over the past two hundred years. Figure 7-1 depicts the estimated power of the United States, Britain, and Russia from 1816 (the end of the Napoleonic Wars) to 1993. It is interesting to see that according to the composite capabilities index, the United States had passed both Britain and Russia in relative power by 1900. Thereafter, Britain's power continued to decline as a proportion of global power, while Russia's, in decline at the outset of these observations until about 1880, turned up and passed Britain's in about 1925. This particular indicator also suggests that Russia briefly surpassed the United States in composite capabilities during the latter part of the 1980s. If power were measured purely in terms of GNP, however, the United States would have clearly remained ahead during this time. This provides us a valuable reminder that any measure of power or of national capabilities is bound to deviate from our expectations, and may in fact be wrong some of the time. Concepts like power, after all, are difficult to measure.

Despite its impressive power position in the nineteenth century, Americans' desire to remain isolated from European conflicts kept the United States from acting like a dominant great power until after World War II. Ironically, America's national capabilities as a proportion of the global total declined almost steadily after the end of that war. Some have pointed to this pattern as an example of hegemonic decline (Keohane 1984; Kennedy 1987), suggesting that after 1950 the United States began to lose its global advantage in economic and military power. Such an inference, however, is misleading. What these scholars perceive as an apparent decline in U.S. power is actually the postwar recovery of European power. America's share of global capabilities was grossly inflated in 1945 because the European economies were largely destroyed during the war. The inflation of American capabilities is evident from looking at the steep spike upward shown for the U.S. graph in Figure 7-1 between about 1940 and 1950. As the Europeans recovered (and as Japan

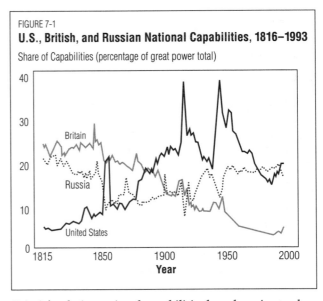

FIGURE 7-1

**U.S., British, and Russian National Capabilities, 1816–1993**

Share of Capabilities (percentage of great power total)

*Britain's relative national capabilities have been in steady decline for two hundred years. The nineteenth century was a period of decline for Russia and ascent for the United States. Russia did not regain its 1815 level of relative national capabilities until well into the twentieth century. The United States appeared to be in a decline during the cold war. How has it fared since the cold war ended?*

recovered as well), America's share of global capabilities returned to its approximate prewar level (Russett 1985; Strange 1987; Kugler and Organski 1989). Figure 7-1 also shows clearly that American and Soviet/Russian capabilities converged during the cold war years, whereas Britain continued in relative decline.

Although Figure 7-1 shows the broad sweep of the U.S. ascent in power from a sleepy backwater in the early nineteenth century to the premier power in the world for much of the twentieth century, Figures 7-2 through 7-5 break that two-hundred-year period into important subdivisions that highlight changing patterns of national capabilities among the great powers of the day.

In the years immediately following the Napoleonic Wars, Britain emerged as the greatest power in Europe and, indeed, in the world. By the 1830s, as is evident from Figure 7-2, British capabilities began to pull noticeably ahead of those of France and Russia, its two main rivals. Germany—Prussia at this stage in history—was a much weaker contender for international preeminence at this time.

It is noteworthy to see how rapidly Prussian resources expanded after 1866, as is evident in the figure. In 1866, Prussia defeated Austria in the Seven Weeks' War. As a consequence of that victory, Prussia unified several northern German principalities under its leadership and established the beginning of what today we call Germany. The absorption of the resources of these principalities, plus its decisive victory over Austria, projected Germany into the first rank of powers (Bueno de Mesquita 1990a). The Germans consolidated their claim to power and completed the unification of their country in a rapid sequence of impressive victories. In 1870, Prussia took on France in the Franco-Prussian War, winning a convincing victory that led to the unification of Germany along contemporary lines.

Germany's quest for global influence expanded apace with its national capabilities. Figure 7-3 shows the distribution of power among the European powers between the start of the Franco-Prussian War and the end of World War I. The most important pattern to note here is the continued rise of Germany and its eventual eclipse of Britain in national capabilities by about 1905. This year marked the true end

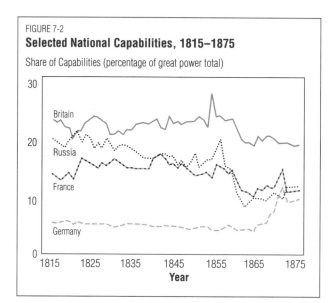

FIGURE 7-2
**Selected National Capabilities, 1815–1875**

Share of Capabilities (percentage of great power total)

*The two major changes in relative national capabilities between 1815 and 1875 are the decline of Russia and the surge in German power toward the end of the period. German unification began with the Seven Weeks' War in 1866 and was completed after the Franco-German War of 1870. Unification put Germany on the path to becoming a challenger for domination of Europe.*

of Britain's nineteenth-century domination of international affairs and the beginning of the turmoil that marked the first half of the twentieth century.

Figure 7-4 highlights the evolving pattern of U.S. and European great power national capabilities during the interwar years. (Japanese national capabilities at this time sit almost exactly on top of the graph for France, reflecting the fact that France and Japan were just about equal in relative power during this period.) It is readily apparent that German capabilities languished after World War I until the rise of Hitler in 1933. From then until about 1943, German power continued to grow, going into eclipse only during the latter years of World War II. During this same period, we can see the rapid expansion of U.S. national capabilities. The United States and Germany emerged as the two most powerful countries during the 1940s, with the Soviet Union not far behind.

The final snapshot of power, depicted in Figure 7-5, reflects the years from 1945 to the present. Britain, the Soviet Union/Russia, and the United States are displayed in this figure. By the end of World War II, Britain and the Soviet Union were about equal in national capabilities. Befitting the emerging bipolar world, however, Britain thereafter continued its long decline while the Soviet Union recovered from its wartime downturn to take its place alongside the United States as one of the two superpowers. By 1970—not coincidentally the very period that the United States and the Soviets pursued a policy of détente—U.S. and Soviet capabilities were nearly equal. The impending implosion of the Soviet Union is not at all evident in the graph shown in Figure 7-5.

A. F. K. Organski and Jacek Kugler, as well as several of their colleagues, have made more precise calculations of national power than those reflected in the composite capabilities index (Arbetman and Kugler 1997) shown in Figures 7-1 through 7-5. They rightly criticize the COW measure and other indicators for making the assumption that all governments are equally capable of mobilizing national resources at all times and across all issues. In fact, some governments mobilize people and resources much more effectively than do other governments of similar size. Organski and Kugler developed an index of relative political capacity (RPC). The RPC index is designed to distinguish between the resources found in a state and the government's ability to mobilize those

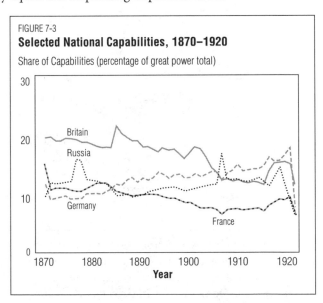

FIGURE 7-3

**Selected National Capabilities, 1870–1920**

Share of Capabilities (percentage of great power total)

*The period 1870 to 1920 culminated in World War I (1914–1918), at which time all of the European powers experienced a significant decline in power. Russia and Germany were the greatest losers in national capabilities.*

resources in pursuit of its foreign policy objectives. Although others have recognized that national security concerns are partially shaped by the government's ability to mobilize domestic support, Organski and Kugler have made the most systematic effort to date to measure this ability (Organski 1958; Waltz 1959; Barnett 1990; Lamborn 1991; Stam 1996; Volgy and Bailin 2003).

The RPC measure is based on the capacity of a government to extract wealth from its citizenry in the form of taxes. A government that has the ability to extract higher taxes from its citizenry than some other government will be better equipped to utilize resources and motivate its population than would that other government, according to Organski and Kugler. This measure asks questions about domestic motivation. The RPC index inflates the power of those states whose income from taxes is above a statistically estimated norm for economies of the size of the country in question and deflates the power of those whose income from taxes is below the norm. The index helps explain how a seemingly resource-rich set of states such as the Arab states can be defeated time and again by a relatively resource-poor state such as Israel. Figure 7-6 illustrates the RPC indexes for a combination of Arab states and for Israel from 1950 through 1974. The figure shows that, taking government efficiency into account, Israel's usable resources exceeded those of Egypt, Syria, and Jordan combined by the mid-1960s. The RPC provides a way to account for Israel's military success over the Arab states.

Unfortunately, the RPC index is unable to distinguish between governments that raise low levels of tax revenue as a proportion of GNP because the population resists paying (as has been true in India for decades and is true in post-Soviet Russia) and governments that raise low levels of tax revenue as a proportion of GNP because the government is philosophically wedded to a low tax policy (as was true in Hong Kong and is currently true, relatively speaking, in the United States and the People's Republic of China). Still, the RPC index does help account for important power-related phenomena, especially as they are associated with the outcome of wars. The composite capabilities index and the RPC index are not the only

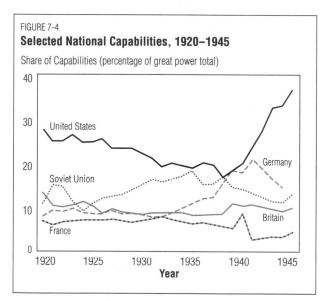

FIGURE 7-4
**Selected National Capabilities, 1920–1945**

Share of Capabilities (percentage of great power total)

*During the twenty-five years from 1920 to 1945 the national capabilities of the European powers declined; in contrast, those of the United States surged far ahead, particularly during World War II. Except for Pearl Harbor late in 1941, the United States experienced no destruction during the two world wars, whereas the continental powers were devastated. With American help, Western Europe was rebuilt after World War II.*

methods by which to estimate relative power. Additional academic and government agency methods have been developed to measure the power of rival states.

## THE FUNGIBILITY OF POWER

Each measure of national capabilities shares a common, although rarely explicit, philosophical view of power. Those who set out to measure national power assume that whatever pool of resources contributes to power, that pool of resources is relevant for all situations that might require the exercise of power. That is, they assume that national capabilities or resources are perfectly fungible. Resources that can be used to build a jet fighter, for example, can just as easily be used to build a negotiating team to resolve a trade dispute. This means that if the resources used by the negotiating team and the jet fighter are equal, then the power of the jet fighter and the power of the negotiating team are equal as well.

In recent years, some scholars have questioned this one-dimensional view of power. Robert Keohane and Joseph Nye (1977) have suggested that power is domain specific. Japan and Germany are very powerful today when it comes to trade negotiations, but they have little power when it comes to foreign military disputes. Religious leaders sometimes exert substantial moral power but can do little to mobilize an army or impose economic sanctions on a foe. Even a wealthy and sovereign religious authority like the Vatican can no longer raise armies as it did during the Crusades. But the pope, even today, is sometimes able to exert such enormous moral authority that he succeeds in neutralizing the threat of armed conflict. It is quite likely, for example, that the army of the Soviet Union or the Polish military would have crushed the anticommunist Solidarity movement in Poland in the 1980s but for the moral power exerted by the Polish pope John Paul II.

In my own research, I have taken the argument that power is not particularly fungible even further (Bueno de Mesquita 1984, 2002; Bueno de Mesquita, Newman, and Rabushka 1985, 1996; Bueno de Mesquita and Stokman 1994). In several studies I maintain that the power of competing interests

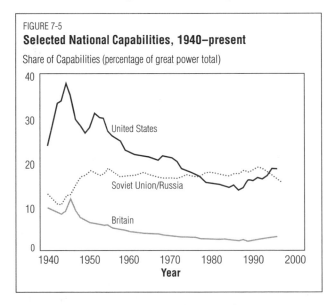

FIGURE 7-5
**Selected National Capabilities, 1940–present**

Share of Capabilities (percentage of great power total)

*The last half of the twentieth century saw the continuation of Britain's decline as a global power and the apparent convergence of American and Soviet capabilities. At the end of the cold war, however, the Soviet Union collapsed and its successor state—Russia—experienced a substantial economic decline while the United States' national capabilities boomed.*

varies from issue to issue and that one really cannot speak effectively about the power of the state. Rather, one must speak of the power or potential influence of competing individuals and interest groups within each state and sometimes across states. On some issues, the influence of these groups may be aggregated so that we can in fact speak in terms of national power; on other issues it makes no sense to aggregate the resources of groups that are competing with one another. This view finds support in the theoretical work of Alan Lamborn (1991, 1997) and is compatible with interest group perspectives as well as the strategic perspective.

When the United States negotiates with China over the balance-of-payments deficit, can we really speak of "American" power? Some American business interests want China to open its markets to more American goods because they stand to profit from such an action. Yet other American businesses stand to lose from such a policy. American firms that manufacture and sell their goods in China surely are not eager to face stiffer competition from American firms that manufacture their goods elsewhere. When the United States negotiates with China over trade relations, we see plainly that power in one setting is not easily carried over to another. American business and labor interests exert pressure and impose costs on political leaders. Yet these interests are likely to be divided in regard to how they want the government to relate to China. Those who do not benefit directly from the use of resources to promote a political agenda between China and the United States will resist the use of resources for that purpose.

Three trade conflicts that occurred between the United States and China in the mid-1990s provide evidence that power is not easily transferable from one sphere to another. The three confrontations occurred in rapid succession. The United States won two of them, and China won the other.

In 1994 the United States demanded that China stop violating textile quotas it had earlier agreed to respect. The Chinese were getting around their commitment by trans-

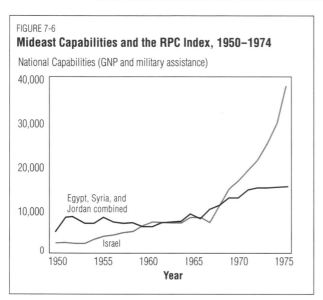

FIGURE 7-6
**Mideast Capabilities and the RPC Index, 1950–1974**

National Capabilities (GNP and military assistance)

*After adjusting for the government's capacity to extract resources from its citizens, Israel's national capabilities appear equal to those of its Arab rivals during their period of greatest conflict. Between the late 1950s and the early 1970s, Israel and its neighbors fought three wars. Following the 1973 war, Israel's power as measured by the relative political capacity (RPC) index soared ahead of its Arab neighbors. The calculations are based on the formula (GNP)(Tax Effort) + (foreign assistance)(Tax Effort of Recipient). GNP and foreign assistance are measured in millions of constant U.S. dollars.*

*Source: A. F. K. Organski and Jacek Kugler, The War Ledger (Chicago: University of Chicago Press, 1980), 92.*

shipping goods destined for the U.S. market through third countries. The United States, in accordance with international free trade agreements stipulated by the General Agreement on Tariffs and Trade and other procedures, threatened sharp retaliatory measures unless China complied with its promises. China quickly agreed to stop the offending policies. In this case the United States used its economic power to threaten an economic punishment.

Later the same year the United States threatened China with revocation of its most-favored-nation (MFN) status unless the Chinese government improved its human rights record. MFN status, granted by the U.S. government to just about every country in the world, entitles its bearer to trade with the United States under the fewest tariff restrictions. U.S. law for many years required that the president decide each year whether China had made progress in respecting human rights as a condition for MFN status. In this instance, the United States tried to use its economic power to change political behavior. The same economic power that had worked when brought to bear in the textile case was now being applied in a different arena, the arena of politics. China stonewalled. Chinese leaders rebuffed and humiliated Warren Christopher, the U.S. secretary of state, when he went to Beijing to impress upon the Chinese government America's determination to carry out its threat to deny China MFN status. When the deadline on the MFN decision arrived, the American government retreated from a confrontation by renewing MFN status for China for another year. The economic clout of the United States did not change China's behavior when the stakes involved human rights violations. The Chinese government was highly motivated to resist American pressure; U.S. leaders, for their part, were concerned about the domestic political fallout if they reduced trade with China.

Finally, the United States and China again collided in 1995 over China's rampant violation of copyright protection of American intellectual property. The brazen violations were carried out by Chinese companies in which relatives of the top Chinese political and military leaders had strong and profitable financial interests. After much teeth grinding, the Chinese in February 1995 capitulated to U.S. demands and reigned in violators of the international copyright protection laws.

How are we to account for the different results of these three confrontations? First, we need to know that in the mid-1990s the United States bought about four times as much from China as it sold to China. What is more, American investment and Chinese sales to the U.S. market kept China's economic growth rate from falling. The Chinese pool of labor, estimated to be between 100 million and 200 million strong, represented a critical economic advantage as long as the economy expanded. But economic contractions would make it impossible for the Chinese economy to absorb the mass of cheap, mobile Chinese rural labor pouring out of the countryside into the urban industrial system. Such large numbers of displaced people might well have destabilized the political system.

Given these facts, surely the United States had by far the stronger hand in its confrontation with China. Yet in the case of MFN status it was the Americans who capitulated. Why? The solution to this riddle speaks directly to the fact that the fungibility of national power is severely limited. In fact, whenever a national elite attempts to use resources derived from one set of relations to control behavior in another set of relations, it runs the risk of fomenting political opposition.

In the present American political environment, the business and labor elite have the upper hand in international economic issues. In the case of China's violation of textile quotas, American business supported the efforts of the U.S. government because the government was applying power on behalf of rules that American businesspeople recognized to be in their interest. Likewise in the case of Chinese violation of copyright protection. If the Chinese were permitted to pirate intellectual property, it was not only the producers of that property that were put in peril. In both cases, Chinese behavior endangered all businesses that were investing capital in China. It could not be tolerated. The U.S. government, in pressing its claims, was carrying water for the entire American business community, and the community clearly was not going to object to having its resource pool used to force the Chinese to capitulate.

In the case of the MFN status, however, business leaders opposed the U.S. government effort for the very reason that it was their trade activity that was the power resource behind the political elite's attempt to win concessions on human rights issues. Although human rights issues were critical to the American administration, they were only secondary to the American business community. Thus, American politicians bore real domestic costs in pressing China on human rights because that pressure had to be enforced at the expense of American investors.

In China, the Chinese business elite certainly did not wish to jeopardize lucrative

*The United States and China frequently find themselves in conflict over trade policy, the protection of property rights, and human rights. Here we see shoppers choosing pirated video CDs on the streets of Beijing. By allowing such infringements of copyright protection, the Chinese government helps stifle incentives to create new ideas and products, and it permits bootleggers to create risks to Chinese-American trade.*

relations with the West, and particularly with the United States, over human rights issues. But the interests of the Chinese business elite could not be separated from the interests of the Chinese political elite. For China's political leaders, questions of political control and law and order were top priority issues not to be exchanged for economic advantages from trade. In such an environment, the Chinese leadership was strongly motivated to resist granting political concessions in exchange for economic gains. And the members of America's political elite were likewise loath to press hard for human rights concessions at the expense of powerful American business constituents. Hence, China's successful resistance to U.S. pressure in the case of MFN status.

In those cases in which the Chinese capitulated to the United States, the reverse held true. In those cases (as in the case it lost), America was the economically stronger party. Given this, all the United States had to do to win was to stand firm. It could do that only if the major foreign policy actors involved—government and business—stuck together and demanded that the Chinese back down on their violations of agreements they had signed. And that is exactly what happened. The major actors did stick together and successfully pressed their advantage.

Our example of the nonfungible nature of power in the case of China can be repeated for Japan (and many other places) as well. In the endless tug-of-war over trade with Japan, the United States tries to convert its political resources into economic gains by inducing Japan to open its markets. American power relative to Japan stems from two sources: first, the United States since World War II has provided Japan with external security and, second, the United States is a critical market for Japanese products. The reasons for America's very modest success in converting its pool of power resources into economic gain stem from the same factors discussed in the case of China. In Japan, the government bureaucracy enjoys a decisive position on trade issues. This bureaucracy is much more strongly allied with Japanese business interests than with Japanese military interests. As such, it is clearly to the government's advantage to fight for every inch of ground it can on trade issues with the United States.

Japanese business interests operating within the United States pose a quandary for the Japanese political elite. To satisfy American trade pressure, and to take advantage of good manufacturing opportunities in the United States, some Japanese companies produce televisions in the United States for the U.S. market. Japanese television manufacturers who produce televisions in the United States have fought hard to prevent other Japanese firms that manufacture televisions in Japan from exporting their products to the United States (Yoffie, Goodman, and Spar 1996). In this situation Japanese government negotiators cannot possibly represent the interests of all Japanese television manufacturers, because those manufacturers obviously have different interests. Some want a quid pro quo in open markets with the United States; others do not. Typically, government negotiators represent only one side in their own domestic debate on the trade issue. And that side is normally the one likely to offer the most votes to government decision makers in exchange for instituting a particular trade policy (McGillivray 1997, 1998; Morgan and Schwebach 1995). But other interests mobilize resources to counter the government's negotiating stance. In such cases it makes no sense to aggregate national resources and to speak of national power. Doing so involves an implicit contradiction. All resources are added together when we assume that they all can be mobilized to work toward a common goal. But if goals differ for different groups in a state, then resources cannot pull toward a common objective, at least not in those states that require the consent of the people to dispose of national resources.

It also makes little sense, as Organski and Kugler's research emphasizes, to treat two countries with equal resources as being equally powerful. Besides variations across governments in ability to mobilize resources through taxation, numerous other factors conspire to influence the fungibility or convertibility of resources into power. We have seen that internal competition over how resources should be used dissipates any government's ability to use all of its resources one way or another. The rate at which resources are dissipated through internal competition depends on how intense that competition is and on how motivated each side is to press its point of view.

## PROJECTING POWER OVER LARGE DISTANCES

Geographic factors also play a part in varying the relative power of states with comparable national resources or wealth. Kentucky is famous for its Kentucky colonels, but what about Nebraska's admiralty? Nebraska, of course, is landlocked. No matter how many resources are poured into building a blue-water navy, it is unlikely that a landlocked country can achieve the naval prowess of even a much smaller state that is not landlocked. Similarly, a nation located on the border of a trouble spot is better able to exert influence over the trouble spot than is a country with comparable resources located thousands of miles away.

Power diminishes as it is projected over long distances. This is true in part because domestic support for foreign enterprises far from home tends to be weaker than support for comparable enterprises in one's backyard. But it is also true simply because resources are expended in moving other resources over great distances. Trucks wear out, soldiers get tired, guns and ammunition get lost or damaged, fuel is diminished, and so forth. All efforts to project power suffer from what is called a loss of strength gradient (Boulding 1963; Bueno de Mesquita 1981a; Diehl 1985; Lemke 2002). This means that the quantity of resources that can be applied to a conflict decays over distance. The rate of decay is almost certainly faster for poorer states than it is for wealthier states because the former lack the most efficient technologies or additional resources that are available to the latter to project power further. It is also almost certainly true that the loss of strength gradient was steeper in the past than it is today because of advances in technology.

The loss of strength gradient provides one explanation of why wars are more often fought between neighbors than between distant powers. We know intuitively that conflict is unlikely between Cuba and the Netherlands, even if their economic and social policies diverge. One explanation for our intuition is simply that neither can project its power effectively over the large distance between them. Yet Cuban soldiers helped in distant Angola during that country's civil war in the 1980s. How can this apparent anomaly be explained? In fact, the explanation is consistent with the idea of a loss of strength gradient. The Soviet Union was willing to foot the bill to have Cuba act as its surrogate in "wars of liberation" in different parts of the world. The Soviet Union, of course, had at its disposal a much vaster pool of resources than did Cuba and thus could comfortably help Cuba cover the costs of projecting power to Angola. Likewise, we know that in the seventeenth century the Netherlands was able to project its power to North America. At that time the Netherlands was a great power, with a vast array of resources available to it compared with those available to its prospective rivals in North America, most notably the Native Americans, with whom they forged many, generally favorable (to the Dutch) treaties. Today, hot disputes far from home are overwhelmingly fought by one or more major powers. Smaller states just do not have the excess resources necessary to project their power effectively over long distances.

Those who have great power but do not suffer greatly from the loss of strength gradient are in a position to influence international politics all over the globe. At one time it was said that the sun never sets on the British Empire. Today, this is no longer true. But as one nation recedes, others come forward to claim their place in the spotlight of world affairs. Now that we are in the twenty-first century, it is compelling to imagine who might join the ranks of the great powers in the near future.

China has a long way to go before it is wealthy enough to compete with the United States, or even Germany or Japan, for influence over global politics. Still, China today has one of the world's largest economies. It is held back only by the vastness of its population. Because that population is so large and poor, the Chinese government is handicapped in its potential to mobilize those resources needed for building a world-class high-technology military or economic capability. The recent slowing of Chinese economic growth, possibly to under 4 percent per year, can only postpone the day when China becomes a great power. If China can resume growth rates in the neighborhood of 9 or 10 percent a year, as it enjoyed during the 1980s and much of the 1990s, then it can accelerate its rise to great power status. Even so, it will take at least fifty or sixty years for China's per capita income to catch up with that of the United States, even under assumptions that are rather favorable for China.

India and Brazil are candidates for great power status, as are Indonesia, Pakistan, and Nigeria. Before any of these countries can assume the mantle of world leader, however, they must achieve substantial improvement in their economic outlooks. For now, they, like so much of the developing world, languish in positions of relative weakness because of their long commitment to inefficient economic systems that have held them back from developing the extra resources needed to acquire great political clout.

Perhaps the twenty-first or twenty-second centuries will see their rise in international influence.

## SUMMARY

Power as a concept is highly variable and complex. Defined as the ability to make others do what they otherwise would not, the exercise of power occurs along four dimensions: persuasion, rewards, punishment, and force. In general, it is cheaper to persuade or reward than it is to punish or coerce with force.

Power is most often evaluated as some estimation of national capabilities. This is the approach taken throughout most of this book. Sometimes national capability estimates are adjusted by taking additional factors into account. The government's ability to mobilize resources is sometimes approximated by evaluating the capacity of the government to raise tax revenues relative to other countries with comparably sized economies. National capability estimates are also sometimes adjusted to take geographic distance into account, because it can be difficult to project power beyond one's borders. Power is also sometimes estimated on an issue-by-issue basis. This reflects limitations to the assumption that national capabilities are perfectly fungible. If we assume that resources are not fungible, then we must look within the state at bureaucratic, interest group, and other factors that make countries more powerful in some spheres and less powerful in others. This view of the nonfungibility of power is consistent with interest group perspectives and the strategic perspective of international politics.

In reviewing the history of the distribution of relative magnitudes of national capabilities among the great powers from 1816 to the present, we saw that the United States rose to a position of preeminence in national capabilities during the nineteenth century but chose not to use those resources to exert global political influence until well into the twentieth century. We also saw that the supposed decline of American influence—the loss of hegemony—often touted to have occurred during the 1980s was in reality no more than the economic recovery of the European (and Japanese) economies that had been devastated during World War II.

# LIMITS TO POWER

Relations between states are commonly thought to be driven by the relative distribution of power. States that are stronger, or that can count on stronger allies, are typically thought to be victors in international disputes and governors of subsequent negotiated decision making. Realist theories draw our attention to the importance of power in directing victory and defeat in international affairs. Many distinguished foreign policy experts and decision makers share the view expressed by historian Sir Eyre Crowe that "history shows that the danger threatening the independence of this or that nation has generally arisen, at least in part, out of the momentary predominance of a neighboring State at once militarily powerful, economically efficient, and ambitious to extend its frontiers or spread its influence" (quoted in Hartmann 1978, 316). If this view is correct, then it provides a parsimonious way to anticipate danger spots in international relations. It suggests that wherever and whenever a state enjoys a power advantage over its neighbors, there is a real danger that those neighbors will lose their sovereignty. Yet, all of us know that most states, most of the time, live in peace with their neighbors. There must be more, then, to how states and their leaders relate to one another than simply asymmetries in power.

In this chapter we investigate conditions that limit the role of power in international relations. We start off by evaluating the empirical validity of the claim that those who enjoy a power advantage inevitably attack their foes and win the wars they fight. Recall

Henry Kissinger's contention, quoted in Chapter 2, that "weakness . . . invariably tempt[s] aggression and impotence brings abdication of policy in its train" (Kissinger 1979, 195). In this chapter we will see that Kissinger's statement is not accurate. We will also explore the idea, touched on in Chapter 7, that the commonly used definition of power can lead to circularity in real-world applications. This may help to explain why power is not as reliable a predictor of behavior as realists would have us believe.

We will then turn our attention to situations in which power is not the only—or even the primary—factor shaping the way people relate to one another. We will examine problems of coordination and distribution of valuable resources and discover some important limitations embodied in the notion of power. We will investigate alternative explanations of how conflicts end. These views help to explain the many instances in which the distribution of power has failed to predict correctly how events turned out. We will also examine the role that asymmetries in motivation play in shaping the resolution of disputes and look at how asymmetries in willingness to tolerate costs distort how disputes get settled. Finally, we will look at intangible factors, such as morale and the quality of leadership, that can give one or another side a boost up in a dispute. Together, these various factors show how the distribution of power by itself provides only a limited explanation of international affairs.

## POWER AND MILITARY VICTORY

The composite capabilities index introduced in Chapter 7 is a useful approximation of relative national power. Here we will apply it to international wars over the past two centuries to assess the association between power on the one hand and the initiation and outcome of wars on the other. For purposes of this evaluation, a war has occurred if each side committed at least one thousand regular troops or suffered at least one thousand battle-related deaths. This is the definition of war used by the Correlates of War Project (Small and Singer 1982) and typically found in research on war. The aim of our evaluation is to uncover how well a commonly used estimation of power predicts war initiation and termination. Later, we will see how adding the effects of other variables or substituting other variables helps improve the predictive capacity of this simple, realist measure of power.

The first thing to note is that war is extremely rare. In principle, any two states could go to war with each other at any time. In the contemporary world, there are about 200 sovereign states. This means that there are currently almost 20,000 pairs of states.[1] Over the span of the last two hundred years, there have been more than 1 million pairs of states if we count each pair once for every year that it existed. Yet, by the above definition,

---

[1] If there are $N$ states, and we are going to choose any two at a time, then there are $(N)(N - 1)/2$ pairs, where the pairs AB and BA are treated as a single pair.

there have been fewer than one hundred wars. Even by a laxer definition, one that treats any reciprocal use of violence between states as war, there have been only two hundred to three hundred wars. Whether we use a stringent definition of war or a lax definition of war, there is no escaping the fact that there have been very few wars. In fact, there has been less than one war per thousand opportunities according to our definition of war. Virtually all of these opportunities involved a pair of states in which one state was stronger than the other. Evidently, the existence of a power advantage by itself rarely prompts a nation to go to war.

Of course, most pairs of states are separated by vast distances and have scant interest in each other. Certainly we would be surprised if Afghanistan and Guatemala fought one another. The idea of a loss of strength gradient helps us see that most states simply cannot project their power far enough to fight with distant states. However, even if we reduce the set of possible confrontations to include just neighbors, war remains a rare event. Note that in this example we have already introduced an additional variable— geographic proximity—that qualifies the notion of realists like Kissinger, Hans Morgenthau, and Kenneth Waltz that imbalances in power produce aggression.

The United States and Canada are neighbors, and the United States enjoys a vast power advantage over Canada. Yet, the United States does not routinely wage war with Canada. Quite the contrary. The two countries have a long history of mutual coopera- tion in foreign policy matters, even though as trade rivals they have motivation for dis- putes. And although the United States and Mexico fought a war in the mid-1800s, throughout most of their long history as neighbors the two countries have coexisted peacefully, even though the United States enjoys a clear advantage in power. Indeed, on some occasions the United States has granted concessions to Mexico. For example, a long-festering dispute over a piece of land along the Rio Grande demarcating the U.S.- Mexican border was resolved when President John F. Kennedy ceded the land, known as El Chamizal, to Mexico (Lamborn and Mumme 1988). Through negotiations, Mexico got what it could not possibly have taken by force.

Asymmetries in power exist in almost every dyadic comparison of states, whether those states are neighbors or not. Although war is more common among neighboring states than among distant rivals, it is clearly still rare in all instances. This observation puts a crimp in the realist argument that power advantages inevitably lead to war. Perhaps realists implicitly assume that the motivation to fight is not always present, but when it is present it is the stronger adversary who first uses force. If this is so, then how well does the realists' focus on power fare in accounting for the initiation of violence?

Over the past two centuries, 59 percent of wars have been initiated by the stronger of the two initial belligerents (Small and Singer 1982). Certainly this suggests that a power advantage helps explain who chooses to resort to force first. But a figure of 59 percent is hardly overwhelming support for the contention that power asymmetries prompt wars. After all, 41 percent of wars apparently are started by a state that is weaker than its adversary. A power advantage is far from decisive in explaining the use of force, suggesting that additional factors are at work in shaping this most extreme of international events.

Does power fare better in explaining who wins wars? As it happens, only 59 percent of wars are won by the initially stronger belligerent, leaving the initially weaker side victorious 41 percent of the time. Interestingly, the initiators of wars emerge victorious 68 percent of the time, yet, as noted above, they are stronger only 59 percent of the time. Clearly, considerations other than just a power advantage calculation enter into leaders' decisions to initiate violence, and these other factors just as clearly improve on leaders' chances of victory. The fact that leaders initiate war when they view their odds of winning as superior to what a pure power calculation suggests encourages us to be on the lookout for those additional, odds-boosting variables on which these leaders apparently rely.

> Disputes between neighboring states are more common than disputes between distant foes. List several examples of wars between neighboring states and wars between geographically distant rivals. Can you identify examples in which the more powerful state lost to the weaker foe? Consult the database at the Web site at http://bdm.cqpress.com to find examples in which the weak defeated the strong.

## POWER CAN BE CYCLICAL

Recall that power is most commonly defined as the ability to make others do what they otherwise would not do. But how are we to know what someone "otherwise would not do"? How can we be sure that a change in behavior has actually occurred, and whose power should be credited with that change in behavior? What conveys the ability to change the behavior of others? Does making someone change behavior require overt exertion, or is an anticipated negative consequence for failure to change behavior sufficient? These are all difficult questions to answer. Consider the following example.

On April 15, 1986, eighteen American fighter-bombers attacked Tripoli, the capital of Libya. The United States launched the attack to punish and deter alleged Libyan support of terrorism and Libyan efforts to deny the United States and others rights in what many considered international airspace. American aircraft took off from bases in Great Britain and flew via an indirect route to Libya because they were denied flyover rights by the French and Spanish governments. The French government's refusal to grant the United States flyover privileges appears to have been motivated by French concern that France would become the target of retaliatory Libyan-sponsored terrorism or of a Libyan oil embargo. In fact, Libyan terrorist acts dropped off dramatically following the bombing raid.

What can we learn from the bombing of Tripoli about the power of the parties involved? The standard definition of power—making others do what they otherwise would not do—treats power as relational, as an asymmetric example of behavioral change. It delineates power as the quantity of relevant resources one state has compared with another and how those relative quantities influence behavior. According to this definition, the statement "I have ten bombers" says nothing about my power; however, the statement "I have ten bombers and you have three" may convey some information about my ability to get you to change your behavior. Then again, it may not. Still, the definition clearly indicates that although you do not have power over me I do have power over you and so can make you change your behavior.

Was the United States more powerful than Libya? The evidence in support of this claim is contained in the observation that Libyan-sponsored terrorism fell off after the bombing raid. If we assume that Libya's past actions could be projected to form an expectation about future terrorism, then the observed drop-off in such acts after the bombing is evidence that Libya's behavior changed. That, of course, would still leave open the question of whether it changed because of the bombing raid or for other reasons entirely. Here, we attribute some degree of causation to the correlation between the American use of force against Libya and Libya's propensity to support terrorism. The hypothesis that the application of force diminished terrorism is consistent with the facts and so supports (but does not prove) the inference that America succeeded in getting the Libyan government to do something (diminish the use of terrorism) that it otherwise would not have done. This argument about changing Libya's behavior depends on counterfactual reasoning. That is, the argument depends on comparing the state of the world (a certain level of Libyan terrorism before the bombing and a different level after the bombing) with a hypothetical, unobservable state of the world (the level of Libyan terrorism after April 15, 1986, if there had not been a bombing) and drawing an inference about the consequences of the bombing (Tetlock and Belkin 1996).

What about the power relationship between France and the United States? The French government made the United States do something it otherwise would not have

> Correlation does not necessarily prove causation. The correlation between Libya's alleged use of terrorism before and after the U.S. bombing raid suggests that the raid caused Libya to change its behavior. But what other explanations might account for the drop-off in terrorism after the bombing? Can you think of other examples where correlation is used to infer causation? Can you offer some examples of causal claims that are wrong even though correlational evidence can be found to support them?

done: it made the United States route its planes so that they did not fly over France. This is consistent with the commonly used definition of power, and yet it offends our intuition to suggest that the United States was compelled by France to change its behavior. We naturally suspect that if the United States had insisted, the French would have succumbed. If this is so, then we must ask, first, why the United States did not insist and, second, what does this suggest about power. For now, in accordance with our common definition of power, we will conclude that France had power over the United States.

What about the relationship between France and Libya? American air force planes are frequently granted flyover privileges by the French government, but on this occasion they were not. Ostensibly, the motivation for France's decision was fear of Libyan retaliation if France acquiesced to the U.S. request. Here, Libya was able to get France to do something that it otherwise would not have done. According to our definition, then, Libya had power over France. The threat of Libyan terrorism and a Libyan oil embargo against France (again, counterfactual conjectures, since France did not help the United States and Libya did not promote terrorism on French soil or cut off France's access to Libyan oil) was sufficient to get France to deny flyover privileges to the United States. Thus, the United States had power over Libya (Libya reduced its terrorism following the bombing of Tripoli), France had power over the United States (France made the United States choose a less efficient attack route), and Libya had power over France (France's reaction to the United States' request was motivated by fear of Libyan reprisals). The common definition of power has taken us full circle.

Figure 8-1 highlights the relational and contextual aspects of power in the Libyan dispute. In one context, a big state like the United States might exercise considerable power over the actions of a smaller state like France; in another context, the power relationship might be reversed. Figure 8-1 illustrates how the commonly accepted definition of power can be circular.

The circularity of power relationships is remarkably common. Indeed, as mentioned in Chapter 7, the children's game of rock, paper, scissors reflects the commonality of the idea that power relations are circular. Of particular significance to matters of international relations, the cyclicity of power points up its essentially nonfungible nature. For years, Germany's economic prowess, for example, put it in a position to determine the value of most European currencies because the French, Italians, and others pegged the value of their money to the value of Germany's deutsche mark. Decisions by the German central bank—the Bundesbank—shaped exchange rates, inflation, and even unemployment in much of Europe throughout the 1990s. Yet Germany exerted relatively little influence over European or NATO decisions to deploy military units to hot spots in and near Europe. In the domain of military power, Britain and France exercised more influence than did the Germans. Thus, in this example we can see that France had some power over Germany in European military matters, and Germany had some power over France in European economic matters. This asymmetry is itself undergoing change. During the war in Kosovo NATO used German troops outside of Germany in combat missions. This was the first time that German military might was used beyond defense of national borders since the end of World War II.

FIGURE 8-1
**Power Relationships in the Libyan Dispute**

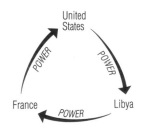

*Because power can be cyclical, it is not always obvious that one state is really more powerful than another. An intuitive sense of power can be risky when applied to real situations.*

## COORDINATION AND POWER

The use of power certainly is one way to resolve problems between different countries or decision makers, but it is not the only way. It may not even be the most common way. For a certain class of problems—those involving coordination—using power to resolve disputes is not the preferred solution.

A coordination problem arises when two or more decision makers have a stake in making a common policy choice but face impediments to coordinating on a common solution (Greif, Milgrom, and Weingast 1994; Morrow 1994b). Why, if each decision maker agrees that she or he will be better off making the same choice as someone else, do decision makers have problems agreeing on a course of action? How do power relationships help or hinder the resolution of coordination problems?

A group of policymakers may have more than one option available to it, each as good as the next for everyone in the group. But uncertainty about which option others in the group are going to take can result in failure to make a common choice. This failure to coordinate can leave each member of the group worse off than if they had shared information and coordinated their decision making. Consider the following example of a pure coordination problem in international relations.

Suppose tank drivers from allied countries find themselves on a battlefield fighting a common foe. This, of course, happened in 1991 during the Gulf War against Iraq and in 2001–2002 during the antiterrorism war in Afghanistan. In the Gulf War, Saudi, British, American, and other allied tank drivers had a profound interest in knowing whether another tank on the same battlefield was a friend or a foe. In modern warfare, the distinction between friend and foe is often made by having each tank emit an agreed-upon electronic signal on an agreed-upon frequency. The signal changes with prearranged regularity, making it difficult for foes to mimic the information and masquerade as friends.

Tank drivers have no reason to prefer one electronic signal to another, but they have a life-and-death interest in coordinating on an agreed-upon signal. Failure to know the right signal heightens the risk of becoming a victim of friendly fire. When a pure coordination issue such as this arises, it is easy to persuade people to agree on a common solution.

Electronic identification of friendly tanks is an example of a solution to a pure coordination problem. All relevant parties agree on the desired outcome. Many options achieve the same desired end, and no one has a reason to prefer one option (one signal) over another. But someone among the commanders coordinating the tank battlefield must

> Can you suggest other examples of pure coordination problems in international relations? What would happen if some trucks in a multinational convoy drove on the right side of the road and others drove on the left side of the road? What are some ways that the international community monitors or detects failures to abide by proposed solutions to coordination problems? Why would any leader have an incentive to violate an international agreement that his or her government had signed?

choose the signal each time it changes. And every recipient must coordinate on the chosen signal, changing behavior in response to the choice made. This guarantees that tank crews will fire only at tanks not emitting the agreed-upon signal. Tanks emitting the signal will automatically be considered friendly. Does the commander who chooses the agreed-upon signal have power over the others? Not in any standard sense of the term, although the commander is able to change others' behavior. Indeed, the commander makes the members of the group do something they otherwise would not have done: without coordination, it is very unlikely that every member of the group would choose the specific signal that is ultimately used. But this is a peculiar way to speak of power. After all, tank crews that coordinate on a common signal do so because they share a common interest. Although each might, by chance, have chosen differently, none is wedded to a particular signal. In this case, we must modify our common definition of power to match the facts better. If we add the word "want" to our common definition of power, we can take into account the importance of preferences in alleviating problems of pure coordination. Thus, our definition now states that power is the ability to make others do something that they otherwise would not *want* to do.

The importance of preferences in international relations is the topic of the next chapter. For now, note that by adding the word "want" to our definition of power we are indicating that the exercise of power itself may depend on preferences or interests. Persuasion and rewards can play upon these preferences and interests to solve problems of coordination. Persuasion is the art of convincing another party that it should want to do the same thing as the persuader is suggesting. Rewards are a recognition that the two parties do not want to do the same thing in the absence of compensation. Persuasion solves the coordination problem by identifying an agreed-upon action that each party is happy to coordinate on. Rewards solve the coordination problem by providing one of the parties with the authority to choose the course of action for both.

## DISTRIBUTION PROBLEMS, COORDINATION PROBLEMS, AND POWER

The basic coordination problem concerns changing behavior when the relevant decision maker cares, not about the choice that is made, but rather that everyone coordinates on that choice. Not all coordination problems are quite so simple, however. Some coordination problems coincide with distributional problems.

A distributional problem involves the allocation of a valuable resource when two or more policymakers disagree about how much of that resource each should receive. Territorial disputes, for example, involve a distributional problem. A piece of territory is valuable because it contains mineral wealth or skilled people or security-enhancing terrain or what have you. Wars are often fought to determine who controls a valuable piece of territory (Vasquez 1993, 1995, 2000; Senese 1995, 1997; Hensel 1996; Huth 1996). In such cases, there is a distributional problem between the combatants, but not a coordination problem. Although power frequently plays a role in resolving distributional problems, we will see that even when a distributional issue is serious enough to result in war, power does not necessarily determine the outcome of that war. Sometimes distributional problems accompany coordination problems. In these cases power is just one means of resolving the problem. Other solutions are available, but they may leave us confused about the nature of power.

A distributional problem that is coupled with a coordination problem arises whenever two or more decision makers agree that they want to undertake a common action—that is, they want to coordinate—but they disagree about which action it is best to take. Consider an example involving the sale of Toyotas in the United States.

The Japanese manufacturer of Toyotas would like to sell as many cars in the United States as it can. It would also like to build as many of these cars as possible in Japan for sale in the United States. The U.S. government, through the office of the United States Trade Representative (USTR), would like cars sold in the United States to be built in the United States. But the USTR also wants American consumers to be able to shop for cars in a competitive marketplace.

To simplify the problem, let's assume that Toyota can follow one of two strategies. It can either build cars in the United States or build cars in Japan for export to the United States. Likewise, the USTR can follow one of two strategies. It can either permit the unrestricted importation of Toyotas made in Japan or restrict the number of Toyotas imported to the United States and encourage Toyota instead to build cars in the United States.

Let us stipulate that the USTR's benefits are greatest (payoff = 1) when Toyota builds autos in the United States, provided the USTR has insisted it do so. In this case, the USTR's policy increases the number of jobs in the United States. The second-best benefit for the USTR (payoff = 0.5) arises when Toyotas are built in Japan and then imported into the United States in accordance with the policies of the USTR. This provides consumers with cheaper cars but does not benefit the domestic auto industry. The worst combination of strategies for the USTR (payoff = 0) occurs if Toyota builds in the United States when the USTR is willing to allow it to import cars or when the USTR precludes Toyota imports, which are then built only in Japan.

The two circumstances that result in a payoff of 0 for the USTR are readily explained. In the first case the USTR suffers politically because it appears to be needlessly permissive and weak in its dealings with Japan. In the second case the USTR angers American consumers because it creates an artificial shortage of new vehicles and thereby limits the competitiveness of the American automobile marketplace. By restricting imports when Toyota builds only in Japan, the USTR causes the price of cars to rise in the United States, as explained in Chapter 13.

In this highly simplified trade story, Toyota's benefits are greatest (payoff = 1) when it builds cars in Japan for sale in the United States, assuming the USTR permits the importation of Japanese-built Toyotas and Toyota does not build cars in the United States. Toyota's second-best benefit (payoff = 0.5) occurs if the USTR restricts the importation of Toyotas built in Japan and Toyota builds cars in the United States. Toyota derives no benefit (payoff = 0) if it builds cars in Japan for export to the United States and the USTR restricts imports or if it builds cars in the United States and the USTR does not restrict imports. Obviously, these strategies represent a gross simplification of what in actuality is a much more complex problem, but they are sufficient to deal with the linkage between coordination and distributional problems and to show the role that power can play in such international political economy situations. (A much more thorough examination of the linkage between distribution and coordination problems can be found in Morrow 1994b.)

The set of payoffs, or utilities, associated with these strategies can be put in a table that reflects what is called the strategic, or normal, form of a game (Morrow 1994a). In this type of game each player is trying to do as well as he or she can. That is, each player is trying to gain the greatest amount of utility possible. What players like Toyota and the USTR gain depends on the choices each makes, not just on the choices any one makes alone. The USTR, for example, can decide to restrict or not restrict Japanese auto imports, but the USTR cannot decide for Toyota whether or not Toyota will build cars in the United States. Because the amount of value each player receives depends in part on what the other player does, both players have a natural incentive to try to influence the other's choice. The game's setting creates an interest in trying to get the other player to do something that she or he might otherwise not do. In this sense, the desire to exercise power is inherent in the strategic situation between the two players.

Table 8-1 depicts the combination of strategies possible in this trade situation. The first number in each cell of the table represents the utility Toyota derives from the specified pair of strategies. The second number in each cell represents the utility the USTR derives from these specified pairs of strategies. Simply stated, Table 8-1 depicts the coordination and distributional problem facing Toyota and the USTR.

The coordination problem is reflected by the fact that both Toyota and the USTR prefer to match strategies so that neither gets a payoff of 0. The distributional problem is reflected by the fact that, although there are two outcomes that both parties like better than two other outcomes, they disagree on which of the outcomes is best. The USTR most wants to restrict imports when Toyota decides to build cars in the United States. Toyota most wants to build cars in Japan when the USTR does not restrict imports.

TABLE 8-1
### U.S.-Japanese Auto Trade: A Simple Game

| Toyota | USTR | |
|---|---|---|
| | Permit Japanese Imports | Restrict Japanese Imports |
| Build in Japan | 1, 0.5 | 0, 0 |
| Build in the United States | 0, 0 | 0.5, 1 |

The Battle of the Sexes game, as this is called (for reasons we need not concern ourselves with here), has three solutions. A solution, recall, requires a plan of action—a strategy—for each player for all possible contingencies in the game. A plan of action for each player is a solution if it forms a Nash equilibrium. (A Nash equilibrium, you will recall, is a set of strategies such that no player has a unilateral incentive to switch to another strategy.) These solutions are either one of two pure strategy equilibria or a mixed strategy equilibrium.

## PURE STRATEGY EQUILIBRIA

In pure strategy equilibria, players do not make moves probabilistically. Rather, each player chooses one, and only one, action at each point in the game when a choice must be made. Of course, the pure strategies are in equilibrium only if no player could be made better off by switching alone to a different strategy.

One solution is for the two players to coordinate on the strategy pair "Build in Japan, Permit Japanese Imports." This would yield a utility of 1 for Toyota and a utility of 0.5 for the USTR. Another pure strategy equilibrium is for the players to coordinate on the strategy pair "Build in the United States, Restrict Japanese Imports." This would yield a utility of 0.5 for Toyota and a utility of 1 for the USTR. Neither player has a unilateral incentive to switch from either of these strategies.

If the USTR switched to a different strategy and Toyota did not, then the USTR would get a utility of 0 (and so would Toyota), which is worse than either 1 or 0.5. Similarly, if Toyota defected unilaterally from either of these pure strategy equilibria, it would get a utility of 0 (and so would the USTR), which is worse than 1 or 0.5. The absence of any unilateral incentive to defect to a different strategy is, as we have seen, exactly what defines these actions as equilibria.

But how will the players choose the strategy pair on which to coordinate? Game theorists sometimes address this question by appealing to a concept introduced by John Nash known as a common conjecture. A shared culture and prior experience interacting with each other are two ways people may develop a common conjecture, or common expectation of how the game will be played. James Morrow (1994a) has offered a particularly good discussion of the ideas behind the common conjecture. He has shown how this concept can be used to connect an approach to politics known as constructivism to the rational choice approach of game theory (Morrow 1997). In constructivism much of what we take for granted in our lives is thought to be part of a socially constructed reality. Beliefs about gender roles is one obvious example. Looking out for the collective welfare of the state might also be viewed as part of a constructed reality. Such an outlook is typical in consensual political systems such as that said to exist in Japan. In contrast, America's constructed reality emphasizes rugged individualism as a guiding principle. Morrow argues that one solution to selecting from among alternative equilibrium strategies is to rely on focal points that are part of our social or cultural makeup. These focal points or social constructions reflect a best guess as to how others with a common background are likely to react. By relying on a common conjecture about the choice that needs to be made, players end up achieving equilibria. In this way, the constructivist focus on a socially or relativistically defined reality is consistent with a core principle of game theory, the common conjecture.

One common conjecture that might help guide decision making in the Battle of the Sexes game or in other distributional situations is to assume that the more powerful of two players will be given the first opportunity to pick an action. Many parliamentary systems use just this rule when no political party wins a majority in an election. The leader of the largest party is given the first opportunity to form a coalition government. Of course, the weaker of the two players will be unhappy with this decision rule and might insist that, as the underdog, he get to pick first. In fact, both are equally compelling arguments in some settings, although the strong often are privileged precisely because they have the opportunity to make the first move. Although a norm of conduct or common conjecture might suggest that the stronger should get to pick first, neither the stronger player nor the underdog can necessarily make the other do what it wants. This is true in situations like Battle of the Sexes because each knows that the other values coordination over disagreement. If the two parties disagree, the distributional issue disappears in that neither gains anything.

Now let's bring power into play as a factor affecting the outcome of the game. Let's assume that the USTR, as an agent of the U.S. government, is more powerful than Toyota. This power is reflected in its ability to inflict costs on Toyota when Toyota does not choose the USTR's preferred strategy. The effect of power is to change the payoffs. Table 8-2 shows a revised set of payoffs. Here, $c$ denotes the costs inflicted on Toyota by the USTR if Toyota does not do what the USTR wants it to do. It is easy to see that if $c = 0$ then we would be back to the game depicted in Table 8-1. With this new strategic form in mind, we can now discuss the third possible solution to the Battle of the Sexes game.

TABLE 8-2

### U.S.-Japanese Auto Trade Game with Costs

| Toyota | USTR | |
| --- | --- | --- |
| | Permit Japanese Imports | Restrict Japanese Imports |
| Build in Japan | 1−$c$, 0.5 | −$c$, 0 |
| Build in the United States | 0, 0 | 0.5, 1 |

### MIXED STRATEGY EQUILIBRIUM

Toyota has an interest in influencing the decision of the USTR and an interest in preventing the USTR from bullying Toyota into always producing cars in the United States. To fulfill these interests, Toyota needs to find a way to make the USTR just as happy to choose to permit Japanese auto imports as to choose to restrict imports. Doing so without changing the payoffs in the game (that would change the circumstance we are studying, and so would be cheating) can be done if Toyota chooses its own strategy probabilistically. This is known as a mixed strategy equilibrium.

Suppose Toyota constructs a dial such as that used in some board games or on the popular television game show *Wheel of Fortune*. One portion of the area under the dial says "Build in Japan"; the remaining portion says "Build in the United States." Suppose further that Toyota publicly commits itself to taking whichever action the pointer on the dial indicates after it has been spun. Let us say that a fair and impartial person is selected to spin the dial and to record the result. One key question is, How large should Toyota make the area that corresponds to the decision to build cars in the United States? (Note that if it makes this area equal to zero, then Toyota is following the pure strategy of always building in Japan.) A second key question arises if the USTR brings forth its own dial and offers to commit itself to whatever the spin of the dial directs. How big should it make the area that corresponds to the decision to restrict (or not restrict) imports?

Let's say that Toyota makes the area labeled "Build in Japan" equal to $p$. If $p$ falls between 0 and 1, then $1 - p$ is the proportion of the dial that corresponds to "Build in the United States." Toyota will build cars in Japan if after it is spun the pointer ends up on the part of the dial that corresponds to this action. This, of course, happens with probability $p$. Toyota needs to determine how large to make $p$ in order for the USTR to become indifferent between the choices "Permit Japanese Imports" and "Restrict Japanese Imports." That is, Toyota needs to assign a value to $p$ such that the USTR's expected utility from permitting Japanese imports equals its expected utility from restricting Japanese imports. In doing this, Toyota takes away the USTR's expectation of doing better by restricting imports and thereby eliminates the distributional problem. Notice that Toyota cannot change the USTR's utility for the different outcomes of the game, but it can change the USTR's expected utility; that is, the utilities

*In May 1995 the United States announced that trade sanctions would go into effect June 28 if Japan did not open its automobile market to the United States and compete more fairly in the United States. On June 27 U.S. Trade Representative Mickey Kantor and Japan's minister for international trade and industry, Ryutaro Hashimoto, point in opposite directions prior to their last-minute negotiations to avoid U.S. sanctions. The two governments perceived trade relations in very different ways, resulting in rancor and brinkmanship. Sanctions were narrowly avoided when an agreement was reached June 28.*

associated with each outcome times the probability the outcome will arise. It changes the expected utility by altering an action within its own control. That change consists of the probability that it chooses one or another action.

At first it might seem odd to think that decision makers choose actions probabilistically rather than just picking the action that is best for them. In strategic situations with more than or less than one pure strategy equilibrium, however, there is no single best action. The best choice for each decision maker is contingent on what other players choose. Consequently, each decision maker has an incentive to try to influence what others will choose. This can be done by keeping the other actors off balance by selecting one's own actions probabilistically. Indeed, many real-life situations call for a mixed strategy approach. Before returning to the Toyota-USTR example let me offer an illustration of the use of a mixed strategy in a historic conflict situation.

Paul Revere gained fame during the American Revolution for spreading the alarm about the direction from which the British would come. His friend mounted the belfry of the North Church in Boston with orders to signal the British strategy, "one if by land, two if by sea," according to Longfellow's famous poem. Notice that the British had kept the Americans off balance by choosing their own action probabilistically. They could have attacked from the sea or by land. Each approach had its advantages and disadvantages. The advantages of either approach would have been diminished if the revolutionaries had known in advance to concentrate their defenses on one or the other route. Thus, the mixed strategy of the British helped improve their prospects for victory by thinning the defenses of the colonists. This is a fundamental advantage of mixed strategies: it forces rivals to thin out their capabilities by not being able to concentrate them in response to a single strategic action. With that in mind, we return to the Toyota-USTR example.

The USTR's expected utility from permitting Japanese imports if Toyota builds in Japan or the United States probabilistically equals $p(0.5) + (1 - p)(0)$. That is, if it happens that the United States does not restrict imports and Toyota happens to decide to build in Japan, the USTR gains 0.5. Japan chooses to build in Japan with a probability equal to $p$ and chooses to build in the United States—not knowing in advance which choice the USTR will make—with probability $1 - p$. If Toyota builds in the United States and the USTR chooses not to restrict imports, then the USTR's utility for the outcome is 0 and that payoff arises with a chance equal to $1 - p$, so that the expected utility for the USTR if it does not restrict imports equals $p(0.5) + (1 - p)(0)$.

The USTR's expected utility from restricting Japanese imports if Toyota builds in Japan with probability $p$ equals $p(0) + (1 - p)1$. Just as in the above expected utility calculation, Toyota does not know the USTR's decision when it makes its own strategic choice, and the USTR does not know Toyota's approach when the USTR chooses whether to restrict imports or not. In either case, however, the relevant decision makers can calculate the probability that the other will select one action or the other, since they know at least all of the information that we know in making that calculation here.

The USTR is equally happy to choose either of its possible actions (restrict imports or do not restrict imports) *if it is true that Toyota picks p such that for the U.S. Trade Representative* $p(0.5) + (1 - p)(0) = p(0) + (1 - p)1$. That is, by picking the right mix between its available actions, Toyota can make the USTR's expected utility for each of its possible actions equal so that the USTR is indifferent between its strategic options. Solving for $p$, we find that if $0.5p = 1 - p$, or equivalently, $1.5p = 1$ so that $p = 2/3$, then the equality of the two choices holds for the USTR. Thus, Japan should construct a dial in which two-thirds of the area says "Build in Japan" and the remaining one-third says "Build in the United States." If Japan does this, the USTR will be equally happy permitting or restricting Toyota imports.

By the same logic, the USTR must design its dial to make Toyota just as happy to build in the United States as it would be to build in Japan. If we let $q$ equal the area of the USTR's dial that says "Permit Japanese Imports," then $1 - q$ would be the area of the dial that corresponds to the decision "Restrict Japanese Imports." Toyota, then, would reach its point of indifference when $q(1 - c) + (1 - q)(-c) = q(0) + (1 - q)(0.5)$. If $c = 0$, then $q = 1/3$. This means that two-thirds of the time when the opportunity presents itself, the USTR should restrict imports (or, perhaps, enforce a preexisting restriction) and the remaining one-third of the time it should not. If $c$ does not equal 0, however, then $q = (0.5 + c)/(1.5) = (1 + 2c)/3$.

If $c$ does not equal 0, then $q$ is greater than 1/3. Thus, the USTR should restrict Japanese imports less than two-thirds of the time and permit Japanese imports more than one-third of the time if $c$ is larger than zero.

> The Battle of the Sexes game has three Nash equilibria, two in pure strategies and one in a mixed strategy. If $c > 0.5$, is the game still Battle of the Sexes? What are the Nash equilibria of the game if $c > 0.5$? How would you characterize the changes in choices players make in this game when $c < 0.5$? When $c = 0.5$? When $c > 0.5$?

Now suppose that the USTR can impose a cost equal to 0.1 on Toyota. In this case, the USTR needs to restrict imports only 60 percent of the time to make Toyota indifferent to the choice between producing in Japan or producing in the United States. This is in contrast to having to restrict imports two-thirds of the time as was required when the costs were equal to zero.[2] As the costs that the USTR can impose on Toyota increase, so too does the attractiveness for Toyota of doing what the USTR wishes. In fact, if $c > 0.5$, then even Toyota would prefer to build cars in the United States. Thus, we can see that if the USTR's power is large enough, the distributional aspect of the problem can be eliminated through the judicious imposition of costs on Toyota. The power to punish Toyota, then, gets Toyota to do something it otherwise would not want to do. In this case, by being able to inflict enough punishment (in the form of tariffs or import quotas, for

---

[2] Remember, $q = (1 + 2c)/3$. So, if $c = 0.1$, then $q = 1.2/3 = 0.4$ and $1 - q = 0.6$. Recall that $1 - q$ is the probability that the USTR restricts Japanese imports.

example), the USTR is able to resolve the distributional problem by changing the game into one of pure coordination. Clearly, the power advantage has helped resolve the distributional problem.

If the punishment inflicted by the USTR is not large enough to eliminate the distributional problem (that is, $c < 0.5$), then an interesting thing happens when the USTR exercises its power. As c increases in size, the probability $q$ that the USTR permits Japanese auto imports will increase as well. Recall that $q = (1 + 2c)/3$. The probability that Toyota sells cars in the United States that were made in Japan equals the probability that Toyota chooses to build in Japan times the probability that the USTR does not restrict imports, or $(2/3)[(1 + 2c)/3] = (2 + 4c)/9$. If $c = 0$, then the probability that Toyota will sell cars in the United States is 2/9. If $c > 0$, however, then the probability that Toyota will sell cars in the United States is larger than 2/9. From the USTR's point of view, then, the power of the United States can provide a disadvantage as well as an advantage. The Japanese, by contrast, never really enjoy an advantage because the value of its most preferred outcome is falling (by $-c$) even as the odds that this outcome will occur increase.

Why does the increased power of the USTR increase the probability that the USTR will not restrict imports? Remember, the reason for selecting a mixed strategy—that is, for picking actions probabilistically—is to make the other player indifferent as to which choices to make so that neither player can be bullied. By spinning the dial and mixing its strategy, the USTR has made the expected utility from making cars in Japan no more (and no less) valuable to Toyota than the expected utility from making cars in the United States. To maintain this equality, what must happen as the value for Toyota drops by c from building cars in Japan when the USTR does not restricts imports? The USTR, to maintain the indifference it contrived to make Toyota feel, must compensate by increasing the odds that it will not restrict imports. Although the USTR's power can make Toyota do something it otherwise would not do, it also can make the USTR do something it otherwise would not do too. Thus, resorting to power as a solution to the distributional problem can be a double-edged sword, especially if the power advantage is not large enough or if uncertainty makes the optimal punishment unknown. Indeed, there are many instances in which the exercise of power to restrict trade has led to perverse consequences, such as an increase in profits for the producers whose trade was restricted (Yoffie 1993; Yoffie and Gomes-Casseres 1994).

## INTERNATIONAL ORGANIZATIONS: AN ALTERNATIVE TO OR REFLECTION OF POWER?

Let's consider one more example of a distributional problem to see how such problems can be resolved without resorting to the exercise of power. The world of international commercial aviation presents coordination and distributional problems just like the ones that might arise in a trade war or even on a battlefield.

English is the language used for all ground-to-air and air-to-ground communications in international aviation. Pilots and ground controllers in Beijing, Paris, Harare, and Bogotá talk to pilots from Germany, Japan, Mexico, and Egypt in English. Even Jordanian pilots, who are native speakers of Arabic, and Egyptian ground controllers, who also are native speakers of Arabic, communicate in English. Of course, each country would prefer that these communications were in its own language, but none wants international commercial aviation to involve the use of multiple languages. Doing so would make the risk of miscommunication and accidents too high. To avoid this, all nations have agreed on a convention as the solution to this particular coordination problem. The solution happens to be the use of English. This could be because the United States, Britain, Australia, or some other English-speaking country pressured others into such an agreement, or it could just be that there was general agreement that English makes sense because it is the world's most commonly spoken second language. If the latter is true, does this imply that an exercise of power by any state over other states has occurred? Behavior changed, but the new, agreed-upon behavior serves everyone's interest.

When you and some of your friends choose sides for a game or divide a cake or pizza, how do you decide on the distribution? Does the solution differ from when there are only two of you dividing a pizza to when there are three or more of you dividing the same pizza? Do you settle these problems by using power or by some other means (for example, choosing sides; flipping a coin; following a rule like "you divide, I choose")?

Solving coordination problems is fundamental to producing cooperative international relations. Imposing costs through the exercise of power is one way of solving such problems, as we just saw in the automobile trade example. But so are several random choice mechanisms like flipping a coin or spinning a dial. These solutions are based not on power but, rather, on recognition of the importance of the problem's coordination aspects. When power cannot ensure one side the ability to impose its will—as when the USTR could not raise costs to Toyota above 0.5—then the exercise of power is not the only way, or even the best way, to resolve these coordination and distributional problems (Brams and Taylor 1996).

When distributional problems are linked to coordination problems, there is a common alternative to the use of power for addressing differences. This alternative means involves the use of international organizations and international laws and norms. I touch on how these organizations influence cooperation here, addressing this matter in greater depth in Chapter 14.

International institutions help states constrain their own actions so that they do not do things that are beneficial in the short term but harmful in the long term. Institutions such as the United Nations, the World Trade Organization, the International Postal Union, and the law of the sea agreement provide a means to solve commitment problems so that the promises leaders make on behalf of their state are credible (North and Weingast 1989; Root 1989). They offer a setting in which agreements to cooperate are brought in line with the self-interest of each of the agreement's signatories. When the issues in dispute are purely about coordination, these institutions can be very effective in apprehending solutions. When they involve both coordination and distributional concerns, such institutions may still be helpful, but they cannot fully resolve members' differences (Morrow 1994b; Simmons 1994). In these cases, the problems of bargaining, especially during a crisis, are more difficult to surmount (Morgan 1984; Banks 1990) and the prospects of only limited or partial coordination are magnified (Downs and Jones 2002).

Formal international organizations or informal regimes—networks of decision makers intended to facilitate coordination and to promote cooperation—provide a routinized means of reducing problems between states. However, they cannot fully resolve coordination and distributional problems because it is simply not possible to do so when there is uncertainty about what it is best to do (Morrow 1994b). And such uncertainty is characteristic of the coexistence of distributional and coordination issues. This is true because the distributional issues disputed between states prompt each state's leaders to provide misleading information. Consequently, one cannot completely trust the information provided as part of any deliberation over an international issue. Leaders lie or bluff in an effort to steer outcomes in a way that benefits them and their country at the expense of others. As in the Battle of the Sexes game, there is no solution that is best for all parties involved.

Some states use environmental policies as a means of erecting nontariff trade barriers to restrict free trade. Although each state benefits from trade that does not limit its own ability to sell goods, there can be substantial political benefits from protecting domestic industries while gaining free access to foreign markets. Therefore, state leaders have an incentive to encourage trade (the coordination issue) while finding ways (such as through use of tariffs and nontariff barriers) to disproportionately benefit their constituents (the distributional issue). The NAFTA agreement, for example, was not signed by the United States until Mexico had made several environmental concessions. Many people see these environmental restrictions as thinly veiled efforts to stymie the flow of business activity and jobs from the United States to Mexico. In another example, European restrictions on irradiated foods may reflect genuine health concerns, but they may also reflect European efforts to limit the amount of American produce that enters into competition with European produce in the European marketplace.

International organizations such as the World Trade Organization help adjudicate these types of differences. Still, the WTO does not have the resources to thoroughly investigate claims independently. It must rely on others for information. As such, the WTO cannot eliminate uncertainty about whether European objections to American produce are motivated by health concerns or, rather, by a desire to get around free trade agreements. Likewise, it is difficult to determine to what extent American environmental restrictions reflect a genuine concern with improving the environment and to what extent they reflect a desire to restrict trade. They may well reflect both concerns. It is just this type of information that interested parties have an incentive to distort. Nevertheless, the threat of exposure and punishment is often sufficient to discipline governments into abandoning or reducing nontariff barriers to free trade (Keohane and Nye 1977; Krasner 1983; Milgrom, North, and Weingast 1990; Greif, Milgrom, and Weingast 1994). In this way, the coordination issue is diminished, facilitating trade, and the distributional issue is at least mitigated.

International organizations, when erected as part of a Nash equilibrium strategy, are a way of promoting cooperation by resolving coordination issues. Equilibria are self-enforcing by definition. After all, when strategy choices are a Nash equilibrium, no one has a unilateral incentive to switch to a different strategy. Therefore, when an institution is erected as part of an equilibrium to solve a coordination problem, the solution is likely to persist and be effective. So, when coordination problems loom larger than distributional problems, we should expect to see international organizations cropping up and proving effective. Unfortunately, there are no foolproof solutions, through international organizations or otherwise, to solve coordination problems that combine with distributional problems.

When distributional issues arise among members of an international organization, a key difficulty in resolving the attendant disputes involves monitoring compliance with the proposed agreement. Recognizing when a member is cheating on an agreement can be very difficult. A cheater has an incentive to hide the fact that he or she is cheating. To be able to monitor compliance effectively, international organizations need the resources to gather information independently of their member states (Axelrod and Keohane 1986). But international organizations receive resources exclusively from their member states. Since cheating can prove beneficial to at least some members of an international organization, few will have the independent means to acquire information, monitor cheating, and enforce punishments. The power of individual self-interest may override the coordination benefits the organization can provide.

A classic example of an international organization that faces both distributional and coordination issues is the oil cartel OPEC. OPEC faces at least two severe strains on its effectiveness. One is that many oil-producing

Does the United Nations have independent ways to enforce the decisions reached by its member states? Can you think of examples of UN resolutions that are strictly enforced and others that are not strictly enforced? How might we explain these differences? Are they related to the relative power of the supporters and opponents of the resolutions in question?

states do not belong to OPEC. Russia (the world's largest oil-producing country), Mexico, Norway, and Britain, for example, are all major producers of oil that do not belong to OPEC. If the OPEC members agree to cut production to raise the price of crude oil, these nonmember countries generally increase production to pick up the slack and thereby make more money. As a result, OPEC has a hard time promoting its objective of providing its members with stable, high oil prices. This difficulty is associated with a second, internal, problem. Many OPEC members cheat. That is, they agree to an assigned production quota and then produce much more. Nigeria, for example, is generally believed to produce and sell far beyond its assigned quota. OPEC simply does not have the means to monitor production adequately and to punish cheaters. OPEC is unable to resolve the distributional problem faced by its member states. In failing to coordinate behavior sufficiently to push the price of crude oil up over the past three decades (except for a few years of "oil shocks" in the 1970s), OPEC has allowed all of its member states to suffer. The real, inflation-adjusted price of oil today is about what it was in 1970.

The failure of OPEC also shows how the strong can be weak. Saudi Arabia is by far the most powerful member of OPEC. That country has more proven oil reserves than its competitors and can extract its crude more cheaply than other countries because its oil is so readily accessible. Yet the Saudis' power has not benefitted OPEC. Saudi Arabia's power to push prices up or down by altering its own production apparently is insufficient to change the behavior of the cartel's other members. Neither power nor an international organization designed to fix oil prices has proven sufficient to overcome market competition and the distributional issues that divide the producer states. Indeed, so strong is the self-interest of each oil-exporting country and its leaders that even with the

*Ali Rodriguez-Araque, the secretary-general of the Organization of Petroleum-Exporting Countries (OPEC), meets with Iranian president Mohammad Khatami to discuss oil policy. By meeting with leaders of OPEC's member states, Dr. Rodriguez-Araque is attempting to resolve distribution issues and create a unified policy to govern oil production and export.*

embargo on Iraqi oil—Iraq was a large producer before the Gulf War—the price of oil dropped almost continuously between January 1996 and December 1998. By late summer 1998, crude oil was selling for about half of what it had cost in 1996. By the end of 1998, it was even cheaper.

The examples discussed thus far reflect problems involving outcomes. International organizations constitute one alternative to power as a means to shape outcomes. But neither international organizations nor power differences alone are sufficient to resolve international issues involving both coordination and distributional problems. We must be careful. Drawing inferences about power from outcomes can be misleading, or at least

MAP 8-1
**How Secure Is the World's Oil Supply?**

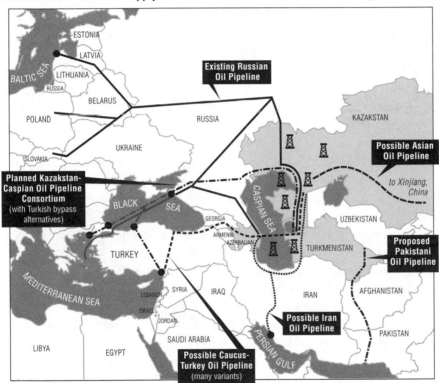

*Azerbaijan, Turkmenistan, and Kazakstan are shaded in gray. These are important oil-producing countries in the Caspian region currently working to expand their access to oil markets by building or improving pipelines and shipping routes. The map shows existing and proposed oil pipelines and shipping ports (denoted with dots). As we think about the importance of Caspian oil in the future it is striking that most of the pipelines run through politically unstable areas. The world's industry runs on oil, and higher oil prices contribute significantly to inflation, especially in the world's poorer countries. What are the likely international consequences if the Caspian governments prove to be unstable or unreliable guarantors of oil contracts in the future?*

may generate an outlook that often offends our intuitive sense of power. The earlier example of the bombing of Tripoli involving the United States, France, and Libya was intended to highlight this fact. Saudi Arabia's failure to reign in the other members of OPEC also illustrates this point. Drawing inferences about power from observing relations or outcomes has still other important limitations. To see why, let's first consider the use of force as the exercise of power and then consider cases in which a seemingly weaker state emerged victorious in war over an apparently more powerful adversary.

## POWER AND MOTIVATION

The Vietnam War is a textbook example of how a weaker power (North Vietnam) can overcome a more powerful opponent (the United States) as a result of asymmetry of motivation. If we take power to mean the relative military capabilities or national wealth of the two combatants, then there can be no real doubt that the United States was much, much more powerful than North Vietnam. Yet it was the North Vietnamese who won. In this case the cost of winning the war was higher than the United States was willing to bear. The costs to the Vietnamese, by contrast, were not higher than they were willing to tolerate. This tolerance for loss favored the seemingly weaker North Vietnamese, even though the costs in lost life and destroyed property were much higher for North Vietnam than for the United States. Simply put, North Vietnam was highly *motivated* to win; the United States was not (George, Hall, and Simons 1971). This is not too surprising. For the North Vietnamese, national survival and national identity were at stake. The United States had nothing of such importance at risk in the war. The example of the Vietnam War proves that it is a mistake to think that power alone determines who wins wars and who loses wars, unless we define power tautologically to mean who wins and who loses.

Stating that the more powerful state always wins is either circular or naive. If it were true without being circular, then we would have to ask why wars even occur. Surely if the weak know they will always lose they will instead negotiate a solution and avoid the terrible costs of war (Fearon 1995; Powell 1999). This is an important point. If it were clear in advance who the winner and loser were going to be, then there would always be a solution to the dispute that for both sides was at least as good as fighting. This solution would require that the prospective loser grant before a war whatever concessions would have been coerced out of it after a war. This is more attractive than fighting because the prospective loser (and winner) saves costs in life, property, and forgone opportunities.

We can easily see why asymmetry in motivation can determine the outcome of a dispute by returning to our examination of the Vietnam War and focusing on national capabilities as a way of thinking about power. As we saw in Chapter 7, capabilities consist of resources relevant to waging war, such as wealth, size of the military, and the like. The GNP of each state in a war is a convenient and frequently used indicator of the potential power or capabilities of each participant (Organski and Kugler 1980; Oneal 1989). To assess the potential capabilities of the three belligerents in the Vietnam War—the United States, South Vietnam, and North Vietnam—we must know their respective GNPs at the time. In 1965 (arguably the first full year of the war) the United States had a GNP of approximately $690 billion, South Vietnam had a GNP of approximately $3 billion, and North Vietnam had a GNP of approximately $2 billion. Clearly, the GNP of the United States dwarfed the combined wealth of North and South Vietnam. We can think of the probability that the combination of the United States and South Vietnam would win the war as being equal to the sum of their GNPs (690 + 3) divided by the sum of all three GNPs (690 + 3 + 2). This is known as an odds ratio and is a common way of thinking about the relationship between relative resources or capabilities and the probability of one or another side winning in a dispute. Using this approach, the probability of a U.S.–South Vietnamese victory can be estimated to equal 693/695, or 99.7 percent. Even if we assume that the marginal value of wealth decreases with each added dollar, so that we take the logarithm of the relevant GNPs, the odds ratio comes out to 91.7 percent.

Two facts are noteworthy about the estimate of the odds that the U.S.–South Vietnam partnership would win the war. First, and most obviously, the United States had the lion's share of national capabilities that could have been brought to bear in the war. Second, even by this crude estimate, there was a small chance that the North Vietnamese would win. Their odds of winning were not zero. However long the odds, North Vietnam had a slim chance of victory—a chance that materialized into fact. With such seemingly strong odds for a U.S.–South Vietnamese rout, it is no wonder that President Lyndon Johnson and Gen. William C. Westmoreland maintained throughout the war that victory was close. Without the contribution of the United States, the comparable estimate of victory by South Vietnam would have been only 3/5, or 60 percent. This tells us that the American contribution was essential to giving the South the (misplaced, as it turned out) confident expectation of a decisive victory.

Although the United States had the lion's share of capabilities, we must recognize that the United States did not mobilize all of its national resources for the war effort. In World War II—a war of much greater import to American interests—the United States mobilized about 46 percent of its GNP at the peak of the war. This was an extraordinary effort. After all, resources must be left for civilian uses as well. People must eat, be clothed, sheltered, and so forth even in the worst of times. In contrast, in Vietnam the United States spent well under 5 percent of its GNP on the war effort. At the same time, North Vietnam was spending every spare dollar.

We can assess the relative motivation of the United States in the Vietnam War by estimating the intensity of its preference for victory much as we estimated Spain and Portugal's motivation to support Columbus's quest for a westward route to the Indies in Chapter 3. In fact, we can state the role of power, measured as relative national capabilities, and of motivation as a general set of principles by constructing a model or simplified representation of the process by which leaders of any state decide to partici-pate on one side or the other in a war or to remain neutral.

Suppose there are three states, called A, B, and C. A and C are fighting a war against each other. B is trying to decide between helping A, helping C, or staying out of the fight altogether. If the national capabilities of A = $a$, of B = $b$, and of C = $c$, then we can say that the probability that A wins if B helps A equals $(a + b)/(a + b + c)$ and the probability that C wins with B's help equals $(b + c)/(a + b + c)$. These are the odds ratios that that partic-ular outcome will occur. We can simplify our notation by substituting $P_{BA}$ for $(a + b)/(a + b + c)$ and $P_{BC}$ for $(b + c)/(a + b + c)$. This notation is the same as writing out the phrases "the chance that nation A will win its war with nation C if nation B helps A" and "the chance that nation C will win its war with nation A if B helps C," respectively. Let's also say that the amount B values a victory by A (B's utility) is equal to $U_{BA}$, whereas the amount B values a victory by C (again, B's utility) is equal to $U_{BC}$. Now let's make $K_{BA}$ the cost B expects to endure in helping A against C and $K_{BC}$ the cost B expects to endure in helping C against A. Note that these two "cost terms" are not the actual costs experienced over the whole war but, rather, the costs anticipated at any given juncture if B helps A or if B helps C. They are expectations because the actual costs cannot be known before the war is over. We will assume that B expects to incur no transaction costs if it stays neutral.

If nation B decides to help nation A, then B's expected utility is

$$P_{BA}U_{BA} + (1 - P_{BA})U_{BC} - K_{BA}.^3 \tag{8.1}$$

This expression is a shorthand way of saying that there is a chance that nation A will win with B's help, and that chance is equal to $P_{BA}$. There is also a chance that A will lose even though it receives help from B. The probability that this will occur is equal to $1 - P_{BA}$. Expression 8.1 takes into account the fact that if A wins, then B derives some value from that outcome and that value is equal to $U_{BA}$. If A loses, B also derives some value (of course, it might be a displeasing value, or loss) and that value is equal to $U_{BC}$. Finally, whether A wins or loses, expression 8.1 reflects the fact that there will be costs associated with B's participation (such as lost property, lost lives, and perhaps lost domestic politi-cal support for the leader). These costs are equal to $K_{BA}$, and they must be subtracted from the utilities expected to be obtained from the war's outcome. The probabilities, utilities, and costs in expression 8.1 are variables—that is, each can take on many differ-ent values. We will be concerned with figuring out what the values and relations among the variables must be to predict that B will help A or that B will help C or that B will stay out of the fight altogether.

---

[3] Here we assume that the decision maker in question (B) neither attaches extra value to taking risks nor attaches extra value to avoiding risks, so that B is assumed to be risk neutral. If this were not so, the expression would be written as follows: $(P_{BA})[U(Join_{BA} - K_{BA})] + (1 - P_{BA})[U(Join_{BC} - K_{BA})]$.

If nation B decides to help nation C, then B's expected utility is

$$P_{BC}U_{BC} + (1 - P_{BC})U_{BA} - K_{BC}. \qquad (8.2)$$

Nation B decides which action to take by comparing these two expected utilities, just as Ferdinand chose between backing Columbus and not backing Columbus by comparing the expected costs and benefits of each of his alternatives. Nation B can take one of the following three predicted actions:

1. If expression 8.1 is larger than expression 8.2, then B should help A in its war effort against C because B expects to end up better off by helping A than by helping C or remaining neutral.
2. If expression 8.1 is less than expression 8.2, then B should help C in its war effort against A because B expects to end up better off by helping C than by helping A or remaining neutral.
3. If expression 8.1 is equal to expression 8.2, then B won't care which outcome occurs and so will remain neutral.

The action that B takes will depend on B's interests (the utility terms), tempered by its ability to impose its will (the probability terms) and the costs associated with promoting its interests (the cost term). Nation B will take whichever of these actions (help A, help C, or remain neutral) that will most enhance its own welfare (B's expected utility).

With the expected utility values stated explicitly, let's rearrange expressions 8.1 and 8.2 by using a little algebra so that we can directly address questions of motivation and power. The decision problem for B can be stated as follows:

What does our discussion suggest about neutrality? Nations often declare themselves neutral during wars, but how likely is it that they are really completely neutral? If a country has a slight interest in seeing one side or another win in a conflict, can it be truly neutral? When a country says it will not sell arms to either side in a war, is this neutrality? What if it had never before sold arms to one belligerent but had in the past sold arms to the other belligerent? Would cutting off arms sales in this case really be an instance of neutrality?

$$P_{BA}U_{BA} + (1 - P_{BA})U_{BC} - K_{BA} > \text{ or } < \text{ or } = P_{BC}U_{BC} + (1 - P_{BC})U_{BA} - K_{BC}.$$

By rearranging the terms we get

$$(P_{BA} + P_{BC} - 1)(U_{BA} - U_{BC}) > \text{ or } < \text{ or } = K_{BA} - K_{BC}. \qquad (8.3)$$

273

If we make use of the definitions given above for $P_{BA}$ and $P_{BC}$ in terms of national capabilities, we can rewrite expression 8.3 as follows:

$$[b/(a + b + c)](U_{BA} - U_{BC}) > \text{or} < \text{or} = K_{BA} - K_{BC}. \tag{8.4}$$

The term in brackets, $b/(a + b + c)$, is exactly equal to $P_{BA} + P_{BC} - 1$ and reflects the proportion of resources that B can bring to bear in the fight. The utility term, $U_{BA} - U_{BC}$, measures B's level of motivation to help bring about a victory for A compared with a victory for C. The right-hand side of equations 8.3 and 8.4 reflects the marginal difference in costs from helping A or helping C. Study this expression for a little while and you will see that it is really not complicated at all. What it says is that the decision to help one side or the other in a war (or any dispute) depends on one's ability to influence the outcome, one's level of motivation, and the costliness of becoming involved. We might look at it in a bit more of a sophisticated way and say that how involved one country is likely to become in a fight between two other countries depends on how big its expectation of gain is from getting involved. In this case, we might be able to predict the degree of involvement as well as the side on whose behalf that involvement occurs (Banks 1990).

Equation 8.4 offers one explanation of the U.S. defeat in Vietnam. It also provides several interesting generalizations that help shed light on how seemingly weak states can succeed against seemingly powerful states. Here we will see that even a simple algebraic representation of policy choices can reveal important ideas that may otherwise be overlooked in the study of power and international relations.

Satisfy yourself that equation 8.3 is just a rearrangement of the difference between expressions 8.1 and 8.2. Then assure yourself that $P_{BA} + P_{BC} - 1 = b/(a + b + c)$ if $P_{BA} = (a + b)/(a + b + c)$ and $P_{BC} = (b + c)/(a + b + c)$ and $(a + b + c)/(a + b + c) = 1$. What does equation 8.4 imply about the importance of national security concerns in a great power's decision to join in a war? What does it imply about the importance of a smaller power's national security concerns?

To simplify the development of useful generalizations, let's assume that nation B prefers to see nation A win the war (that is, $U_{BA} > U_{BC}$). (Of course, we could just as readily assume that B prefers to see C win, or that B prefers neutrality; the generalizations will hold in each case.) If B prefers to see A win, then we should ask under what circumstances will the left side of equation 8.4 be larger than the right side?

What factors increase the chance that $[b/(a + b + c)](U_{BA} - U_{BC}) > K_{BA} - K_{BC}$? To answer this question, let's make use of some hypothetical values. Suppose $K_{BA} - K_{BC}$ is equal to 1. Now suppose that B is a weak country compared with A and C. In fact, B possesses only 10 percent of the total capabilities of A, B, and C combined. This means that the marginal contribution B can make to the war's outcome, $b/(a + b + c)$, is equal to 0.1. In order for $[b/(a + b + c)](U_{BA} - U_{BC})$ to be greater than $K_{BA} - K_{BC}$, or, equivalently, in order for $(0.1)(U_{BA} - U_{BC})$ to be greater than 1, $U_{BA} - U_{BC}$ must be bigger than 10.

Compare this motivation with the same calculation when B's contribution to the capabilities side of the equation is much larger—say, when it is 0.8 instead of 0.1. When B controls 80 percent of the capabilities that influence the war's outcome, then B's motivation for wanting to see A defeat C need only be a little more than 1.25. As B's power (in terms of national capabilities) goes up relative to that of the other belligerents, the level of motivation required of B to see one side or the other prevail can afford to go down. Of course, the actual motivation does not change just because the distribution of power changes among the belligerents, but the threshold value that the motivation must achieve does change. This is a very important point because it suggests some surprises about foreign disputes, power, and national actions.

If a nation is very powerful (in terms of some measure of national capabilities) relative to its foes, then it is comparatively easy to satisfy equation 8.4 and, therefore, to participate in wars even when the nation in question is not highly motivated with respect to the outcome. But when a state is relatively weak compared with its foes, it must be especially motivated with respect to that outcome in order to fight. Thus, a behemoth like the United States could fight in the Vietnam War even though it was not particularly motivated with respect to the war's outcome—that is, even though no vital national security interests were at stake. A country like North Vietnam, by contrast, could only have fought against the United States if it was *very* highly motivated to win. This means that as the costs of a war rise above expected levels, those who are least motivated are more likely to give up the fight before those who are highly motivated.

As the costs in Vietnam mounted, and as political costs at home rose with the increased opposition to the war, the people and the government of the United States gradually shifted their attitude about the war, eventually preferring to lose "with honor" rather than continue to fight and endure costs that exceeded the expected benefits. The Vietnamese could stand higher costs because they were much more highly motivated to win the war. Their high level of motivation compensated for their weakness in tangible national resources such as manpower, guns, food, and so forth.

Now we can make some sense of the U.S. defeat in Vietnam. We have just seen that, contrary to the argument that power can best be evaluated after the fact by looking at who was victorious, the strong can lose to the weak because of asymmetry in motivation (George, Hall, and Simons 1971; Altfeld and Bueno de Mesquita 1979). If the United States had been as motivated as the North Vietnamese, it seems a virtual certainty that the United States would have won because it would have been prepared to endure more costs and because it would have constrained itself less in how it chose to fight. The United States, for example, never even attempted a land invasion of North Vietnam, choosing instead only to fight a war to restore the status quo prior to the onset of hostilities. The United States was not motivated to take over North Vietnam; it was concerned only with preventing North Vietnam from taking over South Vietnam. Of course, there was never an issue of North Vietnam taking over the United States. That surely would have increased America's motivation to win to a much, much higher level than the U.S. motivation just to see South Vietnam win. Apparently, many people confuse defeat with weakness in power. Victory or defeat depends on the power, or resources, to win *and the will to win*. Compared with the North Vietnamese, the United States had plenty of the former, but relatively little of the latter.

The outcome of any dispute, whether it be a military dispute, a trade war, a contract negotiation, or all-out war, depends on the expected costs and benefits. These expectations, in turn, depend on national capabilities (colloquially, power), anticipated costs, and motivation. Powerful states are perfectly prepared to fight in wars about which they do not care much, although they are unlikely to continue to fight if they endure high costs in such wars; relatively weak states are prepared to fight and endure high costs only

*A 1967 protest in Kansas City, Missouri (left), the American heartland, reflects the fact that a cross-section of the American population had turned against the Vietnam War. When protests became broad based and not just limited to Washington, New York, or elite college campuses, the U.S. government began to rethink its commitment to the war. The American population was unwilling to make a large sacrifice to attain victory in Vietnam. In contrast, the North Vietnamese and Vietcong seemed prepared to endure almost any hardship in pursuit of their goals. To the right we see a Vietcong soldier crouched in a bunker with an SKS rifle. Notice how poorly equipped he is. He wears flip flops into battle, rather than combat boots. His Russian-made weapon, inferior to the Russian AK47, had a limited range and was not fully automatic. American soldiers, by contrast, were excellently outfitted, carried the best available weapons, and were supported by an enormous and effective infrastructure. What the Vietcong and Vietnamese lacked in support services they more than made up for by their enormous resolve to fight on at almost any cost.*

in wars about which they care intensely. Knowing the relative power of rivals is not, by itself, sufficient to anticipate the outcome of a dispute. Power is not the only factor that gets one actor to change its behavior to be in compliance with the wishes of another actor. Motivation cannot be ignored in the calculation of outcomes.

The asymmetry of motivation can take on many guises. In the case of the Vietnam War, the motivational advantage of the North Vietnamese was stimulated by the fact that their national survival was at risk. For them, weakness was a regrettable accompanying fact of life. Sometimes, however, weakness itself can be the source of a motivational advantage.

Take, for example, the unusual situation between Prussia (a strong state) and Bavaria (a weak state) in 1850.[4] Bavaria and Prussia were generally on friendly terms. When a dispute arose over access to a strategically important road in the German principality of Hesse, both the Bavarian government and the Prussian government desired a peaceful resolution. The Bavarians, being weak, had little bargaining leverage and so could not anticipate doing very well in negotiations. What is more, they were fearful that if the Prussians chose to take advantage by attacking, then Bavaria would have no choice but to give in to Prussia's demands.

Fearing a crushing defeat and being reluctant to surrender, which would have left Bavaria vulnerable to future crushing defeats, the Bavarians decided that their only viable response was to attack first. It was their hope that the Prussians would not view access to the strategic road to be sufficiently important to justify a war with their German brethren. Indeed, the Bavarians hoped that the Prussians would back down rather than risk having this minor dispute escalate into a larger war involving many of the great powers of Europe. The Bavarian gamble paid off. After one very brief skirmish, the Bavarian military force of well under 10,000 found itself victorious over the Prussians, who had mobilized an army of about 140,000. The Prussians gave in, not out of weakness but out of a lack of motivation. Otto von Manteuffel, the Prussian minister president and foreign minister decided not to escalate hostilities against the Bavarian forces. Rather, he ordered an evacuation, and no further fighting took place. Indeed, Manteuffel's ascent to power was largely sparked by his desire to avoid war—a war described by a London newspaper as "the beginning of a bloody drama that is now unfolding itself, and that nobody will triumph in except Germany's enemies" (*Times of London,* November 13, 1850).

Bavaria's motivation to attack was a product of its weakness. If it had had more power with which to influence negotiations, Bavaria almost certainly would have pursued that course. But, lacking bargaining chips, it created leverage by attacking its stronger rival. Here, then, we have an example in which a motivational advantage is not incidentally associated with weakness; rather, it is the product of weakness. The situation

---

[4] For a more detailed discussion of this dispute, see Bruce Bueno de Mesquita and David Lalman (1992), esp. chap. 4. See also Chapter 10 in this volume.

between Bavaria and Prussia in 1850 illustrates how easily we can be misled by ignoring motivation and considering only capabilities in explaining how power influences the resolution of disputes. It was a situation not unlike that between terrorists, who are weak, and their foes, who are strong.

## ASYMMETRIC MOTIVATION AND COSTS

Asymmetries in motivation can be the product of several factors, each of which may prove large enough in specific instances to overcome an apparent military disadvantage. We have already seen how differences in the perceived importance of the issue in dispute can influence the willingness to resist threats and real punishment. Asymmetries in expected costs can also be critical. Here, however, it is vital to distinguish between costs borne in the form of lost lives and property and costs borne in the form of domestic political burdens. Political costs are frequently overlooked when one examines the outcome of international disputes, although calculations about political costs and benefits can easily outweigh apparent power advantages.

It is evident that expected losses in life and property influence decisions to exercise power. The toll of lost life for America during the Vietnam War was terrible. More than fifty thousand Americans died fighting a war whose very purpose was questioned by the home population. North Vietnam bore a much greater loss of life, both in absolute numbers and as a proportion of its total population. A huge percentage of North Vietnamese who were in or about to enter the most productive years of their lives died in the war. Still, North Vietnam's leaders faced no visible domestic opposition—that, of course, is one of the strengths and weaknesses of an autocratic dictatorship—whereas the American president endured enormous political opposition. It is to this domestic opposition that I now wish to turn.

Leaders inevitably must pay a price to gain support for their decisions from actors whose backing is essential. These costs are the political quid pro quos that leaders extend to followers, to neutrals, to actors on the sidelines of an issue, and even to opponents to entice them to give their support, consent, or neutrality, or at the very least to reduce their opposition to the courses of action the leaders wish to follow. How large this price is, however, varies with domestic political arrangements. In democracies, where opposition is encouraged, the price for disagreeing with the government is relatively low, so leaders must pay more to gain support. In dictatorships, where opponents often find themselves imprisoned, exiled, or executed, the price of opposition is terribly high indeed, so leaders need not make great concessions to muster support.

The political price paid by a leader may include anything potential supporters want that leaders can give. At the crudest level there is what Americans call "political pork"—that is, acquiring resources to build a bridge, factory, road, post office, school, or some other socially or economically desirable project designed to benefit a specific constituency

(Ferejohn 1974; Weingast, Shepsle, and Johnsen 1981). Pork often is given in exchange for support of a policy that a leader wishes to have enacted. A different, possibly more severe political cost involves making policy concessions to meet the objections of the opposition. President Bill Clinton, for example, held up the NAFTA deal negotiated between President George H. W. Bush and the Mexican government until he had succeeded in extracting concessions from Mexico's leaders to satisfy labor unions and environmentalists (Kugler 1994; Conybeare, McCarthy, and Zinkula 1995). These constituents had opposed the NAFTA legislation as it had been negotiated by Bush. Although labor unions and most environmental groups had not given much political support to Bush, they represented important constituencies to Clinton. Naturally, concessions can take many forms, including trade-offs between one issue and another. In exchange for support on one policy, the leaders agree to do what the opposition wants on another policy.

When the political costs of pursuing a particular policy become too high, the policy is likely to be modified or even abandoned. In such cases, even a seemingly weak adversary can emerge victorious. Consider the experience of the United States in Somalia in the 1990s. Gen. Hussein Aidid, the Somali leader in Mogadishu, succeeded in forcing President Clinton to withdraw American troops from Somalia. Clearly, no one thought that Aidid was stronger than the United States. And the financial and human costs of compelling Aidid to bend to the will of the UN and the United States were small. These costs could not explain the American withdrawal and Aidid's apparent victory. What drove the American decision to withdraw were the damaging attacks from domestic political opponents against Clinton's leadership in foreign affairs immediately following the ambush of a group of U.S. soldiers that resulted in casualties. The devastating television images of the body of one American soldier being dragged through the streets of Mogadishu and defiled by a jeering mob gave an opening to Republican opponents and Democratic dissidents to pillory the president's foreign policy leadership, or lack thereof. Foreign policy was not where the American administration wanted the nation's attention focused, so the president decided the attacks engendered political costs that were too high to maintain the U.S. commitment to the UN in Somalia.

Much the same thing happened when President Ronald Reagan decided to withdraw the U.S. military from Lebanon in 1982 after a terrorist ran a truck full of dynamite into the American marine compound, killing more than 240 soldiers. It was a grievous loss, but certainly the United States could still have brought its Syrian adversary to heel. However, midterm elections were looming and Reagan's chief of staff, James Baker, lobbied hard to get America's soldiers out of harm's way before the election. His political efforts won the day. Power politics and foreign policy considerations were set aside to pave the way for Republican electoral victories. Critics could not believe that Syria's President Hafez al-Assad could expel the mighty United States from Lebanon. But America's leaders were simply unwilling to pay the domestic political price necessary to exercise U.S. power effectively.

One could make a long list of examples where a seemingly powerful nation was defeated by an apparently weaker nation. But the two just given sufficiently make the point. Leaders are guided by their calculations of whether the political benefits tied to their policies exceed the political price that pursuing those policies requires. This calculation of political costs is a critical determinant of strategy in decision making and represents a major aspect of leadership. Leaders succumb or triumph on how well they balance their desire to push their policies and their need to compromise to shore up support. These are opposite pressures, each working at the expense of the other, and successful leaders maneuver well within the two extremes. Some tend more to compromise, others to stand firm. In all cases in which the opposition has the potential to block a measure or to extort concessions, inevitably, there is a compromise between the desire for a policy and the need for political support. Such compromises sometimes mean that calculations of political costs and benefits dominate calculations of power politics; in such instances, it is not uncommon for the weak to triumph over the strong.

When politicians emphasize compromise over standing firm, we sometimes describe them as pragmatists; when we support the principles they have abandoned, we call them

*The effective use of power requires enough motivation to endure the hardships that combat entails. Many in the Middle East were surprised when President Reagan ordered the withdrawal of American marines from Beirut, Lebanon, following a terrorist attack on U.S. marine barracks on October 23, 1983. Here we see rescuers preparing to lower an American marine onto a stretcher. The domestic political fallout from costs like this apparently exceeded the expected benefits, leading to the American withdrawal.*

opportunists. The presence of opportunistic politicians creates an interesting anomaly in the conduct of foreign affairs, an anomaly hinted at in our earlier discussion of how a large power can readily participate in disputes in which it has no vital national security interests at stake. Of importance in these instances is that the political costs to leaders who decide to engage in these disputes are low, even if the actual material costs in life and property are relatively high. An example of a very big foreign policy decision that involved very low political costs but terribly onerous implementation costs was the decision of U.S. leaders in December 1941 to enter into war with Japan.

After the attack on Pearl Harbor, the U.S. leadership's decision to prosecute the war was politically cost free, whereas the human and economic costs of staying in that war were inevitably high. So low were the political costs that even today we rarely pause to ask whether or not the Japanese attack represented a fundamental threat to American security. From the Japanese perspective, the attack on Pearl Harbor was designed to keep the United States out of the war and to keep the United States from imposing costs on Japan in the Pacific. Obviously, few Americans saw the event in this light. Yet decades later, American scholars could and did argue that the United States faced no clear and present danger following the attack on Pearl Harbor (Wohlstetter 1962; Russett 1972).

During the decades of the cold war there appeared to be almost no political costs for elites on either side of the Iron Curtain who advocated deterrence policies that were terribly expensive to maintain and that, if acted out, could have cost tens or hundreds of millions of lives. During the Cuban Missile Crisis of 1962 the world came within a hair of worldwide nuclear war. It is now known—although it was not at the time—that the Soviet commander in Cuba had asked Moscow whether to use the nuclear weaponry at his disposal in case of a U.S. invasion, and that Moscow had replied that he should "use his judgment." Evidently, the commander had decided that he would make use of his nuclear arsenal to repel a U.S. invasion. Mercifully for all of us, the United States did not invade, although this option was given serious consideration.

Many of President Kennedy's advisers urged invasion. A taped conversation between Kennedy and Democratic senator Richard Russell of Georgia, a powerful and respected Senate leader at the time, reveals that Russell pressed Kennedy to invade rather than blockade Cuba to show U.S. resolve and protect U.S. credibility. It was a reason frequently given to justify a tough posture toward the Soviet Union. Of course, Russell did not know that the Soviet Union had placed tactical nuclear weapons on the island, and he did not know that the Soviet commander who controlled the use of those weapons had decided to use them if an invasion of the island was launched. But Russell did know, as did so many others who advised the president to invade, how dangerous an invasion was and how uncertain the Soviet response would be following the deaths of Soviet troops. They also knew that an invasion would receive strong political support at home and that the more cautious policy of a naval blockade might not. From this perspective, an invasion seemed to promise lower political costs and so looked more attractive, especially on the eve of elections.

Interestingly, an alternative argument for invasion over blockade also revolved around the presumed higher costs associated with the latter. Democratic senator William Fulbright of Arkansas was also at the meeting with President Kennedy at which he discussed his plan to blockade rather than invade Cuba. Fulbright advised the president to invade. But his reasoning was the polar opposite of Russell's. Fulbright argued plausibly, but incorrectly, that an invasion of Cuba was less dangerous than an open confrontation between U.S. and Soviet ships on the high seas. He argued from the perspective of projected policy consequences rather than projected political consequences. With hindsight we know that it was fortunate for the disputants, and indeed for the world as a whole, that the president rejected the advice of the two senators and other hawkish advisers, regardless of the motivation behind their arguments. At the time, however, the decision could easily have gone either way. The fate of the world can truly rest on the imperfect decisions engendered by imperfect information.

## THE EXERCISE OF POWER

Asymmetries in motivation are one example of how intangible factors can influence international interactions. Asymmetries in domestic political costs represent still another intangible factor that can tip the balance in favor of a seemingly weaker party. Differences in the quality of leadership, in morale, and in preparedness are other examples of intangible elements of power that are difficult to observe before the fact. Yet these factors make understanding the effect of power, evaluated as relative capabilities, difficult to discern.

The better we are at estimating tangible, easily observed factors of power, such as the number of soldiers or bombers a country has or the magnitude of its trade, the more important are intangible considerations in tilting outcomes that depend on power. The effects of power on results in foreign policy are far from simple or determinative. Not only does the "big guy" not always win, but the identity of the big guy is often difficult to discern because the loss of strength gradient and intangible advantages can swamp the easily observed, tangible distribution of power.

The actions that leaders choose to take during international disputes partially depend on their perceptions of the size of intangible, unobservable sources of power in the rival camp. When a leader initiates a dispute and gets a response from the foreign opponent that is inconsistent with expectations based on the observed, tangible elements of power in the rival state, then the leader infers from the unexpected response that the rival must believe it has an advantage in intangible resources. The initiating leader is likely to change her or his mind about pursuing the dispute and to back down.

Figure 8-2 conveys the relationship between tangible power and the likelihood and degree of violence, based on evidence from all disputes in Europe over the past two centuries. The figure challenges many aspects of conventional beliefs about power. The probability that a state will enter into or escalate its participation in a dispute does not increase uniformly with increases in its tangible power advantage. In this sense, morale and guns are fungible sources of power, although morale does not carry over equally to all issues. As a dispute rises up the ladder of escalation, the influence of intangible factors diminishes. This can be seen by examining the change in the shape of the three lines in Figure 8-2. Note that the top line, which refers to any violence between states, curves sharply as the two sides draw equal in observed power. At this point the risk of a violent dispute becomes lowest. Yet the middle line shows a subtle rise in the propensity for both sides in a dispute to use force as the two sides move away from equality in tangible possessions. The bottom line shows a clear and steady increase in the likelihood of war as the distribution of observable capabilities between two foes becomes uneven.

One of the most common assumptions about international relations is that each state wants as much tangible power as it can get. In fact, it is hard to find many instances in which nations obviously and willingly give up military or economic capabilities. No wonder people are quick to leap from this observation to the notion that power—or sometimes security—is the premier goal of states. Is more power always beneficial in regard to a nation's security or its ability to get whatever else it wants? The record of history certainly does not support this point of view.

To demonstrate that tangible power is not all that it is cracked up to be, let's examine the historical relationship between the relative observable, tangible power of pairs of states and the level of conflict in which they found themselves involved. Previously, we saw that higher levels of power do not automatically translate into a willingness to escalate disputes. Now we will see how the frequency of different types of conflict is affected by power differences between adversaries.

If tangible power makes states secure, as suggested by realists, and intangible or unobservable aspects of power are not too important, then we should expect to find that more tangibly powerful states are more commonly engaged in low-level conflicts than their weaker

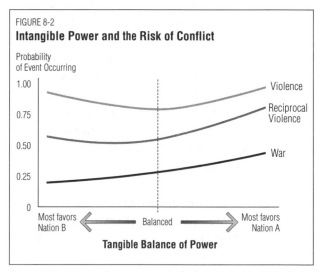

FIGURE 8-2
**Intangible Power and the Risk of Conflict**

Probability
of Event Occurring

*Intangible power plays an especially important role in disputes that do not reach the level of violence conventionally associated with war. One possible reason is that during the early phases of fighting, the superior intangible power of one belligerent is revealed, prompting its opponent to favor capitulation or a quick settlement over risking further losses in a full-fledged war. The horizontal axis shows whether the observed—tangible—distribution of power between nations A and B is more in A's favor or in B's favor. The vertical axis shows how the observed probability of different events responds to changes in the observed mix of power between A and B.*

counterparts. Indeed, we might well think that, if power is particularly desirable, then as states get to be more powerful in readily observed ways they find themselves in fewer and fewer disputes and that the few they do find themselves involved in are resolved in their favor with little resort to force.

Careful reasoning, however, shows that the conventional wisdom that tangible power makes states secure is problematic. All else being equal, tangible power does make it easier for the strong to beat the weak. But it also increases the incentives of the strong to escalate what they demand from the weak. This raises the motivation of the weak to resist the demands of the strong. The weak will give in as long as the cost of the concession does not exceed the expected costs of war, which include the transaction costs associated with fighting and anticipated postwar concessions. If the stronger side demands too much, the weaker side is better off resisting. The strong, then, must be careful and demand from the weak only as much as the weak are willing to give before their costs become too high and they would be better off fighting (Powell 1996a, 1996b, 1999).

We can easily see why this argument supports the expectation that powerful states should get involved only in minor disputes if they get involved at all, provided power is only tangible, readily observed, and common knowledge. If, however, intangible, nonobservable elements of power such as morale and the quality of leadership are important, then there is consequential uncertainty that leads to a breakdown in the conventional wisdom that tangible power makes states secure. Stronger states will want to make demands right up to the limit of what their adversaries will give up without a fight. To ask for less just means that they will have an incentive to come back and get the rest later. To ask for more risks a conflict involving costs that may exceed the benefits being sought. The trouble is, as suggested in Figure 8-2, there is always uncertainty about power because intangible elements are always important. Thus, the conventional, structuralist wisdom about power and security should be problematic as a description of history.

We can test this claim by examining the history of the relationship between tangible power and conflict. We will focus on 707 European pairings between the years 1816 and 1974. In 469 of these pairings, one state initiated a conflict with another state; in the remaining 238 of these pairings, the two states enjoyed a peaceful relationship. We can evaluate each state in each pair of nations along the following five-point scale: (1) the state did not threaten or take action against the other state with which it was paired (no conflict); (2) the state threatened the other but went no further (threat); (3) the state threatened the other and mobilized its armed forces in preparation for fighting (mobilized); (4) the state used at least some force against the other state (force); and (5) the state used a high level of force, involving the commitment of at least one thousand regular troops and inflicting at least one thousand battle-related fatalities (war) (Gochman and Maoz 1984; Bueno de Mesquita and Lalman 1992).

The level of the dispute (or nondispute) between pairs of states that make up the 707 historical circumstances examined here represents the dependent variable—that is, the factor to be explained. The value of the dependent variable can be predicted based on the power of the initiating member of each pair of states as measured by the Correlates of War composite capabilities index discussed earlier.[5] To gain a complete picture of how other variables might influence the level of dispute, we must include the effect of each country's type of political system in our calculus. Here, pairs of countries are divided into three groups. The first includes those in which neither state was a democracy; the second, those in which only one state was a democracy; and the third, those in which both states were democracies. If the importance of tangible power by itself is as great as realists claim, then we should anticipate that countries with more power will find themselves involved in lower levels of conflict. For theories of international relations such as realism or neorealism that view power or security as the primary objective of states, factors like "democraticness" (the degree to which a state's government follows democratic principles) should not be of much interest in influencing security. However, if security is acquired through the selection of domestic political rules such as democracy or autocracy, then those who argue that states want to maximize their security should care more about domestic politics than about power.

Figure 8-3 displays the curves that best describe the statistical patterns behind the association between power and disputes on the one hand and democraticness and disputes on the other. It is evident from the figure that as a nation's power increases, so too does the seriousness of the disputes in which it is involved. Conversely, the seriousness of disputes falls when the adversaries have democratic governments. We can leave for a later chapter the discussion of why democracies live peacefully with one another. For now the important point is that increasing power does not appear to inoculate governments against the threat of violence and instability. Quite the contrary. Power seems to invite trouble.[6] So we can see that the common contention among neorealist theorists that all states want to increase their power to ensure security is problematic. If decision makers pursue increases in national power for this purpose, then they can expect

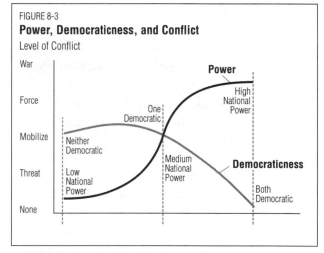

FIGURE 8-3
**Power, Democraticness, and Conflict**
Level of Conflict

*Nonrealist factors such as regime type have a substantial influence over the likelihood that a dispute will escalate or be resolved through negotiations. When two democracies are involved in a dispute with each other, there is little or no chance of escalation, even to the level of a threat. Great advantages in power, however, do not make nations immune to violent conflicts.*

[5] In the 238 cases where states did not become involved in a dispute, one state is randomly designated the "initiator" of the peaceful relationship.

[6] The pattern is similar whether the focus is on the power of the initiator, the target, or both.

to be sorely disappointed. The evidence does not support the contention that increases in power directly increase security. Later, I will suggest that there is scant evidence that national leaders are primarily concerned with increasing national power.

## SUMMARY

In this chapter we have investigated some of the limitations of viewing power by itself as an explanation of the major elements in international relations. We saw that an initial power advantage was not that good at predicting either the initiation of violence or victory. Indeed, initiators of conflict win 68 percent of the time and the initially stronger opponent wins only 59 percent of the time. We learned that the standard definition of power is problematic. It is possible for states to be in a power cycle. This means that A may exercise power over B, and B may exercise power over C, and C may exercise power over A. This circularity contributes to the difficulty in predicting outcomes from standard measures of power.

Our analysis suggested that it is possible for weak states to overcome stronger foes through higher motivation and a willingness to endure costs. We developed a model that offers an explanation of how asymmetries in motivation influence the outcome of disputes (Altfeld and Bueno de Mesquita 1979). The model explains why leaders of powerful states might elect to lose disputes they are strong enough to win. At the same time, leaders in such states may participate in disputes that do not involve a fundamental threat to their nation's interests because their power can help overcome a deficit in motivation.

We found that coordination problems are readily resolved without resort to power. Distributional problems, even when combined with coordination issues, can sometimes be mitigated by exercising power, but at other times alternative solutions are more readily used. Among these, the most important is the creation of international organizations, international laws, and international norms of conduct. When leaders exploit these regimes they can actually benefit by limiting their range of choices. That is, by reducing their power, leaders sometimes can solve problems that would not resolve favorably if they exercised all the power at their disposal.

Intangible considerations such as quality of leadership and level of national morale can offset the impact that raw, observed power exerts in influencing international relations. Observable, measurable power, in fact, turns out not to reduce the risk a nation faces of being involved in security-threatening international disputes. On the contrary, it increases that risk. Although it is an important tool for helping to explain international relations, power by itself cannot predict how international disputes will turn out. The limitations that we have discussed here set the stage for an investigation of the role that preferences and perceptions play in enhancing or diminishing the influence of power.

CHAPTER 9

# PREFERENCES IN INTERNATIONAL POLITICS

Books about international politics almost never discuss preferences. This is odd because variations in preferences are at the root of international controversies. Preferences motivate leaders' domestic and international interactions and direct international bargaining and negotiation. Their configuration helps explain changes in international politics while also explaining periods of constancy. Yet structural theories of international relations simplify the role of preferences until they are all but irrelevant. Bureaucratic and interest group theories give such scant attention to the international consequences of domestic organizational struggles that localized preferences swamp concerns about preferences over international outcomes. Likewise, these theories barely attend to the domestic fallout for bureaucrats from the international circumstances they help trigger. Indeed, by overlooking domestic and international preferences, most international relations theories leave us with a barren account of real-world decisions.

Realism's assumption that all states are interested in maximizing power or national security may well be its greatest weakness. Assuming that all nations are motivated by the same preference, without regard for differences in values, ideas, culture, and ideology, renders realist theories sterile when dealing with problems that do not challenge national survival, and perhaps even when dealing with those that do. Hans Morgenthau, an influential and wise student of international affairs, wrote that "a realist theory of international politics . . . will guard against two popular fallacies: the concern with motives and the concern with ideological preferences" (Morgenthau 1978, 5–6). I believe that Morgenthau's contention that concern for motives and ideological preferences represents a fallacy is wrong. In this chapter we will take a look at just what role these "fallacies" play in international affairs. Two related questions animate our investigation. First, we need to establish whether or not motives and preferences really are relevant to international politics and, second, we need to decide whether or not explanations of international relations that ignore differences in preferences and motives are inevitably inadequate and misleading.

In this chapter I offer a precise definition of preferences. I then assess how preferences and actions are linked to rationality. We will see that people do not always pursue the course of action they most desire. Decision makers face constraints that restrict their choices. We will examine these constraints in depth and identify some important pitfalls associated with inferring preferences from actions and ascribing changes in preferences to circumstances that are more accurately thought of as changes in expectations. We will then identify a particularly important constraint on action in international politics. This constraint is referred to as the social choice problem and is similar to the concern about circularity that was raised when we discussed the limitations of power in Chapter 8. Historical examples, including America's decision to fight in World War I, the decision of the ancient Greeks to resist the Persians at Marathon more than two millennia ago, and the U.S. decision to blockade the Soviet navy in response to the Soviet buildup of nuclear missiles in Cuba in 1962, punctuate our discussion and help illustrate each of the themes introduced here.

## PREFERRED VALUES AND AMERICAN FOREIGN POLICY: AN ILLUSTRATION

When America's doughboys went "over there" in 1917, World War I had been fought to a stalemate. In a fashion consistent with a belief in the balance of power, the power of the Triple Entente (Britain, France, and Russia) on one side and the Dual Alliance (Germany and Austria-Hungary) on the other was almost exactly equal. Of course, many other nations were involved in the fighting, but these were the central actors in the bloody drama of that war. The stalemate was broken when the United States entered the war on the side of the Triple Entente.

Those who believe that a balance of power is a critical feature of international relations often point to World War I as an exemplar of actions consistent with their theory's predictions. And in many ways it is. But in some important respects World War I presents a puzzling development. The United States entered the war ostensibly to "make the world safe for democracy." America's purpose, as articulated by President Woodrow Wilson, was idealistic. The security of the United States was not threatened in any obvious way. None of the combatants showed any inclination or ability to attack American territory, although the German navy did interfere with America's merchant fleet and with America's presumed right as a neutral power to ship people and goods across the Atlantic. Some point to the sinking of the British merchant vessel *Lusitania* on May 7, 1915, by a German submarine as the threat to U.S. security that prompted the American decision to enter the war, but this in reality was more an excuse than a reason.

The sinking of the *Lusitania* was, to be sure, a tragedy. It led to the death of 1,198 people, including 139 Americans. Appropriately enough, the sinking was treated with moral outrage in the United States. President Wilson denounced the attack with strong public language. Still, Wilson's formal note of protest to the German government was more restrained than his public outcry and, after all, the United States did not enter the war within a few days of the event, or even within a few months. Six hundred and ninety-nine days passed between the sinking of the *Lusitania* and the American declaration of war, and that happened only after several American ships had been attacked by German submarines. This stands in sharp contrast to the few hours that elapsed between the Japanese attack on Pearl Harbor on December 7, 1941 (a Sunday), and the American declaration of war on December 8. No, to claim that the American government feared a threat to U.S. security would be stretching credulity. It seems more plausible to believe that President Wilson was genuinely motivated by the idealistic goal he stated: "to make the world safe for democracy." The problem with this is that such a motivation is fundamentally inconsistent with realist or balance-of-power expectations.

The United States in 1917 was in many important respects a sleepy backwater. American governments since the time of George Washington had mostly relished the isolation and protection afforded by the vast oceans that separate the American hemisphere from Europe and Asia. The United States had stood above the fray for years, looking on as people elsewhere in the world struggled against one another. To be sure, the United States occasionally became involved in foreign adventures—in Mexico, Cuba, and the Philippines, for example—but always in places of its own choosing. The United States was a sleepy backwater by choice, not by necessity. Wealth made it possible for it to be a great power, but the United States chose to avoid what Washington had called "entangling alliances" by staying out of European affairs. Although it already had the wherewithal to be the great power that it later became, the American people elected president after president who would avoid U.S. assumption of the role of major actor. There were, of course, occasional lapses. Theodore Roosevelt was eager to expand American influence, and William McKinley had reluctantly presided over America's imperialist Spanish-American War. Adm. Matthew Perry's "opening" of Japan in 1854 and America's failed attempt to "open" Korea to U.S. objectives in 1871 were certainly instances of an expansionist America dabbling in the world of international politics. By and large, however, these expansionist forays all occurred on the periphery of the great power rivalries of the day. The United States generally absented itself from center stage. Its main expansionist focus was on the American continent, where, through conquest and treaties, it seized territory from the American Indians. But in 1917 the United States assumed center stage in the day's most prominent international dispute.

America's departure from Europe at the end of World War I was as remarkable as its arrival in 1917. Throughout history, successful armies followed victory by occupying the territory they had "liberated." Rare indeed was the nation that, having defeated the enemy, restored sovereignty to the conquered people and went home, intentionally going away empty-handed to return to business as usual. But this is exactly what the Americans did at the end of World War I. No occupying army stayed behind to rule Germany or Austria, or to control liberated countries such as Belgium and Holland. Instead, America's army, after defeating the representatives of the authoritarian *ancien regimes*, simply went home, convinced that they had made the world safe (or, anyway, safer) for democracy. Nowhere in Wilson's Fourteen Points (his famous prescription for a new

*As soldiers returned home at the end of World War I, French crowds gathered to welcome them and to celebrate the end of the war. Everywhere we can see the emotional outpouring in support of American efforts in behalf of Europe. A huge sign declares, "Vive Wilson"—"Long Live Wilson"—and is surrounded by Frenchmen flying American flags from their windows and balconies. Certainly the French understood that the United States had truly fought, as Wilson had promised, "to make the world safe for democracy." How ironic, then, that the United States, alone among the great powers, did not ratify the charter of the League of Nations and participate in the organization Wilson envisioned as the cornerstone of a lasting peace.*

world order after World War I) did he call for special rights and privileges for the United States. Nowhere did America forcefully impose its will on a subdued Europe.

The United States of Woodrow Wilson's day was genuinely motivated by goals quite remote from those proffered by theories that assume states are motivated by the desire for power and security. It fought a costly and dangerous war apparently out of principle, not out of some fear for national security. The preferences of the American leader, and perhaps a majority of the American people, were to promote and protect rights and civility between nations and to advance freedom of choice and self-determination. They were not about acquiring power or cultivating security. Indeed, thoughts of American expansion or control in Europe were so remote or so unacceptable to American voters that the U.S. electorate tossed out the internationalists of Wilson's Democratic Party after the war and elected instead the isolationist Warren Harding as Wilson's successor. Keenly tuned in to the political costs associated with internationalism as a foreign policy, the U.S. Senate refused to ratify the Covenant of the League of Nations, leaving the United States outside the very international organization that embodied Wilson's vision for building a safer world. The American people were prepared to fight and sacrifice for freedom in Europe, but they preferred not to accept the role of world leader that seemed to be the inevitable consequence of pursuing an internationalist foreign policy. In a world in which nations seek to maximize power or security to enhance the national interest, it is inconceivable that any country would back away from an opportunity to dominate other states. In 1918 the United States did just that.

The example of American involvement in World War I compels us to come to a better understanding of what preferences and the national interest are all about. The behavior of the United States is too far removed from that which the realist view would lead us to expect for us to ignore the possibility that American leaders wanted something other than greater national power or security. Examples such as this compel us to understand how preferences may shape international interactions.

## WHAT ARE PREFERENCES?

What do we mean by "preferences"? Really, the concept is very simple. If you like chocolate ice cream better than vanilla, then we say that you prefer chocolate to vanilla. If you like them exactly equally, then we say that you are indifferent between chocolate and vanilla ice cream. Naturally, there is no right answer to which ice cream is better, chocolate or vanilla, but there is a right answer to the question, "Which do you like better?" More technically, when we speak of a person having a preference, we mean that the person can connect choices by a relationship that indicates that the person likes one alternative better than, or just as much as, another.

Sometimes people get confused about this point, especially when the choices are not so obviously matters of taste. For example, imagine that we posed the question,

"Which type of government is preferable, democracy or divine right monarchy?" Obviously, very few people today would answer that divine right monarchy is preferable. Indeed, so few would express that preference that we might be tempted to conclude that democracy is a better form of government. This is a dangerous inference; it is not justified by the evaluation of preferences, although it may or may not be justifiable on other grounds. We would do well to recall that at the time of King Ferdinand and Queen Isabella hardly anyone would have thought democracy preferable to divine right monarchy. The notion that the masses, the "rabble," as they might have been described, were qualified to choose the government would have seemed absurd. At the time of Plato it was obvious to most people who thought about such things that democracy was one of the *worst* forms of government. Even at the founding of the United States, the right to vote in most elections was reserved to property holders, with the offices for which one could vote depending specifically on the value of the would-be voter's property.

The objective facts probably have not changed nearly as dramatically as the distribution of tastes or preferences regarding forms of government. Even now there are places in the world where those who advocate democratic forms of government are viewed as enemies of the state, as usurpers of authority, and as fomenters of trouble. There are still places where powerful monarchs hold sway, and the ordinary citizens over whom they rule vehemently defend their system of government.

Preference, then, is not about the superiority or inferiority of one option compared with another. Preferences are an expression of a decision maker's taste, of his or her likes and dislikes. As such, they are strictly subjective. Little attention will be given to evaluating whether people have "good" preferences or even to worrying about whether an international leader has "normal" or "abnormal" preferences. Rather, our concern is to understand how decisions are made in light of alternative preferences.

Our discussion distinguishes between the apparent preferences of a "Hitler" and evaluation of those preferences for their normative content. It is possible to say that Adolf Hitler was a monster who held horrible preferences and, at the same time, that Hitler was a "rational" being who acted on his aberrant preferences in a consistent and predictable way. Indeed, being able to make this distinction will facilitate our ability to lay at the feet of world leaders responsibility for the policies they institute. By focusing on choices given preferences, we will, in essence, deny world leaders an insanity plea as a justification or excuse for horrible actions.

## RATIONALITY AND PREFERENCES

To say that a person has "crazy" preferences and therefore cannot be rational is to excuse such a person's actions. In this book, all that we mean when we speak of people being "rational" is that they act on their preferences so that they do what they think is best with regard to their own welfare. This definition speaks of instrumental rationality. It states that people do what they believe is in their best interest, however perversely they may define those interests. I do not want to deny that decision makers are responsible for what they do, and so I am inclined to assume that decision makers act to try to enhance their chances of achieving their own goals, whatever those goals may be. To say that a particular policymaker is crazy and therefore not responsible for his actions, whether they be innocent mistakes or heinous crimes, is an easy out that I am not eager to provide. A person like Hitler can be held accountable for his actions precisely because he was making rational choices: he knew what he was doing even though it was unimaginably evil.

"Rationality" generally refers to two central conditions: connectedness and consistency (Austen-Smith and Banks 1998). The concept of preference provides a way to connect choices by saying that choice A is more desirable to me than choice B, or choice B is more desirable to me than A, or A and B are exactly of equal value to me. Rational people are, at a minimum, individuals who can connect choices in a transitive or consistent way. This means that if someone likes A better than B and B better than C, then to be rational he or she must also like A better than C. People who can connect choices in a transitive way and who act on their choices to do what they believe is best for themselves are said to be rational.[1]

Connected, consistent (and sometimes convex) preferences are all that is required by our definition of rationality. Any other use of the word, including colloquial, everyday uses that imply sensible or smart or normal, are *not* part of our definition. This is a very important point, and necessary if we are to avoid confusion. If this narrow use of the term makes you uncomfortable, then please substitute some other term. It does not matter what label you attach to the concept, so long as we all mean the same thing—nothing more and nothing less. If we allow "rationality" to mean different things at different times, we will get terribly confused and undoubtedly make mistakes in our reasoning.

> How do expected utility calculations of the type discussed in Chapter 3 incorporate the ideas of connectedness and consistency? Can you think of examples in which individuals violate connectedness or consistency (transitivity) in their decision making? Can you think of examples in which indifference is not transitive? (Hint: think about the desirability of cups of coffee. One cup of coffee has no sugar in it and another has one grain of sugar and another has two grains of sugar, and so forth.)

---

[1] Indeed, rational choices can be made with the conditions of connectedness and consistency (or transitivity) alone. However, the assumption of convexity, a more technical condition, can supplement these two conditions. Convexity means that if A is preferred to B, then there is always a point, or choice, on the straight line connecting A to B that lies between A and B such that A is preferred to the chosen point and the chosen point is preferred to B. And no matter how close the point we choose is to B, there is still always a point that is better than B from the decision maker's perspective and a point that is not as good as A.

## PREFERENCES AND CONSTRAINED CHOICES

You might think that rational people—those with connected, transitive preferences who do what they believe is in their best interest—always choose what they like best. But this is not correct. Choices are not only about what people want; they are also about the options people have. In international politics it is common for rational people to choose that which they do *not* like best. For example, when the Japanese government decided to attack Pearl Harbor they did so not because Japan's leaders liked the idea of going to war with the United States, or liked the idea of killing thousands of people in and around Pearl Harbor; rather, they attacked because they believed it was their best strategic choice given the constraints they faced at the time (Wohlstetter 1962; Russett 1972; Prange 1981). "Constraints" are any factors that limit choices or that influence the expected consequences of alternative choices.

Japan needed many of the natural resources, including rubber and oil, found in those parts of Asia that the United States had promised to protect against Japanese aggression. The Japanese needed these resources to successfully prosecute their war in Asia. They did not have enough of them in part because the United States had cut off Japanese access to alternative sources of these supplies by imposing a trade embargo. The Japanese could not be absolutely sure that U.S. threats to protect parts of Asia were sincere, but they were confident that a war between the United States and Japan fought when and where the Americans chose to fight would mean defeat for Japan. With that in mind, they calculated that their only real hope of prevailing in their ambitions to expand their empire was to knock out the United States in a surprise attack on its navy before it could be mustered. It was a calculated risk made under constrained circumstances. Among the Japanese leaders involved in the decision to attack Pearl Harbor there was considerable concern about whether they could execute their plan successfully and whether it would keep the United States out of the Pacific theater in World War II long enough for Japan to secure its objectives. Far from being Japan's most desired policy, it was entered into with great reluctance and then only once the Japanese leadership was convinced that, as bad as the prospects were, it really was their only chance for success. Having looked over their alternatives, they chose what they thought was best under the circumstances, even though they knew it might lead to very bad consequences (Prange 1981).

Another example of not choosing what they liked best involved Presidents Lyndon Johnson and Richard Nixon. Johnson and Nixon did not want to lose the war in Vietnam. And they did not have to. Few doubt that had the U.S. military been given unfettered authority to do whatever it took to win, the United States could have defeated North Vietnam in the late 1960s or early 1970s. But first Johnson and then Nixon chose to restrict the strategies that the military could employ in response to their own beliefs about what their domestic constituents and foreign adversaries (especially the Soviet Union and China) would tolerate. They refused to allow American troops to cross into and secure permanent control over North Vietnamese territory, making it virtually impossible to stem the flow of personnel and weapons to the South from the North. Given these constraints on military and political strategies, the war apparently could not be won.

MAP 9-1
## Japan's Imperial Expansion before Pearl Harbor

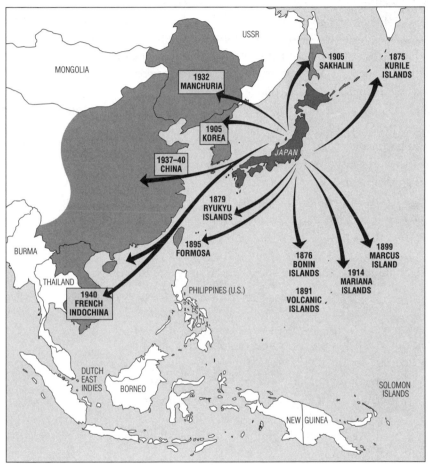

*Beginning as early as the Sino-Japanese War of 1894–1895, Japan began a systematic program of conquest and imperial expansion in Asia. The effort to expand Japan's empire accelerated in the 1930s. The arrows on the map show the directions of that aggressive expansion. The shaded gray areas denote the territory conquered by Japan before the attack on Pearl Harbor on December 7, 1941. The United States imposed an oil embargo on Japan following Japan's invasion of French Indochina in 1940. President Franklin Roosevelt threatened Japan with further serious American reprisals if Japan continued its aggression. Realizing that the United States was likely to defend the Dutch East Indies against Japanese efforts to secure control over their natural resources, the Japanese government decided to preempt the United States by attacking the American naval base at Pearl Harbor. It was a daring gamble that ended in Japan's defeat in 1945.*

The American public did not believe that the war in Vietnam was of sufficient importance to the welfare of the United States to warrant the tremendous cost in American casualties it exacted. Facing public opposition to the war, Johnson and Nixon each attempted to identify strategies that could advance the war effort and control the spread of communism to South Vietnam while still maintaining sufficient public support to fulfill their own ambition to retain hold of the highest office in the land. Nixon, for example, introduced a policy known as Vietnamization. This strategy placed responsibility for air combat on American pilots but left the responsibility for ground combat increasingly to South Vietnamese forces. By using this strategy to reduce the number of Americans being killed and wounded, Nixon hoped to blunt domestic opposition and forge ahead toward victory in Vietnam. Although his policy did greatly reduce the rate of American losses, he nevertheless failed to win popular support for continuing the war. Failing in this, Nixon settled for "peace with honor"; in reality, Nixon's capitulation represented a defeat for American political objectives in Vietnam. A short while after the United States withdrew its forces from the Republic of South Vietnam, the North overran the South and overthrew its government. Today, of course, the North controls all of Vietnam.

The outcome of the war in Vietnam does not imply that the U.S. president or military preferred losing the war to winning it. It does mean that, given the expected costs and benefits of accepting defeat compared with those associated with continuing to pursue victory, Nixon preferred losing—that is, accepting a peace agreement that was not likely to do much more than allow American troops to withdraw in an orderly fashion. Johnson, for his part, gave up the presidency in large measure because his Vietnam policy had cost him too much popular support. Nixon won a second term by promising that peace was at hand. Indeed, the Paris Peace Treaty ending the Vietnam War was signed at the very beginning of Nixon's second term in office.

If outcomes do not always reveal preferences clearly, and if people sometimes pick outcomes they really do not like, how are we to understand the role of preferences in foreign policy decision making? To address the role of preferences and constraints in shaping policy choices and outcomes, let's begin with a simple example about something all of us have faced. We can then generalize from this example to a wide variety of problems in international politics.

## VENDING MACHINES, PREFERENCES, AND DECISIONS

All of you know that sometimes when you put money into a vending machine and press the button for the item you want, nothing happens (except that the machine keeps your money).[2] Perhaps you have even thought from time to time that vending machines are designed to keep a certain percentage of the money put into them without providing a

---

[2] I am indebted to David Lalman, who created this particularly useful illustrative example.

product (probably they are not). What can we learn about preferences from how people use vending machines?

## ORDERING PREFERENCES

Suppose you want a cold drink. The vending machine in front of you offers Coke, Diet Coke, Dr. Pepper, and Fizz, which is a concoction of grapefruit, guava, kiwi, and mango. Let's assume that you prefer Diet Coke to Coke, Coke to Dr. Pepper, and Dr. Pepper to the Fizz concoction (that is, Diet Coke > Coke > Dr. Pepper > Fizz, where > stands for "is preferred to"). Notice that I have connected the choices in what is called a preference ordering. The ordering is not quite complete because I have not specified how you feel about, for instance, Diet Coke compared with Dr. Pepper, or Diet Coke compared with Fizz. I also have not addressed your preference regarding Coke and Fizz.

Perhaps you suspect that I really have. After all, if you like Diet Coke better than Coke and Coke better than Dr. Pepper, then surely you must like Diet Coke better than Dr. Pepper. That is, we naturally expect that a person's preferences are consistent or transitive. If we assume you are rational, then this is not a problem. If the preferences are transitive, then the ordering is complete because from what we have been told (namely, that the ordering is transitive and that Diet Coke > Coke > Dr. Pepper > Fizz) we can infer the preference order between any two of the choices.

## VENDING MACHINES AND INFORMATION CONSTRAINTS

You put your money—the only money you have with you—into the vending machine. If there were no additional constraints, you would push the Diet Coke button, get your can of soda, and go away contented. But right after you deposit the money you notice a little light indicating that the machine is out of Diet Coke. If the machine does not have a coin return button, your next choice would be Coke because Coke is the next best available choice from your point of view. This, after all, is what the preference ordering tells us. But if the machine does have a coin return button, then you have an option that we did not consider in assembling your preference ordering. Thus, if there is a coin return button, the preference ordering is still incomplete. We need to know whether you like Coke better than keeping your money and not having a drink. We need to know at what point in your decision making you would opt to get your money back rather than get a soda from the machine. After all, perhaps there is another vending machine over in the next building, one hundred yards away. Some of us will press the coin return button, get our money back, and invest the time it takes to go over to the other machine to get Diet Coke (with some chance that we will discover that the other machine is out of Diet Coke too, and maybe is out of Coke or out of order). Others will be content to have Coke and not spend any more time looking for Diet Coke. In either case, it does not mean that Coke is preferred to Diet Coke, but it does mean that different people attach a different amount of intensity of preference, or utility, to their desire for Diet Coke over Coke. In a moment we will see that we can calculate how big this difference in preference is, but for now we will continue with our example under the assumption that there is no coin return button. In this case, we do have a complete preference ordering.

Having deposited money into the vending machine, and having discovered that Diet Coke is not available, you must make a constrained choice. Diet Coke is not a feasible alternative. Just as you are about to press the Coke button, resigned to not having a Diet Coke, a friend waiting in line says, "By the way, I saw this machine being refilled this morning. The guy who loaded it was pretty careless. He dropped a bunch of Fizz cans into the Coke slot along with some Coke cans. I'd say that a third of the cans in the Coke slot are that Fizz stuff. He was very careful, though, when he loaded the Dr. Pepper and the Fizz slots. They got exactly what they were supposed to get."

Well, now your choice is constrained even more. The information about your choices has changed. You believe that there is no chance of getting Diet Coke (that is, the probability is zero) because the machine's signal light indicates (presumably in a reliable way) that there is no more Diet Coke. You thought you could get a Coke for sure, but now you believe that if you press the Coke button there is only a two-thirds chance that the machine will deliver a Coke can and there is a one-third chance that you will get the Fizz concoction (presuming that the friend who gave you this information has no reason to lie). Pressing the Coke button involves a risk. What do you do?

## BUYING SODA AS AN EXPECTED UTILITY PROBLEM

To make your choice, you need to think about how much more you like Coke than Dr. Pepper, and how much less you like Fizz than Dr. Pepper. "How much you like" is an expression of utility; it is a statement of your intensity of preference. Merely knowing the order of preferences is no longer sufficient to choose a course of action.

Let's say that $U_{Coke}$ is the utility you attach to getting a Coke, $U_{Dr.\ Pepper}$ is the utility you attach to getting a can of Dr. Pepper, and $U_{Fizz}$ is the utility you attach to getting a can of Fizz. You know that if you push the Coke button there is a two-thirds probability that you will get Coke and a one-third probability that you will get Fizz. Your problem now is to determine whether you prefer to take the risk associated with pushing the Coke button or you prefer to select Dr. Pepper, which you can get for certain. These are problems of the sort we saw earlier when we looked at Ferdinand's choices in Chapter 3 and the choices of Toyota and the U.S. Trade Representative in Chapter 8. Formally, we can say that you will press the Coke button if $2/3 U_{Coke} + 1/3 U_{Fizz} > U_{Dr.\ Pepper}$; you will press the Dr. Pepper button if $2/3 U_{Coke} + 1/3 U_{Fizz} < U_{Dr.\ Pepper}$; and you are indifferent and will just as likely push one button as another if $2/3 U_{Coke} + 1/3 U_{Fizz} = U_{Dr.\ Pepper}$.

The notion here is that each of us will choose the constrained choice that we like best. This allows me to state general rules that serve as predictions about anyone's behavior in this (trivial) circumstance. If I know how much you like one drink compared with another, this is sufficient for me to make a firm prediction about your decision at the vending machine even though I have never met you and I know nothing about your cultural, ethnic, social, economic, or religious background.

Depending on how much more you like Coke than Dr. Pepper, and how much more you like Dr. Pepper than Fizz, you might choose to risk getting something you really do not like in order to have a chance of getting the Coke that you want. People satisfying the first expression like Coke enough to take their chances of getting the Fizz concoction. However, someone else might choose not to gamble and instead settle for Dr. Pepper to avoid getting that awful Fizz drink. Although this should not seem particularly surprising to you, it does remind us that we cannot always infer what people prefer simply by observing what they do, let alone by what happens to them.

All of us, by the assumptions of this simple example, like Coke better than Dr. Pepper, but some of us choose to push the Coke button whereas others of us choose to push the Dr. Pepper button. Constrained choices—and most interesting decisions in international affairs involve constraints—do not necessarily reveal underlying, true (that is, unconstrained) preferences, even when people are not trying to trick or bluff each other into mistaken beliefs. Constrained choices reveal more about people's preferences for certain actions or strategies than they do about their preferences for the outcome of the situation they are in. Inferring preferences based on observation of outcomes can be particularly misleading. You might press the Coke button, having decided to take your chances, rather than have a Dr. Pepper for certain. A can of Fizz might be delivered by the vending machine. After all, the circumstance includes a one-third chance of that happening when you press the Coke button. Seeing you drink the Fizz, I might infer that you prefer Fizz to any other drink. This, of course, would be plain wrong. As we know, you liked Coke so much that you were willing to take the risk of winding up with the Fizz concoction. In the end, you had the misfortune of getting the very drink you like least. Still, you are thirsty and so you drink it. This outcome does not change the fact that you prefer Diet Coke to Coke, Coke to Dr. Pepper, and Dr. Pepper to Fizz.

## CONSTRAINED CHOICE IN INTERNATIONAL RELATIONS: SOME EXAMPLES

Inferring preferences from outcomes is an all-too-common error in international relations. Often we jump to conclusions about rivals' preferences without contemplating under what constraints the rivals operate. We allow careful reasoning to lapse by confusing what people do with what they want to do. Such lapses in reasoning can have dire consequences when they are about momentous decisions in international politics.

Hitler and many of his supporters may have been guilty of just such an error in reasoning. At the end of World War I Germany's armies returned home largely intact. Seeing the army in apparently good condition, some nationalists and militarists like Hitler concluded that the politicians had forced the army from the field before it was defeated.

They said that the army had been "stabbed in the back." They looked at the outcome—surrender although the army was not in ruins—and inferred that the politicians chose to betray the German people; the politicians seemed to prefer some awful deal with the allied nations to fighting on to victory. Hitler's conviction that the German politicians were not to be trusted led, of course, to horrific consequences for Germany and for all the world. He appears to have tragically misjudged preferences by observing outcomes. He may have been unable to take into account adequately the constraints Germany faced (like being outnumbered and industrially outproduced) and to form a rational expectation about what would happen to the German army and to Germany if the politicians insisted on continuing the fight. Because of his poor understanding of constrained decision making, and because of his limited ability to project ahead to consequences from preferences, tens of millions of people suffered and died.

But there is an alternative explanation of Hitler's response to the terms of the Versailles Peace Treaty that ended World War I. Perhaps Hitler fully understood that the politicians had not stabbed Germany in the back. Perhaps he was able to assess the constrained choices they faced and realized that they made the best decision given the circumstances. Why, then, would he have condemned their actions? Contrary to notions about maximizing the national interest, Hitler may simply have been interested in maximizing his own political opportunities, and the national interest be damned. By condemning the German leadership in World War I Hitler created a band of supporters around his own political ideas. He slowly built up the organization and constituency support he needed to become a powerful political figure in Germany. If part of the public was gullible enough to believe Hitler's argument about Germany being stabbed in the back, then he might, quite cynically, have associated himself with that argument just to gain personal power.

Naturally, being forced to make decisions under *uncertainty* about the true preferences or intentions of an opponent, we are tempted to look at the foe's actions and draw inferences about preferences. We act in accordance with our beliefs about those preferences, but, of course, our actions may be based on false inferences. Indeed, these false inferences may become self-fulfilling, prompting false beliefs on the part of our rival and leading to a mistaken, but rational, escalation of tensions.

## COLD WAR PERCEPTIONS AS CONSTRAINTS

Consider a simple, plausible example from recent history. Throughout the decades of the cold war, the United States and the Soviet Union spent vast sums of money arming themselves to the teeth. The Soviets' successes in putting the first Sputnik satellite into orbit in 1957 and then the first man into space in 1961, along with other technological developments, were commonly perceived in the United States as indications of an emerging military disadvantage for America. This was one of the central campaign issues of the 1960 presidential race between John F. Kennedy and Richard M. Nixon. The so-called missile gap prompted a substantial buildup in American nuclear missile capabilities, as well as a fundamental rethinking of America's nuclear strategy. It also contributed to Kennedy's strident, resolute response to the Soviet placement of missiles in Cuba in 1962. From the U.S. perspective, the Soviet Union was an expansionist, hawklike state. The United States acted as if it took literally Soviet premier Nikita Khrushchev's declaration, "We will bury you." Believing that it faced a severe threat, the United States armed itself for protection, perhaps correctly, perhaps mistakenly.

If we put ourselves in the shoes of Soviet leaders, however, we might see the circumstances in a different light. The Soviet Union was devastated by World War II, losing about 20 million of its people and suffering untold destruction to its farms and factories. The United States came out of the war pretty much unscathed. Shortly after the war was over, the United States adopted a foreign policy known as containment. This policy was designed to prevent any expansion of the Soviet sphere of influence beyond those portions of Eastern Europe already ceded to the USSR by the agreement reached at Yalta as World War II drew to a close. Soviet leaders naturally saw the containment policy as a threat to their interests. Well-armed foreign armies surrounded them. Their adversaries in the West were richer and better armed than they were. For their own self-defense it would be necessary to rebuild their strength. Besides, the United States had developed not only the atom bomb but also the hydrogen bomb and was pressing ahead with weapons research and development. The Soviets would have to do the same to remain competitive and viable. U.S. actions in Korea in the early 1950s and later against Cuba at the Bay of Pigs in 1961, when U.S.-backed Cuban forces tried to overthrow the government of Fidel Castro, reinforced Soviet fears that the United States was an expansionist, hawklike state committed to destroying the Soviet Union's communist way of life.

What was the truth? Americans generally, although not universally, perceived their country as a benign, dovelike society that was dragged by circumstances into the unwanted role of superpower. Perhaps the Soviet leaders sincerely held the same view of themselves. From their perspective, they placed missiles in Cuba as a reaction to the Bay of Pigs and other efforts by the United States to depose Castro (including American plots to assassinate him, even down to poisoning his cigars). They were, as they saw it, acting in good faith to help a friend and ally withstand bullying from the United States. From their perspective, the Soviet Union was not trying to gain a military advantage. They built up their missile arsenal in reaction to American and NATO arms levels. Left to their own devices, perhaps the Soviets really were the dovelike, peace-loving people they repeatedly professed to be. And perhaps they were not.

At the time, the American leadership did not know what the true preferences of the Soviet leadership were; nor did the Soviet leaders know the true preferences of the American leaders. Each nation could only make cautious, possibly mistaken, inferences about their opponent's constrained preferences from the actions the opponent undertook. Such inferences are particularly warranted when the cost of such actions to the relevant decision makers was high enough that it is reasonable to assume they would not pay the price if they were not sincere in their action. After all, declarations of love for peace and friendship are easy to make; policies that involve taking big risks to show one's love for peace and friendship are another matter. Talk is cheap, but actions often are not. Thus, maybe both sides were, in fact, doves, spending unbelievable amounts of money needlessly to defend against a threat that was more imagined than real. Or maybe one or both sides were right to fear the other. Maybe the intentions of one or both parties were quite hostile, and disaster was averted only because of the prudent expenditure of great amounts of resources on building weapons capable of scaring the other side into good behavior. In Chapter 10 I discuss a method by which we can learn to read the signals nations send about themselves through their actions (O'Neill 1989; Morrow 1992, 1999). For now, note that it is difficult to know someone's true preferences simply by looking at their actions unless those actions are costly to the people undertaking them.

Decision makers may act out of mistaken beliefs about the intentions of their foes, or they may act by bluffing in the hope of tricking that foe. They may be limited by foreign or domestic circumstances to make choices that they would have preferred to avoid under less restrictive conditions. We must consider the constraints they operate under, whether those constraints pertain to objective realities, such as limited resources, or pertain to imagined realities, such as beliefs about a rival's intentions. In either case, it seems evident that preferences matter and that preferences may be important well beyond the simple notion that all nations desire more power or more security to less. Making careful calculations about how to act given that choices are constrained is very important. This is not something new; it is a universal principle of international politics.

## PREFERENCES AT MARATHON: AN ANCIENT GREEK EXAMPLE

Variations in preferences have been critical at just about every turning point in history. Indeed, it can be argued that the entire history of Western civilization hinged on calculations about preferences and constrained choices at a place called Marathon in ancient Greece. Whether for better or for worse, the spread of Greek values or of Persian values over much of the world at the time depended on the weighing of preferences and constraints by a small group of Greek generals about 2,500 years ago.

In 490 B.C. there was a great war going on between Athens and Persia. The outcome of that war is often regarded as having been determined at the battle of Marathon. Whatever the merits of that claim, we are interested in the international politics of the day and the decisions that proved decisive for the war. The battlefield at Marathon, near Athens, contained a hilly area that sloped down to the edge of the sea. The Persian army landed in great force on the beach, and the Athenians held the high ground. The

Athenians had the advantage of being able to look down and see the Persians' movements without the Persians knowing theirs. The Athenians, however, did suffer from one tremendous disadvantage. They were greatly outnumbered at Marathon.[3] Indeed, the Athenians were so greatly outnumbered that it fell upon them to make a very difficult decision: should they try to fight the Persians, or should they surrender themselves and their city to the Medes (as the Persian combatants were then called)?

The Athenians had a procedure for making such choices. A committee of generals had to vote. If a majority agreed to fight, then it meant war. If a majority voted against fighting, then Athens would be surrendered to Hippias, the Athenian outcast and traitor who had gone over to the Persian side. The Greek historian Herodotus has provided an account of the argument for war offered by Miltiades, an Athenian general who favored fighting. The committee of Greek generals was divided and it fell on Miltiades to try to persuade at least one more general to come over to his way of thinking.

> Never, since the Athenians were a people, were they in such danger as they are in at this moment. If they bow the knee to these Medes, they are to be given up to Hippias, and you know what they then will have to suffer. But if Athens comes victorious out of this contest, she has it in her to become the first city of Greece. Your vote is to decide whether we are to join battle or not. If we do not bring on a battle presently, some factious intrigue will disunite the Athenians, and the city will be betrayed to the Medes. But if we fight, before there is anything rotten in the state of Athens, I believe that, provided the Gods will give fair play and no favour, we are able to get the best of it in the engagement. (Herodotus 1954, bk. vi, sec. 109)

Here we see the essence of a reasoned approach to the fundamental choice between war and peace—an approach that is very attentive to preferences.[4] Miltiades' calculation of the interests at stake boils down to the conclusion that, given the constrained choice facing the Athenians, they should fight and risk defeat at the hands of the much larger Persian army. If the Athenians "do not bring on a battle presently . . . the city will be betrayed to the Medes," whereas by fighting, the Athenians have some chance of winning. For Miltiades, the constrained choice is to surrender and get a terrible outcome or take the risk of defeat in order to have a chance at a desirable result (victory and becoming the first city of Greece). Of course, he also recognized that fighting could lead to defeat and its attendant consequences if, for example, the gods—that is, a chance development—chose to favor the Persians. He notes that defeat would be made more likely

---

[3] At least this is the story as it has been told for over two millennia. Recent research casts some doubts on the history of this event as it has been passed down through the ages, suggesting that the Athenians were not so greatly outnumbered. For our purposes, however, the traditional account of this battle is of interest.

[4] Notice that Miltiades draws attention to the fundamental preference assumed in what today is called neorealist theory: the maximization of security. His speech shows his concern that Athenian independence is at stake, including not only Athenian values but the very survival of the city as an independent city-state.

by delay, giving factious intrigue time to take hold and undermine the political scene in Athens.[5]

Miltiades' oration proved decisive and, fortunately for the Greeks, the Athenians succeeded in defeating the Medes. Certainly, however, we can imagine a different group of decision makers choosing differently. We can imagine that they might have thought the risk of fighting too great and that there was a chance of mercy if they surrendered without a fight. Or we might imagine that they would have made the decision urged on them by Miltiades but that they would have lost the battle and, by resisting, have also lost any chance of mercy from Hippias and the Persians. With hindsight it appears that the Athenian generals made the right choice. Everything turned out as well as it could have for Athens. With foresight, however, they could not have been so sure.

Even if all of the Athenian generals held the same preference order, they might have acted differently if they attached a different amount of intensity to their preferences for victory, unmerciful defeat, or merciful capitulation. If they valued success sufficiently, they would have been willing to take large risks to achieve it. If victory were not that much of an improvement over, for instance, a merciful capitulation or some other intermediate alternative, then they would have been rather cautious in the face of a risky choice.

Figure 9-1 introduces the ideas of risk neutrality, risk aversion, and risk acceptance. To explain these important distinctions, we must make some simple expected utility calculations regarding the choices facing the Greek generals at Marathon. If the Greeks decide to fight the Persians, then there is some chance of victory and some chance of defeat. Defeat means a cruel response from the Medes. Alternatively, the Greeks could capitulate without a fight. Let's

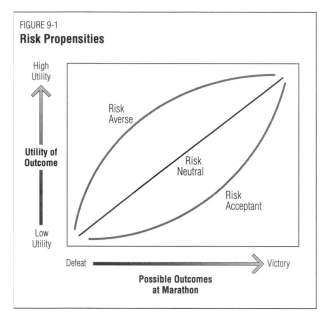

FIGURE 9-1
**Risk Propensities**

High Utility

**Utility of Outcome**

Risk Averse

Risk Neutral

Risk Acceptant

Low Utility

Defeat ——————→ Victory

**Possible Outcomes at Marathon**

*Decision makers evaluate risks differently. Because they ignore variations in risk-taking propensities among decision makers, structural theories leave out an important feature of foreign policy decision making—one that can have great impact on the structure of the international system. Had but one more Greek general sided against Miltiades in his call for action against the Medes, the course of European history might have been entirely different.*

---

[5] Miltiades' concern with factious intrigue in Athens seems inconsistent with the neorealist view insofar as here he emphasizes domestic political differences rather than structural factors in the international system as keys to the Athenian decision. His combined emphasis on international interactions (what will happen between Athens and Persia) and domestic constraints (the undermining of support and hope through factious intrigue) reinforces the perspective of strategic interaction taken in this book.

assume that all of the Greek generals preferred victory to capitulation and capitulation to defeat. The utility for victory ($U_{victory}$) equals 1 for each general and the utility for defeat ($U_{defeat}$) equals 0. Let's assume that the Greeks believe that their chance of victory ($p$) is 0.6, provided they do not wait too long and provided the gods treat them fairly. The chance of defeat ($1 - p$), then, is 0.4. Merciful treatment ($U_{mercy}$) is a sure thing if they capitulate without a fight.

Using the by now familiar tools of expected utility calculations, we can rewrite the above statements as follows:

$$pU_{victory} + (1 - p)U_{defeat} = 0.6(1) + 0.4(0) = EU \text{ of fighting}$$

and

$$U_{mercy} = EU \text{ of capitulation}$$

All we know about the value of $U_{mercy}$ for each general is that it is larger than 0 and smaller than 1. Suppose for some general a merciful outcome following capitulation is equal to 0.6. In this case, the risk associated with fighting is exactly equal to the sure outcome associated with capitulation. Such a general is risk neutral, neither favoring the risky choice—fighting—over the certain choice—capitulation—nor favoring the certain choice over the risky choice. Suppose for some other Greek general $U_{mercy}$ equals 0.5. Such a general prefers the risks of fighting to accepting the consequences of a merciful capitulation. This person is risk acceptant, or risk loving. Finally, a third Greek general attaches a utility of 0.7 to mercy following capitulation. This general prefers to take the sure outcome over the risky choice involved in fighting. He is risk averse. Figure 9-1 displays the shape of these utility curves, reflecting the risk-neutral, risk-acceptant, and risk-averse perspectives of our three hypothetical Greek generals.

Notice that the risk-averse utility function attaches higher utility to intermediate outcomes than do the risk neutral and risk-acceptant utility functions while assigning equal values to the extreme outcomes (victory and defeat). This is equivalent to the statement that the intermediate outcome (such as mercy following capitulation) is preferred to fighting where the best outcome (victory) and the worst outcome (defeat) each occur with some probability. Because the risk-acceptant decision maker places an especially low value on the intermediate outcome—it is not much better than the worst outcome—he prefers to gamble on fighting rather than accept capitulation. As is evident in the figure, a risk-neutral utility function is a straight line, meaning that the gamble (fighting) is equal to the sure thing (mercy after capitulation). Thus, individuals with the same preference ordering over outcomes can nevertheless make quite different choices based on variations in their preference for gambling, known as their willingness to take risks.

Morgenthau's supposition that motives and preferences are fallacies in understanding international affairs is hard to support in light of this and the many other examples I have offered. His view will be even harder to maintain following our discussion of fundamental problems in foreign policy decision making over controversial social choices.

## SOCIAL CHOICE PROBLEMS: IS THERE A NATIONAL INTEREST?

The Greek generals who listened to Miltiades' speech might have faced a still more complicated problem than the one just portrayed. Although each general may have acted rationally, as a group they may have found it difficult, or even impossible, to come up with a collective decision that could be described as rational. They could easily have faced a fundamental social choice problem—namely, that no matter how they weighed their preferences about how best to protect Athens, they could not be sure that their final decision fairly reflected their own sense of what was best for Athens. The problem is that every method of weighing or adding preferences is capable of leading to results that fail

*World history sometimes turns on the brave actions and good political judgment of a handful of people. So it was at the Battle of Marathon at which the Greeks defeated Persia more than two millennia ago. When in World War II Winston Churchill praised the British Royal Air Force with "Never in the course of human conflict have so many owed so much, to so few," he might have had the Battle of Marathon in mind.*

reasonable tests of fairness for the group. Suppose, for instance, that we defined fairness minimally to include just four conditions:

- Universal Domain: Any possible preference ordering of choices can be held—that is, there is no predetermined constraint that stipulates that certain orderings of choices cannot be held.

- Pareto Optimality: If there is a choice that benefits at least one person without harming anyone else, then it is chosen over options that fail to yield that benefit or that harm someone else.

- Independence from Irrelevant Alternatives: If people prefer A to B, introducing some other option C does not alter their preference for A over B.

- Non-Dictatorship: If there are N people and all of them except one (N − 1) like A better than B and 1 likes B better than A, then B—the dictator's preference—is not chosen.

Kenneth Arrow (1951), a Nobel laureate in economics, proved that it is impossible to devise any means of adding up the interests of individual decision makers in a manner that is consistent with these four fairness conditions. That is, there is no method for aggregating individual preferences into a collective choice that *guarantees* that the welfare of the collective group is maximized. This does not mean that group welfare is never advanced in decisions, but it does mean that we can never be sure that such welfare will be promoted by any given rule for counting the relative power or influence of different decision makers. Arrow's impossibility result is one of the most important things we know about politics and it has broad-ranging implications, some of which are explored below. Let's take a look at an example of problems in making social choices—that is, collective rather than individual choices—and then we can reflect on its implications for alternative views of international politics and for the significance of the notion of the national interest.

## SOCIAL CHOICE AND THE CUBAN MISSILE CRISIS

The construction of Soviet missile installations in Cuba was detected by American reconnaissance aircraft in September 1962. By October, President John F. Kennedy was ready to go before the American people and the world community to declare that offensive missiles were being placed in Cuba by the USSR and that those missiles could not remain. As the president delivered his speech on the missiles it became clear to anyone listening that the world was on the brink of a nuclear third world war in which, as the president said, "even the fruits of victory would be ashes in our mouth." Kennedy declared that the United States would use a naval blockade to prevent ships from delivering any more weapons or missile-site equipment to Cuba, leaving open the possibility of further escalation if that proved necessary.

The decision to employ a naval blockade—boarding and searching foreign vessels in international waters—was a carefully made choice. Such a blockade is technically an act of war. As such, it is quite provocative. Still, it is a less forceful action than, say, surgical air strikes designed to destroy the missile sites or an all-out invasion of Cuba. Air strikes or an invasion, however, certainly had a higher probability of reversing the missile buildup before the installations on Cuba could become operational and represent a true military threat to the United States and its allies in Latin America. A blockade, of course, could stop new equipment from getting through, but it could not undo the construction of missile sites already on the island. That would take a political decision by Soviet leader Nikita Khrushchev or by the Cuban leader, Fidel Castro, or a U.S. decision to escalate the dispute to include air strikes or an invasion.

Kennedy appointed an Executive Committee charged with the responsibility of recommending a course of action that would restore the status quo by leading to the removal of the missile installations. At least three alternatives were given prominent consideration by the committee: institute a naval blockade; utilize surgical air strikes, possibly followed by an all-out military invasion; or pursue nothing more than diplomacy. Those who endorsed using diplomacy noted that the missiles did not really represent a fundamental military threat to the United States or a major change in the balance of power insofar as the Soviets already had intercontinental ballistic missiles capable of reaching the United States in just a few minutes.[6]

Robert Kennedy, the attorney general and brother of the president, and Robert McNamara, the secretary of defense, were both strong advocates of the naval blockade as the preferred response to the Soviet missile buildup. They were adamantly opposed to the suggestion that the United States do nothing or that the United States, through diplomatic channels, offer publicly to trade away U.S. Jupiter missiles in Turkey for the Soviet missiles in Cuba.[7] And though fearful of the military option, they seem to have thought it a more sensible approach than doing nothing.

The objections that Robert Kennedy and McNamara raised to the military option were twofold. First, and most important, they felt that a surprise attack by the United States against Cuba would be equivalent to the Japanese attack of Pearl Harbor. In their view, the United States would lose its moral advantage in the dispute, and in the world in general, through such an action. Second, there were considerable doubts about whether the United States could successfully destroy the missile sites, let alone do so without fomenting a massive military response by the Soviet Union. With these considerations in mind, I suggest that the McNamara/Robert Kennedy faction (hereafter I will refer to this

---

[6] Notice how the argument for pursuing diplomacy relied upon the theoretical argument for maintaining a balance of power. One of the arguments against diplomacy was that the missiles *did* change the balance of power by reducing the time available for launching a retaliatory strike from about twenty minutes to only two or three.

[7] In fact, the crisis was resolved by imposition of a blockade in conjunction with a secret deal to remove the Jupiter missiles. The president's concern was not so much the effects of their removal per se as the public appearance of capitulation to the Soviets implied by trading the missiles in Turkey for the missiles in Cuba.

group as the McNamara faction) held the following preference order: blockade > military option > diplomacy.

A second faction on the committee, led by the Joint Chiefs of Staff of the armed forces of the United States (and supported by Dean Acheson, who had been Harry Truman's secretary of state), held a preference order quite different from that held by the McNamara faction. The members of this group believed that a naval blockade was an ineffective strategy because it did not directly address the issue of the missile installations already in place in Cuba. Perhaps they saw this strategy as no more effective than doing nothing other than pursuing diplomatic channels but with greater risks attached to it than were attached to the diplomatic alternative. With this in mind, the Joint Chiefs appeared to hold the following preference order: military option > diplomacy > blockade.[8]

Finally, a third faction, which I identify with Adlai Stevenson, twice Democratic candidate for president and U.S. ambassador to the United Nations at the time, held still different preferences. Members of the Stevenson faction favored doing nothing or pursuing a diplomatic approach. They contended that the missiles on Cuba really were not a major threat to the United States. They felt, and Kennedy agreed, that the U.S. Jupiter missile installations in Turkey were obsolete. They believed these missiles could be traded for the missiles on Cuba. The president, although prepared to trade away the missiles, was prepared to do so only as part of a secret side deal. He was not prepared to remove them as part of the public resolution of the missile crisis, claiming that, although the Jupiter missiles should have been removed long before, still, they should not be bartered away under circumstances that looked like the United States was being blackmailed. In any event, the Stevenson faction most feared the consequences of any military action, such as that proposed by the Joint Chiefs of Staff, although they were presumably more supportive of weaker military action, such as the McNamara faction's naval blockade. For this faction, then, the following preference order was most favorable: diplomacy > blockade > military option.

If these three factions represented all of the interests on the Executive Committee, what would it choose? Consider two plausible strategies by which committees make decisions. In keeping with democracy, we might expect such an important committee to take a vote. First, we will think about what would happen if the committee just voted in round-robin fashion. Then we will consider what would happen if leaders voted on just two of the options at a time. If a majority of the committee was required to carry a

---

[8] Among the preference orders in this example, this is the one that is most problematic. We know that the Joint Chiefs supported the military alternative as the best response, but we are not really sure about how they felt about the blockade compared with doing nothing. Remember, however, that the object in this example is to make a general point about problems of collective action rather than to teach specific details about the Cuban Missile Crisis. Having said this, I believe that all of the other details in this example are accurate, and I suspect that this particular detail is right as well. Those interested in a more detailed examination of the crisis should see Robert Kennedy (1969) and Graham Allison (1972).

recommendation to the president, then its members might simply have voted on each alternative: the military option, a blockade, or diplomacy. Yet no alternative would have received enough support to garner a majority. In each case there would be one vote in favor of choosing that alternative but two votes against.

The second voting option would have been to let each alternative go head to head against the others. By comparing one choice with another, and then comparing whichever of those that won against the remaining choice, the Executive Committee could decide on which alternative to recommend to the president.[9]

The Joint Chiefs might have proposed that the blockade and diplomatic alternatives be considered first. Then, whichever of these two choices prevailed would have been voted on against the possibility of the military option. In the contest between a blockade versus diplomacy, the Joint Chiefs faction and the Stevenson faction would each have supported diplomacy because they preferred it to the blockade, giving diplomacy a clear victory over the McNamara faction's proposed blockade. Then, in accordance with the proposed agenda, the three factions would have voted on diplomacy versus the military option. The McNamara faction and the Joint Chiefs faction each would have supported military air strikes over diplomacy, making the preferred policy recommendation a military assault of Cuba.

But suppose that just before reporting the committee's decision to the president, Stevenson or some other supporter of the diplomacy option had objected to the agenda set by the Joint Chiefs. Suppose that Stevenson or one of his supporters had insisted instead that the following agenda be pursued: vote first on imposition of a blockade versus the military option and then pit the winner of that contest against diplomacy. If the committee had agreed to follow this agenda, then the blockade would have defeated the military option at the first stage of decision making, whereas diplomacy would have defeated the blockade in the second stage of decision making. Following the Stevenson agenda, then, the Executive

*President Kennedy meets with his closest advisers during the Cuban Missile Crisis. The selection of a course of action may have owed as much to strategic maneuvering and agenda control within the executive committee as it did to any well-defined sense of the national interest.*

[9] Of course, formal voting almost certainly did not take place. But the give and take of arguments undoubtedly followed some sequence that influenced the policy recommendation ultimately made by the executive committee and the decision made by the president. It is this sequence of discussion, the agenda, that is the focus in demonstrating how social choice problems can influence even crucial foreign policy decisions.

Committee would have recommended that the president do nothing more than pursue diplomatic solutions.

And what if Robert McNamara had gained control of the agenda? In this case the attorney general and secretary of defense would have preferred that the committee settle between the military option and diplomacy first, and then compare the winner of that contest with their most preferred policy, the blockade option. If this agenda had been pursued, the McNamara faction and the Joint Chiefs faction each would have voted in favor of the military option over diplomacy. This would have been followed by the defeat of the military option in favor of the blockade. In the end, pursuit of the McNamara agenda would have left the naval blockade holding sway as the preferred policy recommendation (and, in fact, this was the policy recommendation ultimately made).

The problem in this hypothetical rendering of the Executive Committee's decision-making process, of course, is that the recommended policy depends on the skill of the participants in manipulating the agenda rather than on any true sense of the national interest. The order in which options were considered would have determined the outcome, even though the preferences of the members of the Executive Committee remained unchanged. In fact, it is very difficult to say that a blockade or a military option or diplomacy was any more in the national interest than any of the other two alternatives, since two-thirds of the factions could be mustered in opposition to any proposal by picking the right sequence of deliberation. If we think of the national interest as the policy supported by a majority, then we have the problem that three radically different policies each enjoyed majority support under the right agenda. The sequence in which these three alternatives were considered, rather than actual preferences for these alternatives, could have determined the U.S. policy.

Although each decision maker in this example behaved rationally, the aggregation of their individual preferences points to a fundamental problem: the aggregated preferences were *not* transitive. The collective preference ordering made a circle such that the military option > diplomacy > blockade > military option > diplomacy > blockade > military option and so forth, cycling on forever. Figure 9-2 displays how this example produces cyclical preferences that reflect the social choice problem: even though each individual has connected and consistent preferences, the group, representing the aggregation of individual objectives, has intransitive or inconsistent preferences.

Aggregating preferences across several decision makers need not always lead to a cycle in which no policy option dominates over all others. But it is very hard to tell in advance when this problem will arise. We know that it is more and more likely to come up as the number of decision makers grows or as the number of choices increases (Niemi and Weisberg 1968). Sometimes the problem is hidden from

FIGURE 9-2
**Cyclical Preferences**

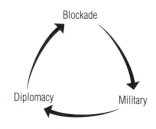

*Decision making by the Executive Committee during the Cuban Missile Crisis illustrates the possibility of cyclical preferences and the importance of agenda control in shaping major international policy decisions.*

view by artificially limiting the number of alternatives considered, but this just sweeps the social choice problem under the rug by violating the fairness condition of universal domain; it does not solve or eliminate the problem (Austen-Smith and Banks 1998).

> Construct an example of decision making in which there are five choices and three decision makers but no cycle. Using the same conditions, construct an example in which there is a cycle. Set out all of the possible ways that five alternatives can be ordered across three decision makers without repeating a preference order for any two decision makers. Now do the same across five decision makers. With five choices and three decision makers, how often does a cycle arise? With five choices and five decision makers, how often does a cycle arise?

## PREFERENCE CYCLES AND STRUCTURAL REALISM

The problems inherent in trying to find rules to connect the preferences of decision makers to the policies of their states are central to the differences between the core perspectives on international relations. Structural theories of international relations focus on factors across states, but not within states. They begin with the view that the nation can be treated as a unitary actor—as a dictator of the national interest, if you will. If the nation is unitary, then individual domestic preferences are irrelevant to international politics and so cannot possibly lead to the social intransitivities suggested by the Cuban Missile Crisis example. By assuming away domestic political differences, structural theories eliminate the social choice problem from their theorizing (but not, of course, from reality).

Although structural theories do not allow for social intransitivities at the subnational level, they must still confront the possibility that they may arise at the international level. In the structuralist's view, the international system is not unitary; it is made up of competing states. Of course, states form alliances in much the same way that domestic factions form coalitions or voting blocs. So, states, in working with or against each other, might also be subject to the social choice problem.

Structural approaches assume away the possibility of the social choice problem at the system level by positing that all nations prefer improving their power to all other possibilities. In effect, the agenda is determined by the structure of the situation. That is, if the agenda is not subject to manipulation but, rather, is always imposed by the stronger on the weaker, then stronger states will simply select the agendas that are best for them. However unpleasant this may be for weaker states, they must accept this as the state of nature in international politics. The structural realist's emphasis on power, in this respect, is decisive.

One of the central hypotheses, or predictions, of structural realism is that alliances are short-lived, temporary arrangements of convenience designed to enhance the security (or power) of their members. The social choice problem suggests that it is easier to put an alliance together to oppose a particular point of view than it is to form one to support a particular point of view. This in fact was true in the Cuban Missile Crisis example. There, in each comparison of alternatives, one faction voted for a policy it did not most desire because it preferred to compromise on its second choice rather than get its least-preferred outcome. This is consonant with the structural view of international politics, which says that alliances are ever-shifting as nations seek to enhance their position in the international system. However, because in structural realism no variation in preference orderings is consequential, no cycles of the sort characterized by the social choice problem can possibly occur. Reality, of course, says differently.

There is nothing wrong with assuming away a particular problem. In fact, this is one of the ways that structural theories simplify reality, a task that every theory must undertake. The relevant question here is whether or not this particular simplification creates more problems than it solves. This is an empirical question, one that asks to what extent the theory's predictions are consistent with behavior in reality. Later, we will find evidence indicating that assuming away the social choice problem is not overly problematic when dealing with major features of international politics such as whether to wage war or sue for peace. It may be more problematic, however, when dealing with lesser problems such as whether to allow free trade or impose quotas and tariffs. In any event, by making assumptions that eliminate the possibility of cycling in the theory, structuralists create an important role for the notion of the national interest. Since cycles are suppressed by assumption, a predominant set of policy objectives and strategies for each nation is implied. These objectives and strategies constitute the ingredients of the realist's notion of the national interest and preclude the necessity of looking at domestic constraints on international politics. In a world without the social choice problem, it is enough to know what is in the best interest of a nation to predict what that nation will do. What is best may be determined by assumption, as is the case in structural theories, or it may be determined by examining the process of decision making when preferences are permitted to vary in theory and in practice.

## INTEREST GROUPS AND THE SOCIAL CHOICE PROBLEM

Approaches to international relations that pay attention to bureaucratic and interest group politics generally are more attentive to the social choice problem than are structural theories. These approaches view international relations in terms of the personal preferences and actions of bureaucrats, interest groups, and the like. Their focus is on the personalities and individual desires of decision makers, not on national characteristics or structural considerations. When people speak of bureaucratic or interest group politics, they are usually reflecting some implicit understanding of how difficult it is to construct policies that really do reflect the national interest on controversial foreign policy questions. It is not because decision makers necessarily have bad or selfish intentions that inadequate policies are adopted. Rather, it is because, whatever policy is chosen, when an issue is controversial it is easy to assemble a majority coalition that opposes that particular policy but difficult to assemble a majority coalition that supports that policy. The most likely scenario will entertain many majorities with partially overlapping memberships, each supporting quite different objectives. We saw in Chapter 6 that a majority of American voters in 1992 may have favored both decreasing the defense budget and, without altering the set of Americans polled, increasing the defense budget. If the individual, competing interests are collectively intransitive, at least over three or more alternatives, so that they produce a cycle of preferences, then really there is no such thing as the national interest on the issue in question. In the absence of a national interest, we should expect individual, selfish motives to dominate decision making, leaving us with the sense that the nation (which now is clearly a metaphor for disparate, unshared interests) is muddling through.

The approaches to international relations that are attentive to domestic political competition over foreign policy decisions remind us that the more groups competing for influence, and the more policy options under consideration, the more likely it is that the social choice problem will crop up. Even in authoritarian societies, bureaucratic or domestic interest group desires can be sufficiently diverse to produce cyclical preferences that lead to the social choice problem. As the Cuban Missile Crisis example illustrates, it takes only three choices and three decision makers for the problem to appear. With more choices or more decision makers, its appearance becomes even more likely.

## COMMON CIRCUMSTANCES WITHOUT THE SOCIAL CHOICE PROBLEM

If preferences are crucial to understanding international affairs, then they should be instrumental in advancing our ability to predict and explain outcomes in foreign policy and international politics. The social choice problem makes prediction difficult. However, there are many situations in which preferences are single peaked, a concept I elaborate below. When preferences are single peaked and issues can be represented as one dimensional, then the social choice problem does not arise. In such special, but common, cases, we can predict outcomes of decisions effectively by using the median voter theorem. The median voter theorem complements win sets, introduced in Chapter 6, and provides a method for predicting important policy decisions. The policy forecaster uses the median voter theorem, and it has a documented track record, which I take up in the last chapter.

### SOCIAL CHOICE AND SPATIAL VIEWS OF POLICY

When groups of people, whether they be voters, a foreign policy elite, military leaders, or what have you, make a collective decision about policy there is always the danger that their individual preferences will add up to form a chaotic, cyclical pattern. In such situations no policy has a solid claim to representing the national interest. Still, the social choice problem is not inevitable; under some circumstances the problem is less likely to arise than under others. To understand real-world conditions that avert the social choice problem, we need to elaborate on the concept of single-peaked preferences.

Individual issues in foreign policy (or in politics in general) can be depicted along a single line, or continuum, with the opposite ends representing the extreme positions taken by competing decision makers as in the discussion of the policy positions of Clinton, Bush, and Perot in Chapter 6. The range of alternatives included on the spatial continuum (whether one dimensional or more) identifies the feasible set of policy choices. For many issues, it is natural to think of preferences as falling somewhere along this single line or dimension. That is, it is natural to represent preferences on a single spatial dimension: a line. In doing this we are assuming that each issue is decided separately. In contrast, linking issues together as we did with win sets in Chapter 6 to capture the notion of trade-offs or interdependency builds on the idea that preferences can be displayed on a line but relaxes the assumption that issues can be treated separately, treating them instead as falling in a multidimensional space.

For many issues it is natural to think that the desirability of alternative choices declines as options move farther and farther away from a decision maker's most desired outcome, or ideal point. The decline in pref-erence as we move farther from a decision maker's ideal point is implied by the assumption of convex preferences intro-duced in Chapter 8. For example, those who want to spend a given amount of money on defense would experience a steady decline in preference as the amount proposed increas-ingly deviated from their desired expendi-ture. Similarly, those who support free trade would be more willing to accept a policy of small tariffs than one of large tariffs, just as those who favor protectionist trade policies would be more willing to tolerate a policy of medium-sized tariffs than one of small tar-iffs and one of small tariffs than one with no tariff at all. You will recall that preferences of this type are called single peaked because they reach one high point on a graph and then fall off continually from there. Specif-ically, preferences are single peaked if they can be drawn on a graph as a line that always rises, always falls, or rises and then falls with-out rising again. If the line falls first and then rises it is not single peaked. Figure 9-3 illus-trates the principle of single-peaked prefer-ences. It also shows how an issue and preferences related to that issue can be

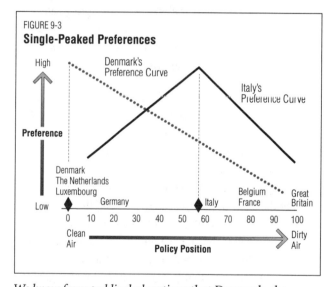

FIGURE 9-3
**Single-Peaked Preferences**

We know from public declarations that Denmark, the Netherlands, and Luxembourg supported a staunch clean air position in the European Community. Britain was will-ing to tolerate much higher levels of noxious exhaust gases, with Germany, Italy, Belgium, and France falling at differ-ent levels in between. Because of the assumption of single-peaked preferences, we can infer that Denmark's opposition to dirty air increased with increases in the quantity of exhaust gases proposed to be tolerated. Likewise, we can infer from single-peakedness that Italy preferred moder-ately clean air policies to policies that favored extremely clean air or extremely dirty air. Single-peaked preferences combined with one-dimensional issues ensure that the social choice problem of cycles does not arise.

depicted on a single line or issue dimension. When preferences are single peaked and issues are decided separately and are unidimensional, a social cycle cannot exist. If we *assume* preferences are single peaked when they really are not, we violate the fairness condition of universal domain.

The specific policy examined in Figure 9-3 is the decision of the European Community (EC) in the 1980s regarding the amount of pollutants it would tolerate from large-sized automobiles (Bueno de Mesquita and Stokman 1994). Low values on the scale refer to support for clean auto exhaust gases, and high numbers indicate tolerance for lots of pollutant (or low demand for clean-burning cars). The members of the EC are situated along the horizontal axis at the position that represents each country's ideal point (that is, its most preferred policy).

Although the figure reveals great diversity of opinion among the EC member states, it nevertheless depicts single-peaked preferences. For example, Denmark prefers position 20 on the scale to position 30, and position 30 to position 40, and so forth. The preference curve for Denmark reaches its high point above position 0, Denmark's ideal point. Italy prefers position 45 (or 65) to position 40 (or 70). This is because Italy's preference curve reaches its maximum value at position 55 before falling off steadily on either side of that value. The policy preference represented by position 80 in Figure 9-3 is the ideal point for Belgium, as well as for France.

The assumption of single-peaked preferences simplifies matters in that it restricts the domain of possible wish lists that leaders might have. Although it is quite natural to think of preferences as having this single-peaked characteristic, we should not lose sight of the fact that it is possible for leaders to have other types of preference orders. Figure 9-4 shows two examples of preference curves from our EC pollution control discussion that

Construct a foreign policy decision-making situation involving three or more decision makers that demonstrates the social choice problem. Satisfy yourself that there is no way to graph these preferences so that they are single peaked. Make sure one axis of the graph represents the array of preferences (try putting them in different orders) and the other axis ranks the choices of each decision maker from most preferred to least preferred. Demonstrate that this ranking produces a cycle. Is there any single ordering that yields a single-peaked graphing for each decision maker? Is the graph single peaked for any one of the decision makers?

are not single peaked. If any decision maker has these preferences, then even though an issue can be depicted on a single policy dimension, it is possible that the social choice problem of cyclical preferences will arise. Single-peaked preferences are a convenience that makes analyzing international politics (or any politics) more manageable, but it is not always the way things are in the real world. For example, when the French and British governments negotiated with one another to build the Chunnel, the tunnel that runs under the English Channel linking England and France by road, non-single-peaked preferences abounded. Each government was subject to pressure from interest groups, some in favor of construction of the tunnel and some opposed to its construction. Among the latter were environmental groups that cited its adverse impact on the channel environment; among the former were business groups, especially in tourism, that trumpeted its positive economic benefits. Preferences on the completeness of the tunnel, however, were not single peaked. None of the interests concerned with influencing the outcome of the tunnel debate preferred to see a tunnel built that was too short to span the channel over seeing one built that was sufficiently long enough or seeing no tunnel built at all. And no tunnel contractor, for its part, would have agreed to build a tunnel that ended under the water. The tunnel builder certainly preferred building a tunnel over not building a tunnel at all and not building a tunnel at all over building one that was too short. Still, there is considerable evidence that many policy choices do involve only single-peaked preferences (Bueno de Mesquita 2002).

If preferences are single peaked, issues fall along a single continuum, and decision makers are fully informed about each other's power and preferences, then the social choice problem cannot arise and the policy outcome may be predicted with significant accuracy. Of course, if decision makers are not fully informed about each other's power, preferences, or perceptions, then the outcome is more complicated. The assumption of single-peaked preferences is common in the study of politics because it appears to be a common property of preference orderings. This assumption has contributed many important insights to the study of international relations. Even so, we must keep in mind that single-peaked preferences do not always characterize real-world conditions. The question of parsimony must be applied to evaluate whether the costs in simplification implied by single-peaked preferences are justified by the gains in accurate empirical insights.

Earlier I noted that structural theories assume away the social choice problem by viewing each state as if it were a single decision maker with connected and consistent preferences. The structural solution to the social choice problem is different from assuming single-peaked preferences even if such preferences were not common. The latter allows for competing domestic (or international) preferences. Decision makers within a state (or in different states) can have diametrically opposed preferences, the same preferences, or preferences that fall somewhere in between these two extremes. Each decision maker's preference ordering, however, is assumed to be single peaked, so that many but not all

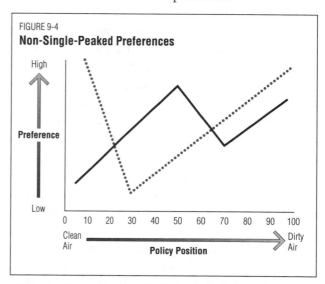

FIGURE 9-4
**Non-Single-Peaked Preferences**

*When preferences are not single peaked, the social choice problem of cyclical preferences will prevail. Real-world preferences are sometimes not single peaked, making outcomes difficult to predict, even for one-dimensional issues.*

In Chapter 3 I asked you to select a current issue to track. You have identified the stakeholders for that issue, and in Chapter 7 you estimated the power or potential influence of each stakeholder. Now I want you to specify the range of possible outcomes that are supported by different stakeholders, and I want you to locate each stakeholder on a line segment that ranges from one extreme outcome to the other. Stakeholder preferences should be single peaked. As it is not possible to know ideal points—most-preferred outcomes—specify each stakeholder's preferred outcome using your best estimate of his or her current position based on what you read in the newspapers or have learned from discussing the issue with experts.

logically possible preference orderings are admissible. By restricting the range of preferences, the social choice problem is avoided (in theory, if not in reality) while still permitting diversity of interests. The structural solution restricts preferences more broadly by allowing no more than one preference ordering in each state. This is one way in which structural approaches make more restrictive assumptions than do theories that allot domestic politics an important role in international affairs. In models that assume single-peaked preferences, fewer logically possible preference orderings are assumed away and so are more likely to mirror reality than are structural theories that assume decision making by a unitary actor.

### PREDICTING POLICY CHOICES: THE MEDIAN VOTER THEOREM

Let's consider decisions in the European Community in the 1980s, considering particularly its decision regarding a European auto emissions policy. Given the preferences shown in Figure 9-3, we need only add an assumption about how much support or power a given policy needs to defeat rival proposals in order to predict which policy fully informed decision makers will choose. Here I assume that the winning policy must be supported by at least a majority of the available power.[10] Given a majority-of-power requirement, it is straightforward to show that the policy preference of the median voter must be the winning position (Black 1958). If we were to assume that more than a majority of power was needed to win, then the location of the winning preference would shift, but the general concept would remain the same. As long as an issue falls on a single dimension, and as long as preferences are single peaked, then a cycle of preferences cannot arise and the outcome will be fairly predictable.

The European Community in the late 1980s did not operate on the principle of equal votes for each member. Instead, it recognized that some members were more influential than others and codified that influence through its distribution of votes. (The European Union of today continues to follow this scheme.) Britain, France, Germany, and Italy were granted ten votes each; Belgium, Greece (not voting on this issue), and the Netherlands had five votes each; Ireland (also not voting) and Denmark had three each; and Luxembourg controlled two. Under majority rule, then, the winning position had to

---

[10] In actuality, this issue was decided by the EC's unanimity rule. For simplicity, our example assumes simple majority rule.

be supported by at least 28 of the 55 votes cast by the members of the EC involved in the decision about auto emission standards.

By summing the power, or votes, of the EC members listed in Figure 9-3, we find that the median decision maker is Italy at position 55.[11] This means that we predict that the policy outcome at position 55 on the scale is adopted by the EC. This assumes that each EC member is completely informed about the power, preferences, and perceptions of all members of the community with respect to auto emissions of large-sized cars.[12] (The actual decision was for a standard equivalent to position 56 on the scale in Figure 9-3.)

Why do we sum votes to determine the winning position? The assumption of rationality and the assumption that preferences are single peaked combined with knowledge of each actor's ideal point are sufficient to reveal all the information we need about preferences to determine how each member of the EC would vote with regard to any two proposed solutions to the policy issue under examination. For example, if a vote were taken on whether to support an outcome at policy position 85 or to support instead policy position 60, we know how each member would vote. Each country's representative would vote for the policy closest to his or her nation's ideal point. We know this because of the assumption of single-peaked preferences. The delegates from Denmark, the Netherlands, Luxembourg, Germany, and Italy all like the policy at position 60 more than they like the policy at position 85 because the policy represented by position 60 is closer to each of these countries' ideal points than is the policy represented by position 85. Because each member, being rational, votes on the basis of its preference, we can add up the votes cast in favor of the policy at position 60 and compare it with the total cast for the policy at position 85 (favored by Belgium, France, and Great Britain). Clearly, the proposal at position 60 will defeat the alternative at position 85. For any pair of proposals, then, we know which of the two available options will win because the assumption of single-peaked preferences gives us the information we need to calculate the complete preference orderings of each member of the EC. No alternative can defeat the proposed policy at position 55; in fact, policy position 55 is unique in that it is the only position for which this holds true. Even if a member (or members) vote strategically rather than sincerely, this fact does not change. Sincere voting involves voting faithfully for your most preferred outcome in any given pair of choices at each stage in an agenda of votes. Strategic voting involves voting for your second choice over your first choice at some intermediate stage in the decision making to steer the subsequent agenda of choices. Decision makers might do this if, for example, they believe that their second choice ultimately has a better chance of winning than does their first choice while also believing

---

[11] It does not matter at which end we choose to start adding votes. The median voter does not change if we sum votes starting on the left side of the issue continuum or on the right side of the issue continuum.

[12] To be a little more precise, our prediction also assumes that the decision makers in the EC have strict preferences. This means that we assume they are never indifferent between two alternatives, such as an outcome at 55 compared with an outcome at 56.

that their first choice could eliminate their second choice from subsequent consideration. Strategic voting does not alter the fact that the median voter's position will be adopted because no alternative can beat the median voter in head-to-head competition. Hence, no strategic sequence of votes can eliminate the median voter's position as a choice. Consequently, we can confidently predict that the median voter's position will be the winning position.

Turn to the Web site at http://bdm.cqpress.com. Select one of the data sets offered there or construct your own estimate of power and preferences for a group of international actors on some issue of interest to you. Use the forecasting model to predict the issue outcome based on the median voter theorem. How well does this prediction fit with what really happened? Is the predicted outcome consistent with the preferred policy of the most powerful decision maker? If not, how does the median voter prediction compare with a realist position?

The ability to predict outcomes allows policymakers to use the concepts of preferences and power in interesting ways. Clearly, the EU has concluded that some of its members are more influential than others. For example, some, like France or Germany, have ten votes each whereas others, like Greece or Belgium, have only five votes each. (And others, of course, have still fewer votes.) The decision maker with a smaller number of votes does not automatically exert less influence on every question, however. In fact, in many EU issues, Greece and Luxembourg are pivotal actors.

Understanding how preferences can alter the calculus of power is extremely valuable when looking at issues in international politics. If the issue in question is unidimensional, a majority rules, and preferences are single peaked, then combining our knowledge about the preferences and power of the relevant actors allows us to predict how that issue will be resolved. This is true even when the issue being looked at does not involve voting. After all, voting is simply a special form of exercising power.

Many issues in international affairs involve the use of power. Resources can be mobilized to coerce a weaker party into doing what a stronger party wants it to do. The more powerful a coalition is, the more likely it is to succeed. Indeed, the probability that an interest group, a leader, a nation, an alliance, an international organization, or any other entity will get what it wants is generally low if it can only muster less than 50 percent of the resources relevant for influencing a decision. Conversely, the probability of achieving a given objective is high if the relevant party can muster more than 50 percent of the resources that confer power. In Figure 9-5 we see that the probability that a player on the international stage will get what it wants is a function of the percentage of relevant resources it can bring to bear on the issue in question. Figure 9-5 reflects the relationship between power (defined here as resources) and the chances for success in any international competition provided all else, such as the intensity of preferences, is equal. Power alone, however, does not determine policy decisions.

The median voter theorem provides a means to predict policy decisions and international outcomes based on the combined impact of power and preferences. As the example of Italy's influence over the EC's auto emission policy illustrates, the median voter perspective differs markedly from the viewpoint of realist theories. These theories assume that the powerful pretty much get to dictate how international affairs unfold at the expense of the weak. The median voter theorem is consistent domestically with the interest group or bureaucratic perspective and both domestically and internationally with the strategic perspective. It takes into account the ability of even a weak decision maker to alter an outcome away from a strict power-dependent result. Strategic positioning, in the median voter view of the world, can confer a powerful role on those who lack power in the form of military might, wealth, or votes. And because the median voter position defeats all rival positions when issues are unidimensional, preferences are single peaked, everybody votes sincerely, and majority rules, the median voter position is the most secure position one can adopt. Even a weak stakeholder located at the median voter position wins under the above conditions. Neorealists, then, ought to expect that states converge on the median voter position, producing a policy of consensus in international politics. That such a consensus does not frequently materialize raises doubts about security being the paramount concern of states.

> Find the median voter position on the issue you selected to focus on. This is the initial prediction of how this issue will be resolved. Does it seem plausible to you as a likely outcome? Are there any stakeholders who have a veto? That is, does an agreement over how to resolve the issue you chose *require* support from one or more particular stakeholders? If they are unhappy with the median voter position, does that change your prediction about the issue being resolved?

## SUMMARY

Preferences are the second pillar in our investigation of international affairs. We have defined preferences and shown that rational decision making requires only that alternative choices be connected consistently to avoid circularity and that people act on their preferences. We saw that acting on preferences does not mean that people always pursue their first choice, nor does it mean that they do not sometimes end up with their last choice. Decisions are almost always made in a constrained environment. Constraints may

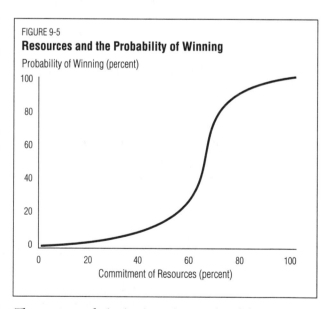

FIGURE 9-5

**Resources and the Probability of Winning**

Probability of Winning (percent)

*The prospects of winning in an international dispute increase rapidly as the level of resources a player commits to that dispute increases up to some threshold. Beyond that threshold, additional resources have a marginally decreasing impact on that player's chances of victory.*

arise because of a lack of power or because of the existence of international organizations, domestic political considerations, or many other factors that rule out some choices.

Because decision makers face constraints, it is risky to judge people's preferences by their actions. What people want and what they do are not always the same. Rational actors do what they believe will lead to the best achievable outcome. It is irrational to pursue one's preferences blindly, without regard to what is feasible.

Even people who share the same preference ordering across alternatives may choose different courses of action. Variations in choice can be caused by differences in access to information and variation in individual predilections for taking risks. Risk-acceptant decision makers are more inclined to risk a bad outcome in order to give themselves the chance of achieving a more preferred outcome. Risk-averse decision makers are more inclined to take an intermediate result rather than risk a bad outcome in an effort to achieve a more preferred outcome. These variations draw our attention to the utility that decision makers attach to each of the elements in their preference ordering.

The social choice problem highlights one of the more critical features of politics. Although individual decision makers may have connected and consistent preferences, when we add up the preferences of a group of decision makers we can end up with a cycle of preferences. That is, the group could prefer option A to B and B to C and C to A, which rounds back to A to B, and so forth. The Cuban Missile Crisis provides an example of the social choice problem. When the number of decision makers in a group is at least equal to the number of choices available to that group, the social choice problem can arise. The larger the number of decision makers, the higher the probability that a social cycle will occur.

The social choice problem alerts us to the difficulties inherent in speaking about the national interest. Not all decisions involve cycles of preferences or social intransitivities, but controversial choices frequently do. The most important problems in international affairs probably are controversial. Several theoretical solutions to the social choice problem are possible in that they allow us to assume the problem away. The notion that the state is a unitary actor with only one decision maker is the most common way that people avoid the social choice problem. This solution makes it easy to talk about the national interest and the state, rather than about competing interests and domestic political competition as elements in international affairs. In the next chapter, we will find that for many problems the unitary actor assumption works pretty well in giving us reliable, though imperfect, predictions. But for other problems, we will find it proves inadequate.

Sometimes issues can be thought of as falling on a single dimension. The median voter approach offers a straightforward way of dealing with the social choice problem for such issues. By assuming single-peaked preferences and majority rule, we can make reliable predictions and offer meaningful explanations about how unidimensional issues will be resolved. We applied these assumptions in our examination of a policy decision on auto emissions made by the European Community in the 1980s. The median voter theorem is not a reliable means of predicting outcomes when issues are multidimensional. Instead, the resolution of multidimensional issues can be predicted through identification of win sets. The basic features of both the median voter theorem and win sets underscore the importance of preferences to the study of international politics.

The entirety of this chapter has focused on a too-little-investigated yet crucial feature of international politics. At the outset, I quoted Hans Morgenthau's view that a focus on preferences or interests was a fallacy. The issues raised here should have dispelled the notion that a concern for preferences is a fallacy. Decision makers act not only in ways dictated by their power, but also use their power in the service of their desires—that is, their preferences.

# CHAPTER 10

# PERCEPTIONS IN INTERNATIONAL AFFAIRS

PERCEPTIONS AND REALITY

PERCEPTIONS AND TRADE SANCTIONS: AN ILLUSTRATION

SUMMARY

If a leader lacks power, there are some things that he or she simply cannot do. The prime minister of Nepal, for example, cannot launch a missile attack against the United States even if he wants to (which he certainly does not). He simply does not have the capability. Power is not the only arbiter of who gets (or who does) what, however. The leader of North Korea, for example, has the wherewithal to extract billions of dollars from the United States. By promising to terminate its program to build nuclear weapons, North Korea gained $4 billion in assistance from the United States in the mid-1990s. The U.S. response to the North Korean nuclear weapons program was prompted by its strong preference that North Korea not become a nuclear power. Strongly held preferences, as we saw earlier, can have a profound effect on international relations. Washington's preference that North Korea be prevented from becoming a nuclear power compensated for North Korea's tangible dearth of resources—that is, for its lack of power. In effect, the U.S. preference gave North Korea considerable power.

Other countries besides North Korea have threatened or are threatening to build nuclear weapons. Despite its policy against nuclear weapons proliferation, the United States assisted Israel in its successful effort to develop a nuclear arsenal. The Indian government tested a nuclear weapon in 1998, as did its rival, Pakistan. In these instances, however, the United States retaliated by imposing economic sanctions. Neither received an offer of substantial U.S. aid to bribe them into giving up their nuclear arsenals. Pakistan, however, did receive substantial U.S. aid in exchange for its support against the Taliban government of Afghanistan during the war on terrorism.

The decision to deter North Korea by offering it economic aid and not doing the same for Pakistan and India when faced with their nuclear programs is based on the U.S. perception that North Korea represents a real threat to America's interests whereas India and Pakistan do not. In particular, Washington is concerned about what a North Korean nuclear arsenal would mean to its close ally, South Korea. In contrast, nuclear weaponry in the hands of India and Pakistan is worrisome but is not perceived to be a major threat to U.S. security. In fact, nuclear weapons capabilities in these two countries are perceived to represent a threat only to the peace between the two of them, although India's nuclear capability could also represent some threat to China. The general perception today is that India and Pakistan, who warred with each other in 1948, 1965, and 1971, will try to resolve their differences now that both countries can threaten nuclear devastation. In fact, in early 1999 they began high-level discussions, including a face-to-face meeting between their two prime ministers. Intense clashes over contested territory in Kashmir later that year highlight both the source of mutual hostility and the importance of renewed efforts to resolve differences. During 2001–2002 the two again came close to war over Kashmir, but again they each backed away from the brink. Perhaps they did so because of the perceived costs of a nuclear exchange and perhaps because of the perception that the U.S. war on terrorism would prompt greater American commitments to promote a lucrative, aid-reinforced peace. Clearly, perceptions about the preferences or power of these nations' leaders have shaped their own and U.S. foreign policy decision making.

In this chapter we will look at questions concerning the role of perceptions in mediating between power and preferences. People's actions are shaped as much by perceptions as by objective reality. Here we will explore how perceptions influence international events, sometimes for the better and sometimes for the worse. It is important to understand that perceptions are neither random nor completely idiosyncratic and not unique to any particular individual. In the world of international relations, perceptions are shaped by events, and events are shaped by perceptions.

I begin by drawing important distinctions between reality and perceived reality. We will then evaluate how these differences influence foreign policy decisions. Using a game involving trade sanctions, I show how different beliefs (that is, perceptions) about reality influence trade policy. I further develop this game to show how beliefs about domestic political consequences influence economic policy decisions. This analysis of trade sanctions serves two purposes. First, it identifies some of the pitfalls associated with using economic sanctions as a foreign policy instrument and, second, it highlights how dependent many foreign policy actions are on perceptions. We will see how perceptions can lead, quite rationally, to outcomes that nobody wants. This does not mean that we should ignore perceptions, as realists urge. Quite the contrary. It teaches us how important it is to understand the real risks associated with alternative foreign policy courses when we live in a world filled with uncertainty. In such a world, decision makers must rely on perceptions whenever they select a course of action.

## PERCEPTIONS AND REALITY

Little that happens in international relations happens purely as a result of objective facts. The manner in which power is distributed, or how well informed foreign policy advisers are, is important, but rarely do such facts determine behavior. Rather, the manner in which relevant leaders think power is distributed, or how well informed leaders believe their advisers to be, is what shapes action. Reality alone cannot explain why, for example, a leader foregoes real opportunities out of a mistaken belief that those opportunities will lead to failure. Understanding such a leader's perceptions is vital to an understanding of his decision making. Any view of international politics that fails to take into account the role of perceptions is inadequate (Jervis 1976).

Consider the experience of the United States during the Vietnam War. Did the United States lose the war in Vietnam because it was weaker than North Vietnam? Certainly not. The United States lost the war in part because of differing perceptions about the importance of the objectives being pursued. Another factor leading to the U.S. defeat was mistaken American perceptions about the resolve of the North Vietnamese.

*Despite Israel's overwhelming military power relative to the Palestinian authority, Palestinian-Israeli fighting has continued for decades. Here the Israelis are seen in December 2001 destroying a Palestinian radio station, perhaps in an effort to silence the "voice" of the Palestinians. While Israel fights with conventional military might, the Palestinians, lacking significant weaponry, fight with terrorist attacks and suicide bombings in their effort to shift perceptions in the United States and elsewhere, so as to gain the sympathy and support of world powers against Israel.*

America's leaders and citizens were surprised when the Vietnamese did not surrender in the face of obviously superior fire power. American leaders believed, mistakenly, that "just a little more" pressure would break the back of North Vietnamese resistance. This mistaken perception dictated a course of action that was different from that which might have been followed had American leaders recognized the willingness of the North Vietnamese to endure such high costs.

The Tet offensive, launched by North Vietnam at the end of January 1968, was a critical event that shifted American attitudes toward the war. In reality, the North Vietnamese suffered a severe military defeat. Yet they won a crucial political victory. By showing that they could still muster the capabilities for an offensive, the North Vietnamese jarred American perceptions about North Vietnam's ability to pursue its objectives. Had the American public and its leaders believed that North Vietnam was capable of such an offensive, then North Vietnam's military defeat would have represented a major setback to North Vietnamese objectives. Instead, because the Americans hadn't thought it possible, the United States was forced to reconsider its war effort, and in so doing handed the North Vietnamese a resounding political victory.

The U.S. experience in Vietnam points to a significant aspect of perceptions—expectations. The American government and citizenry framed the conflict in Vietnam in certain terms. Those terms included a belief that no nation could endure losses as large as those North Vietnam turned out to be willing to suffer. By framing the problem in terms of this conventional expectation, Americans found their reference points badly challenged when the North Vietnamese did not falter. The U.S. belief that any country that loses as large a percentage of its population as had the North Vietnamese could not possibly continue to fight was based on the historical record. But because the Vietnamese were willing to suffer extraordinary losses, this reference point led Americans to form erroneous expectations about their prospects of victory.

A body of theory known as prospect theory examines the relationship between perceptions and how a problem is framed (Kahneman and Tversky 1984; Tversky and Kahneman 1986; Levy 1992; McDermott 1998). Prospect theorists have shown that how a particular problem is framed can affect how decision makers respond to that problem. They have observed that when people perceive an issue in terms of prospective gains, then they are willing to take few risks. However, when problems are perceived in terms of anticipated losses, then many people respond by taking significant risks. These different responses occur even though the objective facts are the same. For example, when patients are told they have a 10 percent chance of not recovering from a medical treatment, they typically decide against treatment. When they are told they have a 90 percent chance of recovering, they usually favor the treatment. Of course, both pieces of information reflect the same objective facts, yet the perception of the facts is quite different depending on whether the information is framed positively or negatively.

Prospect theory draws attention to preferences and to perceptions about the chances for gains or losses.[1] These perceptions form a decision maker's beliefs about the probabilities of acquiring gains and suffering losses. Like all rational choice theories, prospect theory lacks an explanation of the origin of preferences. Unfortunately, it also lacks a theory of framing and so has not yet proven as useful for predicting foreign policy or other behavior as has expected utility theory or the median voter theorem. Even if it develops a theory of framing, prospect theorists will still need to show that decision makers who follow the rules of prospect theory persevere when challenged by decision makers who follow the rules of expected utility. In this regard, it is noteworthy that research by Andrew Farkas (1999) has shown that even initially inefficient decision makers quickly adopt more efficient behavior that produces the same outcomes anticipated for expected utility maximizers. Leaders who do not perceive the advantages of successful choices, and who do not adapt their decision-making style to accept successful strategies and reject unsuccessful ones, tend not to survive politically.

Although perceptions seem clearly important in decision making, such prominent theoretical perspectives as neorealism and balance-of-power theory contend that all that matters is the actual distribution of power and the universal pursuit of security. In the case of the Vietnam War, much of the debate at the time revolved around whether vital American interests were truly at stake. Some leaders and many in the public perceived the war as an unnecessary venture that did not involve American security. Others disagreed, believing that a communist victory in Vietnam would weaken American interests throughout Asia and, perhaps, throughout the developing world. Had the latter view been universally held among American officials, the United States might have applied the higher level of force that was necessary to win. The perception that the stakes were not too high for U.S. security was critical in restraining America's effort.

Today, people still disagree about whether vital American interests were at risk during the Vietnam War. For our purposes it does not matter whether we agree with one side of the debate or the other. We simply need to recognize that differences in perceptions about the importance of the North Vietnamese threat to U.S. security shaped America's foreign policy during the Vietnam War.

---

[1] Sometimes prospect theory is mistakenly presented as an alternative to rational choice theory. In fact, prospect theory is a rational choice theory that rejects the axioms of expected utility theory. Expected utility theory enjoys much broader use than prospect theory. Application of prospect theory is limited because it makes few predictions and is difficult to falsify. Predictions thought to be derived from prospect theory, such as risk aversion for gains, are actually experimental observations that have been used as basic assumptions of the theory. Recently, prospect theory was pitted against the Forecaster expected utility model (available at the Web site for this book: http://bdm.cqpress.com) in analyzing issues about Northern Ireland peace before the resolution of the issues was known. The Forecaster got 100 percent of the predicted results right, whereas prospect theory got less than half right (Bueno de Mesquita, McDermott, and Cope 2001). Perhaps in the future more such tests based on ex ante, real predictions will be undertaken to give a better opportunity to assess the strengths and weaknesses of prospect theory and its rivals.

Understanding the importance of perceptions helps us evaluate the usefulness of alternative explanations of major international events. For example, realist explanations of such events do not take perceptions into account. Wherever a dispute occurs, whether at the heart of the international system or between peripheral, "minor" states, realist theories suggest that all conflicts are about power competition and that clarity and certainty motivate actions.

> In a bipolar world there are no peripheries. With only two powers capable of acting on a world scale, anything that happens anywhere is potentially of concern to both of them. . . . In a bipolar world changes may affect each of the two powers differently, and this means all the more that few changes in the world at large or within each other's national realm are likely to be thought irrelevant. . . . Self-dependence of parties, clarity of dangers, certainty about who has to face them: These are the characteristics of great-power politics in a bipolar world. (Waltz 1979, 171–172)

Such a view leaves little room for the importance of perceptions. Whereas perceptions are the product of uncertainty, the neorealist perspective presumes certainty about interests and risks, at least in a bipolar world. As such, hypotheses about the role of perceptions provide us with a critical test of the merits of alternative perspectives.

## PEOPLE FORM PERCEPTIONS ALL THE TIME

We all form perceptions about facts. We also form perceptions about information that may or may not be factual. Indeed, even when facts are known, identifying which are important depends on perception. Advantages in the possession or interpretation of information can make the difference between success and failure in the making of foreign policy. This is why countries have intelligence agencies sifting through newspapers, television broadcasts, and the public speeches of leaders and their advisers. This is also why intelligence agencies have spies, moles, and double agents who provide them with information believed by rivals to be secrets. This is also why leaders keep some important policy decisions secret. In August 1998, for example, President Bill Clinton ordered missile attacks against a presumed terrorist training ground in Afghanistan and against an alleged chemical weapons factory in the Sudan. Had the military targets been announced in advance, obviously the prospective success of these military missions would have been diminished. Secrecy and uncertainty in this instance were correctly perceived to be the most useful tools of international politics.

Governments devote substantial resources to collecting and interpreting information. They do so because information provides a basis for evaluating how rivals will interpret statements and actions. Information gathering helps reveal concrete facts, but facts alone do not tell the whole story. For example, infrared satellite photographs taken over steel plants in China can reveal approximately how much steel is being produced. Photographic tracking of Chinese freight trains can help reveal where traffic is flowing from and to. Yet these facts must also be interpreted. Do they reflect a change in the level of weapons production or of consumer goods? Do they support the conjecture that government-controlled Chinese industry is sharing in the dramatic economic growth in China, or do they suggest that government-operated industry is lagging behind the private sector? The latter might imply that there is growing tension between those interested in economic growth and those interested in sustaining centralized, autocratic rule. Such an interpretation would likely be of significant interest to the foreign policy decision makers who are accumulating the information. This is why perceptions and interpretations of the meaning of facts are central to planning strategies to deal with contingent developments in China or anywhere else.

Understanding international politics, then, requires that we understand the role of information and perceptions about that information in shaping policy choices and actions. To do so, we must develop a precise understanding of what is meant by "perceptions." We must also understand how to think about the relationship between perceptions and action (Jervis 1976, 1984; Bueno de Mesquita 1985; Kim and Bueno de Mesquita 1995; Gartner 1997). One objective of this chapter is to convey that much can be learned about people's perceptions by observing their actions; what's more, much can be inferred about an appropriate course of action after evaluating the perceptions of others.

## WHAT ARE BELIEFS OR PERCEPTIONS?

Information comes to us from many sources and in many forms. Some information is readily available to everyone. Other pieces of information are known only to some people and not to others. Some information might be known only by a single individual. Advantages or disadvantages in the possession of information often shape how we view situations and how we respond to them. Let's consider a simple example.

Throughout the world there is a shared convention that traffic stops when a traffic light is red and goes when a traffic light is green. In fact, this convention is an example of international cooperation. Imagine how confusing and dangerous it would be to travel from one country to another if the meaning attached to the color of traffic lights varied from place to place. Nations long ago agreed to treat red as the signal to stop and green as the signal to go.

When people are driving they rely on a shared understanding of traffic lights to decide whether to apply the brake or to continue to move forward. I know that if the light facing me is red I am expected to stop. I also know that you know that when my light is red I am expected to stop. You know that I know that fact, and so forth. Simply put, what I am expected to do in the face of a red light is common knowledge. Not only do we share the information, but we also share the fact that we each know the other knows this information. Consequently, if my light is red I stop, and if your light is green you proceed, confident that I will not crash into you.

Of course, you may be wrong. I may not stop. It is common knowledge that I am *expected* to stop, but what I actually will do is probabilistic. Perhaps I am daydreaming or deeply engaged in a conversation and do not notice that the light is red. Perhaps I am color blind and cannot distinguish a red light from a green light. Perhaps I am driving with reckless abandon and don't care if I crash into you. Perhaps my brakes are broken and I cannot stop the car even if I try. All of these factors about me (or my car) are not known for certain by you. Because you have experience driving, you have formed a conjecture about the probability that a car coming down the road will stop at a red light. Your decision to go forward is based on the perception that the risk that I will run the light is low. However, you are acting on your perception of the situation; your belief about what I will do is not a certainty.

My actual state of mind is my private knowledge. I know what I am thinking but you do not. Your belief about my state of mind—the probability you attach to my running the light—could be thought of as common knowledge. After all, experienced drivers know how low the chances are that another driver will run a red light. Thus, I know that you think it is very unlikely that I will drive through a red light, and you know that I think you think it is very unlikely, and so forth. This is common knowledge. However, only I know whether or not I will actually run the light. This is private knowledge.

This time, there is no crash when you enter the intersection. Your belief about the chances that I would run the light, however, may or may not have been right. The facts of this particular encounter reinforce your confidence that I, like other drivers, obey traffic signals. But your belief may still have been wrong. For example, suppose you thought the chances of my running the light were one in a thousand, but in fact I ignore traffic signals ten times out of a thousand. With this being the case, I am ten times more likely to ignore the traffic signal than you thought.

Suppose you had the unhappy experience of encountering me on one of those ten out of a thousand times when I disobey traffic signals. Probably, when you finally drive away from the scene of our crash, you will be more cautious than before. You are fearful that some other fool will be equally reckless. You have changed your conjecture about the risk of someone ignoring a red light. As the day or days wear on, however, you gradually revert to your usual, less tentative driving style. Experience at intersections reinforces your earlier conviction that traffic signals really do provide a reliable basis for deciding whether to proceed or to stop at an intersection.

The traffic light example illustrates several important points about perceptions, points that are crucial to understanding international affairs. First, perceptions are based on experience or expectations. Second, perceptions are concerned with the probability that one or another circumstance will arise. Finally, perceptions change in response to experience. We learn how to respond to a given situation based on our perceptions and the correlation between those perceptions and what actually happens to us. When things happen the way we expect them to, then our confidence in the rightness of our beliefs is reinforced. But if something happens that deviates from our expectations, then we learn to adjust our beliefs, although only if the experience is sufficiently off-kilter with what we expected that we feel compelled to rethink the situation. In essence, perceptions or beliefs lead to predictable actions and therefore can be thought about in quite systematic ways.

## PERCEPTIONS AND INFORMATION

Perceptions matter when decision makers are uncertain about the characteristics of their friends or their rivals, or when decision makers are uncertain about the history of the situation they are involved in. Uncertainty might exist regarding the preferences of other players on the international stage, or it might arise as a result of difficulties in estimating someone else's capabilities. Perhaps uncertainty is an issue when figuring out the costs or benefits that will result from a particular series of actions. All of these are examples of uncertainty about specific attributes of other decision makers. Each falls within the category of information known as incomplete information.

Uncertainty can arise for other reasons as well. Most notably, there can be uncertainty about the past actions of foreign policy leaders or domestic interests. Previous actions reveal information about people's expectations and perceptions. But sometimes we just do not know the history that represents the context for a current circumstance. Difficulties in knowing the history of actions may lead to ambiguous information about someone else's true intentions. Uncertainty about past actions falls within the category of information known as imperfect information.

Foreign policy leaders rarely know exactly and with complete certainty all of the factors that influence the choices of other decision makers. As already noted, some information is private. Sometimes it pays to keep such information private. By doing so, leaders have an opportunity to take advantage of the beliefs held by their foes in a way that will improve their own welfare. In the following section, we will look at an example of such a circumstance and evaluate the importance of perceptions in shaping fundamental aspects of international trade policy. This example demonstrates how perceptions influence the course of international politics and illuminates an important area of the international political economy.

## PERCEPTIONS AND TRADE SANCTIONS: AN ILLUSTRATION

The United States and Japan are engaged in a long-standing dispute over trade policy. Japan exports much more to the United States than the United States exports to Japan. This means that there is a large trade imbalance between the two countries. Many more American dollars flow to Japan than come back through Japanese purchase of American goods.[2] The trade deficit between the United States and Japan has been a thorn in the

---

[2] The trade picture, of course, is more complicated. During much of the 1980s, for example, Japanese investors purchased vast amounts of American Treasury bills and other financial instruments. These are not counted in the balance of trade, but nevertheless represent a substantial economic benefit to the United States. Indeed, Japanese investments in American Treasury bills was a major factor in holding down the national deficit and controlling inflation. Also, we should recognize that the United States has about twice the population of Japan. For the Japanese to buy goods from the United States that are worth as much as the goods Americans buy from Japan, each Japanese citizen would have to spend about twice as much on American goods as individual Americans would have to spend on Japanese goods.

side of American presidents for quite some time. It is a source of political friction between the two countries and is a regular topic of domestic debate in both Japanese and American political circles.

The friction between Japan and the United States over trade policy is part of a larger intellectual debate over free trade and fair trade (Conybeare 1987; Lake 1988; Milner 1988; Milner and Yoffie 1989; Oye 1992; Mansfield 1994). Free traders believe that it does not matter whether imports and exports are balanced between countries. For them, Japanese goods are attractive to American consumers because they combine quality and competitive pricing. They say that we should not punish American consumers by keeping Japanese goods out of the American market. Doing so means that Americans must either pay more for quality goods or buy inferior goods.

Fair traders disagree. They argue that the United States should punish the Japanese with sanctions such as punitive tariffs. According to their perceptions, the trade deficit exists because Japanese regulations are designed to keep American (and other imported) goods out of the Japanese market. This leads to lower wages and unemployment in the United States, which is unfair to American workers.

Fair traders maintain that the playing field is not level. Sanctions are a way to punish the Japanese government into opening its markets to American goods and level the playing field. Free traders, in contrast, believe the field is already level. The problem, as they see it, is that American goods are not competitive in the Japanese market. They note, for example, that American automobiles are designed for driving on the right side of the road. The Japanese drive on the left. American appliances are too large for small Japanese homes. Naturally, American appliances do not sell well in Japan. The fair traders counter that American rice could be sold in Japan for a fraction of what Japanese consumers pay for their home-grown rice. They note that Japanese domestic rice producers are protected from outside competition. This tilts the playing field in Japan's favor. Of course, there is truth to both sides of the argument. If there were no basis for each side's beliefs, then rational free traders and rational fair traders would not be able to sustain their perceptions of the circumstances surrounding U.S.-Japanese trade relations. We look at the political logic behind free and fair trade perspectives in more depth in Chapter 13. For now I just stipulate that this is an important source of political debate.

A fundamental policy issue dividing fair traders and free traders in the United States revolves around the issue of trade sanctions. The question is, would U.S.-imposed trade sanctions lead Japan to open its markets to American goods or would they result in retaliatory tariffs? At the heart of the issue is the basis of the trade imbalance. On the one hand, it might be the case that the trade imbalance is a product of unfair practices, in which case punishment through sanctions could alter behavior. On the other hand, the trade imbalance might be structural. That is, the trade imbalance might result from the mix of goods and services offered by the United States to the Japanese. It might not be the consequence of discriminatory trade policies in Japan at all. Of course, the trade imbalance might also have to do with domestic Japanese politics. Japanese farmers, for example, are influential in Japan's parliament, called the Diet. And farmers, not surprisingly, want the government to protect them from foreign competition. Japanese political leaders who depend on support from farmers are reluctant to sacrifice votes even in the face of national financial losses resulting from American trade sanctions.

The decision on whether or not to impose sanctions depends on the perceptions of U.S. leaders—that is, on whether they believe that sanctions would be effective or whether they believe that tariffs and other sanctions would not be effective because they do not address the real problem. Before choosing a course of action the president cannot know for sure how the Japanese will respond. Perceptions about the effectiveness of sanctions clearly are at the heart of whatever policy is chosen. Let's turn our attention to the strategic calculations behind the policy decision on whether or not to impose sanctions. In doing so, we will examine the integral role of perception in making policy decisions.

*Some in the West perceive whaling as an unnecessary threat to the survival of whales and to biodiversity. In Japan the issue is perceived differently. This image from May 2002 shows demonstrators from all walks of life in Tokyo protesting efforts by the United States and other nations to restrict whaling and to interfere with Japan's cultural, personal, and dietary values. Politicians in Japan who want to be elected need to heed such domestic pressures even if supporting whaling runs counter to the worldview. When domestic political interests run counter to an objective view of the economic national interest, those domestic interests frequently triumph.*

## THE TRADE-SANCTIONING GAME

Suppose that the president must decide whether or not to issue an executive order imposing trade sanctions on Japan. If he decides not to do so, then trade will continue as is and the status quo will prevail. If he does decide to impose sanctions, then the Japanese will respond by either opening their markets (as the fair traders suggest) or keeping them closed (as the free traders suggest). The problem is that the president simply does not know which of these will occur. He perceives that each of Japan's leaders can be either one of two types of people: those who will respond cooperatively to trade sanctions or those who will not. This means that the president believes there is some chance that the Japanese prime minister and Diet will respond in positive (from the U.S. perspective) ways to sanctions by opening Japan's market to American goods. Yet there is also some possibility that they will not. Suppose the president or his trade advisers think that the likelihood that the Japanese will be responsive and open their markets is equal to the probability $p$. Naturally, $p$ is at least as big as 0 but no bigger than 1. The chance that Japan's leaders are the type that will not open Japan's markets in response to U.S. sanctions, then, equals $1 - p$.

What might influence the Japanese decision on whether or not to cooperate? There are many possibilities. One is that each leader's psychological makeup may predispose him to decide one way or the other. Another possible answer points to the effects of culture. Japanese culture emphasizes cooperation and consensus internally although not necessarily with outsiders. The Japanese leaders may also believe that the United States does not have substitute suppliers for the goods and services purchased from Japan and so will not be able to sustain sanctions because they will be too costly to the American economy. Alternatively, the Japanese leadership may believe that the Americans do have substitute suppliers but ones that will charge the United States a higher price than would Japanese suppliers. By switching to these substitute suppliers the Americans may force other buyers out of the markets currently filled by those suppliers. In such a case, other countries may increase their purchase of the very Japanese goods being excluded from the sanction-clouded American market. Unless the international community joined in upholding sanctions against Japan, the Japanese under these circumstances would not be concerned by the imposition of U.S. sanctions (although American consumers would, as they would be forced to pay a higher price for buying from a second-choice supplier) (Martin 1992). From a rational actor perspective, all of these elements can shape leaders' utility functions. These and other factors can be described in terms of the costs and benefits to the Japanese leadership of yielding in the face of U.S. sanctions and opening up markets or continuing to resist American pressure.

The Japanese leaders face three possible consequences, depending on whether or not they are the cooperative type. First of all, the status quo could prevail. In this case, there are no sanctions and the openness of Japan's market does not change. Let's designate the status quo outcome SQ. Second, the United States may change the status quo by imposing sanctions. In this case, the Japanese might decide to open their markets. We will denote the open market outcome with the letters OM. Finally, the Japanese may react to sanctions by retaliating with higher tariffs on American goods. The retaliatory outcome can be designated R. The ordering of preferences for the Japanese leaders will vary depending on whether or not they are the cooperative type. A cooperative Japanese leader will have the following preferences: SQ > OM > R. An uncooperative leader will prefer the following: SQ > R > OM. The U.S. president's preference ordering, naturally, will differ again. His preference ordering will be as follows: OM > SQ > R.

The American preference ordering suggests that sanctions are costly. This is why the United States prefers not to use sanctions if they will not work (SQ > R). If sanctions are doomed to failure, then there is no point in bearing the costs associated with them. That is, the decision whether to impose sanctions is strategically dictated by expectations about consequences in the specific context. In other words, the decision whether to impose sanctions is endogenous.

I suggested above what some of the costs of imposing sanctions might be. The American consumer might have to pay a higher price for substitutes for the goods that previously would have been purchased from Japan or pay higher prices for other Japanese goods because of punitive, retaliatory tariffs. As a result, the president might lose political support from constituents who are hurt by the imposition of sanctions. Certainly the president will consider these ramifications of sanctions before choosing to sanction or not.

Figure 10-1 sketches the problem facing the president. The figure depicts a game tree of the type introduced in Chapter 3. This game, in a sense, is simply a more elaborate model of the Toyota–U.S. Trade Representative game introduced earlier. The actions of each player in the game depend on perceptions and expectations about the responses of other players.

The boxes labeled "United States" and "Japan" in Figure 10-1 denote the points at

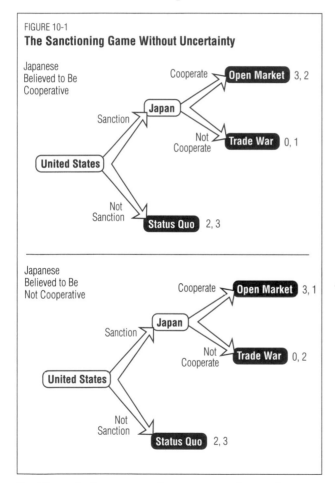

FIGURE 10-1
**The Sanctioning Game Without Uncertainty**

Japanese Believed to Be Cooperative

Cooperate — Open Market  3, 2

Japan

Sanction

Not Cooperate — Trade War  0, 1

United States

Not Sanction

Status Quo  2, 3

Japanese Believed to Be Not Cooperative

Cooperate — Open Market  3, 1

Japan

Sanction

Not Cooperate — Trade War  0, 2

United States

Not Sanction

Status Quo  2, 3

*Deciding whether or not to impose economic sanctions on Japan to force the Japanese government to open its markets would be easy if there were no uncertainty about how Japan would respond.*

which decisions must be made. These are the choice nodes. The arrows coming out of these boxes denote the different actions that could be taken at each choice point. The upper tree shows the game as it is played when the Japanese leadership is of the cooperative type; the lower tree shows the game as it is played when the Japanese leader is of the noncooperative type. The dark boxes labeled "Open Market," "Trade War," and "Status Quo" represent the terminal nodes, or possible outcomes, of the sanctioning problem. Finally, there are two numbers found at each terminal node in each of the two game trees in Figure 10-1. The first number refers to the utility the United States attaches to the outcome at that node. The second number refers to the utility the Japanese attach to the outcome at that node. Higher numbers mean greater value. These numbers are the game's payoffs. Notice that if the Japanese are the cooperative type, as in the upper game tree, then, consistent with the assumed preferences for that type, they attach more value to opening their market (utility of 2) than they do to keeping the market closed (utility of 1). The opposite is true in the lower game tree where the payoffs from the sanctioning game are consistent with the assumed preferences of a Japanese leader of the noncooperative type.

In the games depicted in Figure 10-1, the president has no uncertainty about the Japanese leader's type. If the president is certain that the Japanese prime minister is the cooperative type, then the president (and prime minister) know that the situation can be summarized by the upper game tree. If the president is certain that the Japanese prime minister is the uncooperative type, then the president (and prime minister) know that the situation can be summarized by the lower game tree. In either case, the game is easily solved by using the method of backward induction introduced in Chapter 3 to find the subgame perfect Nash equilibrium.[3] A subgame perfect Nash equilibrium indicates that players give best replies to the actions of other players at each stage of the game, with best replies reflecting the expected utility maximizing choice given the expected actions by the other players from that point in the game forward to its end.

Figure 10-2 shows the solutions to the games in Figure 10-1. By starting at any terminal node, we can work back through the successive choice nodes to establish which sequence of choices will net each player its best outcome. The darkened arrows represent the choice each player is expected to make at each node in the game. An equilibrium outcome is one for which the path of darkened arrows is uninterrupted from the beginning of the game to its end. The description of the full equilibrium includes the moves associated with each darkened arrow, whether or not it is part of a complete, unbroken path from the beginning of the game to the end of the game. The darkened arrows represent the complete plan of action by each player for each contingency in the game, including

---

[3] Recall that a Nash equilibrium is a set of strategies—a complete plan of action for playing the game under any possible contingency—such that no player can expect to improve her or his welfare by switching to a different strategy unilaterally.

those contingencies that ultimately do not arise. For example, the subgame perfect Nash equilibrium in the lower game in Figure 10-2 (where the Japanese leadership is the uncooperative type and the United States moves first) indicates that if the United States chooses not to sanction, then the status quo will prevail, whereas if the United States does choose to impose sanctions, then the Japanese leader will not cooperate. (Recall from Chapter 3 that the utilities of the players are listed in the order in which each makes its first move.) In this game tree, it is clear that if the president chooses to sanction,

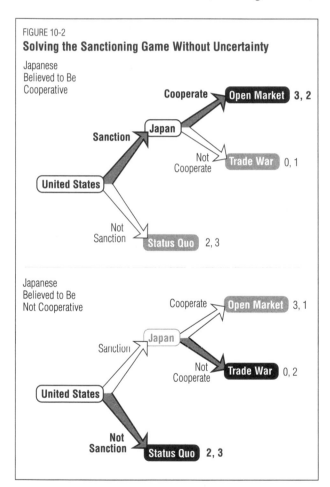

FIGURE 10-2
**Solving the Sanctioning Game Without Uncertainty**

Japanese
Believed to Be
Cooperative

Cooperate — Open Market   3, 2

Japan

Sanction

Not
Cooperate — Trade War   0, 1

United States

Not
Sanction — Status Quo   2, 3

Japanese
Believed to Be
Not Cooperative

Cooperate — Open Market   3, 1

Japan

Sanction

Not
Cooperate — Trade War   0, 2

United States

Not
Sanction — Status Quo   2, 3

*If Japan's leaders value their relationship with the United States sufficiently, then economic sanctions would lead to cooperation from Japan. But if domestic political pressures or other factors make the Japanese leaders willing to retaliate against trade sanctions, then the best course for the United States is to live with the status quo and not sanction Japan for keeping its markets relatively closed.*

the Japanese leader will not cooperate. As a result, the United States will net an outcome valued at 0—that is, it will gain no benefit at all. Clearly, this is not a desirable path for the president to follow. This contingency—which is said to be off the equilibrium path—is a critical element in shaping the president's decision even though it is an action not actually taken when the game is played out. This is why it is so important to look at the entire equilibrium—the complete plan of action for each player—and not just at the moves on the path to the predicted outcome. In the lower game tree in Figure 10-2, an equilibrium outcome can be reached only if the president chooses to allow the status quo to prevail.

The president's decision not to sanction is driven by his calculation of self-interest. He has looked ahead in the game and asked himself, "What will the Japanese prime minister do if I invoke trade sanctions?" He concludes that if the prime minister faces sanctions, Japan will not cooperate and the United States will face the worst possible outcome from the president's perspective, a trade war (Conybeare 1987). Thus, the status quo prevails because the president anticipates that sanctions will make him worse off than the status quo: sanctions are not a best reply in this game. Although the president cannot actually observe the Japanese prime minister's thought processes in this case, the president's expectation of what the prime minister will do is sufficient to help him conclude that he should not use sanctions. The anticipation of a counterfactual state of the world—the trade war that really did not happen—is enough to persuade the United States not to impose sanctions.

If, by contrast, the president were certain that the Japanese prime minister would cooperate in response to sanctions, then the president would choose to impose sanctions on the Japanese. Based on his calculations, represented in the upper game tree in Figure 10-2, he expects that the Japanese prime minister will give in and open up the Japanese market to avert a trade war. Knowing the prime minister's "type" changes the decision made by the president. What the president's best move is depends on how he expects the Japanese prime minister to respond later in the game.

In reality, of course, it is unlikely that the president will know how the Japanese prime minister will respond to trade sanctions. The president will, however, cultivate a certain view on whether or not the Japanese prime minister will cooperate. When we study problems such as the U.S.-Japanese trade-sanctioning dispute we must be able to predict and explain behavior when one or more decision maker faces uncertainty and so must act on his or her perception of the situation. Even though the decision maker faces uncertainty, his or her actions may still be predictable. Indeed, by looking at perceptions in an orderly way we can explain why leaders sometimes end up with foreign policy outcomes that nobody desires. This is one of the great advantages of using an approach like game theory, which focuses our attention on the strategic interplay in international relations. Figure 10-3 expands the game depicted in Figures 10-1 and 10-2 by taking into account the uncertainty over whether or not Japan's leader is the type that prefers to cooperate in a trade dispute or the type that prefers not to cooperate. Figure 10-4 shows the solution to this expanded game.

In this more elaborate rendering of the trade-sanctioning game, the first move is not made by the United States or by Japan, but rather by a participant called Nature. By "Nature" I mean whatever historical, cultural,

The trade game from Chapter 8 is repeated below in its normal, or strategic, form. Remember that there were three Nash equilibria for this game: Toyota builds in Japan and the USTR permits Japanese imports; Toyota builds in the United States and the USTR restricts Japanese imports; and a mixed strategy in which each action is taken probabilistically. Construct an extensive form for this game, under the assumption that the USTR announces its policy before Toyota announces where it will build cars for the U.S. market. That is, construct an extensive form in which the USTR moves first. Using backward induction, solve this game. Are all three of the original Nash equilibria also subgame perfect equilibria? How has the sequence of play changed the expected outcome? Is the expected outcome different if you construct the extensive form of the game so that Toyota moves first by building or not building a manufacturing or assembly facility in the United States before the USTR announces its tariff policy? Notice that the original strategic form assumes that each side moves without knowing the action of the other side. That is, the strategic form implies simultaneous moves or decision making under uncertainty. Such a situation involving uncertainty in the trade-sanctioning game is depicted in Figure 10-3.

or other conditions or circumstances determine whether the Japanese leader is the cooperative or uncooperative type. Nature, in the form of Japanese domestic political circumstances, for example, might force the prime minister to resist sanctions and act tough. In Figure 10-3 we will assume that the probability that Nature has chosen a cooperative prime minister is $p$ and the probability that Nature has chosen an uncooperative prime minister is $1 - p$. The probabilities $p$ and $1 - p$ represent the U.S. president's *belief* about which type of prime minister Japan has. These probabilities are common knowledge so that both the United States and Japan know what the United States believes about Japan's type. The Japanese, of course, also know what their actual type is. This is private information. The U.S. decision on whether or not to impose sanctions in this version of the game depends crucially on the perception that the Japanese prime minister is one or the other type of leader.

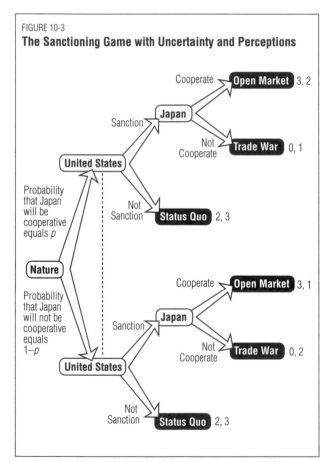

FIGURE 10-3
**The Sanctioning Game with Uncertainty and Perceptions**

*Deciding whether or not to impose economic sanctions on Japan to force the Japanese government to open its markets is a difficult decision if the president is uncertain about the outcome. Will the imposition of sanctions bring about a trade war with Japan, or will it foster greater free trade?*

If the president is certain that the Japanese prime minister is the cooperative type, such that $p$ equals 1 and $1 - p$ equals 0, then the lower portion of the sanctioning game depicted in Figure 10-1 becomes irrelevant and we must solve the upper portion of Figure 10-1. If the president sanctions the Japanese when $p$ equals 1, then we can be certain that the Japanese will choose to open their markets because this is the best reply to U.S. sanctions for the cooperative type of Japanese leader. The fair traders are correct in this case. By sanctioning, the United States can guarantee itself the best possible outcome ($U = 3$). Sanctioning is a best reply because if the president chooses not to sanction, then he would receive a smaller amount of utility (2). For Japan's part, cooperating, in this case, is the best reply to sanctions because the Japanese prime minister derives more utility from opening Japan's markets ($U = 2$) than from enduring a trade war ($U = 1$).

If the president is certain that the Japanese prime minister is the uncooperative type ($p = 0$), then, as we saw in Figure 10-2, he can see that sanctions will lead the

Japanese to retaliate. In this case, the United States gets its least-preferred outcome ($U = 0$). The president would bear the costs of sanctions without getting any benefit. Here, the free traders prove correct, and the president would choose not to sanction Japan. This version of the sanctioning game ends, then, with the president realizing a utility gain of 2 and the Japanese getting their best possible outcome, a utility gain of 3.

In Figure 10-3 a dashed line joins together the two separate games from Figure 10-1. By joining them together in this way, we have created one game with new features. The dashed line joining the two nodes that are labeled "United States" indicates that the president does not know whether he is facing a cooperative or an uncooperative Japanese leader. In other words, when the president must move he does not know whether he is at his upper or lower choice node, something he did know in the two game trees depicted in Figure 10-1. The dashed line describes what is known as an information set and shows us that the game is being played with imperfect information. The imperfect information here refers to the condition that the president does not know whether Nature (that is, Japanese political circumstances) selected a cooperative or uncooperative prime minister. Consequently, the president does not know exactly how the prime minister will respond to sanctions. This is known only to the Japanese prime minister.[4]

What should the president do if $p$ is not equal to 0 or 1 but, rather, falls in between? According to the rules of the game laid down in Chapter 3, the president will choose the course of action he believes is best for him. He must calculate what to do based on his perception about whether the Japanese leader is the cooperative or uncooperative type. The president knows that with probability $p$, imposition of sanctions will lead to open markets in Japan. He attaches a utility of 3 to this outcome. He knows too that with probability $1 - p$ imposition of sanctions will lead to the worst possible outcome for the United States, a trade war ($U = 0$). The president can determine whether or not he expects to be better off by imposing sanctions or by calculating which action is expected to yield a greater return. His calculation depends on how big he thinks the risk is that the Japanese are the uncooperative type.

Of course, the president does not actually sit down and do the algebra that we are now going to perform. He makes his calculations intuitively. We can represent this intuition, however, by calculating the value of each event that can occur, multiplying that

---

[4] Notice that what the president really does not know is the Japanese prime minister's preference ordering at the end of the game. This source of uncertainty would be an example of incomplete information if it were not for a clever "trick" devised by John Harsanyi, a Nobel laureate in economics. Harsanyi saw how to convert games with incomplete information into games with imperfect information by introducing a chance move by Nature, such as is done at the beginning of this game. This chance move, part of the history of the game prior to the move by the U.S. president, makes it possible to talk about a single game even though, in some sense, the president does not know which game he is playing, the upper game in Figure 10-1 or the lower game in Figure 10-1. In Figure 10-3 these two games are now part of a larger game that includes as one of its moves a probabilistic determination by Nature about which game is actually being played. In this way uncertainty about the game's payoffs is turned into uncertainty about Nature's prior move.

value by the probability of its occurring, and adding up the answers under each choice the president could make. We can then compare the value of choosing one action with the value of choosing the other action by seeing which action yields a larger expected utility. You will recall that we used this process in Chapter 3 when we compared the expected utilities of Spain and Portugal from supporting Columbus's venture.

If the president chooses to sanction Japan for alleged unfair trade practices (for example, dumping Japanese products on the American market at below cost while excluding American goods from the Japanese market), there is a chance that the sanctions will succeed in opening the Japanese market to American goods because the Japanese leadership is cooperative ($p$). There is also a chance that sanctions will trigger a trade war initiated by an uncooperative Japanese leadership ($1 - p$). The president's expected utility associated with choosing sanctions is equal to $3p + (1 - p)0$, or $3p$. The expected utility from not sanctioning—that is, from retaining the status quo, equals 2 regardless of how the Japanese would respond to sanctions, because if the president does not sanction, then the Japanese simply do not get an opportunity to respond. We can now predict the president's actions.

If $3p > 2$ or, equivalently, $p > 2/3$, then the president will impose sanctions.

If $3p < 2$ or, equivalently, $p < 2/3$, then the president will not impose sanctions and the status quo will prevail.

If $3p = 2$ or, equivalently, $p = 2/3$, then the president will be indifferent as to whether he imposes sanctions or he allows the status quo to prevail.

It is clear from this discussion that the president's perception of whether or not the Japanese leader is cooperative determines whether or not he will choose to impose trade sanctions. Differences in perceptions in games involving uncertainty lead to results that are not possible if all information is commonly known, as in the games depicted in Figure 10-1. If the president knows the intentions of the Japanese prime minister, then one outcome that could never occur is retaliation in the form of a trade war. Yet in the game depicted in Figure 10-3 and solved in Figure 10-4, we see that if $p$ is greater than 2/3 then the possibility of a trade war does exist. If $p$ equals 3/4, for example, then there is a 3/4 chance that the Japanese will open their markets in response to U.S. imposition of sanctions and only a 1/4 chance that they will refuse to open their markets and retaliate, initiating a trade war. The erroneous perception that the Japanese leader is of the cooperative type, then, can lead to a circumstance that both the president and the Japanese prime minister would like to avoid. In this case, the president makes a carefully calculated decision—one might say a correct decision—but gets a very bad result. This is one of the basic problems in international politics.

Good outcomes sometimes happen by chance to ineffective leaders, and bad outcomes sometimes happen by chance to good leaders. Just because an undesired outcome occurs, we cannot infer that the relevant decision makers were foolish, preferred the bad outcome, or were irrational. After all, we just saw how bad outcomes can arise when leaders do not know for certain what the consequences of their actions will be. Still, they can choose the action that they believe will leave them best off. Sometimes, although probably not often, they will turn out to be wrong. This, you will recall, was one of the lessons from our example in Chapter 9 of buying a soda from a vending machine. The president's perception that the Japanese prime minister was of the cooperative type and would respond positively to U.S. sanctions prompted his decision, and, in this example, his decision reaped an undesired result.

## THE SANCTIONING GAME AND DOMESTIC POLITICS

The only uncertainty the president has to worry about in Figure 10-3 concerns the preferences of Japan's leaders. The figure implies that the personal interests of the president and the welfare of the United States are the same. The example highlights the importance of perceptions, but it is still an incomplete view of international relations and presidential decision making. This is because it leaves no place for domestic politics. In this section we add domestic politics to the mix to show additional effects that perceptions can have on international affairs.

To keep the example manageable I will add only one American domestic interest group (the median voter) to the game. This interest group adds to the game a vote to keep the president in office or to replace him after trade negotiations are finished. If this interest group is happy with the president, it will keep him in office. If it is unhappy, it will vote the president out of office. Naturally, domestic interest groups also play a role in Japan. We can readily imagine that the American electorate is divided into many interest groups. However many of these there may be, let's assume that the preference ordering of the decisive median American voter in

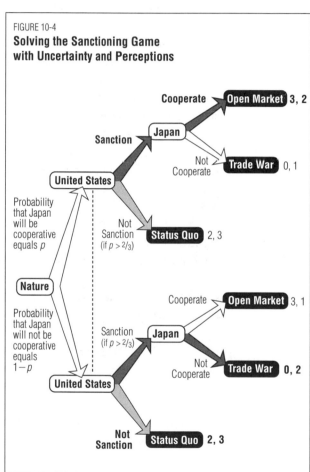

FIGURE 10-4
**Solving the Sanctioning Game with Uncertainty and Perceptions**

*When decisions are made under uncertainty, perceptions about how the Japanese will respond to the imposition of sanctions can lead to unintended consequences. It is possible that a trade war will erupt even though neither the Japanese leadership nor the American leadership wants that outcome.*

presidential elections with respect to trade sanctions is SQ > OM > R. The median voter is someone who does not want to see the president impose sanctions in an effort to open Japan's markets. Perhaps the median voter has a consumer orientation and is particularly nervous about rising prices. If the president imposes sanctions on Japan there is a danger that prices for Japanese goods (or for substitute goods) will rise. This would be harmful to the U.S. consumer. The status quo allows Japanese goods to be sold cheaply in the United States. Japanese manufacturers do not need to pass on any extra cost, which they would have to do were sanctions imposed. Still, this voter prefers opening the Japanese market through the use of sanctions to retaliation; although the median voter does not want to see sanctions imposed on Japan, he or she hopes that if they are imposed they will at least work.

The median voter has a choice to reelect the president or elect someone else. Let's assume that the voter wants to keep the president if he selects the policy favored by the voter. We will assign the voter a utility of 3 if the policy outcome is maintenance of the status quo and the president is reelected. If the policy outcome is maintenance of the status quo but for some reason the president is not reelected (perhaps he does not seek another term), then the voter's utility drops to 2. If the outcome is presidential imposition of sanctions, and the Japanese leadership retaliates, then the voter will punish the incumbent president by electing a new president. The utility for replacing the president is 0. The voter's utility for keeping the president if the United States suffers from retaliatory tariffs is $-1$. If the president imposes sanctions and this leads to an opening of the Japanese market, then the voter is indifferent between reelecting the president or replacing him; the utility in either case is 1. The median voter is happy that there are no retaliatory tariffs but disappointed that the president put his well-being at risk by imposing sanctions rather than accepting the status quo as he desired. In this case, there is a fifty-fifty chance that the president will be reelected.

The preference ordering assumed for the president remains unchanged (OM > SQ > R). However, the president wants to be reelected. To reflect this, let's assume that if he is reelected, his utility increases by 1 compared with its value based solely on his policy preferences. In this way, we can reflect the president's utility for both the policy outcome and his personal political well-being.

The game depicted in Figure 10-5 extends the game tree from Figure 10-3 to take into account both uncertainty about the type of Japanese leader (cooperative or uncooperative) and the effects of domestic politics (median voter preferences).

Is the president's behavior influenced by the desires of the pivotal, median voter even though his preferences over the trade outcomes are unaltered? To answer this question, we must calculate the expected utility for the president under all possible contingencies. First, we must do backward induction to determine what would happen if the Japanese were cooperative and what would happen if they were uncooperative. Then, using the probabilities $p$ and $1 - p$, we need to compute the president's expected utility for sanctioning and his expected utility for not sanctioning. We must also keep in mind that the president is still uncertain about whether the Japanese leadership is going to be cooperative or uncooperative. He still must act on his perception of the situation.

The president knows that he has a fifty-fifty chance of being reelected if he imposes sanctions and the Japanese are cooperative. The fifty-fifty chance reflects the fact that the median voter is indifferent between keeping the president and replacing him under this circumstance. If

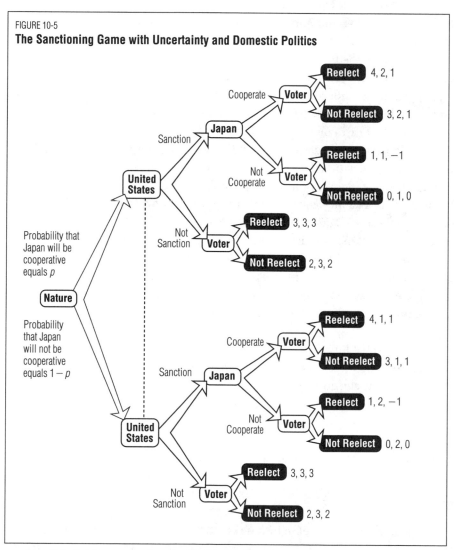

FIGURE 10-5
**The Sanctioning Game with Uncertainty and Domestic Politics**

*Domestic political factors can alter the likelihood that the president will risk the political as well as the economic consequences of trade sanctions against Japan. The president's desire to be reelected can alter his foreign policy decision making from what it would be in a purely international context.*

the president chooses to impose sanctions on Japan and the Japanese retaliate, then the president knows he will be defeated in the next election. He knows this by looking ahead to the election, just as we know it by looking ahead to the relevant terminal node of the game in Figure 10-5. Notice that if the president imposes sanctions and the Japanese retaliate, the voter gets more utility from electing a new president than from keeping the incumbent ($0 > -1$). This means that the president will lose the next election (the median voter's preference is assumed to be decisive) if sanctions fail to open the Japanese market.

If the president does not impose sanctions, then he knows for certain that he will be reelected. The median voter will be happy with the policy choice and will derive more utility from keeping the incumbent than from electing someone new. The voter's utility for keeping the president if the status quo prevails is 3. The voter's utility is only 2, however, if the president is not reelected. The president must take all of this information into account when he decides whether or not to impose trade sanctions on Japan.

If the president cares only about being reelected, he will certainly not impose sanctions on the Japanese, regardless of what he believes their response would be. By choosing not to impose sanctions, the president guarantees himself reelection. Although he values reelection, he is also assumed to have policy preferences. If the president imposes sanctions there is a chance equal to $p$ that the Japanese will open their market. If this happens, then there is a 0.50 chance the president will be reelected and a 0.50 chance that he will be defeated. If the president is reelected he gets utility both for the policy outcome and for his personal political well-being. In this case his total utility equals 4. If he loses the election but succeeds in opening Japan's market his total utility equals 3. If, however, the Japanese retaliate, then the president's utility equals 0. This happens with probability $1 - p$. The president's expected utility for imposing sanctions is

(probability the Japanese are cooperative)[(probability of being reelected)(utility of open markets and reelection) + (probability of losing the election)(utility of open markets and electoral defeat)] + (probability the Japanese are not the cooperative type) (utility of retaliation and electoral defeat).

By substituting the appropriate values we find that

$$p[0.50(4) + 0.50(3)] + (1 - p)0 = 3.50p.$$

If the president chooses not to impose sanctions, he will get reelected for certain. But reelection comes at a price. He will have to give up some personal policy satisfaction because he really does not favor the status quo over opening Japan's market. His expected utility in this case is 3. Thus, the president will sanction Japan's trade policies if $3.50p > 3$ or, equivalently, if $p > 6/7$ or, equivalently, if $p > 0.86$.

Figure 10-6 shows the impact of domestic political concerns on the president's actions in the trade-sanctioning game. Without domestic constituents to worry about, the president chooses sanctions under more circumstances than is true when he is influenced by domestic politics. Recall that in the game without domestic constituents, the president chooses to sanction Japan if he believes the odds are 2/3 (0.67) or greater that the Japanese prime minister is the cooperative type. With domestic constituent constraints, however, he will not impose sanctions unless he believes there is at least a 6/7 (0.86) chance that the Japanese will open their market. Clearly, perceptions influence foreign policy choices, and the impact of those perceptions in turn depends on domestic political factors. Indeed, the president is even unsure of the exact preferences of the median voter; as such, his choice of policies will depend on his perceptions about domestic interests as well as on his perceptions about foreign interests.

Our discussion of extensive form analysis of trade sanction choices has produced results significantly at odds with both the structural and interest group perspectives. The trade sanction example presented here illustrates a realistic situation in which the president is willing to make trade-offs between his personal political well-being and his policy goals. All structural theories look primarily at the international context within which choices are made. The concerns of domestic constituencies are irrelevant. From the perspective of theories concerned with maximizing national wealth, for example, trade sanctions can be assumed to be an avenue to increased wealth. As such, the president should certainly impose sanctions on Japan. From the perspective of these theories, the likelihood of his doing so ought not to be influenced by domestic politics. From an interest group perspective, the expected response from Japan is irrelevant. All that matters are the preferences of the key domestic interests.

The viewpoint set forth in this chapter contrasts sharply with these two points of view. Here, perceptions about both domestic and foreign interests shape decision making. The extensive form game depicted in Figure 10-5 illustrates the approach that dominates the thinking in this book—that is, the strategic perspective. The games depicted in Figures 10-1 and 10-3, in contrast, illustrate

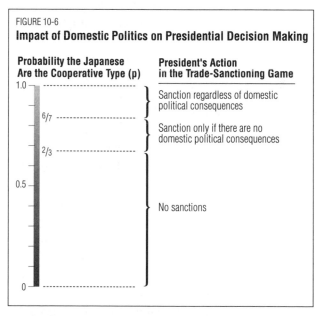

FIGURE 10-6

**Impact of Domestic Politics on Presidential Decision Making**

**Probability the Japanese Are the Cooperative Type (p)**

**President's Action in the Trade-Sanctioning Game**

1.0 — Sanction regardless of domestic political consequences

6/7 — Sanction only if there are no domestic political consequences

2/3 —

0.5 — No sanctions

0 —

*The trade-sanctioning game shows that when the president takes domestic considerations into account, he is less likely to impose economic sanctions on Japan if doing so reduces his chances for reelection. This is true even though the president's preference for open markets, the economic status quo, or retaliatory tariffs is unchanged.*

> Eliminate the Japanese as players in this game and reconstruct it with just the president and the median voter. How does this alter the policy decision? Would the president use trade sanctions under any circumstances if the Japanese were not relevant to his choice? What additional assumptions are needed to reconstruct the game without the Japanese as players?

a structural view that is concerned with international circumstances, but not much, if at all, with domestic politics.

## PERCEPTION, REPETITION, AND REPUTATION

The trade-sanctioning game described above appears as a single, isolated event—that is, as if it were played only once. In reality, the United States and Japan interact repeatedly in the context of threats to impose sanctions and decisions to open markets or leave them as they are. Repetition of the game creates additional reasons to be attentive to the influence that perceptions have on policy choices.

It is instructive to know that the Japanese of either the cooperative or the uncooperative type prefer the status quo over all other possible outcomes. This preference, combined with the structure of the situation, creates incentives for cooperative Japanese leaders to pretend to be uncooperative. These incentives may make it extremely difficult for American leaders ever to figure out what the true inclinations of Japan's prime minister are regarding trade policy.

In the single-shot example, we saw that if the United States imposes trade sanctions then the cooperative type of Japanese leader will open markets and the uncooperative type will not. This means that if American leaders ever implement a policy involving trade sanctions and observe a change in Japanese trade behavior, they would know for certain that Japan's leaders are the cooperative type. This would be true at least for the particular goods or services affected by the sanctions and for the particular leader in power in Japan at the time.

Japan's political leaders presumably realize that American leaders learn by observing Japanese actions. At the outset of the trade-sanctioning game, for example, the U.S. president perceives that the probability that Japan's prime minister is cooperative is somewhere between 0 and 1 (that is, $p < 1$). If the prime minister ever gives in to sanctions, then the president knows that the probability that the prime minister is the cooperative type is equal to 1 (that is, $p = 1$). By observing behavior and evaluating actions in light of expectations, leaders can learn. In the next chapter I introduce Bayes' Rule, which allows us to calculate how much leaders learn under different circumstances based on the logic of conditional probabilities. For now, let's just think about what the awareness of learning does to choices in a repeated version of the trade-sanctioning game.

There are advantages for the Japanese in appearing resolute in their commitment to maintain their present trade policy. This is true even if at any one moment they prefer opening markets to keeping them closed following U.S. punitive actions. At the same time, if the Japanese truly do prefer to give in to sanctions rather than stonewall in the face of punitive tariffs, they will want to hide this fact from the United States. They have an incentive to pretend to be less cooperative than they really are. Consequently, if the costs of enduring the sanctions are not too great, even responsive Japanese leaders might decide to bluff by maintaining their trade policies in the hope of getting the United States to give up on using sanctions. Japan's leaders have an incentive to build a reputation for being uncooperative (that is, decreasing the American perception of the size of p) as long as the costs of enduring sanctions are not too great. If the short-term costs of sanctions are small—including the danger of electoral defeat—relative to the benefits of a return to the status quo, then even the cooperative type of prime minister may bluff and not cooperate. These costs will be more bearable if Japanese resistance is expected to lead the United States to conclude that its sanctions are ineffective so that it gives up using them.

Naturally, American leaders understand the incentives of Japanese leaders. The president must realize that if Japan uses retaliatory tariffs it could, on the one hand, mean that the prime minister really is uncooperative or, on the other, mean that a cooperatively inclined prime minister is bluffing, pretending to be tough when he really is sensitive to the costs American tariffs inflict on him politically and on Japan economically. This means that the United States has an incentive to make the costs of sanctions rather large. By doing so, there is a better chance that for the Japanese leader the cost of bluffing is greater than the expected benefit from bluffing. At the same time, the president is limited in how costly he can make sanctions because he too bears a cost from their imposition. If tariffs raise the price of goods or services, American consumers will become increasingly dissatisfied, leading some of them to withdraw their support for the president. As a result, the president may find that he will not be reelected. Hence, the president cannot pretend that sanctions are acceptable to him at any price. The degree to which the U.S. president can sustain sanctions in the face of retaliatory tariffs from Japan and the extent to which the Japanese prime minister can sustain a policy of retaliatory tariffs against the United States in the face of sanctions are both bounded by tolerance for costs. There are limits to how much each side can bluff or to how effectively they can create a false reputation.

The sanctioning game, when played repeatedly, highlights several aspects of the role played by perceptions in foreign policy. The president may know just how far he can go in imposing costly sanctions. The Japanese do not know precisely what cost the president believes he can bear. Likewise, the president does not know whether the Japanese prime minister really is inclined to be cooperative or not. Furthermore, even after he imposes sanctions, the president cannot be sure about the inclinations of the Japanese prime minister. The president knows that the prime minister has incentives to pretend to be tougher than he may really be. The trouble is, it is costly for the prime minister to pretend too much and it is costly for the president to test the prime minister's true inclinations too much. Thus, trade policy hinges more on beliefs than on reality. If one side believes with sufficient conviction that the other side can tolerate greater costs, then the former may never choose to test the resolve of its opponent. This is exactly the problem in what is called a war-of-attrition model. If each side knew who could tolerate greater costs, there would be no fight. It is uncertainty about tolerance for costs that leads to wars of attrition, whether on the battlefield or in the arena of trade competition (Powell 1990, 1999; Morrow 1994a).

In a trade war, both sides have good reasons to try to hide from their opponent the reality of their situations because each side can gain some advantage by bluffing. Just as in poker, the cards one is dealt may not be nearly as consequential as the way the hand is played. This is a central lesson of the sanctioning game: it is the playing of the game that shapes beliefs, and those beliefs in turn shape the action. Reality per se may never come into play.

## SUMMARY

Historians encourage us to focus on what *really* happened in the past. Advocates of conventional international relations teach us to worry about national capabilities and the distribution of power. Interest group proponents instruct us to attend to competition among groups within a society and to the private preferences of bureaucrats. None of these theorists takes into account the crucial linkages between domestic affairs and international politics. Only the strategic perspective urges us to look at the ways in which domestic and international politics intertwine to produce international interactions. One important linkage concerns how people perceive the situations they find themselves in. Reality may be very different from perceptions. Still, people act on what they believe is true and not necessarily on what actually is true. Consequently, it is impossible to understand international affairs without thinking carefully about how perceptions influence behavior.

People form beliefs based on their experiences and the information available to them. Not everyone has access to the same information. As a result, people can have different views of reality. The realization that not everyone knows the same things about a situation creates opportunities for some decision makers to take advantage of other decision makers. Those opportunities are limited by some important constraints, even in situations in which one decision maker is much better informed than another. The realization that an opponent has better information may itself be sufficient to help a less-informed person make better choices. Therefore, although information advantages are helpful, they are not necessarily definitive.

Decision makers often have incentives to bluff—that is, to pretend their circumstances are better than they really are or to act more resolute than they really are. This means that the declarations of foreign policy leaders should not be taken at face value. Instead, their motives need to be examined. Is there an advantage to be gained by misrepresenting their true circumstances? If the answer is yes, then it is certainly possible that these leaders' declarations are mere bluff. When decision makers state positions that are costly to them, however, their declarations of intentions should be taken more seriously. People do not endure costs needlessly. Knowing this, foreign policy leaders can devise methods by which to test the intentions of their rivals. For example, by challenging the declarations of their opponents from time to time, leaders may force those who are bluffing to back down if the costs of bluffing exceed their true commitment to a position. Tests such as these reveal how credible the commitments or declarations of opponents (or friends) really are. But because these tests are costly, they cannot be undertaken lightly. After all, credibility depends not only on the ability to carry out a declaration but also on the willingness to do so even when it may inflict costs on both sides.

Psychological theories of international relations generally view perceptions as the idiosyncrasies of individual personalities. In this chapter we have seen that actions and experience influence perceptions and that perceptions shape actions. As a result, predicting how people will behave given their perceptions is actually quite straightforward. We have seen that perceptions come into play whenever a situation involves uncertainty, as most foreign policy problems do. Therefore, perceptions form a fundamental aspect of our understanding of how foreign policy is made and what consequences it produces.

We have seen that sensible, rational people acting on their sincerely held preferences can end up with outcomes nobody wants. A trade war, for example, can be the product of differences in perceptions that are based on a careful, even meticulous evaluation of what beliefs are consistent with a person's actions. This means that we cannot fairly judge the correctness of decisions simply by examining outcomes. Instead, we must attend as well to what was known and what was believed before the decisions were made. This too is a fundamental lesson to be drawn from our examination of perceptions.

# Perceptions, Deterrence, and Terrorism

In the spring of 1970 I interviewed an elderly gentleman in Calcutta. A leading politician in one of India's many political parties, the gentleman was eager to be helpful, responding thoroughly to each question about politics in India. He was a gentle soul who expressed deep revulsion toward the political and religious violence occurring in India at that time. I formed the opinion that he must have been a follower of Mahatma Gandhi during India's independence movement. From about 1920 to 1947 Gandhi's strategy of nonviolent resistance to British colonial rule moved India successfully to independence. I couldn't have been more wrong.

When asked about his activities before independence, this soft-spoken, elderly gentleman revealed that he had served many hard years in a penal colony operated by the British on the Andaman Islands. His offense had been blowing up a train carrying British troops and civilians during World War II. He had been a member of the violent anti-British Indian underground that opposed Gandhi's strategy of nonviolent resistance. He was, in modern parlance, a terrorist. How could such a gentle, grandfatherly figure have engaged in acts of wanton violence?

We might similarly ask how the nineteen terrorists who attacked the United States on September 11, 2001, and their backers in al Qaeda, could have justified to themselves the murder of so many innocent people. What beliefs could they have held about the United States or about American citizens that would lead to such heinous and desperate acts of terror?

In this chapter I offer an answer to these questions. The answer will probably surprise you; it will certainly help you to understand better the pitfalls of a too simple view of international affairs and give you a broader view of terrorism in the contemporary world. The answer rests on the fact that policy declarations often shape perceptions in such a way that the policies themselves encourage the very outcomes they are designed to avoid. Before we examine the relationship between perceptions and terrorism, however, it will be helpful to explore other ways in which perceptions influence international affairs.

We will begin by looking at how perceptions influence decisions about whether or not to threaten a rival. Our discussion will focus in particular on one of the more important features of international relations, deterrence. We will then take a closer look at the interactions between the United States and North Korea first introduced in Chapter 10. The willingness of the United States to provide billions of dollars of aid to North Korea to prevent it from becoming a nuclear power illustrates how a foe can manipulate information to gain a real advantage from what may only be a perceived danger. We will then use this information to understand how decision makers can learn to modify their perceptions. The 1991 Gulf War and Saddam Hussein's response to the U.S. threat will provide the backdrop against which to illustrate these points. Finally, we will return to the subject of terrorism to see how policy choices intended to diminish terrorism may actually stimulate it. Coming to grips with terrorism—one of the most disturbing features of contemporary international affairs—requires informed policies that take into account the roots from which such heinous acts spring.

## PERCEPTIONS AND DETERRENCE

Some aspects of international relations simply cannot be understood without considering how beliefs influence actions. Deterrence is an important feature of international interactions that depends on perceptions (Schelling 1960; Kugler and Zagare 1987; Zagare 1987; Powell 1990; Zagare and Kilgour 1993). The underlying objective of deterrence is to persuade an adversary not to take an action that it otherwise would take. We can divide deterrence into three categories: general deterrence, extended deterrence, and extended immediate deterrence (Schelling 1960; George and Smoke 1974; Bueno de Mesquita and Riker 1982; Huth and Russett 1984; Kugler 1984; Huth 1988; Lebow and Stein 1989; Powell 1990; Wu 1990; James and Harvey 1992).

"General deterrence" refers to the actions of one nation when it tries to deter another nation from attempting to alter the status quo. In this case, the first nation directly tries to dissuade the second nation from attacking its homeland. "Extended deterrence" expands this concept to third parties. "Extended deterrence" refers to the actions of one nation designed to persuade another nation not to threaten a third nation. Alliances are a commonly used means to achieve extended deterrence. When the United States built up its military forces during the cold war to prevent the Soviets from attacking the U.S. mainland, the United States was practicing direct general deterrence. By contrast, when the United States extended its nuclear umbrella over Japan and Western Europe, it was practicing extended deterrence.

"Extended immediate deterrence" extends this concept to the final phase in a crisis—that is, to just prior to the outbreak of hostilities. In this situation the protective posture of one state in relation to another persuades a would-be attacker to back down rather than follow through on the threat it has made. Extended deterrence, then, focuses attention on whether or not a threat is made; extended immediate deterrence draws attention to whether or not a threat that has been made is actually carried out. Each form of deterrence is crucially dependent on the creation of certain perceptions.

One question of central importance to our discussion is whether or not deterrence is successful. Successful deterrence depends on persuading a would-be bully not to engage in aggressive behavior. General deterrence and extended deterrence fail when a threat is made. Extended immediate deterrence fails when a threat is carried out. Deterrence depends wholly on whether or not a threat is made and whether or not it is acted on. Whether or not the bully is ultimately defeated is inconsequential. Deterrence has failed if an attack occurs.

A deterrent works as a counterthreat, suggesting the punishment that will be visited on a bullying country if it proceeds in making or carrying out a threat. In order for it to succeed, the bully must believe that the deterrent counterthreat is credible. The credibility of the deterrent counterthreat is facilitated by two factors. First, the party receiving the deterrent counterthreat must believe that the maker of that threat is capable of inflicting a punishment that would exceed the expected gain from whatever it is it may threaten to do. Second, not only must the party making the deterrent counterthreat be capable of successfully carrying through on that threat, it must also be viewed as having the will to carry out the actions specified in the counterthreat. Credible deterrence, then, depends on a party's ability to persuade its opponent that it has both the wherewithal and the will to punish effectively (Starr 1978; Smith 1995, 1996). In effect, persuasion here depends on perception.

## GENERAL DETERRENCE

The United States and the Soviet Union engaged one another in general deterrence throughout the cold war years. Each built weapons of mass destruction to discourage the other from seizing opportunities to alter the status quo in its own favor. The key to successful general deterrence during the cold war years was the creation of the belief that the weapons represented a credible threat of nuclear war. But would either party really commit national suicide by unleashing a nuclear response to any international threat? Possession of the necessary destructive power by itself did not confer credibility. Throughout the cold war years genuine doubt existed about whether either party would use its massive destructive force to unleash a potential nuclear holocaust.

The United States vacillated between two separate methods of deterrence. One, based on the idea of massive retaliation, was predicated on the notion that any act of aggression by the Soviets would prompt in response a U.S. strategic nuclear attack of such proportions that the destruction of the Soviet way of life would be a certainty. The other, known as flexible response, called for a graduated response to threats to U.S. security. It stipulated that the level of force used in reply to an attack be appropriately matched to the level of force applied by the attacker. Each method had its virtues as a credible general deterrent, as well as its limitations. When both the United States and the Soviets designed their deterrence strategies around the idea that each could destroy the other even after being victimized by a nuclear first strike, the two sides adopted the policy called mutual assured destruction, or MAD.

Massive retaliation required a relatively simple force structure with massive destructive capabilities. The development of such a force, however, created a problem. The construction of nuclear weapons and delivery vehicles sufficient to ensure the destruction of the Soviet Union could have been construed by the Soviets as an aggressive act in and of itself. They might have considered the development of such weaponry an attempt on the part of the United States to ensure itself of the ability both to launch an attack and to survive the response. The U.S. policy under MAD was designed to thwart such fears. Consequently, the United States did not merely seek the ability to destroy the Soviet Union but sought as well to provide for *mutual* assured destruction. This was accomplished by leaving American cities vulnerable to Soviet attack.

U.S. missiles were placed in three different delivery systems. They were put in hardened silos capable of surviving all but a direct nuclear hit, on board hard-to-track submarines, and on continuously airborne strategic bombers to protect them from attack. Through these methods the United States ensured that its weaponry would survive a surprise first strike by the Soviets; it could therefore succeed in launching an equally devastating retaliatory attack. The Soviets pursued a comparable approach to protect against a surprise attack by the United States. The decision against an antiballistic missile (ABM) defense system—a decision codified in the ABM treaty signed by both the United States and the Soviet Union at the height of the cold war—guaranteed the vulnerability of the U.S. and Soviet populations. Thereby, the ABM treaty ensured that the Soviets—who also maintained an at-ready, concealed, and mobile strike force—could destroy American cities if the United States launched a surprise first strike, and the United States could do the same to Soviet cities. By agreeing to sign the ABM treaty (and putting aside problems of detecting cheating and punishing it), the Soviets too were leaving their citizens hostage to a potential retaliatory (or first-strike) attack. The mutuality of the situation ensured that each side knew that if it attacked first, the other side would still possess the capability of large-scale retaliation, in effect making any attack too costly for either side.

The vulnerability of American (and Soviet) cities was considered critical to the stability of the relationship between the two superpowers. Indeed, during the cold war the logic of MAD and the ABM treaty was seriously challenged by the United States only during the presidency of Ronald Reagan, which turned out to be the tail end of the cold war, although no one knew that at the time, of course. Inspired by Edward Teller, father of the American hydrogen bomb, Reagan announced a break from the antimissile defense policy. He supported the development of a strategic defense initiative (SDI), popularly known as "Star Wars." The idea behind SDI was to approach general deterrence through defense rather than through MAD. In fact, until the nuclear age, deterrence had relied for centuries on defensive strategies, not just on offensive potential. Mutual destruction was an invention of the nuclear age. By the presidency of George W. Bush, the American government had become committed to abandoning the ABM treaty so that a significant effort could be made to defend the American population against a possible ballistic missile attack by such so-called rogue states as Iran, Iraq, and North Korea. Vladimir Putin, the president of Russia during George W. Bush's term, appeared to agree reluctantly to modification and possible scrapping of the ABM treaty so as to foster greater defense against the proliferating set of nations with ballistic missile capabilities.

The perception that the threat of mutual assured destruction might not be credible was raised early on. The problem with the MAD strategy was that it required that each adversary believe that its opponent would risk national suicide in the event it made even a relatively minor expansionist move. The U.S. MAD policy was predicated on the notion that a massive retaliatory response would follow a nuclear attack against the United States and just about any attack—nuclear or conventional—against Europe. The reason-

*Ronald Reagan and Mikhail Gorbachev sign a treaty to eliminate intermediate-range missiles in 1987. This extraordinary agreement marked a move away from the doctrine of Mutual Assured Destruction that had dominated cold war strategy for several decades. Both sides sought to reduce their defensive reliance on missiles and weapons of mass destruction and to find new solutions to cold war tensions.*

ing behind this strategy arose from the fact that in Europe the Soviet Union had many more ground forces, tanks, armored divisions, and so forth than did the NATO alliance. As such it would be very difficult for the United States and its allies to win a conventional ground war in Europe against the Soviet Union. Consequently, even a conventional attack against Europe by the Soviets had to be deterred with a nuclear retaliatory threat. The danger of not having such a threat, so the reasoning went, was that the Soviets could gobble up Western Europe by using salami tactics. That is, they could take a little slice today and another little slice tomorrow until, one day, there would be nothing left to protect (Zagare 1987; O'Neill 1989; Powell 1996b).

MAD and massive retaliation both lacked a credible punishment strategy precisely because each called for a massive response to even a minor violation of the territorial status quo. The threat of nuclear holocaust simply was not credible when the provocation was small. One solution to the problem of creating a credible punishment strategy in the face of a limited threat against Europe (or elsewhere) was development of the flexible response strategy. Under this strategy, the Soviets would not be subjected to a massive nuclear attack in response to minor infractions. Rather, the degree of the retaliatory response would be pegged to the level of force applied by the Soviets. The difficulty with flexible response, however, was that it deprived America's NATO allies of needed assurance that the United States would adequately defend their territories against Soviet incursions. From their point of view, the flexible response approach invited the salami tactics that could lead to the slow, gradual defeat of Europe. Furthermore, should the NATO alliance retaliate against conventional Soviet forces with its own conventional forces, the response to Soviet aggression would almost certainly occur on European soil. Consequently, the Europeans would suffer the costs of conventional war while American territory would be left unscathed. Flexible response was interpreted by some as an excuse for the United States to avoid involvement in a war centered in Europe. As such it lacked credibility and therefore effectiveness as a deterrent.

Both massive retaliation and flexible response were limited in their ability to resolve the distributional problems between the United States and the Soviet Union through credible sanctions for violating the status quo. Thomas Schelling (1960), a brilliant strategic thinker, suggested a solution to this problem of credible commitment. He saw the nuclear confrontation as a game of chicken. In one version of the game two people drive their cars full tilt toward the edge of a cliff. Whoever swerves first is "chicken." The problem with the game is very much like the credible commitment problem in deterrence. Although you might get close to the edge of the cliff, it is just not credible that you will drive over the brink. Schelling argued that credibility could be guaranteed in the game of chicken if the car drivers were seen to throw their steering wheels out of their windows. Then neither could swerve. Schelling's idea of "brinkmanship" gave credence to the threat that a leader would subject his or her nation to annihilation without blinking. In the real-world context, Schelling's idea was to erect an essentially automatic, fail-safe response to a nuclear threat.[1] Later research showed, however, that the credibility of the threat is undermined by perceptions about the risk of an accidental launch of ballistic missiles or some other event that leaves something (but not everything) to chance (Powell 1990). A fail-safe mechanism, it turned out, was not optimal in supporting deterrent credibility.

Among the foreign policy ideas that evolved from Schelling's notion of throwing out the steering wheel was the doctrine of launch on warning. This concept was predicated on the belief that the U.S. nuclear arsenal might not survive a Soviet attack or, more likely, that the command-and-control structure that would order a retaliatory strike might be destroyed by a Soviet first strike. This led to the idea that nuclear-tipped missiles should be launched when a computer assessment concluded that enemy missiles were on their way to the United States. Of course, launch on warning held one terrifying risk: namely, that a computer error could result in fomenting a nuclear war. In an exaggerated version of this danger, some critics contended that a flock of geese might be mistaken by radar for incoming missiles, leading to nuclear holocaust. Clearly, launch on warning was simply too risky a strategy to be implemented.

## EXTENDED DETERRENCE AND EXTENDED IMMEDIATE DETERRENCE

Extended deterrence "extends" the ideas of deterrence to third parties. Here we are concerned with what happens when a country that is contemplating making a threat against a second country itself faces a counterthreat from a third country.

Some theorists believe that deterrence succeeds or fails because of the *true* intentions of the rivals (Lebow and Stein 1990). This view dismisses the importance of perceptions. It suggests that leaders do not behave strategically. According to this viewpoint, it makes sense for one nation to offer to defend another only if it really intends to do so. In this view, only sincere commitments are made. Likewise, it makes sense for one nation to threaten another only if the former intends to carry out its threat. Uncertainty has no place in this theory.

The problem with this perspective is that a would-be attacker cannot know the true intentions of its target or of third parties when it chooses to act. In fact, prospective defenders may not themselves know what they will do about an attack against a friend until it actually happens. Certainly, Britain's decision to defend Poland following Germany's attack on September 1, 1939, was not known with certainty by either Adolf Hitler or Neville Chamberlain, Britain's prime minister. Hitler was not persuaded that the British cared sufficiently about Poland to come to its aid, and Chamberlain was less than enthusiastic about declaring war even after the attack. He stalled for two days, trying to find a way to avoid a declaration of war against Germany. A famous report covering the deliberations of Britain's Parliament over a possible declaration of war notes

---

[1] You might think about renting the movie *Dr. Strangelove*. The title character is thought to be modeled after a mixture of Thomas Schelling and Edward Teller.

that a member of the opposition party rose to speak against Chamberlain's policy. When he said that he spoke for the Labour Party, another member of Parliament—perhaps from Chamberlain's own Conservative Party—shouted out, "Speak for England." The implication was that even the Conservatives did not support their prime minister. In fact, it was only a few months later that the much bolder Winston Churchill replaced Chamberlain as prime minister (Watt 1989).

In an effort to deter Hitler before Germany attacked Poland, Chamberlain declared in the House of Commons on March 31, 1939, that Britain and France would aid Poland in the event that Poland resisted with force an attempt to threaten its independence. This declaration was intended to convey to Hitler British resolve in stopping an attack against Poland. However, the declaration had several characteristics that made it an unlikely vehicle for deterrence.

One apparent British objective behind its guarantee was to encourage the Poles to negotiate with Germany over giving up Danzig to the Third Reich (Taylor 1961). In actuality, British posturing encouraged Polish intransigence (Newman 1976). Rather than reducing tensions with Germany, the British exacerbated the situation. The declaration ostensibly sent a strong signal that Britain was ready to guarantee Poland's security, but the exact wording of the declaration had the effect of discouraging confidence in British resolve. Chamberlain specifically referred to a threat to Poland's *independence* rather than a threat to Poland's territorial integrity. Indeed, some scholars have expressed the view that Chamberlain was prepared to appease Germany by acquiescing to German territorial demands in Europe, suggesting that Britain's guarantee to aid Poland was a bluff (Thorne 1967; Wandycz 1986).

Whatever Chamberlain's intention, Hitler apparently did not believe the British would take up arms over Poland. Joseph Kennedy, the U.S. ambassador to Britain, reported that "[German foreign minister Joachim von] Ribbentrop was . . . pressing for immediate action against Poland, on the assumption that Britain and France would not support her" (Watt 1989, 183–184). The signal sent by Chamberlain to deter Hitler was instead perceived by the Germans as British weakness, which encouraged boldness on Hitler's part. Even after the British declaration of war on September 3, Albert Speer (1971, 227), one of Hitler's closest advisers, wrote that Hitler did not believe that Britain and France would actually fight.

Hitler's decision to shrug off British resolve did not depend only on his belief about Britain's interest in aiding Poland, a matter that was clearly controversial within the United Kingdom. His doubts were also influenced by his judgments about the relative military preparedness of Germany compared with the Allies. On the eve of the Polish invasion, Hitler could state explicitly great confidence in the power of the German army relative to that of its European adversaries:

> Let us assume that because of our rapid rearmament we hold a four to one advantage in strength at the present time. Since the occupation of Czechoslovakia the

other side has been rearming vigorously. They need at least one and a half to two years before their production will reach its maximum yield. Only after 1940 can they begin to catch up with our relatively large head start. If they produce only as much as we do, however, our proportional superiority will constantly diminish, for in order to maintain it we would have to go on producing four times as much. We are in no position to do so. Even if they reach only half our production, the proportion will constantly deteriorate. Right now, on the other hand, we have new weapons in all fields, the other side obsolete types. (Speer 1971, 225)

Hitler concluded, against the advice of many of his advisers, that the time was right for an invasion of Poland. Apparently, Hitler's belief about the unreliability of British promises helped prompt his decision. He saw concrete evidence that reinforced his belief. Not only had the English been slow to rearm, their government had demonstrated what Hitler perceived as political weakness. Chamberlain's earlier performance at Munich, where Britain agreed to look the other way while Germany took over Czechoslovakia, reinforced the perception that the British government's guarantee of Poland's independence was not credible.

When Churchill was brought into the war cabinet, Hitler's estimate of British credibility changed. Upon hearing the news, he reportedly said, "Churchill in the cabinet? That means that the war is really on. Now we shall have war with England" (Speer 1971, 228). At that point, Hitler's perception of British resolve to protect and aid Poland changed; Hitler now believed that England had the type of government leaders who would defend their Polish ally. Still, he believed that the lack of British military preparedness gave Germany an immediate and substantial advantage.

In Germany, Chamberlain was perceived as a weak leader who preferred appeasement to war. Churchill was perceived as more of a hawk ready to fight Germany. By the time Churchill entered the war cabinet, Hitler had already invaded Poland. Before doing so, as we have seen, he took into account the credi-

*Neville Chamberlain and Adolf Hitler pose for photographs at their meeting in Munich in 1938. Chamberlain returned to England, declaring that the agreement in Munich meant "peace in our time." In 1939, this illusion was dashed as German troops marched into Poland. Chamberlain's agreement with Hitler gave the term "appeasement" a poor connotation from that time forward. Chamberlain's belief that Hitler was sincere contributed to the failure of the British to prepare adequately for the possibility of war. Hitler's perception that Chamberlain was naïve and easily manipulated contributed to Germany's willingness to go forward with Hitler's plans for aggression.*

bility of Britain's guarantee both from the perspective of resolve and preparedness. With Churchill's entry into the cabinet, his judgment about British resolve changed, but his belief in the superiority of the German military did not change.[2] German perceptions of British credibility had not risen enough to reverse the German decision to fight.

Had a hawklike leader such as Churchill become prime minister earlier, it is plausible that Britain would have been committed to a more vigorous early effort at rearmament, perhaps ahead of Germany's efforts. If this particular counterfactual claim is correct (and I offer no evidence here in its favor), then the prospect that Hitler might have been deterred in his actions is supported by the logic of the situation and by the record of Hitler's deliberations.

> How can game theory help us think about counterfactual scenarios? What is wrong with the following hypothetical construction? "What if Napoleon's army had machine guns at the Battle of Waterloo?" How do off-the-equilibrium-path expectations differ from hypothetical circumstances in selecting ways to think about how history *might* have been?

In extended deterrence, the would-be attacker forms a belief, or perception, about the likelihood that a third party truly will help the attacker's target. The would-be attacker must also form an expectation about how well it will do if it must fight against more nations than that (or those) it has initially targeted. If it were all that was necessary to deter a bully, prospective defenders would always declare that they planned to help the target nation. Such declarations would then be made both by leaders who meant what they said and by leaders who were bluffing. It would be no more than uninformative cheap talk unless it was backed up by costly moves, such as mobilizing troops and putting soldiers and materiel on the front line where they would be at risk (Fearon 1997). Naturally, would-be attackers realize this. Consequently, they will attack only when they *believe* that the deterrent counterthreat will not be carried out or when they *believe* that they can defeat their adversary at an acceptable cost even if a third party intervenes. True intentions simply do not affect a decision not to attack or a decision to make a counterthreat. Such decisions are influenced by *perceptions* about what will evolve from either action. A nation with a true and sincere intention of attacking another nation may still be deterred from doing so. All that is necessary is a credible counterthreat that produces an expected outcome more costly to the would-be attacker than the status quo. Simply put, extended deterrence cannot be understood without consideration of the crucial role of perception.

## NORTH KOREA'S ARTFUL USE OF MISCONDUCT

The United States has maintained a large military presence in South Korea since the end of the Korean War in 1953. The purpose of American combat readiness in South Korea

---

[2] Indeed, Hitler's estimate of the time it would take the Allies to overcome German military superiority proved accurate.

has been, and still remains, to deter a North Korean invasion. In fact, the danger of such an invasion is perceived by many foreign policy observers to be higher now than it was during the cold war. During the cold war era, the Soviet leadership viewed North Korea as a client state—an ally—and supported it with massive economic assistance. With the end of the cold war and the demise of the Soviet Union, however, North Korea found itself economically strained. Russia was unwilling to buttress the North Korean dictatorship. North Korea's Chinese neighbors were not prepared to pick up the slack left by the withdrawal of Russian aid. Although they maintained friendly relations with the North, China's diplomatic recognition of the South Korean government in 1992 must have been cause for alarm among North Korean leaders. In such an environment, it is not hard to imagine that the North might believe that its only hope for survival would be to act quickly to remove what it sees as a South Korean threat.

During Bill Clinton's first term as president, U.S. intelligence developed considerable evidence that the North Korean regime had stepped up its efforts to build nuclear weapons. As the North Koreans had already invested heavily in developing their ability to make missiles, many of which they sold to "rogue" states like Syria and Libya, their nuclear research program was perceived as a major threat to peace. This prompted debate among policymakers about the motives behind the North Korean change in policy. Some believed that the North was pumping up its capabilities as a deterrent, fearing an invasion by the South now that the North was economically vulnerable after the loss of its Soviet patron and politically vulnerable after the demise of its longtime dictator, Kim Il-Sung, who died in 1994. Others perceived the situation differently. They believed that North Korea's nuclear weapons program represented an aggressive threat against South Korea. The Department of Defense prepared contingency plans to destroy the North's nuclear weapons research facilities. Satellite photos were used to identify the location of air shafts at the research facility buried deep in a mountain. Smart bombs, it was reasoned, could be dropped down these shafts to destroy the weapons program. Of course, no one knew for sure that work was being done on nuclear weapons. The North maintained—albeit falsely—it was just doing research on peaceful uses of nuclear energy. Perceptions, rather than established fact, ruled the day.

As an alternative to using military force to resolve the potential nuclear crisis, the Clinton administration looked for a diplomatic solution. Former president Jimmy Carter went to Pyongyang to negotiate with the North Korean leaders. He returned with an agreement stipulating that North Korea would stop its weapons research in exchange for assistance from the United States (as well as Japan and, indirectly, South Korea). The North would receive the components necessary to build a clean, light-water nuclear reactor designed to generate energy only. It would turn over to the United States the by-products that could be enriched for weapons use. Additionally, the United States pledged food, medicine, and other humanitarian assistance to North Korea worth about $4 billion.

Since it was made, the North Koreans have repeatedly reneged on aspects of the agreement in an apparent effort to extract additional benefits. They have tried to manipulate perceptions about what they are really up to in order to shore up their regime and, perhaps, replace the aid they had once received from the Soviet Union.

The North Korean example provides a good illustration of how perceptions can be manipulated to gain an advantage. Figure 11-1 links two foreign policy issues of importance to North Korea. The first involves the extension to North Korea of international legitimacy—that is, how well the international community treats a nation by extending diplomatic recognition, foreign aid, and the like. The second involves how North Korea and the international community each view North Korea's nuclear policy. The figure shows policy positions on these two dimensions in regard both to stated policies and to perceived policies. The clear circles represent stated policy objectives for North Korea, South Korea, and the United States. The dark circles reflect the American government's apparent perception of North Korea's actual nuclear policy goals in the mid-1990s and the perceived status quo. The perceived status quo reflects the U.S. belief that the North Korean government was making progress toward building a substantial nuclear capability but had not yet done so.

The hatched area represents the win set formed by the intersection of American preferences relative to the perceived status quo and the perceived policy objectives of North Korea. The clear circle with an arrow pointing to it constitutes American policy objectives and North Korea's claim about where the actual status quo is. What is interesting to note here is that North Korea, by creating—truthfully or otherwise—the perception that it was on its way to becoming a nuclear power, managed to structure perceptions so that the negotiated change from the perceived status quo greatly improved its international position.

The win set reflects significant American willingness to enhance North Korea's

*Poor conduct by North Korea gained valuable concessions from the United States. By developing a nuclear weapons program, North Korea prompted a crisis that led former president Jimmy Carter (center) to go to Pyongyang, the North Korean capital, to negotiate a solution. Here he crosses the military demarcation line in Panmunjom from North to South Korea on June 18, 1994. North Korea was promised substantial financial assistance in exchange for its termination of any further nuclear weapons research. Of course, this still leaves open the question of monitoring compliance and sanctioning violations.*

international legitimacy in exchange for North Korean willingness to pull back on its nuclear weapons program to a point that is substantially higher than the one the United States had tolerated under the old status quo. Thus, by manipulating beliefs about its nuclear intentions, North Korea gained greater international legitimacy, substantial foreign economic assistance, and acceptance of what may be a greater nuclear role than it had perhaps actually been pursuing. North Korea's misconduct proves that perceptions can be manipulated to extract benefits that might otherwise have been forgone.

Several lessons can be drawn from the North Korean–U.S. experience. Because reality is often unknowable, leaders must act on perceptions. Friends and foes have incentives to foster uncertainty about their true intentions and thereby alter perceptions. By manipulating beliefs in this way, they can create negotiating opportunities. If the North Koreans had gone to great lengths to persuade others that the North Korean government had no intention of launching a nuclear weapons program, as it claimed, then North Korea's leaders would only have harmed themselves. By encouraging the United States in its perception that North Korea was pursuing an aggressive nuclear weapons program, North Korea's leaders were able to improve their political prospects. Extremist posturing far from the status quo policy frequently creates large win sets and, therefore, great bargaining latitude with which to extract benefits. North Korea, cut off from its Soviet patrons, showed considerable skill in devising policy concerns that gave it bargaining leverage and yielded improvements in its political situation.

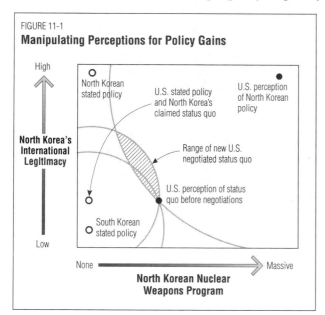

FIGURE 11-1
**Manipulating Perceptions for Policy Gains**

*By misbehaving, North Korea managed to improve its international standing and acquire a greater nuclear capability than it had when its actions were less offensive to the international community. The North Korean case illustrates how the appearance or reality of misconduct can enhance the bargaining leverage of a weak state.*

## PERCEPTIONS AND DETERRENCE: THE GULF WAR

When leaders set out to manipulate or influence perceptions, they run real risks. One of those risks is associated with taking actions that later prove more costly than had been anticipated. Here we can see how perceptions influenced the failure of deterrence during the Gulf War of 1991 and how experience fostered learning on the part of Saddam Hussein.

Recall that the war was fought between Iraq on one side and the United Nations, including hundreds of thousands of American soldiers, on the other side. The threat of war arose when Iraq's army successfully invaded Kuwait in August 1990. President George H. W. Bush responded to the invasion by saying that Iraq must withdraw from Kuwait. Saddam Hussein, president of Iraq, failed to comply with the American demand for a complete Iraqi withdrawal.

Why did Saddam Hussein resist the demands of the United States and the United Nations to get out of Kuwait in the face of the massive military buildup in the Persian Gulf? It seems quite surprising at first blush that Hussein chose to resist. After all, hundreds of thousands of troops and billions of tons of equipment were mobilized to oust his army from Kuwait. He faced about half a million men and women from arguably the best-trained and best-equipped armed forces in the world. Many observers at the time suggested that Hussein must be crazy or irrational to resist such a display of power. What sane person would take the risks he took?

With hindsight, many of these same people declare that Hussein is a brilliant politician and the ultimate victor in the Gulf War. He remained in power years after his country's defeat by the allied forces. He is alive to fight another day. But this kind of Monday-morning quarterbacking is not a useful basis for evaluating foreign policy. No decision maker can know today how things will turn out tomorrow, and so no decision maker can use hindsight to plan a course of action. To understand Hussein's actions, we must start our analysis by asking what he *knew* and what he *believed* before the war started, not what he (or we) know and believe now.

Hussein's choices are not so difficult to understand if you start by asking yourself a few simple questions—questions that are relevant to everyone's experiences. For instance, have you ever told a lie? Of course you have. Who has not? Have you ever told a lie because you thought it would help you more than telling the truth? Naturally. Why else would you lie? Certainly not because you planned on harming yourself. Have you ever told a lie that led to your being harmed? Probably you have. If lying were always more effective than telling the truth, many people would always lie. So, people lie some of the time and tell the truth some of the time. When they lie, they hope to create the belief that they are telling the truth, but they know there is a risk that they will be found out. Everyone knows that. The problem is to figure out when you are being told the truth and when you are not. In politics, bluffing is the polite word for lying. Bluffing is an example of what earlier I called a mixed strategy, choosing responses probabilistically so that sometimes you do one thing and other times you do another. The purpose behind a mixed strategy is to make a rival's expected utilities equal for alternative actions so that the rival becomes indifferent between possible courses of action.

From Hussein's point of view, the United States might have been telling a lie when George H. W. Bush drew a line in the sand and said that Iraq was not to cross that line. Maybe U.S. threats were just a bluff to get a benefit (such as cheaper oil prices following Iraq's withdrawal from Kuwait) without bearing big costs (such as losing American lives during a war). Probably Hussein thought a lot about whether Bush's threat was real or was just a bluff. Of course, now we know and he knows that Bush meant what he said, but this was not obvious before the attack began. Before the attack, Hussein had to form a perception about the credibility of Bush's threat.

Before the war, Hussein could observe that Bush was under a great deal of pressure from the Democrats in Congress who opposed the use of force. The Senate barely passed a resolution supporting the president's Gulf policy at the time. Hussein could note too that since the Vietnam War the United States had seemed reluctant to risk significant casualties in combat.[3] He could detect divisions within the United Nations coalition arrayed against him. The French, with close ties to Iraq, often seemed to prefer a different approach from that supported by the majority of the coalition. The Soviet Union issued statements that seemed divided on whether to back Bush or to try to broker a settlement on its own. Still, Hussein could not ignore the fact that 700,000 allied troops were moved to the Gulf at considerable political and financial cost to his adversaries.[4] The fact that the United States shouldered these costs suggested that, this time, American leaders were not bluffing. But of course, as anyone who plays poker knows, a good bluffer is someone who occasionally risks high losses to trick his or her opponent. We can see that it was certainly possible—perhaps even reasonable—for Hussein to believe that American threats were mere bluffs. In such case, it would be appropriate to respond by standing firm, as Hussein did.

Let's say that at the outset of the Gulf crisis Hussein thought that Bush was a weak type of foreign policy president who would bluff, but who would not fight and risk sustaining heavy casualties. If Hussein were sufficiently confident in this assessment of Bush—say, he felt the probability that Bush was a weak type of president equaled 0.70 ($p = 0.70$)—and if he were sufficiently comfortable with big gambles, Hussein would have stood firm (as he did), even after the allied forces began their massive attack of Iraq with air power. Even then, Hussein could still have believed that the United States was not truly willing to risk the high casualties of a ground war. Why else, he might have wondered, did the allied forces take so long to commit troops to combat on the ground? After all, allied air power took control of the skies within a day or two of the onset of hostilities, and they had proceeded to pummel Iraqi positions relentlessly, day in and day out, for weeks before any ground fighting took place.

Hussein's perception that the U.S./UN threat was not credible was unlikely to be reversed by a sustained air war. No country had ever been forced to give up conquered territory solely as a result of aerial bombardment. Let's say that the probability that a weak president would engage strictly in an air war against Iraq was 0.50 ($p = 0.50$). This

---

[3] Research by Eric Larson (1996), Kiron Skinner (2003), and others casts doubt on the actual existence of this so-called Vietnam Syndrome. The evidence indicates that Americans have been willing to sustain combat casualties when they clearly understand and support the political objectives behind combat.

[4] The allied troops included contingents from a diverse set of nations. Participants included Britain, Egypt, Italy, Saudi Arabia, and 500,000 Americans, among others.

would mean that the probability that a weak president would avoid even an air war would also equal 0.50 $(1 - p)$. This figure, 0.50, is a conditional probability. It is the probability that the president will bomb Iraq, given that the president is the weak type. Let's say additionally that the probability of aerial bombing if the president were the tough type (that is, a leader who is prepared to sustain casualties) equals 1 $(p = 1)$. That is, a tough president would certainly have bombed Iraq.

What might Hussein have learned about Bush once the bombing began? To answer this question, we can use Bayes' Rule. Bayes' Rule states that an initial belief, or prior probability, is changed to an updated belief, or posterior probability, based on the observation of conditional events. The rule is expressed in the following equation:

$$p(C|O) = \frac{p(O|C)p(C)}{p(O|C)p(C) + p(O|\neg C)p(\neg C)}$$

where $O$ reads "the observation," $C$ reads "the condition," the symbol "|" reads "given," and the symbol "$\neg$" reads "not." Thus, in this case Bayes' Rule says that the probability that Bush was the weak type $(C)$ given that he bombed Iraq $(O)$ equals the probability that he would bomb Iraq if he were the weak type times the probability that he was the weak type divided by the same term plus the probability that he would bomb Iraq if he were the strong type times the probability that he was, in fact, the strong or tough type. That is, we evaluate the risk that a weak president would bomb Iraq relative to the probability that a weak or a strong president would bomb Iraq. This tells us the odds that the bombing was carried out by a weak president.

Given our prior assumptions, Hussein believed that there was a 0.70 chance that Bush was the weak type of president who might bluff but who would not sustain substantial casualties. That probability, 0.70, is the probability of the condition "Bush is a weak type." The probability that a weak president would initiate aerial bombing equals 0.50. Thus, $p(O|C) = 0.50$, and $p(C) = 0.70$. The probability that a tough president would authorize aerial bombing equals 1. Therefore, $p(O|\neg C) = 1$. The initial, or prior, belief that Bush was the tough type of leader equals 0.30 because $p(\neg C) = (1 - p)$ $C$. (This is true because we are assuming that there are only two possible types of president: weak or tough.) Solving Bayes' Rule, we find that, after the aerial bombing began, Hussein's updated, or posterior, belief that Bush was the weak type was

$$p(\text{Bush is weak given bombing}) = \frac{(0.50)(0.70)}{(0.50)(0.70) + (1.00)(0.30)} = 0.54.$$

We can readily see that the bombing served to educate Hussein and to alter somewhat his view of the type of leader Bush really was. This, clearly, is very important information. Continuing with our assumptions—which are certainly consistent with the historical circumstances—we can see that although at the outset Hussein had been very confident that Bush was weak (0.70), after the aerial bombing began he had to update his beliefs to take into account the implications of Bush's actions. The odds that Bush was the tough type of leader (0.46) and the odds that Bush was the weak type of leader (0.54) were now almost even. Yet even after the bombing began, it was reasonable for Hussein to believe that Bush was the weak type who would not sustain casualties by fighting on the ground. After all, this, at 0.54, was still the higher of the two probabilities. And so, consistent with what he had learned, he might very well have continued to resist in the hope that the aerial war would not turn into a ground war.

Once the United States actually did launch a ground war, however, it is notable that Hussein gave in almost immediately. Once he saw that Bush was willing to risk significant casualties, the Iraqi president quit rather than fight on and risk more (such as the survival of his regime or, indeed, his own life). It was sensible for Hussein to believe that

*George H. W. Bush joined American forces in Saudi Arabia for Thanksgiving dinner during the 1990 troop buildup leading to the Gulf War. Saddam Hussein did not believe the United States was prepared to sacrifice significant numbers of these soldiers in ground combat and so remained steadfast in his resistance to pressure to give in. America's soldiers, and those of the other UN countries participating, proved up to the task. Indeed, the Iraqi army was unable to inflict significant casualties and surrendered almost as soon as ground fighting began.*

the United States was bluffing and to act tough until the ground war began.[5] Once he saw the U.S. risk significant casualties in a ground war he had to adjust his beliefs once again. American actions were no longer consistent with his initial perception that Bush was the weak type of leader who bluffs. As a result of this updated information, Hussein adjusted his perceptions—and therefore his behavior—accordingly. The Iraqi army surrendered as quickly as it could find someone to surrender to. By holding out as long as he did, rather than caving in at the first threat of air power, Hussein bought time with which to shore up his domestic position. The result: Kuwait was liberated and Saddam Hussein remained in charge in Iraq.

Suppose we assume that the probability of launching a ground war if the president is the weak type is only 0.10 and that it is 1.00 if the president is the tough type. (Notice that even a weak president might be willing to take some risk of casualties if, for instance, he were confident that his forces could elicit a rapid surrender by the enemy.) Then, after the ground war began, Hussein's updated beliefs would have looked as follows:

$$p(\textit{Bush is weak given ground combat}) = \frac{(0.10)(0.54)}{(0.10)(0.54) + (1.00)(0.46)} = 0.11.$$

At this juncture he would have learned that there was very little chance that Bush was the weak type of leader. The decision to bomb Iraq had taught Hussein to view Bush's weakness a bit more skeptically, but still his dominant perception—his updated belief—was that Bush was weak and bluffing. According to Bayes' Rule, and given the numerical assumptions we made, the aerial bombing decreased Hussein's confidence in Bush's weakness from a probability of 0.70 to a probability of 0.54. The ground combat further, and substantially, shook his belief that Bush was weak. The conditional probability fell from 0.54 to 0.11. At that point, Hussein's perception of the type of leader Bush really was changed immediately from weak to tough. Given this, Hussein surrendered rather than risk greater losses.

Had Hussein known U.S. intentions, he might never have invaded Kuwait. Deterrence failed because Hussein did not believe that American threats were credible. Of course, he knew that the United States had the military ability to defeat Iraq. But he did not believe that the president or the American people had the will to use their military prowess. This initial belief proved wrong, but it was, as we have seen, a completely reasonable perception given the most recent examples of U.S. behavior during

---

[5] The Iraqis may have believed that the United States suffered from the Vietnam Syndrome. American leaders appeared extremely cautious about committing troops to combat except against very small adversaries. President Reagan, for example, withdrew American forces from Lebanon immediately after a terrorist bomb killed 241 U.S. marines in Beirut. Even as allegedly tough a president as Reagan had used American troops in combat only against very weak opponents such as Grenada. Iraq, by contrast, had a large army that was battle hardened by a decade-long war with Iran.

Modify the assumed probabilities and then recompute Saddam Hussein's updated beliefs based on the probabilities you have chosen. How might these updated beliefs have influenced the course of the dispute? Make sure that the beliefs are consistent with the observed actions in the game and that the actions of decision makers are consistent with their beliefs.

international conflicts. And, I hasten to note, the calculations we just made still leave open the possibility that Bush was in fact the weak type of leader who would not have continued the ground war if the United States were sustaining significant casualties. Indeed, the probability that he was tough had risen to 0.89, but not even that represents certainty.

Without understanding perceptions we might mistakenly conclude that Saddam Hussein was mad or irrational or a fool. We might also conclude that he was brilliant, wily, and conniving. Such views are almost always shaped by hindsight. If we rely on an analysis of perceptions we are more likely to conclude that Hussein was acting in what he believed to be his own best interest. As things turned out, Saddam's choices were not in Iraq's best interest; nevertheless, they may well have helped the Iraqi leader stay in power.

In Chapter 18 I present the reader with the knowledge necessary to evaluate with great accuracy whether a leader like Saddam Hussein is likely to stand firm or back down in a situation like the Gulf crisis. The U.S. government actually used the approach introduced in the final chapter for just this purpose during the Gulf War.

## BELIEFS ABOUT TERRORISM

I began this chapter by noting the misperception I had developed when interviewing an older Indian politician who had years before committed terrorist acts. Let me return now to the question of international terrorism that my error raised to see how perceptions influence actions and how new experiences change perceptions.

What is a terrorist and what characteristics do such people display? If I were writing a treatise on terrorism I might take up dozens of pages arguing about the definition of the term. Certainly it is a controversial concept. As is frequently observed, one person's terrorist may be another person's freedom fighter. As I am not writing a treatise on terrorism, I offer a straightforward, fairly intuitive working definition of the concept. By "terrorism" I mean any act of violence undertaken for the purpose of altering a government's political policies or actions that targets those who do not actually have the personal authority to alter or enforce governmental policy. The attacks on the United States on September 11, 2001, for instance, clearly meet this definition of terrorism.

Terrorism encompasses all violent acts that are not motivated by a desire to injure the specific individuals actually victimized by the act but rather are designed to influence the behavior of others (typically policymakers). An attack on a military target in wartime is not terrorism. Such an attack is aimed at an organization (the military) that could directly change its policy by, for example, surrendering. In contrast, an attack on random citizens on a busy street targets individuals who do not have direct control over policy. Terrorism aims to spread fear and anxiety (terror) through a population so that it will, in turn, put pressure on its leaders to change policies in a way favored by terrorists. Al Qaeda terrorists, for example, seem to want the United States to withdraw support for the Saudi regime and to get out of the Middle East.

Most people think that terrorists are crazy, irrational fanatics with no sense of morality or decency. Because of this outlook, it is common for people to believe that governments should never negotiate with terrorists. Indeed, the governments of many countries, including Britain, Israel, and the United States, have frequently and openly declared that they would never negotiate with terrorists. The belief that terrorists are unusual types of people with cruel and unbending inclinations is probably behind this particular response to terrorist groups. Yet, it may be that it is this very attitude that precipitates some (although certainly not all) terrorist acts in the first place. There is evidence that retaliation against terrorists has no long-term deterrent effect (Brophy-Baermann and Conybeare 1994). To see how this might be so, let's consider a simple framework based on perceptions that may help us think about terrorism in a new way.

Suppose there are two different types of people who become terrorists. We'll call one type "true believers." These are the unbending, fanatical sort of people most of us commonly think of when we think about terrorists. Probably al Qaeda is made up mostly of "true believers." We'll call the other type "reluctant terrorists." Probably most members of the Palestine Liberation Organization, or PLO, are this type. These are people who would prefer to employ traditional means of being recognized. Both types must make a choice. They can either initiate a terrorist action or try to influence political leaders to change policy through the normal channels of political give and take. True believers prefer to take terrorist actions regardless of how they think the government might respond to their proposals (unless, of course, the government would simply acquiesce to anything they demanded, a possibility so remote that we can

*The terrorist attacks on the United States on September 11, 2001, resulted in the destruction of the World Trade Center, damage to the Pentagon, and the fatal crash of United Airlines flight 93 near Shanksville, Pennsylvania. Over three thousand individuals lost their lives, and many others suffered physical and emotional trauma. In this image, dust and debris from the collapse of one of the twin towers surge down a Manhattan street. The United States and the world community responded to the attacks by declaring war on terrorism.*

371

ignore it here). Reluctant terrorists want to use normal political channels to reach a negotiated compromise rather than engage in terrorism. It is their assumed desire to negotiate in normal ways that encourages me to call them "reluctant" terrorists when they are observed to engage in seemingly wanton violence.

How might a government respond to an agitator's proposal for political change? This, of course, is a fundamental question that those unhappy with government policy must ask themselves before choosing their approach to promoting their own interests. Governments typically take seriously powerful individuals or groups for the obvious reason that powerful adversaries have a lot of leverage with any government. Terrorist organizations just about always start out as very small, weak collections of disaffected people with little influence over government. Such people are usually ignored, or worse, by governments. If these individuals want to see big changes take place in society, and if they are sufficiently weak, it is possible that government leaders will institute repressive policies to thwart them. Thus, governments might be one of at least two types as well. Government leaders might be the sort that bargain in good faith with weak political opponents, taking their wishes into account despite their weakness, or government leaders might be the sort that ignore or even repress weak adversaries, calculating that they probably cannot really threaten the interests of the leaders in any event.

With these possibilities in mind, let's consider a third type of government adversary, a type we'll designate "complacent opponents." Complacent opponents are individuals or groups who would sooner tolerate being taken advantage of by the government than engage in terrorist action. Of course, complacent opponents would prefer to have the government bargain with them in good faith rather than take advantage of them. Table 11-1 spells out the preference orderings of our three types of government adversaries and our two types of governments.

TABLE 11-1
## Preference Orderings for a Terrorism Game

| Player Type | Player Preference Ordering |
|---|---|
| Government Adversary | |
| True Believer | Terrorist act > good faith negotiations > being repressed |
| Reluctant Terrorist | Good faith negotiations > terrorist act > being repressed |
| Complacent Opponent | Good faith negotiations > being repressed > terrorist act |
| Government | |
| Responsive | Good faith negotiations > repression > terrorist target |
| Repressive | Repression > good faith negotiations > terrorist target |

Consider the problem any government adversary faces. The adversary might choose to ask the government's leaders for some political concession, or the adversary might launch a terrorist act in the hope of forcing the government to notice its plight. If the latter course is chosen, then the adversary is, by definition, a terrorist. If the former course of action is chosen, then the adversary risks the possibility that the government will choose repression and punishment rather than bargaining in good faith.

No matter how a true believer thinks the government might respond to an offer to negotiate, the true believer prefers terrorism.

Clearly, when a government confronts such an adversary there is no point in trying to negotiate in good faith or in suggesting that such negotiations are a feasible alternative. As already noted, the posture of nonnegotiation is the declaratory policy of the United States and many other governments toward terrorists. Such opponents are perceived to be unbending and fanatical, which is precisely the case of true believers. Sadly, probably the only way to deal with such people is to punish them whenever the opportunity presents itself, as in the war on terrorism against al Qaeda. For true believers, then, perceptions about whether the government is responsive or repressive are simply irrelevant. They want to either get everything they are after or go out in a blaze of glory.

A complacent opponent, regardless of the government's type, prefers negotiation to engaging in terrorist acts. Indeed, there is no circumstance under which a complacent opponent will choose terrorism over trying to bargain with the government. For complacent opponents, then, it is also true that their perceptions of the government's type— responsive or repressive—are irrelevant.

> Construct a game that reflects the possible moves described here for the three types of government opponent and the two types of government. Be sure to include information sets for each. You may be surprised at how complicated this seemingly simple problem actually is.

For reluctant terrorists, however, the story is entirely different. Suppose that reluctant terrorists attach a utility of 1 to negotiations with the government, a utility of 0.40 to engaging in terrorism, and a utility of 0 for submitting to government repression. Reluctant terrorists, just like everyone else, will do what they perceive to be in their best interest. They know that they can obtain an outcome worth 0.40 with certainty by engaging in terrorist acts. If they offer to negotiate, then they might achieve a much better outcome, an outcome worth 1, if the government is the fair-minded type; if the government is the repressive type, however, then they will suffer a worse outcome, one worth nothing at all. What reluctant terrorists decide to do depends entirely on their perceptions of the government and the probability that it will choose to repress them. The belief that the government will repress "reluctant terrorists" is probably increased by the war on terrorism, as should be clear by applying Bayes' Rule.

If past experiences have taught the reluctant terrorists that the government leaders are fair minded with a probability of 0.50 ($p = 0.50$) and are repressive with a probability of 0.50 ($1 - p = 0.50$), then the reluctant terrorists are better off trying to negotiate and so do not engage in terrorism. We reach this conclusion by calculating the reluctant terrorists' expected utility for trying to negotiate.

$$EU_{Negotiation} = (0.50)(1) + (0.50)(0) = 0.50.$$

The expected utility of trying to negotiate for the reluctant terrorists is equal to the probability the government is fair minded (0.50) times the value of dealing with a fair-minded government (1) plus the probability that the government is the nasty type (0.50) times the value of being repressed (0). The expected utility from offering to negotiate for the reluctant terrorists, therefore, is 0.50. If we calculate the expected utility of engaging in terrorist acts for the reluctant terrorists, we would find it equal to only 0.40. Thus, offering to negotiate is clearly the best choice in this case. Under these circumstances, the reluctant terrorists would not commit terrorist acts and so would never be explicitly identified as terrorists of any sort. But what would happen if our probabilities were slightly different? For example, what would happen if the reluctant terrorists perceived that the probability the government is repressive is 0.65? By refiguring our expected utility, we would find that terrorism becomes the preferred action:

$$EU_{Negotiation} = (0.35)(1) + (0.65)(0) = 0.35.$$

In this instance, we would observe terrorist acts. Significantly, in this case we would not be able to discern the difference between the reluctant terrorists and true believer terrorists, because both kinds are engaging in the same activities.

When a government declares that it will not negotiate with terrorists, how is it affecting the perceptions that would-be terrorists have about the best way to deal with the government? The government is sending the following message: "If the opportunity presents itself, we will punish anyone who has engaged in terrorist actions." This message produces a negative consequence for the government. The reluctant terrorists' beliefs about the government's type are probably being influenced by the government's declaration that it will not negotiate with terrorists. If the government's statement is credible, then in the minds of the reluctant terrorists the probability that the government is the repressive type is likely to increase. The more credible the government's declaration, the greater the potential it has to turn reluctant terrorists down the path of violence rather than down the path of negotiation toward a normal political resolution of differences.

If the reluctant terrorists believe with sufficient confidence that their government adversary will treat them fairly in negotiations, then they, like complacent government opponents, will choose to pursue peaceful solutions to their problems. They would never actually engage in terrorism, and we would never know that they had the potential to commit horrible acts of violence. If, however, the reluctant terrorists were not sufficiently confident of the government's intentions, then depending on just how great their belief is that the government is the repressive type, the reluctant terrorists might choose to negotiate or might choose to use terrorist tactics. The more confident the reluctant terrorists are that the government is the repressive type, the more likely they are to commit violent acts.

If violent acts occur, then the government might infer that the perpetrators are true believers, thereby reinforcing their inclination to convey the message that terrorists will be repressed. Thus, a cycle of reinforced beliefs takes hold. The government's recalcitrance prompts an increase in the frequency of terrorist acts, which in turn reinforces the government's stand on not negotiating, which in turn prompts further terrorist acts, and so forth. This type of situation arises even though both the government and the reluctant terrorists started out with fair-minded intentions. Both have simply perceived incorrectly the true desires of the other.

Our discussion of terrorism highlights several important points related to perceptions. Perceptions can lead people to make choices that in retrospect turn out to be bad. But because we cannot distinguish them from the true intentions of the decision makers (that is, the types pool in game-theoretic terms), we cannot always tell when bad decisions have been made. An act of terrorism might actually be the work of a reluctant terrorist, but we cannot tell from that act alone whether we are dealing with a true believer or a reluctant terrorist (although we can be certain we are not dealing with a complacent opponent). In consequence of this uncertainty, we might choose an improper response, like declaring that we will never negotiate when in fact being open to negotiations is the very thing that would help us distinguish (that is, separate types) between true believers and reluctant terrorists.

Perceptions influence behavior in many other ways. It is possible that reluctant terrorists might overestimate the likelihood that the government is fair minded and so leave themselves open to repression and indeed annihilation. In such cases we would never know that these people had the potential to be terrorists; we might in fact express great sympathy for those individuals or groups so punished by the government. And yet, had those individuals or that group perceived the situation more accurately and engaged in terrorism, we would likely have labeled the very same people fanatic extremists and applauded the government's action in punishing them for their deeds. Notice how much our own response depends on the perceptions we have formed based on what we have observed. We have not adequately taken into account what might have happened had the terrorist or the government behaved differently.

The cycle of terrorism and harsh government reaction has typified the relations between the Arabs and the Israelis for decades. Yet, once an Israeli leader was ready to negotiate, and once the leader of the PLO was ready to believe that the proposed negotiations were being entered into in good faith, it proved possible to interrupt this cycle. Certainly terrorism has not been eliminated in the Middle East—not by a long shot as the sides swing back and forth between negotiation and exchanges of violence, with these cycles fluctuating as a function of rises and declines in trust between the competing leaders. But just as certainly, real progress toward peace was made with the establishment of a semi-autonomous Palestinian Authority. This progress was achieved through a reexamination of perceptions and a concomitant realization that alternative explanations of behavior were more consistent with the facts. As the facts change so, too, do perceptions about the intentions of the rivals, and as these change so does the level of violence.

Indeed, "true believers," like many in Hamas or Islamic Jihad, escalate violence whenever negotiations appear to progress between government and "reluctant terrorists." They do so in the hope that the government will adopt repressive retaliatory measures that scuttle negotiations (E. Bueno de Mesquita 2002). This is the pattern in the Palestinian-Israeli conflict.

The evidence today indicates that PLO leader Yasser Arafat was not a true believer in his terrorist days. Fair-minded Palestinians must recognize that, although some Israeli governments have exhibited the traits of a repressive type of government, others have exhibited the traits of a responsive type of government by making substantial political concessions to advance an agenda aimed at producing peace. Likewise, some Palestinian groups appear to have been reluctant terrorists. They, too, made significant concessions and pursued negotiation rather than violence, even as other Palestinians showed themselves to be true believers who were not interested in a compromise peace. One can only wonder whether the peace process might not have been advanced sooner had foreign policy leaders been better educated to think about perceptions as well as actions. Likewise, one must wonder whether the process toward peace might not advance faster if the two sides did not resort to cutting off exchanges of information between them.

The pattern of violence, progress in negotiations, and heightened violence that has typified the Middle East is also manifesting itself in Northern Ireland. There, too, a shift in the government's openness to negotiations has helped to separate out the reluctant terrorists in the Irish Republican Army (IRA) from the true believers. Once the British government reached agreement with key Northern Irish leaders in 1998, the level of terrorist violence increased. This increase represented the efforts of the true believers, who sought to thwart the compromise struck between government officials and the IRA's "reluctant terrorists."

The challenge to establishing a long-lasting peace, whether in the Middle East, Northern Ireland, or elsewhere, is to identify the reluctant terrorists and enlist their aid in enforcing agreements against the wishes of the true believers. This can be done successfully provided the motivation and resources controlled by the reluctant terrorists and their newfound government allies are sufficient to punish true believers whenever and wherever they are found. By reaching a negotiated compromise and working together, it becomes possible for all parties to separate the various types of opponents from one another so that perceptions are refined, beliefs are updated, and appropriate strategies are chosen. Members of the IRA can tell whether the British government really intends to take advantage of them and crush them or whether it intends to negotiate in good faith. The British government (as well as the British and Irish people) and the reluctant terrorists in the IRA can see who among the members of the IRA really wants a negotiated peace and who will settle for peace only on their own terms. By separating types, the promise of peace can be turned into a reality.

In the Israeli-Palestinian dispute the problems are more difficult. The Israelis are asked to exchange land for peace. The difficulty here is one of the credibility of commitments, given beliefs about the preferences of Yasser Arafat and others in the Palestinian Authority and in Israel. Land for peace calls for sequential strategic decisions. Israel gives up land now in exchange for normalized relations with the Palestinians and other Arab states later. But once the land is given up it is extremely costly to recover it if the Palestinians and Arab states renege on their part of the bargain. Thus, since peace is not expected to come until the land issues are resolved, such proposals rely on the perception by the Israelis that their rivals will subsequently live up to their end of the bargain.

If the Israeli leadership lacks confidence in the commitments of the Arab states, then the Israelis cannot be expected to give up land for the unenforceable promise of peace. From the Arab perspective, however, granting peace before receiving land commitments is equally risky. Although they can retreat from peace back to war if Israel were to renege on promises of land concessions, the move back to a state of war is politically, emotionally, and materially costly. Having conceded peace, they have no assurance that Israel will yield land. Each side is trapped in a bargaining game in which the absence of trust makes reaching a Pareto improving outcome extremely difficult. Here again the problem may well be perceptions rather than reality. It is possible that each side would behave perfectly honorably in enforcing their parts of a peace agreement. The problem is that if either did not, the cost of gambling on the peace agreement may well exceed the cost of maintaining the current state of war.

## SUMMARY

Perceptions change in response to new information. They are not just rooted in personal quirks or biases. If what we observe is sufficiently different from what we expect to observe, we are forced to reconsider our beliefs. The U.S.–North Korean negotiations instruct us that perceptions can be manipulated to promote opportunities to extract concessions that otherwise would not be granted. North Korea created a win set in which it could gain greater international legitimacy and maintain a small nuclear program, whereas before they could do neither. The North Korean example reminds us that apparent policy extremism can provide improved bargaining leverage and that not all observed extremist views are sincere.

The experience of Saddam Hussein during the Gulf War or of Israel provides an example of learning during crises. Often the actions of others are consistent with more than one set of beliefs about their true intentions or capabilities. As events unfold, however, we can sort out the degree of consistency between actions and alternative perceptions of reality. Bayes' Rule provides a direct method for calculating likely changes in beliefs in response to changes in circumstances. We saw, for example, how Saddam

Hussein went from a strong conviction that the United States would not endure substantial casualties in the Gulf War to near certainty that it would. Perceptions change, and they do so in predictable ways.

Sometimes it is possible to distinguish among competing hypotheses by changing our own behavior. This is precisely the process that led to progress toward peace in the Middle East and in Northern Ireland. Our brief examination of terrorism highlighted how perceptions can promote policies that produce unintended consequences. Only through a change in behavior—that is, through a calculated risk—is it possible to break or at least diminish the cycle of terrorist violence. But we cannot blithely call for such a gamble without considering the real risks and costs associated with it. By improving our understanding of how perceptions influence choices, we can help foster progress toward peace throughout the world.

CHAPTER 12

# DOMESTIC INSTITUTIONS AND NATIONAL PERFORMANCE

Do democracies and autocracies behave similarly in international affairs? The answer to this question sheds light on how international politics differs from, or is similar to, domestic politics. If the domestic arrangements of a regime are irrelevant to international affairs, then the strategic perspective is wrong in claiming that international politics is the product of individual national foreign policy decisions. If, however, democracies and autocracies behave differently under the same external circumstances, then structural theories are wrong in denying the importance of the interplay between domestic affairs and international politics. Some logical limitations to the structural viewpoint were suggested in the previous chapter. Here we will extend that logic and also explore the evidence of history.

Italo Calvino observes, in a modern, poetic reverberation of the troubles of King Enrique IV of Spain, with which we began, that

> the throne, once you have been crowned, is where you had best remain seated, without moving, day and night. All your previous life has been only a waiting to become king; now you are king; you have only to reign. And what is reigning if not this long wait? Waiting for the moment when you will be deposed, when you will have to take leave of the throne, the scepter, the crown, and your head. (1988, 36)

*Author's Note:* The material in this chapter draws heavily on pertinent parts of Bueno de Mesquita, Smith, Siverson, and Morrow (2003) and related publications by Bueno de Mesquita, Morrow, Siverson, and Smith. For a comprehensive view of how leadership selection institutions influence political and policy choices, see the work cited here.

What are leaders to do if they want to keep their jobs and their heads? This is no idle question. The answer to it goes to the very heart of politics. If you were king, president, or dictator, what might you try to accomplish? How would you allocate scarce resources to best perform your job and to prevent yourself from being removed from office? What would your friends try to do? Are the answers different depending on whether they aspire to be king, president, or dictator?

I, too, have an answer to suggest to this problem: seek peace and prosperity for your country. Peace and prosperity, after all, enhance the national well-being. Would not peace and prosperity also promote the popularity and longevity of the leadership? In fact, the answer is no. Peace and prosperity would not have saved Enrique five hundred years ago, and they would not save you today.[1] Kings and dictators have no need for peace and prosperity to retain power. Presidents, at least in democracies, can hold on to office a lot longer if they preside over peace and prosperity than if they do not, but they rarely hold on to power as long as kings and dictators, even when the latter create war, poverty, and misery for most of their countrymen.

If peace and prosperity were the recipe for political success, then the structuralist perspective, which contends that states seek to maximize wealth or security; the interest group perspective, which argues that leaders try to promote their own welfare through internal political maneuvering; and the strategic perspective, which says that leaders promote their welfare through internal and external maneuvering, would all be compatible. If all leaders benefited equally from encouraging peace and prosperity, then the structuralist perspective that says all leaders are motivated by a common set of goals is reinforced. Similarly, interest groups and politicians alike would benefit from undertaking policies and actions that are for the good of the nation. Yet such a viewpoint is not correct.

Leaders do not benefit equally from peace and prosperity. In fact, leaders in democracies find it essential to pursue national peace and prosperity, whereas autocrats do not. Democrats who fail to provide peace and prosperity for their constituents are ousted from office with alacrity, whereas autocrats, despite gross failures to provide for the welfare of ordinary citizens, stay in office for a long time. Even in the absence of no term limits, few democratic leaders last as long as autocrats. Over the past 200 years, democratic leaders have remained in office for an average of about 3.7 years. In contrast, autocrats have remained in office an average of 8.6 years. Autocratic leaders suffer relatively few punishments for creating famine, sickness, and misery at home or military defeat abroad. They seem relatively unconcerned with whether or not peace and prosperity are achieved.

---

[1] Indeed, one of Enrique's shortcomings was that he did not wage an aggressive enough war against Granada in his quest to depose its Muslim government. By not mounting a full-fledged campaign, seeking instead to wear his enemy down slowly, Enrique deprived Spanish nobles of the opportunity to enrich and honor themselves on the field of battle. They could not tolerate his approach, which is part of the reason they rebelled against him.

In this chapter, I will summarize a strategic theory that shows how two domestic political institutions shape the motivations of leaders. We will see that some political systems give leaders an incentive to rob and pillage their own countrymen, as well as other countries. Such political arrangements make leaders largely indifferent to whether they produce peace and prosperity or war and famine. Other domestic political arrangements encourage leaders to be attentive to the quality of their economic and military policies by making political survival dependent on successful performance in regard to the nation's well-being. Using game theoretic reasoning to derive hypotheses and extensive historical evidence to test these hypotheses, I will demonstrate that interest group and structural theories are inadequate for dealing with core aspects of international politics. In contrast, the strategic perspective offers a better accounting of the two key features of international affairs under study here: the attainment of prosperity in nations and peace between them.

> Can you find some examples of political leaders who were overthrown by their own citizens during a war or right after a military defeat? Can you think of leaders who were removed from office by a foreign power after experiencing military defeat at the hands of that power? How about leaders who were not deposed either by their own citizens or by their foreign rivals, even following military defeat?

## UNIVERSAL POLITICAL INSTITUTIONS

Every country has fundamental institutional arrangements, or rules, that define interactions within its borders. These include rules that define who is disenfranchised, who is part of the selectorate, and what constitutes a winning coalition. The disenfranchised include all residents without the legal right to participate in choosing the government. Most people throughout history have been part of this group. In monarchies, everyone except a handful of aristocrats were in the disenfranchised group. When John Lackland became King John of England in 1199, only 197 lay barons had a say in his selection. Everyone else in England was essentially disenfranchised. Indeed, in ancient times, most people were not only disenfranchised, they were slaves. The disenfranchised often provide the cannon fodder for war or for domestic revolutions, but they rarely are themselves active in politics, whether domestic or foreign. One of the ongoing, great global political changes that has been taking place since roughly the time of the American Revolution in the eighteenth century is the expansion of the franchise to more and more people. Today much, although by no means all, of the world practices universal adult suffrage—sometimes honestly, at other times dishonestly through rigged elections.

The selectorate is the set of people in a country who have a legitimate say in the selection of the government leadership and who have the possibility (however small) of becoming essential supporters of an incumbent leader. I use the word "selectorate" to draw attention to the fact that the people choosing the government need not do so through voting (Shirk 1993). The selectorate need not be an electorate. As noted above, the selectorate in King John's England consisted of 197 lay barons. In modern Saudi Arabia, the selectorate remains small, as it was in South Africa until apartheid was overturned. The Saudi selectorate includes members of the royal family and, perhaps, some religious leaders. The selectorate in contemporary democracies consists of all adult citizens, although the age of adulthood varies from place to place and from time to time. Until the presidency of Richard Nixon, suffrage extended to all citizens twenty-one years of age or older in the United States. Today, the age for suffrage in the United States is eighteen, representing a consequential expansion of those who enjoy voting rights. Of course, this is a small increase in comparison with that brought about by the extension of the vote to women in most democracies in the early and middle parts of the twentieth century.[2]

The winning coalition consists of those members of the selectorate whose support is essential to the incumbent government. In most presidential democracies, this is effectively a majority of the selectorate. Even in parliamentary systems with proportional representation and many small parties, it is still true that legislation cannot be passed without a majority vote of legislators. Generally, the preferences of a majority of legislators reflect the preferences of a large percentage of voters; sometimes as much as a majority. Whether the winning coalition represents a majority or not, however, in democracies a winning coalition is always a rather large proportion of the selectorate and therefore a large number of people. In contrast, in authoritarian regimes the winning coalition is generally quite a small group of people. In a military junta, for example, it may consist of a small group of colonels or generals who control the armed forces. In the People's Republic of China, Vietnam, or the Democratic People's Republic of Korea (North Korea), it is a tiny subset of the membership of the Communist Party. In Iraq the winning coalition consists of key members of Saddam Hussein's family clan. In Nigeria, under the leadership of Gen. Sani Abacha (1993–1998), the winning coalition was a small set of loyal military officers and bureaucrats. Today, with democracy restored to Nigeria, the winning coalition again can be counted in the millions. Whether democracy will survive in Nigeria, however, is an open question.

Monarchies, authoritarian states, and democracies can be differentiated by variations in the size of their winning coalitions and selectorates. Although not the only difference between them, the size of the selectorate and the size of the winning coalition pretty clearly demarcate different regime types. In monarchies, both institutions are always small. In democracies, both are always relatively large. In some autocracies, both the selectorate and the winning coalition are small; in others, the winning coalition is small but the selectorate is large. Most states with rigged elections, for example, have universal adult suffrage voting rules, but the elections are essentially meaningless because there is

---

[2] Switzerland, however, did not extend the right to vote to women until 1971.

only one viable candidate for each office. This was true in the communist states of the cold war era and remains true in many other authoritarian societies as well. Indonesia under President Suharto; the Philippines during the days of Ferdinand Marcos; Kenya, Nigeria, and Mexico until quite recently; and many other countries combined large selectorates with rigged elections in which the small winning coalition ensures that its candidates remain in power. Many countries in Africa and the Middle East choose their leaders by rigged elections. Sometimes even real democracies devolve into rigged systems. This is what happened in Zimbabwe in 2002 when President Mugabe apparently preferred to abandon true competitive voting in favor of ensuring that he remained in office.

Why would leaders set up a political system with a large selectorate, but a small winning coalition? In the next section we will see that in fact this is the optimal form of government from the point of view of leaders. Such a system maximizes leaders' ability to stay in power and do what they want. However, from the viewpoint of members of the winning coalition, citizens not in the winning coalition, and the disenfranchised, a political system with a large selectorate but a small winning coalition is not optimal. If any of these groups are able to select the institutions of government, they will avoid an

*In the past, Zimbabwe observed free and fair elections. Although opposition candidates still vie for office, it now appears that the government controls the outcome of elections. Here a riot policeman controls voters on March 9, 2002, following riots over unusually long queues at polling stations near the capital city of Harare. Amidst widespread charges of vote-counting fraud, incumbent Robert Mugabe was declared the winner.*

autocratic structure. We will see that for members of the winning coalition, monarchy or democracy, depending on circumstances, is the optimal form of government. If the citizenry at large is able to select its government, it is best off choosing democracy with its large winning coalition and its large selectorate. The disenfranchised always fare best with democracy.

Those who get to pick the institutions of government influence the size of the winning coalition and the size of the selectorate (and, by extension, the number who are disenfranchised). The size of these two institutions, in turn, influences the foreign and domestic performance of the state. The winning coalition and the selectorate help shape the prospects of peace and prosperity and even influence the motivation behind fighting wars or negotiating peaceful solutions to international disputes.

## TOOLS TO REMAIN IN POWER

To hold on to political power, leaders need not satisfy everyone. In fact, doing so is rather inefficient. The disenfranchised, for example, can do little to place the leadership's continuation in office at risk. Leaders should be expected to do what is necessary to satisfy those at whose pleasure they remain in office. Indeed, several researchers (James and Oneal 1991; Morgan and Bickers 1992) have shown that American presidents choose foreign policies with an eye toward the effect those policies will have on their popularity with their supporters rather than with citizens in general. Of course, leaders need to be mindful that they not engage in actions that precipitate their overthrow by foreign adversaries (Werner 1996; Goemans 2000). Trying to select actions to satisfy domestic factions and foreign rivals simultaneously and not always being able to do so is perhaps the fundamental problem of international politics and foreign policy.

Two basic tools allow leaders to influence their prospects of retaining office. These include the distribution of public policies that benefit all in their society and the distribution of private goods that benefit some but not others (Olson 1965, 1982; Ferejohn 1974; Weingast, Shepsle, and Johnsen 1981; Cox 1997; Schultz and Weingast 1998; Bueno de Mesquita and Root 2000; Bueno de Mesquita, Smith, Siverson, and Morrow 2003). Public policies approximate classic public goods. Like public goods, they are nonexcludable and indivisible. We have already encountered many examples of public goods in the area of foreign policy. Private goods are also widespread in the domain of foreign policy. The spoils of war that are distributed only among supporters of the winning regime (Wintrobe 1990, 1998; Lake 1992), trade or tariff policies that benefit key domestic supporters (McGillivray 1997, 2003; McGillivray and Smith 1997) and territory placed under the control of a backer in exchange for support are examples of such private goods. Private goods also abound in domestic politics. These include special tax benefits, access to special goods (for example, special stores open only to party members in communist states), rights to extract bribes, licenses, and the like.

All citizens of a state enjoy the benefits (or suffer the costs) from the public goods component of public policies, regardless of their support for the regime. This is precisely what is meant when we say that public goods are indivisible and nonexcludable. The private goods component of state actions differs from the public policy component in that private goods can be limited to a select set of citizens—that is, to the essential supporters of the regime. This difference is important in regard to the incentives leaders have to produce peace and prosperity, or to take or avoid foreign policy risks.

Time, effort, expertise, and money allocated by the leader as private benefits to constituents are not available to advance public policies. Consequently, leaders must choose how to focus their efforts. Leaders must choose how much of the resources at their disposal to spend on pursuing policy goals and how much to distribute as private goods. After all, resources spent on policy cannot be spent on private goods.

Download the Treaty of Westphalia or the Magna Carta from the Internet. How much of the text deals with the rights of citizens and sovereigns—that is, with general policy issues—and how much deals with the distribution of private goods, like specific castles, towns, and other territorial claims? Did the leaders in Europe in 1648 (when the Treaty of Westphalia was signed) or King John in England in the early thirteenth century face a large selectorate and a large winning coalition, or were both small? Take a look at the Treaty of Versailles, which ended World War I, or the Helsinki Accords, signed in 1975. Do these documents focus on private goods or public policy? Did the signatories generally have large winning coalitions and selectorates, or small ones?

## ALLOCATION OF RESOURCES AND POLITICAL INSTITUTIONS

The manner in which resources are allocated depends on the size of the winning coalition and the size of the selectorate. Leaders depend on support from a winning coalition; that winning coalition is drawn from the selectorate. The defining characteristic of the members of the winning coalition is that together they control the minimum quantity of resources essential to retaining political power, even if they are a minority of the selectorate (Riker 1962; Siverson and McCarty 1978). What is important to realize here is that toppling an incumbent government requires the defection of at least one member of the current winning coalition.

Leaders must retain the loyalty of enough people to maintain a winning coalition if they want to stay in office. Consequently, leaders limit the distribution of private goods to members of the winning coalition—that is, to their essential supporters. If those goods are insufficient to keep their followers happy, then leaders in addition may proffer public policies tailored to satisfy the needs of their supporters. For a given available pool of resources or budget, it is clear that the quantity of private goods received by the average member of the winning coalition shrinks as the size of the winning coalition increases. The more people there are who have a claim on a share of the budget, the smaller that share will be. This suggests that leaders in systems with large winning coalitions, such as democracies, will have a strategy for allocating scarce resources that is different from that of leaders in systems with small winning coalitions, such as monarchies and autocracies.

When does a member of a winning coalition decide that it is time to shift loyalty to some other prospective leader? Naturally, any disgruntled member of a winning coalition must think about the costs and benefits, risks and rewards of political defection. There are many prospective new leaders in any polity and, typically, there are several dissatisfied prospective defectors in the winning coalition, plus members of the selectorate who are not in the winning coalition but would like to be. Individuals who decide to defect from the winning coalition cannot be sure that they will be essential to any new government that forms. If it turns out that the new leadership does not need a defector to form a winning coalition, then the defector will be cut off from access to private goods. This risk is embodied in the ratio of the size of the winning coalition to the size of the selectorate.

When many people are necessary to form a winning coalition, then the chance is high that any member of the selectorate will be essential to that coalition. Put differently, if the support of every member of the selectorate were necessary to form a winning coalition, then there would be a 100 percent chance that each member of the selectorate would also be a part of any successor winning coalition. Unanimity, of course, is rare. What's more, a winning coalition so large as to encompass unanimity is impractical. What is evident, however, is that the odds of continuing to have access to private goods after defecting from the incumbent government depend partly on the size of the winning coalition. As the required size of the winning coalition increases, so do the odds of being included in a successor winning coalition following a political defection. However, as the pool of people increases from whom members of the winning coalition can be drawn— that is, as the size of the selectorate increases—the chances that any given individual will be chosen decreases. The larger the size of the selectorate, the smaller the chance a defector from an incumbent winning coalition will be needed in the successor winning coalition. The simplest way to think about this is to say that the odds of being essential to a new leadership are $W/S$, where $W$ is the size of the winning coalition and $S$ is the size of the selectorate. In effect, the risk of losing access to private goods following political defection increases both as the winning coalition gets smaller and as the selectorate gets larger.

The difference between the certainty of receiving private goods and the risk of being cut off from those goods if the current government falls should give members of the winning coalition pause. In fact, this risk provides an opportunity for the sitting leader to cull some of the private goods budget for his or her own ends. If the incumbent has $1 billion to distribute across the 1,000 members of the winning coalition, then the average member might be expected to receive $1 million. This would certainly be a handsome inducement for supporting the leader. However, there is no need for the incumbent to pay out so much in private goods. He or she can give quite a bit less and still provide enough to keep the winning coalition's loyalty.

Suppose the selectorate includes 100,000 people. In this case there is only a 1 percent chance that any member of the current winning coalition will also be a member of a successor winning coalition, given our odds ratio of W/S (1,000/100,000, or 1/100). If a member of the incumbent's coalition defects, then, he or she has a 1 percent chance of receiving $1 million from the new regime and a 99 percent chance of receiving no private goods whatsoever from that regime. The expected value of the prospective defector's share of the private goods to be dispensed by the successor regime is only $10,000 (that is, $1 million multiplied by 0.01 — the probability of getting private benefits). It is easy to see that as long as the incumbent beats that expectation and provides public policies that are not much worse than those proposed by the challenger, the would-be defector can be kept happy and loyal. The incumbent can keep the difference between the $1 million per supporter that could be distributed and the something above $10,000 per supporter that needs to be distributed. If the incumbent's challenger offers especially attractive public policies, then the incumbent can give up some of the "slush fund" to his or her supporters to purchase their continued loyalty. No wonder so many dictators have fat Swiss bank accounts.

Leaders have a natural preference for providing private goods as a means to retain power. This follows directly from the expected value calculation we have just discussed. The risk to supporters of exclusion from private goods if they defect makes it possible for incumbents always to beat their challengers if the competition is over private goods alone. Challengers recognize their inherent disadvantage in promising private goods and therefore turn to policy to compensate. Thus, incumbents like to reward supporters with private goods, all else being equal, and challengers like to promise improvements in public policy, all else being equal. Of course, all else is rarely equal, and that is at the heart of the matter.

One important way that all else may not be equal concerns the size of the winning coalition and the size of the selectorate. The size of these two institutions varies dramatically from state to state, or, more accurately, from one type of political system to another type of political system. The incumbent's advantage in allocating private goods diminishes rapidly as the size of the winning coalition increases or as the size of the selectorate decreases. Consider our earlier example in which the autocratic incumbent had

> If politics were a cooperative game, prospective new leaders could credibly promise to reward anyone who backs them, including those whose support turns out to be unnecessary to the prospective leader in his or her bid for office. Politics is typically more of a noncooperative game in which promises are not binding. What actions might a prospective leader take to provide would-be supporters with a credible promise that they will share in private goods if the prospective leader in fact comes to power? In answering this question, be sure to consider whether and why the recipients of the promise would or would not believe it. (Hint: Think in terms of costly signals.)

$1 billion to spend on private goods and compare it with the following example: Suppose that the selectorate consists of 1 million people rather than 100,000 people and that the winning coalition requires a simple majority of 500,001 members. These conditions are more like what we would find in a democracy. The average member of the winning coalition could then expect at most $2,000 of that $1 billion the leader has to spend in private benefits. This, of course, is way below the maximum expectation under the terms of our first example. What is more, the incumbent in the second example does not have to promise even this much because even in a democracy there still exists a 50 percent risk that a defector will not make it into the successor winning coalition. And the most the challenger can credibly promise to provide has an expected value of only about $1,000 per coalition member. The upper bound of $2,000 per supporter in the second example compares very poorly with the upper bound of $1 million per supporter in the earlier example. Even the lower bounds are not as attractive; the autocratic leader must provide at least $10,000 per supporter, whereas the democratic leader need only provide $1,000 per supporter. The private goods deal certainly looks a lot better for supporters of an autocrat than it does for supporters of a democratic leader.[3]

The general principle is straightforward. When the winning coalition gets bigger, private goods are spread more thinly and so can less easily make up for failed public policies. As the selectorate shrinks, the risks from defection drop off, making the incumbent's advantage in using private rewards smaller and smaller. Thus, the greatest incumbency advantage in using private goods to satisfy constituents belongs to leaders of political systems that have small winning coalitions and large selectorates. This makes the value of current private goods high for the average supporter and makes the expected value of private goods following a political defection small. It also means that the incumbent can, if so inclined, skim much of the private goods budget for his or her own ends.

## LEADERSHIP INCENTIVES AND POLITICAL INSTITUTIONS

What are the implications for policy of a government's domestic political institutions? How do the incentives produced by those institutions inform a leader's policymaking? We know that when a winning coalition is small and a selectorate is large (as is the case in many authoritarian systems with rigged elections), the essential supporters of an incumbent have good reasons to remain loyal to the leadership even if their leader produces one failed domestic or foreign policy after another. They are loyal for two reasons. First, they are being rewarded with private goods in excess of what they can expect from a challenger. As long as they are being "bribed" sufficiently, they do not really care about the larger national welfare. Second, if they are concerned about the national welfare, then they have

---

[3] Private goods payments are usually subtler in democracies than in autocracies. In democracies leaders promote tax policies or other redistributive programs that benefit their supporters, whereas in autocracies leaders often distribute the right to be corrupt to their cronies.

to worry about being cut out of the successor winning coalition in the event they decide to defect. Because the size of the winning coalition is small, the personal benefits of each of its members, on average, are large; at the same time, because the winning coalition is small and the selectorate is large, the risks from political defection are especially high.

Leaders of authoritarian states with large selectorates and small winning coalitions do not significantly increase their chances of staying in office by spending resources looking for successful public policies. They stay in office by keeping their few essential supporters happy with private goods. Just think of Saddam Hussein's success in holding on to power even after a worldwide trade embargo against Iraqi goods left his nation's economy in a shambles. Those who favor economic sanctions as an instrument to punish recalcitrant foreign adversaries would do well to consider what the effects of sanctions are on essential supporters, rather than on the nation as a whole (Hufbauer, Schott, and Elliott 1990; Tsebelis 1990a; Morgan and Schwebach 1995; Smith 1996; Drezner 1999). As long as Saddam Hussein continues to pay the military well and keep his clansmen happy, he is unlikely to suffer an internal coup. If the Iraqi economy gets so bad that he can no longer muster the resources to pay off this small group of supporters, then he will probably be in political trouble. But so far he has had enough resources to buy off the few people whose support he needs to stay in power. In fact, the economic sanctions have created black market opportunities that Hussein allows his supporters to exploit for personal gain. Mobutu Sese Seko, who held on to power as dictator in Zaire (formerly the Belgian Congo) for decades before finally being toppled while he was near death from cancer, once announced to a rally of supporters: "You who have stolen money and put it into homes here in Zaire and not abroad, I congratulate you" (*The Economist,* September 28, 1996, 53). Here was a man who understood that permitting certain people to steal from his country was the means to stay in office under Zaire's political arrangements. During his more than three decades in power, Zaire went from being one of the most promising economies of Africa to essential bankruptcy. During this time Mobutu's personal fortune grew to somewhere in the neighborhood of $6 billion.

Compare this incentive to provide private goods in authoritarian states with the contrasting incentive to provide successful public policy in democratic states. Democracies

*Iraqi president Saddam Hussein celebrated his sixty-fifth birthday in Baghdad on April 28, 2002. In power since the mid-1970s, President Hussein has gained popularity, especially among Palestinians, because he has provided more than $5 million to the families of those killed during the conflict with Israel. He increased payments to the families of suicide bombers from $10,000 to $25,000 during 2002. Despite this distribution of funds, children in Iraq suffer from malnutrition, poor health care, and a high mortality rate.*

have large winning coalitions and, therefore, also have large selectorates, at least relative to their total population. With a large winning coalition, it is difficult for leaders to provide the average member with sufficient private goods to keep him or her content. In essence, the average member of the winning coalition cannot be "bribed." The democratic leader simply does not have sufficient resources to do so. The promised better policies of a challenger are, at the margin, more attractive and more valuable for members of a large winning coalition (a democracy) than they are to members of a small winning coalition (an autocracy). Remember, everyone derives the benefits from successful public policies because public goods are nonexcludable and indivisible. Furthermore, in democracies the risk associated with defection is low. If an approximate majority is required to stay in office, then the odds of any particular member of the selectorate being excluded from the few available private goods is less than one-half. Thus, relatively speaking, democracy induces a norm of disloyalty from erstwhile backers when a leader fails to provide effective public policies. Defection is low risk and the private goods being doled out to backers are not worth much anyway. As such, the contest for power in democracies is really a contest over public goods. This is why a common theme in democratic politics is "throw the rascals out."

How is a democratic leader to stay in power? What does he or she have to do? Whereas authoritarian leaders hand out private goods to key backers, democratic leaders need to focus their efforts on making good public policy. The result is a high incentive to effect good public policy in democracies but a low incentive to do so in autocracies. Naturally, this has important domestic and foreign policy consequences.

## WINNING COALITION SIZE AND TRADE POLICY

Consider the impact of regime type—specifically the size of the winning coalition—on economic policy, including trade policy.[4] If the institutional argument just made is correct, and if, on average, most citizens value economic growth, then successful economic growth policies should occur more frequently in systems with large winning coalitions than in systems with small winning coalitions. After all, it is in democratic states—those

---

[4] I ignore the selectorate here because the theoretical implications of the selectorate are more complex than those of the winning coalition. The complexity involves the independent effects of the selectorate, which are always predicted to be opposite and smaller than the effects of the winning coalition, even though the size of the selectorate is not independent of the size of the winning coalition. This is true for two reasons. First, the selectorate can be large when the winning coalition is small, but it cannot be small when the winning coalition is large because the winning coalition's membership must be drawn from the selectorate. Second, a common feature of democracy is that the size of the winning coalition is a function of the size of the selectorate. If, for example, the political system requires a majority, then the winning coalition, as defined here, cannot be less than $(S + 1)/2$, where $S$ stands for the selectorate. The size of the winning coalition is not functionally tied to the size of the selectorate in authoritarian and most other systems, although, again, it must logically be smaller than the selectorate.

with large winning coalitions—that leaders must focus their efforts on economic success if they are to keep their jobs. In authoritarian polities (or monarchies), where the winning coalition is small, leaders use private goods rather than public policy to stay in office. They are not opposed to economic success, or to other policy successes. They simply do not have much incentive to put resources into finding effective economic policies because doing so does not advance their political security nearly as much as does spending those resources on private benefits for their most valued supporters. Consequently, we should expect democracies to be wealthier than autocracies, on average, because democratic leaders have stronger incentives to succeed in providing effective economic policies than do their authoritarian counterparts. And effective economic policies produce national wealth.

One foreign policy known to promote wealth is free trade. Free trade involves low or no tariffs as explained in more detail in the next chapter. This policy deprives inefficient domestic businesses of protection against strong foreign competition. In fact, a free trade policy encourages such competition. This means that citizens can choose to buy the products that fill their needs at the best price, whether those products are of foreign or domestic make. Their selection is not limited to domestic products only, which may cost more or may not be as well made as foreign alternatives. As a result, people can buy more goods because they spend less money per good under free trade policies than under protectionist policies. Additionally, and importantly, under a free trade regime domestic industries face added competition. Added competition means that to survive in the marketplace domestic firms cannot be lazy. They must constantly look for ways to make their products as good as or better than their competitors' products and at least as cost effective. Those who do not cannot survive. No government will step in to protect them against their own inefficiency. No government subsidies (which are just private benefits) are offered to prop up firms. In these ways, free trade promotes growth. This is not a particularly controversial viewpoint among economists, yet protectionism continues today. If protectionism is not good for growth, why does it persist?

Trade protection is generally motivated by political considerations rather than economic considerations. Protecting the jobs of voters in democracies or protecting political cronies in authoritarian states helps leaders stay in office (Lohmann and O'Halloran 1994; McGillivray 1997, 2003). Politicians in any political system can be motivated to satisfy the needs of those who suffer adverse consequences from foreign competition. They are less interested in helping those who enjoy diffuse benefits from free trade. Helping those who bear the brunt of the costs of free trade means the politician is more likely to stay in office.

The average consumer sees only small personal gains from each protectionist trade policy that is dropped. The creation of new jobs in diffuse competitive sectors typically is not concentrated in a handful of constituencies so that the newly employed do not represent a focused group of supporters. Workers in inefficient industries, or government

cronies who run such industries, however, feel the concentrated effects of a newly implemented free trade policy. They may suffer a drop in pay, a deterioration of working conditions, and the loss of fringe benefits, or they may lose their jobs or their businesses
altogether. Thus, politicians sometimes opt for protectionist policies in the short run to
gain political support.

For authoritarian leaders, no meaningful offsetting pressure exists to get them to
sacrifice their political cronies to enhance national economic performance. Again, as
long as they can keep their cronies (that is, the members of the winning coalition) happy,
these politicians are secure in office. The economic drag of protectionism need not
burden authoritarian leaders.

Democratic leaders, in contrast, face two problems when they pursue protectionist
policies. First, they need a broad base of support. The votes of producers who gain concentrated benefits from protectionism rarely add up to enough votes to provide the support needed to form a winning coalition. Democratic leaders must look beyond this
small group, which means they must attract support from voters who do not gain from
protectionism. Second, opponents always look for ways to oust the incumbent in the
next election. In a democracy the quality of public policy looms large in the minds of
voters, and therefore looms large in an incumbent's prospects of reelection. Consequently, challengers work at persuading voters that under new leadership, conditions will
improve. One way to make things better for lots of voters is to eliminate tariffs, not on
just one industry but on virtually all industry. In this way the benefits of free trade will be
dispersed across all voters. To counteract such a policy challenge, incumbents must improve their economic policies or face defeat. People generally vote their pocketbooks. In
democratic systems, where a large base of support is needed to succeed, politicians must
meet those pocketbook demands to stay in office. Free trade helps them to do so nation-
ally, although it may work against the politicians' interests in localized regions or districts
(Rogowski 1987, 1989; Alt and Gilligan 1994). Fiona McGillvray (1997, 2003) has shown
that the size of tariffs varies within democracies as a function of the structure of the
electoral system. In systems with district voting, as in the United States, tariffs are concentrated in districts in which voters' support is essential to the national incumbent government. In list voting systems, which are common in many countries that practice
proportional representation, tariffs are not concentrated at all; rather, they are diffuse. In
fact, democracies have been shown generally to engage in trade with fewer barriers than
do their autocratic counterparts (Mansfield, Milner, and Rosendorff 1998).

## THE NEOREALIST, ALTERNATIVE VIEW OF TRADE POLICY

Some scholars take a neorealist perspective and argue that free trade creates what they
call a security externality (Gowa and Mansfield 1993). The argument claims that any relative gain netted by a participant in a trade relationship can be converted into extra military spending. By "relative gain" I mean that one decision maker's utility increases more,

or decreases less, than another decision maker's utility. The extra military spending represents a security advantage for that state relative to its trading partner. Therefore, although trade creates wealth, it also jeopardizes the security of one of the trading partners by creating a relative security loss. In this view, trade decisions are imbedded within a prisoners' dilemma. Take a look at the prisoners' dilemma game depicted in Table 12-1 and consider its implications for trade policy.

TABLE 12-1

**Free Trade as a Prisoners' Dilemma**

| | State B | |
| State A | **Free Trade** | **No Free Trade** |
|---|---|---|
| Free Trade | 16, 12 | 3, 20 |
| No Free Trade | 20, 3 | 5, 7 |

The first number in each cell represents the utility derived by state A from the combination of strategies that defines each cell. The second number represents state B's utility. For example, if both states pursue a strategy of free trade, then state A will derive a value of 16 and state B will derive a value of 12 from that combination of strategies (a relative gain of 4). I have intentionally constructed the payoffs so that they are not identical for A and B in each cell. Remember, the prisoners' dilemma requires only that the temptation payoff (one player does not engage in free trade and the other adopts free trade) be larger than the cooperative, reward payoff (both players pursue free trade); that the cooperative, reward payoff be larger than the noncooperative, punishment strategy (neither player pursues free trade); and that the noncooperative, punishment strategy be larger than the sucker payoff (one player engages in free trade when the other does not).

The payoff matrix in Table 12-1 shows that there are clear gains when each state pursues a strategy of free trade (16, 12). This is in marked contrast to the outcome of the equilibrium strategy when the game is played only once, where each state pursues a strategy of no free trade (5, 7).[5] If states A and B interact repeatedly it is possible for mutual gains to be realized through a combined strategy of joint free trade. In other words, repeated play of the prisoners' dilemma game can support joint cooperation as an equilibrium outcome provided the players follow a strategy or plan of action such as tit-for-tat. Of course, mutual defection (that is, neither player engages in free trade) is also an equilibrium outcome of the repeated game. Neorealists argue that pursuing a strategy of no free trade will be the likely choice of both states A and B in a security-oriented world (Gowa and Mansfield 1993).

Since neorealist theory assumes that all states are security maximizers with a preference for security above all else, it follows that states would not use trade policy to enhance wealth even if they derived an absolute gain from doing so. State A's absolute gain here from practicing free trade over protectionism is the difference between a utility

---

[5] Recall that an equilibrium strategy is one in which no player has a unilateral incentive to switch to another strategy.

of 16 and a utility of 5. What is important to understand according to neorealists is that it is *relative* gains that drive changes in security. In the game depicted in Table 12-1 we can see that free trade gives state A a utility equal to 16, whereas it gives state B a utility equal to 12. A relative gains argument such as that proffered by neorealists compares these two utilities and concludes that state B is made worse off because A's gains are larger relative to its own gains. However, such a conclusion is logically problematic. The utilities 16 and 12 each *encompasses* all sources of utility from the action involved. This includes whatever value a decision maker has placed on relative gain. There is no additional, unaccounted-for utility that can be produced as a result of the fact that the two numbers happen to be different. If there were, then the game being played would be different; it would not be the prisoners' dilemma at all. The relative gains argument sometimes is based on an interpersonal comparison of utility. Such comparisons are illogical because they presume that the metric (that is, the measuring stick) for each decision maker is the same. But in fact, utilities cannot be compared across individuals. They are relevant only with respect to the choices of a single individual. After all, utility does not have a natural scale; one person's 16 is not necessarily larger than another person's 12. For example, if utilities were expressed in dollars, it is unlikely that a rich person would value an extra dollar as much as a poor person. Utility provides a measure on preference. It allows you to say, "I am better off doing X rather than Y because I get 16 [or, equivalently, 160] by doing X and I get 15 [or, equivalently, 150] by doing Y." The utility accrued by someone else is already figured into your utility; it is already part of the valuation of X and Y.[6]

For the moment we will put the illogic of an interpersonal comparison of utility aside so that we can see why neorealists argue that states will select the "no free trade" strategy. To avoid an interpersonal comparison of utilities, we can put the relative gains argument differently. If the decision makers care about relative gains and the utilities in the game matrix somehow do not represent this fact, we can alter the game so that the payoffs do reflect this fact. The payoff matrix depicted in Table 12-2 shows the impossibility of achieving a cooperative, free trade strategy from the relative gains, security-oriented perspective. This payoff matrix was constructed by subtracting B's payoffs from A's, creating purely relative gains estimates. The game depicted here is not the prisoners' dilemma. Notice that for state B, what we earlier labeled as the temptation payoff (B engages in protectionism and A adopts free trade) is still the most preferred outcome, but what we labeled as the reward payoff (both A and B engage in free trade) is smaller than what we earlier called the punishment payoff (neither A nor B pursues free trade). The ordering of preferences (or the utility to be gained) for state B does not meet the cri-

---

[6] Consider the following oddity of relative gains reasoning: If I face a choice where I can win $1 million and you can win $1.5 million or where I can lose $1 million and you can lose $1.5 million, then if I am motivated purely by relative gains, I should prefer to see you lose $1.5 million, and therefore lose $1 million myself.

teria of a prisoners' dilemma. By converting the payoffs we have created a zero-sum game. This means that any gain for state A is always a loss for state B and visa versa.

The equilibrium strategy of the game when it is played only once is the same here as it is in the prisoners' dilemma game depicted in Table 12-1. Neither state engages in free trade. But now, because the states have mutually opposed interests (this is what it means to say that a game is zero sum), no matter how many times the game is repeated, the two states will never have an

incentive to cooperate in free trade. Unlike the prisoners' dilemma, cooperation does not make both states better off than noncooperation, no matter how large the shadow of the future. In fact, the higher the value that is placed on the future, the worse off state B will become if it engages in cooperation. If both states adopt free trade, state A gains 4 points each time there is mutual free trade. According to the neorealist perspective, those points represent extra resources that state A can put toward the pursuit of security. This is better than the 2 points it gains by pursuing the equilibrium strategy. But for state B the situation is different. It loses 4 points each time it cooperates in mutual free trade. This is worse for state B than losing 2 points in pursuit of the equilibrium strategy. Hence, there is no incentive for state B to cooperate. And there is no incentive for state A to cooperate unilaterally because by doing so it loses 17 points. This is the essence of the neorealist argument against free trade. Free trade inevitably gives the advantage to one state at the expense of another, thereby jeopardizing the loser's security. Critics have shown that trade makes up too small a proportion of most economies to have much effect on future security (Morrow, Siverson, and Tabares 1998). Their evidence indicates that although the security externality may exist in theory, it is likely to be inconsequential in practice.

The same neorealist logic should also apply to internal economic policies. If investing in future wealth (that is, economic growth policies) makes states more secure, then all states, regardless of regime type, should do so. If spending on the military rather than on economic growth is the path to security, then all states should invest as much as possible in the military (Powell 1999). That states do not spend as much as possible on the military is evident. For example, over the span of the cold war, major power states spent, on average, about 5 percent of their gross domestic product (GDP) on the military, leaving 95 percent for all other uses. Less influential states put only about 1 percent of GDP toward their military budgets. Some states spent nothing. The highest that any states spent during this time was no more than 7 or 8 percent of GDP. Obviously, much more could have been spent. During wartime, states sometimes apply considerably more of their GDP to military spending. Yet even at the height of World War II, Germany did not mobilize its industry for the war effort to the degree that it had in World War I. One possible explanation for this has been suggested by Albert Speer (1971), who intimates that Adolf Hitler feared he would lose support among the German middle class if he deprived families of consumer goods.

Because some states will enhance security through military spending and others, faced with different circumstances, will enhance security by generating wealth, it's reasonable to believe that structuralists in general would expect to find no particular relationship between regime type and growth policies. Rather, because external circumstances and not internal considerations drive national investment policy decisions, structuralists would predict that no link exists between the size of a country's internal political winning coalition and its economic performance—or, more specifically, its trade policy.

## THE INTEREST GROUP VIEW OF TRADE POLICY

Interest group theories, like structural theories, provide no basis for a clear hypothesis concerning the relationship between winning coalition size and economic growth and trade policy. Some organizations, like the office of the United States Trade Representative, promote free trade policies as part of their mission to improve the American consumer's buying power. Others, like the United Automobile Workers, fight against free trade policies as part of their mission to protect UAW jobs. No theoretical basis exists that would predict that one set of interest groups would predominate over another in organizational and interest group arguments. Rather, each interest group should be expected to provide the selective evidence of policy success or failure that promotes its own well-being in lobbying to influence national debate. Within the logic of organizational theories, the evidence and arguments that interest groups or bureaucrats select to push their case have no reason to be tied to the size of the winning coalition or to regime type (Cyert and March 1963; Sagan 1993; Gartner 1997).

## EVIDENCE: WINNING COALITION SIZE AND ECONOMIC PERFORMANCE

Structural theories and organizational theories produce expectations about economic growth and trade policy different from those of the strategic approach. This difference in expectations provides a basis for testing these competing perspectives on a dimension of considerable importance: economic performance. I begin with three tests. First, how does winning coalition size influence overall economic growth? To see what effect the size of a country's winning coalition has on its economic growth, I rely on data on the annual growth in GDP for all countries from 1961 through 1988 as measured by Richard Summers and Alan Heston (1988, 1991) in their study of comparative economic growth. The size of each country's winning coalition is measured each year as an index derived from indicators in the Polity III data set (Jaggers and Gurr 1996), as described in Bruce Bueno de Mesquita, Alastair Smith, Randolph M. Siverson, and James D. Morrow (2003).

Figure 12-1 indicates that the size of the winning coalition substantially influences growth rates, largely as anticipated by the strategic perspective. The figure shows that those countries with the smallest winning coalitions have an annual growth rate that is substantially below the average for countries with larger winning coalitions. A few percentage points may seem small, but consider what the difference is between the growth rate of the most autocratic systems (indexed as 1 on the measure of winning coalition size) and countries with the second-largest or largest winning coalition size (indexed as 4 and 5, respectively, on the measure of winning coalition size). Over a fifty-year period, equaling approximately the duration of the cold war, the most autocratic systems on average grew about 451 percent, given a yearly rate of increase of 3.06 percent, compounded annually. In contrast, the more democratic systems averaged growth over the same period of between 658 percent and 754 percent. The more democratic systems increased in wealth by 46 to 67 percent more than did their autocratic counterparts.[7]

Economic growth is but one indicator of national policy performance. Our second test of policy performance examines the relationship between winning coalition size and a society's human capital (Barro and Lee 1993; Putnam 1993; Barro 1997; Jackman and Miller 1998). "Human capital" refers to the skills of the population. This represents an important source of productivity for a society, just as do monetary capital (that is, money or wealth) and natural resources like oil or iron ore, fertile soil, and good weather. We have already seen that domestic institutions influence wealth in regard to economic growth. Does winning coalition size also influence the quantity of human capital available? If the argument that leaders need to provide effective policies in more democratic systems but need not worry about the effectiveness of policy in more autocratic regimes is correct, then it should.

Broadly based education is important to systems concerned with effective policy, both as good policy in its own right and as a means of enhancing economic productivity.

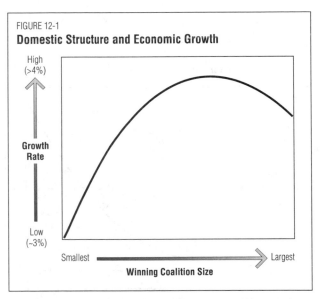

FIGURE 12-1

**Domestic Structure and Economic Growth**

*Note:* The graph is based on a regression analysis of annual growth in GDP with the size of the winning coalition and its square (to capture the nonlinear effects) of 2,798 cases, representing approximately one hundred countries over a twenty-eight year period. The winning coalition index and its square are highly significant statistically. The results are unaltered by controlling for year and total population size.

*Differences in economic growth rates are closely associated with the institutions of government. Domestic political choices affect a nation's ability to compete in the international arena, where democracies have a distinct institutional advantage in generating wealth.*

---

[7] Note that growth rates turn down at the highest level of political openness, when the winning coalition is at a maximum. For an interesting explanation of this phenomenon, see Barro (1997).

I measure human capital with the Barro-Lee human capital stock indicator, which assesses average years of educational attainment of the labor force year by year and country by country. The strategic argument leads us to expect that human capital increases as the size of the winning coalition increases as a result of leaders' increasing dependence on effective public policies.

Once again the expectations derived from the strategic perspective are borne out. Figure 12-2 shows the dramatic impact of winning coalition size on the level of human capital. The most autocratic polities have labor forces with an average level of educational attainment of 3.5 years. This contrasts with an average level of educational attainment of 7.8 years in polities with the largest winning coalitions. System type really matters when it comes to educational attainment by the labor force.

The third test of our evaluation of domestic institutional structure and economic performance relates to trade policy (Milner 1988; Mansfield, Milner, and Rosendorff 1998). We would expect to see systems with larger winning coalitions exhibiting more open, free trade orientations than their autocratic counterparts. We would expect to see the latter engage in protectionism because they do not want their government cronies to suffer at the hands of foreign (or domestic) competition. Protection is a private benefit given to key government backers. It is less generously doled out in more democratic systems because the leaders of those countries have a greater need to rely on effective policies. Figure 12-3 assesses the evidence. The figure is based on Stanley Fischer's data on average tariff rates and economic openness to trade (1993).

Economic policies involving trade are at the heart of international political economies. The record of actual behavior across many states and many years shows that the size of the winning coalition significantly influences policy choices. This directly contradicts structural expectations and is inconsistent with interest group theories. The evidence supports the strategic viewpoint. Trade decisions are not simply driven by the dictates of a security-minded international system; neither are they the result of bureaucratic and interest group "muddling through." Clearly, trade policy depends on the structure of domestic political institutions.

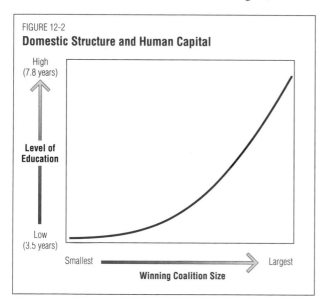

FIGURE 12-2
**Domestic Structure and Human Capital**

High
(7.8 years)

**Level of Education**

Low
(3.5 years)

Smallest ———————▶ Largest

**Winning Coalition Size**

*Note:* The evidence is based on a regression analysis. The measure of winning coalition size and its square are both highly significant, based on 2,399 observations. This remains true after controlling for the year and the total population of each country. This effect is so strong that about 35 percent of all variation in human capital across time and space can be accounted for by the size of the winning coalition.

*Governments that depend on large winning coalitions to stay in office favor policies that promote education and the development of highly skilled and productive populations.*

## WINNING COALITION SIZE AND NATIONAL SURVIVAL

The size of the winning coalition affects a basic aspect of international relations—national survival. Are there differences in the willingness of leaders to put their state's survival at risk, and, if so, do those differences depend on the size of the winning coalition? The answer is a decided yes. Democratic leaders head governments with large winning coalitions. As a consequence, their quests to stay in office are strongly influenced by the quality of their policies. Authoritarian leaders, in contrast, are less affected by policy failure. Their key supporters depend on dispensation of private goods, not effective public policy. Consequently, these supporters are more loyal to the leadership when policies fail than are supporters of leaders of democratic regimes. Naturally, all leaders prefer to see their policies succeed. But, as I have emphasized, some can more easily survive policy failure than others and so are less likely to devote adequate resources to policy pursuits.

One implication of this argument is that democratic leaders are more selective than authoritarian leaders in the wars they are willing to fight. In war, defeat represents a major policy failure; victory, a major policy success. Avoiding war may also represent a policy success. As such, we would expect to find that democratic leaders get involved in fewer wars than their authoritarian counterparts, and, when they do get involved, they are more likely to win. Additionally, we would expect to find that democratic leaders are more likely to avoid the escalation of disputes that can lead to military defeat. Indeed, democratic leaders may make concessions in an international negotiation rather than win outright at too high a cost (Bueno de Mesquita and Siverson 1995; Gelpi and Grieco 1998). Put differently, authoritarian leaders can afford to take bigger policy risks than democratic leaders. Autocrats can more readily engage in wars that they do not have a good chance of winning because the private benefits they dispense to their followers blunt the negative consequences of policy failure. In fact, democracies are disproportionately more likely to win the wars they fight (Lake 1992). This is because democracies are highly selective in deciding whether to negotiate or fight, not because democracies are particularly better at fighting

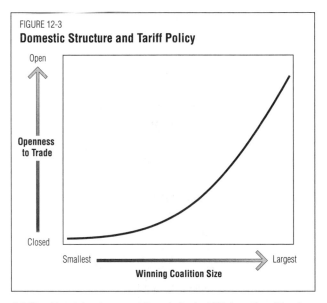

FIGURE 12-3
**Domestic Structure and Tariff Policy**

Open

**Openness to Trade**

Closed

Smallest ——————▶ Largest
**Winning Coalition Size**

*Note:* The evidence is based on a regression analysis using 1,504 observations. Although more data are missing in this test than in the tests depicted in Figures 12-1 and 12-2, keep in mind that we are examining a very large sample. The results are statistically strong in the face of controls for population size and year.

*Governments that depend on large winning coalitions to stay in office favor free trade and low tariffs. Leaders who depend on small winning coalitions are likely to promulgate high-tariff policies to protect the interests of their cronies.*

(Reiter and Stam 1996). This selection effect is strongly associated with prospects of political survival following a war. Democratic leaders are substantially more likely to be overthrown following a military defeat than are their authoritarian counterparts (Bueno de Mesquita, Smith, Siverson, and Morrow 2003).

The evidence that domestic political institutions help shape fundamental features of foreign policy and international politics is strong indeed. James Morrow (1991b), for example, looked at the effect that the domestic economy has had in the United States on the willingness of the president to offer foreign policy concessions during arms negotiations. Morrow demonstrated that when a presidential election was close at hand and the inflation rate was high, the president tended to offer larger arms control concessions to the Soviet Union in a bid to shore up his reelection chances by producing an arms control agreement. Soviet leaders apparently understood this domestic incentive. Their arms control demands escalated when the president was in a relatively weak reelection situation and moderated when he was not.

Kurt Gaubatz (1991, 1999) reinforced the notion that domestic political institutions shape foreign policymaking in his investigation of election timing and war. He showed that democratic states are much more likely to engage in war shortly after an election than shortly before one. Incumbents avoid war, a costly enterprise, just before an election because it might diminish the incumbent's chances of reelection. If a war occurs shortly after an election takes place, and if that conflict results in a defeat, then the incumbent has more time to pursue policy successes and thereby recover any lost popularity that accompanied the military defeat.

Kenneth Schultz (2001) provided still more evidence of the importance of domestic politics in international affairs. He challenged the conventional wisdom that says that partisan politics ends at the water's edge—that is, the notion that domestic political motives do not interfere with the overall national interest. Schultz showed that the empirical evidence indicates that in fact partisan political interests are not set aside in dealings with foreign adversaries.

In democracies, opposition politicians openly compete to unseat the incumbent. Because executive authority resides in the hands of elected officials, the path to incumbency is through popular election. We have already seen that democracies, because of their large winning coalitions, emphasize policy success over private goods distributions in selecting leaders. One consequence of this is that the quality of foreign policy is enhanced by partisan competition (Schultz 2001). Members of the political opposition will not resist effective foreign policy. If they did, their chances of winning election would be diminished. If the opposition believes that a policy will succeed, it will hop onto the bandwagon and support that policy.

At its outset, there was little political opposition in the United States to the Vietnam War. But when it looked as though the war effort would fail, innumerable politicians jockeyed to establish their long-standing opposition to the war. Likewise, prior to the

WINNING COALITION SIZE AND NATIONAL SURVIVAL

Gulf War, Democrats in Congress attempted to block President George H. W. Bush's decision to use force. Once it became apparent that the war policy was proving successful, however, it became virtually impossible to find a member of Congress who did not claim to have favored the war. By war's end, few remembered that even then chairman of the Joint Chiefs of Staff Colin Powell, one of the war's heroes, had initially opposed military action. Following the terrorist attack against the United States on September 11, 2001, no significant political figure in the United States opposed President George W. Bush's war on terrorism. To do so would have been political suicide. In democratic India, by contrast, there were significant divisions among that country's political parties over whether to support the American effort or not. From the Indian context there were political gains to be had from backing the U.S. stance and from opposing it.

Being on the right side of a major foreign policy decision can have important electoral consequences. When domestic rivals believe an incumbent's policy will fail, they scramble to distinguish their own position from the incumbent's. Open articulation of a partisan foreign policy is a signal of discord that can have several consequences that structural theories and interest group theories cannot foresee or explain. First, the opposition will embolden the foreign rival. Just as a high inflation rate stimulated greater arms control concessions by the United States and greater arms control demands from the Soviets, so too can indications of domestic disagreement provide the impetus for a foreign rival to press his or her case. In fact, this is the standard reason for arguments in favor of nonpartisan foreign policy. At the same time, domestic opposition can force the incumbent leader to rethink his or her foreign policy decision making. Knowing that domestic opponents believe they can gain an electoral advantage by challenging the incumbent's policy, the incumbent has incentives to reexamine that policy. The incumbent may conclude that it is still the correct course to follow; alternatively, he or she may decide to make changes based on the challenger's arguments that have until then been given short shrift. The incumbent's reelection motive helps to temper policy decisions, which in turn reduces foreign policy adventurism in democracies.

We can pull all of these disparate observations about regime type and war together within a single framework by taking advantage of the distinction between the size of the winning coalition and the size of the selectorate. A body of empirical observations, known as the democratic peace, notes that liberal democracies rarely, if ever, fight wars with one another (Small and Singer 1976; Rummel 1983; Weede 1984; Doyle 1986; Morgan and Campbell 1991; Kilgour 1992; Bremer 1993; Maoz and Russett 1993; Mintz and Geva 1993; Russett 1993; Farber and Gowa 1995; Kegley and Hermann 1995; Ray 1995; Gates, Knutsen, and Moses 1996; Lemke and Reed 1996; Chan 1997; Gleditsch and Hegre 1997; Oneal and Russett 1997; Russett, Oneal, and Davis 1998; Ward and Gleditsch 1998). So important is this observation that American presidents have made the promotion of democratic institutions a cornerstone of their foreign policy. They believe that democracy promotes peace.

The central empirical regularities that collectively constitute the democratic peace show that democracies typically:

1. do not fight wars with one another (Maoz and Abdolali 1989; Bremer 1992; Maoz and Russett 1993; Russett 1993; Ray 1995),
2. fight wars with nondemocracies with considerable regularity (Maoz and Abdolali 1989),
3. emerge victorious in war (Lake 1992; Reiter and Stam 1996),
4. reach peaceful settlements when disputes arise with other democracies (Dixon 1994),
5. are more likely to initiate war against autocracies than are autocracies to initiate wars against them (Bennett and Stam 1998b),
6. experience fewer battle deaths in the wars they initiate (Siverson 1995),
7. are more likely to fight shorter wars than are autocracies (Bennett and Stam 1996, 1998c),
8. are more likely to fight with one another when they are in transition to democracy (Mansfield and Snyder 1995), and
9. are more constrained as major powers and are therefore less likely to engage in war than are minor powers (Morgan and Campbell 1991).

All of these empirical regularities are consistent with the strategic perspective.[8]

Imagine that two nations find themselves involved in a dispute. They might pursue negotiations or they might use force to achieve their objectives. If they negotiate, they are likely to resolve their argument by striking a compromise that approximates the observable balance of power between them. That is, the existing military balance is likely to give shape to the bargaining leverage of the two sides. If the adversaries fight, the outcome of their war depends in part on the military balance. But it also depends on at least two other factors: intangible assets and the diversion of national resources to the war effort.

In a war, intangible assets such as superior generalship, better morale, and the like can help tilt the military balance one way or the other. Intangible military assets of this type can be credibly revealed only in the course of military action. These intangibles are unlikely to play a role in decision making during negotiations because each side has an obvious incentive to lie, saying that it has a greater store of assets than it really has. In battle, although such claims may still be made, the true facts are quickly revealed (Stam 1996; Gartner 1997; Bueno de Mesquita, Morrow, and Zorick 1997).

Leaders may also choose to reallocate available resources to tilt the balance of power in their favor. Depending on how much of such resources a leader diverts to the war effort, he or she demonstrates a larger (or smaller) commitment to winning the war. One obvious source of additional resources is the reserve normally given out as private bene-

---

[8] For a more detailed explanation of the democratic peace regularities and their relationship to the strategic perspective, see Bueno de Mesquita, Morrow, Siverson, and Smith (1999).

fits to members of the winning coalition. In autocracies, where the winning coalition is small and the share of private goods per member is large, coalition members tend to care less about the quality of public policy—and therefore about the national welfare and winning a war—than they do about safeguarding their own personal, private benefits. In such a system a leader is unlikely to reallocate resources from personal benefit to national benefit. To do so would alienate the leader's key supporters and thereby jeopardize his or her hold on power. In contrast, democratic leaders avidly search out additional resources to bolster their war efforts. They do so because their hold on political power depends on policy success, not on the allocation of private goods. Democratic leaders shift resources into the war effort by taking them away from private goods payments or by taking them out of less important policy pursuits without suffering a marked loss of support from the winning coalition.

In sum, autocratic polities put forth less effort than democratic polities toward winning wars (Lamborn 1991; Levi 1998; Rosenthal 1998; Bueno de Mesquita, Smith, Siverson, and Morrow 2003). The extra effort made by democrats gives them, on average, a military advantage over autocrats in war. This difference in effort directly implies the empirical regularities associated with the democratic peace.

Because democratic leaders try harder to win wars than their autocratic counterparts, democrats make relatively unattractive military targets. In addition, democrats are more selective than autocrats in their choice of targets. Since defeat typically leads to their domestic replacement, democratic leaders fight only those wars that they expect to win. Otherwise, they negotiate.

To go to war, an autocrat does not require a huge military advantage because victory is not as important (except under special circumstances involving all-out war) for survival as is reserving funds to provide future private benefits. Democrats compensate for any initial military disadvantage by devoting additional resources to the war effort; autocrats do not. Democracies typically overwhelm autocracies because they are willing to mobilize more of their resources for the war effort rather than reserve them to reward domestic backers. Wars between democrats and autocrats are generally short in duration and relatively low in cost to the democracy (Bennett and Stam 1996, 1998c). In contrast, democracies find it difficult to overwhelm other democracies. This is because both democracies try hard to win the war.[9] This makes democracies particularly unattractive targets for other democracies. Hence, democratic states rarely attack other democratic states.[10]

---

[9] There is a noteworthy exception. Powerful democracies do not hesitate to fight against weak democracies, because the odds of victory are high and small democracies are reluctant to fight back. Thus, the United States could invade the Dominican Republic in 1965 and overthrow its democratically elected government. The Dominicans were not in a position to fight back. Small autocracies are even less reluctant to fight back against democracies. The example of the Somalis under Gen. Mohammed Farah Aidid against the United States in the early 1990s is a case in point.

[10] It is worth noting that the strategic model does not say it is impossible for democracies to fight one another, only that such conflicts are less likely than those between other polity pairs. The conditions under which democracies would fight one another are particularly difficult to satisfy.

The costs a nation endures in war are inversely related to its military dominance (Bueno de Mesquita 1983). Consequently, those nations that make a greater effort gain an added military advantage that helps reduce the costs they suffer. Democracies make this greater effort. Therefore, on average, we should expect to find that democracies suffer fewer casualties in war than autocracies. In fact, the empirical record supports this expectation.

To examine the democratic transition regularity articulated by the democratic peace, we must first ask what it means to be a state in a democratic transition. Essentially, states in a democratic transition are situated somewhere in between democracies and autocracies in the size of their selectorates and the size of their winning coalitions. These states have selectorates that are proportionately larger than their winning coalitions when compared with those of full-fledged democracies. As such, their behavioral patterns should fall somewhere between that of a full-fledged democracy and that of an autocracy. That is, we would expect to find that transitional democracies are more likely to fight one another or full-fledged democracies than full-fledged, long-standing democracies are to fight with each other. This, in fact, is entirely consistent with empirical observation, as embodied in the democratic peace.

The final empirical observation in our list of regularities—that large democracies are more constrained not to fight than are small democracies—is not stated in regard to relations between pairs of states. As such, it is a bit more difficult to fit within the framework used here. Still, it is consistent with the strategic approach in that major power democracies are generally large countries. In absolute magnitude they have very large winning coalitions. Consequently, their leaders are especially dependent on successful policy performance to retain their jobs and they therefore strongly manifest the expected behavior of democracies (Morgan and Campbell 1991).

## DOMESTIC INSTITUTIONS AND FOREIGN AID

The giving of foreign aid represents another important foreign policy influenced by domestic institutions. At first blush it seems reasonable to think that democratic, large coalition, donor governments are more inclined to help poor democracies than they are to help poor autocracies. Yet this appears incorrect as a matter of empirical record. Democracies routinely give substantial aid to poorly run, corrupt autocracies. The selectorate theory provides an explanation for this aid-giving pattern that, in this case, shares much in common with the realist point of view.

Among the many policy arenas on which large coalition, democratic leaders are judged is the degree to which they successfully gain policy support from foreign countries. American presidents, for example, are partially judged at home by their ability to muster international cooperation against foreign foes. President George H. W. Bush was admired for his success in building a broadly based coalition of support against Saddam

Hussein following Iraq's invasion of Kuwait. President George W. Bush was likewise admired at home for his success in gaining the support of many other states—especially Pakistan—during the war on terrorism. Iran's commitment to the war on terrorism, in contrast, was very limited indeed, and the president was not chastised for failing to attract the support of the Iranian government. Iran is a quasi-democracy that happens also to be classified by President George W. Bush as an evil state.

Democratic leaders in poor states hoping to gain foreign assistance cannot credibly promise to follow the policies desired by a prospective donor if those policies are unpopular among the recipient's constituents. The Iranian government, for instance, cannot easily agree to pursue policies toward Israel or against terrorism that are favored in the United States. Iran cannot back those policies because it is a fairly democratic country and those policies are not popular among Iranians. Because of this fact, the Iranian government is unlikely to get much aid from the United States. When the tight-fisted, autocratic shah of Iran ruled that country (before 1979), Iran received enthusiastic American support. Autocrats, as we know, do not stay in power by satisfying the policy preferences of a large constituency at home. They can credibly promise to follow the policies desired by a prospective patron—as did the shah—in exchange for money with which to continue to purchase loyalty among their core set of cronies. Foreign aid provides added funds to buy support. Thus, democracies can be expected to give lots of direct or indirect aid to autocrats. It is a win-win situation. The autocrat produces policies desired by the donor even if those policies are not a good fit with the preferences of the domestic population in the autocracy. The democratic donor improves the policy satisfaction of his constituents while fulfilling the private benefits requirements of the autocrat. In fact, the average autocrat's political survival prospects are improved more than 30 percent as a result of the typical amount of per capita foreign aid received (that is, about $8 per capita) (Bueno de Mesquita and Root 2002).

## SUMMARY

In this chapter we examined a strategic model of domestic institutions and foreign policy. Leaders, intent on retaining power and authority, must satisfy core constituents identified as the winning coalition. The winning coalition is drawn from the selectorate, or set of people with a legitimate say in the selection of the government leadership. Leaders distribute a mix of benefits in the form of public policies that all enjoy and private goods that only members of the winning coalition enjoy.

We saw that from a leader's point of view the optimal political arrangement is to have a small winning coalition and a large selectorate, as is common in systems with rigged elections. Under such arrangements, supporters receive valuable private benefits that foster loyalty to their leaders even in the face of policy failure. Furthermore, loyalty is reinforced by the high political risks associated with defection to a political rival. Those risks increase as the size of the selectorate increases and as the size of the winning coalition decreases.

Monarchy is often the optimal political arrangement from the point of view of members of the winning coalition (that is, the aristocracy). Under monarchy, which has a small winning coalition and a small selectorate, the current value of private goods is high. This is true as well in autocracies. In monarchies, however, winning coalition members benefit from the fact that the risks associated with defection are not as great as they are in autocracies. This follows from the fact that the ratio of the winning coalition size to the size of the selectorate is larger in monarchies than it is in autocracies with rigged elections.

Democracy is the optimal form of government from the perspective of ordinary citizens. Few private goods are doled out. Instead, public policy is the focus of leadership decisions. Since good public policy benefits all in the polity, even those not in the winning coalition are likely to fare reasonably well. Consequently, the broad mass of the population derives its greatest benefits under democracy. This is in marked contrast to monarchies and autocracies, where the logical focus of leaders is to provide private goods, generally at the expense of seeking out successful public policies.

We saw that as winning coalitions get larger, the rate of economic growth becomes more rapid, slowing down only at the upper reaches of democratic winning coalitions. We also saw that larger winning coalitions promote free trade and the development of human capital. Even the quality of performance in wars and other international disputes is tied to these political institutions, as is foreign aid giving and receiving.

The evidence presented in this chapter, especially regarding free trade and war behavior, directly contradicts structuralist and interest group arguments. At the same time, none of the evidence here falsifies the strategic perspective. Our findings here, which focus on central aspects of international politics—war and trade—compel us to evaluate the usefulness of structural theories, which cannot account for important empirical regularities. It appears that leaving the incentives of individual leaders, the influence of domestic institutions, and the interactions these produce across polities out of a consideration of international politics leads us to overlook fundamental aspects of the explanations of core problems. Taking the incentives of leaders into account, mindful of their domestic institutional and international constraints, seems to offer a better explanation of foreign policy and international politics.

# THE INTERNATIONAL POLITICAL ECONOMY OF TRADE

World leaders gathered in Seattle, Washington, on November 29, 1999, for a meeting of the World Trade Organization. The purpose of the WTO meeting was to further the process of trade liberalization known as globalization. By "globalization" I mean the international process that leads to the worldwide integration of market-driven exchanges in goods, services, and capital.

Thousands of protesters—many peaceful, some violent—also gathered in Seattle in November 1999. They made up a loose coalition of environmentalists, trade unionists, and students opposed to the idea of globalization and to what some perceive as the pro-corporation and antidemocratic processes of the WTO. They were there to stop globalization if they could. Many of these protesters also turned up in Bologna, Italy, in October 2001, once again demonstrating at a WTO meeting in an effort to thwart discussion of trade liberalization.

The WTO's efforts and the opposition those efforts engender raise fundamental questions about trade policy as well as monetary and fiscal policy. As we turn to the issues surrounding trade and currency policies it is important that we sort out purely economic matters from those that are political. International trade, whether in goods, services, or money, does, after all, involve both economic and political considerations.

Trade occurs between businesses or between individuals and businesses or just between individuals. Typically, governments do not themselves engage directly in much international trade other than trade in currencies. The role of governments in the international economy involves taxing and regulating cross-border exchanges and guaranteeing contract enforcement through the legal system. Additionally, governments monitor compliance with international rules, like those accepted by the signatories to such international organizations as the WTO, the European Union, NAFTA, and Latin America's Mercosur, a common market agreement between Argentina, Brazil, Paraguay, and Uruguay. When violations are detected, governments may punish the violators. Furthermore, governments provide the essential infrastructure that supports trade.

For instance, there would be much less exchange of goods and services across borders if governments did not provide for reasonably secure and stable currencies and for well-established means to protect the transfer of payments. One common failing of many autocracies, for instance, is that their leaders gain political advantage by manipulating the value of their country's currency. Because they do not provide secure and stable value for their country's money, they are limited in their attractiveness as trading partners and in their ability to entice investors. This is one of several reasons that people living in autocracies are, by and large, poor. Such seemingly mundane government functions as maintaining a credible currency and currency convertibility or facilitating

*Protesters are arrested on December 1, 1999, during the second day of demonstrations and rioting against the meeting of the World Trade Organization in Seattle.*

currency exchange and repatriation of capital while providing an efficient check-clearing mechanism are essential for trade. We cannot understand trade and trade policies without understanding the foundations of economic exchange and the interplay between government and economics known as political economy.

Governments even routinely influence trade over issues not ostensibly about trade. Consider how governments use punishment strategies like trade sanctions to enforce particular norms or preferences about national and international policies that may be unrelated to trade. Punishment through trade sanctions, of course, is not restricted to violations of trade agreements. The American government, for example, has for more than forty years severely restricted the opportunity of American citizens and businesses to trade with Cuba in an effort to punish the Cuban government for policies of which many political leaders and well-organized constituents in the United States disapprove. The international community has applied trade sanctions—with varying degrees of effectiveness—to Iraq for more than ten years. Those sanctions are designed (poorly) to weaken Saddam Hussein's hold on power and to restrict Iraq's potential to build or acquire weapons of mass destruction. As we will see in the next chapter, using these punishment strategies effectively is difficult.

Globalization draws our attention to the role that government plays in international trade and to the actions that can be taken to advance or retard movement toward greater trade liberalization. The WTO, established in 1995, is the successor organization to the General Agreement on Tariffs and Trade. The GATT was one of the international institutions developed in the aftermath of World War II to promote economic recovery and growth. The WTO, like the GATT, is designed to promote international trade and ensure that it flows as smoothly, freely, and predictably as possible. As such, it is the central international organization responsible for monitoring adherence to a free trade regime and it has important responsibilities as well regarding the enforcement of the terms of agreement. Its membership includes the vast majority of nations in the world, including the very rich, the very poor, and pretty much every nation in between.

The process of globalization promoted by the WTO and the efforts to stymie it represent fundamental puzzles about the international political economy. These puzzles revolve around the domestic political considerations that influence the degree to which different governments subscribe to globalization and the consequences of violations of or the promotion of free trade. Of course, in the previous chapter we already discussed the linkages between trade and security questions. As we go through the political economy behind trade policies, I try to clarify who wins and who loses if globalization progresses and who wins or loses if globalization is stopped or even reversed. To do so I offer a brief historical account of globalization, followed by a primer on some critical insights from economics. When those two tasks are completed, we can turn to evaluating currency and trade policies and their ties to politics.

## GLOBALIZATION IN HISTORICAL PERSPECTIVE

Globalization is not a new phenomenon, nor is it inevitable. To understand current debate about globalization it is useful to begin by considering what the world of commerce was like before the telegraph, the railroad, and perhaps even ships capable of traversing the deep water of the oceans. Earlier we learned of the great secrecy that accompanied the discovery of sea-lanes and the huge importance that Columbus's voyages had in exposing new sources of wealth through expropriation of the resources of "new" lands. Strong economic incentives prompted the secrecy surrounding navigation routes. If one can buy goods cheaply in one place (say gold in America) and simultaneously sell them for more in another place—a process called arbitrage—then there is a great incentive to keep pertinent information out of the hands of competitors. Arbitrage is a way to equalize prices in different places by increasing supply where it is scarce (that is, the price is high) and reducing supply where it is cheap (that is, where supply initially is abundant). It is interesting to realize that price equalization apparently was not terribly different in Europe in the thirteenth century from what it is today. The difference in prices between England and Holland for eight commodities (barley, butter, cheese, eggs, oats, peas, silver, and wheat) in 1273 as reported by Froot, Kim, and Rogoff (1997), is about comparable to price differences observed across the English Channel in the 1990s. Greater price differences—as in textiles, beer, and wine—provided an impetus for the burgeoning trade of the High Middle Ages. International trade is stimulated by the possibility of buying something at a low price in one place and selling it for a higher price in another. This stimulus to trade and price equalization can be and often is stymied by government intervention.

Price differences can be sustained as long as a comparable product cannot be produced competitively in the buyer's locale. As the cost of moving goods from one location to another drops, competition from imports, if unregulated by government or by collusion among domestic competitors of imports, ensures that prices will fall, making access to the goods available to a broader segment of society. If the goods are significantly more expensive in one market than in another, more supply will flow to the higher-priced market. The ensuing competition—again if unregulated by government or by collusion—brings the price down until it is comparable (controlling for differences in shipping costs and product quality) in different markets. This pressure toward comparable prices spreads farther and farther from the point of production as the costs of shipping, storage, and information about goods and services falls, provided government does not intervene to maintain a price differential. The expected price convergence is an important feature of globalization and it is a feature we experience in our everyday lives.

Consider an example. If I know that I can buy television sets in Tokyo for much less than I can buy comparable ones in San Francisco, then I have an incentive to go to Tokyo, buy lots of television sets and bring them to San Francisco to sell at the much higher price. That is, I export television sets from Japan and import them into the United States. As long as the San Francisco price is sufficiently high so that the cost of going to Tokyo and bringing television sets back still leaves me with a large margin, I will want to take advantage of the opportunity. But others who know about the price difference will also want to pursue this opportunity and they will have an incentive to sell for less than I do so that buyers go to them instead of me. I, of course, will respond to this competition by reducing my price, as long as I remain profitable. This process will resolve quickly at a price that is comparable to the cost of television sets in Tokyo, adjusted for the transportation costs involved in getting them to the San Francisco market. This is, in fact, exactly what has happened over the years as shipping costs have dropped and as information about prices in different parts of the world has spread and become common knowledge.

Innumerable examples of price convergence could be provided. Think about the availability of Hong Kong pearls, New Zealand lamb, Swedish automobiles, Mexican tomatoes, Egyptian cotton, English marmalade, French wine, clothing manufactured in Sri Lanka or China, online medical billing services in India, electronics assembled in El Salvador, movies from Italy, and other goods and services available in the American market. Think about American products, including television programming, movies,

*Sri Lankans bring offerings to a Buddhist temple as they pray for successful peace negotiations between the Sri Lankan government and the Tamil Tigers. The two groups have been at war for twenty years over the Tigers' demands for an independent country. The war has cost more than 64,000 lives and has helped stunt economic growth on the island.*

McDonald's hamburgers, Intel computer chips, Boeing airplanes, management consulting services, soybeans, wheat, and on and on, available in much of the world marketplace. A similar story could be told about English textile exports to the European continent in the Middle Ages and the English importation of French wine, Asian spices, and so forth during the same period. When and where trade was unrestricted, goods were exported and imported, prices fell, and consumers had a greater variety of choices. As the economist John Maynard Keynes aptly observed of the nineteenth century—a period of rapid progress toward globalization—by comparison with the world following the start of World War I, "What an extraordinary episode in the progress of man that age which came to an end in August 1914! . . . The inhabitant of London could order by telephone, sipping his morning tea in bed, the various products of the whole earth . . . he could at the same time and by the same means adventure his wealth in the natural resources and new enterprise of any quarter of the world" (Keynes 1920).

The onset of World War I led to a great expansion in protectionism. Although there certainly were many tariffs and other restrictions on free trade in the nineteenth century and before, the degree of protectionism in trade expanded mightily during the years between the two world wars. Indeed, one of the factors that exacerbated the Great Depression that began in 1929 and did not end until the onset of World War II was the decision by the U.S. Congress to pass the Smoot-Hawley Tariff Act in 1930. This legislation imposed the highest level of tariff protection on behalf of American industry in the history of the United States. Import duties increased from 39 to 53 percent. The bill was intended to insulate American farm products and manufactured goods from stiff foreign competition. The idea was to improve the lot of American workers and business owners who were suffering from the onset of the depression. In response to American protectionism, other countries passed retaliatory tariffs. Just as American politicians sought to protect their constituents from foreign competition, so too did foreign leaders try to protect their own constituents from American competition.

Rather than ease the economic pressures from competition, the cycle of protective tariffs severely deepened and extended the depression, pushing unemployment to record heights. By 1932, 13 million American workers (out of a total population of about 123 million) were unemployed, up from 3 million in January 1930, six months after the passage of the Smoot-Hawley bill. American unemployment eventually rose to 30 percent of the workforce. At the same time trade plummeted, falling about two-thirds between 1929 and 1933.

Attitudes toward protectionism underwent a sea change after the end of World War II. Gradually, the U.S. government emerged as a proponent of free trade. To be sure, the United States tried and still tries to protect many of its industries, but the depth and breadth of tariff protection began to diminish. By the late 1970s or early 1980s, the degree of global freedom from tariffs had reached very high levels. Globalization, retarded from 1914 to 1945, was moving forward again. In 1950 about 7 percent of world production was exported. Today about 25 percent of world production is exported. With these facts in mind, we are now ready to explore the ways in which this trend toward renewed globalization is beneficial or harmful.

# AN ECONOMICS PRIMER:
# COMPARATIVE ADVANTAGE, SUPPLY, AND DEMAND

As mentioned, globalization depends on market-driven exchanges. By "market-driven" I mean exchanges that are determined by supply and demand for goods, services, and capital unconstrained by government regulation with the exception of credible government commitments to the rule of law, property rights, currency guarantees, and the adjudication and enforcement of voluntary contracts between buyers and sellers. I add these caveats regarding property rights, rule of law, currency guarantees, and the like because without performing these fundamental functions, government fails to ensure that competition is fair in the marketplace. These conditions are, in essence, the domestic analog of national security; without them, society would be run by bullies. They are among the domestic guarantors of life, liberty, and the pursuit of happiness (or as John Locke put it, the pursuit of property).

## COMPARATIVE ADVANTAGE

A good place to begin our economics primer is with a discussion of comparative advantage. This concept, first rigorously demonstrated by the English economist David Ricardo in the early nineteenth century, is fundamental to understanding trade and to understanding why a country (or a company or a worker) gains from trade even if it is not best in making anything. To understand comparative advantage it is necessary to see how it differs from absolute advantage. By grasping this distinction one gains critical insights into the fundamentals behind how and why competition works to produce economic efficiency and trade. One also gains an appreciation that even if a country is not better than any other at anything it still stands to benefit more from free trade than from trade protectionism.

Imagine two countries, say the United States and India. One, the United States, produces airplanes at a lower cost than the other, whereas the other, India, designs computer software more cheaply than the first. It makes sense, then, for Americans to buy computer software designed in India and for India to buy airplanes from the United States. In fact, India buys many airplanes from the American firm Boeing, and India is a large exporter of software programs to the American market. These countries could have an absolute advantage in what they produce. Trading one country's relatively cheaper good for the other country's relatively cheaper good leads to gains from trade for both the United States and India. Yet, neither the United States nor India nor other countries necessarily choose to focus their efforts on making all the things in which they have an absolute advantage. What is more, not everyone has an absolute advantage; that is, not everyone is best at doing something. Absolute advantage is nice to have but it is insufficient to grasp what different countries produce, buy, and sell.

Let me begin the discussion of comparative advantage with a prosaic, personal example. Then I will turn to a more careful statement of the idea. It just so happens that I type very fast, about 70 words per minute (with just two fingers, I might add). Some professional typists do not type as quickly and accurately as I do, yet I do not choose to compete for their jobs. I do not specialize in typing because, even if I have an absolute advantage in typing skills, it is not my comparative advantage. It is not the activity that maximizes my income or other aspects of my well-being and so I do not specialize in it. This is the kernel of comparative advantage. Resources are put to use in the way that maximizes their return. People specialize in what they are *comparatively* better at even if others are absolutely better than they are at the particular skill. I may be a better typist than many typists, but still they specialize in typing and I do not.

Ricardo provided a clear and useful example of comparative advantage in his book *On the Principles of Political Economy and Taxation,* published in 1817. I use his basic example here because it remains pertinent today. Imagine that England and Portugal each produce two goods, cloth and wine. Furthermore, imagine that the only input in production is labor (ignoring for now raw materials, capital with which to process the raw materials, and so forth). Let us further assume that how much output each worker produces (that is, the productivity of labor) varies both from industry to industry (cloth and wine) and between England and Portugal. To make a sharp distinction between absolute advantage and comparative advantage, let us also assume—as Ricardo did—that Portugal has an absolute advantage over England in the production of both cloth and wine. Table 13-1 provides a numerical example of the assumptions that I will use throughout this discussion.

TABLE 13-1
## Labor Productivity in Making Wine and Cloth

| Country | Available Labor Hours | Hours Needed to Make One Unit of Wine | Hours Needed to Make One Unit of Cloth |
|---------|-----------------------|---------------------------------------|----------------------------------------|
| Portugal | 12 | 1 | 2 |
| England | 12 | 6 | 3 |

It is clear from Table 13-1 that Portugal's labor productivity in making both wine and cloth is higher than England's. Fewer hours of labor are needed in Portugal to produce a unit of cloth or a unit of wine than is true in England. This is how we know that Portugal has an absolute advantage in the production of both goods. Can trade still take place between England and Portugal when Portugal is better at producing both goods than is England? How can England gain from trade in this circumstance? What will the Portuguese buy from England when they both can produce the same two products and Portugal produces both products more efficiently? Ricardo's analysis of comparative advantage nicely shows us that trade will take place and that it makes sense for England to specialize in the production of one of the goods and for Portugal to specialize in the production of the other. Furthermore, he showed that total world output of both goods could rise through such specialization. Indeed, he showed that with free trade and with the right terms of trade—that is, the amount of one good traded for the other—both England and Portugal could end up with more of each good through specialization than they would have in the absence of trade.

How should England and Portugal go about determining which good to specialize in? Random selection would not do. Rather, each should specialize in the good in which the country enjoys a comparative advantage in production. To figure out which good each country has a comparative advantage in we must compare the opportunity cost each pays in producing cloth or producing wine. The opportunity cost, a concept introduced in the Introduction to this book, evaluates how much of the other good is given up in choosing to focus resources on the good being produced. So, it is not how much labor or how much money it costs to produce a good that determines the good in which a country has comparative advantage in production. Opportunity costs are the key. The information in Table 13-1 is used in Figure 13-1 to discover in which good each country has comparative advantage. Figure 13-1 plots what is called the production possibility frontier—that is, the maximum amount of goods that England or Portugal can produce given the available resources (labor in this case) and the cost of production, or labor per unit of cloth or of wine. To calculate the production possibility frontier we solve the following two equations:

Quantity of Wine = (Available Labor/Hours of Labor Needed to Make 1 Unit of Wine) − [(Hours needed to Make 1 Unit of Cloth/ Hours needed to Make 1 Unit of Wine) × Quantity of Cloth]

Quantity of Cloth = (Available Labor/Hours of Labor Needed to Make 1 Unit of Cloth) − [(Hours needed to Make 1 Unit of Wine/ Hours needed to Make 1 Unit of Cloth) × Quantity of Wine]

To solve the first equation, assume that no cloth is made. To solve the second, assume that no wine is produced. Then the production possibility frontier is the line that joins the values (quantity of wine, 0 cloth) and (0 wine, quantity of cloth). We find that for Portugal, the solution to the first equation equals 12 units of wine and no cloth, and the solution to the second equation is 6 units of cloth and no wine. Of course, given the trade-off between labor and production, Portugal can produce any amount of wine and cloth that falls on or below the line that denotes its production possibility frontier. The production possibility frontier, after all, specifies the maximum mix of production if all available labor is used (that is, full employment). For England the comparable values are 4 units of cloth and no wine or 2 units of wine and no cloth.

Several factors are noteworthy in Figure 13-1. If England produces only cloth and Portugal produces only wine, then the market will have 12 units of wine and 4 units of cloth. If, instead, England specializes in wine production and Portugal specializes in producing cloth, then there will be only 2 units of wine and 6 units of cloth in the marketplace.

Try to construct an example in which both cloth and wine production is greater with specialization than without it. Draw the production possibility frontiers for the example you chose. Imagine that a poor country has comparative advantage in labor and a rich country has an absolute advantage both in labor (that is, labor has higher productivity than in the poor country) and in capital. Does it still make sense for the rich country to import labor-intensive goods from the poor country and for the poor country to import capital-intensive goods from the rich country? Can you find examples of such exchanges between the United States and Mexico or between other relatively rich and relatively poor countries?

Obviously that is worse for cloth consumers and wine consumers. Additionally, if both England and Portugal produce both cloth and wine, then if each country applies equal labor to each product, the market will have 7 units of wine (6 Portuguese and 1 English) and 5 units of cloth (3 Portuguese and 2 English). To gain 1 unit of cloth if Portugal produces only wine and England only cloth, the market loses 5 units of wine. The total quantity of products produced (16) is greatest when England specializes in cloth production and Portugal specializes in wine production. Finally, we can see the opportunity costs by examining the slopes of the production possibility frontiers. Although Portugal has an absolute advantage in both, as seen by the fact that its production possibility frontier is always higher than England's (we assume equal labor pools), its slope is flatter and England's is steeper as we move from fewer units of wine production to more units of wine production. This tells us that Portugal has a comparative advantage in wine production and England in cloth production. By each country's specializing in the product in which it has comparative advantage, labor is used most productively to yield the greatest quantity of goods in the global market.

As we have seen, England must calculate how much wine it must give up producing to make cloth and how much cloth manufacture it must give up to make wine, the very calculation facilitated by Figure 13-1. These trade-offs between wine and cloth production are the relevant opportunity costs. Portugal must, of course, make the same calculation. England has comparative

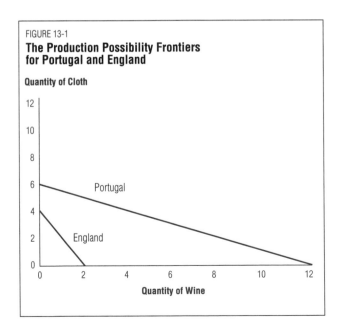

FIGURE 13-1
**The Production Possibility Frontiers for Portugal and England**

**Quantity of Cloth**

**Quantity of Wine**

advantage in cloth production relative to Portugal provided that the amount of wine production it must give up to make one more unit of cloth is smaller than the amount of wine production Portugal would have to give up to make an additional unit of cloth. We can see that this is true in Figure 13-1 even though Portugal makes both wine and cloth more cheaply than does England in terms of the cost of labor (and capital).

Except under unusual circumstances, each country will have a comparative advantage in the production of some good or goods. By pursuing its comparative advantage each country benefits through specialization and trade. Portugal, in the example, has comparative advantage in wine production. By specializing in wine production it frees up resources that would have been used by it *relatively inefficiently* in making cloth. And since England has the comparative advantage in making cloth, it avoids the opportunity cost of spending resources on wine production that could be better used by it to make cloth. Both Portugal and England, then, focus their resources on the use that yields the greatest productivity—the most efficient use—thereby pursuing their comparative advantage. This is just the same as my decision to be a professor rather than a typist.

Sometimes a country (or an individual manufacturer) has both an absolute advantage and a comparative advantage in producing one good over another. There is no problem or contradiction in saying that one's absolute advantage can turn out also to be one's comparative advantage. This just does not have to be so.

Comparative advantage teaches a fundamental lesson about trade. It is a lesson that is especially pertinent in debates about globalization. Some people apparently believe that to benefit from trade a country has to be the best at making something. Those who hold this view believe that an exporter cannot be competitive unless it is better than anyone else in the production of its product or service. Those who hold this belief confuse absolute advantage with comparative advantage. Comparative advantage makes clear that gains from trade follow from specialization. It is not necessary to be best at anything to gain from trade. By specializing in the production of one's comparative advantage—that is, the goods that reflect the lowest opportunity cost to the maker—there are gains from trade even if someone else is absolutely better at making the product. Remember, I might be better than others at typing, but I do not sell this skill in the market for typists.

Just about everyone has a comparative advantage even though they do not have an absolute advantage. As Figure 13-1 makes clear, by specializing in its comparative advantage, both England (the absolutely disadvantaged country) and Portugal benefit. More wine and more cloth are available for purchase as a result of specialization in each country's comparative advantage than would have been true if each produced any other mix of both goods.

## SUPPLY AND DEMAND

Supply and demand together establish the equilibrium price for goods, services, or capital in a market. Producers seek to maximize their total profit. Profit is simply the difference between the total costs of production and the price garnered for the goods (or services) produced. Producers produce until the additional revenue (price times quantity) from the nth unit just equals the cost of production for that unit; that is, until marginal profit equals zero. This determines the amount of the good they supply.

Producers naturally would like to charge the highest price they can for their goods and will stop producing when the marginal cost of the next unit exceeds the price they can get for it. The problem they face in pricing is that as the price for goods or services (or capital and so forth) increases, demand falls. So, they want as high a price as they can get, but, as the Rolling Stones remind us, "You can't always get what you want." This leads to the well-known relationship between supply and demand illustrated in Figure 13-2.

In Figure 13-2 we see the relationship between the quantity of goods (or services or capital or many other things—let's call them widgets) a producer is prepared to supply and the quantity of widgets buyers demand at different prices. The supply curve shows how producers respond (quantity supplied) to changing prices, provided the cost of additional production does not exceed the price. The demand curve is, equivalently, the response curve for consumers to changing prices. Each curve is assumed to be independently determined, the price of the good—widgets in this case—being determined endogenously by the interaction of the two curves as discussed below.

For convenience, let us treat the prices shown in the figure as dollars, although they could be denominated in any currency and any amount of money. As noted, producers will make widgets up to the point at which the marginal cost of producing one more widget equals the marginal gain from that one extra widget; that is, up to the point at which there is no more profit to extract from making another widget. Once the cost exceeds the benefit, producers will not want to make more widgets. A similar argument can be made for buyers. This naturally implies that more widgets can be made if they sell for a higher price than if they sell for a lower price, all else (for example, costs) being equal.

In the illustrative example, we see that suppliers are willing to sell 200 widgets at a price of $7.00 per widget. Buyers, however, would purchase only 100 widgets if they sold for $7.00. There is not much point to supplying so many more widgets than the market demands because it is costly to do so. With a surplus supply (that is, the amount of supply in excess of demand) of 100 wid-

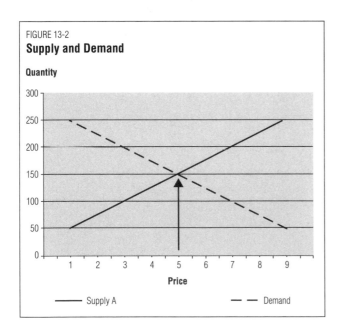

FIGURE 13-2
**Supply and Demand**

Quantity

gets (200 supplied minus 100 demanded at $7.00 per widget), widget sellers have a strong incentive to reduce the price in order to sell their inventory. Conversely, if widgets sold for just $1.00, there would be surplus demand. In this case, there would be demand for 250 widgets, but there would be only 50 widgets supplied in the marketplace. The shortage of widgets would lead buyers to compete for the scarce supply, pushing the price up. By observing where the supply and demand curves cross each other we can estimate just how many widgets will be bought and sold and at what price. The equilibrium between supply and demand arises when the quantity supplied equals the quantity demanded so that there is neither surplus demand pushing the price up nor surplus supply pushing the price down. The equilibrium price is the price for which widgets sell. In Figure 13-2 supply equals demand for 150 widgets at a price of $5.00 per widget. The arrow shows the equilibrium price. Reading across horizontally from the top of the arrow, we see the equilibrium quantity supplied and demanded at that price.

The world of Figure 13-2 has no government intervention to alter the price of goods. In such a world, trade presumably would be limited only by the cost of getting goods from one place to another. In fact, economists have constructed what is called the gravity model of trade. This model seeks to provide a baseline estimate of how much trade is expected between any pair of countries assuming no government restrictions. It says that trade is inversely related to the distance between the countries and is proportional to the product of their sizes. That is, all else being equal, countries that are far apart are less likely to trade with each other than are countries that are close together. Furthermore, the larger the countries are (in population or economic size), the greater the trade expected between them. This simple apolitical model does pretty well at accounting for trade levels, but much still

remains to be explained. In fact, much of what remains depends on domestic political pressure for governments to intervene in international trade. To see how politics can intrude on supply, demand, prices, and trade, let us consider what happens if the government imposes a purely domestic tax on the production of widgets. To illustrate this effect, I relabel the original supply curve, borrowed from Figure 13-2, as Supply A and show a second supply curve, called Supply B in Figure 13-3. In this example, Supply B shows the availability of widgets at different selling prices given a government tax on production.

As can be seen in Figure 13-3, the supply of widgets is decreased as a result of a tax on their production. That is, Supply B is shifted

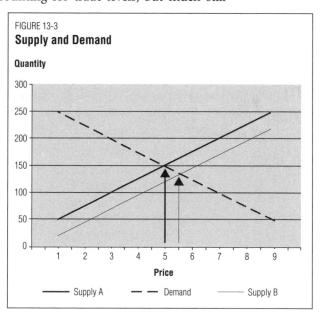

FIGURE 13-3
**Supply and Demand**

Quantity

Price

—— Supply A    — — Demand    —— Supply B

down from the untaxed Supply A curve. Recall that producers produce up to the point at which marginal gains and marginal costs are equal. The government's tax increases the cost of production. Since suppliers produce until the marginal cost of the nth unit equals the marginal revenue for that unit, the added cost from the tax is passed on to consumers. This leads to a higher price that decreases demand. In Figure 13-3 we see how the cost of the tax is passed on to consumers. The darker supply line—Supply A—is the same as the supply line in Figure 13-2, whereas the lighter line—Supply B—shows the decrease in supply due to the tax (that is, an artificial increase in the cost of production). By examining the lighter "taxed supply" line and the demand curve we can see the economic consequences of the government's tax. Whereas without the tax, 150 widgets were produced and sold at a price of $5.00 each (see the dark arrow), now about 136 widgets are made and sold for about $5.50 each (see the lighter arrow to find the new equilibrium price). Consumers are worse off. If producers are initially producing at the efficient market price (zero profit), then the tax must increase the price to consumers, lowering demand and forcing producers to reduce the equilibrium supply. The result is fewer widgets at a higher price than was true before the tax was imposed.

Suppose we now think of the two supply curves in Figure 13-3 in a different way, ignoring the discussion of the effect of a tax on production. Let us say that the two supply curves reflect two different sets of producers—A and B—instead of the same producer with and without a tax on production. Producers in group A, represented by the darker line, can profitably produce more widgets at a given price than can producers in group B, represented by the lighter supply line. That is why curve A is higher than B.

Imagine that A represents all foreign producers of widgets and B reflects domestic producers (or reverse the order if you prefer). Instead of there being a government tax on production, the example in Figure 13-3 has now been turned into a situation in which one

> How many widgets would buyers want to purchase at $3.50 per widget? How many could suppliers in group A provide at $3.50? How many could suppliers in group B provide at $3.50? Make the same comparisons at $8.00 per widget. What would happen to supply, demand, and the equilibrium price if the government imposed a tax on buyers (such as a sales tax or value-added tax)?

set of suppliers—the foreign producers A—apparently have lower costs of production than do the domestic suppliers B. That is, the foreign producers are more efficient in supplying widgets than are their domestic competitors. Clearly, consumers will prefer to buy the less expensive foreign-produced widgets. Up to 150 foreign widgets can be bought for just $5.00 each. To buy 150 domestic widgets, consumers would have to pay $6.00. At that price, there is enough demand for only 125 domestic widgets. At the domestic equilibrium price of $5.50, only 136 widgets would be bought and sold. As long as foreign widgets are on the market, consumers presumably will buy the cheaper, foreign-made product.

Domestic producers are likely to find their situation extremely disturbing. Because of their relative inefficiency, they cannot compete as long as the imported widgets enjoy their price advantage. Domestic widget workers and manufacturers both have incentives to put pressure on the government to exclude foreign widgets from the market. Even though the domestic producer does not seem to have a comparative advantage in producing widgets, the workers and owners in that industry want to maintain their jobs. The domestic producers and workers have votes or other forms of political support to offer government leaders in exchange for help. The government can help. It can provide the domestic widget industry with an equal chance to sell its widgets by imposing on foreign producers a tax known as a *tariff*. If the tariff charged on all imported widgets is priced just right, then the domestic and foreign producers will be in the same boat. A's supply curve will shift down until it sits right on top of B's curve, depriving A of its efficiency advantage. Consumers will pay an average of $5.50 per widget and will be indifferent between domestic and foreign-made widgets. If the tariff is set higher, so that the cost of foreign production plus the tax on importation is greater than the domestic cost of production without a tax, then curve A shifts down below curve B. Under these conditions, consumers will buy only domestic widgets, presumably driving the foreign producer out of the domestic market. Probably the domestic widget industry would lobby for a tariff that high so that they could corner the domestic market and not have to compete with imports. The consequence of a tariff imposed on foreign widgets is twofold: domestic consumers who buy widgets pay more than they would have paid without the tariff protection, and people employed in the domestic widget industry are insulated from the effects of competition. Insulating the industry from competition reduces the incentive for domestic suppliers to become more efficient and so heightens the risk that the industry will need long-term protection. This can have the effect of weakening still further buyer demand in the economy if the indifference curves of supply and demand are not straight lines as in the examples above. If buyers, for example, have a strong need for widgets (that is, they have relatively *inelastic demand*) so that their demand does not drop much as the price increases, then the tariff takes dollars out of the consumer economy that might otherwise have gone to purchase other products.[1] That is, the extra money spent on tariff-protected widgets ($0.50 per widget) is money that can no longer be used to buy other goods and services. So, while domestic widget makers do better, other parts of the economy suffer a loss due to diminished purchasing power created by the tariff.

The examples just completed seem rather simple. Nevertheless, taken together, they tell a fundamental story. In the first example there is no government intervention in the widget industry. Supply responds only to price. Likewise there is consumer demand for widgets. Consumers who need or want widgets respond only to price. The preference of suppliers is to sell more widgets as long as doing so remains profitable. Increasing prices,

---

[1] It is worth noting that elasticities (of demand or supply) are evaluated as the momentary slopes of the supply and demand curves. Thus the elasticity of demand or supply can change constantly, depending on the point on the curve at which the situation is located. Notice that elasticities are constant and equal the slope of the curve if the curve is linear.

if they do not result in diminishing marginal returns, will lead producers to produce more. The interest of consumers is to buy more widgets as the price drops. Widgets are bought and sold at the efficient, market price.

The second example adds government action to the story. The action is either to impose a tax on all producers or to impose a tax only on certain, more efficient producers (who, in the example, happen to be foreign producers whose widgets are subjected to a tariff on importation designed to nullify their comparative advantage). When the government enters the picture, consumers can be made worse off in at least three ways. The price of widgets—but not their quality—increases; widgets become scarcer; and fewer dollars might remain to buy other goods and services after extra money is spent on widgets, thereby harming other parts of the economy. The government's intervention leads the price to rise from $5.00 to about $5.50 and the supply drops from 150 to about 136. This is the direct consequence of government intervention in the market.

Naturally, in the real world there sometimes are good reasons for government intervention. Some of these are discussed later in this chapter. In the example with tariffs, the reason for government intervention is to protect a domestic producer from the competition arising from more efficient foreign producers. There may be good political reasons for doing so. It is a greater stretch to make the case that there are good economic reasons. In fact, virtually all economists agree that free trade improves economic well-being in the aggregate, although, of course, for some—especially holders of domestically scarce factors or members of scarce productive sectors, as explained below—free trade represents a deadweight loss in personal welfare. I reiterate this point. In the aggregate—that is, on average, welfare is improved by free trade. There are, however, winners and losers. Who they are and under what circumstances is fundamental to understanding the arguments for and against globalization. You might make a note now of who you think gains and who you think loses from free trade. You may be surprised by the answer as it unfolds later in this chapter.

## TRADE AS A PUBLIC OR PRIVATE GOOD

If we treat widget production and consumption as indicative of all production and consumption, then we can see that the absence of government intervention in trade (or, put positively, governmental assurance of free trade) is a public good. Everyone is a consumer and therefore everyone derives a benefit from the lower prices that arise without tariffs. Equally, it is important to note that tariffs act as private goods, benefiting (in our example) domestic widget makers at the expense both of more efficient foreign competitors and of domestic consumers (and possibly producers of other products, depending on the elasticity of supply and demand). For many years, for instance, India kept Boeing aircraft out of its domestic market to protect airplanes made by Hindustan Aeronautics, a domestic aircraft maker. Clearly, the trade protection helped the workers and owners in that company, but at the expense of anyone with the resources to fly in India. Likewise, India protected its domestic aluminum industry, providing a private gain for those associated with aluminum manufacture in India, but at the expense of hundreds of millions of people who were compelled to buy relatively low-quality Indian aluminum cookware at inflated—tariff-protected—prices.

Tariffs, or "fair trade," as such policies are sometimes labeled, are classic private goods subject to many of the political considerations discussed in Chapter 12. Unregulated trade is a public good likewise subject to the political considerations addressed in Chapter 12. It should be evident that free trade benefits many, whereas "fair trade" benefits only a few. For the few, of course, the benefit from tariffs may outweigh the value of the public benefit that everyone gets from free trade. Presumably, if no one benefited more from trade protection than from free trade (that is, if the public goods benefit outweighed the private goods component for everyone), then there would be no tariffs or other means of making imports less competitive. In this regard we might note that tariffs arise for more than one reason. Not only might domestic interests benefit from protection against competition, as is commonly the case; it is also possible for tariffs to be used to punish foreign governments that do not observe free trade policies in their own right. President George W. Bush justified his call for a tariff on certain steel products in March 2002 by alleging unfair trade practices by Japan and Europe designed to bolster their steel industries at the expense of American industry. They countered— apparently correctly, given how readily the United States negotiated a resolution relatively favorable to Europe's and Japan's steel industries—by threatening retaliatory tariffs to compel the United States to enforce its free trade obligations under the WTO.

In all these cases, domestic political considerations seem to be behind the use of tariffs as foreign policy maneuvers. One of the central concerns in this chapter is to understand why tariffs exist and who benefits from them and who is harmed by them. Answering these questions will take us a long way to understanding why some people are enthusiastic about globalization and others remain adamantly opposed to it. In thinking about globalization and trade policy we should think expansively. For example, currencies are traded in much the same way as cars, apples, consulting, or other products and services are traded. The number of Japanese yen it takes to buy an American dollar or a British pound fluctuates all the time as the supply and demand for dollars, pounds, yen, and other currencies rise and fall. Globalization raises questions about fiscal and monetary policies that may influence exchange rates and the associated cost to people in developing countries who want or need to buy baby formula, drugs to treat AIDS or to prevent polio, and the like. These concerns are well warranted, although the proposed solutions too often reflect inadequate understanding of either the economics or the politics of trade. Let me touch on currency policy to help clarify how different national currency strategies influence globalization before turning to the consequences of free trade in general.

## CURRENCY, EXCHANGE RATES, AND
## INTERNATIONAL POLITICAL ECONOMY

Governments can adopt a variety of methods of supplying and otherwise regulating the value of their currency. One strategy, for example, is to allow a currency to float. By "float" I mean that the exchange rate fluctuates in response to supply and demand for money. The American dollar, for instance, floats in the world market. The value of the American dollar relative to the British pound, the euro, the yen, the Mexican peso, the Australian dollar, or many other currencies constantly changes in response to the supply and demand for those currencies and for American dollars. You can readily find the exchange rates quoted every day on the financial pages of major newspaper or on the Internet.

The dollar has not always floated. Before President Nixon abandoned the Bretton Woods agreement, for instance, this was not true. The dollar was set to a fixed exchange rate linked to gold. The U.S. government guaranteed to give anyone $35 in exchange for one ounce of gold. Fixed exchange rates are another way to regulate and stabilize currency. When President Nixon broke the link between dollars and gold and allowed the dollar's value to fluctuate in the world market, the dollar's value sank dramatically. After a short while it took more than $350 to buy one ounce of gold. What does such devaluation mean in the context of international relations?

To address this question let us look at the relationship between the U.S. dollar and the Japanese yen. Over the past several years the dollar and the yen have fluctuated dramatically. The range of yen needed to buy a dollar has varied, roughly, from 100 to 140. When more yen are needed to buy a dollar, the dollar is stronger—that is, it is worth more—than when fewer yen are needed to buy a dollar. This fluctuation influences trade and the balance of payments between countries.

Suppose a Honda made in Japan sells for 3 million yen or, equivalently, $25,000 at $1 = ¥120. If the dollar strengthens so that $1 = ¥140, then the exact same car at the exact same yen price could sell in the United States for about $21,400 without any loss in return to Honda because each dollar earned by Honda can now be turned into more yen. Conversely, if the dollar becomes much weaker compared to the yen so that $1 buys only ¥100, then the exact same Honda would need to sell for $30,000 to give Honda the same return. Reality is rather more complicated, but this is sufficient to make the fundamental point. One way a government can manipulate trade without imposing tariffs is to flood the market with its currency by printing more money. In doing so, it weakens its currency, thereby making it harder to buy imported goods.

Suppose an American looking for a new car is torn between a Honda and Ford. If a Ford comparable to the Honda under consideration costs $25,000, then when the dollar is strong against the yen, the Honda looks like a very attractive buy (being $3,600 cheaper if $1 = ¥140). But when the dollar is weak, the Ford looks like a terrific buy (being $5,000 cheaper if $1 = ¥100). So, the American government can protect Ford or other American car makers without imposing a tariff. It just needs to print more money to encourage more consumption of domestic goods and less consumption of imported goods.

American political leaders are constrained in their ability to manipulate the value of the currency for political gain, however, because the Federal Reserve Bank sets interest rates that determine how much it costs to borrow money. The Federal Reserve, like the European Union's central bank and other central banks, is largely autonomous. Its director and other officers serve long terms that extend well beyond any one president's term in office. As a result, the Fed, as it is called, is not easily intimidated by political pressure. When the Fed raises or lowers interest rates it makes dollars more or less expensive, thereby influencing demand for dollars compared, for instance, to yen or euros. The alteration of interest rates is intended to ensure that the price for a dollar—that is, how many it takes to buy something—is kept in check so that inflation is kept under control and the exchange rate is maintained within desired bounds. In this way the Fed helps control the inclination of politicians to use the supply of money as a way to manipulate the economy and trade (Frieden 1987; Simmons 1994; Broz and Frieden 2001; Clark 2002).

If currency manipulation for political ends is not reigned in by a central bank or by some other reliable mechanism (such as a peg, explained below), then politicians have more flexibility to influence their economy. This flexibility comes at a price. They may enjoy few of the benefits of a stable, predictable exchange rate for their currency. Uncertainty is the enemy of investors. Foreign investors with a choice of countries in which to risk their money are reluctant to put it at risk in places where unfettered government control can radically devalue their investment overnight. This is one reason that few investors seem willing to risk their money in most of Africa, Argentina, Russia, or many other places where inflation rates can soar to more than a thousand percent per year or where the government can change the currency's value by fiat.

Consider, for instance, the difference between European Union currency policy in the recent past and the comparable policy in

*As the Argentine peso continues its collapse in June 2002, crowds gather in front of a bank in Buenos Aires. The Argentines are waiting to purchase the more stable U.S. dollar, showing their confidence in the American currency and their lack of confidence in Argentina's currency and its economy.*

Russia. In the 1993 Maastricht Treaty, the members of the European Union agreed to the steps leading to a common European currency. They agreed that the euro would slowly be brought into use (but by a specified time) after the members met requirements to bring inflation under control and to bring the value of their currencies up to particular standards. The euro was introduced for major commercial exchanges well in advance of actual euro currency going into circulation. For several years prices all over the European Union were listed in terms both of the local currency and in euros even though goods could not yet be purchased or sold for euros. Thereby, people became accustomed to thinking about costs in euros. Finally, in 2001 euro currency was introduced into the market to replace local currencies. People were given ample time to convert their francs, guilders, marks, kroner, and so forth into euros. Currency stabilization and lots of information about what was happening and on what schedule facilitated a smooth transition. Uncertainty was kept to a minimum.

Russia also made major changes in its currency several years ago. In 1993 the Russian government removed from circulation rubles from the Soviet era. They did so with only a few days advance notice, leading to panicked spending and runs on banks. Earlier, the Russian government abolished 50 ruble and 100 ruble notes, again with little warning, leaving people with substantial economic losses and with little trust in their government. It is exactly such arbitrary currency policy by government that deters investors, thereby stifling economic growth.

Poor countries face particular difficulties in the global market. As we learned earlier, they just about always enjoy comparative advantage in some aspect of their economy—often in the price of labor—that gives them an opportunity for good terms of trade. Unfortunately, poor countries frequently pursue monetary policies that give the government tremendous flexibility in manipulating the value of their currency and, as a result, the expected terms of trade. Naturally, buyers in the market for the goods or services these countries export recognize the risk associated with doing business under such politically volatile circumstances. There are several solutions to such problems. Sometimes contracts are negotiated in terms of a currency other than the seller's currency. In those instances, the currency chosen is one that is relatively stable so that its value at the close of the contract is predictable. The U.S. dollar is often used in this way even when neither the buyer nor the seller is American. The British pound sterling is another currency that has been widely used for this purpose because it is deemed of trustworthy value.

Other times, the price negotiated between the buyer and the seller takes into account the risk that the exchange rate will be markedly different when the contract is fulfilled from what it is when the contract is entered into. This is known as a risk premium. It is very common for contracts with businesses in developing countries to involve a risk premium. This is a sensible solution to the expectation that the seller may not fulfill his or her obligations. It is also a reasonable way to address concern that the value of payment will be manipulated by the government to assist its cronies. But, if the contract is properly fulfilled and the currency was not manipulated then the risk premium paid up front becomes a deadweight loss for the seller in the impoverished country.

Regina Baker (2002) has demonstrated that poor countries are particularly likely to peg their currency if they are subject to a high-risk premium. That is, they settle on a nearly fixed exchange rate (or one that is constrained to trade in a very narrow range) that determines the value of their currency by linking it to the value of another currency. The Hong Kong dollar, for example, is pegged to the American dollar. It is always the case that it takes about 7.5 Hong Kong dollars to buy 1 American dollar. So, other than small variations, if the American dollar devalues so does the Hong Kong dollar. Likewise, if the American dollar strengthens so does the Hong Kong dollar. This helps establish as much confidence in the Hong Kong dollar as people have in the American dollar. Even after Hong Kong became part of the People's Republic of China on July 1, 1997, the Chinese government maintained the peg for the Hong Kong dollar to try to protect Hong Kong's economy. One concern of some investors is that China will drop the peg just as it has eroded other parts of its assurances regarding Hong Kong's economic autonomy (Bueno de Mesquita, Newman, and Rabushka 1996; Bowring 2002). Some poor countries go even further than pegging their currency to a stable currency from another country. Several countries around the world formally or informally adopt dollarization as a strategy. That means that they use the U.S. dollar as their currency for all or much exchange. Panama and East Timor use the dollar as their currency. Argentina and Ecuador are seriously considering dollarizing their economies. Still others, like Cuba and Russia, maintain their own currency even though a large proportion of economic exchange takes place in dollars and not in their local currency. This happens because people lack confidence in the trustworthiness of their own currency, preferring the dollar.

There are several reasons for such distrust. One is currency manipulation, as already discussed. Another is that many currencies cannot be converted. Convertibility ensures that people can, on demand, change their money for another currency. Anyone who has traveled outside the United States knows that it is easy to buy euros or Mexican pesos or Japanese yen for dollars and it is just as easy to buy dollars with euros, pesos, or yen. There is no problem turning one currency into the other. Equally, travelers in China or India or many other countries know that local citizens cannot readily turn their money into dollars or, if they can legally, only at exchange rates that bear little relationship to the supply and demand for the currencies involved. This is one of the reasons that black markets for money develop in such societies.

Nonconvertibility is a nontariff barrier that can keep foreign products and foreign investment out of a country. When currencies are not readily converted, there is no easy way for foreign investors to repatriate their profits or for people or firms to be paid in a currency that is of use to them except in the country to which they are selling. These losses in flexibility for investors or manufacturers mean increases in the price of selling or investing, and so fewer people pursue the opportunity. Naturally, this hurts not only the prospective sellers and prospective investors but also the local population, who are deprived of the opportunity to buy imported goods or to take advantage of the economic growth opportunities promoted by foreign investment.

Currency is used in still other ways to restrict trade. Before leaving this subject, let me touch briefly on capital markets. Companies often look for investment to fund expansion. One common way for larger companies to raise new investment money is to sell stock—an equity stake—in the company. Many governments erect elaborate rules to protect prospective investors from unscrupulous businesses. But sometimes these rules are used to restrict access to potential stock buyers; that is, to the capital markets. Consider the American Securities and Exchange Commission (SEC). No business can list on an American stock market without adhering to the SEC's financial reporting rules. These rules are much more stringent than those required by Britain, France, Germany, Japan, or any other capital market. This helps protect American investors, but it also helps exclude non-American firms from access to America's huge capital markets. Most non-American firms simply find it too expensive to maintain two sets of books, one to meet their government's regulatory and reporting requirements and another to satisfy the SEC. The SEC's rules, whether intentionally or not, serve to keep non-American firms from having easy access to listing on America's stock exchanges. It is noteworthy that there have been efforts for years to establish international accounting standards. These efforts routinely fail because the SEC refuses to compromise on any reporting standards short of those they have established. So here, too, we have an example of how government regulation of the flow of money can interfere in free exchange, protecting local interests at the expense of aggregate economic welfare.

## POLITICAL ECONOMY AND TRADE

We have seen that free trade, on average, provides cheaper goods and services to consumers. It also provides more abundant goods and services both in quantity and in diversity. Yet free trade has not been the norm of conduct throughout history. I have already hinted at why this is so. Free trade is a public good, but the effects of trade involve both public and private goods components. Trade affects domestic producers and sellers differently from importers, exporters, or consumers, and government trade policies affect the wealth of each of these groups differently. So, the distribution of wealth in a society depends, in part, on governmental approaches to trade. If trade is unrestricted, then domestic producers for the domestic market are at a potential disadvantage and foreign exporters and domestic importers could have an advantage.

Imports can be restricted through such means as tariffs or nontariff barriers. Nontariff barriers—some were alluded to earlier—are a more subtle way for governments to limit imports. They have become increasingly popular among members of the

WTO as the political means to limit imports. The WTO (and some other regional trade organizations like NAFTA) has strict rules about tariffs and somewhat harder-to-enforce rules about nontariff barriers to trade. Examples of nontariff barriers can include exchange rate manipulation, environmental or health standards that exclude foreign-made products; quotas that restrict the quantity of an item that can be imported; and restrictions on the movement of people or capital to where they can command the highest price. The use of nontariff barriers has come under

> Provide a list of ten nontariff barriers that influence whether you or your family have access to particular goods and services. Think broadly about this question. For example, does the requirement of a passport or visa to travel to or from the United States act as a nontariff barrier? What effect does the Internet have on trade barriers? Besides the examples I give here, how do health, environmental, safety, or cultural restrictions (for example, movie ratings and censorship) create nontariff barriers? Can you give examples of such barriers imposed on American goods and services by other governments?

increasingly close scrutiny by the WTO and other international trade organizations because these barriers have assumed a major role in keeping goods and services from flowing freely across national borders despite the absence of protective tariffs.

For instance, France makes some extraordinarily fine cheeses from raw, unpasteurized milk. These soft cheeses (for example, true Camembert) are at their peak flavor when they are less than sixty days old. France is a country with excellent health standards and a high standard of living. The French have been enjoying these cheeses for centuries with no discernible ill effects. Nevertheless, such cheeses cannot be purchased in the United States. Among unpasteurized (raw-milk) cheeses, only those that are more than sixty days old are permitted to enter the United States. Why? Ostensibly to protect Americans from health risks. In reality, the nontariff barrier on these cheeses just protects American cheese makers and, perhaps, helps stimulate American tourism in Normandy.

Similarly, it is difficult to bring into the United States an automobile that was purchased elsewhere. Chrysler-Benz (formerly Mercedes Benz) offers many models in Germany that cannot be bought in the United States. These vehicles can enter the United States only if they are retrofitted with expensive equipment to protect the environment. Of course, protecting the environment may provide a public good that justifies the nontariff restrictions imposed on some foreign cars, but nevertheless we should not lose sight that these restrictions also serve to limit consumer choices and to raise prices. Here we have an instance of a trade-off between environmental concerns and consumer interests that is resolved by government restrictions in favor of the environment. This, of course, can be a very good thing. But the U.S. government fails to show an equal commitment to the environment when it comes to imposing restrictions on popular but gas-guzzling and polluting SUVs manufactured in the United States. Whether the actual trade-off adopted in the United States (or elsewhere) between the environment and free trade is motivated primarily by a desire for cleaner air or a desire for fewer imported vehicles is an issue worth close exploration.

Under the terms of NAFTA, the United States is expected to permit Mexican trucks to cross the border and proceed to their destinations within the United States. The U.S. Congress has been successful for many years in restricting Mexican trucks from going more than twenty miles from the border. One effect of this nontariff barrier is that Mexican goods coming into the United States by truck must be unloaded near the border and reloaded onto American trucks. This, of course, delays (and, therefore, harms) the delivery of perishable food stuffs, increases the cost of shipping goods to the United States, and so harms the consumer. It also raises the price of electronics and any other goods shipped from Mexico to the United States, again harming the consumer. Mexico reciprocates by imposing restrictions on American trucks crossing into Mexico, thereby harming Mexican consumers.

In contrast, environmentalists can sensibly argue that the price distortion for Mexican products trucked into the United States is created by unfair trade practices originating in Mexico. The argument is that Mexican trucks are artificially cheap because their prices do not reflect the social cost of the pollution they generate, and the proper route to free trade would be to adjust Mexican environmental policy. Thus far, however, adjudication of claims on both sides of the border regarding obligations under NAFTA do not support this contention.

President George W. Bush has pushed for greater implementation of the NAFTA requirements even as Congress has pushed to maintain restrictions on Mexican trucks. The ostensible justification for these restrictions is environmental and highway safety, although little evidence has been mustered to support the claims of those who favor the restriction. Some American truckers, manufacturers, and growers and packers of fruits and vegetables benefit from these nontariff barriers. Despite these barriers to trade, the years roughly between 1994 (when NAFTA went into effect) and 2000 saw tremendous expansion in trade between Mexico and the United States, up from about $250 billion to $850 billion per year. Even with nontariff barriers, Mexico has surged in a few years to become the second-largest trading partner of the United States, only behind Canada. It is quite possible that by the time you read this book, Mexico will have surpassed Canada and be the largest trading partner of the United States. It already is a more significant trading partner than China, England, or Japan.

Before leaving the issue of nontariff barriers we should be careful to recognize that eliminating these barriers to free trade is controversial precisely because of the difficulty of distinguishing such cynical ploys from policies sincerely aimed at protecting consumers, the environment, and workers. Consider the Environmental Protection Agency's (EPA's) prohibitions against importing foods grown with certain pesticides like DDT. Many Latin American farmers view this restriction as an unfair trade practice. Reasonable people can reasonably disagree whether the price distortion induced by the ban outweighs the negative health and medical care externalities associated with the use of these pesticides. How appealing the trade-off is between higher food prices and fewer pesticides in fruit, vegetables, and meat products versus lower prices and more pesticides is sure to vary from society to society and across individual consumers.

Each of these and many, many more examples—involving not only the United States but almost every country in the world—reveal a common pattern of influence over trade protectionism. Again, free trade is a public good. Yet trade restrictions create private—usually income—benefits to only a few people. Add to this the fact that public goods are generally underprovided because people free ride (Olson 1965). Individuals have incentives to consume the benefits from public goods while letting others bear the cost of their provision, since, once they are provided, public goods benefit everyone. It is therefore difficult to motivate a large group of people—say consumers—to take action to protect their interests when their collective action will yield each one only a small gain relative to the costs of being an activist for free trade. This is a fundamental coordination problem that inhibits consumers from fully exercising their collective influence over government policies. Conversely, it is not so difficult to mobilize small groups of producers or workers whose incomes are significantly diminished if their jobs disappear because of foreign competition. For them, the stakes are high; for the average individual consumer the gain from reversing any particular trade restriction tends to be small. To summarize, private benefits arise from trade protectionism that can be distributed to certain domestic producers or workers. Consumers derive public goods—not private goods—from free trade. Therefore, the strategic problem in trade policy is a classic coordination and distribution problem. The asymmetry between diffuse collective (or public) benefits and concentrated costs (through lost private benefits) associated with trade is a substantial factor contributing to the existence of trade protectionism. In general, the greater the private benefits from protection, the more likely are interest groups, lobbyists, or other coalitions of affected individuals to mobilize to exercise their political influence over leaders. To the extent that a leader's hold on political office requires support from those who seek protection from foreign competition we can expect that protection will be forthcoming. As we learned earlier, less democratic political systems, in which leaders rely on a small coalition to stay in office, use private benefits to reward backers more than do more democratic systems, in which leaders require a large coalition of supporters. So, we should expect more trade protectionism in autocracies than in democracies. This is, in fact, the case. The average democratic regime is about 25 percent more open to trade than is the average autocratic regime, a difference that is extremely unlikely to be the result of chance (Bueno de Mesquita, Smith, Siverson, and Morrow 2003). Not all seekers of protection can expect to have their wishes fulfilled. They may not be essential supporters of the leadership. In that case, their appeals for protection are likely to fall on deaf ears. They may be in a relatively weak position to advance their cause, making it hard to get the attention of leaders.

## FACTORS OF PRODUCTION

People's interests regarding trade are shaped both by their economic interests and by their political interests. Whether our emphasis is on economic or political interests, we are still addressing politics. Trade policies, after all, are set by government and so are political.

Let us divide all people in any given country into two basic economic groups; those who provide labor and those who provide capital. Labor and capital are called factors of production. Let us also assume that a country has two industries, say, widgets and gadgets. Widget manufacturing is capital intensive whereas gadgets are labor intensive. By this I mean that the ratio of capital used to labor used for widgets is larger than it is for gadgets. In plain English, the widget business relies more heavily on capital (loosely, money) than on labor (again loosely, workers) to produce its product, and the gadget industry uses labor more intensively than it does capital to make its product. We will also assume that everyone has the same preferences when they are in the role of a consumer so that variation in preferences is due to considerations other than the consumer's role. As consumers, everyone wants a large selection of high-quality goods and services at low prices. By assuming that all consumers have the same preferences we can evaluate how a tariff influences the return on labor and capital. By knowing the relative economic returns on the factors of production, we can infer how a tariff affects the interests of people based on their particular factor endowments (that is, the extent to which they offer more in the form of capital or in the form of labor).

One place to begin our analysis is by asking whether a given country is more likely to export labor-intensive products or capital-intensive products. Imagine, for example, a rich country, such as France, Germany, Japan, Singapore, or the United States, and a poor country, such as China, Ghana, India, or Peru. Can we say anything about their exports based on the relative abundance of the two factors of production, capital and labor? The Hecksher-Ohlin theorem allows us to do so. This theorem, or logically proven proposition, addresses the mix of a country's exports and imports based on the relative abundance of the factors of production in an economy. Specifically, if there are two factors of production, a country will export products that are based on the intensive use of its relatively abundant factor and will import products whose production is based on the intensive use of the relatively scarce factor in its own economy. That is, countries with a relative abundance of capital, like many rich countries, will tend to export products that

> Using the Web or an annual yearbook, find a list of the leading exports and imports of Brazil, China, the Netherlands, Nigeria, and the United States, or select your own list of countries to look up. In each case see if you can find out whether the exports or imports are relatively labor-intensive or capital-intensive. How open are each of these economies to free trade? What trade protection, if any, is there against foreign imports in these countries? Are the countries you selected members of the WTO?

are capital intensive and import labor-intensive products. Poor countries tend to have a relative abundance of labor and so use labor intensively in production. They will tend to export labor-intensive products and import capital-intensive products. The link between this idea and the concept of comparative advantage should be evident.

The dichotomy I have drawn between rich and poor countries is a bit simpler than reality, but it is essentially right. The complicating factor is the word "relative" when speaking about the abundance of different factors of production. The Hecksher-Ohlin theorem, for instance, can also be readily applied to trade between two wealthy economies or two poor economies, since in each case, one factor will be *relatively* more abundant in one country than in the other.

Returning to the world of widgets and gadgets, let us imagine that there are two countries, Richland and Poorland, and that capital is relatively abundant in Richland and labor is relatively abundant in Poorland. The Hecksher-Ohlin theorem leads us to expect that Richland will want to export widgets to Poorland and Poorland will want to export gadgets to Richland. I say "want" because we have not yet considered whether labor, capital, or both in some industry will seek government protection in either Richland or Poorland. If the government acted purely on the basis of a policy in favor of free trade, then we could say, based on the Hecksher-Ohlin theorem, that Richland *will* export widgets and import gadgets while Poorland *will* export gadgets and import widgets.

Who will seek protection depends on several considerations. One is related to the economic return on widget and gadget production. Another is the preparedness of individuals to organize to press for the private benefits that could be derived from protection or to try to protect the public goods that could be derived from a free trade policy. Still another consideration is how the institutions of government—particularly dependence on a large coalition (as in democracy) or dependence on a small coalition (as in autocracy) influence the responsiveness of political leaders to pressure for or against protection. A good place to start our investigation of economic returns to factors of production is to think about how easily capital or labor can be shifted from one industry to another, because this significantly influences who wants protection. This is the topic of the next section.

## MOBILITY OF FACTORS OF PRODUCTION

Capital and labor can both be mobile. That means in the context of our hypothetical example that workers and capital can move easily from one job to another. Workers, or labor, for instance, might move from producing widgets to producing gadgets or other goods within their own country or they might even move to jobs in another country. Naturally, all else being equal, they would want to move only if they expected to be better off as a result of changing positions. Likewise, if capital is mobile this means that capital can move freely between businesses or even across country boundaries, so that capital could shift from Richland to Poorland (or visa versa). Like labor, all else being equal, owners of capital would not move their resource unless they expected a better return by moving it than by keeping it where it is.

To illustrate, consider why many relatively unskilled Mexican workers migrate to the United States. Their labor is mobile to the extent that they can perform unskilled jobs anywhere. Although poorly paid by U.S. standards, these Mexican workers get paid considerably more in the U.S. market than they do in the Mexican market. Consistent with the Hecksher-Ohlin theorem, Mexico exports labor-intensive products, including labor itself, to the United States. Mexican workers, when they can, exercise their labor mobility by seeking a better return on their labor by coming to the United States. Many, of course, save their money and return to Mexico, where they help improve their family's welfare as well as that of their country. Many more cannot enter the United States because the American government restricts the mobility of labor across the national frontier.

Consider also why many corporations, including many American corporations, invest in businesses in Mexico or China or India. These economies, starting from a low baseline, appear to have better growth prospects than does the United States over the next several years. Higher growth is likely to mean a better return to capital in those markets than in the United States. So, again consistent with the Hecksher-Ohlin theorem, American firms export capital by investing in places with high growth prospects when they can, moving capital to where it is expected to produce the best return. Not all governments, however, permit capital mobility across their frontiers. They restrict the movement of capital by limiting the ownership rights and opportunities of foreign investors seeking to enter their marketplace.

The two examples help clarify what is meant by labor and capital mobility, but they also highlight two (of many) reasons that labor or capital might not be mobile. In addition to the government restrictions alluded to, it is also possible that neither labor nor capital is mobile because either or both might be useful only in so specialized a way that the productive capacity in one sector does not translate into comparable productive capacity in another sector. Skilled carpenters, for example, cannot easily move to positions as design engineers creating new automobiles and neither can automobile design engineers move easily into positions as carpenters. Neither engineers nor carpenters have the requisite specialized skills to do the other's job productively. Of course, they are not completely immobile in reality. People can and do retool, but this is expensive in time and money and so is done only if the expected benefits from learning new skills outweigh the expected costs. It is likely, for example, that many blacksmiths in the early twentieth century retooled to do new jobs as the automobile supplanted the horse-drawn technology of the nineteenth century. More recently, we can see that many people in the typewriter manufacturing and repair industries retooled as typewriters were supplanted by personal computers. Typewriter repair shops used to be commonplace; now there are hardly any.

Still another possible scenario is that one factor of production is substantially more mobile than the other. Whether capital is likely to be more mobile than labor or vice versa depends on how specialized the use of labor is in a given economy and on how specialized the use of capital.

The economic incentives to seek protection depend, in part, on whether both labor and capital are mobile, only one is mobile, or neither is mobile. I proceed by examining these three situations, starting with mobile factors of production.

## INTERINDUSTRY FACTOR MOBILITY

If both labor and capital are mobile, then we know from what is called the Stolper-Samuelson theorem that a change in the price of a product is more than proportionally reflected in the return to the factor that is used (more intensively) to produce that product. This is a fairly complicated statement, so let's break it down into its important parts. To do so, I return to our Richland and Poorland example.

The widget industry is capital intensive. Richland is more competitive at making widgets than gadgets. As the price of widgets increases, the economic return (profit) to widget producers in Richland increases at a faster rate than does the return in Richland from making gadgets. That, however, is not all the Stolper-Samuelson theorem tells us. The proportional return to capital relative to labor increases across the entire Richland economy if the economy emphasizes the production of capital-intensive goods. Even in the gadget industry, the return to capital increases proportionally more than the return to labor in Richland, a place that focuses on capital-intensive production. Equivalently, and this is very important in understanding the policy debate over globalization, in Poorland there is a more than proportional return to labor as the price of gadgets—the labor-intensive product—increases in Poorland's labor-intensive economy.

Now, let us suppose that for some reason (for example, a policy shift to favor free trade) the price of imports—gadgets—falls in Richland. One consequence of the drop in price is that Richland's domestic gadget producers will make fewer gadgets (see Figure 13-3) and so will need less labor. Another consequence is that the relative price of Richland's widgets, its capital-intensive export good, will rise. The rise in the relative price of widgets leads to increased demand for capital because any expansion in widget production is capital intensive. This means that labor in Richland is in relatively abundant supply following the change in the price of gadgets, and capital is in relatively short supply following the increase in the price of widgets. The widget makers do not pick up the slack in labor because, after all, widget making is capital intensive. They need relatively more capital to exploit the increased price, not more labor. In fact, because the demand for capital in Richland rises in this example while the demand for labor falls, the relative price for all labor drops, provided that both labor and capital are mobile across the economy. At the same time, the relative price of capital rises across the economy—not just in the widget business—as long as it is mobile. This is because if there is interindustry mobility, capital will move from one industry to another to find its highest price. Labor will do the same. Because demand for capital has grown, the only way to attract new capital is to pay more for it by giving higher returns. Because the demand for labor has dropped relative to capital, the only way for labor to be utilized more is to reduce its relative price so that it becomes more competitive. So, in Richland we can expect the relative return to capital to rise and the relative return to labor to fall.

In Poorland it is likely that the opposite effect will be observed under a free trade regime. That is, the return to labor is likely to increase relatively more than the return to capital because in Poorland labor, not capital, is the more intensively used factor of production. Gadget makers will need more labor and so will bid up the price of labor across their economy. They will not need more capital, and so capital will chase possible users and its price will drop as those who provide capital compete to find uses for their less-in-demand factor of production.

The argument thus far shows us that in a country with relatively more capital-intensive industry—like Richland—free trade makes the owners of capital winners and the owners of labor, relatively speaking, losers. But in a country where industry is relatively labor intensive—like Poorland—free trade is a winning strategy for labor and a losing strategy for capital. So, to the extent that both factors of production are mobile, globalization of free trade has four economic effects (Magee 1978; Hill and Mendez 1983; McKeown 1984; Rogowski 1989). Generally, with interindustry factor mobility:

1. workers in poor countries become wealthier;
2. owners of capital in rich countries become wealthier;
3. owners of capital in poor countries do relatively worse with free trade; and
4. labor in rich countries does relatively worse with free trade.

*Among the primary beneficiaries of free trade are poor laborers in poor countries—workers like this Costa Rican banana picker. The nation's exports have increased due to free trade, creating more opportunities for its citizens.*

Recall that at the beginning of this chapter I listed labor unions, environmentalists, and students as among the opponents of globalization who demonstrated in Seattle, Bologna, and elsewhere. Now we can pause to think about their opposition in the context of mobile factors of production and the economic returns from free trade or trade protectionism.

The group of demonstrators against globalization can be described as people living in wealthy countries who share a dislike for big business. To be sure, they are right in believing that if capital and labor are both mobile, then in countries with an abundance of capital, capital-intensive big business is a winner from free trade. The losers in a capital-intensive economy—most prominently labor—are most likely to exercise their political clout to try to stop free trade and promote protection. Debate over free trade or trade protection is extremely salient for them because its outcome directly influences their welfare. But the anti–free trade demonstrators are mistaken about the effects on workers in poor countries that tend to emphasize labor-intensive industry. In those countries we should expect labor's relative return to improve disproportionately as a result of free trade while the return to capital does not. That is, rich businesspeople in poor countries with mobile factors of production can be expected to oppose free trade.

The discussion here helps us understand why trade policy outcomes have a different salience for different groups or individuals. In fact, the salience of issues varies among stakeholders regardless of the issue. Return to the issue you selected in Chapter 3 and specify the salience of the issue for each of the stakeholders. Think of salience as a value between 1 and 100, where values of 90–100 indicate that the issue is the most important concern of the stakeholder, so important, in fact, that the stakeholder would drop whatever he or she was doing to attend to the issue whenever it came up. A score of 80–90 suggests a somewhat reduced willingness to attend to the issue on demand. The closer the salience of an issue is to zero, the less likely the stakeholder is to attend to it rather than attend to other issues that are competing for his or her attention.

Multiply each stakeholder's power by its salience and divide by 100. Treat the resulting values as the expected power contributed to the issue by each stakeholder and use this value to find the salience-adjusted median voter position. Is this a better prediction of the likely resolution of the issue you chose?

Laborers and unions can be expected to support free trade in poor countries with interindustry factor mobility. So, if both factors of production are mobile, it is incorrect to think that free trade helps the rich (or the poor) across the board and harms the other economic class. Rather, free trade allows each economy to pursue its comparative advantage in labor or capital so that it competes as efficiently as it can in the worldwide market. Where labor is the abundant factor—as in much of the developing world—protectionism as a trade policy harms workers and benefits "capitalists."

In a world with perfect interindustry factor mobility we can see that political pressure will arise for protection against foreign competition among those whose factor of production—whether it be capital or labor—is relatively disadvantaged by free trade. This conclusion helps us understand opposition to globalization by labor and students in wealthy countries. Students typically are not yet significant owners of capital and, on average, they do not yet have skills that allow them to command a high price as labor. They naturally identify with the relatively worse off in their society. Labor unions have as their mission to improve the conditions for labor *in their industry or community*. They are not as interested in the welfare of laborers in other countries or other industries than their own. The opponents of free trade in the United States align with the interests of labor at the expense of capital; that is, they side with workers *in their country* at the expense of business owners. However, they are also siding against poorer workers in poor, labor-intensive countries and, probably without realizing it, they are siding with the big businesses of developing countries.

The big magnates in developing countries may be disadvantaged in their ability to compete with capital-intensive goods made in wealthier countries, and so they seek protection against capital-intensive imports. In India, for example, the only available automobile for many years was the Hindustan Ambassador. It was basically a twenty-year-old model that could not compete with foreign imports. Until relatively recently, the Indian government's solution was to bow to political pressure (in the name of national self-sufficiency) to make it prohibitively expensive to import foreign cars into India. This was equally true for the availability of aluminum, many types of iron and steel, foodstuffs, medical supplies, and on and on. The upshot was great distortion of the economy to the benefit of wealthy Indian producers and at the expense of Indian consumers, helping to make the rich very rich and the poor exceedingly poor. Since India shifted to somewhat freer trade (although it still is far from having a free trade policy), its economic growth rate has skyrocketed, providing improved opportunities for its poor workers.

## THE CASE WITH NO INTERINDUSTRY FACTOR MOBILITY

Perfectly mobile factors of production are an ideal. Such perfection may be achieved in the long run, but it is not an accurate description of the mobility of capital or labor on the ground. Since the true adjustment of prices and returns resulting from free trade is not instantaneous without perfect factor mobility, the predictions of the Stolper-Samuelson theorem need also to be examined in regard to their effects in the shorter term. In the short run, factor mobility might be quite limited. To assess the short-run effects I now examine what happens following the introduction of a tariff when neither labor nor capital is mobile at all.

If factors are completely immobile, a new equilibrium price cannot be achieved, as it was in the Stolper-Samuelson world, by having capital and labor move from one industry to another to seek their best return. That is what it means to say they are immobile; they are stuck where they are and cannot move from one industry to another. North Korea comes close to the "ideal type" of a society in which labor and capital are both immobile. The authoritarian government of North Korea does not permit people to move from one part of the country to another, nor does it allow people to change jobs at will. Rather, labor mobility is strictly determined by the whim of the government. Being a communist state, North Korea also does not promote capital investment by its citizens and permits capital movement by foreigners only within a narrow special economic zone. It is, in short, a society basically without labor or capital mobility. In this case, if a tariff is imposed, inflating the price of one good compared with another, then price adjustments can occur only through changes in the price of the factors of production. There is no additional effect arising because of labor or capital mobility. Therefore, the effects of price changes for factors of production are localized to specific industries rather than across the economy. Any effect felt from a tariff will be industry specific without factor mobility.

Let us assume that factor prices are completely flexible so that they can change readily. Let us also assume that the economy had full employment prior to the introduction of a tariff (as is nominally true in North Korea). This means that there is no elasticity in the supply of either factor, because both factors are fully utilized. With these conditions in place, the introduction of a tariff will not lead to a change in the quantity produced by either industry. In North Korea's case, however, trade is almost completely quashed by government action. North Korea exports missiles to some Middle Eastern states, but otherwise it has no export market for any other consequential goods. It imports little as well, so I return to the hypothetical world of widgets and gadgets.

Without factor mobility, relative returns to factors do not change, unlike in the world with complete interindustry mobility. However, an important change does occur. The amount paid for capital and labor in an industry that is protected by a tariff increases relative to the unprotected industry. If a tariff is imposed on gadgets, for instance, everyone (that is, capital and labor) in the gadget industry will benefit relative to everyone in the widget industry (again, both capital and labor). With factor mobility, we saw that policy preferences over protection were factor dependent. With immobile factors of production, policy pressures for trade protection arise on an industry-by-industry basis rather than a factor-by-factor basis. So, with immobile factors, labor and capital in the gadget business would seek government protection and be pitted politically against labor and capital in the widget industry. In this case, some of the relatively well-off people and some of the relatively poor people will benefit from trade protection, just as some of each group, in unprotected industries, will be losers. Thus, who tries to organize for protection differs depending on factor mobility. With full mobility we might expect, all else being equal, to see "class warfare" over trade policy. With immobility, we might expect to see interindustry warfare. In this environment, the relatively wealthy and the relatively poor in a given industry win as a result of the imposition of a tariff, but other relatively wealthy and relatively poor people employed in other, unprotected industries suffer. Consumers in general, of course, are harmed, as are labor and capital in Poorland's export industry, having become victims of a tariff (Alt and Gilligan 1994).

## THE CASE WITH SPECIFIC FACTOR MOBILITY

Perfectly immobile factors, like perfect interindustry factor mobility, are the extremes and therefore unrealistic. Trade policy is completely driven neither by factor mobility nor by immobility. Before turning to other considerations, we examine what happens when one factor is perfectly mobile and the other is not. Under the specific factor approach one factor of production is specific to a particular industry whereas the other factor is mobile. To say that a factor is specific to a given industry means that it cannot be moved to improve the return from it; rather, it can be moved only to another industry at a cost. For convenience I will assume that labor is perfectly mobile whereas capital is tied to its specific industry. The conclusions, however, are equally applicable if we reverse this convenience as long as you keep track of your assumptions of which factor is mobile and which is specific.

The implications of tariffs depend on whether they are applied to the specific factor's industry or to the mobile factor of production. Imagine that each person in an economy possesses only one of these two factors of production. Then, as in the immobile factor world, those who own the specific factor will form views about tariff protection based on the circumstances in the industry in which they work. If those with the specific factor are at a competitive disadvantage to foreign producers, then they will want protection from imports in their industry, although they may readily oppose tariff protection in other industries. Those who possess the mobile factor of production will form views regarding tariff protection based on the circumstances affecting their mobile factor. If the mobile factor is not intensively used in their economy, they will want protection from foreign competition. If their factor is intensively used in their economy, then they will prefer free trade to tariffs (Hillman 1982; Grossman 1983; Rogowski 1989).

Let us imagine in Richland that capital is industry specific so that capital used in producing widgets is costly to move to the gadget industry and visa versa. The labor used in making widgets and gadgets, in contrast, is assumed to be mobile across industries. We will assume comparable facts in Poorland. In Richland, gadgets are an import industry and widgets are an export industry. If Richland does not impose a tariff on Poorland's gadgets, the price of gadgets will fall as a result of import competition. The domestic production of gadgets will also fall in response to the price drop brought on by the free importation of Poorland gadgets. Labor will respond by moving away from domestic gadget production and seek employment in the export-oriented widget business. Capital, being immobile (specific) in this example, will not be able to move. Although capital remains in the import-competing gadget business, it can no longer attract sufficient labor, and so the domestic gadget makers become less productive. The result is that the income from capital in the domestic gadget industry will drop both with respect to the price of Richland's export good—widgets—and the price of Poorland's gadgets imported into Richland. Meanwhile, mobile labor is moving from the domestic gadget industry into the export-oriented domestic widget business, where prices are rising relative to domestic, import-competing gadgets. The extra labor made available to capital in the export widget industry in Richland improves the productivity of capital in that business. Consequently, the return on capital (the immobile or specific factor) used to make widgets will rise relative to the price of widgets and relative to the price of imported gadgets. In summary, under this scenario, the return on capital (assumed to be the specific, or immobile, factor) under free trade is industry specific. In an export-oriented industry, capital does especially well. In an industry with import competition, capital does especially poorly. Labor, being mobile, moves to the industry in which it can command its highest return. That is the export-oriented industry. Naturally, those who face import competition and who own the specific factor of production will be more inclined to pressure government to impose a tariff than will those who own the specific factor in the export-oriented industry or those who own the mobile factor of production. So, the owners of capital devoted to making gadgets in Richland (or aluminum, cars, or airplanes—all requiring vast commitments of hard-to-move capital—in India) will seek government protection. Labor does not need protection because it can move to the more productive, export-oriented widget business. Those with capital invested in making widgets (or computer software in India) likewise will not want protection. Under these circumstances, protection helps immobile capital in the import-competing industry. This industry is a winner with protection whereas just about everyone else is a loser. If the tables were reversed and there were free trade, then only capital in the import-competing gadget business would lose and everyone else would win.

## THE CONSEQUENCES OF FREE TRADE: SOME EVIDENCE

Logic tells us that free trade creates many more winners than losers. Trade protection distorts the economy by insulating relatively inefficient industries from competition. Trade protection arises to protect the few with political clout at the expense of the many. The few who press for protection can exercise their political influence effectively for two reasons. Those who benefit from protection have a focused interest in persuading government to protect them. As mentioned earlier, this focus makes it easier for them to overcome coordination problems. They are more likely to avoid the problem of free riding than are the many who benefit from the public good of free trade. A second factor that plays into the hands of those seeking protection is the extent to which the domestic political environment rewards leaders with long tenure in office if they compensate their backers with private goods.

Autocrats rely on private benefits to stay in office. Democrats are more reliant on providing public goods. I have already mentioned that autocratic governments are substantially less supportive of free trade than are democrats. Now we can ask whether the preference for free trade translates into improved social well-being.

We can think of social welfare in two distinct ways. Governments routinely must choose between policies that advance efficiency and policies that advance equity. By efficiency is meant policies that do not interfere with the smooth working of a free market. In free markets producers and consumers all seek their own comparative advantage. As a result, resources are used in the most efficient way possible, avoiding waste and distortions that arise from regulation. But efficient markets can be cruel. Those who are less competitive suffer. Without a social safety net like social security, unemployment insurance, progressive taxation, and the like, they might not be able to survive. Markets are often regulated and resources redistributed to improve equity; that is, the more equal treatment of all citizens.

Much of the debate about globalization is really a debate about equity. Opponents of globalization may accept, along with virtually all economists, that free trade promotes efficiency, but they fear that it is inequitable. We have seen that in theory trade protectionism creates winners and losers. Who wins and loses is not systematically related to whether they are relatively wealthy or poor but, rather, to who has incentives to press for protection and who is in a good position to overcome free-rider problems and organize to use their political clout to get protection. Now I summarize some historical evidence about the equity effects of trade policy.

Governments can be evaluated in terms of their receptivity to trade. For example, we can assess the percentage of a country's gross domestic product that comes from exports and imports (measured in 1985 international dollars). A data source called Penn World Tables has just such information in a variable called OPENC (http://pwt.econ.upenn. edu/frontpage.html). Likewise, we can evaluate how evenly or unevenly income is distributed in each country. The standard way of evaluating income inequality is through something called a GINI index. The higher the value of the GINI index, the less equally distributed is income in a country. Essentially, the GINI index compares the percentage of the population, ranked from lowest income to highest, against the percentage of total income accounted for at each level. If, for instance, the top 10 percent of the population accounts for 30 percent of income while the bottom 10 percent accounts for, say, only 1 percent, then income is pretty unevenly distributed. The closer the cumulative percentage of the population is to the cumulative percentage of income, the more equally—or equitably—income is distributed.

If receptivity to trade—OPENC—is inequitable, then we will observe that the more open a country is to trade, on average, the larger is its GINI index score. Conversely, if openness to trade promotes more equal income distributions by helping to lift the poor to narrow the gap with the rich, then globalization promotes improved equity as well as improved efficiency. In evaluating the relationship between trade openness and income inequality, I control for the independent impact of per capita income levels to make sure that whatever we discover is not simply a product of differences in wealth across countries. This speaks directly to the worry of those opposed to globalization that it is just a means to make the rich richer at the expense of the poor and that the idea of free trade has been hijacked by large corporations to enrich themselves at the expense of workers. Naturally, large corporation executives, if left to their own devices, would try to maximize their personal welfare, just as workers, if left to their own devices, would do the same. Free trade, however, ensures competition that makes any such inefficient exploitation of resources exceedingly difficult.

With the statistical control for per capita income in place, we can see the independent impact that trade openness has on income equality. To assess this impact I use all available data. This includes the years 1950–1992 and all countries for which data are available. The available number of countries varies from year to year between about twenty countries and more than fifty. These countries differ markedly in income levels, with the lowest in per capita income being Ethiopia in 1984 ($318) and the highest being Switzerland in 1989 ($16,304). The United States—which has relatively equal income distribution—is missing from the data.

Wealthy countries enjoy greater income equality on average than do poor countries. In fact, every doubling in per capita income is associated with 1.5 percent less income inequality on average. If, however, we investigate the magnitude or percentage change in income inequality looking three years ahead of when we observe per capita income, we discover that income levels do not significantly influence changes in inequality one way or the other.

With the assessment of income levels in mind, we can now evaluate the impact on income inequality that results from the degree of receptivity to trade. Countries vary in their income inequality from a best-case GINI score of about 20 to a worst case score of about 60. Remember, the closer the GINI index is to zero, the more equally income is distributed, and the closer it is to 100, the more income is in the hands of only a small segment of the population. The trade openness measure varies from a low of about 8, meaning that 8 percent of gross domestic product comes from imports and exports, to a high of over 200, reflecting an economy that is completely dependent on trade. Such an economy produces and consumes very little that is not imported or made for export. The statistical evidence tells us that the average country that is closed to trade (that is, OPENC equals about 8) can expect an income inequality equal to 54. The evidence also tells us that an economy that is most open to trade (that is, OPENC equals about 212) can anticipate a GINI index of about 43. In other words, those who use the most trade protectionism also promote income inequality, keeping the poor poor and keeping the rich rich. The probability that this relationship arose by chance is less than one in one thousand. What is more, if we ask what happens to income inequality in the future as a result of openness to trade now, we discover that strong equity effects persist. Whether we look at the GINI index three years after observing openness to trade, or we look at the magnitude or percentage change in income inequality, we continue to find statistically significant equity benefits from free trade.

Before closing, I think it is worthwhile taking one more statistical look at the effects of free trade. We now know that trade improves income equality, but what specifically does it do for labor and for capital? To evaluate the effect of openness to trade on labor, I assess labor's share of value added in manufacturing as measured by the World Bank. To evaluate the effect of openness to trade on capital I examine real gross domestic investment (private and public) as a percentage of GDP (both in 1985 international prices) using Penn World Tables data. Again I control for the independent effect of per capita income levels.

Not surprisingly, the higher a country's average income level, the smaller the contribution that labor makes to value added in manufacturing. This is a significant effect that is consistent with our Richland example, in which the wealthier country tends to be more capital-intensive in its industries. Openness to trade, however, has a huge impact on labor's contribution to the value added through manufacturing. The significance level is off the charts. Those countries that offer the most trade protection can anticipate that labor's share of value added in manufacturing is only 41 percent. Those that are most open to trade can anticipate that labor's share is 59 percent. Clearly, a greater commitment to free trade is beneficial to labor.

Equally, a commitment to free trade is beneficial to capital. Higher-income countries have only a marginally better prospect of attracting investment than do poorer countries. The strength of the statistical relationship is weak enough that it would happen in 7 out of every 100 samples. Trade openness, in contrast, is again off the charts in terms of statistical significance. Those countries least open to trade have, on average, about 12 percent public and private investment as a share of GDP. Those most open to trade average investments equal to 18 percent of GDP, or 50 percent more than those closed to trade. So we can see that those nations that favor free trade policies promote greater income equality (equity) and better returns to labor, and they attract more capital. Those that eschew free trade protect special domestic interests, but they foster inequity, poor returns to labor, and low investment in the society's future growth.

## SUMMARY

Trade is a vital and growing area of international interaction. Efforts to promote globalization are supported by many governments around the world and, equally, are opposed by other governments and by well-organized interest groups. Free trade is good for everyone in the role of a consumer but can harm particular industries or those who own particular factors of production. Who is harmed depends on the mobility of labor and capital and on the ability of interested groups to overcome free-rider problems by organizing to pressure government for protection. If both labor and capital are pretty mobile, then over the long run, free trade is relatively beneficial for capital in capital-intensive economies (like many wealthy countries) and is beneficial for labor in labor-intensive economies (like many poor countries). I say "over the long run" because given sufficient time, both labor and capital are likely to find ways to move if they want to. In the short run, mobility is more difficult, because investments are tied up, workers have family commitments, the government might restrict mobility, and so forth. In the long run, free trade is relatively disadvantageous for owners of capital in poor countries and for labor in rich countries.

The evidence across many countries over the past fifty years shows us the effects of different trade policies. Countries that restrict trade so that it is a small part of their economic picture tend to have relatively unequal income distributions; tend to provide relatively little value added to labor; and tend to attract relatively small amounts of investment. Countries that have been open to trade tend to have relatively equal income distributions; tend to provide a relatively large value added to labor; and tend to attract relatively large amounts of investment. Apparently those governments that interfere least in foreign trade produce the best outcomes, on average, for most of their citizens.

# CHAPTER 14

# INTERNATIONAL ORGANIZATIONS AND INTERNATIONAL LAW

The end of World War II produced renewed vigor and interest in promoting cooperation among the world's nations. This interest is manifest in the explosion of international organizations dedicated to creating rules designed to coordinate and regulate behavior. Such rules and regulations are prominent in almost every domain of international inter-action. Some multilateral organizations or agreements and the rules they promulgate have been dedicated to conflict resolution, including, for instance, the United Nations and the Nuclear Nonproliferation Treaty. The World Trade Organization and regional organizations—including, for instance, NAFTA, Mercosur, and the European Union—regulate trade. Bodies like the G8, the International Monetary Fund (IMF), the World Bank, and the Asian Development Bank help govern other forms of economic interaction.[1] The Red Cross and the Red Crescent, Amnesty International, and other non-governmental organizations (NGOs) focus on a variety of social, environmental, informational, and human rights issues. These issues likewise are the focus of international law, multilateral agreements, and a host of other international organizations. In

---

[1] The G8, called the G7 before the addition of Russia, is a regularly scheduled summit of leaders from Canada, France, Germany, Italy, Japan, Russia, the United Kingdom, and the United States to coordinate economic policy.

fact, virtually every aspect of international interactions has been the subject of the burgeoning body of international law and international institutions. The prominence of these institutions and their rules and regulations raises fundamental questions about international politics. Those questions are the subject of this chapter.

Several puzzles revolve around the proliferation—or even the existence—of international law and international organizations. Foremost among these is whether they make a difference. Certainly the events of September 11, 2001, compel us to wonder about the efficacy of international law. Do these organizations and regulations alter behavior or merely codify existing interests and actions? Are they effective in promoting cooperation where otherwise private interests would prevail over collective welfare? Do they undermine sovereignty to the advantage of intergovernmental organizations like NATO or the United Nations, or of nongovernmental organizations like the World Economic Forum (consisting of 1,000 multinational corporations), or do they protect states against the erosion of their sovereignty by the Internet—which makes government restrictions on the flow of information difficult to enforce—or by a few powerful predatory states or businesses? There are no generally accepted answers to any of these questions. The competing perspectives of international relations prompt different conclusions, and the body of evidence remains too incomplete to reach firm judgments.

## INTERNATIONAL LAW, ORGANIZATIONS, AND REGIMES: DEFINITIONS AND DISTINCTIONS

Before turning to the specifics of international law, international organizations, and international regimes, we should be clear about how these categories differ and how they overlap. This is especially important because I will sometimes treat them in common and other times make sharp distinctions among the three categories.

### INTERNATIONAL LAW

International law consists of a body of treaty obligations that states enter into. Because they are treaties, rather than lesser agreements among states or subnational or non-national actors, they carry the force of law. This often means that independent, nonstate bodies—such as certain international organizations—have the authority to adjudicate disputes and, at least in principle, to punish violations. This also often means that signatory states can press legal claims against alleged violations within the court system of member states.

Consider the importance assigned to treaties in the American Constitution. The Constitution designates treaties as special arrangements. It explicitly forbids individual states within the United States from entering into treaties or alliances. This is exclusively the domain of the federal government. Within that domain, the president is given the power "by and with the advice and consent of the Senate, to make Treaties, provided two

What are the implications of the Constitution's discussion of treaties for understanding the obligations of the U.S. government toward Native American tribes as a result of peace treaties signed between these tribes and the American government in the nineteenth century? Do these obligations differ legally from the obligations of the U.S. government under the Versailles Treaty that ended World War I or the Paris Peace Treaty that ended the war in Vietnam? What does the existence of such treaties with Native American tribes indicate about their legal status as recognized by the U.S. government? Is the treatment of Native Americans a purely internal affair or is it subject to scrutiny under international law?

thirds of the Senators present concur" (Art. II, Sec. 2, Cl. 2). The adjudication of disputes involving treaties is also given a special place in the legal structure of the United States. Article III, Section 2, Clause 1 of the Constitution stipulates that "[t]he judicial Power shall extend to all Cases, in Law and Equity, arising under this Constitution, the Laws of the United States, and Treaties made, or which shall be made, under their Authority, . . . and between a State, or the Citizens thereof, and foreign States, Citizens, or Subjects." Here the Constitution places the status of treaties on a par with the laws promulgated within the United States and on an equal footing with the Constitution itself so that treaties cannot be voided purely on the basis of a judgment that they violate other aspects of the Constitution. They become part of the core law and commitments of the nation once they are ratified in accordance with the procedures set out in the Constitution.

International law includes treaties about such diverse topics as fishing and exploration rights within the world's oceans; protection of human rights; prohibitions against torture; the treatment of prisoners of war; regulation of international commerce; copyrights and other intellectual property rights; the nonproliferation of nuclear weapons; the use of land mines; and so forth. States can opt out of the obligation to obey a given international law by failing to endorse the law. In this way, international law can be very different from laws within states. People living in a given state do not have the option of picking and choosing the laws they are obligated to obey. To a much larger degree, nations do have this choice. That is one indication that international politics is anarchic, as suggested by realists.

One central question about international law that clearly separates approaches to international relations is whether such law is binding, is not binding but alters behavior, merely codifies existing norms and beliefs, or is irrelevant to the actions of nations. Constructivists, as discussed in Chapter 8, for instance, see international law as reshaping the internal perception of national interests and, thereby, changing how states behave. In their view and as a central tenet of constructivism, law helps to create norms of conduct. Legalistic observers, in contrast, perceive international law as binding rather than as reflecting accepted norms of conduct. International lawyers, for example, do not think of law as reflecting strategic interactions but, rather, as a body of legally binding obligations to which signatory states have subjected themselves. The strategic perspective views treaty obligations as costly signals that constrain the range of choices leaders can make, allowing one generation of leaders to tie the hands—limit the freedom of action—of future leaders. If the restraints imposed by international law deviate too greatly from a leader's interests, then the strategic point of view suggests that the leader will opt out of the law because the costs of doing so are smaller than the gains. Such breaks with prior treaty agreements being costly, they are expected to be infrequent. Realists consider international law largely as the codification of current interests and, therefore, as easily altered or violated when the nation's interests are no longer served by the existing treaty obligations. Realism, then, suggests more frequent breaks with international law than is implied by the strategic perspective or a constructivist viewpoint. Liberal theorists perceive international law as a foundation on which nations build cooperative arrangements that facilitate coordination in the areas covered by the law. As such, they anticipate infrequent departures from such law because its purpose is to facilitate the advancement of shared national interests in creating a cooperative environment. Liberal theorists share with constructivists the conviction that international law fosters the creation of new norms of conduct among states (Keohane and Nye 1977; Goldstein and Keohane 1993; Clark 2003).

## INTERNATIONAL ORGANIZATIONS

International law is sometimes enforced within national courts, and other times it is enforced within bodies specifically created for that purpose. Some international organizations (for example, the World Trade Organization) fall into this latter category. That is, these are institutions created by participating states for the purpose of enforcing, elaborating, and modifying international laws much as a state's legislature reviews and alters law from time to time. Just as laws within a state are binding only on citizens and residents within the state, so international laws generally are enforceable only against signatories to the treaties that created the law. This means that international organizations created to enforce certain rules and regulations generally have no standing with nonsignatory states. This restriction on enforceability is itself an area of considerable discussion among students of international organizations. As we will see later in this chapter, there are benefits and costs associated with making an international organization more or less inclusive in its membership.

---

### Perspectives on International Law

**Constructivism:** International law creates norms of conduct. For many governments, it alters their perception of their own national interest.

**Liberalism:** Creates norms of conduct. Promotes shared values in favor of cooperation among states. Norms of conduct are often promulgated and protected by a hegemonic power.

**Realism:** Codifies current perceptions of the national interest, especially for powerful states. Relatively frequent violations by the powerful are expected when interests in specific circumstances are not advanced by existing international law or agreements.

**Strategic Approach:** Acceptance of international law creates costly signals that constrain a state's future range of actions. Because the hands of future leaders are tied by international commitments, expect relatively few violations of international law and agreements.

Perhaps the most prominent international organization in today's world is the United Nations. The United Nations, with its main headquarters in New York City, was created at the end of World War II. It was designed as an organization that would be as universal in membership as possible and that would establish and enforce international law across a wide area concerned with preserving or restoring peace and protecting human rights. Its largest body, the General Assembly, includes almost every state in the world. The General Assembly passes resolutions and debates many of the fundamental international policy questions of the day.

The Security Council is the most powerful body in the United Nations. It is made up of fifteen countries, five of which are permanent members with veto power. The remaining ten slots rotate among member states based on regional associations, like the Arab League or the Organization of American States. All questions concerned with international security and peace are in the domain of the Security Council if it chooses to consider them. The Council has the power to implement resolutions of the United Nations with force if necessary, provided the permanent members all agree to do so.

The International Court of Justice, located in The Hague in the Netherlands, has responsibility for adjudicating cases involving alleged violations of member obligations under the United Nations Charter, with the Charter being the UN's equivalent to the American Constitution. That is, the Charter is the fundamental law that all member states agree to abide by when they become members of the United Nations. Later in this chapter I examine how well these and other aspects of the United Nations work in practice.

Not all international organizations exist to create or enforce laws that are, in principle, binding obligations among signatory states. Some international organizations exist to facilitate coordination and cooperation among members, although they lack the standing of law. The World Bank and the Asian Development Bank, for example, are voluntary organizations designed to facilitate economic assistance among member states. The Asian Development Bank makes loans and sometimes provides economic advice to member states so as to facilitate economic growth. The World Bank does much the same. OPEC is designed to help member states coordinate their production and sale of petroleum so as to influence and stabilize the price of crude oil around the world. OPEC members agree to produce no more than their assigned quota of oil, but OPEC has virtually no mechanisms to enforce compliance with its quotas. In fact, some member states—most notably Nigeria—are believed to cheat almost all the time, producing more oil than was authorized by OPEC. Doing so, of course, reduces the overall price of oil (as supply increases beyond demand) while potentially improving the market share of the cheating state. Depending on how quickly a state's market share expands through cheating (that is, selling more than its authorized quota of oil) compared with how much the price of crude oil drops in the market, cheating can allow a state to come out ahead financially. Naturally, if a state expects to lose money by cheating, it is unlikely to do so.

International organizations are formally established bodies designed to facilitate coordination among member states or nonstate actors. Some international organizations involve nongovernmental members. A few of the better known such organizations are the Red Cross, the Catholic Church, CARE, and Amnesty International. Although each of these organizations has operations based in specific countries, these members normally are not operated, controlled, or organized by governments. Rather, they are nongovernmental organizations. They exist to help facilitate the promotion and fulfillment of their mission on a regional or global basis without the intervention of national governments. Of course, they are restricted to operate within the laws of the states in which they perform their services, but otherwise their members choose their own rules and regulations.

The number of international organizations, and particularly the number of NGOs, has grown tremendously over the decades since the end of World War II. There are many possible explanations for this proliferation. Constructivists and liberal theorists suggest, for instance, that the growth in such bodies is the result of a shared realization that the world could avoid disaster only through better mechanisms for coordinating action, creating shared values, and promoting cooperation. The end of World War II and the subsequent decades of cold war both served to increase these concerns.

The strategic perspective, although not in disagreement with the above viewpoint, also suggests that the proliferation of democratic governments after World War II—and especially since the end of the cold war—fostered the emergence of more international organizations and NGOs. Because democracies experience high turnover in leaders, their governments have especially strong incentives to reduce the inherent policy uncertainty created by such turnover. One way to do so is by limiting the freedom of action of future leaders through public, explicit international commitments. Violating such commitments can be politically costly, as discussed later. Therefore, membership in international organizations helps promote compliance, especially for democratic leaders who are vulnerable to the domestic political costs associated with rapid reversals in policy, making such organizations an attractive vehicle for reducing uncertainty and promoting stability in foreign affairs.

## INTERNATIONAL REGIMES

International regimes—defined as international institutions, rules, regulations, and norms—subsume international law and international organizations. Thus, international regimes constitute a generic category intended to promote the importance of ideas in international politics (Goldstein and Keohane 1993). States and their leaders respond not only to explicit legal obligations through law, but also through informal understandings and expectations resulting from norms of conduct. Norms of behavior change and these changes result in altered patterns of international interaction. In the Middle Ages, capturing and ransoming foreign leaders was a legitimate aspect of warfare. Today's norms of conduct prohibit targeting specific political leaders for capture or assassination. Ransoming prisoners of war for money is widely regarded as inappropriate and inhumane today. During the Hundred Years' War, in the fourteenth and fifteenth centuries, it was not only normal conduct; it was the basis for relatively humane treatment of prisoners. Torture, although still used frequently enough to have prompted an international treaty against torture, violates contemporary norms of behavior, whereas in the twelfth century the Catholic Church saw torture as a means to save souls, rescuing people from eternal damnation. In those days it was perceived as a good thing, and today it is perceived as evil conduct.

When norms of conduct are insufficient to promote cooperation, then more formal arrangements become important as means to reduce international conflict. Thus, informal regimes get replaced by formal international organizations or by codified laws of conduct when norms alone prove insufficient to achieve the desired ends. When and why any of these mechanisms work is the focus of the remainder of this chapter.

## CAN WE EVALUATE THE EFFECTS OF INTERNATIONAL REGIMES?

The degree of influence that international law and international organizations exert on the actions of nations is difficult to resolve, primarily because institutions, rules, and regulations are endogenous. That is, neither international law nor any specific organizations arise spontaneously or by chance. They are the consequence of negotiated agreements among leaders of states. It is difficult to separate the interests these leaders represent from the choices they make regarding the structure of international organizations and rules. Certainly it is unlikely that they agree to structures that constrain their behavior in ways that are contrary to their interests. But if that is so then international regimes, rather than influencing national actions, just reflect "national interests." There are, however, counterarguments that support the conclusion that international law, organizations, rules, and regulations alter behavior rather than just reflecting national interests.

### CONSTRUCTIVIST CASE

Constructivists argue that the very content of a country's national interest can be redefined by membership in an international organization. This is hypothesized to happen as a result of three factors: legitimation, role redefinition, and reflection. The argument for regime legitimation maintains that when members comply with an organization's mission the members endow the regime's rules and regulations with authority and legitimacy. Oren Young and M. A. Levy (1999), for example, maintain that organization members do not engage in the kind of cost-benefit calculations that characterize strategic behavior because they have internalized the regime's routines and they have been socialized to accept them. Little evidence, however, is offered to bolster this claim. It remains a question for future research to resolve. Among the unanswered questions is why a member of an international regime would see the regime's rules and regulations as being either legitimate or authoritative if they run counter to the interests of the state. George Downs (2000) suggests evidence to the contrary in the case of environmental regimes.

Role redefinition is also hypothesized to be a factor in redefining national interests. Organizations, being complex, assign different roles to different actors. Japan, for example, was thrust into a leadership role during the environmental negotiations over what came to be called the Kyoto Protocols. Japan seemed to take a stronger pro-environmental stance than it had in earlier negotiations, perhaps because its new role gave it a new identity or, from a strategic perspective, perhaps because it realized that U.S. opposition would defeat the Kyoto proposals and so Japan did not have to go out on a limb by declaring itself to be opposed. Alexander Wendt (1994) contends that the roles nations play in international organizations gradually create new identities for the state as it associates itself with the role in which it has been placed. New identities, in turn, promote new interests, thereby redefining the national interest. Of course, organization members agree to accept particular roles. This means that it is difficult to distinguish between a true change in national identity and the acceptance of roles as part of an endogenous, negotiated process that reflects national or individual leader interests. The idea of role redefinition is intriguing, although it has yet to be subjected to rigorous empirical scrutiny beyond selected case studies (Weiss and Jacobson 1998).

The idea that member states, through the process of interaction within an organization, learn to see themselves as others see them is called reflection. In part this is hypothesized to be a direct process and in part an indirect process. The more one realizes that others perceive one as cooperative or as obstreperous, for example, the more that reflected perception leads to reinforced or changed behavior. Furthermore, the more one behaves cooperatively, the more likely it is that others change their views and reflect back the actor's new image as a cooperator. That reflected improvement in perceptions, in turn, is hypothesized to lead to or to reinforce changes in behavior and in self-definition. Such a psychological process may go on, but we do not yet have sufficient evidence to conclude that reflection takes place and changes self-identity or interests (Wendt 1994). George Downs (2000), in fact, provides a thoughtful review and critique of the contructivist perspective about international organizations and their prospects for promoting changes in the national interest and in cooperation. He shows example after example in which such changes do not appear to have occurred. Furthermore, even if such changes in outlook occur for the agent representing a given government in an organization, it is not clear why the leadership of the country maintains the representative in office.

If a representative's orientation is out of alignment with the national leadership's perception of the "national interest," then it seems likely that the representative will be replaced. In such a circumstance the nation's leaders would retain such a representative only if the representative's actions did not deviate so much from their own interests that they felt the cost was too high. In that case, however, the national interest has not been materially changed. Thus, the constructivist notion of reflection could be true in influencing small, marginal changes within the confines of what the principal-agent relationship will tolerate. It cannot be true as regards a material shift away from the "national interest," however the national political leadership defines that interest. It is hard to tell empirically whether any change in the "national interest" has taken place, because reflection must fall within the principal's presumably narrow bounds of tolerance for shifts in approach by his or her agent in an international organization. Testing whether such reflection occurs at all or whether deviations from the wishes of the leadership back home are just indicative of the routine latitude of agents with special knowledge is a daunting empirical question. In this particular instance, neither the constructivist nor the principal-agent account can easily be falsified.

## THE STRATEGIC CASE

The strategic perspective helped us see that what constitutes the national interest can be manipulated by individual political leaders. They build coalitions around interests and can link issues together so that many different winning coalitions can be formed. As we saw in Chapter 6, a super-majority of relevant constituents can be assembled in favor of widely divergent and even contradictory policy stances through skillful political maneuvering. Observers might mistake the policies of any of these coalitions as being deviations from the national interest, but then such deviations can arise only if the national interest is assumed to have some specific content as opposed to being viewed as a product of strategic maneuvering and bargaining.

Skillful political leaders can shape the focus of the national interest on issues and policy positions that are advantageous for them because many different majority coalitions can be assembled by using linkage politics, that is, tying choices together across multiple issues as in win set analyses. This suggests both strengths and limitations to the influence that international agreements or organizations can have. Leaders come and go. Few leaders of democracies last even as long as five years. Autocrats last longer, but few even among autocrats survive in office beyond a decade or two. International organizations commonly survive several generations of national leaders. NATO, for example, was formed in 1949. Each member country has undergone many, many domestic turnovers in political leadership during the more than half century since NATO's creation. Yet NATO's fundamental rules remain the same. The Treaty of Westphalia was signed more than 350 years ago, yet many of its specifications regarding sovereignty, as discussed below, remain relevant to international interaction today. These examples remind us that international law and international organizations are not as ephemeral as are the terms in office of political leaders or as their view of the "national interest."

Organizations and law are sticky. By this I mean that it takes large changes in the interests of member states before it is possible to make substantial changes in the structure of law and organizations. The transaction costs associated with change often exceed the expected benefits. In this way international bodies are much like a factory. No business owner tears down a factory and rebuilds every time there is an improvement in technology. The cost of doing so is just too high. They live with some inefficiency in their factory rather than bear the cost of change. Only when the inefficiency becomes too costly does a business tear down and rebuild.[2] So it is with international organizations or law. New leaders come to power and find that some of the organizations or rules their predecessors endorsed are not optimal for their purposes. Still, the organizations may provide enough benefits that they live with them rather than trying to make politically costly changes or withdrawing.

The stickiness of international organizations has a deeper strategic implication. The decision to form or belong to international institutions is, as noted, endogenous. That is, political leaders make a strategic choice, presumably designed to enhance their own or their political party's prospects to remain in office and to ensure that, should they lose office, their policy preferences will persist. By forming or accepting the rules of an international organization or by endorsing a body of international law, current leaders impose these rules and laws as constraints on subsequent leaders. The value in imposing constraints on subsequent leaders, according to the strategic perspective, depends on the expected frequency, intensity, and uncertainty about deviations in the ideal points of future leaders. As we know, political leadership turns over more frequently in democracies. There are, therefore, more opportunities for someone to come to power whose coalition's interests deviate markedly from those currently in place. Autocrats, in contrast, tend to stay in office considerably longer than democratic leaders. Consequently, autocrats face less uncertainty about policy shifts because they will be in office longer to sustain their own policy objectives. International organizations—and international laws—are arguably more valuable to the leaders of democracies because the cost of abandoning the law or organization in the future constrains future leaders to adhere to the policies, rules, and regulations already in effect (Gartzke and Gleditsch 2002).

The bureaucrats who make up the "civil service" of a large international organization can play an active role as well in preserving

*The U.S. secretary of state, Dean Acheson, signs the NATO treaty on April 4, 1949. Standing to the immediate left of Acheson is President Harry Truman; Vice President Alben W. Barkley stands to the far left. The NATO treaty served as the foundation of American security policy throughout the cold war.*

---

[2] I am indebted to Barry Weingast for this argument.

such institutions even when the institution's reasons for existing may be ended or greatly altered. Interested agents may inflate the expected cost of doing away with an organization to give the appearance that getting rid of it is just not cost effective. This possibility alerts us that international regimes can be critical sources of conflict between the bureaucrats who run them and the leaders of member states (or NGOs). The former are in the role of agents and the latter are in the role of principals. To the extent that international regimes foster principal-agent problems, it is likely that such regimes only partially reflect national interests and so may be ineffective in promoting the goals of the membership. If principal-agent problems are prominent in international regimes, then we may indeed observe organizations adopting policies that deviate from the national interests of some member states as suggested by constructivists and neoliberal theorists. In such cases, if the strategic perspective is correct, the organization should prove to be unsuccessful in extracting meaningful compliance from the affected members.

## NATO AND ORGANIZATIONAL INERTIA: AN ILLUSTRATIVE CASE

NATO was created in 1949 to provide security for Europe and North America against the threat of Soviet expansion. NATO erected a large, complex bureaucracy, currently situated primarily in Brussels, Belgium. The armies of the member states are highly integrated, using common weapons and a common command structure. This and many other complex features of NATO were designed to make it an efficient and effective fighting force against the often-superior numbers of the Soviet military.

Many credit NATO with playing a central part in maintaining peace during the cold war and probably rightly so. But NATO did not cease to exist after the Soviet Union collapsed. Now, more than a decade after the Soviet Union's demise, NATO is still a large and powerful international organization. It has broadened its scope—of course it had to do so because its original purpose no longer exists—to include peacekeeping missions in, for instance, central Europe and to protect and defend the membership's shared democratic values. The mission is much broader and more vague than it was in 1949, but then, the membership has been expanded to include former members of the Warsaw Pact, NATO's long-time adversary. Even Russia, the successor state to the Soviet Union, is spoken of as a prospective member of NATO. The change in mission, indeed, is not unique to NATO. It is typical of alliances and other international organizations that they tend to persist beyond the issues for which they were formed (Bennett and Tarry, 1996).

When bureaucratic inertia helps an organization survive, it is likely that the organization will become less effective in pursuing its mission. It is also likely that compliance with the new activities of the organization will diminish as members contend over exactly what their obligations are. Such divisions were evident throughout the Bosnia and Kosovo crises of the 1990s. NATO's members were not of one mind with regard to whether they should or could intervene in these violent disputes. As a consequence, NATO was slow to act and failed to achieve consensus on how it ought to act. Although the organization was created to coordinate defense policies, divisions among the member states arising from NATO's uncertain mission during the war in Kosovo and its aftermath diminished the effectiveness of the fighting forces. Edward Luttwak, a foreign policy analyst, reported on April 11, 2000, that

> [t]he Albanian terror campaign against Serb and Roma civilians started as soon as the Serb forces withdrew. General Clark and the British Kosovo Force Commander therefore urged NATO forces to deploy as quickly as possible, and to patrol intensively to stop the mayhem. British troops maximized control of their sector by patrolling on foot in half squads by day and by night. But the U.S. Joint Chiefs insisted that the first priority was to ensure the protection and comfort of the U.S. garrison. While $36 million was being spent to erect the defenses and comfort facilities of Camp Bonesteel (complete with two PX stores, fast-food cafeterias, etc.), U.S. troops were only sent out on patrol in large detachments mounted on vehicles, which remained on the main roads. Albanian ethnic cleansing was virtually unopposed in the U.S. sector, in which no Serbs or Roma now remain. French patrol practices at first resembled those of the British. Once the French realized that the other NATO forces were avoiding effort and risk, they too stopped their intensive patrols. The phenomenon of "multi-national troop degradation" had set in. (http://www.theatlantic.com/ unbound/roundtable/goodfight/luttwak2.htm)

The circumstances described by Luttwak highlight a crucial issue for all international organizations. International regimes are erected to coordinate cooperation among members *especially when individual interests dictate that some members are better off not cooperating.* Yet, as the example of American and then French forces makes clear, the member states of NATO faced the prisoners' dilemma in the aftermath of the Kosovo war. The objective of NATO's forces was to act aggressively to stop ethnic cleansing. All members would benefit if the ethnic cleansing ended and the situation were stabilized. But members would also benefit by free riding on the efforts of others, avoiding the risks inherent in aggressive military patrols. As we know, if the prisoners' dilemma is not indefinitely repeated, players are most likely to choose to defect; that is, in this case they are likely not to patrol. The United States engaged in lax patrols while the British and French for a time took greater risks. Realizing that the Americans were avoiding circumstances that put them in harm's way, France reciprocated by also choosing a low-risk patrol strategy. The consequence was that

*Former Yugoslav leader Slobodan Milosevic, tried as a war criminal for his policies in Bosnia, Croatia, and Kosovo, is seen by most of the world as a heinous killer. Here we see a woman kissing his photograph. Obviously, not everyone was opposed to his policies or his tactics.*

457

I described the game between France and the United States over patrols in Kosovo as a prisoners' dilemma. Can you make the case that this is the wrong game to represent that situation? Might Battle of the Sexes better reflect the situation? Can you design your own simple game to capture the dynamics of the military patrol problem discussed by Luttwak? Consider a three-player game including the British, French, and Americans, or even a four-player game that expands the set to include Albanians engaged in ethnic cleansing.

NATO was poorly positioned to implement its objective effectively. This illustrative case points to the heart of the problem for international organizations: to enforce actions when in the immediate circumstance those actions are contrary to the interests of some members. With the NATO example of failed compliance in mind, I now turn to an example of a successfully implemented set of treaty obligations.

## SOVEREIGNTY: A SUCCESSFUL INTERNATIONAL INSTITUTION

In earlier chapters we saw some of the important aspects of the Treaty of Westphalia and noted that this treaty established many elements of international law regarding sovereignty. Here I quote in detail two articles of that treaty. Article 64 states:

> And to prevent for the future any Differences arising in the Politick State, all and every one of the Electors, Princes and States of the Roman Empire, are so establish'd and confirm'd in their antient, Prerogatives, Libertys, Privileges, free exercise of Territorial Right, as well Ecclesiastick, as Politick Lordships, Regales, by virtue of this present Transaction: that they never can or ought to be molested therein by any whomsoever upon any manner of pretence.

Article 67 says:

> That as well as general as particular Diets, the free Towns, and other States of the Empire, shall have decisive Votes; they shall, without molestation, keep their Regales, Customs, annual Revenues, Libertys, Privileges to confiscate, to raise Taxes, and other Rights, lawfully obtain'd from the Emperor and Empire, or enjoy'd long before these Commotions, with a full Jurisdiction within the inclosure of their Walls, and their Territorys: making void at the same time, annulling and for the future prohibiting all Things, which by Reprisals, Arrests, stopping of Passages, and other prejudicial Acts, either during the War, under what pretext soever they have been done and attempted hitherto by private Authority, or may hereafter without any preceding formality of Right be enterpris'd. As for the rest, all laudable Customs of the sacred Roman Empire, the fundamental Constitutions and Laws, shall for the future be strictly observ'd, all the Confusions which time of War have, or could introduce, being remov'd and laid aside.

These two articles provide, in modern parlance, that states are secure within their borders. The sovereign government within a state is free to make its own rules and regulations regarding virtually every aspect of life. Some of the examples enumerated in these articles include the rights of the sovereign to establish religious practices within the bounds of his or her territory and to raise taxes to advance the policies and programs to which the sovereign—that is, the governing authority—subscribes. Regardless of how repugnant these internal activities are to outsiders, the expectation established in these articles is that outsiders have no right to interfere in the domestic affairs of other states. What are the consequences, if any, of these stipulations? How have they shaped international politics? Is it likely that international politics would have looked the same whether these two articles of the Treaty of Westphalia had been formally written down or not?

## INTERNATIONAL BORDERS AS INSTITUTIONS

The two articles quoted above establish essential principles of international law and practice as still observed to this day. Article 64 is intended to bar foreign rivals from interfering in the sovereign's rights within his or her territory. Article 67 reinforces this point, emphasizing that the sovereign has full jurisdiction over all matters within the borders of the state. In this way territorial borders are created as an institution of international politics, an institution with standing in international law. That law, of course, is the treaty itself.

States are granted the right to defend their actions and privileges within their borders. Other states do not have the right to cross a country's border and impose their will on the sovereign territory of another government and people. Even today, more than three and a half centuries after the Treaty of Westphalia was signed, this has profound implications.

There are, of course, the obvious implications regarding war and aggression. The Treaty of Westphalia set out rules and regulations restricting the rights of states to use force against one another. These rules are generally obeyed. Aggression is regarded in principle as unacceptable conduct in international affairs and it is relatively rare. The relations among few states can long be characterized by the presence of aggression. Yet, territorial issues, especially the location of borders, are the most frequent sources of war (Vasquez 1995; Huth 1996). The body of international law that has grown up around the enforcement of territorial sovereignty accurately characterizes most international relationships most, but not all, of the time. Whether the enforcement or respect for borders is a consequence of the restrictions imposed by international law or the restrictions of international law reflect the interests of powerful states is difficult to sort out. Doing so requires that we assess how frequent territorial disputes would be in a counterfactual world (or a pre-Westphalian world) in which international laws and regulations regarding borders did not exist. Whatever effect international law has had on the sanctity of borders, it is clear that most people most of the time oppose on principled, normative grounds the violation of sovereignty by using aggression to cross national frontiers. In this way, the law has created a norm of conduct. So strong is the normative belief that the citizens of a state have the right to be secure within its borders that the violation of such borders is perceived generally as unwarranted aggression. Yet the law regarding sovereign rights within borders has a less obvious and perhaps morally reprehensible consequence, a consequence that suggests that the norms surrounding the sanctity of borders are gradually changing.

Consider the case of ethnic genocide. Under the leadership of Pol Pot (1976–1979), the Cambodian government engaged in genocide against its own people. Nearly two million Cambodians were killed during Pol Pot's reign of terror. Neither the United Nations nor the United States, nor anyone else other than Vietnam intervened against Pol Pot's genocide, ostensibly because they had no basis in international law to do so. The reason was as simple as it was troubling. The Pol Pot regime was exercising its right to do whatever it chose within its own borders. The Cambodian government, in keeping with Article 67 of the Treaty of Westphalia, was acting with "full Jurisdiction within the inclosure of their Walls, and their Territorys." The United Nations, then, seemingly had no jurisdiction. Just as law gave Pol Pot his rights in Cambodia, law denied the right to the nations of the world to intervene to save the people of Cambodia. Vietnam eventually intervened, deposing Pol Pot in the process and receiving condemnation from the United States and elsewhere for violating the sovereign territory of Cambodia.

*The United Nations Charter was signed in San Francisco's War Memorial on June 26, 1945. The Charter specifies the mission of the United Nations, creates its organizational structure, delineates the obligations of the member states, and carries the weight of international law.*

The United Nations, however, could have provided a legal basis to intervene in Cambodia had it been willing to interpret its authority a bit more broadly. The UN Convention on the Prevention and Punishment of the Crime of Genocide was approved by a vote of 55 to 0 in December 1948. The Convention defines genocide as the commission of certain acts with the intent to destroy, wholly or in part, a national, ethnic, racial, or religious group and deems it a crime under international law, whether committed in war or peace. Here, then, we have another difficulty with international law. The legal status of sovereignty protects states from foreign intervention in their domestic affairs. The law regarding genocide since 1948 theoretically empowers states to intervene in the domestic affairs of another state to prevent or stop genocide.[3] In fact, this contradiction was much on the mind of American senators who were responsible for ratifying the Convention. Although President Truman signed the Convention on December 12, 1948, the U.S. Senate did not ratify it until 1988. The Senate's hesitation was precisely concern over the Convention's prospects of leading to interference in American domestic affairs and the erosion of sovereignty.

The right of foreign governmental and nongovernmental interests to interfere in the internal actions of sovereign states, then, is changeable to reflect changing interests, sensibilities, and power. Perhaps, as constructivists argue, experience and reflection led participants in the Convention against genocide to internalize stronger norms about the value of human life, norms sufficiently strong that they could overcome the earlier norm against intervention in the internal policies of a state. Why one norm usurps another is a question unanswered by constructivism but may be answered by the strategic perspective.

Constructivism, as discussed earlier, is about the formation of preferences and not about the actions expected, given preferences. The strategic perspective does not explain where preferences come from, but it offers an equilibrium basis for thinking about how people act on their preferences. Together they may provide a coherent explanation of changing values and actions in international affairs.

As the world becomes more democratic it may be that it is harder to sustain old norms that favored thinking of states as unitary sovereigns. The more we think about state policies as the aggregation of individual interests, the more likely we are to elevate the importance of individuals over collective ideas like "the state." Thus, newly constructed values in favor of individual welfare over the collective national welfare might gain greater importance. Democratic practices place great emphasis on individual interests, whereas authoritarian arrangements compress the state and the dictator into a single actor. When the state is seen as a unitary actor, it is difficult to sustain a norm that addresses the welfare of individual constituents. When we think of state policies as

---

[3] I say, "theoretically empowers states to intervene in the domestic affairs of another state" because when the genocide convention was established the members had the holocaust of World War II in mind. It is not evident that they envisioned a circumstance in which a government committed genocide exclusively against its own people.

reflecting aggregated individual preferences, then the constructivist focus suggests that norms and values are likely to be reshaped. They are expected to become attentive to individual welfare. The strategic perspective then identifies the circumstances under which governments that are so inclined can act to enforce these reshaped norms that place value on individual welfare. The genocide Convention, of course, is illustrative of just such a set of normative values.

International law has frequently been changed and its domain expanded. The Convention on genocide, signed by the vast majority of the world's nations, was not actually used as a basis for an international legal action until September 1998 when Rwanda's Hutu leaders were charged with genocide in connection with their actions against Rwanda's Tutsi population. This marked an important shift in the use of international law to deal with gross misconduct within a nation's borders. A different example may be even more significant because it shows the use of international regimes to alter the behavior of a great power. Consider how the Helsinki Final Act of 1975 expanded the rights of a few nations and private organizations to interfere in the domestic affairs of the signatory states, including the Soviet Union.

## THE EXPANSION OF INTERNATIONAL LAW:
## THE EXAMPLE OF HELSINKI

The Soviet Union agreed, along with thirty-four other states, to the Helsinki Final Act in order to ensure recognition of the independence of its ally, the German Democratic Republic, then known in the West as East Germany. In exchange for this recognition, the Soviets probably unwittingly set the stage for tremendous international pressure designed to foster democratization and the spread of freedom across the Soviet empire. The Helsinki Final Act expanded international law to permit governmental and non-governmental interference in the face of human rights violations in any of the signatory states. Without the agreement in Helsinki, it would have been difficult—as it had been for decades prior to the Final Act in Helsinki—to speak out authoritatively against the internal policies of the Soviet Union and its East European satellites.

The thirty-five signatories to the Final Act reached seemingly innocuous agreements stipulating that

> [t]he participating States will respect human rights and fundamental freedoms, in-cluding the freedom of thought, conscience, religion or belief, for all without dis-tinction as to race, sex, language, or religion.
>
> They will promote and encourage the effective exercise of civil, political, economic, social, cultural, and other rights and freedoms all of which derive from the inherent dignity of the human person and are essential for his free and full development. . . .
>
> The participating States recognize the universal significance of human rights and fundamental freedoms, respect for which is an essential factor for the peace, justice and well-being necessary to ensure the development of friendly relations and co-

operation among themselves as among all States. (http://www.civnet.org/resources/historic/helsinki.htm)

Through these seemingly innocent terms, the Helsinki Final Act permitted Western states and nongovernmental organizations like Amnesty International to assert something approximating a right to oversee and to influence domestic policies regarding human rights in any or all of the signatory states (Clark 2003). The act authorized them "to promote and encourage the effective exercise of civil, political, economic, social, cultural, and other rights and freedoms," and so they promoted and encouraged these rights and freedoms with vigor. Because the Soviet Union and its allies in the Warsaw Pact agreed to the Final Act, the other signatories had a legitimate basis to question human rights policies in those states without being accused of infringing on the internal sovereign rights of the Soviets and their allies in Europe. After all, the Soviets and their allies agreed to these conditions by signing the act. Signing the act, then, proved to be a costly action for the Soviets (Thomas 2001).

Human rights watchdog groups (NGOs) sprang up almost immediately within the Warsaw Pact countries and in the West. Both the former and the latter groups reported on human rights violations in the Soviet Union and especially in its allied states. They fomented government-to-government pressures to improve human rights conditions. Movements such as Solidarity in Poland and equivalent forces for free expression throughout Eastern Europe were bolstered by intense, legitimate scrutiny from the outside world, scrutiny fostered by the Final Act. Whereas the Soviets easily argued against foreign intervention during similar efforts to promote freedom in Hungary in 1956 or Czechoslovakia in 1968, their signature on the Helsinki Final Act made such arguments hollow in the late 1970s and early 1980s. Thus, the Helsinki Final Act established the foundation for international pressure to see democratic principles spread to the Soviet Union and Eastern Europe. Just how successful these pressures were perhaps can be gleaned by looking at how the world has changed since 1975. Of course, many other considerations contributed to the downfall of the Soviet Union and to the end of the cold war, some of which were discussed in Chapter 6. Still, the Helsinki Final Act stands out as an example in which international regulations and agreements seem to have influenced significantly the course of international relations in a manner not easily accounted for by a neorealist focus on international power and bipolar structure. Nor is it easily explained by constructivism's reliance on redefinition of the national interest or neoliberal theory's emphasis on hegemony. Indeed, at the time of the Helsinki Act, neoliberal scholars were arguing that American hegemony was in decline (Keohane 1984).

From the strategic perspective we can infer that the Soviets either were willing to make a costly commitment regarding human rights oversight in exchange for the recognition of East German sovereignty or they believed that once such sovereignty was granted it would be costly for the Western democracies to renege. They may have believed it would be less costly for them to renege on their side of the bargain. Soviet and

East European leaders ruled in autocracies, which were not subject to severe internal political sanction—such as the loss of reelection—if they violated agreements, so they may have believed they were free to continue business as usual in their approach to human rights. That the West was prepared to make it costly for Soviet regimes to back down on their commitment may not have been adequately foreseen or may have been a price the Soviets and their allies were prepared to pay. That is, they may have perceived the benefits of East German recognition as larger than the costs of permitting greater external intervention in internal affairs. This calculation may have been correct as far as it went. Of course, other developments, such as the incredibly poor performance of the Soviet economy, may have soaked up any surplus benefits the Soviets anticipated from the Final Act. Poor economic performance by the Soviets and their client states may have left them more vulnerable to external pressure than would have been the case had their own and their client states' economies been doing better. The United States, in particular, had the leverage that came from contracts to sell large quantities of agricultural products—essentially subsidies—to the Soviet Union to help prevent serious shortfalls in grains.

Helsinki is an exemplar for those who believe that international law makes a difference on important matters. For those more focused on a strategic perspective it is an example of how international law can be used to create trade-offs and gambles that can prove highly productive or that can backfire. It is likely that the United States and its allies at Helsinki agreed to recognize East Germany because doing so had little cost and because they attached great value to the possibilities created by the right to challenge East European and Soviet human rights practices. The Soviet leadership may have gone along because they thought the human rights elements would prove harmless and they could diminish their spending on the defense of East Germany against the threat of a West European or American incursion while gaining a propaganda coup. In the end, the Soviet leaders proved to have made a bad choice, but of course they could not have known that at the time. Coupled with their declining economic strength and America's military expansion under President Reagan a few years later, the Soviet Union's leaders were struggling on so many fronts that they could no longer resist the pressures for change (Gorbachev 1996; Skinner, Kudelia, Bueno de Mesquita, and Rice 2002).

With the examples of Westphalia and Helsinki in mind, we can now examine more closely the purposes of international law and international organizations. We can also investigate the conditions under which international rules and regulations are likely to matter.

## THE PURPOSE OF INTERNATIONAL RULES AND INSTITUTIONS

We learned about coordination and distribution problems in Chapter 13. Now we return to those topics for a look at how they might be solved through international rules and institutions. Sometimes it is politically beneficial for leaders of different countries to find a way to coordinate their activities. When issues involve only coordination, without any differences in the benefits to be derived from cooperating with others, then reaching international agreements to regulate behavior is rather easy. Air traffic control, as mentioned earlier, is a good example of an international agreement that no one has a strong incentive to violate. Cooperation is easily achieved when it is in everyone's interest and when no one has an incentive to cheat; that is, when no one can get extra benefits by free riding or by secretly breaking the agreement. The interesting challenge for those who hope to promote international cooperation is to design agreements and institutions to enforce them when incentives exist to cheat or to free ride. The Soviet Union, for instance, had strong incentives to renege on its promise to promote and respect human rights even though it wanted other nations that signed the Helsinki Final Act to respect East German sovereignty. Iraq's invasion of Kuwait in 1990 to gain control of some Kuwaiti oil fields apparently reflected Saddam Hussein's incentives to violate borders and the international laws and norms that grew up around the Treaty of Westphalia. Members of OPEC want to coordinate in increasing the price of oil by keeping supply down, but inevitably some members cheat by producing more than their quota to reap the economic advantages that follow from gaining more market share. They rarely incur punishment for cheating.

International institutions are sometimes established to resolve problems in which individual interests lead to inefficient outcomes. Consider the difference between markets and situations regulated by an international organization. Markets provide an efficient means to solve many forms of competition in international affairs. For instance, as we saw in the previous chapter, free trade generally leads to efficient pricing and efficient supply of goods. The problem that confronts the marketplace for trade is that politicians often protect domestic businesses and labor from competition so as to gain domestic political advantage. One potential solution to that problem is for politicians to limit their own freedom of action by joining international organizations that promote free trade and that punish states for violating international rules that favor free trade. The marketplace differs from a free trade international organization in that the market is not capable of restraining a politician's temptation to gain political advantage from protectionism; an international organization may have that capability. I illustrate this point by reflecting on how NAFTA may serve this purpose.

Because the United States belongs to NAFTA, American presidents might successfully shift responsibility away from themselves for the free trade policies they apply to Canada and Mexico as dictated by NAFTA. The president can reasonably argue that it would be costly to America's reputation as a country that respects the rule of law if the United States were to withdraw from NAFTA or if it were to selectively enforce or violate the terms of NAFTA. Thus, the president can insulate himself from political accountability for free trade with Mexico or Canada by pointing to his predecessors who signed and abided by NAFTA. Their actions created precedents that now are part of American practice and that, if violated, could jeopardize America's *reputation* and America's ability to invoke NAFTA if another signatory violates its terms. In this way, the international agreement would have altered the short-term actions of the president by providing a way for him to liberate himself from political accountability for what might be an unpopular policy. The same, of course, also holds true for the president of Mexico or the prime minister of Canada.

Leaders, however, are unlikely to concern themselves with matters of "national reputation" if the costs for maintaining such a reputation are high. Tying hands through precedent is unlikely to carry much weight when doing so harms the leader's political interests. America's reputation for cooperation in NAFTA may carry weight in influencing how others think about the United States when it comes to trade agreements in other arenas, like the WTO. However, it is unlikely that a reputation in one arena carries over as a generalized national reputation. This is so for several reasons. National civil service bureaucracies tend to have slow turnover in personnel. As a result, it is likely that the same people will help shape and implement policy in the bureaucracy's arena for many years. Therefore they are likely to form a reputation that is tied to a set of people that changes only slowly. But there is no special reason to think that the policies formed in the trade arena and the policies formed, say, in the national security arena are made by the same people with the same interests at stake. Thus it is unlikely that a nation has a reputation overall for cooperation or anything else.

Furthermore, leaders at the national level turn over with much greater rapidity on average than do civil servants. This is especially true in democratic polities. As a consequence, some portion of what is thought of as national reputation adheres to the individual leader rather than the state. That part of "national" reputation changes when leaders change. It is unlikely, for instance, that America's reputation in foreign policy is the same under George W. Bush as it was under Bill Clinton or any earlier president. Of course, any president inherits treaty commitments that ties his hands, but he also has latitude to negotiate changes in prior agreements, much as George W. Bush decided that the United States ought not to adhere to the Anti-Ballistic Missile Treaty that was promulgated during the cold war. Creating a national reputation is a weak thread on which to build organizational commitments. Reputations limited to specific agencies of government, however, may provide a sounder basis for influencing national decisions about organizational regulations in specific, circumscribed issue areas.

I have mentioned that the president's hands can be tied by the prior actions of past presidents. This is especially true when foreign policies are enshrined as law by signing a treaty. The president (or other executive) is legally bound to enforce the terms of treaties. In fact, in the United States, treaty obligations take precedence over other restrictions in the American Constitution. Interests that benefit from NAFTA, for example, can bring suit in U.S. courts if they believe that the executive branch is not properly following the law. This means that the executive branch must convince the judicial branch that its actions do not violate the law. At the same time, if the president wants to change the law, he has to renegotiate the treaty with a foreign power and, if he succeeds in doing so, he then must get the modified treaty ratified by Congress. These are difficult, time-consuming steps. Consequently, the executive is likely to enforce the current provisions of the treaty to the degree that his— or his constituency's—ideal point does not differ dramatically from the treaty's obligations and to the degree that he expects to be challenged in court for failing to do so.

International organizations are sometimes formed to promote efficient market outcomes where otherwise individual incentives lead to less efficient solutions. Not all problems, however, have a market solution as the alternative. Consider the problem of war. International conflict is always inefficient ex post (that is, after the fact) but does not easily fit into a market-oriented account of the world. States go to war presumably because the leaders in the belligerent countries believe that it serves their best interest to fight rather than give in to the other side. That is, ex ante (before the fact), they expect that conflict or even war will prove to be an efficient way to reduce uncertainty about what the resolution of a dispute should be. Yet it is likely that each potential belligerent also realizes that there are better ways to solve problems. Imagine, for instance, that Israel and the Palestinian Authority are on the verge of war over their respective territorial claims in Jerusalem, an all-too-common occurrence. Each side surely recognizes that whatever settlement they ultimately reach after decades of violence is not as good as reaching the exact same agreement right now without violence. One problem faced by each side is that there is insufficient trust to make transparent the information needed to determine what the contents of such an agreement might be. Neither side can credibly commit to reveal reliable information to the other side. Another problem, pertinent to the current discussion, is that neither side seems willing to trust the role of an international organization like the United Nations to help discover and enforce the as-yet undiscovered prospective agreement.

The Palestinian Authority's leaders might want to appeal to the United Nations General Assembly for its judgment on the contents of an agreement. That body makes decisions based on a majority vote of the member states. The General Assembly can pass resolutions that specify expected conduct. A majority of General Assembly members seem sympathetic to the plight of the Palestinians. So, too, do many members of the Security Council, although that body is more guarded in what it is prepared to approve, for reasons explained below. A problem for the Palestinians arises, however, if they turn to the UN for help. The issue is unlikely to remain before the General Assembly. The Palestinian leaders are much less confident of a supportive outcome in the Security Council.

Let us consider as an example of UN decision making regarding the dispute between Israel and the Palestinians the oft-invoked and never enforced Resolution 242 passed on November 22, 1967. It states:

> The Security Council,
> Expressing its continuing concern with the grave situation in the Middle East,
> Emphasizing the inadmissibility of the acquisition of territory by war and the need to work for a just and lasting peace in which every State in the area can live in security,

Emphasizing further that all Member States in their acceptance of the Charter of the United Nations have undertaken a commitment to act in accordance with Article 2 of the Charter,

1. Affirms that the fulfillment of Charter principles requires the establishment of a just and lasting peace in the Middle East which should include the application of both the following principles:

(i) Withdrawal of Israel armed forces from territories occupied in the recent conflict;

(ii) Termination of all claims or states of belligerency and respect for and acknowledgment of the sovereignty, territorial integrity and political independence of every State in the area and their right to live in peace within secure and recognized boundaries free from threats or acts of force;

2. Affirms further the necessity

(a) For guaranteeing freedom of navigation through international waterways in the area;

(b) For achieving a just settlement of the refugee problem;

(c) For guaranteeing the territorial inviolability and political independence of every State in the area, through measures including the establishment of demilitarized zones;

3. Requests the Secretary-General to designate a Special Representative to proceed to the Middle East to establish and maintain contacts with the States concerned in order to promote agreement and assist efforts to achieve a peaceful and accepted settlement in accordance with the provisions and principles in this resolution;

4. Requests the Secretary-General to report to the Security Council on the progress of the efforts of the Special Representative as soon as possible.

Adopted unanimously at the 1382nd meeting.

This resolution provides the foundation in international law for the idea that the Israeli-Palestinian conflict can be resolved through a deal of land for peace. The resolution specifies that Israel must return to its borders as they were before the Six-Day War fought between Arabs and Israelis in 1967, when Israel was a much smaller country (with not only less territory but also far fewer people). Israel seems unwilling to abide by Resolution 242 because each of its governments since 1967 has thus far concluded that some of the territory captured by Israel during the 1967 war—such as the Golan Heights between Israel and Syria—is vital to providing Israel's citizens with secure borders. Further, it remains unconvinced that a promise of peace in exchange for land reflects a *credible commitment* for peace from the Arab states. Israel's government points to the many occasions on which, from its perspective, Yasser Arafat has reneged on promises and infers from these occasions that he and his Arab backers do not value a reputation for reliability in fulfilling international commitments. The United Nations membership and its secretary general are powerless to enforce this or any resolution if enforcement does not have the support of the five permanent members of the Security Council. Thus, although the UN—especially the General Assembly—provides an opportunity for deliberations and a place where world leaders can exchange views, it lacks the teeth to enforce its judgments.

Israel might be willing to refer its grievances to the Security Council provided that it is confident the United States (or some other permanent member) will veto any action called for by that body that is contrary to Israel's interests. The United States did not veto Resolution 242, but then, neither has it taken action to enforce Israeli withdrawal from the territories captured during the 1967 war. Nor, for that matter, does the resolution speak clearly with regard to another fundamental issue in dispute: the Palestinian Authority's leaders claim of a "right of return" for all Palestinian refugees. The Israelis refuse to recognize this claim because it could mean that Israel would be deluged by millions of Palestinians, the majority of whom never actually lived in what is today's Israel.

The Palestinian Authority might be reluctant to rely on the Security Council, where it has no staunch friends among the permanent members. They might point to the failure of the United Nations to enforce Resolution 242 as evidence that the Security Council's permanent members—especially the United States—are not serious in their claim to seek peace. For the Palestinians (or the Israelis), the Security Council's decisions seem more important as propaganda tools in their conflict than as genuine means of resolving the dispute.

The Security Council includes rotating membership from each region of the world plus five permanent members. The rotating members are selected by regional organizations of countries. This means, in effect, that Israel is the only country in the world with no prospect of selection for a term of membership. The Arab states constitute the geographic region Israel naturally falls in, but they do not collectively recognize Israel's existence and so never select Israel for membership in the Security Council. Any one of the five permanent members—China, France, Russia, the United Kingdom, and the United States—can veto any proposal before the Security Council. Israel, of course, might choose to resist an action approved by the Security Council. Even if a majority of the Council, including the five permanent members, voted to enforce Resolution 242 (as they did), Israel could still balk and refuse to turn over any territory to, for instance, Syria. Ultimately, the ability of the United Nations to enforce its will depends on the preparedness of each of the five permanent members to support the mobilization of a military force under United Nations command to enforce the Council's decisions.

The Security Council's effectiveness is seriously limited by its structure. Its limitations, of course, are by design; they are not an accident. The right of each permanent member to veto any Security Council decision ensures that such decisions can be meaningful only if they serve the interest of each permanent member. This suggests that national interests (that is, the interests of the leaders of the moment) and national power, and not the United Nations itself, is the mechanism by which international policies are enforced. But if that is the case, then why bother to have an international organization in the first place? This is the most crucial question regarding international organizations and international law when issues involve more than just coordination. The Palestinian-Israeli case highlights how cooperation can break down when cooperation requires that one or both sides to a dispute also sacrifice individual gains. The purpose of international rules and regulations and the organizations that promulgate them is to promote international cooperation, sometimes by acting as an impartial mediator and sometimes by acting as an interested party with authority to mete out punishment to violators. Cooperation is difficult to achieve when distributive issues crop up that make the benefits from cooperation greater for some than others. In such cases, as may be true of the Security Council's permanent members' commitment to Resolution 242, rules and regulations may be little more than cheap talk.

Because cooperation is difficult to achieve when organizations face distribution issues, at the outset an organization's design must reflect the best judgments of the members regarding how to address the problems that are likely to arise, keeping in mind that their best judgment reflects what is best for them within the organization rather that what is best for everyone. That is, in designing the structure of an international organization, members must be strategic about the choices they make. In particular, there are five primary factors that must be considered when designing an international organization. These are:

*The population of East Timor, a former territory of Indonesia, suffered during a genocidal war before falling under the protection of the United Nations. The new nation is an example of a successful intervention by the UN. In May 2002 people throughout East Timor celebrated their independence.*

1.  How inclusive is the organization's membership?
2.  How are decisions made?
3.  How likely is compliance with the organization's decisions?
4.  How is punishment imposed for noncompliance?
5.  How effective are the rules and regulations established by the organization?

I now address each of these concerns.

## HOW INCLUSIVE SHOULD AN INTERNATIONAL REGIME BE?

Some international organizations, like the United Nations, are extraordinarily inclusive. Almost every state in the world is a member of the UN, although the Republic of China on Taiwan, for instance, is not, because the People's Republic of China claims it as a breakaway province. Other organizations, like NAFTA, have an exclusive membership consisting of very few participants. Still others fall everywhere and anywhere in between. The WTO is very large; OPEC is of moderate size, as is NATO and the Organization of American States; the European Union is smaller, although still significantly larger than NAFTA or Mercosur.

Larger organizations leave less leeway for states to avoid punishment if they are caught cheating, but they also make it more difficult to establish rules that effectively alter behavior than do smaller organizations. In general, organizations achieve high levels of compliance when their decisions are shallow (Downs, Rocke, and Barsoom, 1996). By "shallow" I mean that the decisions do not much constrain actions by the member states so that the problem addressed by the rule or regulation is not effectively resolved. Larger organizations are more likely to make shallow decisions than are smaller, more selective organizations. It is easy to comply with rules that do not demand a costly change in behavior, and it is difficult to get many states to agree to rules that require significant and costly changes in behavior. Likewise, we generally can expect that decision rules are easier to satisfy when decisions are less likely to be enforced than when they are more likely to be enforced or when, even with enforcement, the decisions are not particularly effective. Let us consider each of these factors in turn.

The inclusiveness or exclusiveness of an international organization is a design issue that turns out to be controversial. Consider the implications for decision making that arise as the size of the decision-making body increases. An international organization with a small membership, like NAFTA, limits participation to governments or private organizations with little diversity in their preferences for organizational policy. As more members are added to an organization, the expected diversity in policy preferences increases. Indeed, there is a real risk as an organization becomes larger that new members with preferences far from those of the founding members will block progress toward cooperation that might more easily have been achieved with just a few members

(E. Bueno de Mesquita and Stephenson 2002). Larger membership, then, diminishes the chances that the participants will reach agreement on rules and regulations to promote meaningful steps toward international cooperation.

Consider the exclusion of Britain from the original Coal and Steel Agreement that served as the forerunner to the European Union. Britain was opposed to virtually every important decision made by the Coal and Steel Community and then the European Community (EC) during the first twenty or so years of the existence of these organizations. Had Britain been brought in as a member at the outset in 1951 it is likely that the British—because of domestic political concerns about their coal and steel industries—would have disrupted progress toward European integration. It is difficult to imagine that the 1957 Treaty of Rome, signed by Belgium, France, Germany, Italy, Luxembourg, and the Netherlands, could have gained British approval. The Treaty of Rome propelled European integration forward, adding the European Atomic Energy Community (Euratom) and the European Economic Community (EEC) to the Coal and Steel Community. Furthermore, the treaty explicitly promoted the idea of closer integration across Europe's states and singled out national exchange rate policies as a matter to be worked on, presumably with an eye toward creation of a single currency (as occurred finally in 2002). Even after Britain joined the EC in 1972, it acted against the policy wishes of a significant number of member states and probably succeeded in diminishing the effectiveness of the organization on important decisions, especially those regarding currency integration. Indeed, currency integration was a major issue that split the British Conservative Party in the early 1990s and contributed to the party's decision to oust Prime Minister Margaret Thatcher—who opposed currency integration—in favor of John Major.

Whether larger or smaller organizations are preferable is openly debated. A constructivist perspective differs sharply from the realist view that large membership in an organization reduces effectiveness. Realists maintain that inclusiveness waters down decisions by allowing too much diversity in policy preferences. After all, from the realist perspective, states act on their national interest and the more states that are included in an organization, the less likely it is that the organization can reflect the national interests of its member states. Constructivists, in contrast, maintain that cooperation is stimulated by participation in international organizations. From this perspective, inclusiveness is a highly desirable property of international organizations. Constructivism suggests that preferences are not exogenous to the situation in which decision makers find themselves. Rather, constructivists believe, preferences are shaped and reshaped by participation in and deliberation with alternative viewpoints, as suggested earlier in the discussion of identity formation and the redefinition of the national interest. Wendt (1994), recall, suggests that members of an international organization learn to see themselves as others see them through the process of interaction such as is promoted by an inclusive international organization. The effect of such interactions on self-perception is strongest in situations involving dependence on the views of other actors, again as can be true in large international organizations. From this point of view, organizations like the UN General Assembly might be expected to be especially effective in fostering cooperation by exposing representatives from so many states to the perspectives of others. Although constructivists and realists each muster case studies to support their own point of view, neither the hypothesis in favor of inclusiveness nor that in favor of exclusiveness has been subjected to rigorous analysis.

At first blush one might infer that the strategic perspective favors inclusive organizations. As we saw earlier, systems that rely on a large coalition drawn from a large selectorate tend to produce more public welfare. In the international context it is sometimes true that cooperation among member states is a public good for all the participants in an international organization. But that claim assumes that members of an organization agree on what policies contribute public goods. That is, it assumes that the preferences of the median "voter" are the goals that leaders must fulfill. This makes perfectly good sense in settings in which members of the selectorate cannot easily withdraw and cannot freely violate the policy decisions made by their leaders. States can and do, however, sometimes withdraw from international organizations, and they decidedly can and do violate the policies of those organizations. Violations of the law probably are more easily detected within a state than they are among the members of an international organization. This is true because the amount an organization spends on detecting violations is likely to be smaller the more diverse the interests of its membership. Punishment is also difficult to mete out in international organizations, as discussed below. On balance, then, the strategic perspective favors inclusiveness of membership (the selectorate) only if the rules also ensure inclusiveness in the winning coalition of members whose support is needed to keep the leadership of the organization in office (the winning coalition). The United Nations, for example, fails to meet these requirements. Its leadership in the Secretariat requires broad support among the membership, but as a practical matter, no one can be effective as secretary general without the support of an oligarchy of permanent members of the Security Council. Thus, it has characteristics similar to those of an autocracy in which many have a chance to join a winning coalition, but a small group is essential and is guaranteed a primary role in choosing leaders and, therefore, policies. In such an environment, the organization is likely to be ineffective in promoting policies that are contrary to the interests of the oligarchs who occupy a privileged position. As Ethan Bueno de Mesquita and Matthew Stephenson (2002) show, informal networks or formal organizations bound by costly contract rules have an optimal size. If they are too large, the costs of monitoring and punishing deviant behavior become large as the expectation of deviant behavior increases with the variability in preferences. If they are too small, then there are few "gains from trade" or economies of scale in coordinating cooperative behavior so that the benefits are inadequate to sustain cooperation. What constitutes the optimal size of an organization depends in an identifiable way on trade-offs between the costs, benefits, and risks created by the organization.

## ORGANIZATIONAL DECISION-MAKING RULES

In any international regime, decision rules are likely to be chosen strategically. The more consequential the policy being regulated, the more stringent the decision rule is likely to be. Consider once again the example of decision making in the UN General Assembly and in the Security Council.

### THE UNITED NATIONS AND DECISION-MAKING RULES

A simple majority of member states in the General Assembly can pass resolutions on any policy question that comes before them. The secretary general of the United Nations might point to these resolutions as demonstrations of the UN's ability to form international policy regarding human rights, the environment, security issues, or just about anything else. Yet, we have also seen that the General Assembly is not endowed with the means to enforce its resolutions so that achieving compliance could be a difficult problem in the case of resolutions that demand significant changes in behavior by member states. As a result, we can expect that most resolutions passed by the General Assembly are shallow, are passed by a huge margin, and experience a high degree of compliance; or they are deep, important policy statements with no teeth behind them to ensure compliance. The vast majority of General Assembly resolutions are unlikely to be effective either because they do not call for a substantial change in behavior over what individual national political calculations already call for or because they are unenforceable. These claims imply that the decision rule is endogenous; that is, it is strategically chosen, taking into account the depth of the issues to which it is likely to be applied.

The decision rule in the Security Council is much more demanding than that used by the General Assembly. The Security Council has fifteen members, five of whom are permanent members. The Charter of the United Nations gives the Security Council primary responsibility for maintaining international peace and security. It therefore has the right to order economic sanctions, send peacekeepers, or take other actions to protect or restore peace. Because of its primary responsibility for promoting peace and security, the United Nations requires that a representative from each of the Security Council's member states be present at all times at UN headquarters in case the Council is compelled to meet unexpectedly in response to a crisis. Because the issues that come before the Council are often of profound consequence, its rules are constructed to ensure that its actions are based on a strong consensus.

If a simple majority were all that was required for decisions in the Security Council, then the Security Council would operate the way the General Assembly operates. The Security Council, however, has the opportunity to make much more consequential decisions. If the Security Council votes to enforce its decisions, then the UN can raise an "army" of peacekeepers or peacemakers and put them in harm's way in combat situations. It has done so in Kosovo to try to maintain peace in that embattled land. It has done so in numerous disputes in Africa, Asia, and elsewhere around the world. Most notably, it did so in Korea during the Korean War (1950–1953) in a successful effort to push the North Koreans back to the prewar boundary between North and South Korea—that is, to the 38th parallel.

Security Council decisions require a majority of all its voting members and no dissent among the five permanent members. This means that fourteen of the fifteen members at any one time could vote for an action and still the action could be defeated if one permanent member voted against it. Thus, the Security Council's rules require unanimous assent or abstention among the permanent members. Because it can be difficult to get unanimous approval (or abstention) among the five permanent members, we can expect that considerable horse-trading takes place before a vote, watering down proposals until no permanent member will exercise a veto. The unanimity rule for permanent members, then, ensures that Security Council decisions have teeth behind them and, therefore, on controversial matters Security Council decisions are likely to be shallow. They will enjoy compliance among the members but prove ineffective. When Security Council decisions are not shallow they can be effective. If the permanent members are genuinely behind a UN resolution and the resolution is not the product of a substantial compromise, then compliance with the resolution is likely and the resolution itself is likely to be effective. Of course, in such cases, the decision of the Council is in the interest of the five permanent members. Otherwise it would be vetoed. This suggests that the Security Council can effectively perform a coordination/facilitation function, but it is unlikely to redefine the policies of the permanent members.

Consider the UN Security Council decision in June 1950 to mount a force to engage in what was called a "police action" in Korea. This action constituted the United Nations first consequential multilateral military mission. As such it is an important case to understand because it both set precedent and created deeper awareness among member states about how to use and how not to use the Security Council.

One might well wonder how the Security Council could approve this use of force when the Soviet Union—a permanent member with a veto—was allied with China, the key backer of the North Korean invasion of the South. At the time, China's seat as a permanent member was occupied by the Republic of China on Taiwan and not by the People's Republic of China (PRC), then sometimes referred to as Mainland China or Red China. The PRC did not displace the government on Taiwan as China's permanent member until 1971. Had the PRC been a permanent member (it was not even admitted to membership in the United Nations until 1971) in 1950 it certainly would have vetoed the United Nation's use of military force to counter the invasion of South Korea by North Korea, an invasion fully supported by the PRC. The only friend communist North Korea had at the time among the Security Council's permanent members was the Soviet Union. In a remarkable blunder, the Soviet delegate was under orders to boycott meetings of the Council to protest the PRC's exclusion and the inclusion of Taiwan. Apparently the

Soviets believed that a failure to vote carried the same weight as a veto. The absence of the Soviet delegate opened the door for a vote without a Soviet veto, a mistake the Soviets would not make again. Because of the Soviet ambassador's error, the Security Council was able to put a policy in force that had real teeth, and because any other permanent member could subsequently veto any Soviet effort to undo their error, the UN could sustain its "police action." In essence, the Security Council resolution made it possible for the United States and its allies to wage a war against North Korea to restore the status quo prior to the North Korean invasion of South Korea and to do so under the UN's umbrella.

Even here, then, we must question the effectiveness of the Security Council's action. Had the Security Council failed to support military action in defense of South Korea, the United States probably would have committed its own troops anyway. The UN provided greater apparent legitimacy to the U.S. action, but it probably did not alter what the United States and its allies did. In that sense, the Security Council did not alter behavior so much as it provided a gloss of international legitimacy to the action that would have been taken in any case.

We have seen that the decision rules in different parts of the UN are different and that they almost certainly represent negotiated deals among the members. That the rules are endogenous seems a certainty. That this means they cannot influence future behavior is less clear. Let us now consider some of the ways that organizational decision rules influence action and how they can be more than just a codification of the intentions of powerful organization members.

## THE CHERNOBYL DISASTER AND STRUCTURE-INDUCED EQUILIBRIUM

Realists maintain that the rules and regulations promulgated by international organizations reflect the distribution of power among member states. If an organization calls for action contrary to a powerful member's interests, then, according to realists, the organization either will be changed or ignored. Liberals disagree. They contend that such organizations are developed to facilitate coordination among member states, with the most powerful member—sometimes referred to as a hegemon—providing the public good of assuming the costs of coordination. If that is right, international organizations at least can promote cooperation when their most powerful members bear the costs of coordinating behavior. In this view, the role of the hegemon can help alter the expected utility calculations of member states, making the expected utility from cooperation larger than it would be in the absence of a coordinator. Constructivism contends that the very preferences or interests of member states are reshaped by their participation in an international organization. The organization reconstitutes the initially divergent interests of members, creating a desire for cooperation even in situations in which, left to their own devices, individual states would be in contention with one another. Organizations achieve cooperation in this view not just by altering the probability that cooperation can be achieved, as is argued by liberals, but by changing the desire for cooperation among the members. Each of these arguments sounds plausible, although the evidence for each is scattered and tentative, depending generally on case studies selected to reinforce a particular point of view rather than selected with an eye to falsifying a perspective's claims. Still, let us see how rules might help to reshape behavior. To do so, I take an example from an environmental policy decision made by the European Community in the wake of the nuclear accident in Chernobyl, Ukraine, in 1986. The decision concerns limitations on the level and type of radioactive contaminants in food that would be tolerated by the EC.

A combination of staff conducting an unauthorized experiment, poor reactor design, and poor emergency-preparedness training of the on-site staff led in April 1986 to a near meltdown of the nuclear reactor in Chernobyl. The result was an explosion and an improper shutdown that sent a cloud of radioactive dust across most of Europe. Although the United Nations now attributes about forty deaths to the Chernobyl accident, the UN Scientific Committee on the Effects of Atomic Radiation reported the following on June 6, 2000:

> There is no scientific evidence of increases in overall cancer incidence or mortality or in non-malignant disorders that could be related to radiation exposure. The risk of leukaemia, one of the main concerns owing to its short latency time, does not appear to be elevated, not even among the recovery operation workers. Although those most highly exposed individuals are at an increased risk of radiation associated effects, the great majority of the population are not likely to experience serious health consequences from radiation from the Chernobyl accident.

The specter of nuclear disaster understandably heightened concern in Europe for the risks of radioactively contaminated food products being imported from Eastern Europe and the Soviet Union. It took the then twelve members of the European Community—Belgium, Denmark, France, Germany, Greece, Ireland, Italy, Luxembourg, the Netherlands, Portugal, Spain, and the United Kingdom—just one month to reach an interim agreement in the European Community's Commission on how much radioactive contamination they would tolerate. This agreement called for tolerance of not more than 370 becquerels of cesium radioactive contamination per liter of milk or kilogram of children's food and 600 becquerels per kilogram of other foods (Van den Bos 1994). Although this compromise was to be in effect only until November 1986, agreement on a long-term policy took nineteen more months to resolve.

The case of limitations on radioactive contaminants in food products raises several fundamental issues about international organizations and the specific decision rules they use to choose policies. For instance, the EC Commission, consisting of delegates from each of the twelve member states, required unanimity to extend the temporary agreement beyond November 1986. The French viewed the temporary regulation as too restrictive, whereas the Dutch not only wanted to continue the temporary arrangement, they wanted as tough a permanent arrangement as possible. A tough policy would have calmed concerns over environmental consequences in the Netherlands and would have helped protect Dutch farmers from East European competition. Extension of the temporary agreement was achieved only after the French agreed to abstain. What might have happened had the decision rule been less demanding than unanimity?

Table 14-1 displays data on the voting power of each member state in the European Community other than Belgium as of December 1987, when this issue was resolved. The Belgians did not stake out a position on this question.[4] The voting power levels are precisely the weighted voting scheme used by the EC and its successor, the European Union, to determine the relative influence over policy choices exercised through voting by each member state. The table also shows the policy, or position, supported by each member state at the outset of the deliberations. The policy scale has been calibrated so that the lower numbers reflect lower tolerance for radioactive contaminants and the higher numbers reflect higher tolerance. Finally, the table shows the level of salience attached to the question of tolerable radioactive contaminants for each member state.

As is evident from Table 14-1, France, the UK, and Spain favored lax standards. Germany, with its proximity to Eastern Europe and presumed heightened exposure to radiation, supported especially tough standards against radioactive contaminants in agricultural products. Italy and Greece were prepared to live with weak standards, whereas the Netherlands, Portugal, Ireland, and Luxembourg were almost as tough-minded as the Germans. Surprisingly, the Danish government—normally a country

TABLE 14-1

**European Community Preferences Regarding Tolerable Radiation Levels, December 22, 1987**

| Stakeholder | Power | Position | Salience |
|---|---|---|---|
| France | 10 | 100.0 | 100 |
| UK | 10 | 100.0 | 75 |
| Spain | 5 | 100.0 | 50 |
| Italy | 10 | 81.3 | 60 |
| Greece | 5 | 81.3 | 10 |
| Denmark | 3 | 25.0 | 100 |
| Portugal | 5 | 10.8 | 25 |
| Ireland | 3 | 10.8 | 70 |
| Luxembourg | 2 | 10.8 | 80 |
| Germany | 10 | 10.0 | 100 |

Source: Bruce Bueno de Mesquita and Frans Stokman, *European Community Decision Making* (New Haven: Yale University Press, 1994), tables 3.4 and 3.7.

with extremely pro-environmental policies—took a somewhat middle-of-the-road position. This was possibly because Denmark's own large agricultural industry might have been adversely affected by tougher regulations. Whatever the reasons for the relatively moderate position of Denmark, it is worth noting that Danish policies in the European Union are generally more sensitive to domestic political considerations—especially on environmental issues—than are those of any of the other member states. Of course, domestic political considerations play a part in the policies adopted by each and every

---

[4] Belgium had a statutory right to a weighted vote equal to 5.

member state. The Danish referendum procedures to ratify or reject European Community decisions at the time, however, gave unusually large weight to domestic Danish politics in determining whether Denmark would agree to and comply with policy choices. With the information from Table 14-1 in hand, by asking what the emissions standards probably would have been under different rules, we can see how the EC's decision rules influenced policy. We can see how the rules actually chosen might have influenced the outcome, creating a structure-induced equilibrium (Shepsle and Weingast 1981).

Suppose preferences regarding radioactive contamination were single peaked, as is likely, and that the decision over contaminants was not linked to any other policy decision in the EC. If a plurality of votes were needed for the EC Commission to adopt one standard or another, then the standard associated with more votes than any other standard would have been chosen. If that were the case, then the lowest standard—100 on the position scale—would have been chosen. It had the backing of twenty-five votes, whereas the moderately lax standard (81.3 on the position scale), backed by Italy and Greece, and the pretty tough standard (10.8 on the scale), backed by the Netherlands, Portugal, Ireland, and Luxembourg, would have tied for second place with fifteen votes each. The seemingly weakest position was that endorsed by Denmark (25.0 on the position scale). It had only Denmark's three votes. Yet, as we will see, under the rule actually used, the policy chosen came closer to Denmark's position than to any other state's expressed preference.

If plurality voting were not used and simple majority rule prevailed instead, the choice would not have been for the most lax radioactive contamination standard. Rather, the median voter position would have carried the day among the eleven members engaged on this issue. The median voter in this case was in favor of the somewhat tougher standard equal to 81.3 on the policy position scale.

In actuality, neither plurality voting nor simple majority rule was in use in the EC Commission at the time. The commission had two voting rules; each invoked under different circumstances. One called for a "qualified majority," defined by the European Community to be 71 percent of the weighted votes, with that 71 percent representing 58 percent of the population of the EC Commission's member states.[5] The other rule called for unanimity.

The eleven members voting on radioactive contamination had a combined total of sixty-eight votes. Under the qualified majority voting rule (and assuming Belgium abstained), for a policy to win it needed forty-eight of the sixty-eight votes to be cast.

---

[5] An EC policy established that it would revisit the definition of a qualified majority once its membership exceeded twenty, so as to adjust the weighted voting to represent its new reality. In 1997 the member states, now called the European Union, designated Cyprus, the Czech Republic, Estonia, Hungary, Poland, and Slovenia as prospective new members. Expansion to include these countries was to be completed in 2002. Earlier additions included Austria and Sweden, with four votes each, and Finland with three. Others aspire to join in the near future.

Looking at Table 14-1, and remembering that we are assuming single-peaked preferences, we can see that none of the initially stated positions readily attracts a qualified majority. To get a qualified majority, it would be necessary to draw at least one state supporting 10.8 on the scale into a coalition that included Denmark and the members supporting a standard of 81.3 or of 100.0. Portugal, with enough votes and very low salience might have seemed like the best target among those at 10.8 to be attracted to a compromise.

Assuming that Portugal (or any other vote combination in the "10.8" coalition that could produce five votes in favor of a compromise) was willing to compromise, what might the agreement have looked like? To answer this question we must think about the swing voters. The status quo going into the deliberations was 10.8, the temporary measure that the Netherlands wanted to see maintained. France had allowed this temporary measure to continue for a while but was unlikely to continue to do so. The coalition in favor of the weakest standard would have to remain united, however, in order to deprive all the other members of the opportunity to combine in a compromise that controlled a qualified majority. Assuming that France, the UK, and Spain remained united (possibly a strong assumption), they could exert considerable bargaining power in constructing a compromise. By the same token, without Denmark and a five-vote combination from the "10.8" coalition, a qualified majority could not be assembled. The most likely deal lay somewhere between Denmark's position and the Italian and Greek position. If the two sides split the difference they would have compromised somewhere around 54 on the scale. Assuming that such a resolution was better than no resolution for the groups at the extremes of this compromise (that is, a weighted vote worth five from the 10.8 coalition plus the votes of all members of the "100.0" coalition and everyone in between), a qualified majority could be assembled toward the middle of the scale. This analysis indicates that a shift from simple majority rule to the qualified majority would have produced a change in standards from 81.3 (the median voter position) to somewhere between 25.0 and 81.3, perhaps in the neighborhood of 54. When the issue was finally resolved, the agreement was to tolerate a modest level of radiation contamination equal to 35.6 on the position scale.

If the unanimity rule were invoked, then it appears that France, Denmark, or Germany—with their intense salience for this environmental issue—might have rejected any policy far from their preferred outcome. The unanimity rule could have provoked a severe problem. France favored the weakest radioactivity contamination standard, and Germany supported the toughest standard. They were as far apart as possible, making the likelihood that they would come to an agreement fairly small. It is unclear whether, given the salience of the other decision makers, any felt strong enough to veto a compromise standard if it were proposed under the unanimity rule. For many EC members other issues were more important than the concerns over radioactive contaminants in agricultural products, despite the initial alarm following the Chernobyl accident. Perhaps the scientific evidence that was emerging helped quell their fears. Whatever the reasons, it is apparent from the data in Table 14-1 that Greece and Portugal cared little about this question and that Spain and Italy gave it only modest attention. Belgium, of course, did not even involve itself in the debate.

It is worth noting that the Forecaster model at www.bdm.cqpress.com, when applied to the data for the radioactive contaminants issue, makes a prediction very close to the actual outcome. That model, approaching the question from the perspective of a weighted version of the median voter theorem, concludes that the issue would be resolved somewhere between 28 and 32 on the position scale (within the "2" range in the software), which is very close to the actual resolution.[6] The Forecaster model does not consider the organizational structure of the European Union. Rather, it assumes that the stakeholders engage in negotiations based purely on calculations of their own self-interest. That it also produces a rather accurate prediction about the outcome of this issue raises questions about the extent to which organizational structure leads decision makers to change their behavior in a way that alters policy out-

> It is likely that members of the European Community lobbied one another over standards for radioactive contaminants. Imagine that the influence they exerted over one another depended, not only on how many votes each member had, but also on the salience or focus each member brought to this issue. One way to reflect that focus is to discount the total number of votes—or leverage—that could be exercised by the willingness to focus time and effort on this issue rather than other issues. You can estimate this leverage by multiplying power times salience and then dividing by 100. Do that using the data in Table 14-1 and recalculate the plurality policy preference, the simple majority policy position, and the qualified majority policy positions that could win.

comes. After all, the policy choice is accurately predicted using a dynamic model concerned only with relative bargaining power, coalition formation, and individual risk taking and not concerned at all with the specific institutional constraints operating on the decision makers.

We have now seen that different decision rules could have had a dramatic impact on Europe's tolerance for radioactive contaminants in food products. The EC commissioners really had a choice only between two rules, the qualified majority and unanimity. Which of these two rules would be made applicable to the particular decision we are examining surely would itself have been a matter for negotiation and strategic maneuvering. For the German government, for instance, passage of anything other than a stringent standard might have alienated their environmentally sensitive constituents at home, perhaps even jeopardizing the political survival of the incumbent German government in the face of Green Party swing votes. The Germans, then, would have had strong reasons to press for the unanimity decision rule. If, however, they and other like-minded members thwarted all decisions with which they disagreed, they could have anticipated

---

[6] Of course, we can neither definitively judge the accuracy of the Forecaster model nor the reliability of bargaining in an international organization from a single example such as is provided here.

the collapse of the EC as an organization. In that case, they would have had essentially no influence over the domestic environmental policies of any other member state in the future. This calculation about future consequences for the organization may help restrain the use of the unanimity rule or the exercise of vetoes except under extreme circumstances. In that sense, the expected cost of losing the benefits that follow for member states from the existence of the EC as a functioning organization may have been sufficient for them to tolerate some decisions that they opposed. If that is the case, then the institution's rules can be expected to be sticky, as suggested earlier. The cost of constantly altering the rules could easily exceed the benefits derived from the European Union as a body that coordinates policy across many countries and many issue areas.

## COMPLIANCE AND EFFECTIVENESS

In actuality, the European Community adopted 35.6 as the radioactive contaminants standard for agricultural products. This is a less demanding standard than was proposed by half the members. It is a far more stringent standard than was favored by three of the four most powerful member states. Obviously the decision was a compromise designed to mollify the opposition on both sides of the issue. Such compromises often are constructed to ensure a high level of compliance. That is, members of the organization can be expected to adhere to the chosen policy. That does not mean, however, that the policy is effective in reducing radioactive contamination of foods. Consider the post-Chernobyl experience in Europe.

The United Nations Food and Agriculture Organization sponsored a study that evaluated the risks to the food chain from post-Chernobyl radioactive fallout. The study also compared effects with those resulting from atmospheric nuclear tests. Among the key findings were claims that the radioactive fallout from Chernobyl was likely to have little impact on crops—possibly no higher than background radiation levels—and also little impact on grazing animals or other elements of the land-based food chain. It was possible, however, that the fallout might have some debilitating consequences for foods that were part of the aquatic food chain (Winteringham 1989). With that in mind, it is evident that the high standards adopted by the European Community immediately after Chernobyl were important and effective in reducing a risk commonly agreed upon by the members of the European Union. However, it is also evident from this report that the monitoring infrastructure was already in place within the individual member countries. In that sense, it also seems apparent that the negotiated compromise standards that were subsequently passed to replace the temporary standards were weaker and made little difference in the actual behavior of members of the European Union.

International regimes face many obstacles to achieving compliance when countries find it costly to cooperate with the regime's rules and regulations. A good rule of thumb when examining international organizations is that the more effective an agreement is in addressing costly distribution issues, the harder it is to get compliance. The reason for this is easily seen.

Two tasks that confront international organizations are monitoring and punishing behavior that deviates from agreed principles. Several difficulties surround efforts to detect cheating or deviations. Naturally, cheaters have an incentive to hide their behavior. Because it is not out in the open it can be difficult to prove that a member cheated. For instance, OPEC assigns oil production quotas to the member states. Nigeria is believed to sell more oil than is permitted under its quota. Following oil from the wellhead to a pipeline to a tanker and then to the marketplace can be very difficult. OPEC does not have monitors who can go to Nigeria and count how many barrels are produced or sold each day. OPEC has been wise enough under Saudi leadership to avoid such heavy-handed monitoring practices. If they had not been so wise, they would face stiff resistance from Nigeria (or many other member states alleged to cheat). The Nigerian government probably would not allow inspectors to monitor oil production and sales so closely. That is one reason Saudi Arabia and other OPEC members are wise not to insist too strongly on compliance with assigned quotas. To do so would just invite some members to leave the organization, further weakening its already limited long-term ability to influence world oil prices.

*Mobile radiological laboratories from seven European countries evaluate soil for radioactive contamination in the area around the Chernobyl nuclear plant. The international community continues to monitor closely the effects of the Chernobyl nuclear accident. Fortunately, the effects to date have been far smaller than was feared initially.*

Effective monitoring and punishment confronts a host of information problems. A member may be thought to be cheating but the member may deny this, claiming instead that its seemingly aberrant behavior was an error on its part or that the claim that its behavior is aberrant is a misinterpretation of the situation. Consider the decision by President George W. Bush in 2002 to impose a tariff on certain steel imports. Tariffs are not permitted by the WTO unless they are approved as a response to unfair trade practices by the target of the tariff. President Bush's tariff is aimed at European steel producers. The European governments, defending their own steel industries, maintain that Bush's action is nothing more than trade protectionism designed to shelter uncompetitive American steel producers from free and fair European and Japanese competition. Bush, however, counters that the tariff is nothing more than an effort to redress fifty years of unfair European and Japanese government intervention in the worldwide steel industry. In Bush's stated view, the tariff is designed to make the "playing field" level, exactly the opposite claim of the Europeans. The WTO must evaluate the merits of the case on each side. The most likely sources of information, alas, come from the parties to the dispute: the American, Japanese, and European steel industries. The WTO has limited ability to make its own independent judgment when the parties to the dispute are its biggest members who are most active in worldwide trade. Still, the WTO will need to adjudicate the case and assign a punishment to whomever is found in violation of WTO rules, unless the dispute is resolved among the aggrieved parties. The WTO, for example, has permitted European governments to impose retaliatory tariffs on the United States to counter American tariffs deemed to be unjustified by the WTO. The United States appears to have capitulated to avoid stiff penalties.

Even if behavior that deviates from international agreements is detected, designing effective punishment strategies can be difficult. One solution, known as the *grim trigger strategy,* is to have members agree that they will never again cooperate with anyone who cheats. This policy, if implemented, certainly makes deviant behavior potentially very costly. But, then, it also makes punishing the culprit costly for the punishers. Just imagine two trading partners. Trade often arises under conditions very much like those in the prisoners' dilemma. If both parties adopt free trade, both benefit from the jointly cooperative outcome. But each player knows that if it persists in cooperating by not adopting tariffs while the other cheats, then it suffers a severe loss. This was the exact issue before the WTO in 2002 regarding American steel tariffs. Cutting off trade forever with the cheater, however, means that both the buyer and the seller will suffer. Eventually the cost of maintaining the punishment exceeds the benefit, and the punisher seeks to renegotiate the relationship with the cheater. A cheater, of course, can calculate how much cost the "enforcer" will tolerate before renegotiating away from the grim trigger. As a consequence, the grim trigger is not a credible punishment strategy.

Temptation is generally the root cause of cheating on an agreement, but then it is not evident that an organizational structure is essential to control cheating. Consider a frequent source of difficulty; that is, problems surrounding common pool resources (Ostrom 1999). Common pool resources, like fisheries, grazing land, and water energy, have in common with public goods that they are nonexcludable and they have in common with private goods that they are divisible and consumable and, therefore, can be depleted. Imagine a fishing area in international waters. Fish come into and go out of the waterway. The resources of the waterway represent a common pool. Anyone has the right to fish in the waters. If the waterway is overfished, too few fish will remain to replenish the supply and everyone will lose out. However, if a fisherman exceeds the permitted quota, he or she has more fish to sell and so makes more money in the short run. In the long run, the fisherman's overfishing means that he or she, like everyone else, can no longer catch fish economically and so suffers a loss. This is a problem known as the tragedy of the commons. All benefit from using restraint, but if everyone else uses restraint, then cheating is attractive. But if everyone (or many) cheat, then everyone loses. As Ostrom (1999) and her collaborators have demonstrated, it is not essential to have a complex organization monitor and punish cheating. Often if the group of fishermen (or other users of a common pool resource) is not too large, it is perfectly capable of arriving at a cooperative norm that minimizes, but usually does not fully eliminate, cheating. The problem is solved, in essence, by the anticipation of market forces. When the magnitude of cheating is high, the supply of the common pool resource is large and so commands a relatively low price. This makes excessive exploitation of the common pool resource relatively unattractive compared with investing one's time and resources in other income-generating opportunities. The more people who divert their energy and time away from exploiting the common pool resource, the less of it that finds its way to market. With supply to the market reduced, the price rises, making it attractive for more time and energy to be devoted to using the resource than to putting time and energy into some other activity. Thus, there is a long-term equilibrium use of the resource that stabilizes price and supply, provided people have relatively attractive next-best alternative uses of their time and energy (that is, their factors of production are mobile). What this means is that the users of a common pool resource have a good prospect of avoiding the tragedy of the commons even without developing an elaborate oversight organization. This is akin to the observation that if people are engaged in an indefinitely repeated prisoners' dilemma situation, there are cooperative equilibria that emerge and can be sustained by individual actions without the benefit—or costs—of introducing organizational structure into the mix.

## SUMMARY

The central theme of this chapter has been that international rules, regulations, and organizations may help induce cooperative behavior, but they cannot be counted on to do so. Rules, regulations, and structure are likely to be the product of strategic maneuvering. As such they are more likely to reflect national or individual interests as defined at a given moment than they are to define those interests. Still, organizations are sticky. Once created, they are hard to get rid of, so they can help tie the hands of leaders or increase the costs of deviant behavior.

A high level of compliance with an organization's rules and regulations should not be mistaken for evidence that the organization is effective in altering behavior. The level of compliance is likely to be endogenous. Organizations are unlikely to pass rules that members are unwilling to follow unless the organization does not bother with effective means to monitor and punish deviant behavior. As a consequence, many organizational decisions are likely to be shallow, making compliance easy. Decisions that would effectively alter behavior undoubtedly exist, but they may be relatively rare.

Compliance may be seen as a way to establish a national reputation. A reputation for cooperative behavior may make it easier to reach cooperative arrangements with other states in the future. However, reputation should be thought of as being divided into at least three important constituent parts. Nations may have reputations in general, but it is more likely that individual leaders develop reputations and that those reputations do not adhere to the state when they are gone from office. Individual government agencies with persistent civil service bureaucracies may develop reputations that are issue-area specific. These are likely to matter and to persist over time, but they are unlikely to carry over into arenas outside the purview of the government organization or agency.

CHAPTER 15

# ALLIANCES

People in different states cooperate with each other in many ways. Trade, investment, travel, telecommunications, and the like all provide opportunities for cooperation. Governments set the terms of international cooperation by establishing policies concerning virtually every aspect of interaction. In the previous chapters, we explored many of the factors influencing cooperation. We saw that many international organizations and regimes represent agreements between states that are designed to foster cooperation among their citizens. But some international cooperation occurs strictly at the government-to-government level. Military alliances are an example of international agreements that are designed to foster only direct government-to-government cooperation. In this chapter we examine how, when, and why military alliances work.

First we will look at what an alliance is. Then we will turn our attention to the factors that lead alliances to form—that is, to the purposes they are designed to fulfill. Of course, the intended purpose of alliances and their actual performance may differ. We will investigate in some detail the issues affecting alliance reliability and how best to predict which alliances will prove reliable and which will not. Among alliances that prove unreliable, a particularly pernicious group involves those cases in which allies fight with one another. We will probe this phenomenon and develop a general theory to help us understand why some alliances break down into internal combat.

## WHAT IS A MILITARY ALLIANCE?

A military alliance is an agreement between two or more sovereign states concerning the actions each will take in the event that a specified military contingency occurs. A contingency generally involves the violation of one party's sovereignty by some other state. Alliances are rarely pertinent in civil wars or internal coups d'état. Although the leadership in one country might decide to step in to protect friendly leadership in another country if there is a civil war or a coup, such action typically would not be in response to an alliance commitment.

Military alliances come in a handful of varieties. They may be bilateral or multilateral. A bilateral alliance, like the Japanese-American alliance signed following World War II (and still in force today), is made between two states. The Japanese-American agreement is unusual because it is not mutual with regard to defense. The United States has promised to defend Japan, which is precluded from having armed forces (beyond those necessary to protect its own territory) by the Japanese Constitution, drafted with American help after Japan's defeat in World War II. Japan, however, is not obliged under the terms of the agreement to defend the United States.

Multilateral alliances such as the North Atlantic Treaty Organization (NATO) involve more than two states. As of early May 2002, NATO's membership included Belgium, Canada, the Czech Republic, Denmark, France, Germany, Greece, Hungary, Iceland, Italy, Luxembourg, the Netherlands, Norway, Poland, Portugal, Spain, Turkey, the United Kingdom, and the United States. NATO appears on the verge of considerable expansion to encompass many more states in eastern Europe, including probably Bulgaria, Estonia, Latvia, Lithuania, Slovakia, Slovenia, and Romania. In addition, following an agreement between the United States and Russia to reduce substantially their nuclear weapons stockpile, NATO has entered into a new partnership with Russia.

By joining NATO, each member is making a promise to every other member that it will defend that member in the event it is attacked by an outsider. Even those members who, on occasion, have fought against each other, like Turkey and Greece, promise to defend one another.

Military alliances typically spell out what is to be done in the event a member is attacked. They are anticipatory, tied to expectations concerning what might happen. They are not binding commitments. Sovereign states and their leaders can and do renege on promises. Rather, they are signals of intent designed in part to deter prospective foes and in part to facilitate preparedness by coordinating the actions of the signatories under specific contingencies. More often than not, alliances are costly signals. When nations incur real costs, whether material or political, as a consequence of signing an alliance agreement, they show greater commitment to their promise than would be true if they bore no material or political conse-

In what sense are alliances costly signals? Why are the promises that alliances engender not cheap talk? What are some of the costs members bear? Why is it that some nations that seem very close to each other politically (like Israel and the United States before the 1979 Camp David Accords) do not sign formal alliance agreements? Does the United States seem more or less closely associated with Israel today than it was before the Israeli-Egyptian peace agreement of 1979?

quences for making that promise. This is one reason why alliances sometimes involve explicit obligations even when the military threat they have been created to deal with has not materialized.

The most common contingency plans in alliances distinguish three types of agreement: mutual defense agreements, neutrality and nonaggression agreements, and consultation agreements, also called ententes. In the nineteenth century, defense pacts were typically couched in very specific language that laid out exactly what circumstances had to arise before the alliance promise of mutual defense would be invoked. Today, defense pacts, such as NATO and ANZUS (between Australia, New Zealand, and the United States), are much broader with few narrowing contingencies.

Neutrality and nonaggression pacts involve a promise by each signatory that in the event one is attacked, the others will not join against it on the side of the attacker. The Soviet Union was particularly fond of such agreements during the cold war, usually referring to them as friendship treaties. They signed bilateral nonaggression agreements with Afghanistan, Bulgaria, Egypt, Poland, and Syria, among other states.

Ententes involve an agreement or, literally, an understanding, between member states to consult with one another on a course of action in the event that any one of them is attacked. Probably the most famous entente in history is the Triple Entente. This was the alliance between Britain, France, and Russia that decided to wage war against Germany following the Austro-Serbian crisis in 1914. The Triple Entente was the bulwark of the allied effort in World War I.

Ententes were a fairly popular form of alliance in the nineteenth century. Neutrality and nonaggression pacts were rare at that time. In the twentieth century, especially after World War I, nonaggression pacts supplanted ententes. In both the nineteenth and twentieth centuries, defense pacts were common, representing the most serious of agreements between states. Perhaps the twenty-first century will see the invention of some other form of alliance. The final decades of the second millennium saw greater use of collective

*Army medics carry wounded personnel to waiting ambulances during the Korean War. This UN police action involved soldiers from all over the world. The C-124 troop transport pictured here, for instance, belonged to the Royal Thailand Air Force. The wounded soldiers were flown to Camp Drew Hospital in Tokyo. Truly this was a multinational effort.*

security arrangements in which all participants agree in principle to defend any state that is the victim of aggression. The United Nations police action against North Korea and China in defense of South Korean sovereignty in the 1950s and the Gulf War in 1991 are examples of collective security efforts. Of course, collective security is complicated by the need for many to agree on who is an aggressor and who is a victim. And quite often, one person's aggressor is another person's victim.

## THE PURPOSE OF ALLIANCES

The fact that alliances take a variety of forms suggests that states join alliances for different reasons. Alliances may provide security against threats from foreign adversaries or they may provide the wherewithal to make threats. As such, they can be defensive or offensive. Alliances can be a substitute for buying and developing weapons. They can facilitate the standardization of weaponry across nations and establish a common chain of command. Alliances can be large or small, be focused on narrow or broad issues, and be long lived or of short duration. Which of the many forms an alliance takes depends on the interests of the leaders who make them.

Collective security arrangements are predicated on the idea that massive force deters prospective aggressors from launching military threats. They are designed to convince prospective aggressors that they cannot bully weak states into submission. As such, these alliances are large (that is, they include many participants) and long lasting. Because of their breadth, however, collective security agreements suffer from problems associated with the credibility of promises to honor broad-gauged and far-ranging demands. Often they are shallow.

An alternative to vast collective security agreements such as the United Nations are minimal winning coalitions—that is, alliances that are just large enough to achieve their security or other foreign policy objectives and no larger (Riker 1962). These alliances are more likely to be effective in that they are able to maximize the share of prospective benefits to each member while keeping costs in line with the specific objectives for which they were formed. But what are those objectives?

Structural theories generally view alliances as quick, inexpensive methods of accumulating power and security. By forming alliances, states pool their resources in an effort to enhance one another's security (Waltz 1979; Walt 1985). Thus, the main function of alliances, from a structural point of view, is to deter attacks and provide mechanisms for states to coordinate with one another in the event of an attack. The deterrence quality of alliances in promoting security is important, but it immediately poses a puzzle. It is easy to see that the American defense pacts with Canada, Luxembourg, Mexico, New Zealand, and Uruguay can help deter attacks against these states, but can these states really help deter attacks against the United States? Probably not. One reason that the United States has such a large military establishment is that it cannot readily rely on the strength of its allies to deter trouble. If this is so, why does the United States bother to ally with such obviously weaker states?

James Morrow (1991a) has offered an intriguing answer to this question. Imagine that leaders are interested in maintaining sufficient *security* so that they need not worry about any deterioration in the international status quo. Imagine too that they are interested in maintaining sufficient *autonomy* so that they have enough freedom of action that they can exploit favorable shifts in the international status quo to enhance their influence. Although leaders do not want to see any shifts in the international status quo affect them negatively, they certainly would welcome any shift that places them in a position more favorable than where they stood before the shift. But autonomy might come at a price—namely, a loss of security. The opposite may be true as well. Security may be gained, but only with a loss of autonomy. To achieve their goals, leaders may trade away some autonomy for security or some security for autonomy, depending on their domestic and international circumstances.

Great powers like the United States today, Britain in the nineteenth century, and Spain in the sixteenth century tend to be secure. The international environment is favorable to them because they play an important role in giving shape to the international status quo (Organski 1958; Organski and Kugler 1980; Gilpin 1981; Tammen et al. 2000). Still, great powers always have rivals; therefore, as far as the leaders in powerful states are concerned, the status quo can always be improved. In effect, although they might not gain much from added security (since they are already very secure), they could gain from added autonomy of action. To gain this, leaders in great power states may trade away some of their country's security by aligning with weaker states that could entangle them in conflicts (Iusi-Scarborough and Bueno de Mesquita 1988). In return, increased autonomy in the form of rights to base their own military capabilities on the ally's territory, for example, may be achieved. Thus, a secure state may seek the ability to project its interests into new arenas through the acquisition of military bases and other benefits that alliances can provide.

According to this security-autonomy outlook, the smaller states in an alliance enhance their security and the more powerful states gain additional freedom of action in the international arena. Each member gains on a dimension that is beneficial to it, and each sacrifices on a dimension that is less critical to its overall well-being. Leaders in weaker states, perforce, do not concern themselves so much with changing the world as they do with protecting themselves against unpleasant changes. More powerful nations have the luxury of looking for ways to shift the status quo to improve their well-being.

Morrow's theory does not, of course, suggest that weaker states have more autonomy than stronger states. Rather, it suggests that, relative to the amount of security they would like, weaker states have autonomy they are willing to give up. Consequently, weaker states are willing to allow powerful friends to station troops on their territory or otherwise influence their freedom of action in order to gain greater protection from foes.

Likewise, because powerful states have so much security, they are willing to risk some of it through entanglement with weaker states in order to gain more foreign policy latitude.

Figure 15-1 depicts hypothetical indifference curves and status quo points for a powerful state and a much weaker ally. As you can see, the marginal rate of substitution—that is, the rate at which autonomy will be substituted for security or visa versa—favors giving up more autonomy for a smaller amount of security in the case of the weak state and favors giving up a relatively larger amount of security for a smaller amount of autonomy in the case of the strong state. The figure illustrates that two states endowed with different levels of autonomy and security can readily form an alliance in which each state finds itself better off than if it were not involved in an alliance. Notice that the status quo of a weak state with an alliance places it on a higher indifference curve than it was on without the alliance, even though in the process of forming the alliance it loses some degree of autonomy. Likewise, the powerful state also finds itself on a higher indifference curve after forming an alliance even though it has given up some of its security. In both cases, then, the state is better off. Notice too that the weaker state has less autonomy and less security than the more powerful state, both at the outset and after it joins in the alliance. This is not always the case, but it is the most typical scenario. The weak state, though giving up some autonomy, never had more than the powerful state in the first place. Figure 15-1 suggests another implication of Morrow's model of alliance formation. Although it is not impossible to form a symmetric alliance—that is, an alliance in which both parties gain autonomy or both parties gain security—it is harder to do than it is to form an asymmetric alliance—that is, an alliance in which each party gains on a different dimension.

Alliances that are asymmetric cannot long survive if the realist view is correct in its assertion that alliances are only about pooling and augmenting capabilities against a common foe (Bennett 1997c). Yet, on average, asymmetric alliances last 15.7 years, whereas symmetric alliances last, on average, just 12.2 years (Morrow 1991a). This difference is statistically significant, with asymmetric alliances lasting almost 30 percent longer than their symmetric counterparts. Additionally, symmetric alliances occur more frequently over time, not because they are a stronger motivation for alliances, but because they collapse more quickly and so

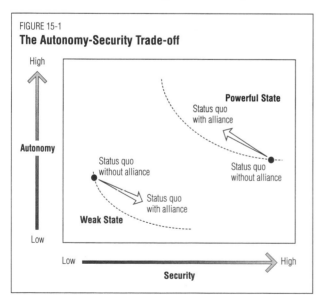

FIGURE 15-1
**The Autonomy-Security Trade-off**

High

Autonomy

**Powerful State**
Status quo
with alliance

Status quo
without alliance

Status quo
without alliance

Status quo
with alliance

**Weak State**

Low

Low    High

**Security**

*Alliances between states with different objectives are more easily formed and longer lasting than are alliances based only on mutual quests for security or on mutual quests for autonomy.*

turn over with greater regularity. In contrast, asymmetric alliances exhibit remarkable durability. Evidence from studies not directly focused on Morrow's theory provide further support for it. Douglas M. Gibler and John A. Vasquez report that "alliances that are war prone have two notable characteristics: they are made by states that have been successful in their last war, and they consist of major states" (1998, 803–805). This latter result highlights the difficulties encountered by symmetric alliances (comprised of two major powers in the Gibler and Vasquez example).

Morrow's theory of asymmetric alliances and the empirical evidence he presents help resolve a fundamental puzzle. It is obvious that small states can gain security by placing themselves under the protective wing of a powerful ally. The puzzle has been why would a powerful state risk being dragged into the problems of a smaller state through an alliance commitment? Morrow has provided a convincing explanation of why an asymmetric alliance is in the interest of the powerful state as well as the weaker state. The powerful state takes a calculated risk by opening itself up to the possibility that it will become entangled in the affairs of the smaller partner (or partners). But at the same time it gains the ability to project its influence in new parts of the world. For example, the United States helped protect the Philippines during and after World War II and in exchange gained access to important military bases, including a major naval base. The United States has, however, now lost access to those bases. Morrow's distinction between symmetric and asymmetric alliances provides an explanation for the existence and durability of those alliances that cannot be easily explained by realist (or interest group) theories and provides a way to understand the differing motivations behind alliance formation.

> Use indifference curves to construct an example in which both parties to an alliance gain security and at least one party loses autonomy. Construct an example in which both parties gain security and autonomy. What has changed? Can you infer anything about the ease or difficulty of forming symmetric alliances compared with that of forming asymmetric alliances from the indifference curves that you drew?

## WHEN ARE ALLIANCES RELIABLE?

Just because two states agree to ally does not mean that either or both are prepared to honor their commitment. Consequently, one issue that is often debated by foreign policymakers, as well as by students of international relations, is the reliability of alliances. In his farewell address, George Washington warned against becoming involved in what he called entangling alliances. He believed that the promises made in alliances constituted meaningful commitments that might harm the young country by dragging it into the wars of other countries. For more than a hundred years, American leaders heeded Washington's admonition.

Adolf Hitler had a different view of alliances. He reportedly told his advisers that the promise he made to Britain's Neville Chamberlain at Munich in 1938 to seek no more territorial gains in Europe was meaningless and that they should not worry that the piece of paper he signed would limit Germany's freedom of action in the future. Unlike Washington, Hitler viewed the promises embedded in this alliance to be worth no more than the paper on which they were written.[1] Whether alliances are costly commitments that limit action or are worthless promises remains today a question that is much discussed and debated (Altfeld and Bueno de Mesquita 1979; Siverson and King 1980; Iusi-Scarborough and Bueno de Mesquita 1988; Morrow 1994c; Smith 1995; Gaubatz 1996; Reed 1997).

To ascertain the reliability of alliances, statesmen and scholars alike have looked to the historical record for answers. From the record of the past, we might be able to draw inferences about what to expect of alliances in the future. Alan Sabrosky (1980) reported that in the years between 1816 and 1965 alliances were not honored fully 73 percent of the time when an attack took place. His findings have been reinforced by additional studies (Vasquez 1987; Wayman 1990). Others have cautioned that the actual rate of reliability is probably higher than that reported by Sabrosky (Moul 1988; Leeds, Long, and Mitchell 2000; Leeds, Ritter, Mitchell, and Long 2002).[2] Whatever the actual level of reliability is or however broadly or narrowly we specify the intent behind an alliance agreement, clearly it is not a certainty that allies will aid each other even under the contingent conditions of their agreement. What can we infer from this important fact?

We might conclude that alliances are not reliable. After all, the record of history shows that perhaps as many as three-quarters of all alliance agreements are not fulfilled after an ally has been attacked. By taking the analytic perspective common to historical research—that is, by focusing exclusively on what actually took place—we would surely conclude, along with Sabrosky and many others, that alliances are not worth the paper on which they are written. In fact, this is the conclusion generally reached by realists and neorealists. They hypothesize that alliances are short-term, unreliable arrangements. They are short-term because their signatories have only a momentary shared interest in pooling their military power against a common foe. They are unreliable because in the long term each state has an adversarial relationship with every other state. According to this view, alliances are not about sustained interests; they are only about a temporary balancing of power (Walt 1985).

---

[1] Not only did Hitler not take his own promises seriously, he viewed British promises to defend Poland as equally untrustworthy.

[2] I am indebted to Jeffrey Ritter for bringing to my attention the frequency with which alliances are incorrectly reported to be unreliable, especially in the nineteenth century, when the terms of alliances were typically quite detailed, even though the actual terms of the treaty were not in fact violated. For example, although the 1879 treaty between Austria and Germany obliged the partners to aid each other "with the whole war strength of their Empires" if either was attacked by Russia, it otherwise indicated that an attack by any other state required only that the partner maintain benevolent neutrality (Pribram 1920, 27–29; Hurst 1972, 2:590).

Leaving realist and neorealist arguments aside, what view does the strategic perspective take? In fact, the strategic viewpoint leads to an entirely different conclusion. It provides a coherent basis for declaring that alliances are really quite reliable. With a bit more information and a little more reasoning, we will find that *if alliances generally are reliable, we should expect to observe that most alliances are not honored when an attack takes place even if mutual defense is the action called for by the agreement.* This claim may seem puzzling at first glance, but a straightforward hypothetical example will help to clarify the issue.

Suppose that nations A and B are rivals. Suppose further that nation B has an ally in nation C. Consider the following two possibilities: A can choose to attack B or A can choose not to attack B. In either case we will assume that A's motivation to attack B is the same; the only thing that is different is whether or not A decides to attack. Nation A believes it can defeat nation B and gain a benefit that exceeds the anticipated costs of the fight. However, nation A does not believe that the expected benefits warrant the expected costs of a fight against the combined forces of nation B and nation C. As such, if A believes that the alliance between B and C is reliable, it will not attack B because a war with B and C will be too costly. If, in contrast, A believes that the alliance is unreliable, A will attack B. Naturally, some of the time A's beliefs will be mistaken, but we should expect that A's beliefs will generally be consistent with the subsequent behavior of C.

The mistaken beliefs in nation A can have two consequences, only one of which will actually be observed in the historical record. If A attacks, thinking incorrectly that C will not aid B, we would expect that A would be defeated. Essentially, when one state attacks a second state that has allies, and the allies help their partner, then the attacker may have made a mistake and so is relatively likely to lose (Gartner and Siverson 1996).

In the 598 militarized disputes in Europe between 1816 and 1984 for which we have data, we find that when the initiator of a militarized dispute acting alone fought a single adversary, the initiator won 74 percent of the time ($N = 328$). When the initiator acting alone ended up fighting against its adversary and its adversary's allies, the initiator won only 40 percent of the time ($N = 60$). This is what we should expect to see happen if nation A, in this case the initiator, attacks nation B, its adversary, under the assumption that nation C, B's ally, will prove unreliable, only to discover that it was mistaken. These are the attacks that in the end nation A probably wishes it had not launched.

To continue, when the initiator fought with the help of allies and the opponent did not, the initiator was victorious an impressive 80 percent of the time ($N = 138$). Finally, when both sides fought alongside allies so that the dispute was multilateral on both sides, the initiator won just 44 percent of the time ($N = 72$).

But what happens if nation A does not attack nation B because A mistakenly believes that B's allies are reliable when in fact they are not? The answer, of course, is that we do not observe anything. In particular, we do not observe the probable victory that nation A would have gained against nation B. Thus, mistaken attacks leave a record in the ledger of history, whereas deterred attacks leave no readily observed record at all. This suggests a bias in the inferences drawn from historical analysis, one that we should keep in mind whenever we examine case studies or statistical assessments, like Sabrosky's, that look at only one side of the ledger.

Figure 15-2 depicts a game in which nation A is uncertain whether or not nation C is reliable. Nation A does not know whether or not C, when faced with war, will defend B. Following the game theory methods introduced earlier, A believes that there is a chance, equal to $p$ that C is reliable. C is unreliable, then, with a probability equal to $1 - p$. C's actual type—its and B's private knowledge—is reflected by the payoff ($c$ or $d$) that C receives if it chooses to help B. If the payoff for helping B is greater than the payoff for not helping, then C is reliable. A's problem is that it cannot know which type of ally C is (that is, reliable or unreliable) when it chooses to attack or not attack. According to the payoffs listed at the end of each terminal node of the game (A's are listed first, C's are

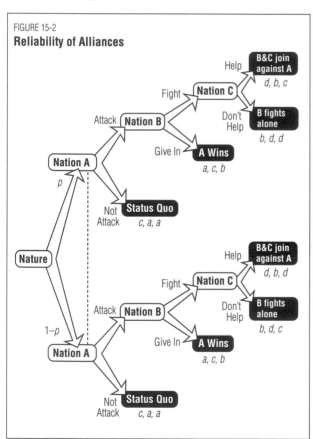

FIGURE 15-2
**Reliability of Alliances**

*The reliability of alliances cannot be judged simply by the actions of states with alliance commitments that are tested in war. Alliances create selection effects. The most reliable alliances are not tested by foreign foes.*

listed last, and $a > b > c > d$), it is important to A that it guess correctly about C. If C is known to be reliable then C will help B if it is called upon to do so, B will choose to fight back against A if attacked, and A, anticipating an unfavorable outcome if it attacks, will choose not to attack in the first place. If, however, C is known to be unreliable, then C will not help B if B is attacked. In anticipation of C's unreliability, B will give in to A rather than fight against A alone. A, knowing that C will not fight and that B will thus give in, will attack.

By examining only those cases in which an attack takes place, per the historical perspective, we fail to evaluate the reliability of alliances adequately. If A takes the expected response of nation C into account in its decision making, then, as we just saw, we would expect that those alliances that are tested by an attack will in fact generally prove to be unreliable, exactly as Sabrosky reports. After all, nation A has already taken into account which type of ally it believes nation C to be, reliable or unreliable, as part of its strategic decision making. A will attack B only when it expects C to remain out of the fight or when it believes that it can beat

B and C at an acceptable cost relative to the prospective gain. C's anticipated response to the contingent, hypothetical attack is sufficient to deter A if A expects C to be reliable. In such a case, C is not called upon to act in B's defense because B is not attacked. A, unwilling to face both B and C in battle, chooses instead to live with the existing state of affairs.

Figure 15-2 suggests that because they succeed in *deterring* attacks, the most reliable alliances do not get tested, whereas the less reliable alliances are more likely to be tested and prove wanting. Militarily unreliable alliances may serve functions other than pro-

> What is A's expected utility if it chooses to attack, where the chance that C will help B is *p* and the chance that C will not help B is 1 − *p*? What is A's expected utility if it chooses not to attack? How small must *p* be before A will choose to attack B?

viding deterrence, but they are not evidence that alliances *in general* are militarily unreliable. Quite the contrary. From the strategic perspective, reliable and unreliable alliances alike respond in expected ways. What "really" happened includes events that never actually took place and so could never be observed, such as nation A attacking nation B when nation A expects nation C to be a reliable ally. A focus on observable facts alone misleads us about the cooperative commitment of allies. A selection effect is clearly at work (Zagare 1987; Morrow 1989, 1991b, 1993; Fearon 1994; Wagner 1994; Smith 1995; Powell 1996a). The behavior under study—namely, the reliability of allies—leads would-be attackers to select their targets carefully. They choose to attack only when they believe their rival's allies do not intend to honor their commitment or when they believe that the combined ability of their adversaries is insufficient to inflict costs that will exceed the expected gains from their action. Under any other circumstances, they choose not to attack.

The historian's perspective, with its primary emphasis on observable facts, leads to a conclusion about alliance reliability that is opposite to that arrived at if we assume decision makers, like chess players, take anticipated responses into account. The strategic perspective, which emphasizes expectations, leads us to ask questions about alliances that are different from those that arise with the historical approach. And whereas the evidence cited earlier is consistent with expectations derived from the strategic point of view, it is *not* in fact consistent with the expectations derived from a historian's perspective. Historians are interested in what is on the equilibrium path—that is, in the sequence of observable events that lead to an outcome. The strategic perspective compels us to consider the entire equilibrium, including both what is on and what is off the equilibrium path. Off-the-path expectations reveal events that are counterfactual (that is, events that did not take place) but that actually explain why a particular outcome occurred. They remind us that leaders choose courses of action (including inaction) aimed at avoiding alternatives that are expected to yield worse results. Off-the-path expectations help us to see alliances in a completely different light.

One last point is worth noting here. As we have already claimed, some states enter into alliances in a quest for security, whereas others enter into alliances to gain added autonomy. If a nation belongs to an alliance in order to acquire protection, and offers freedom of action to its partners in return, then we should not expect that nation to fight on behalf of its ally. Security is not the valuable resource they are bringing to the table. As such, they cannot really be considered unreliable. In fact, they are doing precisely what is expected of them, no more and no less.

## PREDICTING THE RELIABILITY OF ALLIANCES

In Chapter 8 I introduced ideas about how motivation and power interact. We saw that a high degree of motivation can help compensate for military weakness just as military strength can bolster a leader's willingness to engage in a war that he or she is not strongly motivated to win. The simple model suggested in Chapter 8 provides a useful tool for anticipating third-party choices in international disputes. As such, it is a vehicle for assessing and predicting the reliability of alliances. Certainly would-be attackers seem to behave as if they make calculations of the sort suggested by this model.

Recall that the model proposed in Chapter 8 argued that the decision to join one side or the other in a dispute, or the decision to remain neutral, depends on the expected costs and benefits associated with joining one or the other side. Neutrality, which is the most common choice, reflects (approximate) indifference over seeing one side or the other win.

Expression 8.4 stated that if $[b/(a + b + c)](U_{BA} - U_{BC}) > K_{BA} - K_{BC}$, then state B should be expected to join an ongoing dispute on the side of A; if $[b/(a + b + c)](U_{BA} - U_{BC}) < K_{BA} - K_{BC}$, then B is expected to join an ongoing dispute on the side of C; and if $[b/(a + b + c)](U_{BA} - U_{BC}) = K_{BA} - K_{BC}$, then B is expected to remain neutral. Recall that $a$, $b$, and $c$ are the respective national military capabilities of nations A, B, and C (or groups or coalitions or alliances A, B, and C). The $K$ terms refer to the expected costs and the $U$ terms to the utilities of the outcomes A wins or C wins. Finally, recall that expression 8.4 says that the decision to help one side or the other is driven by the strength of motivation (the difference in the $U$ terms), the wherewithal to exert influence over the outcome (the ratio $b/[a + b + c]$), and the prospective costs (the $K$ terms).

Since expression 8.4 predicts what choice a third party will make in an ongoing dispute, it represents one way to evaluate the expected reliability of alliances. For example, if nations A and C are at war, and nation B is allied with one of them, we can predict the reliability of that alliance by using expression 8.4 to estimate the likelihood that B will join A, B will join C, or B will remain neutral.

To do this, however, we must first calculate how much each prospective participant in a war values victory by one side or the other and how valuable the military contribution of each participant will be. The military contribution of each participant can be estimated using the Correlates of War composite capabilities score discussed in Chapter 7. Calculation of the value of victory relies on an evaluation of the similarity in alliance portfolios to establish the extent to which interests are shared between nations (Altfeld and Bueno de Mesquita 1979). The evaluation of shared interests is relatively complex and warrants a more detailed discussion here.

## MEASURING SHARED INTERESTS

To measure shared interests across states, we can evaluate the similarity in alliance portfolios. An alliance portfolio is defined as a nation's complete array of alliance commitments. Thus, in comparing alliance portfolios we are assessing the degree to which the full array of alliance commitments of one nation matches that of another nation. For example, Great Britain on the eve of World War I had defense pacts with Japan and Portugal and ententes with France, Russia, and Spain. Britain had no other alliances. These five agreements comprised Britain's alliance portfolio in 1914. Germany, for its part, had defense pacts with Austria-Hungary, Italy, and Romania. The Germans had no other military alliance commitments. Finally, France in 1914 had a defense pact with Russia, a neutrality pact with Italy, and ententes with Britain, Japan, and Spain. How might we think about the shared interests of these three states, as reflected in their alliance portfolios?

One way to think about shared interests, or at least shared security interests, is to examine the commonalities in the alliance portfolios of states. Just looking at states'
bilateral relationships can be misleading. Two nations that have a defense pact with each other may actually share little else. Two other nations that have no mutual alliance between them may in fact share a similar perspective on security interests. Consider the two hypothetical international systems of alliances in Figure 15-3. In System I, nations A and B have a bilateral defense pact with one another. A, in addition, is aligned with states C, D, E, F, and G. Nation B has no alliance ties to these states, but it does have defense pacts with H, I, J, K, and L. A does not. We can see, then, that nation A has no alliances with any of the states with which B is aligned and nation B has no alliances with any of the states with which A is aligned. Although A and B share a bilateral commitment, it appears that they do not share similar security interests in System I. In System II, the opposite is true. Nations A and B are

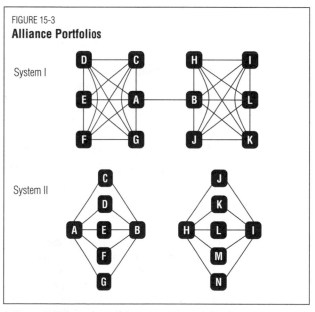

FIGURE 15-3
**Alliance Portfolios**

System I

System II

*Bilateral alliance agreements can be misleading in terms of the depth of commitment of the allied states. Patterns or profiles of alliance commitments reveal more about the reliability of allies than do bilateral ties.*

not committed to a bilateral alliance, but all of their alliance commitments are otherwise alike. If a war were to take place between A and H in the first system, we would be hard-pressed to judge whether B would help A, help H, or stay neutral. In the second system, we can confidently predict that B would help A and not H, even though states A and B are not directly allied in System II.

Curtis Signorino and Jeffrey Ritter (1999) have developed a measure of shared interests that uses the logic of a technique I developed in 1975 while solving some problems in the original method of computation.[3] Measures or indicators of the similarity in alliance portfolios are designed to take the guesswork out of determining the likelihood that one ally will help another in the event that the contingency for which the alliance was signed occurs. Let's calculate the Signorino-Ritter score, the S-score, for the two hypothetical systems in Figure 15-3.

To calculate S, we will assign a score of 0 points to defense pacts, 1 point to neutrality or nonaggression pacts, 2 points to ententes, and 3 points to situations in which two countries maintain no alliance at all. This scale captures the idea that defense pacts require a promise that, in principle, sacrifices more freedom of action than does a nonaggression pact, and a nonaggression pact requires a promise that sacrifices more autonomy of action than does an entente. Naturally, no promise at all involves no sacrifice in choices of action. Scoring each type of alliance relationship is analogous to assigning a spatial location to ideal points or policy positions on a continuum, as we did in our discussion of the median voter theorem with single-peaked preferences.

The formula for measuring the S-score is

$$1 - 2\ \frac{\sum_{i=1}^{n}\left| C_{Ai} - C_{Bi} \right|}{n D_{max}}$$

where $C_{Ai}$ equals the alliance score that nation A has with nation $i$, $C_{Bi}$ equals the alliance score nation B has with nation $i$, $i$ stands for each country in turn, and $n$ indicates the total number of countries in the sample. The term $D_{max}$ is the maximum possible differ-

---

[3] My method is based on Kendall's tau-b statistic and is much more difficult to calculate. The two methods often, although not always, produce similar scores. In both cases, all calculations assume that each country has a defense pact with itself—that is, both methods assume that governments promise to defend their own country if attacked. The Signorino-Ritter method appears to resolve potential—although empirically infrequent—anomalies in my original approach. However, their method introduces new problems when applied to alliance portfolio patterns calculated over a very large set of nations. My method tends toward zero from the negative side as more unallied states are included in the sample, whereas the Signorino-Ritter S-scores tend toward their upper bound of 1.0. Using all countries in the world, for example, the S-score in 1960 between the United States and Britain—two close allies—and the S-score between the Soviet Union and the United States—two staunch adversaries—are almost equal and are close to 1. This is not true for my application of tau-b. I am indebted to Joseph Gochal for bringing this anomaly to my attention.

ence in the relationship between the alliance commitment of any one country $i$ to A and the alliance commitment of that country $i$ to B. In our sample, the maximum is 3, as this is the difference between a defense pact (0 points) and no alliance at all (3 points).[4] The denominator, then, for the cases in Figure 15-3 is equal to the number of countries multiplied by 3.

Although the calculation of $S$ looks complicated, it is really quite straightforward. Essentially, we are calculating how far apart nation A's alliance commitment with nation $i$ is from nation B's alliance commitment with that same nation $i$, adding up all of these absolute values (each will be somewhere between 0 and 3), and then dividing the summed total by the number of countries times three. We then multiply the answer by 2 and subtract that answer from 1. In this way we generate an index that ranges between $-1$ and $+1$. When the score is $-1$, the alliance portfolios of nations A and B are as different as possible. When the score is 1, the alliance portfolios of nations A and B are as similar as possible. Scores falling in between these extremes reflect varying degrees of alliance similarity.

Using the formula, we can now figure out the $S$-score for nation A and nation B in hypothetical System I. The difference between nation A's commitment and nation B's commitment to nations C, D, E, F, and G is the difference between A's defense pacts with these states (worth 0 points each) and B's nonalignment with these five states (worth 3 points each). The sum of that difference then is $(5)(0) + (5)(3)$, or 15. Likewise, the difference

Have a look at the Web site called EuGene at www.eugenesoftware.org. This site allows you to download lots of useful data, including the Signorino-Ritter $S$-scores and my tau-b scores for any combination of countries you choose. Compare the scores for the United States and Britain and the United States and the Soviet Union based on the global population of all states in 1960. Repeat this process but now limit the computation to be based only on states in Europe. How do the scores differ? Repeat this process for other combinations of states. These values could, with a little bit of effort, be used as estimates of country policy positions on a security continuum. Try to do that. Then, using COW capability scores locate the median power based on the scale you constructed. Enter the data into the Forecaster (and set salience to 100) at http://bdm.cqpress.com. What does the Forecaster software predict? For more ideas on how to use these and other data to estimate power, position, and salience, see Bueno de Mesquita (2002).

between nation B's defense pacts with nations H, I, J, K, and L (worth 0 points each) and A's nonalignment with these five states (worth 3 points each) is $(5)(0) + (5)(3)$, or, again, 15. The A-B defense pact contributes 0 points. Summing these totals $(15 + 15 + 0)$ and multiplying by 2 gives us a numerator of 60. Since there are twelve countries in System I, the denominator is $(12)(3)$, or 36. $S$, then, equals $1 - (60/36)$, or $-0.67$. Although A and B share a common defense pact with one another, their alliance portfolios are dissimilar. In contrast, in hypothetical System II, A and B do not share a common defense pact. Yet in this

---

[4] The $S$-score can also be weighted by some measure of national capabilities or power, but this adds more complexity than we need here.

system $S$ equals 0.71, suggesting that A and B share similar security interests. In confirming our intuition that B is more likely to help A against H in System II than it is in System I, the S-score provides a replicable tool, so we do not have to rely on intuition alone.

Examine real world alliances or construct a few hypothetical alliance systems of your own. Calculate the S-scores for several pairs of states. What other indicators might you use to evaluate the shared interests of states? See if you can estimate S-scores for one or more dyads based on some alternative source of data. Try applying this method to a current international problem to see if you can predict how helpful some allies might be compared with others.

Now that we have a method for taking the guesswork out of estimating similarity in foreign policy commitments, we can return to the alliance portfolios of Britain, France, and Germany on the eve of World War I. Calculating the S-score for these countries within the pool of politically relevant states in 1914, we find that $S$ for Britain and Germany equals 0.24; for Britain and France, 0.59; and for France and Germany, 0.40.[5]

We can easily see from these scores that Britain favored France over Germany and that France favored Britain over Germany. Comparison of the S-scores indicates that

$$S_{UK-France} - S_{UK-Germany} = 0.59 - 0.24, \text{ or } 0.35,$$

and that

$$S_{France-UK} - S_{France-Germany} = 0.59 - 0.40, \text{ or } 0.19.$$

This indicates that France was less concerned about Britain's chances of success over Germany than Britain was about France's chances of success over Germany. Britain's military capabilities in 1914 equaled roughly 33 percent of the combined capabilities of Britain, France, and Germany; France's capabilities equaled about 22 percent of the three; and Germany held the remaining 45 percent. Returning to the model introduced at the beginning of this section, we can say that the value Britain placed on helping France rather than Germany in the war (0.35) multiplied by Britain's expected military contribution (0.33) equals 0.12. In other words, Britain's expected utility for upholding its alliance commitment to France is 0.12. In contrast, France's expected utility for helping Britain (that is, honoring its alliance commitment) based on this model is just 0.04. If our metric for measuring shared interests has produced a reasonable approximation, then we would expect to see Britain do more and endure more on France's behalf than would France on Britain's behalf.

---

[5] The "politically relevant" states, a concept utilized by Zeev Maoz and Bruce Russett (1993), for this analysis includes Albania, Austria-Hungary, Belgium, Britain, Bulgaria, Denmark, France, Germany, Greece, Italy, Japan, the Netherlands, Norway, Portugal, Romania, Russia, Spain, Sweden, Turkey, the United States, and Yugoslavia. This means that the denominator of our alliance similarity formula is (3)(21), or 63.

## TESTING THE PREDICTIVE MODEL

Now that we are able to assess the value of victory, and combine it with our measure of military capabilities to establish utilities, we can apply expression 8.4 to determine the reliability of alliances. Although we do not have a good way to predict expected costs, we do know that the probability of honoring an alliance commitment, according to this model, increases with the expected benefits, provided that those are not highly correlated with the expected costs.[6] Michael Altfeld and I (1979) developed a model that applies this method to predict third-party decisions to join with the stronger or weaker side in a war or to remain neutral. That is, we predicted the reliability of alliances. Our empirical results appear in Table 15-1 (Altfeld and Bueno de Mesquita 1979).

The table shows that when a third party joined the weaker side in a war, the model correctly predicted that it would do so in 80 percent of the cases. What's more, the

TABLE 15-1

### Predicted and Actual Third-Party War Choices

| Actual Choices | Predicted Choices | | |
| --- | --- | --- | --- |
| | Join weaker side | Stay neutral | Join stronger side |
| Join weaker side | 16 | 4 | 0 |
| Stay neutral | 1 | 104 | 3 |
| Join stronger side | 1 | 5 | 10 |

Source: Michael Altfeld and Bruce Bueno de Mesquita, "Choosing Sides in Wars," International Studies Quarterly (March 1979): 106.

model never predicted that the third party would join the stronger side when it actually joined the weaker side. The model does even better at predicting decisions to remain neutral. The model correctly predicted that the third party would stay out of the fray in 96 percent of the cases. Finally, the model correctly predicted that a third party would join the stronger side in 63 percent of the cases.[7] These results are statistically significant. We can see just how important they are substantively by applying a simple measure called the proportionate reduction in error (PRE) measure.

PRE measures establish how much additional information we gain from using a theory that makes accurate predictions compared with knowing only the distribution of the data or the information to form the null hypothesis. In this case, the null hypothesis

---

[6] For a systematic assessment of a method for estimating costs, see Bueno de Mesquita (1983). For a theoretical demonstration that we should not expect costs and benefits to be highly correlated, see Todd Flynn (1994).

[7] For the purposes of this test, nation A was designated as the weaker of nations A and C, and nation C was designated as the stronger of the initial belligerents. This distinction is simply a convenience to give some systematic, politically interesting meaning to A and C.

predicts that everyone remains neutral because neutrality is the most frequent choice. To find the PRE, all we have to do is calculate the percentage of cases predicted correctly minus the percentage of cases in the modal category (that is, the category that occurs most often) of known outcomes and divide that answer by the quantity 100 minus the percentage of cases in the modal category of known outcomes. The resulting percentage is the proportion of cases that we now have gotten right above the percentage that we would have gotten right just from always predicting the modal category. If the theory did not reduce predictive errors at all, then the PRE measure would be zero. If all predictive errors were eliminated, then the PRE measure would be 100. Hence, the closer the PRE is to 100, the greater the substantive advantage in regard to accurate predictions to be gained from the theory in question.

The three rows in Table 15-1 represent our knowledge after the fact about the distribution of decisions by aligned third parties to join one side or the other or to remain neutral. If we knew only the number of cases in each row, but not in each cell, our best guess about any one case, in the absence of any theory, would be that the state in question will remain neutral. This is obviously the best guess, given that we at least know that in 75 percent of the cases the state did remain neutral. The purpose of our theory is to improve on the null prediction that everyone stays neutral. Improvement on the null prediction is one way we can assess whether the theory provides part of the explanation of when alliances are reliable. That is, the object of the theory is to discriminate among categories of choices sufficiently so that we would get more cases right by using our theory than we would get right just by predicting the modal or most common category.

The best we could possibly do is to predict the choice correctly in each and every case. In this circumstance, we would guess correctly in 100 percent of the cases. Of course, this would be wonderful. Suppose I told you that on some problem we had a theory X that made a correct prediction in 96 percent of the cases and for another problem we had a theory Y that made a correct prediction in 65 percent of the cases. You would likely infer that theory X is a better theory than theory Y. In fact, you may be wrong. If the modal category for the first problem includes 94 percent of all cases, then theory X eliminates at most only an additional 2 percent of the cases beyond the modal category out of the total 6 percent of the remaining cases to be explained. The PRE of theory X is equal to 33 percent. If, however, the modal category for the second problem includes just 25 percent of all cases, then the fact that theory Y provides an accurate prediction in 65 percent of the cases eliminates error in 40 percent of the remaining 75 percent of cases to be explained. Theory Y's PRE, then, is 40/75, or 53 percent. Theory Y does better at improving predictions than does theory X.

Returning to Table 15-1, we can establish that the PRE for our theory is 61 percent. How does this compare with other efforts to evaluate the reliability of allies? Table 15-2 summarizes a study done by Randolph Siverson and Joel King in 1980. They predicted war participation by third parties using data similar to that used in my study with Altfeld.

In Siverson and King's analysis, however, choices to participate or not in an ongoing war were made in accordance with realist criteria. Siverson and King considered power relationships alone; alliances were viewed as nothing more than augmentations of power. Estimates of preferences over the outcomes of the dispute played no role at all in their calculations. Siverson and King treated the effects of each variable as separate and additive, whereas Altfeld and I placed the data in an expected utility framework and so looked at the interaction of probability terms and estimates of preferences or utility.[8]

The PRE in the realist-oriented view of alliance reliability equals 34 percent. The

TABLE 15-2

### War Participation and Alliance Attributes, 1815–1965

|  | Predicted to Participate | Predicted Not to Participate |
|---|---|---|
| Actually Participated | 211 | 12 |
| Actually Did Not Participate | 32 | 35 |

*Source:* Randolph M. Siverson and Joel King, "Attributes of National Alliance Membership and War Participation," *American Journal of Political Science* 24 (February 1980): 10.

realist perspective does only about half as well as the perspective reflected in Table 15-1, which takes preferences as well as power into account. My model with Altfeld gives us encouragement that the reliability of alliances is predictable. In addition it reminds us that, in keeping with Morrow's theory of the trade-off between autonomy and security, some alliances are not expected to be reliable in a military sense and this can reliably be anticipated by prospective aggressors.

## ALLIANCES, COORDINATION, AND COMPETITION

When nations sign an alliance, they typically agree on methods to deter aggressors and to coordinate military efforts in times of war. The members of NATO, for example, coordinate military exercises, armament use, battle strategies, lines of command, and so forth. Likewise, members of the Organization of American States (the OAS) work closely together to protect the Western hemisphere and to help resolve internal differences among member states. Yet sometimes conflict arises among members of alliance organizations such as NATO and the OAS. For example, Greece and Turkey, both long-standing members of NATO, have fought with each other over their respective influence in Cyprus. Nicaragua and Honduras, members of the OAS, had several limited military

---

[8] Siverson and King's dependent variable was concerned only with whether third parties participated in war, regardless of which side those parties joined. Thus, the one egregiously wrong prediction in my study with Altfeld, where a country was predicted to join the weaker side when it actually participated on the stronger side, would have been counted as a correct prediction in the Siverson and King analysis. That is, the country was predicted to participate in the war, and it did. Treating this prediction as correct in Table 15-1 would increase the PRE from 61 percent to 64 percent. (The error in my study with Altfeld involved a case in the Second Balkan War, fought in 1913, in which two countries had a secret alliance between them. Because others did not know about the alliance, we did not take it into account in our investigation. Had we included knowledge of the secret alliance, we would have gotten that case right.)

confrontations with one another during the 1980s. El Salvador and Honduras, also members of the OAS, fought what has come to be called the Soccer War in 1969. The United States invaded Panama in 1989 and the Dominican Republic in 1965. These states, too, are members of the OAS. It is evident, then, that alliances contain not only elements of cooperation but elements of competition as well, both in theory and in reality.

**Disputes within the Americas since 1948**

| | Combatants | Year |
|---|---|---|
| 1 | Peru–Ecuador | 1951 |
| 2 | U.S.–Ecuador | 1954 |
| 3 | Mexico, U.S.–Guatemala | 1958 |
| 4 | Paraguay–Argentina | 1959 |
| 5 | Paraguay–Argentina | 1962 |
| 6 | U.S.–Cuba | 1962 |
| 7 | Honduras–Nicaragua | 1962 |
| 8 | Chile–Argentina | 1965 |

MAP 15-1

**Conflict between Members of the Organization of American States**

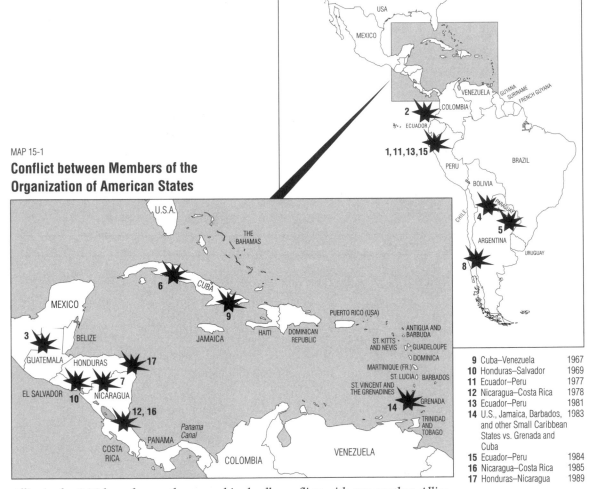

| | | |
|---|---|---|
| 9 | Cuba–Venezuela | 1967 |
| 10 | Honduras–Salvador | 1969 |
| 11 | Ecuador–Peru | 1977 |
| 12 | Nicaragua–Costa Rica | 1978 |
| 13 | Ecuador–Peru | 1981 |
| 14 | U.S., Jamaica, Barbados, and other Small Caribbean States vs. Grenada and Cuba | 1983 |
| 15 | Ecuador–Peru | 1984 |
| 16 | Nicaragua–Costa Rica | 1985 |
| 17 | Honduras–Nicaragua | 1989 |

*Allies in the OAS have frequently engaged in deadly conflicts with one another. Allies, like married couples, often squabble and sometimes turn violent. Although allies usually remain allied even after a war with each other, this is not always true. Since 1962, for instance, Cuba, under the Castro regime, has been excluded from participation in the OAS in accordance with the decision of the eighth meeting of consultation of ministers of foreign affairs.*

The competition that sometimes arises among alliance members and the failure of some allies to honor their promises can weaken alliances. When the costs of adhering to an alliance exceed the expected benefits, we expect the alliance to come apart. It is significant that the interests of member states are never identical. If they were, the members would not need to signal their shared interests to others through an alliance. As a result, alliance membership is fluid. A nation that joins an alliance to gain military security, for example, may use the alliance to buy time while it develops its own military capabilities (Altfeld 1984). When these capabilities are sufficient to satisfy the security concerns of the nation's leaders, then the country is likely to weaken its commitment to the alliance or even withdraw altogether (Berkowitz 1983). Similarly, alliances are weakened when a shift in interests takes place among the member states. For example, if one member experiences a revolutionary change in leadership, it may no longer consider itself to be among friends within the context of that alliance. In such an instance, the alliance is a burden rather than an asset. This is the type of change that took place among the East European states between 1990 and 1991 as the Soviet Union unraveled. No sooner did the Soviet Union come apart than the members of the Warsaw Pact withdrew and that alliance collapsed. By 2002, four former members of the Warsaw Pact (East Germany, Hungary, Poland, and the Czech Republic) had joined NATO, and another ten east and central European states were on the verge of doing so. NATO had been their archenemy just a decade or so earlier.

Ideally, in a well-functioning alliance, the parties do not resent, question, or even notice the control exercised over each of them by the other members because they consider it entirely appropriate in view of the collective interests of the alliance. When coordination veers into a relationship in which one or more members suspects that another member is using the alliance to enhance its own position primarily at the expense of its "partners," as was the case in the Warsaw Pact, then the alliance is likely to unravel. Resentment or friction among allies is especially likely when one state in the alliance dominates all of the others. This, of course, was precisely the problem with the Warsaw Pact. The Soviet Union dominated the alliance and dictated policy to its members. Although in principle every alliance is a voluntary agreement in which each signatory chooses to participate, in reality nations are sometimes coerced into joining. In some instances, the government in power has been imposed from outside; it has not been freely chosen by the population. The leaders of such nations freely join the alliance, but the outside power responsible for placing them in office must continue to exert complete control or else the alliance organization will collapse.

Alliance cohesiveness can be shaken under less dramatic circumstances. Resentment among members can arise when an alliance is dominated by an especially powerful state, even if that state does not engage in the type of extreme behavior exhibited by the Soviet Union in the Warsaw Pact. For example, France in 1961 pulled out of NATO's joint military command. Charles de Gaulle, the leader of France, felt that it had become an instrument of American domination of Western Europe. De Gaulle wanted France to be free of U.S. control. Of course, the United States offered protection against a putative attack from the Soviet Union. Avoiding such an attack was a primary element in the common interest of the member states. As far as de Gaulle was concerned, however, such an attack was unlikely. He calculated that the political costs to France from U.S. control through NATO were greater than the benefits France accrued from the protection NATO afforded. What is more, de Gaulle anticipated confidently that regardless of France's pullback from NATO, the alliance would continue to protect Western Europe from any Soviet threat and that, therefore, French security could free ride on NATO's efforts. In effect, de Gaulle understood that France could gain security from NATO without having to bear the full political and economic costs of membership.

> Over the past several decades, France has followed a foreign policy strategy that has often differed from that of the United States and much of western Europe. Can you find examples in which France opposed NATO or American foreign policy initiatives in recent years? Can you find examples in which France coordinated its policies with those of other western European countries? Make a list of ten major foreign policy actions involving NATO over the past twenty years. How many times did Britain go along with these initiatives? How often did other NATO members go along with them? How many times did France?

De Gaulle freed France to pursue a more independent foreign policy line. American foreign policy decisions under President Dwight Eisenhower had twice left France facing military defeat unassisted by the United States. De Gaulle attributed significant responsibility for the defeat of France, Britain, and Israel in the Suez War against Egypt in 1956 to America's unwillingness to come to their aid. Likewise, France's defeat at Dienbienphu in Vietnam in 1954 followed on the heels of Eisenhower's decision not to assist the French. In this instance, the Eisenhower administration had initially decided to back the French but later reneged.

The chairman of the Joint Chiefs of Staff of the American armed forces, Arthur Radford, went so far as to advocate a nuclear strike against the Vietminh (as the pro-Communist forces in Vietnam were then known). This proposal did not receive support, but a proposed massive air strike, called "Operation Vulture," did. The decision to provide a massive air strike was approved by the National Security Council on March 25, 1954, just five days after news reached Washington of the impending collapse of France's hold on Dienbienphu. The French must have been greatly encouraged if they knew of the American decision. The decision surely spoke of America's commitment to aid its French ally.

A major intervention by the United States would have strengthened France's hand at the upcoming Geneva Peace Conference, aimed at resolving the French-Indochinese war. As preparations for the Geneva Conference went forward, and as the siege of Dienbienphu continued, Prime Minister Winston Churchill in Britain informed the

American government on April 25, 1954, that Britain rejected the planned air strike. Four days later, on April 29, President Eisenhower denied that there had ever been a planned massive air strike by the United States against the Vietminh. Imagine French dismay at seeing American support evaporate into thin air. Dienbienphu fell to the Vietminh on May 7, 1954.

The French, who suffered 35,000 killed and 48,000 wounded in the Indochina war, reasonably inferred that the United States was not an ally that could be counted on, at least not outside of Europe. De Gaulle, reflecting on France's unhappy military history with the United States since the end of World War II, concluded that the United States was committed to using NATO for its own advantage. In his view, France would be better off withdrawing from NATO, building its own nuclear force, strengthening its defense industry, and following its own independent foreign policy. This, in fact, is precisely what France did.

The fact that allies cooperate and coordinate with one another and also sometimes fight with each other or pull apart highlights the complexity of alliances. Although

*Charles de Gaulle, as France's leader, would never forget how the United States forsook France at Dienbienphu in May 1954. The sight of French and Vietnamese prisoners loyal to France under guard of communist Vietminh troops left a bitter taste in his mouth. Years later, France weakened its ties to NATO by withdrawing from the unified military command. De Gaulle was convinced that NATO was an instrument to advance American interests and that it would readily sacrifice French interests if they conflicted with the goals of the United States.*

unaligned nations coordinate military planning less often and come to blows more often, it would be a mistake to believe that alliances are either necessary or sufficient for coordination between states. The armed forces of the United States and Israel have long shared ideas and training, as well as equipment. Yet it was not until the 1979 Camp David Accord between Israel, Egypt, and the United States that Israel and the United States entered into a formal military alliance. Their shared interests were so strong that a formal agreement simply was not necessary. Often an alliance is required to shore up an emerging relationship when the basis for that relationship is not well established.

Alliances can be viewed as costly signals (Morrow 1994c). The United States and Israel did not need to establish a formal alliance agreement because doing so would not have conveyed any additional information to would-be foes. The level of coordination on security matters between the two states was already so high that adversaries could readily infer America's commitment to Israel by its actions. The U.S.-Egyptian agreement following the Camp David meeting, by contrast, conveyed new information. In this way, the alliance, and the coordination it implied, communicated that the United States was prepared to endure costs to promote Egypt's new foreign policy course once Egypt had agreed to make peace with Israel. The U.S. agreement with Egypt also introduced some ambiguity into the American-Israeli relationship. Thus, having signaled a shift in policy toward Egypt, the United States needed also to signal more clearly its continued commitment to Israel, thereby resulting in a formal alliance between them.

Alliances like NATO and the Warsaw Pact are good examples of how an alliance can be a costly signal, at least for some signatories. The unified NATO military command involves an unusually high level of coordination between the military services of the member states. This is a very costly endeavor. It signals significant resolve on the part of the NATO members to defend one another. After all, they each spend considerable resources on military coordination, an expenditure that would make little sense and serve little purpose if they were not resolved to carry out their commitments. They train together, they use many weapons in common, they share commanders, and so on. Soviet resolve in the Warsaw Pact was evident in the significant military costs Moscow bore to defend itself and its allies against prospective encroachments by the United States and its West European allies. Just how strong that resolve was, however, was not signaled as clearly as in the case of the United States and NATO. This is because the Soviet Union had its own incentives, quite apart from the interests of the other Warsaw Pact countries, to invest in forward-based divisions. It did so as much to defend itself from internal East European efforts to overthrow Soviet domination as to defend its allies against NATO encroachments. In fact, during the cold war, Soviet troops were used in combat only against states with which it was aligned (for example, Afghanistan, Czechoslovakia, Hungary). An important difference between the Hungarian or Czech experiences in the Warsaw Pact and France's experience in NATO is readily discernible. When de Gaulle decided to pull France out of NATO's military structure, the other members of NATO did nothing to stop the French. When Hungary in 1956 and later Czechoslovakia in 1968 attempted to pursue more independent courses, they suffered Soviet invasions and were forced to follow the Soviet foreign policy

I have given numerous examples from the twentieth century of allies who came to blows with one another. Can you find additional examples from the nineteenth century? Do alliances tend to survive the use of force by one member against another? Why do you think this is so?

line. This crucial difference is worth further study so that we can better understand those singular cases in which one ally fights another.

## CONFLICT AMONG ALLIES

Although an alliance engenders a promise by its members to cooperate with one another, these agreements sometimes provoke conflict among their signatories, as we have just seen (Bueno de Mesquita 1981a, 1985; Ray 1990; Bremer 1992). It seems paradoxical that allies should fight with one another, and we must hasten to note that, more often than not, they do not. Still, allied states do on occasion fight. As such, it would be beneficial to develop an explanation of such an odd circumstance. We can readily do so by appealing to the median voter theorem.

Recall that the median voter theorem tells us that for an issue situated on a continuum, when preferences are single peaked and a majority rules, we can predict the outcome of that issue if we know the preferred choice of the median voter. Voting is just one form of exercising power, so we can speak of the median voter as the actor on the international stage who occupies the position that balances the power of all other actors to the right and to the left on the issue continuum of interest. This median position has a characteristic that neorealists and others believe is the major objective of all states: it is the position that maximizes a state's security.

The median position maximizes security in that if the median state were involved in a conflict with any actor to its left, all of the states to its right would prefer to see the median state win so that, together, these states and the median state would control a majority of available power. Likewise, if the median state were involved in a conflict with any actor to its right, all of the actors to its left would prefer to see the median state win so that, again, these states together with the median state would control a majority of the available power.[9] If states truly cared only about security, per the neorealist view, then they would all cluster at the median voter position.

Variations in preferences over fundamental foreign policy issues *other* than security help explain why all states are not located precisely at the median voter or median power position on every issue. This is not to say that national leaders do not care about security.

[9] Note that these preferences are singled peaked.

In fact, when states shift position on a policy question, they do so in part to improve their security. If a shift a little bit to the left or a little bit to the right leaves them equally well off in regard to the policy they are pursuing, but a shift to the left makes them more secure than a shift to the right, or visa versa, then we would expect national leaders to move their policies in the direction of enhanced security. Thus, when states shift their policy stances on fundamental issues, we should expect them generally to move toward the median voter position, unless coerced to do otherwise. Figure 15-4 depicts the policy positions and capabilities of the United States, NATO, France, Czechoslovakia, the Soviet Union and other Warsaw Pact countries, and East Germany in 1968 on the eve of the Soviet invasion of Czechoslovakia. At the time of the invasion, Czechoslovakia and the Soviet Union were both members of the Warsaw Pact.

Select some data sets on our Web site. Using the model found there, find the median power. Which actor or actors are associated with this position? Are such actors always powerful, or can they be individually weak but supported by a strong coalition? What does this suggest about the argument that to become more secure nations need to increase their power?

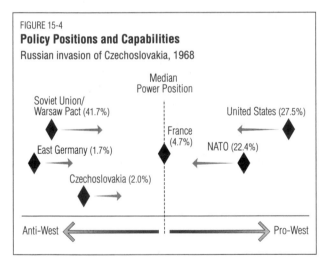

FIGURE 15-4
**Policy Positions and Capabilities**
Russian invasion of Czechoslovakia, 1968

Median
Power Position

Soviet Union/
Warsaw Pact (41.7%)

United States (27.5%)

France
(4.7%)

East Germany (1.7%)

NATO (22.4%)

Czechoslovakia (2.0%)

Anti-West        Pro-West

*Note:* Percentages of power resources are Correlates of War composite capabilities. In the case of the United States, capabilities are adjusted for the distance between the United States and Europe. The adjustment follows the procedure described in Bueno de Mesquita (1981a).

*One reason a state might attack its own ally is to prevent the erosion of friendly ties by a shift in leadership or a shift in policies in the ally's government. The Soviet Union frequently used force to keep its allies in check, but never used its military forces openly in combat against avowed enemies. The United States also used military force against its own allies from time to time during the cold war.*

Notice that in Figure 15-4 France is the median power. The states to France's left (East Germany and the Soviet Union and the rest of the Warsaw Pact countries) together control 45.4 percent of available power resources. The states to France's right (the NATO countries and the United States) control 49.9 percent of available power resources. The remainder is held by France.[10] In a conflict between France and NATO, France can count on support from East Germany and the Soviet Union and the other Warsaw Pact countries, including Czechoslovakia. NATO, in such a dispute, can rely only on the United States. This leaves France with a slim advantage. This may be one reason why France felt comfortable pulling out of the NATO joint command in the early 1960s and why it has been willing to pursue a fairly independent foreign policy course since

[10] This is a bit of a simplification. Europe's neutral powers—Austria, Sweden, and Switzerland, for example—are not included here to keep the example uncluttered.

then. If France and the Soviet Union become involved in a dispute, and if everyone pitches in to back up one or the other, then the Soviets will get help from East Germany and Czechoslovakia, their allies, whereas France will be assisted by NATO and the United States. France, again, would then have the advantage. Looking at the distribution of power and interests within Europe, it is little wonder that the cold war was a stalemate for so long. Now, as Russia continues to improve its ties to NATO, it will be interesting to see if France's policies become less independent, as the location of the median power may well have shifted.

Suppose we define allies as states that are close to one another on the issue continuum. Then, relatively speaking, East Germany, the Soviet Union, and the other Warsaw Pact countries, and Czechoslovakia are seen in Figure 15-4 as more closely allied than are the Soviet Union and NATO or the Soviet Union and the United States. This, of course, was precisely the case. If we define enemies as states that are far apart on important policies, and if the continuum in Figure 15-4 represents an important policy dimension in 1968, then we can say that, relatively speaking, the Soviets and their allies were enemies of NATO and the United States, and visa versa.

The arrows next to country names in Figure 15-4 show the Soviets' best guess as to the direction (and distance) that East Germany, Czechoslovakia, NATO, and the United States would shift on the policy question, if they were to shift at all. Notice that the Soviet Union assumes that any shift will occur in the direction of the median power position (that is, toward France). The Soviets are not assuming that these shifts will certainly take place, only that probabilistically they might take place. What the Soviets are assuming is that no state will move away from the median voter position, thereby diminishing its security, when any move in either direction from its preferred policy means some loss on the policy dimension anyway. Remember, the position that each country occupies is its ideal point—that is, the policy outcome each desires most. Thus, the Soviet Union assumes that there is no chance that either the East Germans or the Czechs will move farther to the left on their own. Doing so would make these countries worse off, both in regard to the policy issue at hand and in regard to their overall security. Likewise, the Soviets assume that neither NATO nor the United States will move farther right if either decides to modify its policy stance. Any compromises in policy resulting from international negotiations are presumed to shift the relevant actors toward the median voter position—that is, toward a sort of "convergence" of views.

A fight initiated by the Soviets against NATO or the United States would presumably be motivated by the Soviet desire to coerce either of them into accepting a policy more to the Soviets' liking. However, given the assumed Soviet belief that any policy shift by NATO or the United States will be toward the French at the median power position, the Soviets could hope to gain some policy concessions for free just by being patient. Likewise, the United States could expect that any change in policy by the Soviet Union would likely move them toward the French position and, therefore, toward a policy friendlier to the United States at no negotiating or coercive cost to Washington. Because the nations on opposite sides of the median power position each have reason to hope for a "free" policy shift by an enemy, the incentive to get into a hot fight is diminished and the prospect of apparent cooperation between foes is improved.

The Soviet Union did not have a similar offsetting incentive to avoid fighting with Czechoslovakia. If the Czechs were going to compromise their policy stance to improve their security, then the Russians knew that the Czechs would move farther away from the Soviets and closer to the French. This, in fact, is just what the Czechs were trying to do in the spring of 1968. If the Soviets anticipated a shift by Czechoslovakia, and if they believed they were strong enough to coerce the Czechs into not shifting (or into shifting in the direction of the Soviet Union), then the Soviets had a reason to attack their ally, Czechoslovakia. To succeed, the Russians had to be confident that France, NATO, and the United States cared sufficiently little about the benefits they might gain from a shift by the Czechs relative to the costs of helping them that their efforts on Czechoslovakia's behalf would be severely attenuated. This is precisely what happened when the Soviets and their allies invaded Czechoslovakia in August 1968. Mitigating circumstances reduced the incentive of the Soviets to fight with NATO or the United States. In the case of Czechoslovakia, no such mitigating circumstance existed.

Note that the Soviets' concern about the Czechs was entirely anticipatory. What they were worried about is what the Czech government might do in the future, not what it had actually done. Wars between enemies often take place over *current* differences in foreign policy perspectives. In contrast, wars between allies usually take place over *anticipated* future differences in policy. In these cases, one partner is seeking to prevent the other partner from changing course. These wars are initiated to avert a future change in policy by the target, not to correct a past or present discrepancy in interests. Thucydides wrote of such a case in his *History of the Peloponnesian War*. Speaking through the ambassadors of the Mytilenaeans, he explained their betrayal of their allies, the Athenians, by saying:

> The relationship between the Soviet Union and East Germany in the example here is more complicated. Under what conditions would the Soviets have favored a shift in East German policy and under what conditions would they have found a shift a potential reason for war?

> We held them not any longer for faithful leaders. For it was not probable when they had subdued those whom together with us they took into league but that, when they should be able, they would do the like by the rest. . . . Now the reason why they have left us yet free is no other but that they may have a fair colour to lay upon their domination over the rest and because it hath seemed unto them more expedient to take us by policy than by force. . . . So it was more for fear than love that we remained their confederates; and whomsoever security should first embolden, he was first likely by one means or other to break the league. Now if any man think we did

unjustly to revolt upon the expectation of evil intended without staying to be certain whether they would do it or not, he weigheth not the matter aright. For if we were as able to contrive evil against them and again to defer it, as they can against us, being thus equal, what needed us to be at their discretion? But seeing it is in their hands to invade at pleasure, it ought to be in ours to anticipate. (1959, 3:10–12)

The invasion of allies by allies has, as the passage from Thucydides makes clear, an ancient lineage. Such wars, based as they are on "the expectation of evil intended," have continued throughout history. The Soviet invasion of Afghanistan in 1979 is a particularly unambiguous modern example. Beginning on Christmas day tens of thousands of Soviet troops began pouring into Afghanistan to overthrow the regime of Hafizullah Amin. The Soviet attack precipitated a decade-long struggle between the Soviets and the Afghani rebels to whom, so the Soviets feared, Amin might cozy up. Just two days before the invasion, the Soviet state-controlled newspaper *Pravda* praised Amin, a hard-line Marxist, and denied reports of any Soviet intention to place troops in Afghanistan. Afghanistan, under Amin, had become a Soviet client state and ally in 1978. Amin's principal failing was his inability to quell a Muslim rebellion, a rebellion that, if successful, was expected to completely eliminate the Soviet Union's influence in that country. Rather than risk such a fate by continuing to support the unpopular and apparently incompetent Amin, the Soviets overthrew his government, executed him, and installed Babrak Karmal as the new chief of state. Presumably, the Russians expected Karmal to be more compliant. In other respects, however, there was little reason for them to believe that the placement of Karmal would represent a significant change in policy from Amin. Had not Afghanistan been a client state, it is difficult to imagine that the Soviets would have taken such a bold step to quell the nascent Muslim rebellion. Other states might have been more likely to intervene had not the government the Soviets knocked down already been its puppet.

In the end, the Soviet decision appears to have been based on a correct concern about "the expectation of evil intended." After bleeding in Afghanistan for a decade, Soviet troops were finally withdrawn during the leadership of Mikhail Gorbachev. Although civil war continued in Afghanistan after the Soviets withdrew, the war then was among competing fundamentalist groups, all with policies antithetical to Russian interests. By the late 1990s, the rigidly fundamentalist Taliban had taken control of Kabul and imposed a government that adhered to an extremely strict interpretation of the Koran. In addition to remaining hostile to the Russians, the Taliban also banned the education of girls and women. They were, from the Russian point of view, the very "evil" that the Soviet invasion was intended to prevent. What is more, the United States had provided economic assistance to many Taliban rebels in their war against Russia only to have these same people, once in power, become enemies of the United States. The Taliban, as we know, were important protectors of al-Qaeda terrorists who attacked New York and Washington, D.C., in 2001, launching the American war on terrorism.

Having dwelt on wars among allies, we should not lose sight of the fact that alliances more often involve or prevent, and even sometimes provoke, conflict with those outside the alliance. The promise to cooperate with alliance members is often seen by a third party as a competitive, aggressive move that threatens its security. After all, the alliance may make it harder for a third party to persuade one of the allying states to correct some prior misconduct because now that allied state has the promise of extra help with which to enforce its viewpoint. Certainly the Soviet Union and its allies in the Warsaw Pact viewed the NATO alliance as a deliberate threat to their security. Indeed, America's post–World War II policy of containment, aimed at encircling the Soviet Union to prevent it from expanding its sphere of influence, was a central feature of NATO. Of course, the members of NATO viewed the Warsaw Pact as a prospective threat to their security. This view was bolstered by the series of crises over access to Berlin precipitated by the Soviet Union from the late 1940s through the 1960s.

Finally, we cannot conclude this discussion without some comment on how domestic political institutions influence the reliability of alliances. Kurt Gaubatz (1996), Scott Bennett (1997c), and William Reed (1997) show that alliances with more democratic members last longer than alliances with fewer democratic members. As with so many

*Since the defeat in 2002 of the Taliban regime in Afghanistan, women are again permitted to hold jobs and girls can once again go to school. Boys and girls go to school together now, as seen in this photograph of women teachers with their students in outdoor classrooms in Kabul in March 2002. The school building was destroyed during the Afghan civil war.*

other empirical results discussed thus far, this observation contradicts the fundamental tenets of structural theories and reinforces the strategic perspective.

## SUMMARY

A military alliance constitutes an agreement between two or more states stipulating a specified response on the part of the signatories in the event that one or more parties to the agreement are attacked. Sabrosky (1980) has demonstrated that about three-quarters of allies fail to honor their promises when an attack occurs. Alastair Smith (1995) has shown, however, that Sabrosky's finding is likely the consequence of a selection effect. The alliances that get tested are typically those that the attacker believes are unreliable or, in other words, are alliances that have been formed for some purpose other than *mutual* defense. Morrow (1991a) provides a theory that predicts the formation of long-lasting, asymmetric alliances that involve security gains for one party and autonomy gains for the other. Morrow's theory provides an explanation for the existence of alliances between strong and weak states, where it is unlikely that the weak state can really augment the security of the strong state. Such asymmetric alliances typically prove unreliable when tested. And it is these that are especially likely to be tested.

In contrast, reliable alliances are disproportionately symmetric and are designed specifically for mutual security gains. These types of alliances rarely get tested. Altfeld and I (1979) have shown that it is possible to predict which alliance partnerships are likely to be reliable and which are not. Our model of alliance reliability accurately predicted whether or not an ally exhibited reliability in just over 90 percent of the cases examined and reduced predictive errors by more than 60 percent. The cumulative body of knowledge presented here explains fundamental aspects of the workings of alliances and provides the tools necessary to predict which alliances will be reliable and which will not in the event of war.

George Washington, more than two centuries ago, warned his countrymen to avoid involvement in entangling alliances. He was worried that the young American republic would be swept away in the larger battles of Europe. America heeded Washington's advice, eschewing almost all alliances until the twentieth century. Today, we know much more about the risks and rewards of alternative forms of alliances. In this area of international relations, the application of the scientific method has yielded real benefits. The policymakers of Washington's day lacked specific methods for telling which alliances were likely to be entangling and how entangling they were likely to be. The benefits of our systematic knowledge of today, however, allow us to leave Washington's concerns behind and embrace alliance opportunities with confidence.

# THE CAUSES OF WAR: STRUCTURAL ACCOUNTS

Two thousand years passed between the biblical departure from Eden and the first recorded war. Never again would two thousand years go by, or even two hundred, without a recurrence of humankind's worst invention. The perfection of the means of warfare has critically affected the ebb and flow of civilizations over the millennia. Those early hunters and gatherers who learned to use a club or stone as a weapon against wild beasts experienced the first human use of power as a means of control. They then applied their weaponry to gaining control of one another until today the technology of warfare is so advanced that weapons of mass destruction are capable of destroying civilization as we know it.

Warfare represents the most egregious breakdown of international cooperation. Yet even during wars there are numerous examples of cooperative behavior. Of course allies sometimes assist one another in defeating a foe. But even enemies engage in cooperation. The Geneva Conventions, for example, establish rules of war. Although not always obeyed, these rules do help control wartime excesses. The conventions on warfare proscribe the unnecessary and wanton killing of innocent civilians, provide rules for handling prisoners of war, and impose limits on the uses of certain types of weapons (for example, poison chemicals and gases). International agreements discipline behavior in wartime. This is accomplished by creating clear expectations about what is or is not acceptable behavior and by reinforcing the expectation that the loser will be held accountable for wartime misconduct (Ash 1997; Morrow 1998). Proscribed behavior reflects rules or institutions that limit leaders' freedom of action. This, in fact, is the purpose behind such institutions. Thus, even at the height of war, some international cooperation is evident between adversaries. Still, the fundamental feature of warfare is the breakdown of cooperation and its replacement with violence and destruction.

Because war is so destructive, its causes have occupied generations of researchers. Some early ideas about the causes of war have been disproved or have been shown to be so weak as to be unworthy of continued consideration. For example, in the 1920s some observers maintained that war was caused by a virus. They observed that railroads, having made it easy for large numbers of people to travel all over Europe, helped to spread the "World War I virus" throughout Europe in 1914, just as four years later they contributed to the spread of the deadly flu virus. Thus it was, they claimed, that a larger, more destructive war than had previously been known erupted in 1914. Although the metaphor of war as a contagious disease has persisted (Beer 1981), no one any longer takes seriously the idea that war is literally a disease. There just is no evidence to support the claim. But many other theories persist as plausible explanations of warfare. The most prominent and most promising of these will occupy our attention here.

In this chapter we investigate the two most prominent structural theories of war: neorealism and power transition theory. First, we will examine the logical foundations undergirding neorealism's key hypotheses, and then we will evaluate the historical record to see if it is consistent with realist predictions. Next, we will examine the power transition theory. This, too, is structuralist in its perspective, but it assumes that international politics are organized hierarchically rather than anarchically. Again, we will discuss the assumptions of the theory and then review its empirical performance. Our conclusions will help us assess whether or not a balance of power and bipolarity promote international stability.

## REALIST THEORIES OF WAR

Realist and neorealist theorists believe that the distribution of power in the international system is a major factor in determining whether international affairs are stable or unstable. "Stability" refers to circumstances in which the sovereignty of key states is preserved (Gulick 1955). "Instability" refers to changes in the composition of the international system, especially changes involving the disappearance or emergence of consequential states following large wars. Consequential or key states are those whose assistance might be necessary to counteract a threat from a rival grouping of states. Sometimes I refer to these states as essential actors to highlight their ability to turn a potentially losing situation into a winning one, or at least into one that blocks adversaries from victory.

Since war represents a potential threat to sovereignty, realist theorists are concerned with the causes of war, especially big wars capable of jeopardizing the survival of great powers. In addressing war and instability, neorealist theories start with the following four assumptions:

1. International politics is anarchic.
2. States, as rational unitary entities, are the central actors in international politics.

3. States seek to maximize their security above all else, considering other factors only after security is assured.
4. States seek to increase their power so long as doing so does not place their security at risk.

Anarchy, you recall, means that there is no supernational authority that can enforce agreements between states. Consequently, in the international arena every state must look out for its own well-being. International politics involves self-help above all else. The second assumption implies that domestic politics is largely irrelevant to international politics. Because of this, foreign policy should be considered separately from international politics. The third assumption establishes the primacy of security. It also establishes that states are not willing to trade away their security for other benefits. Other possible goals are pursued only after security has been assured. This assumption should lend considerable predictability to states' behavior. Because all states have the same goal, we need not worry about idiosyncratic factors such as the personalities of individual leaders or the domestic political institutions that govern state behavior. Every state is a role player, with the role dictated by its security needs.

The final assumption tells us that states are always interested in increasing their influence over other states. No state is content to be weak, but states accept being weaker than they might otherwise be if pursuit of greater power would place their security at risk. This assumption places restrictions on the pursuit of power. If a state becomes sufficiently powerful that other states foresee the possibility that their security will be threatened by it in the future, then they will join together to deprive the growing state of the power to threaten them. Thus, an increase in a state's power can actually make the state weaker in the long run. This happens if the increase in power alarms rivals and mobilizes them to form an opposition alliance. A coalition or alliance of states will come together to beat back a growing state if that state's power threatens to become large enough that others face a possible loss of sovereignty. This phenomenon is sometimes known as the security dilemma.

These four assumptions provide a parsimonious and potentially powerful view of international politics. Several important hypotheses are said to follow from them. In Chapter 15 we looked at hypotheses that have to do with alliances. In this chapter we will examine those hypotheses that directly concern the risk of war. The most important structural neorealist hypotheses about the threat of war or instability are as follows:

1. Bipolar systems are more stable than multipolar systems.
2. States engage in balancing behavior so that power becomes more or less equally divided among states over time.
3. States mimic, or echo, each other's behavior.

## HOW WELL DOES NEOREALISM DO IN EXPLAINING WAR AND INSTABILITY?

Our examination of neorealist theory and the risk of war will proceed in stages. First, we investigate whether the three primary neorealist hypotheses are logically implied by the four assumptions of neorealist theory. Then we examine how well those hypotheses describe historical circumstances. In this way we can assess the logical and historical significance of the neorealist view of war and international politics.

If the neorealist hypotheses are not accurate descriptions of international affairs, then their logical status is unimportant. Hypotheses that are logically implied by the assumptions of a theory but that are inconsistent with observed behavior serve to falsify that theory's predictions. If the neorealist hypotheses are consistent with observed behavior but do not follow from the assumptions, then we will need to alter the assumptions to account for the observed facts. In this case, a different set of implications will likely follow from these new assumptions. We will want to know whether those new implications are also consistent with the facts. It is through this process of evaluation and alteration that theories grow and we achieve a better understanding of how the world works. Finally, if the hypotheses follow logically from the assumptions, and if the hypotheses accurately account for observed behavior, then neorealist theory is a powerful tool for understanding international politics.

### BIPOLARITY AND STABILITY

A bipolar international system is dominated by two very powerful states, with weaker nations clustered around each of the two power poles. A multipolar system consists of more than two very powerful states. The great powers in a multipolar environment may also attract the support of other, lesser states. In a multipolar system, there must be more than two such concentrations of power.

The argument that bipolar structures are more stable than multipolar structures is built on the claim that there is more uncertainty in a multipolar system than there is in a bipolar system. In a multipolar world it is difficult to anticipate how nations will organize themselves in the event of a threat by one nation against another. There are so many possible linkages between different blocs of nations that the commitments of third parties not directly involved in a confrontation become difficult to predict.

Suppose the international system consists of five powerful nations, A, B, C, D, and E, each of which is the leader of a bloc. If A and B get into a squabble, each will be relatively uncertain about what C, D, and E will do. In contrast, if the international system consists of only two big powers, A and B, then there must be less uncertainty. Each is the adversary of the other, and neither needs to worry about anyone else. Neorealists conclude that because there is less uncertainty in a bipolar world, fewer errors are made by the leaders of states in bipolar international politics. Therefore, they claim, bipolar systems are more stable than multipolar systems.

We can see how this argument about polarity and uncertainty works by considering the configuration of international military commitments shown in Figures 16-1 and 16-2. Figure 16-1 displays the military commitments of the major powers on the eve of World War I. Six major powers were actively engaged in European diplomacy in 1914. They included Austria-Hungary, Britain, France, Germany, Italy, and Russia. The United States and Japan were also great powers at that time, but their foreign policies, although actively promoting trade, generally reflected a desire to stay out of European security questions.

It is evident from Figure 16-1 that there was considerable uncertainty about how the great powers would respond to hostilities between Austria-Hungary and Russia over the future of Serbia. The future of Serbia was the immediate issue that led to World War I. It is notable that the combinations of states that eventually formed the two sides in World War I did not make up obviously distinct sets of interests before the war. England, France, and Russia stuck together in fighting against Austria-Hungary and Germany, but that they would do so was neither inevitable nor obvious before the war. Italy, with ties to both camps, held back, waiting to see how the war was going. It finally came in on the side of the Triple Entente in April 1915. Figure 16-1 reminds us that explanations of World War I that say the alliances worked like trip wires, making a massive war inevitable, rely more on hindsight than on the actual prewar facts.

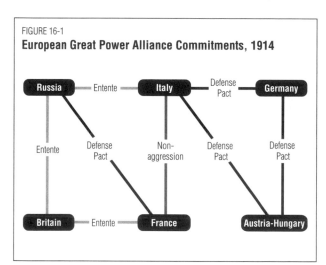

FIGURE 16-1
**European Great Power Alliance Commitments, 1914**

*After World War I was over, many experts maintained that rigid alliance commitments created a trip wire that allowed the 1914 crisis between Austria-Hungary and Serbia to escalate into a global conflict. However, looking at the great power alliance ties in June 1914, just before World War I erupted, suggests that in fact the boundaries demarcating commitments were far from clear.*

England had revealed itself to have weak ties to France and Russia, promising only to consult with them and no more. One might have readily imagined that Britain would stay out of the war altogether. In fact, that's just what the Germans thought the British would do. France, for its part, was closely aligned with Russia but also had a neutrality pact with Italy. Italy, in turn, was strongly associated with Austria-Hungary and Germany through an alliance that promised mutual defense. The sides that appeared to be polar opposites after the war began, seemed to be intricately intertwined beforehand. Certainly, the war would have been much more limited had Britain stayed out of it and had France participated only half-heartedly.

The ambiguous alliance commitments of 1914 stand in sharp contrast to the structure of major power commitments in European affairs during the cold war. As shown in Figure 16-2, European security affairs were dominated by five major powers: Britain, France, Germany, the Soviet Union, and the United States. China had emerged as a great Asian power, but it was little involved in European security questions. Likewise, Japan was a great economic power but not a major player on the European or world security stage.[1]

The major power system during the cold war years was unambiguous. The United States led the NATO alliance, which included all of the European great powers other than the Soviet Union, and the Soviets led the Warsaw Pact countries. No alliance commitments ran from one bloc to the other to create ambiguities about who was committed to whom. The cold war bipolar structure contained very little uncertainty indeed.

We can see that a system in which two states are dominant is unlikely to contain much uncertainty. Likewise, a multipolar system with more than two important centers of power can easily contain uncertainty. It appears that neorealists are correct in their contention that in multipolar systems decisions are made under greater uncertainty than in bipolar systems. But there is a considerable logical leap from the association of uncertainty with multipolarity to the association of multipolarity with instability and bipolarity with stability. Indeed, some have argued that multipolar systems are more stable than bipolar systems precisely because multipolarity produces uncertainty (Deutsch and Singer 1964). Others have argued that there may be no relationship at all between polarity and stability (Bueno de Mesquita 1978).

There are several problems with the argument that because bipolar systems encompass less uncertainty than multipolar systems they yield greater stability. To start with, this argument is not implied logically by the four key assumptions of neorealism. In fact, those assumptions say nothing at all about uncertainty or how uncertainty affects stability. To conclude that there is a relationship between uncertainty and the stability of the international system, we would need to make additional assumptions.

In particular, we would need to make some assumption about how states (or decision makers) respond to uncertainty. Here we run into disagreement about what uncertainty implies about decision making and

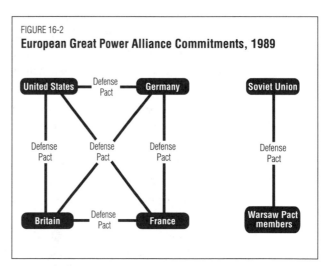

FIGURE 16-2
**European Great Power Alliance Commitments, 1989**

*The bipolar structure of major power alliances during the cold war contained little ambiguity.*

---

[1] Germany's primary strategic importance during the cold war lay in the fact that both the United States and the Soviet Union had stationed large numbers of troops on German soil. Germany was the point at which a war between the United States and the Soviet Union was most likely to begin.

stability. For example, uncertainty may prompt states (or their leaders) to behave cautiously. At the same time, powerful nations may attempt to eliminate or diminish a rival precisely because greater certainty makes evident the opportunity to do so. If uncertainty promotes caution and certainty encourages opportunism, then bipolarity in fact encourages instability. This is essentially the argument that led Karl Deutsch and J. David Singer (1964) to conclude that multipolar systems are more stable than bipolar systems.

In order to support the argument that bipolarity fosters stability, then, we might assume that certainty makes states cautious, whereas multipolarity and uncertainty make states somewhat reckless or risk seeking. That is, we must logically exclude the possibility that uncertainty breeds caution. If this is true, then all states are risk averse in the face of certainty. Although this is a strong assumption, it does solve the logical dilemma we face and it is consistent with the third neorealist hypothesis, which holds that states echo one another's actions. Whether it solves the logical problem we are confronted with at the price of departing too much from reality is an empirical question to be resolved by examining evidence rather than making a judgment of whether we think the assumption is realistic or not.

The fix I have just proposed precludes the possibility that different leaders or different states respond in different ways to uncertainty and is consistent with the system-level view of neorealism. Indeed, the notion that leaders in different states react to uncertainty each in his or her own way presents three immediate problems. First, it violates the unitary rational actor assumption of structural theories, including neorealist theory, which contends that important choices in international politics are driven by structural factors, not by considerations internal to the state. All structural or system-level arguments ignore variation in leader proclivities. Second, if different decision makers respond to uncertainty in different ways, then there is no reason to expect any empirical relationship between bipolarity and stability at all. Some leaders might be cautious when faced with an uncertain situation whereas others might be reckless. If there is a roughly equal mix of states (or leaders) with reckless and with cautious reactions, then, on average, uncertainty would not have any systematic effect on stability. Half the time uncertainty would prompt cautious, stability-enhancing actions and half the time it would prompt reckless, instability-producing actions. Third, if leaders differ in how they respond to uncertainty, then the third hypothesis, which maintains that states mimic one another, does not hold up. Clearly, neorealist theory equating bipolarity with stability cannot tolerate the possibility that individual decision makers vary in their response to uncertainty.

The bipolarity argument is problematic even if we ignore the fact that it offers no explanation of how uncertainty or certainty affects international stability. The deeper problem is that the hypothesis that stability is fostered by bipolarity is inconsistent with the four assumptions of neorealism. In fact, taking neorealist assumptions into account, we can show that it is logically true that more distributions of power are stable in a multipolar world than in a bipolar world.

To prove this claim, let's suppose that there are 300 units of power in the international system. Two distributions of power are of interest when it comes to a bipolar world. If the distribution of power for bloc A and bloc B is exactly 150–150, then neither state can destabilize the system by trying to take power away from the other bloc. Each is exactly powerful enough to prevent a victory by its rival. Such a bipolar balance-of-power system would be very stable indeed, as hypothesized by neorealist thinkers. If, however, the distribution of power differs at all from that perfect 150–150 split, then the system *must* be unstable according to neorealist assumptions, if not neorealist conclusions (Niou, Ordeshook, and Rose 1989).

Suppose, for example, that nation A has 151 units of power, whereas nation B has 149 units of power. The system is practically balanced, but not quite. According to assumption 3, nation A wants more power but, per assumption 4, will not seek it if doing so puts nation A's security at risk. Since power is the ability to make a rival do something it otherwise would not want to do, A has the absolute ability to force B to give up all of its resources (that is, the 149 units of power). A is stronger than B. If B does not willingly give up its resources, A can just take them. In a bipolar world, nation B cannot turn to anyone else for help because there is no one else. By taking B's resources, A increases its own power and does not place its sovereignty or its security at risk because it knows that it can beat B. This is what it means to say that A is more powerful than B in the terms of structural perspectives. Therefore, except in the unlikely event that power is perfectly balanced, or *perceived* to be perfectly balanced, bipolar systems are unstable according to neorealist logic.

Unbalanced bipolarity results in the destruction of one big state or bloc of states by the other, bigger state or bloc. This argument holds even after introducing uncertainty about the exact distribution of power or accounting for a range of costs associated with war. The introduction of uncertainty in the bipolar setting, in fact, turns the argument for the stability of bipolar systems on its head. Remember, bipolar systems are supposed to be less uncertain than multipolar systems.

> I have been careful to say that the distribution of power is precisely equal, or is perceived to be precisely equal, when bipolarity implies stability. What if the real distribution of power in a bipolar setting is 120–180 and the perceived distribution is 150–150? Is this system likely to foment an attempt by one bloc to take power from another? What if the real distribution of power is 150–150 but the perceived distribution is 120–180? In this case, is one bloc likely to try to take power away from the other? Think about the answer to these questions strictly in regard to the assumptions of neorealism. What does the theory logically imply? What does the theory say about perceptions? Are the implications consistent or inconsistent with the hypothesis that bipolarity leads to stability?

Now let's consider two different multipolar systems. Each system consists of five nations (or blocs of nations), A, B, C, D, and E. System I contains the following possible power distributions: A = 75, B = 74, C = 75, D = 74, and E = 2. System II's power distribution differs slightly. It is as follows: A = 78, B = 74, C = 73, D = 73, and E = 2.

According to the assumptions of neorealism, what can we say about the stability of these systems?

System I (75, 74, 75, 74, 2) is a stable system. No state can be eliminated from the international system given the current distribution of power—not even state E, although E holds only 2/300 of the total power. In fact, state E is an important stabilizing element in this system because it can join with some combination of states to build a coalition strong enough to protect itself from the remaining combination of rivals. State E helps itself and other states enhance security.

According to neorealism, any combination of states with power totaling more than half the available capabilities can defeat any combination of opponents. For hypothetical systems with 300 units of power, then, any combination of states that controls greater than 150 units of power can defeat the remaining states. As such, each state has an incentive to prevent the formation of such a coalition if the alliance excludes that state. By forging a blocking coalition that itself holds 150 units of power, states can ensure their security. Viewed mathematically, we can say that, where $R$ = resources (that is, power), the blocking coalition must equal $R/2$. Recall that in our earlier, bipolar system stability was achieved when each pole formed a blocking coalition with $R/2$ units of power.

In System I, nation E might align with nations B and D ($74 + 74 + 2 = 150 = R/2$) against A and C. This arrangement is stable in that neither side is strong enough to eliminate any one state. Each state in the system is essential because each state can turn a losing coalition into a winning coalition or a blocking coalition. Notice that if A attacks E, other states will join to defend E and defeat A. They will do so because if they do not, their own security will be diminished by the lost opportunity to form a blocking coalition with E or a subsequent winning coalition against A. By ignoring E's plight, C and D place their own future security at risk. This is something they would not do according to the assumptions of neorealist theory. Less obviously, B's security will be at risk. Under the assumptions of neorealism, there is no sustainable additional benefit in regard to security for B (or anyone else) once a coalition with $R/2$ resources has formed. The power distribution may or may not remain stable, but all of the states will survive because they all play a crucial role in helping to preserve someone else's security. There is no need to redistribute power to ensure security, although security could be ensured even if the power were to be redistributed. For example, a redistribution to 75, 75, 70, 70, 10 would also engender stability, as would a redistribution that gave any one state 150 units of power.

Notice that in System II (A = 78, B = 74, C = 73, D = 73, E = 2) there is no combination of states that cares to ensure the survival of nation E because no state requires E's assistance to form a blocking or winning coalition. Nation A can form a winning coalition just by joining with B, or, if B is not willing, by aligning with C or D. Adding E to any of these coalitions is superfluous. B likewise can forge winning coalitions by aligning with A or with C and D. No winning or blocking coalition that would otherwise be a losing coalition can form by adding nation E to it. Consequently, E is expendable. Should any of the remaining states (or all of the remaining states) defeat and seize E's two units of power, this will not change their ability to form winning coalitions. Thus, A, B, C, and D have ensured security for themselves by being an essential component of at least one blocking or winning coalition; in contrast, E is inessential.

We can see how System II might evolve by applying to it the rules of neorealism. States A and D might threaten to gobble up states B, C, and E, provided that A and D agree to evenly split all available resources at the war's end. If no power is dissipated in war costs, each would require 150 units of power at the end of the fighting. If either accepted anything less, it would quickly succumb to its erstwhile ally. States B, C, and E would obviously be unhappy with this state of affairs. States B and C might therefore head off such a threat to their security by approaching A and offering it a deal that is at least as good for A as the one it could have by forming an alliance with D to destroy B, C, and E. B and C might suggest to A that it destroy E and thereby gain E's 2 units of power (so it now has 80 units of power instead of just 78) and, in addition, take 35 units each from B and C, each of whom would give it willingly—say, by transferring territory or some other tangible source of power—so that A will end up with 150 units of power without ever having to fight a big war against B, C, and E and without having to take the risk that D might come out ahead of A in the war. Under this arrangement, while B and C sacrifice power, they ensure their survival because once A has 150 units of power ($R/2 = 150$), the surviving states are all essential. The new distribution of power might be A = 150, B = 39, C = 38, D = 73 or, perhaps, A = 150, B = 74, C = 3, D = 73, or any of a number of other possibilities.

In summary, state E is an essential actor in the first hypothetical multipolar system. In System I, no one can afford to see state E eliminated. Its demise would needlessly place someone else's future security at risk in direct violation of neorealist assumption 4. In this system, for any winning alliance that could form, some other state can offer a better deal (that is, more security) to some member of the winning combination in exchange for their support in a blocking coalition. Because of the possibility of switching alliances to get a better deal, no state is expendable in this system. Thus, System I is stable, although the distribution of power may be subject to change.

The second hypothetical multipolar system, although similar to the first, is not stable according to neorealism because there is no circumstance in which E can survive that is consistent with neorealist assumptions.

Construct ten hypothetical multipolar systems with five blocs each that are stable according to neorealist criteria. Does this come close to exhausting the number of possible stable, multipolar power configurations? If power is equally distributed in a multipolar system, how might a blocking coalition be formed? Does an exactly equal distribution of power ensure the survival of all states? Does it prevent any redistribution of resources? A survey of systems over the past five hundred years makes clear that, contrary to the claims of neorealists and other structural theorists, the bipolar major power system that began in 1945 and ended in 1989 was not especially long lived.

Other states can increase their power by destroying E without placing their own security at risk. The key to stability, at least in regard to the survival of states, is that each state be essential to the formation of at least one winning or blocking coalition. Although some states remain essential through a transfer of power to rival states, they at least survive. But states that are inessential cannot survive. As such, any system containing an inessential state must be unstable (Niou, Ordeshook, and Rose 1989).

It should be evident that many different distributions of power in a multipolar system can be stable, and as many others cannot. Among potentially stable multipolar systems, one in which every state can survive, are those in which power is perfectly evenly distributed among the member states. Such a system, however, is subject to power redistributions that shift the equilibrium away from perfect equality. This is so because a blocking coalition with power equivalent to $R/2$ that ensures the survival of all states can be formed without redistributing resources only if the system is multipolar, has an even number of members, and resources initially are equally distributed between two camps.

Stability in a multipolar world is not limited to the situation of exact power equality. This is in marked contrast to the bipolar world, where stability can be achieved only through a perfectly equal division of resources between two blocs. Thus, it appears that the neorealist hypothesis that bipolarity promotes stability and multipolarity promotes instability is logically false given the assumptions of the theory. Further, it seems that a true balance of power is essential for stability in a bipolar world, but not in a multipolar one, contradicting the second hypothesis. A vast array of power distributions produce stability so that in a multipolar environment, an exact balance of power is irrelevant. Either the balance of power does not matter in multipolarity or the term is defined to mean any system in which each actor is essential. In the latter case, the concept is so broad as to be vacuous. Too many systems would then qualify as a balance-of-power system to give the concept much meaning in our search for answers.

## BIPOLARITY AND STABILITY: A SECOND LOOK

You might object that the portrayal of the relationship between polarity and stability is too simple. After all, war or any other means of taking away a rival's power and threatening its sovereignty is a risky business. Success is not a certainty. More powerful states or alliances of states cannot be sure of their advantage unless that advantage is very large indeed (Morgenthau 1978). The risk associated with war may mean that a bipolar system will still be stable even though power is not divided exactly equally between the rival camps. Although this argument seems appealing at first blush, it actually contradicts fundamental aspects of neorealist theory. We will return to the bipolar example of instability to see why this is so. But before doing so, let me remind you again that the basis for the claim that bipolar systems are more stable than multipolar systems hinges on the contention that multipolarity encompasses greater uncertainty than does bipolarity. In an effort to save the logical foundation of this hypothesis, I am now going to turn this contention on its head by asserting that uncertainty is especially a problem in bipolar systems.

Suppose nation A thinks there is some chance, $p$, that it can defeat nation B. If this is so, then there is also a chance, equal to $1 - p$, that A will be defeated by B. For convenience, we can define $p$ so that it equals the ratio of A's power to the sum of A's and B's power, as we have done before. A will not try to take advantage of B if the following is true:

$$p(U_{A\,winning}) + (1 - p)(U_{A\,losing}) < U_{A\,status\,quo},$$

where $U_{A\,winning}$ is the utility for A of capturing B's power, $U_{A\,losing}$ is the utility for A of losing its sovereignty to B, and $U_{A\,status\,quo}$ is the utility for A of the status quo in terms of maintaining its level of security.

Suppose that A attaches a utility of 1 to capturing all of B's power and a utility of 0 to losing its sovereignty. In addition, we know that in accordance with neorealist assumptions A prefers capturing B's power to losing its own sovereignty or maintaining the status quo and that A prefers the status quo to losing its sovereignty. With these conditions in mind, we can develop rules for A that will guide its decision on whether or not to go after B's power. First we need to rearrange the terms so that

$$p > (U_{A\,status\,quo} - U_{A\,losing})/(U_{A\,winning} - U_{A\,losing}),$$

and then substitute our given values so that

$$p > (U_{A\,status\,quo} - 0)/(1 - 0),$$

to establish that

$$\text{if } p > U_{A\,status\,quo}, \text{ then A will attack B} \qquad \text{(Rule 1)}$$

and that

$$\text{if } p \leq U_{A\,status\,quo}, \text{ then A will not attack B.} \qquad \text{(Rule 2)}$$

It is clear that the decision A makes depends on how much it likes or dislikes the status quo in regard to its security. States that are very unhappy with the status quo might, under rules 1 and 2, attack the rival pole in a bipolar system, even though the rival pole is much stronger. That is, $p$ could be quite small and still be bigger than the value such states attach to the status quo. Imagine, for example, that the value of the status quo is 0.1. This is more than the value of losing sovereignty (0) and less than the value of gaining B's power (1). If $p$ is 0.2, then the rule for attacking B is satisfied. This is equivalent to saying that it is possible in a bipolar world for nation A to attack nation B when A's power is 60 and B's power is 240. This is what is implied by the measurement of $p$ and the stipulation that $p = 0.2$ and that the utility for the status quo equals 0.1. In this example, $p = A\text{'s power}/(A\text{'s power} + B\text{'s power}) = 60/(60 + 240)$. Here we have an example in which A attacks B even though A's chance of success in gaining power is very small.

States that are happy with the status quo might not attack B in a bipolar system, even if B is much weaker. That is, $p$ could be very large and still be smaller than the value these states attach to the status quo. For example, suppose that the value of the status quo is 0.9. Even if $p$ were equal to 0.8, rule 1 would not be satisfied. A would not attack B. Even though A's power equals 240 and B's power only totals 60, A still would not feel confident enough to seize B's capabilities, given the high value of the status quo for A relative to a potentially disastrous defeat.

Such conclusions make a lot of intuitive sense. The problem is that they contradict realist assumptions. The fourth neorealist assumption limits the pursuit of increased power to just those situations in which national security is not at risk. As Kenneth Waltz has aptly noted in explaining neorealism,

> In anarchy, security is the highest end. Only if survival is *assured* can states safely seek such other goals as tranquility, profit, and power. Because power is a means and not an end, states prefer to join the weaker of two coalitions. They cannot let power, a possibly useful means, become the end they pursue. The goal the system encourages them to seek is security. Increased power may or may not serve that end. . . . The first concern of states is not to maximize power but to maintain their positions in the system. (1979, 126, emphasis added)

Since an anarchic world almost never ensures survival, it is rarely possible from the neorealist point of view for states to trade between security and other desirable goals. Yet, by assuming that the outcome of a contest for power is probabilistic rather than certain, we necessarily introduce trade-offs between security (that is, the preservation of sovereignty) and the quest for power. With probabilistic outcomes we can imagine a probability of success large enough to warrant putting security at risk (I gave an example where that probability of success might be quite low). In doing so we violate assumptions 3 and 4 and so are no longer examining the logic of neorealist theory but, rather, the logic of some other theory in which security need not take precedence.

The first hypothesis of neorealism, that bipolarity leads to stability, does not follow from the stated assumptions of the theory. Still, we can save the hypothesis logically by introducing an assumption that says that states always behave with caution in the face of certainty and generally behave recklessly in the face of uncertainty. Whether or not such an assumption is consistent with observed behavior is, of course, another matter. At the same time, we cannot save the argument by allowing the outcome of competitions for power to be probabilistic because this requires that we contradict some of the core assumptions of the theory. Doing so also contradicts the hypothesis that states mimic one another's actions and discounts the importance of the balance of power in the calculations of decision makers. Although it is perfectly acceptable to develop additional assumptions to rescue a theory, no theory can be rescued by contradicting its basic assumptions or by contradicting other important aspects of the argument. Therefore, we cannot maintain the neorealist argument by acknowledging that leaders might make different choices about whether or not to try to gain power at the possible expense of security. Calculations concerning the value of the status quo versus the risks inherent in pursuing more power fly in the face of neorealist views about how states behave.

## HISTORY AND NEOREALIST EMPIRICAL CLAIMS

Is it worth our while to try to save the bipolarity argument of neorealism? That is, does the record of history work out to be sufficiently consistent with the hypothesis that we should care to find some logical explanation for the stability produced by bipolarity? There are many ways to go about figuring out whether a strong historical relationship exists between the international system's level of polarity and its stability. I address several of these now, mindful of Waltz's admonition that all theory, including neorealism, should be subjected to distinct and demanding tests (1979, 13).

One perspective that seems to make sense in light of neorealist arguments is to evaluate how long the structure of the international system remained unchanged under different configurations. According to neorealists, the modern international system, which is dominated by sovereign states, began in 1648 with the end of the Thirty Years' War. The international system was multipolar in structure from 1648 until the defeat of Germany in 1945. Thus, between 1648 and 1945 there were many major powers, with no one or two predominating. The multipolar system lasted for 297 years, although many internal changes took place during that time, with great powers rising and falling along the way. The bipolar system began in 1945 and lasted until about 1989 when the Berlin Wall was torn down, symbolizing the end of the bipolar cold war. The bipolar system lasted just forty-four years. The international system has now entered a new phase of multipolarity, or perhaps unipolarity. Of course, we do not know how long this will last. It is evident, however, that the first multipolar period lasted much longer than the first bipolar system. In this sense, it would appear that multipolarity is more stable than bipolarity.

Neorealists, however, might object that the above assessment is not correct. We have already noted that internal changes occurred during the 297 years associated with the multipolar system. Spain, for example, was one of the great powers during the sixteenth and seventeenth centuries, but it certainly was not among this elite group of states in the nineteenth or twentieth centuries. The United States is the most powerful state in the world today, but it did not even exist in 1648 and remained a sleepy backwater at least until the Spanish-American War in 1898. If stability requires that the set of great powers remain unaltered, then each time the list of major powers changes we can say that a new system has emerged. Using Jack Levy's (1983) classification of great powers since 1492, we can determine whether the longevity of the bipolar system was comparatively long or short.

Figure 16-3 shows the longevity of each system defined as the period during which the makeup of the major powers remained unaltered. It is evident that the forty or so years of the bipolar international system was neither unusually long nor unusually short. Many multipolar great power systems lasted longer; many lasted a shorter time. We cannot conclude on the basis of the longevity of the major power system that multipolarity produces less stability than the one instance of bipolarity.

Of course, the longevity of a given international structure is not the only way to think about system stability. Another way to evaluate the stability of the international system is to examine the frequency of wars among the most influential states in the world, the major powers. During the bipolar years, there were two dominant powers: the United States and the Soviet Union. It is noteworthy that no war erupted between these two dominant states during those years. Still, although the superpowers never engaged in battle against each other, both fought several wars against other states, and there was at least one war between a major power and a superpower during the bipolar years. The Korean War (1950–1953) saw combat between the United States and China. In addition, China and the Soviet Union fought sporadically along their extensive border. Many casualties and deaths resulted, but the Sino-Soviet conflict is rarely elevated to the status of war.

The peace between the two superpowers has been described by the historian John Gaddis (1987) as "the long peace." Just how long it was and whether or not it was due to bipolarity are both tricky questions. Numerous changes in international affairs can be singled out to explain the long peace. Bipolarity is one, but there is no reason to think it a more or less plausible factor than several others possibilities. Consider, for example, the advent of nuclear deterrence. Nuclear deterrence tends to push the international system toward multipolarity, especially when several well-endowed nuclear powers make the costs of an attack excessive relative to the prospective benefits. Nuclear

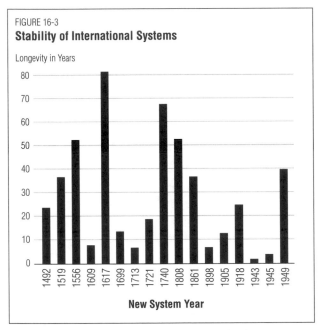

FIGURE 16-3
**Stability of International Systems**

Longevity in Years

*A survey of systems over the past five hundred years makes clear that, contrary to the claims of neorealists and other structural theorists, the bipolar major power system that began in 1945 and ended in 1989 was not especially long lived.*

weapons may have raised the anticipated costs of war well beyond the level of any fore-seeable benefits.

Some might point to the creation of the United Nations as a significant improvement over the prewar League of Nations in helping to limit superpower warfare. Certainly the United Nations has been involved in numerous peacekeeping missions that have helped contain and resolve disputes that might have otherwise entangled the great powers. The United Nations' most powerful arm is the Security Council. As you know, five great powers (Britain, China, France, Russia, and the United States) are permanent members of the Security Council. Each can veto any resolution brought before the council, and pretty much all major security issues do come before it. The UN Security Council, then, by institutionalizing a multipolar decision-making structure, has provided a counterweight to bipolarity. This too may be an explanation for the long peace.

Numerous other explanations for the peace between the great powers have been put forth (Mueller 1989). The advent of commercial television and the increasing frequency

*During the post–World War II "long peace" there were numerous wars involving at least one major power and surrogate forces for another major power. Fidel Castro of Cuba salutes the Grenadian army at the Port Salines airport upon his arrival in Grenada on August 2, 1998. He unveiled a plaque commemorating Cuban workers who built the airport that was the site of fighting between U.S. and Cuban troops during the 1983 U.S. invasion of Grenada. Castro's Cuba, a satellite of the Soviet Union, fought in many parts of the world during the cold war's "long peace," sometimes on its own and sometimes as a substitute for Soviet troops.*

of intercontinental air travel, for example, have both been claimed as pacifying developments. Each brings people closer together and fosters greater cultural understanding. Of
course, it also could be said that familiarity breeds contempt. We should not leap too
quickly to endorse these or many other explanations of the long peace, because each has
counterarguments. Still, we have already seen that bipolarity as an explanation of stability has counterarguments that are at least as persuasive as the arguments in its favor.

Just how long has the long peace really lasted? Of course, the easiest answer is that
during all forty-four of the years between the end of World War II and the tearing down
of the Berlin Wall there was no war between the superpowers; there was peace in a limited but important sense. But only thirty-six years passed without a war between two
major powers (excluding the Sino-Soviet border fighting), and there was barely a moment without some smaller war going on, wars often involving a major power. Recall
that the Korean War pitted the United States against China. Additionally, the French
fought in Indochina in the early 1950s; the French and the British fought in Egypt in the
Suez War in 1956; the United States fought in the Dominican Republic, Grenada, Panama, Vietnam, and elsewhere; the Chinese fought in India and Vietnam, among other
countries, and along the Soviet border; and the Soviet Union engaged in combat in
Afghanistan, Czechoslovakia, Hungary, and along the Chinese border. It is reasonable to
ask whether forty-four years or even thirty-six years (or less) is really an unusually long
time without a major power war. Again, we can turn to Levy's compilation to assess
whether or not the long peace was really all that long.

Levy's data show that thirty-eight years passed without a major power war from the
end of the Napoleonic Wars (1815) to the beginning of the Crimean War (1853). Forty-
three years passed between the end of the Franco-Prussian War (1871) and the beginning
of World War I (1914).[2] Other lengthy intervals between major power wars can be found
scattered throughout the past several centuries. Levy identifies seven general wars since
the Treaty of Westphalia: the Dutch War of Louis XIV (1672–1678), the War of the
League of Augsburg (1688–1697), the War of the Spanish Succession (1701–1713), the
Seven Years' War (1755–1763), the French Revolution and Napoleonic Wars
(1792–1815), World War I (1914–1918), and World War II (1939–1945). The average
interval between general wars has been thirty-four years; the longest interval was ninety-
nine years, well above the current period of peace. It appears, then, that the so-called
long peace cannot be considered unusually long after all.

In the previous chapter we studied alliances and learned that allies sometimes fight
wars with each other. These conflicts generally are about expected changes in one or

---

[2] One might object that the Russo-Japanese War qualifies as a major power war. Japan's status as a potential factor in global power politics, however, was established by its performance in that war and did not pre-
date the event. Still, in some respects Japan had already attained great power status. If we include it among our
list of great power wars, then the interval between the Franco-Prussian War and the Russo-Japanese War was
thirty-three years.

another ally's policies in the future. That was, for instance, the cause of the Soviet Union's invasions of Afghanistan and Czechoslovakia and of the U.S. incursion in the Dominican Republic in 1965. These wars speak to a problem in the neorealist contention that bipolar systems inherently contain less uncertainty than do multipolar systems. Since wars among allies are not rare, it seems that poles or blocs of nations cannot be thought of as a cohesive, unitary whole. Each member of a pole, even in a bipolar world, must be uncertain about the future policies of its friends and the effect any changes in policy might have on its own security. The median power argument made in Chapter 15 about allies at war emphasizes that uncertainty about future policy shifts by allies is more problematic than potential policy shifts by enemies. If this is correct, then whether the system is bipolar or multipolar is irrelevant for uncertainty. Every state is, according to this reasoning, uncertain about every other state and especially about the states within its own pole. Then there is no reduction in uncertainty through bipolarity and there might even be an increase in uncertainty.

## OTHER NEOREALIST HYPOTHESES AND THE HISTORICAL RECORD

Another way to assess the predictive accuracy of the neorealist structural perspective involves careful examination of what does follow logically from neorealist assumptions. We can then determine whether or not the hypotheses that follow logically from the theory are historically accurate. Several careful studies of the logic of neorealism have been conducted. Emerson Niou, Peter Ordeshook, and Gregory Rose (1989) carefully traced out the logic of neorealism and reached four central conclusions based on neorealist assumptions. These implications of neorealism, proven as theorems within a neorealist framework, are as follows:

1. Essential states never become inessential.
2. Essential states are never eliminated from the international system.
3. Inessential states never become essential states.
4. Inessential states are always eliminated from the international system.

An essential state, you will recall, is any state that can join a losing coalition and, by dint of its membership, turn that coalition into a blocking coalition or a winning coalition. Inessential states are states that are unable to turn even one losing alliance into a winning or blocking coalition.

### THE SURVIVAL OF ESSENTIAL AND INESSENTIAL STATES

Each of these propositions is historically false. Austria-Hungary was an essential state at the outset of World War I. By war's end it had not only become inessential, it was completely eliminated from the international system. Likewise, the Soviet Union was an essential state throughout the cold war. Indeed, it was a superpower. Today it does not exist.

In fact, the Soviet Union willingly and peacefully gave up its sphere of influence and its status as a great power. It is not yet clear whether any of its successor states have willingly reduced their power to ensure their survival or are themselves inessential and possibly doomed to extinction. The United States in the nineteenth century was an inessential state. Obviously, today it is an essential player on the world stage; it is the lone super-power. Many other examples can be given to show that the four hypotheses identified by Niou, Ordeshook, and Rose from neorealist logic are simply not consistent with history.

## UNCERTAINTY AND WAR

David Lalman and I also constructed a formalized version of neorealist theory (Bueno de Mesquita and Lalman 1992). We focused attention on the competing demands of states. These demands form the core of international disputes. According to neorealist logic, a state makes demands based on its need to protect its security and enhance its power. Therefore, what is demanded (and what is not) depends on the structure of the situation in which the state finds itself. Demands in the international arena are the result of strategic choices—that is, they are endogenous. Because demands are developed based on the logic of the situation at hand, nations would never knowingly choose actions that lead to war and risk their sur-

> Can you add to the list of once-essential states that are now inessential or that no longer exist? Can you identify once-inessential states that are now essential or that still exist but remain inessential? See if you can list states in each of these categories over the span of the past three or four centuries.

vival. Lalman and I demonstrate this within the context of what we call the realpolitik version of our international interaction game (IIG). In the international interaction game, rival heads of state choose whether or not to make foreign policy demands, whether or not to respond with counterdemands, and whether or not to negotiate, fight, or appease adversaries. Numerous other game theoretic examinations of war (Powell 1990, 1999; Fearon 1995; Morrow 1997) within a structural perspective have confirmed that war does not arise without uncertainty. These findings appear to support the neorealist claim equating bipolarity with stability. (Remember, bipolarity is really a surrogate for the absence of uncertainty, and multipolarity is really a surrogate for the presence of uncertainty.) In fact, if states lived within a neorealist world and were faced with no uncertainty, then they would knowingly choose only those actions that protected the status quo or that led to a negotiated resolution of differences.[3] Lalman and I

---

[3] Lalman and I measured uncertainty in several different ways. One measure indicates that uncertainty increases as the variation in risk-taking inclinations of state leaders increases. In the neorealist view, remember, bipolar systems have little uncertainty and everyone responds to risks by being cautious. A second measure of uncertainty compares the probability of victory for side A and the probability of victory for side B in any dispute. The more unequal the distribution of power between sides A and B (and therefore the more likely one side is to win than the other), the less uncertainty there is about the outcome of a dispute.

identified three hypotheses that follow directly from this representation of the logic of neorealism.

1. Uncertainty promotes war and certainty promotes negotiations or the status quo.
2. Regardless of information circumstances (uncertainty or certainty), no nation will ever acquiesce peacefully to the demands of another state.
3. A necessary, but not sufficient, condition for war is that both parties to the war believe their chances of winning are better than 50 percent.

The record of history does not support any of these hypotheses either. Figure 16-4 shows that there is no straightforward historical relationship between uncertainty and the risk of war. At low levels of uncertainty there is a statistically significant increase in the likelihood of war as uncertainty itself increases. This is followed by a significant decrease in the risk of war at moderate to high levels of uncertainty. At extremely high levels of uncertainty, the probability that disputes will turn into war turns sharply upward. For most of the range of degrees of uncertainty, the probability of war stays well below 20 percent, rising above that level only under truly extreme conditions. The two periods during which the level of uncertainty was so high that it predicted war with near certainty are 1866, when Prussia, Austria, and several smaller German states fought the Seven Weeks' War, and 1966–1968, when mounting cold war tensions culminated in the Soviet invasion of Czechoslovakia. In the mid-1860s, as in the mid-1960s, long-established ties among nations were under great strain, making leaders more uncertain than usual about on whom they could and could not count. In both general instances of extremely high uncertainty it is interesting to note that the associated conflicts were among states allied to one another. The states involved in the Seven Weeks' War were all members of the same mutual defense pact. This was also true in the cases of tension under high uncertainty during the period 1966–1968. Because allies typically share similar foreign policy commitments, it is difficult to discern how states will line up behind belligerents. This difficulty reflects uncertainty in the international system (Bueno de Mesquita 1981a).

That the risk of war is linked to changes in uncertainty is not straightforward.

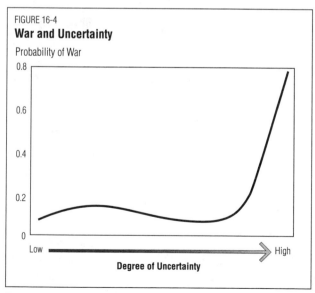

FIGURE 16-4
**War and Uncertainty**

Probability of War

Degree of Uncertainty

Low → High

*Except at extreme levels, it is not true that uncertainty increases the risk of war. Moderate levels of uncertainty actually produce less war than do low levels of uncertainty.*

Neither is the prospect that the status quo will persist or that disputes will be resolved through negotiations. James Fearon (1994) has shown that with just one exception war will not arise without uncertainty. His general argument, then, supports Waltz's narrower claim equating bipolarity with stability. The one circumstance in which war can arise under complete and perfect information involves situations in which one or both parties to a dispute cannot credibly commit themselves to a course of peaceful resolution. In the next chapter we will see that tests of such conditions reinforce Fearon's contention and further undermine neorealist arguments.

Lalman and I examined the role of uncertainty in promoting peaceful dispute resolution using data from 1816 to 1974. Our realpolitik deduction—that diminished uncertainty should increase the odds of peaceful dispute resolutions—is a more general form of Waltz's contention that bipolarity reduces the threat of instability and presages Fearon's rationalist explanation of war. The failure of Lalman's and my neorealist proposition to find support in the historical record is quite troubling, especially in light of all the other evidence against the hypothesis that bipolarity promotes stability.

## ACQUIESCENCE AND NEOREALISM

The second hypothesis derived from Lalman's and my realpolitik variant of the IIG contends that a state will never choose to give in to the demands of another state without first either negotiating a compromise or fighting to protect its interests. This hypothesis is also historically false. That nations do acquiesce to the demands of others is evident. During the Fashoda Crisis between Britain and France in 1898, for example, Britain sought control of as much of the Upper Nile as possible. The French-held town of Fashoda in the Sudan lay exactly in the path of British ambitions. The British were unyielding in their demands. They wanted nothing less than a full acquiescence by the French and were prepared to go to war to pursue their ends. The French were in a militarily weak position. What's more, domestic dissatisfaction with the French cabinet at home left the government in a vulnerable political position. Rather than resisting and provoking a British attack that would almost certainly lead to a humiliating military defeat and most probably as well to the downfall of the government, France's leaders gave in to British demands. They recognized that they were better off acquiescing in this case than adding fuel to domestic political dissatisfaction with an international crisis.[4] Contrary to the logic of neorealism, then, acquiescence is not impossible; in fact, it happens quite often in international affairs.

## BALANCE OF POWER AND NEOREALISM

Perhaps the most common claim among neorealist theorists is that war occurs only when both sides believe that their chance of winning is greater than 50 percent. This is a

---

[4] Although the government did avoid adding fuel to the fire, it was not enough. The French government fell soon after in the face of overwhelming domestic opposition.

partial statement of what has come to be known as the balance-of-power theory. Many eminent scholars and statesmen have suggested that when power is fairly evenly distributed peace is likely to prevail; when power is unevenly distributed, however, they contend that the risk of war increases. Still, these scholars and statesmen sometimes disagree on exactly what is meant by an even, or balanced, distribution of power. Some emphasize the effects of the distribution of power among influential states; others emphasize the effects of the distribution of power among coalitions or blocs of states. These two emphases can mean two very different things.

Consider the estimates of national power depicted in Table 16-1. The table shows estimates of the national capabilities of the seven states that were major powers in 1896. It also shows the capabilities of the three blocs of nations that represented the major power blocs in 1896, based on calculations of similarity in their military alliance commitments. The data are drawn from the Correlates of War project. The list of capabilities of each of the major powers presents quite a different picture from that of the three major power blocs. The individual states were quite unequal in their relative power. Britain alone controlled over 28 percent of the capabilities of the major powers. Japan controlled less than 5 percent and Italy just barely more than 5 percent of the major power capabilities. Yet, the bloc that Italy belonged to, which included Germany and Austria-Hungary, possessed almost 35 percent of the total capabilities of the major powers. A second bloc, including Russia, Japan, and France, controlled just under 37 percent of total capabilities. Britain, in a "bloc" of its own, possessed the remaining 28 percent.

One way to measure the extent to which power is unequally divided is to add up the absolute difference between the power of the average nation (or coalition of nations) and the power of each individual nation (or coalition of nations).[5] If every unit has exactly the same amount of power, then our measure of the balance of power would equal 0 (that is, the total absolute deviation from the mean equals 0 percent). If one state (or coalition) had all the power and the others had none (the most unbalanced system possible), then the balance-of-power measure would be 100 (that is, the total absolute deviation from the mean equals 100 percent). If we focus on the individual major powers

TABLE 16-1

## The Major Power Balance of Power in 1896

| Country | Power (percent) | Bloc | Power (percent) |
|---|---|---|---|
| Germany | 21.4 | Germany, Austria-Hungary, and Italy | 34.9 |
| Austria-Hungary | 8.4 | | |
| Italy | 5.1 | | |
| Russia | 17.3 | Russia, Japan, and France | 36.9 |
| Japan | 4.6 | | |
| France | 15.0 | | |
| Britain | 28.2 | Britain | 28.2 |
| Total | 100.0 | Total | 100.0 |

___

[5] $Balance\ of\ Power = 100 \sum_{i=1}^{n} \left| Capabilities\ of\ i - \frac{1}{n} \right|$

in Table 16-1, we find that the balance-of-power measure equals 49.5, reflecting great inequality in the distribution of power among the major states in 1896. In contrast, if we focus on the major power alliance blocs of 1896, we find a more balanced system. In fact, the sum of the absolute deviations from the mean for each bloc is only 15.3 percent. Clearly, the manner in which we group power (that is, by states or by blocs) profoundly influences whether or not we define a system as balanced or not. Whichever measure we use, however, it turns out that there is no systematic relationship between the likelihood of war and the balance of power (Singer, Bremer, and Stuckey 1972; Organski and Kugler 1980; Bueno de Mesquita and Lalman 1988b).

Neither is there a significant association between estimates of the probability of victory for either side in a war and the likelihood that there will be a war, as shown in Table 16-2. The evidence fails to support the neorealist hypothesis that it is necessary (but not sufficient) that each side in a dispute thinks its chance of victory is greater than 50 percent before war will occur. If the neorealist hypothesis were correct, then the entry in the cell that corresponds with the row labeled "Yes" and the column labeled "Initiator's Probability of Victory < 50 percent" would be zero because that cell violates the hypothesized necessary condition for war. Not only is it not zero, but it is not meaningfully closer to zero than the cell that corresponds to the row labeled "Yes" and the column labeled "Initiator's Probability of Victory > 50 percent." The data in Table 16-2 take into account all disputes within Europe between 1816 and 1974. As such, the table presents a broad-based test of this neorealist claim.

TABLE 16-2

### Is a Greater than 50–50 Chance of Victory a Necessary Condition for War?

| Did War Occur? | Initiator's Probability of Victory > 50 percent | Initiator's Probability of Victory < 50 percent |
|---|---|---|
| Yes | 52 (13.1%) | 37 (11.9%) |
| No | 345 (86.9%) | 273 (88.1%) |

*Source:* Bruce Bueno de Mesquita and David Lalman, *War and Reason* (New Haven: Yale University Press, 1992), 70.

After applying the very standards for evaluating theories that leading neorealists suggest (Waltz 1979), we must conclude that neorealism's central empirical claims are false. As directed in Chapter 4, we have subjected these claims to numerous distinct and demanding tests and found that the central hypotheses do not follow from the stated assumptions. In an effort to save the theory, we have modified it and then retested our refined proposition while still faithfully applying the definitions of terms used in stating the theory. However, these either contradicted core assumptions or failed to meet the test of the empirical record. In light of this, it is difficult to see how we can avoid the conclusion that the neorealist and realist views are falsified. Still, there is the first rule of wing-walking. We should not abandon neorealist theory unless we can offer a demonstrably better alternative. In the section that follows, we will examine a structural alternative that does in fact do better. And in Chapter 17 we will examine a strategic approach that does better still.

## THE POWER TRANSITION:
## A STRUCTURAL ALTERNATIVE TO NEOREALISM

Building on the work of Edward Carr (1939, 1945), A. F. K. Organski (1958) constructed what was perhaps the first challenge to realism that was neither idealistic nor normative. Organski's power transition theory shares with realism a focus on the importance of power in international affairs. However, it breaks with the "balance of power" realism of Morgenthau and Waltz, most notably by maintaining that the international system is not anarchic. Instead, foreshadowing the later development of neoliberal theory and the study of international political economy, Organski suggested that the international system is hierarchically organized. Figure 16-5 depicts the power triangle that Organski suggested captures fundamental elements of international affairs. The triangular shape reflects the observation that the more powerful and influential a category of states is, the fewer the states in that category. Many nations are small, with few resources with which to influence international relations. Some examples of such states include Chad, Haiti, Laos, and Liechtenstein. Middle powers are less numerous, as reflected by the smaller area of the power triangle given over to them, but they are generally more influential than the small states. Examples of middle powers include Mexico, the Netherlands, Nigeria, and Pakistan. The great powers, such as Britain, China, France, and Russia, exert substantial influence over international affairs. The dominant state throughout the post–World War II years has been the United States. Its position at the pinnacle of the power triangle is ensured by a combination of great national wealth, great per capita wealth, and overwhelming military prowess. According to Organski's power transition viewpoint, there is only one dominant state at any given time. That state establishes the fundamental rules and norms of behavior in the international arena.

Figure 16-5 also hints at another assumption of Organski's power transition theory and also of Robert Gilpin's similar theory of hegemonic stability (1981). The shaded area in the power triangle indicates that there is a set of satisfied states, content with the international order. However, the larger, unshaded area indicates that most states are dissatisfied with the international order. In this view of the world, rather than wishing to maximize security or power,

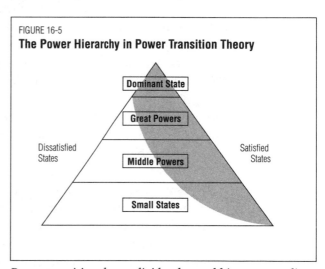

FIGURE 16-5
**The Power Hierarchy in Power Transition Theory**

Dominant State

Great Powers

Dissatisfied States

Middle Powers

Satisfied States

Small States

*Power transition theory divides the world into two coalitions: satisfied states and dissatisfied states. The stronger a state is, the more likely that it is satisfied with the organization of the international system and the status quo that reflects that system's rules. Weaker states are more likely to be dissatisfied.*

nations are interested in maximizing their control over the rules and customs that govern international interactions so that they can define the status quo according to their interests. Dissatisfaction, then, is most prevalent among those least content with the existing status quo. However, it is the more powerful dissatisfied states that represent the biggest threat to international peace and stability. If they have the wherewithal, they will, according to power transition theory, try to alter the hierarchy to put themselves at the top.

Returning for a moment to a topic from Chapter 15, we can now see that James Morrow's theory of alliances combines aspects of neorealism and power transition theory (1991a). Neorealism contends that states are always seeking security; power transition theory contends that states are always seeking control over the status quo (autonomy, in Morrow's terms). In Morrow's view, states are seeking a mix of security and autonomy that will allow them to alter the status quo in their favor.

The rules of the international system are selected by the dominant state and enforced by that state and other members of the satisfied coalition. System-transforming conflicts occur when a dissatisfied state gains sufficient power to challenge the existing order. Thus, we can see that the focus of hierarchical theories like the power transition is very much on the rules and norms that govern behavior, rather than on the distribution of power or state security per se.

The supposition that the dominant state determines rules and norms of action is an important departure from realist or neorealist thinking. This feature of power transition theory places it somewhat closer to liberal or neoliberal theory. Although power transition theorists share the realists' view of the state as the central actor in international affairs, they disagree with the realist assumption that all nations are trying to maximize power and security (Organski 1958; Organski and Kugler 1980; Lemke 1995b, 1996, 2002; Kim and Morrow 1992). Rather, power transition theorists argue that states have policy objectives that they wish to impose on other states. These goals or objectives can best be imposed by establishing rules and norms that govern international interactions. Control over the rules and norms, then, is tantamount to control over the course of international politics.

The very fact that a dominant state can impose rules suggests that it has the means at its disposal to enforce those rules. Enforcement depends on power. As such, power transition and hegemonic stability theorists consider power to be the essential instrument of international affairs. In this way they differ markedly from the so-called idealists, who dominated thinking about international relations before World War II. For idealists, ethics, morality, and maximizing collective welfare rather than individual national well-being were the normative guideposts for international intercourse. Their views are currently enjoying a renaissance in more sophisticated theories of the role that ideas play in international affairs (Katzenstein 1985; Goldstein and Keohane 1993; Wendt 1999). For power transition theorists, however, normative concerns or social constructions are not central to understanding international relations.

## EXAMPLES OF INTERNATIONAL RULES AND NORMS

What are the rules and norms governing international politics? Examples abound both in the domain of international economic exchange and in that of security. After World War II, the United States promoted a currency regime known as the Bretton Woods Agreement. At Bretton Woods the United States dollar became the currency against which the value of all other currencies was pegged. Before Bretton Woods, much of the world was on the gold standard, meaning that the price of an ounce of gold was fixed, but the amount of a given currency that was needed to purchase that ounce of gold fluctuated. The gold standard began to crumble during the interwar years with international financial interests looking for a substitute (Simmons 1994). Under the Bretton Woods Agreement, the American dollar took over the role of gold, becoming the fixed standard against which other money was valued. This meant that the dollar became the most desired means of exchange in international markets, and hence that the United States would be at center stage in economic dealings. The abandonment of the Bretton Woods Agreement by President Richard Nixon led some observers to speak of a decline in American hegemony (Keohane 1984; Kennedy 1987). Whether there was a decline in American hegemony or not (Russett 1985; Strange 1987; Kugler and Organski 1989), what is important to recognize here is that the Bretton Woods Agreement represented a new set of rules imposed on the international community after World War II by the hegemonic United States.

Over the past several decades the United States has been the world leader in pressing for the establishment of a free trade regime, through the GATT (the General Agreement on Tariffs and Trade) from 1947 to 1995 and then through the World Trade Organization (WTO). Although, as we saw in Chapter 13, the United States has not always practiced free trade itself, it has steadfastly promoted its practice among other nations. The free trade regime enforced by the GATT and now the WTO and other trade arrangements such as NAFTA establish rules for judging whether or not specific trade practices are protectionist. Even though their enforcement powers are limited, these agreements still maintain a significant rule-based and normative influence on the trading practices of their members. For example, tariff levels are today only about one-tenth of what they were in 1947, when the GATT first began to operate (*The Economist*, May 16–22, 1998, 21).

Perhaps the most visible norm engendered by America's international leadership has been the promotion of democratic institutions and the protection of human rights. These ideas are clearly imbedded in the American perception of what constitutes an appropriate basis on which people should be governed. Long before the United States emerged as a hegemonic power, it was touting the benefits of democratic practices. Most visible among its early efforts was the inclusion of self-determination as one of Woodrow Wilson's famous fourteen points, articulated at the end of World War I.

Although the United States has from time to time collaborated with nondemocratic and even antidemocratic states, its closest ties have always been reserved for like-minded governments. It is unlikely that NATO, for example, would have remained as cohesive as it did throughout the cold war if the members shared only a common fear of the Soviet Union. Surely, if that were the only glue holding NATO together, some members would have defected and made separate arrangements with the Soviets. All of the members of NATO, however, shared a common commitment to democracy and human rights. Indeed, some West European states, like Spain and Portugal, were prohibited from joining NATO or the European Community until their dictatorships (under Gen. Francisco Franco in Spain and Antonio de Oliveira Salazar in Portugal) were replaced by democratic systems. Likewise, NATO expansion to include eastern European states formerly in the Warsaw Pact depends in part on the ability of those states to demonstrate a commitment to democratic norms of conduct.

On the security front, the United States was a prime mover behind the establishment of the United Nations as an institution designed to promote peace throughout the world. Although the UN General Assembly has frequently voted in support of points of view opposed by the United States, the United States remains an active UN participant. The United States, especially during the presidencies of George H. W. Bush and Bill Clinton, steadfastly looked to the United Nations to provide legal, political, and moral support for major international military interventions. It has relied on UN coalitions to justify war against Iraq and Afghanistan and military actions against Somalia, Haiti, and others. To be sure, American financial support of the United Nations has waxed and waned, but the United States today remains a promoter of a peacekeeping, security-providing role for the United Nations.

Britain is often thought of as having been the hegemonic power of the nineteenth century. What rules or norms of international conduct did Britain try to enforce around the world? Can you give examples of changes in conduct imposed by the French under Napoleon on their far-flung empire? Had Germany won World War II, what might it have introduced as the norms and rules of international relations? When the Catholic Church was Europe's hegemonic power, did it impose rules of behavior on other states? How was the church's hegemony challenged and ultimately defeated? Look back still further to ancient Rome or Greece. What rules did they impose? Examine Edward Creasy's *Fifteen Decisive Battles of the World* (1960). He has chosen his "decisive" battles precisely because they represented turning points in international norms and rules.

It is not difficult to imagine that many of the rules and norms promoted by the United States would have been discarded had the Soviet Union won in the competition to become world hegemon. Certainly the Soviets were interested in promoting socialist economic systems rather than the free trade, market-oriented regime espoused by the United States. The Soviets would have promoted authoritarian governments, as they did throughout their sphere of influence, to protect and enhance the control of Communist parties around the world. They probably would not have supported the United Nations politically if it routinely opposed their point of view.

## DISSATISFACTION, THE STATUS QUO, AND WAR

When their perspectives on the rules governing international interactions differ markedly, dominant states and those in the groupings below them in the power triangle

*Britain was content to develop democratic practices at home, without showing much enthusiasm for promoting them abroad. In contrast, the United States aggressively pursued the installation of a democratic system in Japan following World War II. Here we see a British gentleman (above), attended by Indian servants at the beginning of the twentieth century. The British, except when under pressure from the Indians, were oblivious to developing India's political institutions. By contrast, General Douglas MacArthur (below right), shown here witnessing the Japanese signing of the surrender agreement at the end of World War II, surprised the conquered Japanese by the respect he accorded them and by his and America's commitment to help Japan rebuild itself as a prosperous, democratic society after the war.*

may clash. Dissatisfaction with the status quo becomes the principal source of international tension. Conflict arises when a powerful, dissatisfied state grows strong enough to challenge the authority of the hegemon. Because such a challenge concerns the very way in which international affairs are conducted, the ensuing conflict is fierce and costly. Wars over changes in the rules have the potential for transforming the international system.

But when do such wars occur? The dominant state will not sit by and permit the challenger to pass it by in power. It will not peacefully concede control to the upstart. At the same time, the challenger is reluctant to start a fight before it has enough power to give it a credible chance of defeating the hegemon. The conjunction of these conditions arises, according to power transition theorists, when the two rivals are just about equal in power. This time period—the period during which the challenger roughly comes to equal and then surpass the dominant state in power—is the period known as the power transition. It is the time when the threat of a major war is at its peak. Contrary to the balance-of-power perspective, power transition and hegemonic stability theorists believe that major wars are most likely to occur when the power of the opposed states is about equal. According to these theorists, a balance of power *promotes* war. They maintain that system-transforming wars—that is, wars that lead to a new power hierarchy and to new rules and norms—will occur only when the power of a challenger and the dominant state are about equal and the power of the challenger is increasing faster than that of the dominant state. These claims have been extended and shown to have empirical bite at the regional as well as the global level, so that regional hegemons apparently face the same pressures and the same sources of war as their global counterparts (Lemke 1996, 2002).

How does a threatening balance of power develop in the first place? It should be evident from the power triangle that it is virtually impossible for transition-inducing conflict to emerge as a result of alliances. After all, satisfied states are concentrated at the upper reaches of the power triangle; they are not likely to join forces with a powerful, dissatisfied state intent on challenging the hegemon because satisfied states, by their very definition, prefer the rules and norms of the existing status quo to those of a potential hegemonic rival. Thus, we must look elsewhere for the source of shifts in power that create a transition-inducing balance of power.

For power transition and hegemonic stability theorists, a threatening balance of power emerges as a result of differing rates of internal growth between a dominant state and a challenger state. These theories still give little attention to domestic politics per se, but they do recognize that internal factors shape rates of growth. In fact, power transition theory defines domestic affairs as those issues pertaining to economic matters such as the skills of the population, the quality of infrastructure, and the value of national resources such as labor, capital, and natural assets. Domestic politics affects these matters only in that polities vary in their ability to mobilize their society's wealth for foreign (or domestic) policy purposes. Growth rates themselves are not a product of strategic decision making or internal politics. Quite the contrary, the leading power transition theorists maintain that the long-term rate of economic growth is inevitable and cannot be altered, even by such massive shocks as national defeat in war (Organski and Kugler 1980; Kugler and Lemke 1995).

The likelihood of war, as predicted by the power transition and hegemonic stability theories, is summarized in Figure 16-6. When a dissatisfied state lags far behind the dominant state in power, war is not expected to occur. Likewise, if the rising challenger state overtakes the dominant state by a substantial margin of power, then war again is unlikely. In this case, a peaceful transition takes place. But when the challenger's power rises quickly, first to equal and then to overtake the dominant state, a wrenching, system-transforming power transition war is likely to occur.

Organski and Jacek Kugler (1980) have subjected the power transition's core war hypothesis to empirical testing. They noted that there are three different types of power distributions that can arise between states. The challenger can be significantly weaker than the dominant state; the challenger can be about equal in power to the dominant state but not growing so fast as to appear to be overtaking the hegemon; or the challenger can be about equal in power to the dominant state and be growing so fast that it appears to equal and then overtake the dominant power. Organski and Kugler hypothesize that major wars can occur only in this last circumstance. Table 16-3 shows the results of their examination of interactions between major powers from 1815 to 1980. The table indi-

cates that there is a statistically significant probability that the power transition's main war hypothesis is accurate, although some critics have raised questions about the method of case selection (Siverson and Sullivan 1983).

The power transition argument has been formalized to tease out its precise logical implications. Woosang Kim and James Morrow (1992), for example, show that although some of the core hypotheses stated by Organski and Kugler are in fact borne out by precise logic, other important hypotheses are not and must be modified. Kim and Morrow show that there is a critical time during which the risk of war is at a maximum. This occurs when the challenger feels that the costs of deferring an effort to defeat the existing status quo are equal to the benefits that would be obtained from proceeding

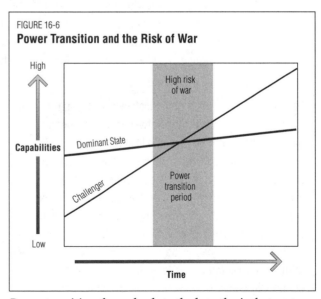

FIGURE 16-6
**Power Transition and the Risk of War**

*Power transition theory leads to the hypothesis that system-transforming, high-cost wars are especially likely when a dissatisfied challenger state achieves approximate power parity with the dominant, status quo–defending state.*

TABLE 16-3

## Empirical Evidence for the Power Transition Theory, 1815–1980

| Does War Occur? | Power Is Unequal | Power Is Equal and Challenger Is Not Overtaking Hegemon | Power Is Equal and Challenger Is Overtaking Hegemon |
|---|---|---|---|
| No | 4 | 6 | 5 |
| Yes | 0 | 0 | 5 |

*Source:* Adapted from A.F.K. Organski and Jacek Kugler, *The War Ledger* (Chicago: University of Chicago Press, 1980), 52, Table 1.7.

*Note:* The table shows a $\tau_c$ statistical test, which is a test of correlation for ordinal data that evaluates the magnitude of deviations in an asymmetric matrix for the data from the diagonal running from the upper left cell to the lower right cell. Here, $\tau_c = 0.5$ and probability $< .05$.

with such an effort and when the dominant state believes that the costs of fighting are less than the costs of granting concessions to the challenger. However, the emergence of that critical interval during which both states are prepared to fight does not depend on an equal distribution of power (Kim and Morrow 1992; Powell 1996b).

Kim and Morrow have shown that the distribution of power at which the foes will fight depends on their willingness to take the risks of waiting. The longer the challenger waits to attack, the higher is its probability of victory. This is true because the challenger's power is growing faster than the dominant state's power. Thus, the longer the challenger puts off a war, the greater will be the odds in its favor. However, the longer it waits, the longer it must endure the rules of international intercourse with which it is dissatisfied.

Table 16-3 shows a statistical test, called tau-c, that assesses the correlation between the conditions of the power transition theory and the likelihood of war. It is statistically significant and so lends consequential support to the power transition's most important hypothesis. What is the PRE (proportionate reduction in error) gained from the power transition theory, as indicated by the evidence in Table 16-3? Recall that the PRE equals the sum of the maximum cell value in each column of the table minus the maximum row total divided by the number of observations minus the maximum row total. What should we infer when different statistical tests legitimately lead to different conclusions about a theory's explanatory and predictive potential?

The challenger's decision about whether or not to attack the dominant state, then, depends on its inclination to take risks, on how quickly it is growing in power, on how costly the war is expected to be, and on how unhappy it is with the status quo. Kim and Morrow have shown that the interval during which the challenger is willing to fight expands as the expected costs of the war increase, as the challenger's dissatisfaction with the status quo increases, as the challenger's relative growth rate declines, and as the challenger becomes more risk acceptant.

Conversely, the longer the dominant state waits, the worse its political and military prospects will be. The difference in their respective growth rates places the dominant state increasingly at a disadvantage relative to the challenger. For the hegemon, then, waiting is risky business. But it does forestall the day when the hegemon loses control over the rules of the game. The dominant state's willingness to fight is postponed as the expected costs of war decrease and as the growth rate of the challenger increases. Under these circumstances, the hegemon becomes increasingly risk averse. How long the challenger and the dominant state will wait, then, depends on their respective responses to risk, their relative rates of growth, the expected costs of the war, and their respective degrees of satisfaction with the status quo. The empirical evidence generally supports the core claims of power transition theory. These claims are logically coherent. Although some empirical expectations have been borne out by the evidence, others have failed the empirical test. For example, differences in growth rates turn out not to be crucial empirically. Power transitions need not occur at the time of equality in power. Indeed, power transitions per se cannot explain especially costly wars. As Paul Huth has observed, "no state initiates war if it expects the war to be long and bloody" (1988, 74). In fact, although there is a critical time during which wars are more likely to occur, that period of time is not a function of the distribution of power and can fluctuate widely to either side of a power balance, depending on the specific, risk-taking proclivities of the relevant leaders, the magnitude of dissatisfaction with the status quo, the anticipated costs of war, and the precise growth rate differential between the challenger and the hegemon.

Unlike neorealism, power transition theory and hegemonic stability theory are not falsified by the evidence. Their core argument concerning dissatisfaction with the status quo (which is a measure of preferences or interests) is logically consistent and their central hypotheses, with significant modification, are supported by the evidence. These modifications do not contradict other core assumptions. Thus, the deficiencies in the theory can be fixed, precluding the need to discard it. These arguments can be held up as contenders for effective explanations of a specific class of wars. As we now know, the same cannot be said of neorealist theory. In the spirit of the first principle of wing-walking, the power transition theory provides a viable, superior alternative to neorealism's account of how international politics operates, at least with regard to the most wrenching sources of instability: system-transforming wars.

## SUMMARY

In this chapter we have examined the central hypotheses of two major structural theories of the causes of war. Neorealism's claims that bipolarity promotes stability, that uncertainty provokes instability, that states routinely mimic each other, and that a balance of power fosters stability are logically flawed and unsupported by the historical record. In contrast, an alternative structural explanation, the power transition theory, is consistent with the historical facts.

As the balance-of-power explanation of war is a venerated and widely believed explanation of war and peace, we cannot take these findings too lightly. So little evidence exists with which to sustain confidence in neorealist and balance-of-power predictions that the time has come to recognize the inadequacy of neorealist theory.

Scientific progress in understanding how the world works is made by building progressively on the ideas we inherit and discarding those parts that clearly fail us in exchange for superior alternatives. Much valuable debate has been stimulated by structural theories, and many useful insights have been gleaned from these approaches. However, the first rule of wing-walking compels us to abandon balance-of-power and polarity arguments and adopt a worthy alternative. The logic behind the refinements of power transition theory and, as we will see in the next chapter, several game theory treatments of war provides just such alternatives. These theories account for those facts that are successfully explained by neorealist and balance-of-power theories, but they also account for many facts that such theories do not adequately explain.

CHAPTER 17

# STRATEGIC THEORIES OF WAR

THE INTERNATIONAL INTERACTION GAME AND WAR

ARMS RACES, DETERRENCE, AND WAR

OTHER HYPOTHESES ABOUT WAR

SUMMARY

In March 1999, NATO forces, including American, British, Dutch, and German troops, among others, began a campaign of bombing against Serbia in the heart of Europe. The purpose of this action was to force Serbian president Slobodan Milosevic to abandon his push to drive the Albanian population, of which 90 percent were Muslims, out of Christian Serbia's Kosovo province. President Milosevic's policy of ethnic cleansing was, and is, abhorrent.

The military campaign against Serbia was not motivated by any concerns for the general security of the United States or even of the European NATO countries. Although it is true that conflict in Serbia, and the Balkans in general, was at the root of World War I and that the area remains a tinderbox today, few observers believed that by driving the Albanian Kosovars out of Kosovo and into Albania, Macedonia, and other neighboring states, the Serbs would destabilize Europe, although the flow of refugees certainly posed an immense burden on the surrounding states. If security concerns were not a major issue, how can we explain the willingness of the NATO countries to wage war against Serbia? For that matter, how can we explain NATO's efforts to put an end to Serbia's earlier foray into ethnic cleansing in Bosnia, or its efforts to put an end to the rule of warlords in Somalia in the early 1990s? These questions are the companions to our earlier discussion of America's decision to participate in World War I.

The proposed answer to these questions is that the political leaders in NATO in 1999, leaders in other countries on earlier occasions, and more recently, leaders of the war on terrorism found their most basic values so offended by the policies of foreign powers that they were compelled to take a forceful stand. These leaders calculated that the domestic and international repercussions of doing nothing were worse than the expected consequences of going to war. At the same time, leaders like Milosevic calculated that such foes did not have the resolve to endure the high human and political costs that came with fighting. They believed that if they just stood firm, their rivals would ultimately seek a negotiated means to bringing the war to a close. Thus, in these cases domestic and foreign strategic factors rather than global structural factors alone came together to create a conflict that culminated in war.

We begin this chapter by examining the domestic version of the international interaction game introduced in Chapter 16. We will see what this theory predicts about the relationship between uncertainty and war as well as about the relationship between power and aggression. We will examine two hypotheses, the resurrection hypothesis and the pacific doves hypothesis, that suggest that weakness and domestic considerations can encourage aggression. In addition, we will evaluate theories that link arms races to war and theories that explain war as a diversion from domestic difficulties. In each case, we will examine the logic and the evidence behind the arguments.

## THE INTERNATIONAL INTERACTION GAME AND WAR

In Chapter 16 I introduced the neorealist, or realpolitik, version of the international interaction game (IIG) developed by myself and David Lalman (1992). We also proposed an alternative to the neorealist version, one called the domestic IIG. According to this theory, policy demands and threats are motivated by domestic political considerations, whereas choices of action are shaped by the international context. Figure 17-1 shows the fundamental sequence of interactions in international relations in the extensive form of IIG. The game indicates that international interactions have eight possible generic outcomes: maintenance of the status quo, negotiation, acquiescence (giving in without offering armed resistance) by one side (called A) or the other (called B), capitulation (giving in immediately after sustaining an armed attack) by A or B, or war (the mutual use of force) initiated by A or B. In the domestic version of the IIG, Lalman and I make seven assumptions. These assumptions define restrictions over the possible ordering of preferences for each decision maker across the eight outcomes. The seven assumptions of the domestic version of the IIG are as follows:

1. Each decision maker is rational in the sense that he or she chooses actions so that the strategies played are subgame perfect Nash equilibria. (Recall that a subgame perfect Nash equilibrium is a Nash equilibrium for every subgame of the larger game so that each player selects a best reply to the anticipated actions of the other from that stage of the game forward.)
2. The outcome of any acquiescence or capitulation is known with certainty so that the probability of success in these instances is $p = 0$ or $p = 1$, depending on whether a state is giving in or being given in to. The acquiescing or capitulating state loses and the state acquiesced or capitulated to gains its demand for certain. The status quo also does not have a probabilistic outcome.
3. Disputes that are resolved through negotiations or through war involve a lottery in which each player has a chance of gaining his or her objective ($p_A$ and $p_B$ for players

A and B, respectively) and a chance of losing ($1 - p_A$ and $1 - p_B$, respectively), with $0 < p < 1$.

4. Each state prefers to resolve disputes through negotiation rather than through war, and this preference for negotiation over war is common knowledge.

5. Violent disputes involve costs not involved in negotiations. In war, a would-be attacker expects to lose fewer lives and less property if it attacks rather than if it is attacked so that there is a first-strike advantage. A capitulation involves being attacked and giving in without retaliating. The state that gives in absorbs the costs inflicted in the initial attack. Any state using violence pays a domestic political cost for failing to resolve the dispute through peaceful means.

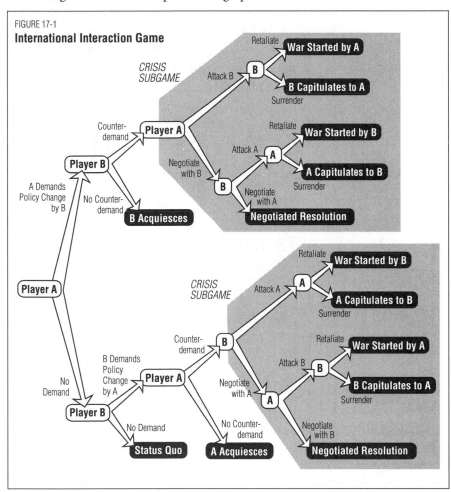

FIGURE 17-1
**International Interaction Game**

*The international interaction game offers a scaffolding from which to investigate international interactions. The game identifies eight generic outcomes of international interactions and emphasizes both international and domestic factors that influence the course of international events.*

6. Each decision maker prefers to gain any policy change he or she has demanded from the rival rather than have the status quo persist; at the same time, each decision maker prefers that the status quo persist rather than acquiesce to the policy demanded by the rival.

7. Foreign policy demands are shaped by domestic political considerations that may (but need not) take into account international constraints.

As should be evident from these assumptions, this theory models international relations as a process of strategic interaction involving external and domestic considerations. Without the seven assumptions, it would be logically possible for each of the two players in the IIG to prefer the eight possible outcomes of the game in any order. For example, without the restrictions imposed by the assumptions, a state might prefer capitulating to its adversary over the status quo, the status quo over a war it starts, a war it starts over negotiating, negotiating over acquiescing to its adversary, acquiescing to its adversary over having its adversary acquiesce to it, having its adversary acquiesce to it over fighting a war started by its adversary, and fighting a war started by its adversary over having its adversary capitulate to it. Obviously, some of these are very strange preferences indeed. Without these restrictions, there are 8! possible orderings for each player, or $(8!)^2$ possible pairs of preferences for the two players.[1] This equals 1,625,702,400 possible pairs of preference orderings. By making these assumptions, Lalman and I have greatly reduced the logically permitted set of preference orderings. With the assumptions in place, there are $52^2$, or 2,704, admissible pairs of preference orderings. Table 17-1 summarizes the limitations imposed by the assumptions of the domestic IIG in regard to how preferences over possible outcomes are restricted. Clearly, the assumptions greatly simplify the world; they eliminate 99.9998 percent of all possible pairs of preference orders. Perhaps this is too drastic a reduction, and perhaps it is not. This can be determined only by seeing what follows logically from the theory and then testing our results against the empirical evidence. Despite the huge reduction in possible pairs of preference orders, the theory remains rich (more than 2,700 pairs of preference orderings) in possible combinations of player interactions.

The domestic version of the IIG assumes that leaders select policy demands for their state based on domestic political pressures—that is, on the needs of those key domestic supporters who maintain them in office. This produces one fundamental difference between the IIG's neorealist variant and its domestic variant. In the neorealist version, it is not possible for a decision maker to prefer to compel a rival to capitulate rather than to negotiate with that rival. This is because demands are shaped by the structure of the international situation, without regard to domestic politics. At all times states seek to

---

[1] The symbol "!" means to calculate the factorial value of a number. The factorial is the product of the sequence of whole numbers from 1 to the specified number. Thus, $8! = 8 \times 7 \times 6 \times 5 \times 4 \times 3 \times 2 \times 1$.

TABLE 17-1

## Restrictions on Preferences for Decision Maker i in the IIG

| Outcome | Restriction on Ordering | Possible Preference Rank [a] |
|---|---|---|
| Status Quo | > Acquiescence by i, Capitulation by i | 7 to 3 |
| Acquiescence by j | > All other outcomes | 8 |
| Acquiescence by i | > Capitulation by i | 5 to 2 |
| Negotiation | > Acquiescence by i, Capitulation by i, War started by i, War started by j | 7 to 5 |
| Capitulation by j | > War started by i, War started by j | 7 to 3 |
| War started by i | > War started by j | 5 to 2 |
| Capitulation by i | > None assured | 4 to 1 |
| War started by j | > None assured | 4 to 1 |

[a] Rank order runs from 1 (lowest) to 8 (highest).

minimize any risk to their security. Because capitulation following an attack reduces a state's security by compelling it to give in to whatever its adversary has demanded and to bear the cost in lost lives and property, each state structures its response to its adversary's demand in a way that allows it to avoid such losses. That is, each state will offer just enough in concessions to make the would-be aggressor decide to negotiate a compromise settlement rather than use force. In effect, each state hones its demands to steer its adversary toward indifference. By negotiating, the would-be attacker gains less of whatever it demanded (such as territorial or policy concessions from the foe) than it might have had it used force, but it conserves resources by avoiding the costs it must endure as a consequence of its attack. As long as the expected utility from negotiating is at least as large as the expected utility from attacking, the rival will negotiate rather than attack.[2] This leaves the would-be attacker no worse off and the would-be target better off.

By contrast, in the domestic version of the IIG, although it is possible for one side to persuade the other side to negotiate rather than attack, the assumptions of the theory do not preclude the possibility that one state's leader will prefer to force a capitulation rather than negotiate. Therefore, the domestic IIG allows some preference orderings that the neorealist version does not—namely, any orderings in which forcing a capitulation is preferred to negotiating.

Be careful not to get confused here. In either version of the IIG, any state prefers to negotiate rather than capitulate. The difference is not in choosing to capitulate or to negotiate. The difference is that in the domestic version a state can want to make another state capitulate, whereas in the realpolitik variant it cannot. In the realpolitik version of the IIG,

---

[2] The procedure for identifying endogenously chosen demands is explained in chapter 3 of Bueno de Mesquita and Lalman (1992).

negotiation will always win out over a forced capitulation. In the domestic IIG, actors who prefer to negotiate with a rival rather than force the rival to capitulate are labeled doves; actors who prefer to force a rival to capitulate rather than to negotiate are labeled hawks.

The existence of hawks as well as doves in the domestic version of the IIG produces predictions about war fundamentally different from those produced by the neorealist version of the IIG. Lalman and I prove what we call the IIG's basic war theorem. This theorem, or logical implication of the game, states that war can be a subgame perfect Nash equilibrium of the IIG. This means that the game contains conditions that are both necessary and sufficient for war under complete and perfect information. In other words, when there is no uncertainty, war can occur if and only if these conditions hold true. In the absence of uncertainty, war cannot occur at any other time. This is a very powerful prediction. War is the complete and perfect information equilibrium outcome of the domestic IIG provided four conditions are fulfilled that are logically permitted, but not required, by the assumptions of the game. That is, these conditions define a subset of the 2,704 admissible pairs of preference orderings over the game's outcomes. They are as follows:

1. Player A prefers to initiate a war rather than acquiesce to the demands of player B.
2. Player A prefers to capitulate if attacked rather than retaliate and fight a war in which player B has gained the advantages of a first strike.
3. Player B prefers to fight a war started by player A rather than acquiesce to the demands of A.
4. Player B prefers to force player A to capitulate rather than negotiate with A.

As we know from our previous discussion, condition 4 is not possible under the neorealist version of the IIG. When demands are chosen strategically within the international framework, condition 4 is the preference that each actor worries about most and so takes action to offset. That action, again, is to make a demand or offer concessions that persuade the would-be aggressor that negotiating is at least as good for it as is trying to force capitulation. Negotiation is always better for the state that otherwise has to capitulate. Negotiation not only allows that state to avoid the physical costs of being attacked but also provides it with some chance (remember, $0 < p < 1$) of getting at least part of what it wants. When a state is compelled to capitulate, there is no such chance.

The logical possibility of war under complete and perfect information is consistent with James Fearon's observation that only one

> Use Figure 17-1 to satisfy yourself that the basic war theorem leads to war in the IIG. To do so, start at any terminal node, identify the choice of each player at each terminal node, and work your way up the game tree. Be sure not to violate any of the theory's assumptions in determining the choice of moves at each node in the game, and be sure to adhere to the theorem's conditions. Note that if a player prefers to capitulate rather than retaliate, then it must also prefer to acquiesce rather than retaliate, because the latter involves the same policy outcome as capitulation, but with no loss of life or property.

circumstance can lead rationally to war in the absence of uncertainty (1994). That one condition, as noted in Chapter 16, is when it is not possible for the players to commit credibly to negotiation. A simple way to think about how such a situation could arise is to think of a situation similar to a prisoners' dilemma occurring in the "Crisis Subgame" part of Figure 17-1. What happens, in essence, is that the threat of being forced to capitulate can lead a state to initiate war if it has a large enough first-strike advantage. Knowing that its rival will take advantage and force a capitulation if it offers to negotiate, a state that has a valuable first-strike advantage of its own may decide to initiate a fight rather than cede the first-strike advantage to a foe. Even if the prospective target of the preemptive strike professes that it will negotiate in good faith, the existence of a first-strike advantage prevents the professed commitment to negotiate from being credible.

The derivation of conditions under which war is logically possible with complete and perfect information also implies important differences between the domestic IIG and structural theories. We have already seen that neorealist theory suggests that uncertainty in the form of multipolarity increases the risk of instability (and war is often both a source and symptom of instability). Liberal theory, such as that developed by Robert Keohane (1984) and discussed in Chapter 4, makes a similar claim. Keohane's structural argument indicates both that uncertainty is destabilizing and that the spread of information fosters cooperation and stability. In contrast, Lalman and I report conditions under which uncertainty promotes peace and stability while certainty (or improved information) promotes war and other conditions under which uncertainty promotes instability.

If the IIG's logically necessary and sufficient conditions for war are met, then war is expected to take place. That is, if preferences are common knowledge, and the four basic conditions of the basic war theorem are met, then the conditions for war would be satisfied. Suppose, however, that because of uncertainty rivals do not know the preferences of their adversaries (that is, there is incomplete information). This uncertainty reduces the likelihood that the choices that are made will lead to war. If at least one leader mistakenly perceives that a rival's preferences are anything other than what is stated in the basic war theorem, then the risk of war is reduced by uncertainty. This must be true if the theorem is correct because the probability that an action will be taken when its necessary and sufficient conditions are met is, by definition, 1. The theorem, of course, stipulates complete and perfect information. If complete information is absent but the rest of the theorem's conditions hold, the necessary and sufficient conditions for war as stated above are no longer satisfied. In such case, the probability of the relevant event or action occurring can only decrease as a result of the decision maker's uncertainty.

For example, player A might mistakenly believe that B is a dove who prefers to negotiate rather than exploit his or her first-strike advantage to attack A. Consequently, A might offer to negotiate rather than grab the military initiative. If B really is a hawk, B will attack and A will find it necessary to capitulate. But if B mistakenly believes A is the type who will retaliate if attacked so that B thinks his or her choice is between negotiation and war, then B will respond to A's offer to negotiate by negotiating as well. In this instance, uncertainty about the preferences of the adversary can avert a war that would have occurred if the players were less uncertain about their rival's preference ordering over outcomes. More complete information would have made the risk of war greater, not smaller.

Similarly, it is possible for decision makers to mistakenly perceive that the conditions for war are met so that their interaction is ripe for war. If the conditions for war under complete and perfect information are not met, but because of uncertainty leaders believe that those conditions have in fact been met, then uncertainty increases the risk of war, because without uncertainty there would be no chance of war at all. Thus, uncertainty does not always have the same effect on the risk of war-created instability in the international system. In effect, uncertainty can both increase the risks of a destabilizing conflict and decrease that risk, each under specific, identifiable circumstances.[3]

## WAR AND UNCERTAINTY: THE IIG AND STRUCTURAL THEORIES

The results of the domestic IIG can be compared directly with the hypotheses of neorealism or liberalism. In liberalism and neorealism, uncertainty makes war (and other sources of instability) more likely, and certainty makes war less likely. Put more broadly, the greater the degree of uncertainty, the higher the probability of destabilizing events like war. By contrast, the domestic IIG identifies conditions under which increases in uncertainty make war more likely (that is, at least one of the four conditions are not met, but decision makers mistakenly perceive that all four are satisfied because each has incomplete information about the preferences of the other) and conditions under which increases in uncertainty make war less likely (that is, the four conditions are met but uncertainty about the preferences of an opponent lead to choices that do not result in war). If the IIG's necessary and sufficient conditions for war under complete and perfect information are not met and there is complete and perfect information, the probability of war (or instability) should be zero. Predictions made under these conditions are consistent with those made with the bipolarity hypothesis of neorealism. When the necessary and sufficient conditions for war under complete and perfect information are not met, and there is not complete information (that is, there is uncertainty), then the IIG predicts that the probability of war increases. This prediction is consistent with that made by neorealism and liberalism.

Under two conditions, then, neorealism and liberalism and the IIG make the same predictions about the likelihood of war (or other forms of instability), and under two other conditions the two structural theories make predictions opposite to those of the IIG. Of course, we cannot choose among theories on the basis of cases that make the

---

[3] This general result does not depend on what theory is used to identify the necessary and sufficient conditions for war. The result depends only on the existence of necessary and sufficient conditions under which an action or event is certain to happen and the existence of uncertainty.

same predictions. In those cases, if one is right so is the other, and if one is wrong so is the other. But when two different theories make different predictions, we have an opportunity to conduct a critical test of the accuracy of the alternative explanations of instability and conflict.

Evidence from European disputes since 1816 supports the domestic IIG's hypotheses about war and uncertainty and refutes those of the structural alternatives. Figures 17-2 and 17-3 show the relationship between the probability of war and the level of uncertainty in the European system for all disputes in that part of the world between 1816 and 1974. In Figure 17-2, the IIG's necessary and sufficient conditions for war under complete and perfect information are met, and in Figure 17-3 they are not. In both figures, uncertainty varies from very low levels to very high levels. If neorealist and liberal predictions are supported, then both graphs should slope upward because these theories predict that uncertainty is destabilizing and less uncertainty produces greater stability. If the IIG is supported, however, then the first graph should slope downward and the second graph should slope upward.[4] In contradiction to structural theories, the two figures clearly support the expectations deduced from the domestic version of the IIG. Reevaluations of the claims of the IIG that use more advanced statistical methods or control for more potentially confounding factors and that are conducted on a larger sample of countries generally reinforce these findings, although in some cases with significant qualifications and modifications (Gelpi and Grieco 1998; Signorino 1999; Smith 1999; Bennett and Stam 2000a, 2000b).

## WEAKNESS AND WAR: RESURRECTION AND PACIFIC DOVES

Before leaving the domestic IIG, two other results are worth discussing. Belligerence is often thought to increase as a state becomes

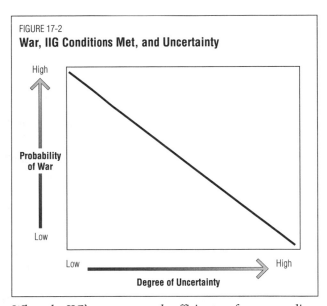

FIGURE 17-2
**War, IIG Conditions Met, and Uncertainty**

*When the IIG's necessary and sufficient preference conditions for war are met, but there is uncertainty about the preferences of rivals, then war is less likely to occur than in the case where there is no uncertainty. This result contradicts the predictions of liberal and neorealist theory, which contend that increases in uncertainty always increase the risk of instability. The IIG accounts for cases not explained by structural theories.*

---

[4] The figures are based on a statistical test called Logit analysis that estimates the likelihood of a binary dependent variable (in this case, "War" or "No War") as a function of a set of independent variables. The actual statistical test as well as a more demanding version of the test can be found in Bueno de Mesquita and Lalman (1992, at 77 and 216, respectively). All relevant variables are statistically significant and in the direction predicted by the domestic version of the IIG.

more powerful. Recall the words of Henry Kissinger quoted in Chapter 2: "In the final reckoning weakness has invariably tempted aggression and impotence brings abdication of policy in its train" (1979, 195). Kissinger's view that aggressiveness increases irreversibly with power is widely shared, and yet it is probably incorrect. There are several reasons why a weak state or nonstate actor such as a terrorist might, *because of its weakness,* be more aggressive than a stronger counterpart. Let me suggest two.

**THE RESURRECTION HYPOTHESIS.**    George W. Downs and David M. Rocke (1995) developed what they call the resurrection hypothesis. This hypothesis begins with the now familiar premise that leaders want to keep their jobs. Downs and Rocke show that when a leader faces a military defeat and can anticipate being ousted as a result, he has a strong incentive to fight on in the hope that serendipity will turn events in his favor. The leader's only hope of political resurrection is to fight on despite great military disadvantage. In essence, the resurrection hypothesis implies that the extreme efforts of apparently defeated leaders do not reflect a loss of rationality under extreme stress, which has been the more common explanation of such efforts among psychologically oriented arguments (Gurr 1970). Extreme efforts in the face of defeat are actually a rational response. Such a leader loses nothing by fighting on and stands to gain much if luck should turn his way.

Adolf Hitler launched the Battle of the Bulge after the rapid advance toward Germany of the Allied armies following the invasion of Normandy in June 1944. Hitler's action appears to have been an instance of the resurrection hypothesis at work. The Battle of the Bulge was a desperate attempt to save Germany from an Allied invasion. Although it failed, the Germans were able to mount a much tougher campaign than the Allies believed was still possible. The Tet offensive undertaken by the North Vietnamese on January 31, 1968, is another example of the resurrection hypothesis at work. America's military and political leaders believed that they had already so punished the North Vietnamese that they would no longer be capable of launching a military offensive. Likewise, the American public had

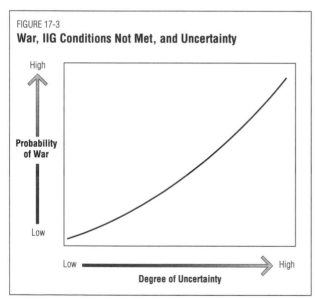

FIGURE 17-3
**War, IIG Conditions Not Met, and Uncertainty**

*When the IIG's necessary and sufficient preference conditions for war are not met, but there is uncertainty about the preferences of rivals, then war is more likely than in the case where there is no uncertainty. This result also supports the predictions of liberal and neorealist theory, which contend that increases in uncertainty always increase the risk of instability. The IIG accounts for cases also explained by structural theories.*

become convinced that the war in Vietnam was virtually won. And in fact, the Tet offensive was a considerable military rout—of the North Vietnamese by the Americans. But just by the very fact that they were able to launch the offensive at all, the North Vietnamese pulled off a stunning political and propaganda victory that resurrected their hopes.

The resurrection hypothesis provides an important lesson about foreign policy. During wartime, and during the diplomatic negotiations preceding a war, leaders commonly demonize their foes. George H. W. Bush, for example, referred to Saddam Hussein of Iraq in 1990 and 1991 as another Hitler, thereby casting Hussein in the eyes of the American public as a major menace to world peace. Bush may well have been right about Hussein. Whether he was right or not, however, demonizing Hussein may have actually had the effect of making him even more dangerous than he already was and thus helped to ensure his political survival. If Hussein believed, rightly or wrongly, that the United States was committed to marching into Baghdad and overthrowing him, a threat resurrected in 2002 by George W. Bush, then he was unintentionally encouraged to take great risks to resurrect himself politically. How he did this in 1991 is a complex story told brilliantly and convincingly by Avigdor Haselkorn (1999). Here I will only summarize the highlights of his account.

On the morning of February 25, 1991, the Iraqis fired a Scud missile into a sparsely populated area of southern Israel. The missile was remarkable in several respects. Unlike the other missiles Iraq launched against Israel during the Gulf War, this one apparently was not aimed at a population center. This is all the more remarkable because only by aiming at a population center could the Iraqis have hoped to gain the terror advantage that Scud missile attacks provided. Additionally, the missile carried no payload. There apparently were no explosives on board, although the evaluation of the missile by the Raytheon Corporation, which was charged with responsibility for assessing the Scuds as part of its evaluation of the performance of the American Patriot missile defense, stated that it was not a dud. Finally, the missile, unlike all other Scuds used during the Gulf War, had a concrete casing warhead. Such a warhead is designed for chemical or biological weapons and not for explosives, but no such weapons were on board.

Haselkorn draws an eminently plausible inference: the missile was a signal from Hussein. The Iraqis were unlikely to have Scud missiles with concrete casing warheads if they did not have operational chemical or biological weapons. We now know that they had nearly two hundred warheads containing such unconventional weapons as anthrax bacillus, botulin toxin, and nerve gas. Hussein seemed to be sending a signal. He was warning the United States and its allies that if they marched on Baghdad to overthrow him, he was prepared to use chemical or biological weapons against Israel. Since it was widely speculated that the Israelis would retaliate with nuclear weapons in reply to such an attack, he apparently was prepared to provoke the Israelis into a nuclear strike, with all that that implies. President Bush called for a ceasefire a day later and negotiated a settlement of the war on terms relatively favorable for Iraq given the utter defeat of its forces in the field.

Just months after demonizing Hussein and depicting him as another Hitler, the United States found itself giving up any chance at an unconditional surrender such as it had extracted from Nazi Germany in 1945. Having built a record of extremely dangerous behavior, including the use of mustard gas and nerve gas against Kurdish Iraqis and against Iranian forces in the nearly decade-long war between Iran and Iraq, Hussein had established the credibility of his threat to engage in unconventional warfare. Haselkorn concludes that Hussein resurrected himself politically, having been left no way out of the war that would ensure his own political or even physical survival. Rather than negotiate an agreement to move into exile, an avenue that was cut off to him by the United States's persistent portrayal of Hussein as a demon, he dangerously but effectively raised the stakes by sending the signal that he was prepared to escalate and possibly provoke a nuclear strike. In the process, he showed that even the greatest power in the world could be deterred if the benefits of continued action were no longer worth the anticipated cost of acquiring them. Pushing leaders to the point where they need to resurrect themselves, leaving them no graceful way out of a dispute, increases the risk of carnage and the prospects of watching a victory be snatched away in the jaws of defeat. The resurrection hypothesis highlights a difficult political trade-off. Demonizing an adversary helps mobilize political support for the use of force, thereby increasing the chances of victory. But demonizing an adversary also motivates that foe to try harder to win, raising the specter of increased loss of life and the possible necessity of negotiating a settlement on terms that belie the heinous charges leveled against the opponent. Demonizing an adversary also makes it harder for the victor to sell at home the idea of negotiating with the "evil" foe.

*Demonized leaders facing desperate straits may seek to resurrect themselves politically by engaging in extremely risky behavior. Sometimes, as appears true for Saddam Hussein, doing so builds their clout and saves them politically—which, after all, is what politics is all about. The risk that adversaries will resurrect themselves should make victors cautious about describing their foes as demons with whom one must not negotiate or compromise.*

**THE PACIFIC DOVES HYPOTHESIS.** The IIG yields its own brand of the resurrection hypothesis. It states that under certain circumstances a weak state—or terrorist—has incentives to initiate a war or other violent dispute against a stronger state even if the weak initiator strongly prefers a negotiated, compromise resolution of differences. As in the resurrection hypothesis, such a circumstance arises when conditions become so extreme as to compel a state, in desperation, to act in an unexpected, some would even say irrational, manner.

As noted earlier, a dove is a leader who prefers to negotiate with a rival rather than force that rival to capitulate. Lalman and I identify a special type of dove we call a pacific dove. Not only does a pacific dove prefer to negotiate rather than force the opponent to capitulate, but a pacific dove itself prefers to capitulate if attacked rather than retaliate. We demonstrate that if a state is a pacific dove,

> There have been calls for the establishment of war crime trials to punish those guilty of atrocities during the Bosnian-Serbian conflict and the Kosovo conflict in the former Yugoslavia. In fact, such war crimes tribunals have commenced under the aegis of the United Nations. Such trials provide an opportunity to obtain justice, but at the expense of possibly triggering more intense fighting as nearly defeated leaders attempt to resurrect themselves. Consider the circumstances under which the threat of such trials might prevent atrocities in the first place and the extent to which they might provoke war criminals into committing additional atrocities to gain sufficient leverage to negotiate their way out of punishment. What policies strike the right balance between the desire for justice and the desire to avoid further carnage?

and if it is uncertain of its foe's type, then the weaker it is relative to its opponent, the higher is the probability that it will launch a preemptive attack in an effort to extract a capitulation from that opponent.

The intuition undergirding this phenomenon is similar to that undergirding the resurrection hypothesis. In the IIG, when a dispute arises between a weak state and a strong state, the strong state's advantage in negotiations is proportional to its relative strength. The weaker a state is relative to its opponent, the less attractive is negotiation precisely because the weaker state does not bring much leverage in the form of power to the negotiating table. Still, a pacific dove prefers to negotiate rather than force the rival to capitulate, even if that rival is itself willing to give in. The trouble is, if the initiator in any dispute tries to negotiate, there is a danger of being attacked by the foe if that foe turns out to be a hawk. Thus, the extra leverage a weak state gains from seizing a first-strike advantage may for it be well worth the attendant risk of severe defeat by its more powerful adversary.

The weak pacific dove is uncertain as to whether his or her opponent is a hawk or a dove and also as to whether the opponent is the type that will retaliate if attacked or will view the issue as not worth the costs of a fight. The weak pacific dove simply does not know whether or not he or she will be forced to cave in if he or she does not attack in the hope that the foe will also do nothing and allow the status quo to persist. Negotiations do not look that attractive to the weak pacific dove because he or she lacks leverage. Giving up first-strike advantage and facing the danger of being forced to cave in looks bad too. For the weak pacific dove, then, the best chance for gain is to attack and hope that the stronger rival is not motivated to fight back over the issue in dispute. This is the only way that the weak pacific dove can derive benefits from the situation.

A numeric example may help make the intuition behind this claim clear. Let me stipulate payoffs for A in the crisis subgame depicted in Figure 17-1. Consistent with the idea of A being a dove, let A's payoff for negotiation equal 5 and A's payoff for making B capitulate equal 4. Additionally, let A's payoff for capitulating to B equal 2, for starting a war against B equal 3, and for retaliating if B attacks A, 1. Since A prefers capitulating to retaliating, A is pacific as well as being a dove. Suppose A is uncertain of B's preferences. Let $Q$ equal the probability with which A believes B is a dove (that is, B prefers negotiation to forcing A to capitulate) so that $1 - Q$ is the probability that, if A offers to negotiate, B is expected to attack, forcing A to capitulate. To keep the example relatively simple, assume that A—who prefers to negotiate rather than attack, forcing B to capitulate—is certain B would capitulate if attacked. Then A will attack if the expected utility from offering to negotiate is worse than the expected utility from attacking. In this case, that means that $5Q + 2 \times (1 - Q) < 3$. That is, A attacks B if $Q < 1/3$ and offers to negotiate if $Q > 1/3$. Now, suppose some state A' is in the same situation but is considerably more powerful than A so that A' expects to gain more utility from negotiation than does A. Suppose the payoff A' for negotiation is 20 rather than 5. Since A' is also certain that B will capitulate if attacked (a condition not required for the generalization about pacific doves, but convenient to keep the example simple) nothing else of relevance changes when A' calculates its expected utility for negotiating versus attacking B. A' attacks B if $20Q + 2 \times (1 - Q) < 3$. That is, A' attacks if $Q < 1/18$ and offers to negotiate if $Q > 1/18$. In other words, A is weaker than A' and, as a result, expects fewer benefits from a negotiated settlement and, therefore, attacks under more circumstances than does A'. If A' believes that there is only a 1/18 chance that B is a dove, that is sufficient to gamble on negotiation, but A must be more confident that B is a dove to undertake the gamble. A attacks unless there is at least a 1/3 chance that B is a dove who will, by definition, negotiate rather that attack A.

Although there are just forty instances of pacific doves in my analysis with Lalman, we can see clearly in Figure 17-4 that they behave as predicted by the IIG. The figure depicts the significant statistical relationship between the probability of victory, estimated

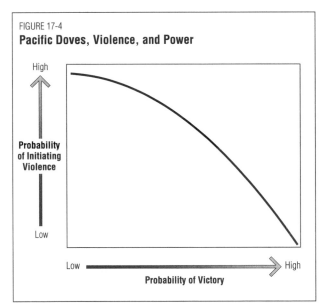

FIGURE 17-4
**Pacific Doves, Violence, and Power**

*Pacific doves—that is, leaders who prefer to negotiate rather than force a rival to give in but who would themselves rather give in than retaliate if attacked—are especially likely to initiate violence when their chances of winning are low. Here, then, is a case in which weakness fosters violence in otherwise peace-loving leaders.*

as an odds ratio, and the likelihood that a pacific dove will initiate violence. Contrast Figure 17-4 with Figure 17-5. The latter shows the same statistical analysis for initiators who were not pacific doves. The difference is stark and completely in line with the domestic version of the IIG. This result, like the earlier results regarding uncertainty, illustrates the importance of identifying the contingent conditions under which one or another relationship is expected to hold. Although the standard view that more powerful states are also more violent states is often true, it is not always true. For pacific doves, grabbing the initiative and engaging in violence helps make their demands more credible in a negotiation, but it also makes getting negotiations under way more difficult.

That pacific doves are more likely to engage in violence when they are weak rather than strong raises difficult questions about conflict resolution. Terrorist organizations, for example, typically are small and weak compared with the military might of their enemies. We observe terrorists as terrorists only when they engage in violent action. In such circumstances, we cannot tell them apart from hawks. Both hawks and weak pacific doves (but not powerful pacific doves) behave in the same way if they are sufficiently uncertain of the response they can expect if they try to pursue peaceful solutions to their disputes. A fundamental problem in crises is that it is dangerous for weak parties to gamble on trying to negotiate if the foe is a hawk who will seize the initiative and try to destroy them. Gambling on negotiation can be fatal. Yet, failing to gamble on negotiation can mean giving up the opportunity for a peaceful and successful end to the dispute. In thinking about conflict resolution we must always be careful not to underestimate the risks associated both with aggression and with gambling on peace. Either can be deadly.

## VIOLENT PACIFIC DOVES: A CASE HISTORY

The statistical evidence in Figures 17-4 and 17-5 shows that the contingent relationship identified by the domestic IIG between power and the initiation of force is consistent with the historical facts. In Chapter 8 I introduced briefly the decision by the Bavarians to fight the Prussians in 1850. As that case is a near-perfect example of violent action by a pacific dove, I return to it here to illustrate the logic of the IIG claim with a case history.

In 1850, when Germany was still organized into semisovereign princely states that

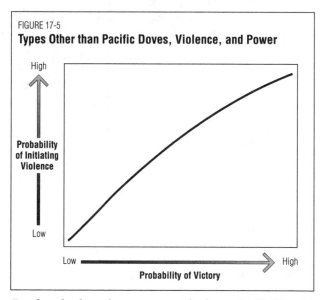

FIGURE 17-5
**Types Other than Pacific Doves, Violence, and Power**

*For those leaders who are not pacific doves, the likelihood that they will initiate violence increases as their power increases relative to that of their opponents.*

collectively made up a confederation with policies coordinated through the German parliament, called the Diet, Prussia was one of the world's great powers and Bavaria was a weak German princely state. In that year these two states confronted one another over disputed access to a strategically vital road in another German princely state, Hesse Electoral. Each of these states and a long list of other German principalities plus Austria made up the German Confederation.

Following the revolutions across Europe in 1848–1849, Prussia found itself compelled to take a backseat to the Austrian Habsburg monarchy in the newly restored German Diet, which had been allowed to lapse during the revolutionary period. The Prussians viewed the restoration of the German Diet as provocative. Gen. Joseph Maria von Radowitz, a key adviser to King Frederick William IV of Prussia, pressed firmly for Prussian pursuit of parity with Austria, the dominant member, in the newly constituted German Confederation (Mowat 1932). Although his approach was popular with the king, Radowitz's position was opposed by leading Prussian conservatives, including the young, rising star Otto von Bismarck.

Restitution of the pre-1848 organization of German states and other actions by Austria led to growing animosity between Prussia and much of the rest of Germany. These tensions escalated and reached a head when Austria and its allies confronted Prussia over a dispute centered on Hesse Electoral. The Hessian elector was locked in a struggle with the Hessian parliament. In a contest of wills, the Hessian parliament was dissolved before it had even authorized a budget. In consequence, Hessian officers, judges, and other key officials resigned, precipitating a power vacuum. Fearing for his security, the Hessian elector sought military assistance from the German Diet. This provoked a strong negative reaction in Prussia, which feared that the circumstances in Hesse would be used to consolidate the role of the Austrian-dominated German Confederation at Prussia's expense. Prussia declared that it did not recognize the Diet's authority to support the Hessian elector with military assistance and that Prussia would not permit the Hessian frontier to be closed.

On October 8, 1850, the Erfurt Union, which included several German states as well as Prussia, formed an alliance to back Prussia in its struggle.

*Prussia's capitulation to the weaker Bavarians in 1850 became a rallying cry for Prussian politicians who were not pacific doves. Otto von Bismarck rose to political prominence on the slogan that never again would Prussia suffer the "shame of Olmütz." During his leadership Prussia showed no reluctance to fight fellow Germans as Bismarck waged war against Austria and many smaller German states in 1866.*

This action provoked the kings of Austria, Bavaria, and Württemberg—the so-called Kings' Alliance—to pursue the interests of Austria and her allies in the German Confederation. They agreed that Bavarian troops and an Austrian rifle battalion would march into Hesse. By late October 1850, Bavarian troops had entered Hesse to protect against a Prussian incursion.

At the same time, Prussian forces approached Hesse, making it look as if war was imminent. So dangerous had the situation become that Russia, trying to mediate the dispute in a conference at Warsaw, declared that any armed resistance by Prussia to any other German troops in Hesse would constitute a declaration of war against Russia. Nevertheless, 140,000 men in the Prussian army were mobilized (*Times of London*, November 4, 1850).

To make matters still more threatening, there were indications that the dispute would spread. The French also appeared willing to enter into the conflict, although there was some ambiguity as to which side they actually favored. *The Economist* reported on November 2 its expectation that the French were prepared to assist the Russians in "dismembering" Prussia. Indeed, by November 23 it was reported that the French had called up an additional 40,000 conscripts and were amassing a large army on the Rhine. However, historians, with the benefit of hindsight, have suggested that in fact the French tried to negotiate a treaty with Prussia (Mowat 1932). In either case, it was widely believed that should a war begin, it would involve Russia, France, and England as well. By November 1850, then, there was serious danger of a general European war.

By November 1, 8,000 Bavarian troops and 1,000 Austrian Rifles had entered the town of Hanau in Hesse; about half that force was sent to occupy the neighboring province of Gelnhausen. With Prussian troops close at hand, an accidental, if not intentional, confrontation seemed inevitable. The immediate Prussian reaction to the incursion was to issue orders not to resist the occupation of Hanau but not to permit the occupation of the provinces of Cassel or Fulda, areas that were of strategic importance to Prussia. On November 8, Bavarian troops, under the leadership of Prince Paul von Thurn and Taxis, advanced against Fulda. In the village of Bronzell the Bavarian troops encountered Prussian troops, and the greatly feared collision of the two armies took place. Shots were exchanged and several soldiers were seriously wounded and some others killed. It appeared that war had broken out. Yet, Otto von Manteuffel, the new Prussian minister president and foreign minister, did not press the Bavarian forces. Instead, he ordered an evacuation, and no further fighting took place. Manteuffel's decision to order the withdrawal of the Prussian army was consistent with his well-known dovish desire to avoid war.

Following Manteuffel's display of restraint, Prince Felix Schwarzenberg, Austrian minister president, offered Manteuffel guarantees concerning Prussia's right of way over the military road of the Electorate and also regarding the duration of the occupation of Hesse Electoral. Manteuffel rejected these promises, requesting instead a meeting. A meeting was agreed upon at Olmütz, where a settlement was reached on November 29, a settlement that largely represented a capitulation by Prussia. As Agatha Ramm (1967, 221) explains it, the capitulation at Olmütz arose because "the King's fundamental wish for peace [brought] Prussia to concede the whole of Schwarzenberg's demands."

The events leading up to Prussia's capitulation fit the conditions of the pacific dove argument. It is important to recognize that events such as these are scarcely noted by historians.[5] This is because little comes of such disputes. Historians focus on explaining what did happen; they rarely draw attention to what could have happened. Strategic perspectives, like the IIG, help us understand why little came of the dispute over Hesse Electoral, even though the event looked quite threatening to its contemporaries.

It is apparent from the contemporaneous journalistic accounts, which did not have the benefit of hindsight, that the events leading up to the capitulation threatened a European great power war. The representatives of Austria, Bavaria, and Württemberg demanded Prussian acquiescence to the authority of the German Diet, but they were uncertain as to how Prussia would respond. Prussia's true intentions were not known. On the one hand, it was possible that Prussia was a hawk bent on exploiting the lesser German states. Such a view squared with the formation of the Erfurt Union and its accompanying efforts to deny Austria its historic hegemonic position in Germany. On the other hand, the Prussians acted in a restrained manner while pursuing a reconciliation through the Russian-sponsored discussions in Warsaw. Indeed, on November 2, 1850, the *Times of London* reported:

> The ceremonious attention shown to the Austrian Emperor [during the meetings in Warsaw] must have made an unusual impression on public opinion.... Prussia exhibited a disposition to mediate and come to a better understanding with the Government of Vienna, although it adheres firmly to its protest, on principle, against every general interpretation of the Austrian Bund.

Furthermore, it was clear that there were divisions within Prussia over how to approach the crisis. Even Radowitz, a hawk, had declared that Prussia's displays of armed power were meant only as a demonstration to encourage negotiations. Here, then, was the crux of the matter. From the perspective of Prussia's adversaries, it was not clear whether Radowitz's actions and those of Manteuffel following him were intended to encourage negotiations or were preparatory to an attack against the German Confederation's army (known as the Federal army) consisting of Austrian and Bavarian soldiers. If the latter turned out to be the case, then it would be better for the Federal forces to move first.

---

[5] Of course, the so-called *Punktation* of Olmütz (an agreement not quite as strong as a treaty) is much more extensively discussed by German and Austrian historians than by historians writing in English. Even among German and Austrian scholars, however, Olmütz is discussed much more in regard to its impact on subsequent German policy than in regard to the events in Hesse per se.

The Prussians also must have been uncertain of the intentions of the Federal army. On the one hand, these troops were undeniably placed to prevent Radowitz and Frederick William from realizing their goals in regard to Hesse Electoral and, more broadly, to Germany. On the other hand, the pro-Austrian factions in greater Germany had gone to great lengths in Warsaw and later to provide Prussia with a face-saving way out of the impasse. Perhaps the Confederation was only trying to gain additional leverage in future negotiations—behavior consistent with dovishness—or, more ominously, perhaps it believed that Prussia was only bluffing and sought to exploit Prussian reluctance to fight other Germans.

The Prussians did not acquiesce. After all, Prussian forces were much stronger than the primarily Bavarian force sent to resist them. Rather, the Prussians demanded their rights as they understood them. That is, the Prussians believed that they were strong enough to gamble on the dovish orientation of the Federal army, even at the risk of having to capitulate later. There was not sufficient evidence that the Confederation's forces would actually fight to warrant a Prussian decision to acquiesce without first testing the waters.

The mobilized Austro-Bavarian force was weaker than the mobilized Prussian army.[6] What is more, the Austrians had been careful to minimize their own military involvement. The overwhelming bulk of the Federal forces in fact consisted of Bavarian troops. Apparently, the Federal forces were less well prepared to cede the first-strike advantage by gambling on Prussia's good intentions. Not being sure of Prussia's true "type," and knowing themselves to be too weak in the field to relinquish whatever small advantage was to be had by seizing the initiative, the Bavarian forces struck out, leading to the violent collision in Bronzell.[7]

By Lalman's and my estimation, the confrontation between the German Federal forces and the Prussians was a confrontation between two pacific doves. When faced with a military confrontation by the Bavarians, Prussia capitulated. With some befuddlement, the *Times of London*, a source generally hostile to Prussia's ambitions and sympathetic to those of the German Confederation, summarized the unfolding events of the conflict in this way:

> There remains still a subject of mortification in the fact that Bavaria should now be playing the part of an intervening Power, even though it is manifestly under the wing of Austria. That Bavaria, the subordinate state, which [sic] wishes to assert its

---

[6] The Prussians did, of course, worry about the threatened intervention of Russia. Still, that intervention might have been offset by anticipated support for Prussia's claims from other powers.

[7] The exact details of the confrontation are unclear. Pro-Austrian reports indicate that the Bavarian soldiers marched with their muskets unloaded and with their swords sheathed, whereas Prussian accounts state that the Prussians had their swords sheathed and their muskets unloaded. It is also unclear who fired the first shots. Some accounts indicate that the Prussians fired some volleys *over* the approaching troops, presumably to signal them to halt or retreat. Others indicate that the Bavarian troops shot at the Prussians as soon as they saw them in Bronzell. In either case, the Bavarians certainly knew that in approaching Fulda they were proceeding into sensitive territory. It was inevitable that they would come face-to-face with Prussian forces.

place as one of the first rank. According to the theory of the Confederation, its army, formed of the contingents from the several states, is considered as one, and it is difficult to discover how, in this case, Prussia is entitled to resolve the occupying force now in Hesse into its national elements, and attribute the entry to the "too great haste" of the least influential of them. (November 8, 1850)

In fact, the theory of pacific doves provides an accurate description of how "Prussia is entitled to resolve the occupying force . . . in Hesse." Manteuffel simply was not prepared to fight a war against fellow Germans over so small an issue. Consequently, he ordered the Prussian forces to capitulate in the face of the use of force by the weaker Bavarians—the precise action anticipated by the propositions regarding pacific doves.

The domestic variant of the international interaction game accounts for facts explained by neorealism and other structural theories. It also accounts for facts of history that neorealism and other structural theories are unable to explain. In the domestic variant of the IIG, we have an alternative that seems to be logically and empirically superior to its main theoretical rivals. In keeping with the first principle of wing-walking, then, theories based on structural or system-level arguments should be discarded in favor of those based on strategic considerations such as the domestic version of the IIG.

## ARMS RACES, DETERRENCE, AND WAR

One of the great debates among foreign policy leaders and scholars is whether arming to the hilt increases the prospects of peace or the prospects of war. The fourth-century Roman military expert Vegetius said that those who desire peace must prepare for war. In our own time, Albert Einstein argued that you cannot simultaneously prepare for war and make peace. For those who share Einstein's view, vigilant efforts at arms control; prevention of the proliferation of nuclear, biological, and chemical (sometimes known as NBC) weapons; and, ultimately, disarmament are the surest path to peace. For those who take Vegetius's view, peace is promoted by developing weapons that are so destructive as to deter foes from seeking an advantage through the use of force, encouraging them instead to look for ways to resolve differences through negotiations. These two perspectives are so different that they define a political divide. Often, political liberals, or doves, are associated with the perspective that promotes arms control and fears the consequences of arms races, whereas political conservatives, or hawks, are associated with the perspective that promotes deterrence and fears military unpreparedness. How these alternative outlooks are linked to war is the subject we now examine.

After World War I, Lewis Fry Richardson, a brilliant meteorologist by trade, set out to understand arms races and their relationship to war. As a scientist, he was eager to construct and test a logically rigorous theory of arms racing. He argued that nations acquire arms in response to the hostility they perceive in a foreign adversary, the rate at which that adversary is arming, and the "fatigue" a nation feels in devoting economic resources to arms rather than to goods for domestic use. By "fatigue," Richardson had in mind the idea that the domestic population would eventually grow tired of postponing material improvements so that the government could buy more weapons. For example, Mikhail Gorbachev's quest for an arms control agreement with the United States may well have been motivated by his concern that the Soviet citizenry was tired of paying for weapons. In Richardson's model (1960), which is based on differential equations, fatigue slows arms races, whereas a rival's hostility and acquisition of arms accelerate arms purchases. He described an arms race as a situation in which the fatigue factor is weak relative to the accelerating purchase of weapons to offset the perceived threat implied by an opponent's choices. Richardson concluded that if hostility intensifies to the point where it overcomes the fatigue factor, then arms purchases will spiral out of control, with each side buying more and more arms until a war erupts (Siverson and Diehl 1989).

Richardson's model fit brilliantly with the data he amassed about World War I. His theory, however, failed to predict or account well for the advent of World War II. One possible reason lies in an intellectual leap of faith in Richardson's argument. The dependent variable in what has come to be known as the Richardson model is the change in arms expenditures of each participant in the alleged arms race. However, the argument that war results when the race spirals out of control is not grounded in the mathematical structure or logic of the theory. Also, why nations do not eventually become exhausted is not evident in the theory. Nor is it evident why, if states do fear exhaustion but are not yet exhausted, they turn to war rather than to some other means of redressing their frustration and concern over being outspent by the other side. Finally, because the Richardson model contains no uncertainty, it is not evident why the parties to an arms race cannot foresee the consequences of their spending and find a solution short of war before the situation "spirals out of control."

The argument for an arms spiral is, in the parlance of mathematical modelers, a hand wave. It seems like a sensible conclusion and it might be true, but it does not follow from the theory. In fact, the Richardson model assumes a knee-jerk, stimulus-response, action-reaction environment, with no strategic interaction at all. His arms racers were not selecting actions strategically. Neither was assumed to consider the effects of its own actions on the subsequent decisions of its adversaries. Consequently, the participants in a Richardson arms race have no basis on which to look ahead, consider the consequences of their decisions, and avoid having circumstances spiral out of control.

Richardson is not to be faulted for this. After all, he developed his arms race model two decades before the first formal inklings of game theory were set down and five decades before game theory was capable of dealing with the complex strategic interactions involving uncertainty that characterize efforts at deterrence. Furthermore, as a physical scientist, he was trained to think about interaction among particles, not about strategic interaction. This, after all, is one of the major differences between the physical sciences and the social sciences. In the purely physical world, particles—whether molecular, atomic, or subatomic—are not sentient. They do not prepare themselves for collisions or attempt to maneuver away from or toward collisions. People and other sentient agents do, and so they interact strategically.

Despite the nonstrategic foundations of Richardson's model, the idea of arms races as sources of war persists, and considerable effort has been expended to refine Richardson's core ideas. The notion that each side in a pair of adversarial states is arming in reaction to the arms decisions of the other immediately raises a problem in that there is an observationally equivalent explanation for escalating arms expenditure. Figure 17-6 illustrates the difficulty of distinguishing an actual arms race from a situation in which two national defense establishments are each arguing on a domestic level for greater budgetary authority. Organizational theorists have noted that bureaucracies and their leaders measure their success in part by the size of their budgets (Niskanen 1973; Wildavsky 1979). The more they have to spend, the more sway they have over people and policies. This means that leaders of organizations, including those in the military who argue for ever-expanding defense budgets and weapons procurement, have an incentive other than concern for the national well-being to seek more resources. Military leaders may be agents of the national government, but they often pursue their own interests, especially in light of the legitimate basis for debate over whether arms acquisition or arms control is in the national interest.

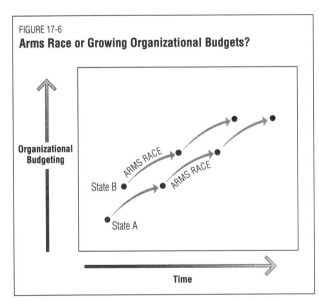

FIGURE 17-6
**Arms Race or Growing Organizational Budgets?**

*Arms racing and bureaucratic competition for budget increases create observationally equivalent predictions about the trajectory of arms expenditures. This means that it is difficult to tell arms races apart from ordinary internal budget competition.*

Figure 17-6 depicts two alternative causal relationships that account for the arms possessed by two nations at different moments in time. Since the length of the observed intervals between periods of weapons acquisitions is arbitrary, we cannot tell which of the time intervals in the figure represent budgetary growth for weapons through bureaucratic competition within each state (and possibly involving complicity by bureaucrats in "competing" states) and which signify the series of action and reaction that characterizes arms races between states. No wonder there is so much rhetoric and so little solid evidence about whether arms acquisitions programs are motivated by national security concerns or by everyday bureaucratic and interest group infighting.

Figure 17-6 alerts us to the concern expressed by President Dwight Eisenhower on the occasion of his farewell to the American people. Eisenhower warned of the growing influence of what he termed the "military-industrial complex." The military-industrial complex reflects the shared interests that weapons manufacturers and military leaders have in expanding their respective budgets by persuading Congress to spend more on weapons and defense. The military-industrial complex had an interest during the cold war in promoting the belief that the Soviet Union was accelerating its weapons capabilities while the United States was falling farther and farther behind.

During the 1960 presidential campaign between Richard Nixon and John F. Kennedy, one of the most hotly debated topics was the alleged missile gap. Kennedy argued that the United States lagged far behind the Soviets; Nixon was confident that American military capabilities were ahead of those of the Soviets. We know today that there was no missile gap. It was a political perspective that served the defense establishment well but that did not reflect reality. We now know that the CIA, for example, routinely and systematically overestimated Soviet capabilities. These overestimates helped fuel congressional willingness to invest large sums in expensive defense projects. Today, with military spending greatly reduced from its cold war high, it is common for the military-industrial complex to argue that the United States needs to produce more new submarines and massively expensive aircraft like Stealth bombers so that it will be prepared for as-yet unforeseen enemies and threats. Such arguments might, should a real threat emerge swiftly and menacingly, seem prescient. Based on what we know of the military capabilities of other states around the world, however, they only serve to underscore the contemporary relevance of Eisenhower's decades-old warning. These arguments are consonant with the bureaucratic and interest group perspective that favors a domestic explanation of growing arms budgets.

Considerable effort has been devoted to measuring arms races and then to seeing how they correlate with the escalation of disputes to war. Michael Wallace (1979, 1982) constructed a measure of arms races that proved to be strongly associated with the escalation of disputes to war. However, his analysis also proved highly controversial. His procedure for measuring an arms race is difficult to replicate. Others (Altfeld 1983; Sample 1996) have tried to implement his methods but have failed to produce estimates or results that reproduce those reported by Wallace. Furthermore, Wallace's approach to arms races allows for some odd

> Identifying arms races is difficult. How might you go about identifying an arms race without relying on hindsight? What criteria might you look for? Make a list of criteria and then look at the historical record to see if your criteria separate arms races from domestic bureaucratic efforts by the military to expand their budget. See if your criteria help predict whether a violent conflict subsequently arose between the racing states or not.

circumstances. For example, Michael Horn (1987) has shown that some cases that Wallace classified as arms races actually involved situations in which one of the two parties to the alleged race was slowing down in its arms acquisitions throughout the period described as an arms "race." It turned out that as long as one of the members of a pair of hostile states was spending enough on arms so that the average of the two was rising rapidly, Wallace called it a race.

In an effort to improve on Wallace's conceptualization, Paul Diehl (1985), Horn (1987), and Susan Sample (1998) each devised a procedure for defining and measuring an arms race while making a concerted effort to remain faithful to the logic underlying the Richardson model. Horn, for example, insisted that an arms race required accelerating arms expenditures, as was claimed by Richardson. Diehl, Horn, and Sample each found some support for Wallace's contention that arms races lead to war. Further, they and others (Altfeld 1983; Sample 1996) note that the direction of causality is problematic. Even if we ignore the budgeting issue raised in Figure 17-6, there is the problem that an apparent arms race may represent a buildup of weapons during a prolonged period of tension between states in anticipation of the need to be prepared to fight. In this case, the arms buildup does not cause war; the buildup is caused by the anticipation of a high risk of war. The causality runs opposite to the notion of an arms race that has spiraled out of control.

We can examine some of the data on arms acquisition for ourselves. Figure 17-7 displays a series of graphs showing arms expenditures for six different pairs of states over the period 1961 to 1990. Each graph has been normalized so that the dollar amount of expenditures cannot be seen but the change and acceleration in expenditures over time can. It is these last two elements, of course, that supposedly reflect an arms race. One of the pairs is the United States and the Soviet Union. Another is India and Pakistan, rivals that fought wars with one another in 1948, 1965, and 1971, and came close to doing so again in 1999 and in 2002. A third pair is Israel and Syria, long-standing adversaries in the Middle East. The remaining three pairs include Canada and Mexico, Belgium and the Netherlands, and Australia and New Zealand. Each of these last pairings involve states that are themselves closely allied or that at least do not harbor any security concerns about one another. The puzzle is to identify which graph goes with which pair. Although hardly a scientific survey, I suspect few readers will successfully or easily identify the U.S.-Soviet, India-Pakistan, and Israel-Syria pairings, because they do not look appreciably different from the others. For all of the scrutiny applied to the Soviet-American "arms race," there in fact seems to be scant evidence that one actually existed.

Arguments in favor of arms control to prevent war represent the flip side of arguments in favor of deterrence. The idea behind arms control is that the risk of war is reduced if adversaries have fewer weapons. Little systematic empirical research has been done to evaluate the actual impact that arms control agreements have on conflict. One substantial investigation of this subject, by Vasiliki Koubi (1993), shows that arms control agreements, like the Washington Naval Conferences of the 1920s that restricted the number of battleships in the fleets of the world's key naval powers, reduce hostility briefly but have no consequential effect in diminishing the threat of war beyond a brief period after signing. Indeed, many arms control agreements either codify decisions to limit the pursuit of an already obsolete technology or, by limiting known technologies, push countries in the direction of spending on weapons innovation. The Washington Naval Conference, for example, actually produced an agreement by which participants sank some of their own battleships (or dreadnaughts as they were then known). It did not limit the construction of aircraft carriers or submarines, the two new technologies that were rapidly making the battleship a highly vulnerable, largely obsolete weapon.

Negotiations between the United States and the Soviet Union in the late 1960s and early 1970s to limit the number of missiles available to deliver nuclear weapons led to the

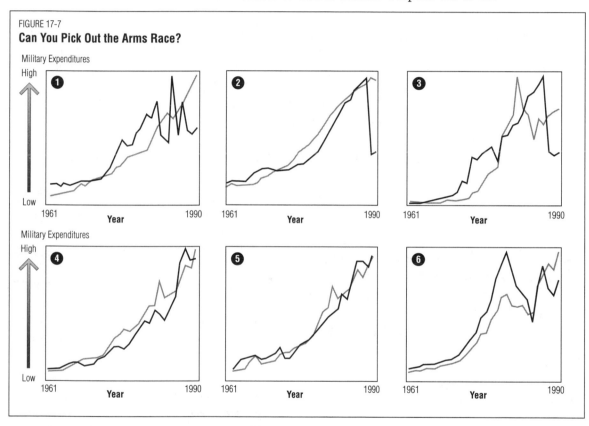

FIGURE 17-7
**Can You Pick Out the Arms Race?**

*Arguments that arms races lead to international tension and even war are very common. Yet arms races are exceedingly difficult to discern. Here we have six pairings of states, three of which were thought to have been involved in an arms race and three of which were not at all thought to have been engaged in an arms race. Can you pick out the three pairs purportedly involved in an arms race?\**

\* The military expenditures graphs are as follows: (1) Canada and Mexico, (2) the United States and the Soviet Union, (3) Israel and Syria, (4) Australia and New Zealand, (5) India and Pakistan, and (6) Belgium and the Netherlands.

introduction of MIRV technology. MIRV stands for multiple independent reentry vehicles. In effect, the agreement resulted in the greatly improved efficiency of individual missiles to deliver warheads. Before SALT I (Strategic Arms Limitation Talks) and the resultant Antiballistic Missile Treaty (ABM), each missile carried only one warhead. After, with the number of missiles allowed to each side limited by treaty, a single missile could carry multiple warheads. In 2002 the United States and Russian governments agreed to massive reductions in nuclear warheads, with each side free to choose which particular warheads or weapons systems to curtail and which to maintain. This

> Abandonment of the ABM Treaty is a source of controversy between the United States and Russia. George W. Bush wants to scrap the ABM Treaty and Russia's Vladimir Putin prefers to keep it. Draw up lists of advantages and disadvantages that are likely to result from abandonment of the treaty from the American perspective and from the Russia point of view. Would these lists have looked different during the cold war?

arms reduction agreement was relatively easily reached, reflecting more that the relations between the United States and Russia have changed rather than that they are trying to diminish the threat between them. That is, this latest arms control agreement seems more designed to codify the friendship emerging between these former enemies than it is to mute the remaining tensions. Still, it probably also helps pave the way for the American effort to develop antimissile defenses while abandoning the cold war–inspired ABM treaty.

Arms control is an idea with great public appeal. James Morrow (1991b), for example, has demonstrated that when American presidents were at risk of losing their reelection campaigns during the cold war, they were likely to make extra concessions to the Soviets in order to get an arms control agreement. These agreements boosted their popularity, helping improve their reelection prospects. But what should we logically expect the consequence of an arms control agreement to be in regard to the risk of war? Arms reduction agreements never roll arms back to zero. Even if they did, we should remember that ancient humans managed to fight one another with sticks and stones before the invention of the

> What does our earlier discussion of supply and demand curves in Chapter 13 suggest about how arms control agreements influence the price of war? What does this suggest about the expected frequency of war among signatories to arms control agreements? How would you design a study to see whether arms control agreements influence the risk of war, keeping in mind possible endogenous links between such agreements and the risk of war?

spear, hammer, bow and arrow, catapult, crossbow, canon, repeating rifle, machine gun, bomber, and so forth. Of course, cruder weapons meant fewer deaths, a very good thing indeed. The question is, however, did fewer or lesser-advanced weapons mean less war?

We know that as the centuries have unfolded, war has become less frequent but more deadly (Levy 1982; Levy, Walker, and Edwards 1999). When rivals reduce their arms, they reduce the expected costs of war. If they do not simultaneously resolve the issues creating tension between them, then arms control creates a situation in which the prospective benefits from war remain unaltered while the anticipated costs go down. In such circumstances, arms control acts like a sale on war. The price has been lowered, although the value of victory to the belligerents remains unaltered. The reduction in expected costs is precisely the feature that makes such wars less deadly and more likely.

The logic in support of deterrence is stronger than that in support of arms control. With deterrence, vast amounts of money may be wasted on building defensive military capabilities in response to a perceived threat that may not be real. The problem is, of course, to differentiate real threats from imagined ones before the fact. Trust in promises made by the other side is difficult to sustain when survival is at stake, as we saw in the analysis of the behavior of pacific doves. This is the problem of credible commitment that we have examined repeatedly throughout this volume and that has occupied much research on international security (Fearon 1994; Gaubatz 1996; Reed 1997; Morrow 1999). Although deterrence does raise the expected costs to an adversary of undertaking an attack, deterrence does not remove the issues in dispute. Like arms control, deterrence does not reduce or resolve the benefits side of the war-making calculation. It does, however, make war more costly. By doing so, it reduces the incidence of war and thereby reduces overall deaths by warfare. After all, had deterrence not been in place, war, and all that it entails, would likely have occurred. The benefits of deterrence come at a price, however. Should the deterrent threat prove inadequate, and war ensue, then the level of bloodshed is likely to be elevated by the greater stock and quality of weapons available to the belligerents.

The empirical evidence supports the notion that deterrence decreases the likelihood of war relative to arms control. Alastair Smith (1995) has shown that cases in which attacks did not take place were those in which alliance reliability was high, serving as an effective deterrent against aggression. William H. Riker and I have shown that the probability that a dispute will escalate to include violence and death increases as one moves down the deterrence ladder in the nuclear age (Bueno de Mesquita and Riker 1982). We found that while nuclear powers are involved with one another in many disputes, they do not engage in war. Rivals that are protected under nuclear umbrellas but that lack nuclear deterrents of their own were only slightly more likely to engage in war. Rivals with only conventional weapons at their disposal were the most likely to engage in war.

## OTHER HYPOTHESES ABOUT WAR

I have touched on some of the most prominent perspectives on the causes of war. There are, however, many other interesting approaches to this important topic. I mention some briefly here, but leave their detailed exploration to you.

### THE SCAPEGOAT HYPOTHESIS
One of the most enduring claims about the causes of war is the scapegoat hypothesis. When a leader is in domestic political trouble—because of a bad economy, a scandal, or

what have you—he or she may precipitate an international conflict, perhaps even a small war, to command the nation's attention and thereby divert it from the leadership's domestic failings. It is certainly well documented, at least for American presidents, that an international crisis creates a "rally-'round-the-flag" effect that boosts popularity for a short while (Mueller 1973; Brody and Page 1975; Norpoth 1987; Brody 1992; Morgan and Bickers 1992). Whether or not the increase in popularity helps with reelection, however, has not been ascertained. The rally-'round-the-flag effect is not necessarily tied to the creation of a bogus dispute to gain popularity. The scapegoat hypothesis, by contrast, is focused exclusively on the initiation of a dispute to gain political security.

A case that drew attention as a possible effort at scapegoating should help make the hypothesis clear. In August 1998 President Bill Clinton was compelled to give testimony before a grand jury investigating his personal conduct. Following his testimony, he gave an address to the American people in which he apologized for having had an illicit affair in the White House. A few days later, while discussions of possible impeachment swirled around Washington, the president returned from his vacation retreat to oversee an American military attack on alleged terrorist targets in Afghanistan and the Sudan.

There was immediate speculation about whether the missile attacks were an effort to divert attention from the president's personal and political problems or whether these were legitimate retaliatory strikes for the bombing by terrorists of the American embassies in Kenya and Tanzania a few weeks before. The speculation was heightened by the president's declaration that he had "convincing evidence" that the selected targets were in the first instance a terrorist training camp and in the second a factory manufacturing precursor chemicals for use in chemical weapons.

Clinton's failure to provide details about what evidence he had fueled talk that the attacks were an effort to use terrorism as a scapegoat, or diversion, to draw attention away from the president's problems. American presidents had in the past displayed what evidence they had gathered to justify their harsh reactions to foreign events. President Kennedy's ambassador to the United Nations during the Cuban Missile Crisis, Adlai Stevenson, showed satellite photographs of Soviet missile installations in Cuba to prove that Russian denials were false. President Ronald Reagan ordered the release of air-to-air recordings of conversations among Soviet pilots before they shot down a Korean commercial airliner that had strayed over Soviet territory. It was not widely known prior to the release of the recordings that the United States was able to monitor such conversations. The president compromised this intelligence source to prove convincingly that Soviet denials were false.

Whether the American attacks in Afghanistan and Sudan were motivated primarily by legitimate foreign policy objectives or by a president seeking to divert attention from his difficulties, we will probably never know. In any event, Clinton's antiterrorist actions had little sustained effect on foreign or domestic opinion of the president. It seems, in light of the tragic events of September 11, 2001, that the antiterrorist actions had little beneficial effect on the risk of terrorism. But it is just these types of questions that are at the heart of the scapegoat hypothesis.

The scapegoat argument finds mixed empirical support. Although many people subscribe to the idea, no convincing evidence exists beyond anecdotes of the sort just reviewed, to support the claim (Levy 1989; Leeds and Davis 1997). This is not too surprising. In essence, the scapegoat hypothesis relies on an argument that politicians are clever, their constituents and domestic opponents are naive, and observers, such as social scientists, are smart. Politicians are clever because they figure out how to use foreign policy to promote their popularity. They do this without jeopardizing their welfare, because the concocted conflict is one they do not expect to lose. Their adversaries, apparently, are not so clever, because they willingly engage in a dispute or small war that is designed specifically to end in their defeat. The citizens are naive because they cannot figure out that the little dispute their country is involved in is meaningless and is trumped up. And it would have to be pretty meaningless or else the leader might land in deep political trouble. After all, the whole idea behind a scapegoat is to focus blame elsewhere. We must also wonder why citizens and the political opponents of the incumbent cannot figure out that the dispute is being used to deflect attention from the leader's very real domestic problems. In effect, the scapegoat must be important enough that people will set aside their concerns about the leader's domestic failings but not so important as to represent a real domestic or international threat to the leader's well-being. This is a very tall order. Still more remarkable, while political opponents and citizens apparently cannot figure out what is going on, social scientists looking at the same information apparently are smart enough to recognize scapegoating when they see it. Generally it is a good idea to be skeptical of arguments that require the assumption that one or another key participant in decision making is just plain stupid. There is too much evidence that even seemingly inattentive citizens are quite savvy about the most complex issues once those issues impinge on their well-being.

## STATUS INCONSISTENCY

A variety of psychological theories draw attention to the well-documented psychological link between frustration and aggression. One common claim in this literature is that status inconsistency leads nations to fight wars (Galtung 1964; Wallace 1973; Ray 1974; Midlarsky 1975). The core of this argument is that frustrated leaders become aggressive. One source of frustration arises when a state has considerable power but low international status. The powerful, low-status state believes that it should receive rewards and recognition in international affairs that are commensurate with its power. Yet others treat it in accordance with its low status. Some argue that this was a major factor that drove Adolf Hitler to initiate World War II. Germany became powerful through Hitler's rearmament program yet continued to be treated as a pariah state, forced to pay war reparations for its role in World War I and denied an influential part in determining international norms of conduct. Others point to China before Richard Nixon's overture in 1972. Although powerful by dint of its huge population and massive economy, China, albeit poor on a per capita basis, had the world's second largest economy in the 1890s and still does today, but it was treated as a pariah by the United States. On the opposite side of the ledger, Britain and Switzerland are accorded high status in international circles despite their lack of real power.

As with so many other theories of war, the status inconsistency argument, although appearing to make sense, musters little evidence in support of its predictions. Upon reflection, the reasons for this failure to explain events is not too difficult to discern. The hypothesis that frustration breeds aggression and that status inconsistency is an important source of frustration is well demonstrated by psychologists who study the individual. The hypothesis that frustration foments war, however, requires several huge logical leaps. Nations do not have psychological states. We may speak metaphorically of a nation's psyche, but metaphor is not reality. Leaders, like all individuals, do have psychological states. They may feel frustrated and they may become

> Can you name other states with high prestige but low power or with high power but low prestige? Are there any discernible patterns to the behavior of these states that makes them different from other states? Why might such inconsistency between power and prestige arise? Looking back over the past couple of centuries, can you draw any generalizations about status inconsistency and foreign conflict involvement?

aggressive. It is entirely possible, although it has not been demonstrated, that the status inconsistency of a particular nation may be a source of frustration for that nation's leader. But why should we expect leaders to act out their frustration through international aggression? Is there any more reason to believe that leaders will manifest their frustration through warfare rather than by hitting their heads against a wall, yelling at their spouses or children, beating their underlings, or hitting their golf balls too hard?

Geoffrey Best (1994, 362) reports on having seen covert footage of senior Iraqi officers hitting helpless prisoners captured during Saddam Hussein's campaign to recover control of southern Iraq, which was lost in the wake of his massive defeat in the Gulf War. The American general George S. Patton famously struck one of his own soldiers during World War II. Such acts are clearly aggressive, and they are just as clearly linked to frustration. Yet they did not lead the generals involved or their political leaders to go out and redress their personal frustration through warfare. Is there any more logical reason to expect frustrated leaders to wage war than to expect them to try harder to implement successful policies that remove the source of frustration or that shift their own attention to other challenges, suppressing their frustration over the nation's status inconsistency? The obvious answer to these questions is that all of these psychological responses are plausible. The empirical record simply does not support the contention that leaders systematically respond to status inconsistency with frustration and international aggression.

## WAR IN CYCLES

A substantial literature contends that war comes in cycles. These cycles are typically long, varying from about fifty years to well over a century (Doran and Parsons 1980; Rasler and Thompson 1983; Thompson, Rasler, and Li 1986; Modelski 1987; Goldstein 1988; Modelski and Thompson 1994). In the most sophisticated accounts of war cycles, states rise, reach a power peak when their influence is at a maximum, and then gradually decline as others rise to supplant them. War is most likely to occur at turning points in this cycle of growth and decay. At these junctures, leaders hold mistaken views of their prospects. The state that has been on the upswing, but that has now in fact reached its apex—that is, the turning point leading to its downswing—remains focused on its growth in power and fails to adjust to its new reality. It continues to expect to be accorded more respect (that is, influence) than other states are willing to give it (Doran and Parsons 1980).

Much of the long-cycle literature is empirically driven. It relies on the examination of long series of data, trying to discern patterns and then fitting an explanation to those patterns. But the length of a cycle is often within the eyes of the beholder. Some systematic tests for the presence of cycles of recurring length fail to support the claims (Singer and Cusack 1990). Charles Doran and Wes Parsons's thesis (1980), however, is theoretically grounded and seems to find some empirical support. Their argument leaves open some important puzzles for future investigation. For example, why can the rest of the countries in the world tell when a state has reached its downturn inflection point, but the leaders in that country cannot? It is understandable that they might not recognize their changed circumstances right away, but as more and more unsuccessful interactions take place, why doesn't the theory allow for the possibility that leaders will learn from their failures, adjust their expectations, and thereby avert disastrous mistakes? Indeed, some recent, highly innovative organizational theory research by Scott Gartner (1997) shows that leaders make these types of adjustments as they figure out which of their strategies and tactics are successful and which are not.

## SUMMARY

In this chapter we have seen how uncertainty promotes international instability, but also how it can promote international stability as well. We tested the logic undergirding these claims and found them to be consistent with the historical record. We also saw that conditions exist when the weak are expected to be belligerent, perhaps even more belligerent than the strong. The resurrection hypothesis helps explain why leaders who face severe military defeat fight on in the hope that luck will turn the tide their way. We saw that demonizing an enemy leader may encourage his or her efforts at resurrection through accelerated violence, thereby possibly creating a worse situation than might otherwise have materialized. We found that a particular type of state or terrorist-actor, pacific doves, are especially likely to initiate violence when they are much weaker than their foes. The likelihood that pacific doves will be peaceful increases as their relative power increases.

We also examined several theories linking arms levels to war and found them wanting either in logical rigor or empirical support, or both. The record indicating that arms races are a cause of war is weak at best. The claim that arms control treaties reduce the threat of war is mistaken. Although arms control does reduce the deadliness of war, it appears to increase—or at least not to decrease—its frequency. Deterrence, for its part, does reduce the likelihood that disputes will escalate into violence; however, when deterrence fails, the ensuing conflict is likely to be much bloodier than would otherwise have been the case.

War is so terrible a feature of international relations that I cannot leave the subject without emphasizing the importance to all of us of improving our understanding of this deadly phenomenon. The last few decades have seen real progress in our theoretical and empirical understanding of the logic behind warfare, but much remains to be done.

CHAPTER 18

# A PREDICTIVE MODEL OF INTERNATIONAL AFFAIRS

Ideas about international politics are well and good, but do they really help us predict and explain future events? Are the tools developed in this book sufficient to provide real insight, or are they simply ways of making sense of the past? In this chapter I pull together the ideas and tools introduced earlier to provide practical guidance on how to explain events in contemporary international relations and to predict how they will unfold. I will do so by using a practical model of political decision making, alternately known as the expected utility model and the rational actor model, with, as we shall see, a proven track record of real-world predictions.

The model that is presented here can be accessed and used on the World Wide Web at http://bdm.cqpress.com. You have already been asked to use parts of it throughout earlier chapters. As an example of *applied* modeling, it makes some sacrifices in theoretical or analytic purity in order to gain empirical leverage. At the same time, the model remains faithful to the strategic perspective that has been discussed throughout this book. The representation of decision makers in this model, however, assumes that individuals are bounded in their rationality. This means that they are not able to look ahead across a limitless time horizon but, instead, can see only the move that lies directly ahead of their current choice. Furthermore, although they update information and so learn, they do so crudely. They are not as efficient as fully rational Bayesian decision makers, who follow Bayes' rule, introduced earlier. Andrew Farkas (1999) has shown that inefficient decision makers with limited time horizons, who are rewarded for success and punished for failure, quickly fall into patterns of choice that mirror expectations for rational actors. The model introduced here is dynamic and makes specific, detailed predictions about policy processes and outcomes.

The model sees policy choices as the product of competition between decision makers; as such, it is a noncooperative game. Players put forward alternative policy solutions that attract a certain amount of support (or opposition) from other players. Sometimes decision makers (individuals or coalitions) are powerful enough to coerce one or more of their rivals into accepting major shifts in policy position. Other times the actors reach more modest compromises. And still other times decision makers exchange proposed solutions, disagree with one another, and perceive their relative influence differently. Such circumstances can result in intense conflict, or even war. Finally, decision makers may believe that they lack sufficient influence to alter another actor's point of view. Indeed, they may believe that any effort to do so will only result in a costly defeat. In such situations, decision makers prefer to accept the status quo over trying to alter it by proposing a policy shift. Decision makers' perceptions are based on their estimates of the expected utilities to be gained from choosing alternative policy proposals and the anticipated personal and policy consequences of those proposals.

The bargaining process over policy decisions is dynamic. Decision makers exchange ideas and proposals about how to resolve issues and adjust their views of the situation based on what they observe. They may decide to make a particular proposal, or they may realize that they cannot muster sufficient support to change the status quo. Ultimately, their maneuvers result in specific, predictable policy decisions for the issues in question or in outright failure to reach agreement.

The predictive model simulates the bargaining process while adhering to a fixed set of assumptions. It assumes that decision makers are trying to maximize their expected utility with regard to both policy and personal security satisfaction. The simulations assume that each player's actions are informed by what that player expects to see happen in the next round of play and by what happened in the round immediately preceding. The model proceeds through a potentially large number of rounds of negotiation until the model estimates that the expected cost to the players of continued negotiation exceeds the anticipated benefit. At this point the simulation ends. The model assumes that the cost of bargaining rises at an increasing rate as the simulations continue through successive rounds. The predicted final policy outcome is equal to the position of the median voter in the last round of simulation, if there are no veto players. If there are veto players, then the predicted outcome is the policy, if any, that those actors agree to in the final round. If they do not converge on a common position, then the model predicts that the issue debate will end without agreement.

In essence, the model, when applied to any policy issue, identifies the simulated round-by-round sequence of expected conflict, compromise, acquiescence, or stalemate between each pair of decision makers. In discussing players in this model, I use the terms "actor," "decision maker," "stakeholder," and "player" interchangeably. Each of these terms can refer to an individual, a group, an entire nation, a bloc of alliances, an international organization, or anything in between. For clarity, I use the impersonal pronoun whenever I mean to refer to more than a single person. The model identifies the median voter in each round and the process by which some players may be persuaded to shift their policy stances from one side of the median voter to the other. It identifies the final bargaining round and predicts that the outcome is the median voter position in that round unless there are veto players or the rules require a supermajority. The model focuses attention on the application of power in pursuit of decision makers' preferred policy outcomes and the dynamics of bargaining as shaped by each actor's perception of its negotiating leverage with each other actor.

## LOGICAL FOUNDATION OF THE MODEL

The predictive model explains how the stated policy positions of competing decision makers evolve over time. It makes predictions about policy outcomes and identifies strategic opportunities for altering them. As such, it can be used to explain and predict political decisions at any level of analysis. The model has been described more fully elsewhere (Bueno de Mesquita 1984, 2002; Bueno de Mesquita, Newman, and Rabushka 1985, 1996; Bueno de Mesquita and Stokman 1994). Here, I concentrate on the underlying logic of the model and only sketch its technical features.

The Forecaster model applies Duncan Black's median voter theorem (1958), which we have already explored at length, and Jeffrey S. Banks's theorem about the monotonicity between certain expectations and the escalation of political disputes (1990), that is, as a decision maker's expected gains from a dispute increase, so too does the decision maker's willingness to use force in pursuit of those gains. These theorems, along with ideas from bargaining theory, foster the development of a quasi-dynamic political model that includes detailed expectations about the agreements or compromises that various players are willing to make over time and an assessment of the anticipated resolution of the issues in question.

Two constraints facilitate prediction and explanation. First, issues are unidimensional such that preferences can be represented on a line segment and, second, preferences (and associated utilities) for potential outcomes diminish steadily the farther in Euclidean distance a possible settlement is from one's preferred outcome. These two constraints, as we know from our earlier discussion, are requirements of the median voter theorem. Black's theorem proves that the median voter's preferred outcome is the winning position under the two constraints noted above, provided that a simple majority is required for victory. Of course, many important political problems do not involve voting per se. As such, in this model it is assumed that the exercise of power through the mobilization of resources is the nonvoting equivalent of votes in most political interactions, the same assumption you were asked to make in the issue example on which you chose to focus. Unlike in Black's theorem, the decision rule used in this model need not require a majority of power in support of a particular position and can be adapted to require a supermajority (for example, two-thirds or three-quarters or unanimity) or to empower one or more stakeholders with a veto.

The model deviates from the median voter theorem in one other important way. Black assumed that all voters vote and that they do so strictly and sincerely according to their preferences. Although this is a natural way to look at decision making in democratic systems, it is not the only way. Black's theorem certainly has much to tell us in nonvoting situations. In applying the median voter theorem, however, we must recognize that not everyone is free to "vote" or act according to his or her own preferences as to outcomes. Indeed, Black's theorem does not allow for the possibility that votes are coerced, but coercion is a distinct possibility in most political settings, especially in international politics. Black's theorem also does not deal directly with sequential decisions in which the choices of decision makers at one stage may alter the range of options available to other decision makers at a later stage in reaching a final resolution of a policy question. The model discussed here recognizes this sequential element and the possibility that some decision makers can be coerced. It allows for the possibility that under some circumstances decision makers may be compelled to throw their support behind a less-preferred alternative.

Through coercion, or in response to the sequential character of decisions, it is possible for players to cross over the median voter position. In such case, a decision maker has been compelled, or has chosen strategically, to back an outcome farther away from his or her true wishes in a direction opposite to the median voter position. This creates the possibility that the median voter outcome will shift over time even though "voters" neither enter nor leave the system and even though their preferences regarding outcomes do not change.

The monotonicity theorem provides a basis for predicting whether policy debates will produce negotiated settlements or lead to an escalation of tension between competing decision makers. Banks's monotonicity theorem highlights an important feature of all politics. It tells us that in any asymmetric information game—that is, in any game in which some player or players know information that other players do not know—the more one expects to gain from challenging a rival's perspective, the more likely one is to undertake that challenge. This simple statement turns out to have interesting and sometimes surprising implications for political intercourse. In particular, Banks's monotonicity result provides insights into how to expand the analysis of decision making into arenas in which rational actors can be compelled to back policies that in less constrained environments they would prefer to oppose.

By using the monotonicity result and the median voter theorem, I suggest a model of perceptions and expectations. This model helps us comprehend bargaining and understand the conditions that can lead to increased tension or even a complete breakdown in negotiations. I capitalize on the perceptual features of the model to simulate the process by which negotiations unfold, moving from one set of circumstances (and outcomes) to another, and then another.

The model is a game in which players simultaneously make proposals to each other about how to resolve a policy issue and exert whatever pressure they can to get their rivals to accept their proposals. Proposals consist of suggested new positions on a policy continuum. The game is essentially a multiplayer version of the domestic international interaction game introduced in Chapter 17. Players evaluate options and build coalitions by shifting positions on the issue in question. The above steps are repeated sequentially until the issue is resolved or until the costs of continuing to negotiate exceed the benefits.

In the game, each player knows three factors. Each knows (1) the potential influence of each actor on each issue examined, (2) the current stated policy position of each actor on each issue examined, and (3) the salience each actor associates with those issues. The stakeholders do not know how much value their rivals place on alternative outcomes or what perceptions those rivals maintain about their risks and opportunities. Each decision maker chooses based on his or her perceptions and expectations, with these perceptions and expectations sometimes in error.

Of the infinitely many possible proposals available to resolve an issue, how are we to predict which proposal will ultimately be chosen? To answer this question, let's first learn a little more about each actor. In this analysis, each decision maker is endowed with three and only three characteristics. Each player (1) has a stated or inferred position on the issue at any time, (2) is endowed with resources with which to exert some influence over decisions, and (3) has a personal agenda of priorities or salience attached to the issues at hand.

A player's stated position reflects the current policy choice that represents that player's utility-maximizing mix of policy satisfaction and personal security. The stated position, then, is not a policy ideal point but is the policy satisfaction–personal security ideal point for that player, as discussed in Chapter 5. A player's resource endowment represents the pool of potential power that that player can draw on during negotiations or conflict over the issue resolution. Thus, the resource variable reflects potential power, as discussed in Chapters 7 and 8. The third critical variable, which I call salience, concerns a player's preferences concerning how to distribute resources across issues. This model, then, builds on the discussion in Chapter 9 by recognizing that stakeholders have preferences over outcomes within issues as well as over the issues themselves.

Any aggregation of individuals with identical values on all three variables can constitute a stakeholder for the purposes of this model. Differences in the available pool of resources, in preferred outcomes, or in salience mean that the aggregation of individuals makes up more than one group and must so be treated in any analysis. Players are defined only by the three characteristics of potential influence (capabilities), stated policy preferences, and salience. The predictive model is quite generic, equally applicable to interpersonal decision making, group decision making, and interstate interactions. Its application recognizes no level of analysis restrictions.

When alternative courses of action are pitted against each other, the array of forces of the competing interests influences which interest (if any) will win. Of course, this array depends on more than just the relative power of the actors involved. It also depends on each actor's willingness to spend influence on the issue in question (salience) and the intensity with which it prefers one proposed settlement over another. Each actor has a total number of potential "votes" that is equal to its capabilities, a factor that may be influenced by external considerations, by the institutional arrangements that impose structural constraints on the decision-making process, or by both. Where structural constraints are relevant, as in qualified majority voting in the European Union, voting in the U.S. Congress following a presidential veto, choices made by the UN Security Council, and so forth, the model can be readily adapted by changing its key decision rule—the median voter rule—to reflect the operative rules of the institutional setting.

The "votes" cast by any actor depend on the extent to which an actor prefers one alternative to another, the depth of the pool of resources at its disposal, and how deeply the actor is willing to draw from that pool to spend on the issue in question. This means that an actor's "vote" (the amount of influence it is willing to mobilize) in support of a specific policy choice is equal to its potential capabilities multiplied by the importance of the issue to the actor multiplied by how much the actor prefers one proposal to another. If you pause for a moment to think about this statement, you will recognize it. This "voting" component is equivalent to the model by myself and Michael Altfeld used to test alliance reliability in Chapter 15 and to evaluate the effect of motivational differences on power in Chapter 7 (Altfeld and Bueno de Mesquita 1979).

This "voting" scheme reflects what takes place inside the proverbial smoke-filled room before the formal, visible decision-making process occurs. It assumes that any formal process echoes the agreements reached beforehand. Put differently, it assumes that stakeholders anticipate only the next stage of decision making, using the process of backward induction first introduced in Chapter 3. The decision makers anticipate how the formal decision-making setting will influence all actions and pick policy proposals in the negotiating process that they believe will survive within that structure. Stakeholders, however, are bounded in their rationality. That is, they are able to look ahead only as far as the next stage of decision making and no farther. Their choices, then, although locally rational, may turn out to be inefficient two or more steps down the road.

The prospect that a proposal will succeed depends on how much support it can muster compared with that garnered by each of the feasible alternatives. In any negotiation, there are likely to be many proposed settlements. By pitting all alternatives against one another, two at a time, as in the Condorcet voting method introduced in Chapter 6, the preference of the median voter (weighted by power, salience, and intensity) is found. Absent any uncertainty or coercion, which may lead an actor to switch position, the median voter position is the predicted outcome (Black 1958). In practice, perceptions or beliefs often lead decision makers to grant concessions or to give in to a rival's point of view, sometimes needlessly. Such concessions or capitulations can change the location of the median voter and, therefore, the predicted outcome. Consequently, the initial median voter prediction is not the final prediction of the model. The beliefs and perceptions of the relevant actors frequently suggest compromises and concessions that one or another actor is willing to pursue and that the other actors involved are willing or compelled to accept. These beliefs and perceptions may influence the array of interests sufficiently to require a reestimation of the median voter position, perhaps across several simulated rounds of bargaining, until perceptions and positions stabilize around the "dominant" outcome. To undertake this type of before-the-fact analytic updating, we must first develop the means to estimate each actor's relevant beliefs and perceptions.

## PERCEPTUAL ANALYSIS

The forecasting element of the model reveals what decision makers should expect if everyone acts sincerely according to their current stated policy position at the time a choice has to be made. They may have been forced to accept their current stance, but, once they have taken it, the players renege only if they see an opportunity to form a credible winning coalition closer to their initial position. What can decision makers do if the predicted outcome is not to their liking? Are there strategic maneuvers that can improve the expected outcome?

It is possible, and indeed likely, that actors will engage in private, strategically sophisticated deals to rearrange the prospective resolution of a controversial issue. These deals may result from cooperation and coordination among a subset of stakeholders, or they may be the product of conflict and coercion. Deal making that arises as a result of coordination among actors reflects the essence of negotiations. The perceptual model guides decision makers in understanding which deals are feasible and which are not. It points out how to construct an outcome with strategically sophisticated approaches to resolve a policy issue. Actors who are dissatisfied with the expected outcome can take one of four courses of action to improve their prospects. They can alter their own level of effort (that is, effect a change of salience); shift their revealed position so that their stated position is altered; influence other actors, either cooperatively or coercively, to make concessions that result in an altered level of effort (effect a change in salience); or influence other actors, either cooperatively or coercively, to make concessions that result in altered stated policy positions.

Here we will focus only on the last of these four strategies whereby actors persuade or coerce other actors to switch positions, with the direction and size of a change in position dictated by the logic of the model. Changes in salience are treated analogously. That is, an actor might be persuaded to make more or less effort if doing so improves the outcome sufficiently from the actor's point of view. If a greater effort is required, then the stakeholder must also believe that the cost of extra effort (that is, higher salience) is acceptable, given the expected impact it will have on the resolution of the issue. Increasing someone's salience is likely to be much more difficult than persuading a player to reduce his or her salience.

By estimating the beliefs of the other actors involved in an issue, decision makers can decide what type of leverage to exert to gain their own ends. These beliefs allow decision makers to estimate each player's expected utility from challenging or not challenging the various policy proposals. At the same time, decision makers can calculate the expected consequences of challenging and not challenging alternative proposals and of resisting and not resisting proposals made to them. By estimating a rival's expected utility for the different responses to challenges to their policy position or personal security, decision makers form beliefs about how rivals will respond to different levels of pressure.

One of three contingencies may arise if the stakeholder levels no challenge at its rival. First, the rival may not alter its policies during the period of concern so that the status quo between the stakeholder and its rival will prevail. Second, the player may anticipate that its rival's position on the issue in question will change in a way that is beneficial. Thus, without taking any overt action, the actor can gain further support for its position. Finally, a rival may shift its position in a way that is harmful to the decision maker. To summarize the point, if you do not try to change someone else's behavior, then that person may, on his or her own, not change at all, change in a way that is better for you, or change in a way that is worse for you, just as we saw in our analysis of relations among allies and enemies in Chapter 15.

Rational decision makers will want to weigh the expected costs and benefits of not directly challenging another actor's preferred policy against the costs and benefits of challenging that actor in the hope of coaxing it to shift its policy position. If a policy challenge is made, there is some chance that the rival will not care enough about the issue to resist the proposed settlement—that is, the rival may simply acquiesce to whatever is demanded. Of course, it is also possible that a rival will resist. If there is resistance, then there is some likelihood that the decision maker demanding a shift in policy position will prevail; there is also some probability that the decision maker will not prevail. Compromise is another possibility. In such case, the decision maker will achieve neither complete success nor complete failure but, rather, will engage in some form of give and take.

If a decision maker makes a demand and the target of that demand acquiesces, then the decision maker derives the utility he or she attaches to gaining the rival's support. Should the demand fail, then the decision maker confronts the prospect of being coerced by the rival into supporting the rival's preferred policy outcome. In the event of a compromise, less utility is gained than would have been the case had there been an outright victory; at the same time, however, less utility is lost than if there had been an outright defeat.

Once the players have estimated the relevant expected utilities, we can describe the relationship between each pair of stakeholders. If a player believes it stands to gain from challenging a rival and also believes that the rival concurs in this assessment, then the challenger expects the rival to either compromise or simply give in to coercion. A compromise occurs if the challenger's demand is larger than what the rival thinks it is necessary to give. Coercion occurs if the challenger's demand represents a smaller utility loss for the rival than the rival is expecting. Of course, the rival's actual expectations may not match up with the challenger's beliefs. If they do match, then the challenger will realize the outcome it expects. If they differ, however, a more modest compromise, or some other outcome altogether, will arise.

A stalemate leading to the expected continuation of the status quo occurs if a player believes that it stands to lose by making a demand and if it believes as well that its rival also expects to lose by making a demand. In this situation, as in the situation in which a player expects to be forced into an undesired policy if it makes a demand, the player will not propose a shift in policy—that is, the player will not challenge its rival. The rival may see things differently. It may calculate that it can obtain a favorable compromise, or even compel its opponent to accept its point of view. In such case, the rival will propose that its opponent adjust its policy position.

In the event a decision maker thinks he or she stands to gain from challenging a stakeholder and believes as well that the rival expects to win, the challenger and the rival can anticipate a tense and conflictual relationship. Sometimes when a challenge is made under these circumstances the rival turns out to believe that it should compromise or give in, leading to a lower-cost confrontation than expected. At other times the actual response to a policy demand is as anticipated, and the relationship becomes strained.

The possible relationships between decision makers are summarized visually in Figure 18-1. The horizontal axis measures the difference between player A's expected utility for challenging the policy position of each other stakeholder and A's expected utility for not challenging that position. Positive values (located to the right of the vertical axis) denote that player A expects more from challenging (making a policy proposal to) a given player than from not challenging that

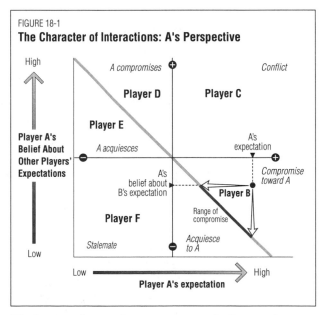

FIGURE 18-1
**The Character of Interactions: A's Perspective**

*The impact of perceptions on outcomes is direct and predictable.*

player. Negative values (located to the left of the vertical axis) denote that A expects more from not challenging a given player than from challenging that player. In this case, A prefers to accept the status quo in relation to the other player over trying to alter the other player's policy stance. Naturally, A's expected utility for challenging one player could be positive, and its expected utility for challenging another player could be negative.

The vertical axis denotes A's belief about the value of each other player's expected utility for challenging or not challenging A's policy position. In other words, the vertical axis is A's perception of each other decision maker's view of its own situation in relation to A. Positive values (located above the horizontal axis) indicate that A believes that the other player expects to gain more from challenging A than from not challenging A. Negative values (located below the horizontal axis) indicate that A thinks that the other player expects to gain more from not challenging A (that is , from accepting the status quo) than from challenging A. If A believes another player prefers to accept the status quo over challenging A, then A does not expect to receive a policy proposal from that player. Of course, A's perceptions may prove mistaken and the other player may make a challenge; in so doing, it provides A with new information about how it (A's rival) sees the situation.

Labels in each section of Figure 18-1 give the expected consequences of different combinations of expectations on the horizontal and vertical axes. For example, the solid dot in the lower right quadrant of Figure 18-1 shows a situation in which A expects to gain from challenging B. A thinks that B expects to lose utility in a confrontation with A. A thinks that B believes it will lose less than A is demanding, with the difference reconciled through a compromise that shifts B's policy stance toward A's. The model calculates how large the anticipated policy shift will be. In the software available to you at the Web site, policy issues are situated along a five-point scale. A compromise might, for example, require a shift in position from the lowest end of the scale to the third-highest swath when the two players start out at opposite ends of the issue continuum. Of course, the compromise might require a larger or smaller movement.

Similar figures can be drawn for each stakeholder. When a stakeholder believes its relationship with a rival is in one part of the graph, and the rival believes it is in another part of the graph, one of these two players may have an opportunity to exploit the belief of the other. Whether or not the opportunity is worth pursuing depends on the nature of the difference in their perceptions.

A verbal summary table is part of the model's output. For example, Table 18-1 shows Austria-Hungary's verbal summary table for the first round of negotiations during the June 1914 crisis between Austria-Hungary and Serbia that led to World War I. The first column in the table indicates what relationship the prospective challenger (in this case, Austria-Hungary) anticipates it will have with the listed rival; the second column shows what relationship the rival anticipates; and the third column indicates the predictive model's assessment of the type of relationship that will arise as a result of the interac-

TABLE 18-1

## Austria-Hungary's Verbal Summary Table, Round 1 (June 1914)

| Rival | Focal View (Austria-Hungary's) | Rival's View | Joint View |
|---|---|---|---|
| Germany | No Issue | No Issue | No Issue |
| Italy | No Issue | No Issue | No Issue |
| Rumania | No Issue | No Issue | No Issue |
| France | + Stalemate | + Stalemate | + Stalemate |
| Russia | + Stalemate | + Stalemate | + Stalemate |
| Turkey | + Stalemate | + Stalemate | + Stalemate |
| England | + Stalemate | + Stalemate | + Stalemate |
| Bulgaria | + Stalemate | + Stalemate | + Stalemate |
| Belgium | + Compel | + Compel | + Compel |
| The Netherlands | + Compel | + Stalemate | + Compel |
| Switzerland | + Compel | + Stalemate | + Compel |
| Sweden | + Compel | + Compel | + Compel |
| Denmark | + Compel | + Compel | + Compel |
| Norway | + Compel | + Compel | ı Compel |
| Albania | + Stalemate | + Stalemate | + Stalemate |
| United States | + Compel | + Compel | + Compel |
| Portugal | + Compel | + Compel | + Compel |
| Spain | ı Compel | + Compel | + Compel |
| Japan | + Compel | + Compel | + Compel |
| Greece | + Stalemate | + Conflict | − Compromise |
| Serbia | + Compel | + Conflict | − Conflict |

*Note:* "+" indicates that the focal group is expected to have the advantage; "−" indicates that the rival is expected to have the advantage. "Conflict" indicates that the focal groups and the rival expected to gain from challenging the other's policy stance, resulting in a conflict between them; "Compromise" indicates that either the rival (+) or the focal group (−) is expected to shift its policy stance toward the position of the other player (i.e., the player that has made a demand); "Compel" indicates that either the rival (+) or the focal group (−) is expected to acquiesce by accepting the policy stance of the other player (i.e., the player that has made a demand); "Stalemate" indicates that neither the focal group nor the rival is expected to propose a change in the status quo.

tions of the two players when each player acts according to its expectations. There is one verbal summary table for each decision maker in each bargaining round of the model.

In Table 18-1, Austria expects Serbia to feel compelled to accept Austrian demands. The plus sign in front of the word "Compel" tells us that the focal group (Austria-Hungary) expects Serbia to acquiesce. If there were a negative sign preceding the word "Compel," then the implication would be that Austria-Hungary thinks that Serbia can compel it to give in to Serbian demands. This latter scenario, of course, is not the case in Table 18-1, nor was it the case in 1914. Note that the model predicts that Serbia expected a conflict in which Austria-Hungary would have the upper hand (+Conflict) and that the interaction between the two states would lead to a conflict in which Austria-Hungary would not come out on top (−Conflict).

## ESTIMATING THE MODEL

The various components of the model must each be measured if the model is to have any practical value. The measurement procedures are explained in considerable detail elsewhere (Bueno de Mesquita and Stokman 1994; Bueno de Mesquita 2002) and at www.bdm.cqpress.com. Here I provide only brief, summary descriptions of the methods used for estimating each of the key variables.

The estimation of the subjective probability of success for any actor A in a competition with any other actor B uses my model with Altfeld (1979) with just two modifications. First, the predictive model adds a denominator that normalizes values between zero and one. Second, the numerator is modified in that the "Altfeld–Bueno de Mesquita" equation is now summed across all third parties that prefer the outcome desired by the actor on whom we are focusing, as perceived by that actor. This gives a fairly refined odds ratio measure of the probability of victory in a contest between any two stakeholders. Unlike the odds ratio measures introduced in Chapter 7 that looked only at capabilities, this indicator not only takes into account capabilities but also takes into account the willingness of decision makers to spend their resources on the issue in question (salience) as well as on the specific proposed resolutions (stated positions).

The numerator and denominator have straightforward political interpretations. The numerator calculates the support actor A can expect to receive in a confrontation with actor B. This support depends upon the capabilities of each actor that prefers A's policy objective to B's. However, capabilities alone are not sufficient information to estimate the value of the support of each third party. Those capabilities are diminished by the degree to which the issue in question is not salient to the actor whose support level is being estimated. The lower an actor's salience score, the less likely that actor is to spend resources on the issue in question. Finally, capabilities must also be discounted by the intensity of preference of the actor in question for the outcomes under contention. If a third party is just about indifferent between supporting what A wants and supporting what B wants, then it is unlikely to put much effort behind helping A. If, however, a stakeholder intensely favors A's objective over B's, then it will place proportionately more of its capabilities at A's disposal. Thus, the numerator is the expected strength of the coalition (or the "votes") supporting player A. The denominator reflects the sum of the support for A and for B so that the overall expression shows the gambling odds for player A.

The probability calculation is subjective because player A's estimate of its chances for success may be quite different from player B's estimate of the same value. The subjective component is introduced by using estimates of the individual risk-taking profiles of each decision maker. In particular, the utilities for the specific proposals that enter into the calculation are evaluated so that we can approximate the size of the trade-off made by each decision maker between what I described earlier as the pursuit of political satisfaction and policy satisfaction (Lamborn 1991).

By "political satisfaction" I mean the value a player attaches to seeing an issue resolved even if the resolution of that issue is not the outcome the stakeholder desires. By "policy satisfaction" I mean the value a player attaches to supporting a substantive policy outcome close to his or her desired choice, even if that outcome is inferior to the player's preferred outcome. I assume that all decision makers make trade-offs at some rate in their pursuit of policy goals and political goals. Decision makers differ, however, in the rate at which they are willing to give up one form of utility for the other, because they value the two dimensions differently. This difference across actors means that purchasing policy support from some players is easier than purchasing it from others.

The political satisfaction that arises from getting a deal done is, of course, a central idea in much of politics, but what does it mean in this context? The closer in expected utility an actor's public position on a policy issue is to the median voter position, the more secure the actor is. After all, the key characteristic of the median voter position is that in head to head competition it beats all alternatives. The decision to locate close to the median voter reflects a fear of vulnerability or a tendency to be risk averse.

This presumption of risk aversion follows from the notion that the actor has chosen a position that minimizes threats to its desire to "do a deal" at the expense of pursuing what it really wants. The farther the decision maker's expected utility score is from its possible maximum (while still remaining within the feasible set of alternative proposals), the more risk acceptant the decision maker is presumed to be. Thus, we find that there are three different expected utility values of interest. One is the player's expected utility on the issue, given the player's stated position. The second is the player's expected utility had the stakeholder been located at the position of the median voter. And the third is the player's hypothetical expected utility had the player chosen a policy stance that minimized its prospects of being a member of the winning coalition. With three points we can plot a curve on a graph with one axis being the utility the player associates with alternative policy outcomes and the other axis being the utility the player associates with its role in helping to forge a winning coalition to resolve the issue in question.

The measure of risk taking explained in *War and Reason* (Bueno de Mesquita and Lalman 1992) provides one perspective on how much each decision maker appears to have exchanged personal political security for policy goals or vice versa. The risk-taking measure also provides a basis for estimating the value each player attaches to the overall policy status quo. The stated position leads to a set of expectations about how others will respond to the player in question, as indicated in Figure 18-1. Thus, the sum of a player's expected utilities in relation to that of all the other players, given stated positions, assesses the value of the status quo from each decision maker's perspective.

The model's assessment of the willingness to take risks can be evaluated empirically. I have looked at the estimated risk scores for eighty war initiators over the past two hundred years (Bueno de Mesquita 1985). I calculated the risk scores using data on alliance portfolios that were knowable prior to each war so that no hindsight entered into the analysis. In this way the accuracy of the risk indicator in sorting out the likelihood that a war initiator would end up winning or losing the war it started could be assessed. The expectation was that risk-averse war initiators would choose disputes that they were especially confident of winning, whereas risk-acceptant war initiators would be more willing to start wars in cases in which the odds of victory were not as good. In fact, this proved to be the case, as can be seen in Table 18-2. Another way to assess the accuracy of the risk indicator is to look at the measure of the probability of success and the risk score together. Nearly two-thirds of the militarized disputes initiated by risk-acceptant leaders were undertaken when the probability of success was less than 0.5. In contrast, 53 percent of the disputes initiated by risk-averse leaders were undertaken when the probability of success was greater than 0.5. This difference is so statistically significant that it would have occurred by chance fewer than two times in a hundred samples.

TABLE 18-2

## Relationship between Risk Taking, War Initiation, and Victory or Defeat

|  | Initiator Won | Initiator Lost |
|---|---|---|
| Risk-Acceptant Initiator | 27 (68%) | 13 (32%) |
| Risk-Averse Initiator | 38 (95%) | 2 (5%) |

## WHY DOES THIS MODEL HELP?

What information does the perceptual model reveal? Recall that every decision maker is assumed to know the array of potential power, positions, and salience of each other decision maker. This information is common knowledge. The private information possessed by each decision maker involves the shape of his or her own utility function and the beliefs he or she holds about the expected utilities of every other actor. Thus, every actor is assumed to know the basic information that goes into the expected utility model. Every actor knows the shape of his or her own utility function but can only form a belief, not a certainty, about the shape of the utility functions of the other decision makers. The model offers an empirical advantage over the methods of real decision makers. If it is a reliable description of how decisions are made, then it mirrors how real decision makers think about problems. Real decision makers, however, almost certainly take intellectual shortcuts. With ten, twenty, thirty, or more stakeholders involved in a particular decision, it is too difficult for them to keep track of all of their expected actions and interactions. As a result, decision makers in the real world tend to focus on the five or six most important actors (besides themselves).

Computers are not as smart as people, but they have much better memories. The computer has no problem keeping track of the calculations for the interactions among any number of stakeholders. By not taking intellectual shortcuts, it is likely to uncover information that real-world decision makers miss. This provides a distinct advantage in developing accurate predictions and in designing effective strategic responses to difficult situations. You will see shortly how well this model has fared in helping policymakers in making real decisions.

## INTUITION BEHIND THE MODEL'S DYNAMICS

The beliefs of each actor imply actions. These actions, which involve the extraction or granting of concessions over support for this or that specific position, lead to a reevaluation of the situation by each decision maker. As stakeholders respond to revised proposals, with their responses supported by their beliefs and expectations, the prospects for a favorable or unfavorable settlement change for many participants. Beliefs and expectations provide the foundation for a quasi-dynamic assessment of the evolution of issue positions and recalculations of the location of the median voter.

When actors are persuaded or coerced into accepting a proposal different from their initial (or current) position on an issue, the decision process enters a new phase. Coalitions change and the support or risks associated with alternative proposals vary. New proposals are brought forward as revised beliefs and expectations open new possibilities or foreclose old ones. Each such sequence of revised stances is called an iteration, or bargaining round. The model computes as many iterations as it takes for the policy issue to resolve itself. Issues are resolved when they reach a stable, equilibrium outcome—that is, an outcome from which there seems to be no meaningful possibility of change, given the estimated expectations of the actors. The model assumes that continuous bargaining is costly. As such, it determines when bargaining should come to an end by calculating how large the change in the median voter position is from round to round relative to its built-in, assumed cost function. Once the cost exceeds the benefits for all of the players, the game ends.

Each player would like to choose the best offer made to it, and each proposer enforces its bids to the extent that it can. Actors that are perceived to be capable of enforcing their wishes make their proposals stick. Given equally enforceable proposals, players will move the least distance possible from their original stated positions. In effect, each actor selects from among the bids it makes and the bids it receives. The bid chosen is that which is optimal, given the constraints under which the player is operating. These constraints include its own perceptions and the reality of which proposals turn out to be enforceable and which turn out to be effectively resisted or rejected outright by rivals.

At the end of a round of proposal making, players have learned new information about their opponents. If, for example, a player finds that some proposals it thought of as enforceable are successfully rejected, then it has learned that these proposals were in fact unenforceable (that is, the player has less support than it thought). By monitoring responses to its proposals a player learns how much leverage it actually has. If a proposal is accepted, then a player learns that it made the best offer among all the proposals made to the recipient of its accepted bid. Furthermore, at the end of each round, the players are atop a new political landscape. This landscape consists of a revised distribution of resources times salience across the issue continuum. Because players may have changed positions by the end of any given bargaining round, this distribution of resources times salience is altered, reflecting the new distribution of positions along the issue continuum.

When the players have finished sorting out their choices, each shifts to the position contained in the proposal it accepted. Of course, when a decision maker agrees to a compromise with another actor, it hopes that that actor will live up to its end of the compromise bargain. But this is a game in which promises are not binding. Proposals are enforceable only if a decision maker has the means to make sure that the other actor does what it says it will do. But each player is free to renege on a proposed deal so long as it can enforce another agreement or so long as someone else can enforce an agreement on it.

What are the consequences of the actions implied by the model's first iteration? How do these actions influence the location of the median voter? How do we decide when the median voter outcome at a particular iteration is to be taken as the actual resolution of the issue at hand? If no stakeholder believes it has a remaining credible proposal, then the game ends. Similarly, if the value of remaining proposals is sufficiently small such that the cost of continuing to bargain outweighs the value to each player of the expected improvement in the outcome, then the game ends. The median voter at that stage of the game is the predicted policy outcome, barring the caveats about veto players or supermajorities discussed earlier. If, however, it is believed that credible proposals remain—proposals that can change the outcome sufficiently given the assumed cost function for continued bargaining—then the game will continue to the next round (Bueno de Mesquita and Stokman 1994; Bueno de Mesquita 2002).

## DEVELOPING THE DATA

Political outcomes, whether they involve intra- or intergovernmental relations, negotiations between public and private organizations, or even negotiations within a single organization, can be explained and predicted using the model described here. To do this, however, theoretical concepts must be converted into practical application. Although this can be a difficult task, there is, fortunately, a body of knowledge that we can call upon to help us estimate the variables. By combining the perspective of this rational actor model with the knowledge of issue experts, it is possible to estimate the variables of interest and to solve the perceptual and "voting" components of the model.

The model requires the identification of the groups or actors interested in influencing a policy outcome on the issues in question. For each actor, data can be estimated on the three variables that are necessary to developing a prediction: capabilities, stated policy position, and salience. In institutional settings we would also need to take into account any structural constraints shaping outcomes. As noted earlier, the predictive model is readily adapted to reflect requirements other than simple majority rule. Supermajorities and veto power, both of which are found in institutional settings, can also be accommodated. With just this minimal information in hand, it is possible to predict what the likely actions and outcome of an international relations issue will be. Information such as the history of a situation, the history of relations between particular actors within that situation, and cultural factors is unnecessary. Even an interview of the actors involved to assess their own judgments about their beliefs and expectations will add no benefits.

Where do the necessary data come from? The best source is individuals with area or issue expertise. Through them we can identify which players are likely to be involved with any given issue. What is more, although these experts themselves often doubt that they possess the essential information to quantify capabilities or salience, careful interactive techniques generally allow us to elicit this crucial information. It is critical to realize that the area experts need not be asked what they think will happen on a given issue. Remember, the only information that we need is the numerical estimation of the three required variables. Usually, issue experts find this process helpful because it distills the process down to very specific, structured considerations.

The essential feature behind the development of the data estimates is, to begin with, the following precise operational definitions of each variable:

*Salience*

90–100: This issue is of the utmost importance. I would drop whatever I am doing and turn immediately to this issue whenever asked.

70–80: This issue is very important to me. I would try very hard to reschedule to handle this issue when it arises.

50–60: This is one of several important issues. Others are more important. I would have to drop this if one of those more important issues arose. Otherwise, I will focus on this issue.

30–40: This is an issue that I care about but that is not very important to me. I have many more important issues to deal with and so generally would not drop what I am doing to deal with this one.

10–20: This is a minor issue. I rarely make much effort to deal with it, or for that matter even pay attention to it.

Less than 10: I really don't care about this issue.

*Resources*

100: I am the most powerful stakeholder on this issue. [There can be more than one group at this score or at any other score.]

All other values (positive only) are evaluated relative to 100 and to other stakeholders. Thus, two stakeholders with 40 and 60 equals a single stakeholder at 100 in a head-to-head contest where no one else is involved and all three stakeholders try as hard as they can. Two groups at 15 and 30, if they share a common position, are very close in potential influence to a group at 40 and will probably just barely persuade the group at 40 to accept their point of view where no other players are involved. The resource scores should not be thought of as percentages. A decision maker with a score of 100 does not have 100 percent of the resources; in fact, it may have only a small percentage of the total. The total is the sum of all the resources across all the groups or decision makers.

*Stated Position*

The stated position is the current negotiating position on the issue for each stakeholder. This position is not the outcome the stakeholder expects, or is prepared to accept, but is the stakeholder's current negotiating stance. When the position has not been stated, it is best thought of as the answer to the following mind experiment: If a stakeholder were asked to write down his or her current position on the issue continuum without knowing the positions of any of the other stakeholders concerned with that issue, what would he or she write? To place a numeric value on the stated position, the investigator must first define the issue continuum. The continuum will either have a natural numeric interpretation, such as the percentage or speed of reform on privatization policy, or the analyst will need to develop numeric values that reflect the relative degree of difference across policy stances that are not inherently quantitative. It is important that the numerical values assigned to different positions (and they can range between any values) reflect the relative distance or proximity of the different solutions to one another.

Sometimes the information required to analyze a policy choice can be gleaned from the careful reading of newspaper and journals. This is one common method used by experts to develop their expertise. It is worth noting that it is possible (and not very difficult) to achieve a high level of accuracy and cross-expert agreement on the essential information. This is true even when the experts you interview (such as professors at your school) disagree markedly on the likely outcome or evolution of the issue. The greatest power and insight from such an approach can be obtained by combining the analytic consistency of models such as those explained here with the nuanced and rich insights of area or issue experts.

It is when issue experts combine their skills with the analytic strengths of these models that accurate and subtle predictions are most likely to be attained. To be sure, an abstract model such as the one proposed here is of no value without the needed information to turn its abstractions into practical estimates. Expert knowledge is invaluable.

Even without a model, issue experts can suggest what information is critical and how that information should be organized. Controlled experiments show, however, that predictions extracted from the model using information from area experts are substantially more reliable than predictions made by the experts alone. After all, most area specialists have invested heavily in learning critical facts about the issue they study. They have invested less time in developing expertise in theories of decision making under uncertainty. It is insights from just such theories that this model incorporates and routinizes. By combining the advantages of expert knowledge with the advantages of a systematic codification of how decisions are made, it is possible to develop analyses that are considerably more informative than can be achieved using either type of expertise alone.

One question frequently asked about this methodology is how sensitive is it to the biases or perspective of the particular experts who provide the data? It is surprising to most people to learn that the outcomes predicted by the model are quite uniform across different experts. Upon reflection, however, this should not be too surprising, since experts are not asked their opinion but rather are asked for very basic information: who are the stakeholders? what do they say they want? how influential could they be and how much do they care about the issues in question? It turns out that the vast majority of specialists view this basic information in the same way. Naturally, different specialists will give different labels to some stakeholders (especially when the stakeholder is a group and not an individual), but the underlying structure of the data turns out analytically to be remarkably similar from specialist to specialist. Indeed, in some sense, simply knowing the basic information necessary to activate this model is a minimal condition for being a specialist.

That the predicted results are not terribly sensitive to which issue specialist provided the input information is evident if we examine the model's track record, an endeavor we will undertake in a later section. For now, I will simply point out that independent audits of the accuracy of this model in making real-time predictions (that is, predictions about events that had not been resolved at the time the prediction was made) indicate that it has achieved an accuracy rate of about 90 percent. It is very unlikely that the users of this model, who generally lack substantive expertise in the problems to which they apply it, will be fortunate enough to pick just the right experts to get the right information that will lead to the right prediction. Indeed, the experts often disagree with the very predictions produced through the modeling process. It is more likely that the results are not as sensitive as one might think to variations in the personal perspectives of the experts. In fact, because it contains so many nonlinear feedback elements, the model describes a complex system whose path is difficult to anticipate. The model's complexity precludes the

Construct a data set that addresses a foreign policy issue in today's newspaper. What do the journalists predict will happen? What is your prediction? Look at the data and then try to predict the outcome based on the model on the Web. Look over these predictions again when the issue is resolved. Which prediction was most accurate?

possibility that experts will be able to manipulate the model in a credible way to produce the outcome they want. Even someone intimately familiar with the model cannot guess what it will predict. Although I developed the model and have used it thousands of times, I cannot look at an input data set and guess accurately at its outcome.

## MODEL OUTPUT

Our discussion to this point has provided an abstract sense of how expected utility is incorporated into the modeling process to develop accurate predictions of the outcomes of international relations disputes. To put a bit more flesh on this process, I will now apply the model to the case of Europe in June 1914 on the eve of World War I. You will find additional data sets at the Web site, where you have the opportunity to analyze issues for which you will need to develop the necessary data. Using the Web software, you can assume the role of key decision makers in many major foreign policy disputes from history and see how well you would have done in handling those situations.

The essential question being asked here is, "What is the consequence of each stakeholder's point of view regarding resolution of the Austrian-Serbian Crisis of June 1914?" Table 18-3 contains the data required by the model to help us answer this question. The stated preferred position of each player is expressed in terms of the degree to which the country in question favored Austria-Hungary or Serbia. On the issue continuum, scores closer to 100 are more favorable toward Austria-Hungary, and those closer to 0 are more favorable toward Serbia. The stated positions on the issue are derived from the alliance portfolios of the states active in the European political system in 1914. The data were created by using the Signorino-Ritter S-score discussed in Chapter 15. These data are only a crude approximation of the policy positions of the governments of the day. More precise estimates, including the positions of individual leaders, ministries, and so forth could be collected through careful historical research or by interviewing experts on World War I. Here I have chosen to use these more basic data for three reasons. First, these estimates are derived from readily available information that anyone can obtain simply by researching published alliance data. Second, the information used to develop these estimates is based on knowledge that any of the relevant decision makers could have possessed in 1914 as the crisis was unfolding. Third, although these data do not lead to an exact replication of the facts of World War I, they do yield results that are similar in fundamental ways to what actually happened and thereby reinforce the notion that outcomes can be predicted even with the use of rather crude data. This is all the more instructive because the decision makers in 1914 were surprised to find themselves in a major war and almost certainly would not have put themselves in such a situation if they could have foreseen the consequences of their actions. You have already seen in Table 18-1 that the model's simulation of the beginning of the 1914 crisis predicted that Austria-Hungary misperceived the likely development of its relationship with Serbia.

TABLE 18-3

## Data for the Austro-Serbian Crisis, June 1914

| Code | Resources | Position | Salience | Country Name |
|------|-----------|----------|----------|--------------|
| AUH | 0.0467 | 100.0 | 0.9 | Austria-Hungary |
| GMY | 0.1425 | 100.0 | 0.8 | Germany |
| ITA | 0.0333 | 100.0 | 0.5 | Italy |
| RUM | 0.0056 | 100.0 | 0.7 | Romania |
| FRN | 0.065 | 44.5 | 0.6 | France |
| RUS | 0.105 | 38.2 | 0.7 | Russia |
| TUR | 0.0163 | 33.6 | 0.75 | Turkey |
| ENG | 0.095 | 33.6 | 0.6 | England |
| BUL | 0.0027 | 33.6 | 0.75 | Bulgaria |
| BEL | 0.0136 | 33.6 | 0.3 | Belgium |
| SWZ | 0.0062 | 33.6 | 0.4 | Switzerland |
| NTH | 0.0068 | 33.6 | 0.3 | Netherlands |
| SWD | 0.005 | 33.6 | 0.2 | Sweden |
| DEN | 0.0024 | 33.6 | 0.2 | Denmark |
| NOR | 0.0015 | 33.6 | 0.2 | Norway |
| ALB | 0.0001 | 33.6 | 0.7 | Albania |
| USA | 0.11 | 33.6 | 0.1 | United States |
| POR | 0.0035 | 32.7 | 0.3 | Portugal |
| SPN | 0.01 | 32.7 | 0.2 | Spain |
| JPN | 0.01 | 32.7 | 0.1 | Japan |
| GRC | 0.0031 | 0.0 | 0.6 | Greece |
| SRB | 0.0016 | 0.0 | 0.95 | Serbia |

The resource values are the Correlates of War project's composite capabilities scores for the relevant states, adjusted to reflect the distance to the scene of the dispute. The adjustments follow the procedure delineated in my book *The War Trap* (1981a). Again, I have chosen data that are readily available to anyone interested in understanding the outbreak of World War I.

Unlike the position and resource scores, the salience scores are judgmental. There is no ready-made source for this information. The scores listed in the table represent the collective "wisdom" of myself and the two colleagues in international relations whom I surveyed to gain estimates of salience values. You could repeat this process by asking an international relations professor to guestimate the salience scores for each government at the *outset* of the Austro-Serbian crisis following the assassination of the Archduke Franz Ferdinand. My colleagues and I have been careful not to allow our knowledge of how things turned out to interfere with our judgments. Basically, we assumed that governments close to the scene (such as Albania, Bulgaria, and Rumania) were very attentive to the growing crisis because they well remembered the Balkan Wars and were themselves in danger of getting caught up in the conflict. We assumed that the European great powers were also attentive, increasingly so the closer they were geographically to the prospective action. Other governments, in our view, did not overly concern themselves with the Austro-Serbian dispute before fighting broke out.

Find the median voter position for the data in Table 18-3. (Remember, "votes" are equal to resources multiplied by salience.) Through your library, check the *New York Times,* the *Times of London,* and other newspapers of the day to learn what journalists reporting on the Austro-Serbian crisis anticipated in 1914. How well does the median voter position fit with these expectations?

In the case of this data set, I am not especially interested in the position of the median voter, except in terms of seeing how wide the gulf is between the states on either side of the median voter divide. We care more about whether or not the positions of the veto players (Austria-Hungary and Serbia) converge than we do about the median voter position. Of most intense interest is to see how the model simulates the responses of each of the governments to the unfolding crisis when the only information the model receives is

*The immediate event that triggered the Austro-Serbian crisis that led to World War I was the assassination of Archduke Franz Ferdinand, heir to the Austro-Hungarian throne. He is seen here with his wife Duchess Sophie, minutes before his assassination by Serbian nationalists on June 28, 1914. June 28 was the anniversary of Serbia's most famous military battle and so carried great symbolic weight at the time, much as this same anniversary loomed over the resolution of the Kosovo War in 1999.*

the data in Table 18-3. I am especially interested to see if the model predicts a high probability of war and, if so, to see how the great powers align themselves.

Using just the data reported in Table 18-3, the model simulates the unfolding crisis. Table 18-4 indicates the dynamics in terms of policy positions of the major powers and the Serbs through five bargaining rounds. Several interesting factors emerge from this part of the simulation. Note the dramatic shift in the situation during the third round. Italy moves sharply away from the Austrians and the Germans, apparently trying to broker a settlement. If the crisis had continued without a major change, then the Russians, French, and English would likely have gradually accepted Serbia's defeat even as Serbia itself continued to offer only small concessions. Had the crisis gone beyond Round 3 without further incident, it appears likely that the dispute would have been resolved among the great powers, albeit at the expense of Serbia's sovereignty. However, the model shows that in fact the Serbian crisis will evolve into something quite different.

The fundamental change that occurs during Round 3 can be seen by looking at

TABLE 18-4

## Predicted Dynamics of the Austro-Serbian Crisis, June 1914

| Country | Bargaining Round | | | | |
|---|---|---|---|---|---|
| | 1 | 2 | 3 | 4 | 5 |
| Austria-Hungary | 5 | 5 | 5 | 5 | 5 |
| Germany | 5 | 5 | 5 | 5 | 5 |
| Italy | 5 | 5 | 2 | 5 | 5 |
| England | 2 | 2 | 2 | 3 | 4 |
| France | 3 | 2 | 2 | 2 | 4 |
| Russia | 2 | 2 | 2 | 4 | 5 |
| Serbia | 1 | 1 | 1 | 1 | 1 |

Note: The numbers represent policy positions across the rounds. Position 5 is the position that is most pro–Austro-Hungarian and most anti-Serbian; position 1 is the position that is most pro-Serbian and most anti–Austro-Hungarian. Values below 3 reflect policy positions that increasingly favor Serbia; values above 3 reflect policy positions that increasingly favor Austria-Hungary. Position 3 reflects strict neutrality.

the model's output using the opportunity summary tables for Germany, Belgium, and Serbia shown in Tables 18-5, 18-6, and 18-7. These tables show the proposals made by the focal state (Germany, Belgium, and Serbia, respectively) to each of the listed players and whether the proposal was perceived by the recipient to be credible or to be a bluff. If no proposal was made according to the model, then the "recipient" country is not listed. If under "Credible" the model indicates "None," then the relevant actor received a proposal but did not believe the proposal to be credible, leaving the two actors either at a stalemate or in conflict. As will be evident when you examine the stability summary table depicted in Table 18-8, in this case most of the instances in which no proposal was credible reflect a heightened state of confrontation likely to lead to war.

Germany actively demanded significant concessions favoring the pro-Austrian position that it had staked out alongside Austria-Hungary. These two countries were at 5 on the policy position scale. This position represented the strongest endorsement of the Austro-Hungarian point of view. In Round 3 Germany sought compromises that would put Serbia almost at Germany's position so that Serbia would almost acquiesce to Germany's demands. It also pursued large compromise concessions from France, Russia,

TABLE 18-5

## Opportunity Summary for Round 3, Germany (June 1914)

| Recipient | Original Position (Germany = 100.0) | Germany's Proposal | Credible [a] |
|---|---|---|---|
| France | 44.5 | 5 | 4 |
| Italy | 100.0 | 5 | 4 |
| Russia | 38.2 | 5 | 4 |
| Albania | 33.6 | 5 | 5 |
| Turkey | 33.6 | 5 | 4 |
| Bulgaria | 33.6 | 5 | 4 |
| England | 33.6 | 5 | 4 |
| Greece | 0.0 | 5 | None [b] |
| Serbia | 0.0 | 5 | None [b] |

*Note:* Germany's proposals indicate the model's prediction of what policy position Germany demanded support for from the listed stakeholders; stakeholders not listed are predicted by the model not to have received a proposal from Germany in Round 3.

[a] Shows what each stakeholder is predicted to have considered as the most it would concede to Germany in Round 3 (for example, France would have taken a German proposal to move from position 2 to position 4 seriously).

[b] Indicates that no German proposal was credible at this juncture.

TABLE 18-6

## Opportunity Summary for Round 3, Belgium (June 1914)

| Recipient | Original Position (Belgium = 33.6) | Belgium's Proposal | Credible |
|---|---|---|---|
| 0 | 0 | 0 | 0 |

*Note:* Belgium seeks to preserve the status quo and so challenges no one.

TABLE 18-7

## Opportunity Summary for Round 3, Serbia (June 1914)

| Recipient | Original Position (Serbia = 0.0) | Serbia's Proposal | Credible |
|---|---|---|---|
| 0 | 0 | 0 | 0 |

*Note:* Serbia seeks to preserve the status quo and so challenges no one.

and England as well as from other states. This can be discerned from the relevant verbal summary table (Table 18-1). It is harder to see in the German opportunity summary table (Table 18-5) because the original 100-point policy scale has been divided into five swaths of 20 points each. Germany's actions represented a meaningful diplomatic shift for the German-Austrian axis, which had demanded capitulation in the second round. The model estimates that the Austrians will continue to demand that the other actors acquiesce and fully accept the Austrian view. Thus, the simulation clearly distinguishes between the hard-line Austrian position and the somewhat softened German position.

In the third round, France, Russia, and England were trying to consolidate support behind a weakly pro-Serbian position. France and England did not shift their own positions in the simulation, indicating that they rejected the German overtures for compromise. Serbia made no proposals and saw none as credible. Table 18-9, Serbia's verbal summary for Round 3, makes it clear that the Serbians expected war. The same was true for the Belgians and other nonaligned powers.

By Round 3, the situation had deteriorated markedly. At the outset of the crisis, according to the model's simulation, 33 to 35 percent of the relationships between these actors were conflictual. This is somewhat elevated above normal, which tends to be in the 20 to 25 percent range. By the second round, this indicator of tension had risen to 44 percent. And by the third round the level of conflict among the contending states had risen to encompass roughly 73 to 75 percent of all the

TABLE 18-8

## Stability Summary for Round 3

| Perceptions (percent) [a] | | | | | Interaction of Perceptions (percent) [b] | | | | |
|---|---|---|---|---|---|---|---|---|---|
| No Issue [c] | Conflict | Compromise | Status Quo | Compel | No Issue [c] | Conflict | Compromise | Status Quo | Compel |
| 7.4 | 72.7 | 15.4 | 0.0 | 4.5 | 7.4 | 74.5 | 14.7 | 0.0 | 3.5 |

[a] Expected proportion for relationship between actors based on perceptions.
[b] Predicted proportion for relationship between actors based on interaction of perceptions.
[c] Percentage of relationships in which actors already agree on policy position.

TABLE 18-9

## Serbia's Verbal Summary Table, Round 3 (June 1914)

| Rival | Focal View (Serbia's) | Rival's View | Joint View |
|---|---|---|---|
| Austria-Hungary | – Conflict | – Compromise | – Conflict |
| Germany | – Conflict | – Compromise | – Conflict |
| Rumania | – Conflict | – Compromise | – Conflict |
| Switzerland | – Conflict | – Conflict | – Conflict |
| Sweden | – Conflict | – Conflict | – Conflict |
| Denmark | – Conflict | – Conflict | – Conflict |
| Norway | – Conflict | – Conflict | – Conflict |
| The Netherlands | – Conflict | – Conflict | – Conflict |
| Belgium | – Conflict | – Conflict | – Conflict |
| United States | – Conflict | – Conflict | – Conflict |
| Portugal | – Conflict | – Conflict | – Conflict |
| Spain | – Conflict | – Conflict | – Conflict |
| Japan | – Conflict | – Conflict | – Conflict |
| France | – Compromise | – Compromise | – Compromise |
| Italy | – Conflict | – Compromise | – Conflict |
| Russia | – Compromise | – Compromise | – Compromise |
| Albania | – Compromise | – Compromise | – Compromise |
| Turkey | – Compromise | – Compromise | – Compromise |
| Bulgaria | – Compromise | – Compromise | – Compromise |
| England | – Compromise | – Compromise | – Compromise |
| Greece | No Issue | No Issue | No Issue |

*Note:* "+" indicates that the focal group is expected to have the advantage; "–" indicates that the rival is expected to have the advantage. "Conflict" indicates that the focal groups and the rival are expected to gain from challenging the other's policy stance, resulting in a conflict between them; "Compromise" indicates that either the rival (+) or the focal group (–) is expected to shift its policy stance toward the position of the other player (i.e., the player that has made a demand); "Compel" indicates that either the rival (+) or the focal group (–) is expected to acquiesce by accepting the policy stance of the other player (i.e., the player that has made a demand); "Stalemate" indicates that neither the focal group nor the rival is expected to propose a change in the status quo.

Imagine that you are the leader of one of the major powers during the crisis that led up to World War I. Did you have any opportunities to change the viewpoint of any other decision makers to avert war? Might a change in your initial position or a change in salience have helped to defuse the crisis? Simulate such changes and solve the model with the modified data to see if you could have avoided war without giving in to the other side.

relationships (see Table 18-8). This represents an extraordinarily high level of conflict that must almost inevitably lead to war.

Figure 18-2 displays graphically the information contained in the model's verbal summary table (column 1) for Germany in Round 3 (see this table by solving the World War I dataset at http://bdm.cqpress.com). Together with Figure 18-3, the Serbian viewpoint in Round 3 (Table 18-9), these two figures tell a remarkable story of the tragic escalation of the crisis. They show that Germany expected Serbia to compromise substantially (also seen in Table 18-9, the column labeled "Rival's View" in Germany's row), whereas Serbia expected war with Austria-Hungary and Germany (as seen in Table 18-9, the column labeled "Focal [Serbia's] View" in the rows for Austria-Hungary and Germany).

Returning to Table 18-4, we see that in the third simulated round of the crisis, Italy sought a genuine compromise resolution, shifting its position to endorse the French point of view. Had the war not expanded at that point, the model's counterfactual prediction is that Italy would have returned to the Austro-German fold. However, the war did expand, for reasons anticipated in the model's simulation of the crisis. It is worth mentioning that Italy joined the allies against Germany and Austria-Hungary on April 26, 1915. The model gets the timing of the Italian decision a bit wrong, but it does foreshadow the Italian shift to the allied side. This is noteworthy, since Italy had mutual defense treaties with Germany and Austria-Hungary. Nevertheless, the model picks Italy out as the likely defector from what at the time was called the Holy Alliance.

The real June crisis leading up to World War I ran its course through July, culminating in the violation of Belgian neutrality at the beginning of August. Although the simulation has missed a critical event—the Russians went to war against Germany in defense of Serbia before Germany invaded Belgium—it has correctly captured German

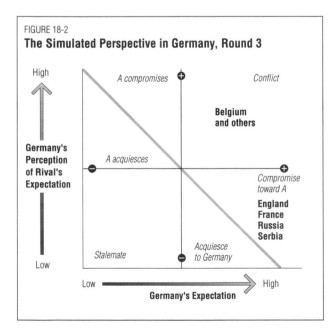

FIGURE 18-2
**The Simulated Perspective in Germany, Round 3**

*Germany anticipated a violent conflict with Belgium and others, but expected England, France, Russia, and Serbia to accept a compromise favorable to Germany.*

efforts to compromise with the allied powers in an attempt to contain the dispute and Germany's ultimate and fateful decision to escalate the crisis by attacking Belgium. The model also correctly concluded that the allies resisted making concessions to Germany, thereby ensuring that the crisis could evolve only into a stalemate or into a war. It has also captured Germany's frustration with its inability to reach an agreement with the English, French, and Russians. Taking the model's estimate of the probability of confrontation into account, it is evident that war should be expected.

## PREDICTION AND INTERNATIONAL RELATIONS

Ultimately, the best way we have to evaluate the explanatory power of a model is to assess how well its detailed analysis fits with reality. This is true whether the reality is about a repeated event, like the price of a commodity, or about important, one-time political decisions. This can be done with retrospective data or prospective data. In the latter case, when actual outcomes are unknown at the time of investigation, there is a pure opportunity to evaluate the model, independent of any possibility that the data have been made to fit observed outcomes. Indeed, perhaps the most difficult test for any theory is to apply it to circumstances in which the outcome events have not yet occurred and where they are not obvious. Of course, predicting that the sun will rise in the east and set in

the west is not terribly interesting. Neither is the prediction of a U.S. presidential election on the Tuesday after the first Monday in November every fourth year. The prediction of uncertain events is demanding precisely because the researcher cannot fit the argument to the known results. This is a fundamental difference between real-time prediction and post-diction.

The model discussed in this chapter has been tested in real time against problems with unknown and uncertain outcomes thousands of times. Many of the applications have been conducted by Decision Insights Incorporated (DII), a private company that owns the proprietary software associated with this model, including the student version available to you at the Web site. Few applications from DII or its predecessor firm, Policon, have been widely available for public scrutiny. However, the

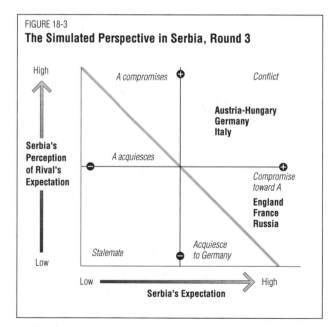

FIGURE 18-3
**The Simulated Perspective in Serbia, Round 3**

*Serbia expected war with Austria-Hungary, Germany, and Italy and so was unprepared to fulfill Germany's expectation that Serbia would agree to compromise.*

Central Intelligence Agency has declassified its own evaluation of the accuracy of this model, which it has used in various forms since the early 1980s.

According to Stanley Feder (1995), formerly a national intelligence officer at the CIA,

> Since October 1982 teams of analysts and methodologists in the Intelligence Directorate and the National Intelligence Council's Analytic Group have used Policon to analyze scores of policy and instability issues in over 30 countries. This testing program has shown that the use of Policon helped avoid analytic traps and improved the quality of analyses by making it possible to forecast specific policy outcomes and the political dynamics leading to them. . . . Political dynamics were included in less than 35 percent of the traditional finished intelligence pieces. Interestingly, forecasts done with traditional methods and with Policon were found to be accurate about 90 percent of the time. Thus, while traditional and Policon-based analyses both scored well in terms of forecast accuracy, Policon offered greater detail and less vagueness. Both traditional approaches and Policon often hit the target, but Policon analyses got the bull's eye twice as often.

Feder goes on to report that "[f]orecasts and analyses using Policon have proved to be significantly more precise and detailed than traditional analyses. Additionally, a number of predictions based on Policon have contradicted those made by the intelligence community, nearly always represented by the analysts who provided the input data. In every case, the Policon forecasts proved to be correct" (p. 292).

A similar view was expressed by Charles Buffalano, the deputy director of research at the Defense Advanced Research Projects Agency.

> [O]ne of the last (and most successful projects) in the political methodologies program was the expected utility theory. . . . The theory is both exploratory and predictive and has been rigorously evaluated through post-diction and in real time. Of all quantitative political forecasting methodologies of which I am aware, the expected utility work is the most useful to policy makers because it has the power to predict *specific* policies, their nuances, and ways in which they might be changed. (June 12, 1984, private correspondence, emphasis in original)

Feder (1995) has conducted a systematic assessment of the accuracy of the predictive model. In it he notes which types of issues the CIA has analyzed using these models. Some examples of the array of policy questions to which the model has been applied follow:

What policy is Egypt likely to adopt toward Israel?
How fully will France participate in SDI?
What is the Philippines likely to do about U.S. bases?
What stand will Pakistan take on the Soviet occupation of Afghanistan?
How much is Mozambique likely to accommodate the West?
What policy will Beijing adopt toward Taiwan's role in the Asian Development Bank?

How much support is South Yemen likely to give to the insurgency in North Yemen?

What is the South Korean government likely to do about large-scale demonstrations?

What will Japan's foreign trade policy look like?

What stand will the Mexican government take on official corruption?

When will a presidential election be held in Brazil?

Can the Italian government be brought down over the wage indexing issue?

As is evident from this sampler, the modeling method can address diverse questions. Analysts have examined economic, social, and political issues. They have dealt with routine policy decisions and with questions threatening the very survival of particular regimes. Issues have spanned a variety of cultural settings, economic systems, and political systems.

Feder's assessment compares the forecasts based on the expected utility model with more conventional approaches used by the intelligence community. Feder notes that the model makes specific, detailed predictions 60 percent of the time. Such specificity is found only 33 percent of the time in "traditional" intelligence analyses (Feder 1995). Perhaps more important, Feder reports that although the data for the model generally are obtained from area experts, the predictions frequently differ from those made by the very experts who provide the data, and the model proves to be right in all such cases. Feder cites numerous examples of government applications in which the model and the experts who provided the data disagreed. His discussion makes clear that the model is not a Delphi technique—that is, one in which experts are asked what they believe will happen and then these beliefs are reported back in the form of predictions. Rather, the expected utility model provides added insights and real value above and beyond the knowledge of the experts who provide the data.

Government assessments are not the only basis on which to evaluate the predictions made by the rational actor model. Stokman and I have examined five competing predictive models (Bueno de Mesquita and Stokman 1994). These include an improved version of the expected utility model and models developed by James Coleman, Stokman, Reinier Van Osten, and Jan Van Den Bos. All of the models were tested against a common database of policy decisions taken by the European Community. Statistical tests were used to compare the accuracy of the alternative models with the now-known actual outcomes on the issues examined. Results from the expected utility model exhibited a statistically high probability of matching the actual outcome of the relevant issues, outperforming the other models evaluated in the book on this criterion. On other criteria, such as the average size of the errors of prediction, the Stokman–Van den Bos exchange model, which looks at logrolling across issues, did about as well as the expected utility model (Bueno de Mesquita and Stokman 1994). That, plus recent evidence of improved performance of the exchange model, encourages me to believe that the study of international negotiations has reached a stage at which several practical and reliable tools for prediction are becoming available. Knowledge is truly moving beyond the speculative into the realm of scientifically rigorous assessments.

Additional evidence for the reliability of the expected utility model can be found in the published articles that contain predictions based on the rational actor model. James L. Ray and Bruce M. Russett (1996) have evaluated many of these publications to ascertain their accuracy. Motivated by the claim of John Gaddis (1992) that international relations theory is a failure at prediction, they note that the

> "expected utility" forecasting model has now been tried and tested extensively. [T]he amount of publicly available information and evidence regarding this model and the accuracy of its forecasts is sufficiently substantial, it seems to us, to make it deserving of serious consideration as a "scientific" enterprise.... [W]e would argue in a Lakatosian fashion that in terms of the range of issues and political settings to which it has been applied, and the body of available evidence regarding its utility and validity, it may be superior to any alternative approaches designed to offer specific predictions and projections regarding political events. (Ray and Russett 1996, 1569)

Ray and Russett (1996) report on specific studies as well as on general principles. They note that the model was used to predict that Ayatollah Khomeini would be succeeded by Hasheimi Rafsanjani and Ayatollah Khameini as leaders of Iran following Khomeini's death (see Bueno de Mesquita 1984). At the time of publication, Khomeini had designated Ayatollah Montazari as his successor so that the predictions were contrary to expectations among Iran specialists. Khomeini died five years later, in 1989. He was succeeded by Rafsanjani and Khameini. Ray and Russett also note that in 1988 the model correctly predicted the defeat of the Sandinista government in elections; the elections were held in 1990.

Gaddis (1992) has specifically claimed that international relations theory failed to predict three critical events: the Gulf War, the collapse of the Soviet Union, and the end of the cold war. In fact, the model discussed here had previously correctly predicted in advance two of these three critical events. In May 1982 in an interview with *U.S. News and World Report*, I noted that war was likely to occur "between Iraq and Saudi Arabia or between Iraq and other states on the Arabian Peninsula once the Iran-Iraq war is settled" (May 3, 1982). And in 1995 the Russian newspaper *Izvestia* reported that the forecasting model, demonstrated to them by officials from the U.S. government, predicted in May 1991 the putsch in August 1991 that precipitated the downfall of the Soviet Union.

At Gaddis's suggestion, the predictive model has since been used to examine the likelihood of American victory in the cold war. The model was used in a simulation environment to test alternative scenarios to determine if the end of the cold war could have been predicted based only on information available in 1948. The simulations show that there was a 68 to 78 percent probability that the United States would win the cold war peacefully within fifty years, given the conditions in 1948 and plausible shifts in the attentiveness (salience) of each state to security concerns over time. Again, no political information or data that were unknown in 1948 were used in this study (Bueno de Mesquita 1998).

Other predictions over the years can be found in articles dealing with a peace agreement in the Middle East, political instability in Italy over the budget deficit, the dispute over the Spratly Islands, Taiwanese nuclear weapons capabilities, the Maastricht referendum in Europe, and admission of the two Koreas to the United Nations, among other topics.[1] Each of these instances includes accurate predictions that were surprising to many at the time. For example, in 1990 the model predicted that Yasser Arafat would shift his stance to reach an agreement with the next Labour government in Israel by accepting very modest territorial concessions that would not include autonomy (Bueno de Mesquita 1990b). The prediction was made and published well before the Gulf War and yet foreshadowed rather accurately the steps Arafat took when the next Labour government came to power in Israel. Francine Friedman has demonstrated that the model indicated in December 1991 that the Croat-Serbian conflict "would in the end settle for Croatian independence with some Croation (territorial) concessions to Serbia but also that the Bosnian Muslims were the next likely target for extremist Serbian forces" (1997, 55). At the time, this seemed an unlikely event. As with the applications within the U.S. government, the accuracy rate across all of the published work is about 90 percent.

To be sure, some predictions have been wrong or inadequate. The expected utility model successfully predicted the break of several East European states from the Soviet Union, but failed to anticipate the fall of the Berlin Wall. The model predicted that the August 1991 Soviet coup would fail quickly and that the Soviet Union would unravel during the coming year, but it did not predict the earlier, dramatic policy shifts introduced by Mikhail Gorbachev. To be fair, the expected utility model was not applied to that situation, so such predictions could not have been made. This, of course, is an important difference between prediction and prophecy. The first step to a correct—or incorrect—prediction is to ask for a prediction about the relevant issue.

The predictive model has limitations. It is inappropriate for predicting market-driven events not governed by political considerations. It is imprecise with respect to the exact timing behind decisions and outcomes. The model can have timing elements incorporated into it, by including timing factors as contingencies in the way issues are constructed, but the model itself is imprecise with regard to time. The dynamics of the model indicate whether a decision is likely to be reached after very little give and take or after protracted negotiations. Nevertheless, it cannot say how long in clock-time a round

---

[1] For a sampling, see Bueno de Mesquita and Berkowitz (1979); Bueno de Mesquita and Beck (1985); Bueno de Mesquita (1990b); Morrow, Bueno de Mesquita, and Wu (1993); Organski and Bueno de Mesquita (1993); Wu and Bueno de Mesquita (1994); Kugler and Feng (1997); and Williams and Webber (1998). The work by Kugler and Feng (1997) appears in a special issue of the journal *International Interactions* that contains a wide variety of applications of the model conducted by many different authors.

of negotiations will last. Most important, the model by itself is of limited value without the inputs from area or issue experts. Although the views of experts are certainly valuable without the model, in combination the two are substantially more reliable than are the experts alone. The limitations remind us that scientific and predictive approaches to politics are in their infancy. Still, some encouragement can be taken from the fact that in many domains it has already proven possible to make detailed, accurate predictions accompanied by detailed explanations.

## USING THE MODEL

You can use the Web site software to make your own predictions about current events. Select an issue from the newspapers and carefully define the continuum that reflects the range of choices on the issue. Read current and back issues of *The Economist*, the *New York Times*, the *Financial Times*, the *Wall Street Journal*, and *U.S. News and World Report* and investigate Internet sites and other sources of information to gather data on the issue under study. You may want to identify a professor with expert knowledge and interview

*The remains of nearly four thousand murdered Bosnians have been exhumed from mass graves in northeastern Bosnia. Former Yugoslav president Slobodan Milosevic was brought to trial for his part in the genocide of non-Serbs. A study conducted by Francine Friedman with the forecaster model indicated as early as 1991 that, after the Croats, Bosnian Muslims were the next likely target of Milosevic's Serbian extremists. This forecast proved all too correct.*

him or her on the problem you have selected. Either through your own careful reading of news sources or by interviewing an expert, list the individuals and groups with an interest in trying to influence the policy decision on the issue in question. For each stakeholder, estimate their relative resources or potential influence, their salience for the issue, and their current stated position. Enter these data into the software and solve the model. The output is an ASCII file that can be read by any word processor. Open up the output and examine the results. Find the predicted outcome and also look for alternative strategies that could steer the results in another direction. Reopen the data file that you created and saved. Modify it to reflect the predicted positions of actors in a round in which you think a sensible strategic shift in position or salience could alter the outcome. Enter the new positions of the actors. Resolve the model to find out whether this strategic maneuver is sufficient to change the predicted results. Imagine the influence you could have as a decision maker if you could simulate events in advance and experiment with opportunities to change the course of history.

In doing this exercise, based on your own data or using data found at our Web site, you will have begun a new journey of exploration not so different from that undertaken by Christopher Columbus five centuries ago. You will have begun to learn how to anticipate events in international politics and how to alter those events in ways that promote peace and prosperity around the world.

# Glossary of Key Terms

**Anarchy.** A structuring of the international system in which no supranational authority exists to enforce agreements between states so that international affairs becomes a self-help system dependent on individual national interests. Anarchy is equivalent to the conditions of a noncooperative game in which promises are not binding and actions are based on self-interest.

**Arms race.** A competition between two or more states characterized by a reciprocal and everincreasing acquisition of arms by each state in response to the arms procurement or foreign policy actions of the other state or states engaged in the competition.

**Autonomy.** The degree to which a state can exert influence to change the status quo to be more in its favor.

**Backward induction.** A method for solving extensive form games. An individual interested in solving an extensive form game through backward induction must begin at the terminal nodes and work his or her way back to the beginning of the game, identifying at each node the response that is the best choice at that juncture for the relevant player given what that player can anticipate about the subsequent choices of all other players.

**Balancing.** Joining the threatened (and usually weaker) of two sides in a dispute to gain leverage and bring the two sides into balance.

**Bandwagoning.** Joining the threatening (and usually stronger) of two sides in a dispute to gang up on the threatened (and usually weaker) side.

**Battle of the Sexes.** A game that highlights the mix of coordination and distribution problems. *See* Coordination problem; Distribution problem; Game theory.

**Bayes' Rule.** The rule by which an initial belief, or prior probability, is updated to a posterior probability based on the observation of conditional events. The rule is

$$p(C|O) = \frac{p(O|C)p(C)}{p(O|C)p(C) + p(O|\neg C)p(\neg C)}$$

where "O" is the observation, "C" is the condition, the symbol "|" indicates the word "given," and the symbol "¬" indicates the word "not."

**Beliefs.** Probabilistic information possessed by one or more players about the characteristics, payoffs, or preferences of another player in any situation with uncertainty.

**Benefits.** The things of value, both tangible and intangible, that actors receive as a consequence of their actions.

**Bipolarity.** A structuring of the international system in which international politics is dominated by two powerful states, with all other states associated with one or another of these two poles.

**Blocking coalition.** A coalition strong enough to prevent the formation of a winning coalition but not strong enough to win on its own. *See* Winning coalition.

**Bounded rationality.** The inability of leaders to evaluate all of the information that is available to them in making choices. They may do what they believe is best given what they have taken into account, but their rationality is limited by the fact that they do not take into account everything that is available to them.

**Bretton Woods Agreement.** The backbone of the international economy from the end of World War II until it was dismantled by Richard Nixon in 1971. The agreement pegged the dollar to gold so that one ounce of gold was fixed at $35.00. The United States guaranteed that it would exchange dollars for gold at this rate. Bretton Woods also established the International Monetary Fund and the International Bank for Reconstruction and Development, which evolved into the World Bank.

**Bureaucracy.** The organizations and individuals who are responsible for evaluating or implementing government policies or the policies of other, usually large, organizations.

**Capitalism.** Economic system in which investment in and ownership of the means of production, distribution, and exchange of wealth are made and maintained chiefly by private individuals or corporations.

**Cartels.** Groups of organizations, including firms or nations, that coordinate policies to influence the production or price of particular products.

**Cheap talk.** Actions or signals in a game that are costless.

**Collective action problem.** Difficulties associated with coordinating activities when many can benefit from a common effort but each can benefit more by avoiding paying for the effort, allowing others to pay the associated costs. Collective action problems are most likely to occur when organizations provide their members with public goods rather than private goods. *See* Collective goods; Free riding.

**Collective goods.** Goods that are indivisible and nonexcludable so that everyone in a relevant class shares equally in the benefits of such goods.

**Collective security agreement.** An agreement between states specifying that each participant will come to the assistance of any other participant if it is attacked.

**Common knowledge.** This is an information condition that says I know something and you know something, you know that I know that something, I know that you know that I know that something, you know that I know that you know that I know, and so forth.

**Composite capabilities score.** A commonly used measure of national power that is the average of six scores, including the percentage of the world's total population, urban population, military expenditures, military personnel, iron and steel production, and commercial fuel consumption. The indicator was created by the Correlates of War Project.

**Concordat of Worms.** An agreement reached in 1122 between the Holy Roman Emperor and the Pope that resolved the investiture controversy and gave the Catholic Church the right to nominate its own bishops. This agreement may have created one of the first property rights adhering to the state and thereby initiated the beginnings of the modern sovereign state.

**Condorcet winner.** An alternative that defeats all others in head to head competition.

**Connectedness.** The ability to link alternatives by a relation of preference or indifference. Choices A and B are connected if a decision maker can order them such that A is preferred to B, B is preferred to A, or the decision maker is indifferent between A and B.

**Consistency.** A circumstance in which if someone prefers A to B and B to C, then they must necessarily prefer A to C. Sometimes referred to as transitivity.

**Contract curve.** The set of all points that pass through the points of tangency between two decision makers' indifference curves.

**Convexity.** A preference wherein A is preferred to B and a point or choice on the straight line connecting alternatives A to B can be found that lies between A and B such that A is preferred to the chosen point and the chosen point is preferred to B. No matter how close the chosen point is to B, there is always a point that is better than B from the decision maker's perspective and a point that is not as good as A.

**Cooperative game.** A form of game theory in which players can make binding commitments and in which promises are both credible and enforced. *See* Game theory; Noncooperative game.

**Coordination problem.** Situation in which two or more decision makers have a stake in making a common policy choice but face impediments to doing so because of information or other limitations that make it difficult for them to recognize or act on their shared interest.

**Costly signal.** Action or signal in a game that is costly to the sender because in taking the action the sender gives up or spends something she or he values.

**Counterfactual reasoning.** An argument about causality that depends on comparing the state of the world to a hypothetical, unobservable state of the world. For example, if A causes B, then the counterfactual claim that if A does not occur then B will not occur is implied.

**Cultural norms.** Behavior that tends to be acceptable within a certain population but may not be acceptable within other populations.

**Decision theory.** The representation of choices through the calculation of costs and benefits and the comparison of those costs and benefits across alternative actions.

**Defense pact.** An agreement between states to provide for each other's defense in the event that any of the signatories is attacked.

**Democratic peace.** A body of empirical regularities that indicate that democracies tend not to fight wars with one another but do fight with nondemocratic states.

**Dependent variable.** Variations in values that one is trying to explain. For a theory of war outcomes, for example, a likely dependent variable would be whether one won or lost or how much a nation gained. For theories about trade, a likely dependent variable might be how much trade increased or decreased between particular nations or between particular regions over time.

**Deterrence.** The ability to convince an adversary not to take an action because the adversary anticipates adverse consequences from doing so.

**Dissatisfaction.** The degree of displeasure one attaches to a given state of affairs.

**Distribution problem.** Situation in which two or more decision makers prefer to allocate valued resources differently, creating at least a partial conflict of interests.

**Dominant strategy.** A strategy a player prefers to pursue no matter what response other players are anticipated to make. *See* Strategy.

**Endogenous choice.** A choice within the control of an actor. This is in contrast to a choice determined by circumstances beyond the actor's control. *See* Exogenous circumstance.

**Entente.** An agreement between states to consult with one another before choosing a course of action in the event that one is attacked.

**European Union.** An organization of European states founded to advance free trade among its members and to build a political and economic infrastructure to further advance their integration.

**Exogenous circumstance.** Factor that is beyond the control of decision makers and so is treated as given or assumed. *See* Endogenous choice.

**Expected utility.** The value attached to a particular action or decision discounted by the chance that the prospective outcome of that action or decision will arise.

**Extended deterrence.** The process by which one nation's supportive relationship with another is designed to convince a would-be aggressor that it should not threaten the defended nation. Extended deterrence focuses attention on whether a threat is or is not made.

**Extended immediate deterrence.** Circumstance in which the protective posture of one state vis-à-vis another convinces a would-be attacker to back down rather than carry out the threat it has made. Extended immediate deterrence draws attention to whether a threat that has been made is carried out.

**Extensive form game.** A game depicted as a tree in which the sequence of moves is displayed. Any number of choices can emanate from any branch of the tree, but only one branch can enter a choice point or choice node. The tree ends in terminal nodes that represent end points in the game.

**Fair trade.** Economic exchange between nations regulated by the principle that one nation should not sell goods to another nation at a price below the price at which the goods are sold in the producer country. Fair trade also includes the idea that countries should try to achieve a rough balance or equality in their trade with one another.

**Falsifiability.** A condition whereby a test or a body of evidence that would lead to the conclusion that a theory is wrong can be specified. Falsifiability is a controversial aspect of the philosophy of science in view of the fact that an entire theory may be rejected on the basis of a falsifying test. Critics argue that falsifiability is all but impossible because tests generally address ancillary conditions of a theory rather than its core tenets.

**Fixed exchange rate.** Rate that values currencies based on a fixed standard, for example, gold or the value of the U.S. dollar.

**Flexible response.** The process of using graduated responses to potential threats to security.

**Floating exchange rate.** Rate that values currencies based on the market forces of supply and demand and resulting in exchange rates that fluctuate from moment to moment.

**Foreign policy.** The decisions of governments that are designed to influence how they relate to individuals, groups, and nations outside their own borders.

**Free riding.** Enjoying the benefits of collective goods without undertaking any costs toward their provision.

**Free trade.** Economic exchange between nations unencumbered by tariffs, quotas, or other rules and procedures designed to limit the flow of goods from one country to another.

**Game theory.** A mathematical means to evaluate strategic interaction in which the choices of any individual are contingent on expectations about the choices of other individuals.

**General deterrence.** Circumstances in which one nation tries to dissuade another from undertaking an effort to alter the status quo between them.

**Grim trigger strategy.** A punishment strategy in which a player who has defected or otherwise punished a second player is itself punished by that player throughout the remainder of the game no matter what type of behavior the first player displays thereafter.

**Hegemony.** A distribution of power in which one state dominates international interactions and possesses so much power that no credible combination of states can expect to defeat it.

**Hypothesis.** A proposition that predicts the effect of one or more independent variables on a dependent variable.

**Ideal point.** The most-preferred resolution of the issue or issues for a single decision maker. The ideal point is the policy position at which a decision maker would receive the most utility.

**Imperfect information.** Uncertainty in a game created by not knowing the complete history of play.

**Imperialism.** The policy of extending the rule or authority of an empire or nation over foreign countries, or of acquiring and holding colonies and dependencies for the purpose of economic gain.

**Incomplete information.** Uncertainty in a game created by not knowing the payoffs for one or more players at the terminal nodes of the game.

**Independent variable.** The variable or variables hypothesized to influence the value of the dependent variable.

**Indifference.** The relationship characterized by two choices that are considered to be equally good by a decision maker. That is, the outcome of choice A is just as good as the outcome of choice B—no better and no worse.

**Indifference curve.** The set of points in a policy space such that every point is just as good for the decision maker in question as every other point.

**Information set.** The information known to a player at a given choice point. If the information set is a singleton, then the player knows the history of prior moves that brought the game to the particular choice point. If the information set is not a singleton, then the player does not know the entire history of prior play and therefore does not know which choice point he or she has reached.

**International political economy.** The study of the politics regulating or otherwise influencing economic exchange relations between states.

**International system.** The interdependent parts of the set of nations; the interdependencies among all of the nations that make up the global or regional communities of nations.

**Investiture struggle.** The controversy between the Catholic Church and the Holy Roman Emperor (and other kings) during the latter part of the eleventh century and the early part of the twelfth century over who should have authority to nominate and elect Catholic bishops. This controversy may have planted the seeds for the emergence of the modern sovereign state. *See* Concordat of Worms.

**Issue space.** The representation of preferences on a line, plane, or higher-order spatial array.

**Loss of strength gradient.** The idea that national power declines with distance so that a nation is not as powerful far from its home base as it is at home.

**Marginal gain or loss.** The added benefit or loss associated with one decision or action as compared to another.

**Marginal rate of substitution.** The rate or multiple at which a person will substitute one good for another given that he or she holds a specific quantity of each good.

**Median voter theorem.** Theorem that posits if preferences are single peaked, an issue is unidimensional, and a majority is required to win, then the position of the median voter is the winning position in a contest with any alternative.

**Mixed strategy equilibrium.** A Nash equilibrium in which players choose actions probabilistically so as to make other players indifferent among their strategy choices.

**Multipolarity.** Domination of the international system by three or more great powers, each of whom is supported by weaker states that cluster around it.

**Mutual assured destruction (MAD).** A deterrence doctrine that reflects the belief that each party to a dispute would be deterred from using force if each believed that its own annihilation or destruction is the guaranteed result of using force.

**Nash equilibrium.** A set of strategies in a game such that no player has a unilateral incentive to switch to another strategy. Every finite game has at least one Nash equilibrium in mixed strategies and may have more than one.

**National interest.** The set of objectives that enhances the welfare of the state. Usually the national interest is thought of in terms of protecting sovereignty, maximizing security or power, and improving national wealth.

**Nonaggression pact.** An agreement between states stipulating that if one of the signatories is attacked the other signatories will not join with the belligerent against their co-signatory. Nonaggression pacts indicate that the signatories will not attack each other.

**Noncooperative game.** A game in which promises between players are not binding and actions are based on self-interest.

**Normal form game.** A game that depicts payoffs in a matrix, showing the costs and benefits associated with the alternative strategies of the game while not showing the sequence of moves in the game. *See* Game theory.

**Nuclear deterrence.** The ability to dissuade an adversary from using force against one's own state through the threat of nuclear retaliation; the ability to dissuade an adversary from using nuclear weapons by threatening a punishment sufficiently destructive so as to convince the adversary that use of its nuclear weapons would be too costly. MAD (mutual assured destruction) is one form of nuclear deterrence, but nuclear deterrence can be achieved without reaching the level of assured destruction for either side, let alone both sides. For deterrence to succeed, it is only necessary that the rival believes that the costs of using force exceed the expected benefits.

**Off-the-equilibrium-path expectations.** The components of an equilibrium strategy that do not lead directly to the equilibrium (predicted) outcome. Off-the-path expectations are the counterfactual expectations about what would happen if some other action were chosen so that what is on the equilibrium path is chosen because other actions are anticipated to yield worse outcomes.

**Opportunity cost.** The cost associated with foregoing alternative uses of resources once those resources have been put to a specific use.

**Outcomes.** The results or consequences of choices.

*Pareto optimality.* The best attainable outcome without disadvantaging at least one group.

**Parsimony.** A fundamental principle of science that is satisfied when a theory produces more information (i.e., results) than it has assumptions or constraining conditions. In general, the more parsimonious a theory is, the better it is.

**Payoffs.** The costs and benefits associated with alternative outcomes resulting from one or more choices.

**Perceptions.** The subjective interpretation of events and actions.

**Policy risks.** The probability that the substantive policy goal of a leader will fail to be achieved.

**Political risks.** The probability that policy choices will harm the political position and well-being of a political leader.

**Power.** The ability to make others do something they otherwise would not do.

**Preference ordering.** An ordering of preference that stipulates the connection between choices for all relevant pairs of alternatives.

**Preferences.** The ordering of choices according to their desirability.

**Preferred-to set.** The set of all points closer to a decision maker's ideal point than the indifference curve that is tangent to a specified point (e.g., the status quo).

**Principal-agent problem.** The problems that arise because of asymmetries in information that allow agents of principals to pursue their own interests rather than those of the principal. The principal has insufficient information with which to ascertain whether a deviation from its desired course is due to the interests of the agent or due to external constraints.

**Prisoners' dilemma.** A game with a dominant strategy equilibrium that is not *pareto optimal* — that is, it will end by disadvantaging at least one player. The game is indicative of problems of mistrust in which promises are not credible.

**Private knowledge.** Information known to one player in a game but not known to other players in that game.

**Probability.** The chance or likelihood that a particular action or event will take place. If all possible events or circumstances are specified, then the sum of the probabilities of the events or circumstances must be 1.

**Proportionate reduction in error (PRE).** A measure of how much a theory reduces errors of prediction over the null hypothesis, with the null hypothesis usually evaluated as predicting the modal category of the dependent variable.

**Public goods.** *See* Collective goods.

**Rationality.** Characteristic that enables individuals to connect choices transitively, take constraints into account, and choose the course of action that they believe will give them the best result.

**Regime.** A set of rules or norms governing how members of a group, community, or system interact with one another; an agreement among states to constrain their behavior within some well-specified domain.

**Relative gains.** Evaluating costs and benefits solely by comparison to how others are doing rather than based on the magnitude of gains or losses to oneself.

**Resource stability.** A circumstance in which capabilities are distributed among states or blocs of states in such a way that the distribution remains unaltered across time.

**Risk.** The probability that an event occurs.

**Risk acceptance.** A preference for a lottery or risky choice over a sure outcome when the expected value of the two are the same.

**Risk aversion.** A preference for a sure outcome over a risky choice or a lottery when the expected value of the two are the same.

**Risk neutrality.** Indifference between a lottery or risky choice and a sure outcome when the expected value of the two are the same.

**Satisfaction.** The degree of pleasure, preference, or utility one attaches to a given state of affairs.

**Security.** The condition of being able to preserve a desirable status quo; the ability to fend off external threats to one's territory, one's sovereignty, and the welfare of one's citizens or to other desired values.

**Security dilemma.** Situation in which a nation's increased military capabilities or enhanced alliance ties improve national security but at the same time lead other nations to perceive it as becoming a threat, thereby prompting those nations to make countermoves that diminish that state's security.

**Security studies.** The investigation of relations between states that influence their vulnerability to military incursion, coercion, or the loss of sovereignty.

**Selectorate.** The citizens of a state with a legal say in choosing the leadership.

**Shadow of the future.** The value a person attaches to future benefits as compared to present benefits.

**Sincere voting.** Situation in which a decision maker chooses its more-preferred alternative in any vote even though in subsequent votes it may end up with a worse outcome than it would have achieved by not voting for its true preference at every stage in the process. *See* Strategic voting.

**Single-peaked preferences.** Arrangement where alternatives can be ordered spatially such that the farther a choice is from an actor's ideal point, the less preferred that choice is to the actor; preferences as a group that decline with Euclidean distance from an actor's ideal point.

**Social choice.** Choice made by one or more decision makers on behalf of a group.

**Social choice problem.** Situation in which the preferences of a group, when aggregated, violate consistency (or transitivity, as it is sometimes called). This may occur even though the individuals involved have connected and consistent preferences. In such case, a cycle may arise in which A is preferred to B, B is preferred to C, and C is preferred to A. In this instance, it is difficult to say whether A, B, or C is a better social choice.

**Sphere of influence.** The set of countries whose foreign policies (and perhaps whose domestic policies) are dominated or even determined by a foreign power.

**Standard Operating Procedures (SOPs).** A set of predefined, routinized responses to classes of events.

**Strategic Form Game.** *See* Normal form game.

**Strategic voting.** Situation in which a decision maker chooses its less-preferred alternative in a vote so that in subsequent votes it will end up with a better outcome than it would have achieved by not voting for its true preference at every stage in the process. *See* Sincere voting.

**Strategy.** A complete plan of action for a game that takes into account all known or anticipated contingencies.

**Structure of the international system.** All exogenous attributes of the international system, especially including the distribution of power and the degree of security among the set of states (and their alliances) that comprise the interacting parts of the international system.

**Subgame perfection.** A refinement of Nash equilibrium in which each choice is a best reply from that stage in the game onward. *See* Backward induction.

**System stability.** A distribution of resources or capabilities such that the survival of all states is assured so that, even if resources are redistributed, the membership of the international system remains constant.

**System-transforming war.** A war that leads to fundamental changes in how nations relate to each other by sharply redistributing power or resources among states, by changing the organizing principles that influence how states relate to each other, or by fundamentally changing the objectives that nations pursue through their foreign policies.

**Tit-for-tat.** A strategy in which a player echoes whatever its opponent did in the previous move of the game.

**Transaction costs.** The ex ante and ex post costs directly linked to the negotiation, implementation, and enforcement of a particular transaction or decision.

**Treaty of Westphalia.** Treaty that in 1648 marked the resolution of the Thirty Years War and codified the characteristics of what today is considered the modern sovereign state.

**Uncertainty.** The condition under which the probability of an event or condition is unknown.

**Utility.** A cardinal measure of the degree to which one choice is preferred to another as measured by risks.

**Variables.** Concepts, including attributes (e.g., height or weight, GNP, size of army), events (e.g., going to the prom, waging war, negotiating treaties, joining alliances), relations (e.g., friendship, satisfaction, hegemony, equality), and so forth that can take on more than one value across time or across units of observation (e.g., people, interest groups, organizations, nations, systems).

**Westphalia.** *See* Treaty of Westphalia.

**Winning coalition.** A group of individuals that controls sufficient resources to defeat rival combinations.

**Win set.** The set of all points that represent the intersection of preferred-to sets for enough decision makers so that their combined influence constitutes a winning coalition.

**Zero-sum game.** A game in which the value of the gains to one or more players is exactly equal to the value of the losses for the other players. Zero-sum games do not require that any player loses everything, but just that the sum of gains and losses is zero.

# BIBLIOGRAPHY

The Bibliography contains not only all the works referenced in
the book but also others to help you explore research on international
relations more thoroughly. Examine the Bibliography for
other readings that interest you.

Allison, Graham. 1972. *The Essence of Decision: Explaining the Cuban Missile Crisis.* Boston: Little, Brown.

Allison, Graham, and Morton H. Halperin. 1972. "Bureaucratic Politics: A Paradigm and Some Implications." In *Theory and Policy in International Relations,* edited by Raymond Tanter and Richard Ullman. Princeton: Princeton University Press.

Almond, Gabriel A. 1960. *The American People and Foreign Policy.* New York: Praeger.

Alt, James E., and Michael Gilligan. 1994. "The Political Economy of Trading States." *Journal of Political Philosophy* 2:165–192.

Altfeld, Michael. 1983. "Arms Races? And Escalation?" *International Studies Quarterly* 27:225–232.

———. 1984. "The Decision to Ally: A Theory and Test." *Western Political Quarterly* 37:523–544.

Altfeld, Michael, and Bruce Bueno de Mesquita. 1979. "Choosing Sides in Wars." *International Studies Quarterly* 23 (March): 87–112.

Arbetman, Marina, and Jacek Kugler, eds. 1997. *Political Capacity and Economic Behavior.* Boulder, Colo.: Westview Press.

Arrow, Kenneth. 1951. *Social Choice and Individual Values.* New York: John Wiley.

Art, Robert. 1973. "Bureaucratic Politics and American Foreign Policy." *Policy Sciences* 4:467–490.

Ash, Timothy G. 1997. *The File: A Personal History.* London: HarperCollins.

Austen-Smith, David, and Jeffrey Banks. 1998. "Social Choice Theory, Game Theory, and Positive Political Theory." In *Annual Review of Political Science,* edited by Nelson Polsby. Palo Alto, Calif.: Annual Reviews.

Axelrod, Robert. 1984. *The Evolution of Cooperation.* New York: Basic Books.

Axelrod, Robert, and Robert Keohane. 1986. "Achieving Cooperation under Anarchy: Strategies and Institutions." In *Cooperation under Anarchy,* edited by Kenneth Oye. Princeton: Princeton University Press.

Baker, Regina. 2002. "Market Realism: Political Development, Currency Risk, and the Gains from Trade under the Liberal International Economic Order." Ph.D. dissertation, University of Michigan.

Baldwin, David. 1995. "Security Studies and the End of the Cold War." *World Politics* 48:117–34.

Baldwin, John W. 1986. *The Government of Philip Augustus.* Berkeley: University of California Press.

Banks, Jeffrey S. 1990. "Equilibrium Behavior in Crisis Bargaining Games." *American Journal of Political Science* 34:599–614.

Barnett, Michael. 1990. "High Politics Is Low Politics: The Domestic and Systemic Sources of Israeli Security Policy, 1967–1977." *World Politics* 42:529–562.

Barro, Robert J. 1997. *Determinants of Economic Growth: A Cross-Country Empirical Study.* Cambridge: Harvard Institute for International Development, Harvard University.

Barro, Robert J., and Jong-Wha Lee. 1993. "International Comparisons of Educational Attainment." National Bureau of Economic Research (NBER) Working Paper No. w4349.

Beer, Francis A. 1981. *Peace against War: The Ecology of International Violence.* San Francisco: W. H. Freeman.

Bennett, D. Scott. 1996. "Security, Bargaining, and the End of Interstate Rivalry." *International Studies Quarterly* 40:157–183.

———. 1997a. "Democracy, Regime Change, and Rivalry Termination." *International Interactions* 22:369–397.

———. 1997b. "Measuring Rivalry Termination, 1816–1992." *Journal of Conflict Resolution* 41:227–254.

———. 1997c. "Testing Alternative Models of Alliance Duration." *American Journal of Political Science* 41:846–878.

Bennett, D. Scott, and Alan C. Stam III. 1996. "The Duration of Interstate Wars: 1812–1985." *American Political Science Review* 90:239–257.

———. 1998a. "Comparative Theory Testing: Expected Utility versus All Comers." Paper presented at the annual meeting of the International Studies Association, Minneapolis, Minn., March 18.

———. 1998b. "Conflict Initiation and Escalation." University Pork: Pennsylvania State University, Department of Political Science.

———. 1998c. "The Declining Advantage of Democracy: A Combined Model of War Outcomes and Duration." *Journal of Conflict Resolution* 42:344–366.

———. 2000a. "A Universal Test of an Expected Utility Theory of War." *International Studies Quarterly.* 44:451–480.

———. 2000b. "A Cross-Validation of Bueno de Mesquita and Lalman's International Interaction Game." *British Journal of Political Science* 30:541–61.

Bennett, D. Scott, and S. E. Tarry. 1996. "Self-Perpetuation or Rational Choices? A Model of Rationality and Hysterisis in International Alliances." Paper presented at the annual meeting of the Midwest Political Science Association, Chicago, April 18–20.

Berkowitz, Bruce. 1983. "Realignment in International Treaty Organization." *International Studies Quarterly* 27:77–96.

Best, Geoffrey. 1994. *War and Law since 1945.* Oxford: Clarendon Press.

Binmore, Ken. 1990. *Essays on the Foundations of Game Theory.* Cambridge, Mass.: Blackwell.

Black, Duncan. 1958. *The Theory of Committees and Elections.* Cambridge: Cambridge University Press.

Blainey, Geoffrey. 1973. *The Causes of War.* New York: Free Press.

Bolks, Sean M. 1998. "Security Policy Choices: Foreign Policy Behavior as a Function of Threat, Capability, and Governmental Structure." Ph.D. dissertation, Rice University.

Boulding, Kenneth. 1963. *Conflict and Defense: A General Theory.* New York: Harper and Row.

Bowring, Philip. 2002. "Accountability—but not to the people," *International Herald Tribune.* May 4. See www.iht.com.

Brams, Steven J. 1985. *Superpower Games.* New Haven: Yale University Press.

———. 1990. *Negotiation Games: Applying Game Theory to Bargaining and Arbitration.* New York: Routledge.

Brams, Steven J., and Alan D. Taylor. 1996. *Fair Division: From Cake-Cutting to Dispute Resolution.* Cambridge: Cambridge University Press.

Brehm, John, and Scott Gates. 1997. *Working, Shirking, and Sabotage: Bureaucratic Response to a Democratic Public.* Ann Arbor: University of Michigan Press.

Bremer, Stuart. 1992. "Dangerous Dyads: Conditions Affecting the Likelihood of Interstate War, 1816–1965." *Journal of Conflict Resolution* 36:309–341.

———. 1993. "Democracy and Militarized Interstate Conflict, 1816–1965." *International Interactions* 18:231–249.

Brody, Richard A. 1992. *Assessing the President: The Media, Elite Opinion, and Public Support.* Stanford: Stanford University Press.

Brody, Richard A., and Benjamin Page. 1975. "The Impact of Events on Presidential Popularity." In *Perspectives on the Presidency,* edited by Aaron Wildavsky. Boston: Little, Brown.

Brophy-Baermann, Bryan, and John A. C. Conybeare. 1994. "Retaliating against Terrorism: Rational Expectations and the Optimality of Rules versus Discretion." *American Journal of Political Science* 38:196–210.

Brown, Frederic J. 1968. *Chemical Warfare: A Study in Restraints.* Princeton: Princeton University Press.

Broz, Lawrence, and Jeff Frieden. 2001. "The Political Economy of International Monetary Relations." *Annual Review of Political Science,* edited by Nelson Polsby. Palo Alto, Calif.: Annual Reviews.

Bueno de Mesquita, Bruce. 1975. "Measuring Systemic Polarity." *Journal of Conflict Resolution* 19:187–215.

———. 1978. "Systemic Polarization and the Occurrence and Duration of War." *Journal of Conflict Resolution* 22:241–267.

———. 1981a. *The War Trap.* New Haven: Yale University Press.

———. 1981b. "Risk, Power Distributions, and the Likelihood of War." *International Studies Quarterly* 25:541–568.

———. 1983. "The Costs of War: A Rational Expectations Approach." *American Political Science Review* 77:347–357.

———. 1984. "Forecasting Policy Decisions: An Expected Utility Approach to Post-Khomeini Iran." *PS* (Spring): 226–236.

———. 1985. "The War Trap Revisited." *American Political Science Review* 79:157–176.

———. 1990a. "Pride of Place: The Origins of German Hegemony." *World Politics* 43 (October): 28–52.

———. 1990b. "Multilateral Negotiations: A Spatial Analysis of the Arab-Israeli Dispute." *International Organization* 44:317–340.

———. 1996. "Counterfactuals and International Affairs: Some Insights from Game Theory." In *Counterfactual Experiments in World Politics,* edited by P. Tetlock and A. Belkin, 211–229. Princeton: Princeton University Press.

———. 1997. "A Decision-Making Model: Its Structure and Form." *International Interactions* 23:235–266.

———. 1998. "The End of the Cold War: Predicting an Emergent Property." *Journal of Conflict Resolution* 42:131–155.

———. 2000. "Popes, Kings, and Endogenous Institutions: The Concordat of Worms and the Origins of Sovereignty." *International Studies Review* 6:93–118.

———. 2002. *Predicting Politics.* Columbus: Ohio State University Press.

Bueno de Mesquita, Bruce, and Douglas Beck. 1985. "Forecasting Policy Decisions: An Expected Utility Approach." In *Corporate Crisis Management,* edited by S. Andriole. Princeton: Petrocelli Books.

Bueno de Mesquita, Bruce, and Bruce Berkowitz. 1979. "How to Make a Lasting Peace in the Middle East." *Rochester Review* (Spring): 12–18.

Bueno de Mesquita, Bruce, and David Lalman. 1986. "Reason and War." *American Political Science Review* 80:1113–1131.

———. 1988a. "Arms Races and the Opportunity for Peace." *Synthese* 76:263–283.

———. 1988b. "Systemic and Dyadic Explanations of War." *World Politics* 40:1–20.

———. 1990. "Domestic Opposition and Foreign War." *American Political Science Review* 84:747–765.

———. 1992. *War and Reason.* New Haven: Yale University Press.

Bueno de Mesquita, Bruce, Rose McDermott, and Emily Cope. 2001. "The Expected Prospects for Peace in Northern Ireland." *International Interactions* 27, no. 2, 129–167.

Bueno de Mesquita, Bruce, and Jongryn Mo. 1996. "North Korean Economic Reform and Political Stability." *Hoover Essays in Public Policy.* Stanford, Calif.: Hoover Institution Press.

Bueno de Mesquita, Bruce, James D. Morrow, Randolph M Siverson, and Alastair Smith. 1999. "An Institutional Explanation of the Democratic Peace." *American Political Science Review* 93:791–807.

———. 2000. "Political Institutions, Political Survival and Policy Success." In *Governing for Prosperity,* edited by Bruce Bueno de Mesquita and Hilton Root. New Haven: Yale University Press.

Bueno de Mesquita, Bruce, James D. Morrow, and Ethan Zorick. 1997. "Capabilities, Perception, and Escalation." *American Political Science Review* 91:15–27.

Bueno de Mesquita, Bruce, David Newman, and Alvin Rabushka. 1985. *Forecasting Political Events.* New Haven: Yale University Press.

———. 1996. *Red Flag over Hong Kong.* Chatham, N.J.: Chatham House.

Bueno de Mesquita, Bruce, and William H. Riker. 1982. "Assessing the Merits of Selective Nuclear Proliferation." *Journal of Conflict Resolution* 26:283–306.

Bueno de Mesquita, Bruce, and Hilton Root, eds. 2000. *Governing for Prosperity.* New Haven: Yale University Press.

———. 2002. "The Political Roots of Poverty." *National Interest.* May 22.

Bueno de Mesquita, Bruce, and Randolph Siverson. 1995. "War and the Survival of Political Leaders: A Comparative Study of Regime Types and Political Accountability." *American Political Science Review* 89:841–855.

Bueno de Mesquita, Bruce, Alastair Smith, Randolph M. Siverson, and James D. Morrow. 2003. *The Logic of Political Survival.* Cambridge: MIT Press.

Bueno de Mesquita, Bruce, and Frans Stokman. 1994. *European Community Decision Making.* New Haven: Yale University Press.

Bueno de Mesquita, Ethan. 1996. "Bargaining over International Accounting Standards: An Empirical and Game-Theoretic Examination." Honors thesis, Department of Political Science, University of Chicago.

———. 2002. "An Adverse Selection Model of Terrorism: Theory and Evidence." Ph.D. dissertation, Harvard University.

Bueno de Mesquita, Ethan, and Matthew Stephenson. 2000. "Order and Law: A Formal Model of the Effect of Legal Institutions on Informal Trade Networks." Paper presented at the annual meeting of the American Political Science Association, Washington, D.C., September.

Calvert, Randall L. 1985. "The Value of Biased Information: A Rational Choice Model of Political Advice." *Journal of Politics* 47:530–55.

Calvino, Italo. 1988. *Under the Jaguar Sun.* Translated by William Weaver. New York: Harcourt Brace Jovanovich.

Campbell, John C., ed. 1976. *Successful Negotiation: Trieste 1954.* Princeton: Princeton University Press.

Carr, Edward Hallett. 1939. *The Twenty Years' Crisis: 1919–1939.* London: Macmillan.

———. 1945. *Nationalism and After.* London: Macmillan.

Caspary, William. 1970. "The 'Mood Theory': A Study of Public Opinion and Foreign Policy." *American Political Science Review* 64:536–547.

Chan, Steve. 1997. "In Search of the Democratic Peace: Problems and Promise." *Mershon International Studies Review* 41:59–91.

Christensen, Thomas J., and Jack Snyder. 1990. "Chain Gangs and Passed Bucks." *International Organization* 44:137–168.

———. 1997. "Progressive Research on Degenerate Alliances." *American Political Science Review* 91:919–922.

Clark, William Roberts. 1998. "Agents and Structures: Two Views of Preferences, Two Views of Institutions." *International Studies Quarterly* 42:245–270.

———. 2003. *Capitalism, Not Globalism: Capital Mobility, Central Bank Independence, and the Political Control of the Economy.* Ann Arbor: University of Michigan Press.

Cohen, Youssef. 1989. *The Manipulation of Consent: The State and Working-Class Consciousness in Brazil.* Pittsburgh: University of Pittsburgh Press.

Conybeare, John A. C. 1987. *Trade Wars: The Theory and Practice of International Commercial Rivalry.* New York: Columbia University Press.

Conybeare, John A. C., Hayes McCarthy, and Mark Zinkula. 1995. "NAFTA and the Strange Coalition of Environmentalists and Protectionists." *International Executive* 37:211–224.

Cox, Gary. 1997. *Making Votes Count.* Cambridge: Cambridge University Press.

Creasy, Edward S. 1960. *Fifteen Decisive Battles of the World.* 2d ed. Harrisburg, Pa.: Stackpole Books.

Croxton, Derek, and Anuschka Tischer. 2002. *The Peace of Westphalia.* Westport, Conn.: Greenwood Press.

Cyert, Richard M., and James G. March. 1963. *A Behavioral Theory of the Firm.* Englewood Cliffs, N.J.: Prentice-Hall.

De Santillana, Giorgio. 1955. *The Crime of Galileo.* New York: Time.

Deutsch, Karl W., and J. David Singer. 1964. "Multipolar Power Systems and International Stability." *World Politics* 16:390–406.

Diehl, Paul. 1985. "Contiguity and Escalation in Major Power Rivalries." *Journal of Politics* 47:1203–1211.

Dixon, William. 1994. "Democracy and the Peaceful Settlement of International Conflict." *American Political Science Review* 88:14–32.

Doran, Charles, and Wes Parsons. 1980. "War and the Cycle of Relative Power." *American Political Science Review* 74:947–965.

Downs, Anthony. 1957. *An Economic Theory of Democracy.* New York: Harper.

Downs, George W. 2000. "Constructing Effective Environmental Regimes." In *Annual Review of Political Science,* edited by Nelson W. Polsby. Palo Alto, Calif.: Annual Reviews.

Downs, George W., and Michael A. Jones. 2002. "Cooperation and Reputation." Department of Politics, New York University.

Downs, George W., and David M. Rocke. 1990. *Tacit Bargaining, Arms Races, and Arms Control.* Ann Arbor: University of Michigan Press.

———. 1995. *Optimal Imperfection? Domestic Uncertainty and Institutions in International Relations.* Princeton: Princeton University Press.

Downs, George W., David M. Rocke, and Peter N. Barsoom. 1996. "Is the Good News about Compliance Good News about Cooperation?" *International Organization* 50:379–407.

Doxey, Margaret P. 1996. *International Sanctions in Contemporary Perspective.* 2d ed. New York: St. Martin's Press, 1996.

Doyle, Michael. 1986. "Liberalism and World Politics." *American Political Science Review* 80:1151–1161.

Drezner, Daniel. 1999. *The Sanctions Paradox: Economic Statecraft and International Relations.* Cambridge: Cambridge University Press.

Duverger, Maurice. 1955. *Political Parties.* Translated by Barbara North and Robert North. New York: John Wiley.

Elman, Colin, and Miriam Fendius Elman. 1997. "Lakatos and Neorealism: A Reply to Vasquez." *American Political Science Review* 91:23–26.

Farber, Henry S., and Joanne Gowa. 1995. "Polities and Peace." *International Security* 20:123–146.

Farkas, Andrew. 1999. *State Learning and International Change.* Ann Arbor: University of Michigan Press.

Fearon, James D. 1994. "Domestic Political Audiences and the Escalation of International Disputes." *American Political Science Review* 88:577–592.

———. 1995. "Rationalist Explanations for War." *International Organization* 49:379–414.

———. 1997. "Signaling Foreign Policy Interests: Tying Hands versus Sinking Costs." *Journal of Conflict Resolution* 41:68–90.

Feder, Stanley. 1995. "Factions and Policon: New Ways to Analyze Politics." In *Inside CIA's Private World: Declassified Articles from the Agency's Internal Journal, 1955–1992,* edited by H. Bradford Westerfield. New Haven: Yale University Press.

Feng, Yi. 1991. "International Trade and Coalitional Conflict." Ph.D. dissertation, University of Rochester.

Ferejohn, John A. 1974. *Pork Barrel Politics.* Stanford: Stanford University Press.

Fischer, Stanley. 1993. "The Role of Macroeconomic Factors in Growth." *Journal of Monetary Economics* 32:485–512.

Flynn, Todd C. 1994. "Limited War and Regional Conflict Escalation." Ph.D. dissertation, Stanford University.

Frieden, Jeff. 1987. *Banking on the World: The Politics of American International Finance.* New York: Harper and Row.

Friedman, Francine. 1997. "To Fight or Not to Fight: The Decision to Settle the Croat-Serb Conflict." *International Interactions* 23:55–78.

Friedman, Milton. 1953. "The Methodology of Positive Economics." In *Essays in Positive Economics,* edited by Milton Friedman. Chicago: University of Chicago Press.

Friedman, Thomas. 1995. *From Beirut to Jerusalem.* New York: Doubleday.

Froot, Kenneth, Michael Kim, and Kenneth Rogoff. 1997. "The Law of One Price over 700 Years," National Bureau of Economic Research (NBER) Working Paper w5132.

Gaddis, John Lewis. 1987. *The Long Peace: Inquiries into the History of the Cold War.* New York: Oxford University Press.

———. 1992. "International Relations Theory and the End of the Cold War." *International Security* 17:5–58.

———. 1997. *We Know Now: Rethinking Cold War History.* Oxford: Clarendon Press.

Galtung, Johann. 1964. "A Structural Theory of Aggression." *Journal of Peace Research* 1:95–119.

Gartner, Scott S. 1997. *Strategic Assessment in War.* New Haven: Yale University Press.

Gartner, Scott S., and Randolph Siverson. 1996. "War Initiation and War Outcome." *Journal of Conflict Resolution* 40:4–15.

Gartzke, Erik A., and K. Gleditsch. 2002. "Regime Type and Commitment: Why Democracies Are Actually Less Reliable Allies." Columbia University.

Gasiorowski, M. J., and S. W. Polachek. 1982. "Conflict and Interdependence: East-West Trade and Linkages in the Era of Détente." *Journal of Conflict Resolution* 26:709–729.

Gates, Scott, Torbjo L. Knutsen, and Jonathan W. Moses. 1996. "Democracy and Peace: A More Skeptical View." *Journal of Peace Research* 33:1–10.

Gaubatz, Kurt Taylor. 1991. "Election Cycles and War." *Journal of Conflict Resolution* 35:212–44.

———. 1996. "Democratic States and Commitment in International Relations." *International Organization* 50:109–139.

———. 1999. *Elections and War.* Princeton: Princeton University Press.

Gelpi, Christopher, and Joseph Grieco. 1998. "Democracy, Crisis Bargaining, and Audience Costs: Analyzing the Survival of Political Elites." Paper presented at the annual meeting of the American Political Science Association, Boston, September 3.

George, Alexander L. 1980. *Presidential Decisionmaking in Foreign Policy: The Effective Use of Information and Advice.* Boulder, Colo.: Westview Press.

George, Alexander L., David K. Hall, and William E. Simons. 1971. *The Limits of Coercive Diplomacy.* Boston: Little, Brown.

George, Alexander L., and Richard Smoke. 1974. *Deterrence in American Foreign Policy.* New York: Columbia University Press.

Gibler, Douglas M., and John A. Vasquez. 1998. "Uncovering the Dangerous Alliances, 1495–1980." *International Studies Quarterly* 42:785–808.

Gilchrist, John. 1969. *The Church and Economic Activity in the Middle Ages.* New York: Macmillan.

Gilpin, Robert. 1981. *War and Change in World Politics.* Cambridge: Cambridge University Press.

Glaser, Charles. 1992. "Political Consequences of Military Strategy." *World Politics* 44:497–538.

Gleditsch, Nils Peter, and Havard Hegre. 1997. "Peace and Democracy: Three Levels of Analysis." *Journal of Conflict Resolution* 41:283–310.

Gochman, Charles S., and Zeev Maoz. 1984. "Serious Interstate Disputes, 1816–1976." *Journal of Conflict Resolution* 28:585–616.

Goemans, Hein. 2000. *War and Punishment.* Princeton: Princeton University Press.

Goertz, Gary, and Paul Diehl. 1995. "The Initiation and Termination of Enduring Rivalries: The Impact of Political Shocks." *American Journal of Political Science* 39:30–52.

Goldstein, Joshua A. 1988. *Long Cycles: Prosperity and War in the Modern Age.* New Haven: Yale University Press.

Goldstein, Judith, and Robert O. Keohane, eds. 1993. *Ideas and Foreign Policy: Beliefs, Institutions, and Political Change.* Ithaca: Cornell University Press.

Gorbachev, Mikhail. 1996. *Memoirs.* Translated by Georges Peronansky and Tatjana Peronansky. New York: Doubleday.

Gowa, Joanne. 1983. *Closing the Gold Window: Domestic Politics and the End of Bretton Woods.* Ithaca: Cornell University Press.

———. 1994. *Allies, Adversaries, and International Trade.* Princeton: Princeton University Press.

Gowa, Joanne, and Edward Mansfield. 1993. "Power Politics and International Trade." *American Political Science Review* 87:408–420.

Greif, Avner, Paul Milgrom, and Barry Weingast. 1994. "Coordination, Commitment, and Enforcement: The Case of the Merchant Guild." *Journal of Political Economy* 102:745–776.

Grieco, Joseph M. 1988a. "Anarchy and the Limits of Cooperation: A Realist Critique of the Newest Liberal Institutionalism." *International Organization* 42:485–507.

———. 1988b. "Realist Theory and the Problem of International Cooperation: Analysis with an Amended Prisoner's Dilemma Model." *Journal of Politics* 50:600–624.

Grossman, Gene. 1983. "Partially Mobile Capital: A General Approach to Two-Sector Trade Theory." *Journal of International Economics* 15:1–17.

Gulick, Edward Vose. 1955. *Europe's Classical Balance of Power.* Ithaca: Cornell University Press.

Gurr, Ted Robert. 1970. *Why Men Rebel.* Princeton: Princeton University Press.

Haas, Peter M. 1992. "Introduction: Epistemic Communities and International Policy Coordination." *International Organization* 46:1–35.

Hacking, Ian. 1981. "Lakatos's Philosophy of Science." *Scientific Revolutions.* New York: Oxford University Press.

Hagan, Joe D. 1993. *Political Opposition and Foreign Policy in Comparative Perspective.* Boulder, Colo.: Lynne Rienner.

Haggard, Stephan, and Robert R. Kaufman. 1995. *The Political Economy of Democratic Transitions.* Princeton: Princeton University Press.

Hartmann, Frederick H. 1978. *The Relations of Nations.* 5th ed. New York: Macmillan.

Haselkorn, Avigdor. 1999. *The Continuing Storm: Iraq, Poisonous Weapons, and Deterrence.* New Haven: Yale University Press.

Hensel, Paul. 1996. "Charting a Course to Conflict: Territorial Issues and Militarized Interstate Disputes, 1816–1992." *Conflict Management and Peace Science* 15:43–73.

Herodotus. 1954. *Histories of Herodotus*. Translated by A. de Selincourt. London: Penguin Books.

Hill, John, and José Mendez. 1983. "Factor Mobility and the General Equilibrium Model of Production." *Journal of International Economics* 15:19–25.

Hillman, Ayre L. 1982. "Declining Industries and Political Support for Protectionist Motives," *American Economic Review* 72:1180–1187.

Hollick, Ann L. 1991. *Global Commons: Can They Be Managed?* Cambridge: Center for International Affairs, Harvard University.

Horn, Michael. 1987. "Arms Races and the Likelihood of War." Ph.D. dissertation, University of Rochester.

Hufbauer, Gary Clyde, Jeffrey J. Schott, and Kimberly Ann Elliott. 1990. *Economic Sanctions Reconsidered*. 2d ed. Washington, D.C.: Institute for International Economics.

Hurst, Michael. 1972. *Key Treaties for the Great Powers, 1814–1914*. 2 vols. New York: St. Martin's Press.

Huth, Paul K. 1988. *Extended Deterrence and the Prevention of War*. New Haven: Yale University Press.

———. 1996. *Standing Your Ground: Territorial Disputes and International Conflict*. Ann Arbor: University of Michigan Press.

Huth, Paul K., and Bruce M. Russett. 1984. "What Makes Deterrence Work? Cases from 1900 to 1980." *World Politics* 36:496–526.

Iusi-Scarborough, Grace, and Bruce Bueno de Mesquita. 1988. "Threat and Alignment Behavior." *International Interactions* 14:85–93.

Jackman, Robert, and Ross Miller. 1998. "Social Capital and Politics." In *Annual Review of Political Science*, edited by Nelson Polsby. Palo Alto, Calif.: Annual Reviews.

Jaggers, Keith, and Ted Robert Gurr. 1996. *Polity III: Regime Change and Political Authority, 1800–1994*. Computer File Study 6695. Ann Arbor, Mich.: Inter-University Consortium for Political and Social Research.

James, Patrick, and Frank Harvey. 1992. "Nuclear Deterrence Theory: The Record of Aggregate Testing and an Alternative Research Agenda." *Conflict Management and Peace Science* 12:17–45.

James, Patrick, and John Oneal. 1991. "The Influence of Domestic and International Politics on the President's Use of Force." *Journal of Conflict Resolution* 35:307–332.

James, Robert Rhodes, ed. 1974. *Winston S. Churchill: His Complete Speeches, 1897–1963*. "Imperium et Libertas," March 15, 1945. Speech to the Conservative Party Conference, Central Hall, Westminster, vol. 7, pp. 7128–7135. London: Chelsea House.

Jervis, Robert. 1976. *Perception and Misperception in International Politics*. Princeton: Princeton University Press.

———. 1978. "Cooperation under the Security Dilemma." *World Politics* 30:167–214.

———. 1984. "War and Misperception." *Journal of Interdisciplinary History* 18:675–700.

Kahneman, Daniel, and Amos Tversky. 1984. "Choices, Values and Frames." *American Psychologist* 39:341–350.

Kantorowicz, Ernst. 1957. *The King's Two Bodies*. Princeton: Princeton University Press.

Katzenstein, Peter J. 1985. *Small States in World Markets*. Ithaca: Cornell University Press.

Kegley, Charles W., and Margaret G. Hermann. 1995. "Military Intervention and the Democratic Peace." *International Interactions* 21:1–21.

Kennedy, Paul. 1987. *The Rise and Fall of the Great Powers: Economic Change and Military Conflict from 1500 to 2000.* New York: Random House.

Kennedy, Robert. 1969. *Thirteen Days: A Memoir of the Cuban Missile Crisis.* New York: W. W. Norton.

Keohane, Robert O. 1984. *After Hegemony: Cooperation and Discord in the World Political Economy.* Princeton: Princeton University Press.

Keohane, Robert O., and Joseph S. Nye. 1977. *Power and Interdependence: World Politics in Transition.* Boston: Little, Brown.

Keohane, Robert O., and Elinor Ostrom, eds. 1995. *Local Commons and Global Interdependence: Heterogeneity and Cooperation in Two Domains.* Thousand Oaks, Calif.: Sage.

Keynes, John Maynard. 1920. *The Economic Consequences of the Peace.* New York: Harcourt, Brace, and Howe.

Kilgour, D. Marc. 1992. "Domestic Structure and War: A Game Theoretic Approach." *Journal of Conflict Resolution* 35:266–284.

Kim, Woosang, and Bruce Bueno de Mesquita. 1995. "How Perceptions Influence the Risk of War." *International Studies Quarterly* 39:51–66.

Kim, Woosang, and James D. Morrow. 1992. "When Do Power Shifts Lead to War?" *American Journal of Political Science* 36:896–922.

Kissinger, Henry. 1979. *White House Years.* Boston: Little, Brown.

Koubi, Vasiliki. 1993. "International Tensions and Arms Control Agreements." *American Journal of Political Science* 37:148–164.

Krasner, Stephen D. 1978. *Defending the National Interest: Raw Materials Investments and U.S. Foreign Policy.* Princeton: Princeton University Press.

———. 1983. "Structural Causes and Regime Consequences: Regimes as Intervening Variables." In *International Regimes,* edited by Stephen D. Krasner. Ithaca: Cornell University Press.

———. 1984. "Approaches to the State: Alternative Conceptions and Historical Dynamics." *Comparative Politics* 16:223–246.

———. 1991. "Global Communications and National Power: Life on the Pareto Frontier." *World Politics* 43:336–366.

———. 1995/96. "Compromising Westphalia." *International Security* 20:115–151.

Kreps, David M. 1990. *A Course in Microeconomic Theory.* Princeton: Princeton University Press.

Kugler, Jacek. 1984. "Terror Without Weapons: Reassessing the Role of Nuclear Weapons." *Journal of Conflict Resolution* 28:470–506.

———. 1994. "The NAFTA Bargain: Forecast of a Political Decision." Paper presented at the University of California, Irvine, May 27.

Kugler, Jacek, and Yi Feng, eds. 1997. *International Interactions* 23.

Kugler, Jacek, and Douglas Lemke. 1995. *Parity and War: Evaluations and Extensions of the War Ledger.* Ann Arbor: University of Michigan Press.

Kugler, Jacek, and A. F. K. Organski. 1989. "The End of Hegemony?" *International Interactions* 15:113–128.

Kugler, Jacek, and Frank Zagare, eds. 1987. *Exploring the Stability of Deterrence.* Boulder, Colo.: Lynne Rienner.

Lakatos, Imre. 1976. *Proofs and Refutations: The Logic of Mathematical Discovery.* Cambridge: Cambridge University Press.

———. 1978. *The Methodology of Scientific Research Programmes.* Vol. I. Cambridge: Cambridge University Press.

Lake, David. 1988. *Power, Protection and Free Trade.* Ithaca: Cornell University Press.

———. 1992. "Powerful Pacifists: Democratic States and War." *American Political Science Review* 86:24–37.

Lalman, David, and David Newman. 1990. "Alliance Formation and National Security." *International Interactions* 16:239–254.

Lamborn, Alan C. 1991. *The Price of Power.* Boston: Unwin Hyman.

———. 1997. "Theory and the Politics in World Politics." *International Studies Quarterly* 41:187–214.

Lamborn, Alan C., and Stephen P. Mumme. 1988. *Statecraft, Domestic Politics, and Foreign Policy Making: The El Chamizal Dispute.* Boulder, Colo.: Westview Press.

Larson, Eric V. 1996. *Casualties and Consensus: The Historical Role of Casualties in Domestic Support for U.S. Military Operations.* Document MR-726-RC. Santa Monica, Calif.: RAND Corporation.

Laudan, Lawrence. 1977. *Progress and Its Problems.* Berkeley: University of California Press.

Lebow, Richard Ned, and Janice Gross Stein. 1989. "Rational Deterrence Theory: I Think, Therefore I Deter." *World Politics* 41:208–224.

———. 1990. "Deterrence: The Elusive Dependent Variable." *World Politics* 42:336–369.

Leeds, Brett Ashley, and David R. Davis. 1997. "Domestic Political Vulnerability and International Disputes." *Journal of Conflict Resolution* 41:814–834.

Leeds, Brett Ashley, Andrew G. Long, and Sara McLaughlin Mitchell. 2000. "Re-Evaluating Alliance Reliability: Specific Threats, Specific Promises." *Journal of Conflict Resolution* 44:686–699.

Leeds, Brett Ashley, Jeffrey Ritter, Sara McLaughlin Mitchell, and Andrew G. Long. 2002. "Alliance Treaty Obligations and Provisions, 1815–1944." *International Interactions* 28:261–284.

Lemke, Douglas. 1995a. "Toward a General Understanding of Parity and War." *Conflict Management and Peace Science* 14:143–162.

———. 1995b. "The Tyranny of Distance: Redefining Relevant Dyads." *International Interactions* 21:23–38.

———. 1996. "Small States and War: An Expansion of Power Transition Theory." In *Parity and War,* edited by Jacek Kugler and Douglas Lemke. Ann Arbor: University of Michigan Press.

———. 2002. *Regions of War and Peace.* Cambridge: Cambridge University Press.

Lemke, Douglas, and William Reed. 1996. "Regime Types and Status Quo Evaluations: Power Transition Theory and the Democratic Peace." *International Interactions* 22:143–164.

Lepgold, Joseph, Bruce Bueno de Mesquita, and James D. Morrow. 1996. "The Struggle for Mastery in Europe, 1985–1993." *International Interactions* 22:41–66.

Levi, Margaret. 1998. "Conscription: The Price of Citizenship." In *Analytic Narratives,* edited by Robert H. Bates et al. Princeton: Princeton University Press.

Levy, Jack S. 1982. "Historical Trends in Great Power War, 1495–1975." *International Studies Quarterly* 26:278–301.

———. 1983. *War in the Modern Great Power System, 1495–1975.* Lexington: University Press of Kentucky.

———. 1989. "The Diversionary Theory of War: A Critique." In *Handbook of War Studies,* edited by Manus Midlarsky. Boston: Unwin Hyman.

————. 1992. "An Introduction to Prospect Theory." *Political Psychology* 13:171–186.

Levy, Jack S., Thomas C. Walker, and Martin S. Edwards. 1999. "Continuity and Change in the Evolution of War." In *War in a Changing World*, edited by Zeev Maoz. Ann Arbor: University of Michigan Press.

Lohmann, Susanne. 1997. "Linkage Politics." *Journal of Conflict Resolution* 41:38–67.

Lohmann, Susanne, and Sharon O'Halloran. 1994. "Divided Government and U.S. Trade Policy." *International Organization* 48:595–632.

Lumsdaine, David H. 1993. *Moral Vision in International Politics: The Foreign Aid Regime, 1949–1989.* Princeton: Princeton University Press.

Magee, Stephen. 1978. "Three Simple Tests of the Stolper-Samuelson Theorem." In *Issues in International Economics*, edited by Peter Oppenheimer. Stocksfield, UK: Oriel.

Mansfield, Edward. 1994. *Power, Trade, and War.* Princeton: Princeton University Press.

Mansfield, Edward, Helen Milner, and B. Peter Rosendorff. 1998. "Democracies, Autocracies, and International Trade Negotiations." Paper presented at the annual meeting of the American Political Science Association, Boston, Mass., September 3.

Mansfield, Edward, and Jack Snyder. 1995. "Democratization and the Danger of War." *International Security* 20:5–38.

Maoz, Zeev. 1990. "Framing the National Interest: The Manipulation of Foreign Policy Decisions in Group Settings." *World Politics* 43:77–110.

Maoz, Zeev, and Nazrin Abdolali. 1989. "Regime Type and International Conflict, 1816–1976." *Journal of Conflict Resolution* 33:3–36.

Maoz, Zeev, and Ben Mor. 1996. "Enduring Rivalries: The Early Years." *International Political Science Review* 17:141–160.

Maoz, Zeev, and Bruce M. Russett. 1993. "Normative and Structural Causes of the Democratic Peace." *American Political Science Review* 87:624–38.

March, James G. 1976. *Ambiguity and Choice in Organizations.* Bergen, Norway: Universitetsforlaget.

————. 1993. *Organizations.* Cambridge, Mass.: Blackwell.

Margolis, Howard. 1993. *Paradigms and Barriers: How Habits of Mind Govern Scientific Beliefs.* Chicago: University of Chicago Press.

Martin, Lisa L. 1992. *Coercive Cooperation: Explaining Multilateral Economic Sanctions.* Princeton: Princeton University Press.

————. 1994. *The Influence of National Parliaments on European Integration.* Cambridge: Center for International Affairs, Harvard University.

McDermott, Rose. 1998. *Risk-Taking in International Politics.* Ann Arbor: University of Michigan Press.

McGillivray, Fiona. 1997. "Party Discipline as a Determinant of the Endogenous Formation of Tariffs." *American Journal of Political Science* 41:584–607.

————. 1998. "How Voters Shape the Institutional Framework of International Negotiations." In *Strategic Politicians, Institutions, and Foreign Policy*, edited by Randolph M. Siverson. Ann Arbor: University of Michigan Press.

————. 2003. *Fighting for the Marginals: Political Institutions and Industry Handouts.* Princeton: Princeton University Press.

McGillivray, Fiona, and Alastair Smith. 1997. "Institutional Determinants of Trade Policy." *International Interactions* 23:119–143.

McGinnis, Michael D. 1986. "Issue Linkage and the Evolution of International Cooperation." *Journal of Conflict Resolution* 30:141–170.

McKelvey, Richard. 1976. "Intransitivities in Multidimensional Voting Models and Some Implications for Agenda Control." *Journal of Economic Theory* 12:472–482.

———. 1979. "General Conditions for Global Intransitivities in Formal Voting Models." *Econometrics* 47:1085–1112.

McKeown, Timothy. 1984. "Firms and Tariff Change: Explaining the Demand for Protection," *World Politics* 36:215–33.

Mearsheimer, John J. 1990. "Back to the Future: Instability in Europe after the Cold War." *International Security* 15:5–56.

Mercer, John. 1995. "Anarchy, Self-Help, and Relative Gains." *International Organization* 49:229–252.

Midlarsky, Manus. 1975. *On War: Political Violence in the International System.* New York: Free Press.

Milgrom, Paul, Douglass North, and Barry Weingast. 1990. "The Role of Institutions in the Revival of Trade: The Law Merchant, Private Judges, and the Champagne Fairs." *Economics and Politics* 2:1–23.

Milner, Helen. 1988. *Resisting Protectionism.* Princeton: Princeton University Press.

Milner, Helen, and David Yoffie. 1989. "Between Free Trade and Protectionism." *International Organization* 43:239–272.

Mintz, Alex. 1993. "The Decision to Attack Iraq: A Noncompensatory Theory of Decision Making." *Journal of Conflict Resolution* 37:595–618.

Mintz, Alex, and Nehemia Geva. 1993. "Why Don't Democracies Fight Each Other? The Political Incentives Approach." *Journal of Conflict Resolution* 37:487–503.

Modelski, George, ed. 1987. *Exploring Long Cycles.* Boulder, Colo.: Lynne Rienner.

Modelski, George, and William R. Thompson. 1994. *Innovation, Growth and War: The Co-Evolution of Global Politics and Economics.* Columbia: University of South Carolina Press.

Moore, Barrington. 1966. *Social Origins of Dictatorship and Democracy.* Boston: Beacon Press.

Morgan, David. 1986. *The Mongols.* Oxford: Blackwell.

Morgan, T. Clifton. 1984. "A Spatial Model of Crisis Bargaining." *International Studies Quarterly* 28:407–426.

———. 1990. "Issue Linkages in International Crisis Bargaining." *American Journal of Political Science* 34:311–333.

Morgan, T. Clifton, and Kenneth Bickers. 1992. "Domestic Discontent and the External Use of Force." *Journal of Conflict Resolution* 36:25–52.

Morgan, T. Clifton, and Sally H. Campbell. 1991. "Domestic Structure, Decisional Constraints and War: So Why Kant Democracies Fight?" *Journal of Conflict Resolution* 35:187–211.

Morgan, T. Clifton, and Valerie Schwebach. 1995. "Economic Sanctions as an Instrument of Foreign Policy: The Role of Domestic Politics." *International Interactions* 21:247–264.

Morgenthau, Hans J. 1978. *Politics among Nations.* 5th ed. Revised. New York: Knopf.

Morison, Samuel Eliot. 1955. *Christopher Columbus: Mariner.* Boston: Little, Brown.

Morrow, James D. 1989. "Capabilities, Uncertainty, and Resolve: A Limited Information Model of Crisis Bargaining." *American Journal of Political Science* 33:941–972.

———. 1991a. "Alliances and Asymmetry: An Alternative to the Capability Aggregation Model of Alliances." *American Journal of Political Science* 35:904–933.

———. 1991b. "Electoral and Congressional Incentives and Arms Control." *Journal of Conflict Resolution* 35:243–263.

———. 1992. "Signaling Difficulties with Linkage in Crisis Bargaining." *International Studies Quarterly* 36:153–172.

———. 1993. "Arms versus Allies: Tradeoffs in the Search for Security." *International Organization* 47:207–233.

———. 1994a. "Alliances, Credibility, and Peacetime Costs." *Journal of Conflict Resolution* 38:270–297.

———. 1994b. *Game Theory for Political Scientists.* Princeton: Princeton University Press.

———. 1994c. "Modeling the Forms of Cooperation: Distribution versus Information." *International Organization* 48:387–423.

———. 1997. "A Rational Choice Approach to International Conflict." In *Decision-Making on War and Peace: The Cognitive-Rational Debate,* edited by Alex Mintz and Nehemia Geva. Boulder, Colo.: Lynne Rienner.

———. 1998. "The Laws of War as an International Institution." Hoover Institution, Stanford University.

———. 1999. "The Strategic Setting of Choices: Signaling, Commitment, and Negotiation in International Politics." In *Strategic Choice and International Relations,* edited by David A. Lake and Robert Powell. Princeton: Princeton University Press.

Morrow, James D., Bruce Bueno de Mesquita, and Samuel Wu. 1993. "Forecasting the Risks of Nuclear Proliferation: Taiwan as an Illustration of the Method." *Security Studies* 2:311–331.

Morrow, James D., Randolph M. Siverson, and Tressa Tabares. 1998. "The Political Determinants of International Trade: The Major Powers, 1907–1990." *American Political Science Review* 92:649–661.

Most, Benjamin, and Harvey Starr. 1989. *Inquiry, Logic, and International Politics.* Columbia: University of South Carolina Press.

Moul, William B. 1988. "Great Power Nondefense Alliances and the Escalation to War of Conflicts Between Unequals, 1815–1939." *International Interactions* 15:25–44.

Mowat, R. 1932. *The States of Europe: 1815–1871.* London: Edward Arnold.

Mueller, John E. 1973. *War, Presidents, and Public Opinion.* New York: John Wiley.

———. 1980. "The Search for the 'Breaking Point' in Vietnam: The Statistics of a Deadly Quarrel." *International Studies Quarterly* 24:497–519.

———. 1989. *Retreat from Doomsday: The Obsolescence of Major War.* New York: Basic Books.

Neack, Laura, Jeanne A. K. Hey, and Patrick J. Haney, eds. 1995. *Foreign Policy Analysis: Continuity and Change in Its Second Generation.* Englewood Cliffs, N.J.: Prentice-Hall.

Newman, S. 1976. *March 1939: The British Guarantee to Poland—A Study in the Continuity of British Foreign Policy.* Oxford: Oxford University Press.

Niemi, Richard, and Herbert Weisberg. 1968. "A Mathematical Solution for the Probability of the Paradox of Voting." *Behavioral Science* 13:317–323.

Nincic, Miroslav, and Barbara Hinckley. 1991. "Foreign Policy and the Evaluation of Presidential Candidates." *Journal of Conflict Resolution* 35:333–355.

Niou, Emerson, Peter Ordeshook, and Gregory Rose. 1989. *The Balance of Power.* Cambridge: Cambridge University Press.

Niskanen, William A. 1973. *Structural Reform of the Federal Budget Process.* Washington, D.C.: American Enterprise Institute for Public Policy Research.

Norpoth, Helmut. 1987. "Guns and Butter and Governmental Popularity in Britain." *American Political Science Review* 81:949–959.

North, Douglass C., and Barry R. Weingast. 1989. "Constitutions and Commitment: The Evolution of Institutions Governing Public Choice in Seventeenth-Century England." *Journal of Economic History* 49:803–832.

Nye, Joseph. 1988. "America's Decline: A Myth." *New York Times.* April 10, 1988, E31.

O'Callaghan, Joseph F. 1975. *A History of Medieval Spain.* Ithaca: Cornell University Press.

Olson, Mancur. 1965. *The Logic of Collective Action.* Cambridge: Harvard University Press.

———. 1982. *The Rise and Decline of Nations.* New Haven: Yale University Press.

Olson, Mancur, and Richard Zeckhauser. 1966. "An Economic Theory of Alliances." *Review of Economics and Statistics* 48:266–279.

Oneal, John. 1989. "Measuring the Material Base of the East-West Balance of Power." *International Interactions* 15:177–196.

Oneal, John, Frances Oneal, Zeev Maoz, and Bruce M. Russett. 1996. "The Liberal Peace: Interdependence, Democracy, and International Conflict, 1950–1985." *Journal of Peace Research* 33:11–28.

Oneal, John R., and James L. Ray. 1997. "New Tests of the Democratic Peace Controlling for Economic Interdependence, 1950–1985." *Political Research Quarterly* 50:751–775.

Oneal, John R., and Bruce M. Russett. 1997. "The Classical Liberals Were Right: Democracy, Interdependence, and Conflict, 1950–1985." *International Studies Quarterly* 41:267–294.

O'Neill, Barry. 1989. "Game Theory and the Study of the Deterrence of War." In *Perspectives on Deterrence,* edited by P. Stern, R. Axelrod, R. Jervis, and R. Radner. New York: Oxford University Press.

Organski, A. F. K. 1958. *World Politics.* New York: Knopf.

Organski, A. F. K., and Bruce Bueno de Mesquita. 1993. "Forecasting the 1992 French Referendum." In *New Diplomacy in the Post–Cold War World,* edited by R. Morgan, J. Lorentzen, and A. Leander. New York: St. Martin's Press.

Organski, A. F. K., and Jacek Kugler. 1980. *The War Ledger.* Chicago: University of Chicago Press.

Ostrom, Elinor. 1990. *Governing the Commons: The Evolution of Institutions for Collective Action.* Cambridge: Cambridge University Press.

———. 1999. "Coping with Tragedies of the Commons." *Annual Review of Political Science,* edited by Nelson Polsby. Palo Alto, Calif.: Annual Reviews.

Ostrom, Elinor, Roy Gardner, and James Walker. 1994. *Rules, Games, and Common-Pool Resources.* Ann Arbor: University of Michigan Press.

Oye, Kenneth. 1992. *Economic Discrimination and Political Exchange.* Princeton: Princeton University Press.

Palmer, Glenn. 1990. "Corralling the Free Rider." *International Studies Quarterly* 34:147–164.

Polachek, S. W. 1980. "Conflict and Trade." *Journal of Conflict Resolution* 24:55–78.

Pollins, Brian M. 1989a. "Does Trade Still Follow the Flag?" *American Political Science Review* 83:465–490.

639

———. 1989b. "Conflict, Cooperation, and Commerce: The Effect of International Political Interactions on Bilateral Trade Flows." *American Journal of Political Science* 33:737–761.

Popper, Karl. 1963. *Conjectures and Refutations: The Growth of Scientific Knowledge.* New York: Basic Books.

Posen, Barry. 1984. *Sources of Military Doctrine.* Ithaca: Cornell University Press.

Powell, Robert. 1990. *Nuclear Deterrence Theory: The Search for Credibility.* Cambridge: Cambridge University Press.

———. 1991. "Absolute and Relative Gains in International Relations Theory." *American Political Science Review* 85:1303–1320.

———. 1996a. "Bargaining in the Shadow of Power." *Games and Economic Behavior* 15:255–289.

———. 1996b. "Uncertainty, Shifting Power, and Appeasement." *American Political Science Review* 90:749–764.

———. 1999. *In the Shadow of Power: States and Strategy in International Politics.* Princeton: Princeton University Press.

Prange, Gordon W. 1981. *At Dawn We Slept.* New York: Penguin Books.

Pribram, Alfred Francis. 1920. *The Secret Treaties of Austria-Hungary, 1879–1914.* Translated by Archibald Coolidge. Cambridge: Harvard University Press.

Przeworski, Adam. 1991. *Democracy and the Market.* Cambridge: Cambridge University Press.

Putnam, Robert. 1988. "Diplomacy and Domestic Politics: The Logic of Two-Level Games." *International Organization* 42:427–460.

———. 1993. *Making Democracy Work: Civic Traditions in Modern Italy.* Princeton: Princeton University Press.

Ragin, Charles, and Howard Becker. 1992. *What Is a Case? Exploring the Foundations of Social Inquiry.* Cambridge: Cambridge University Press.

Ramm, Agatha. 1967. *Germany, 1789–1919: A Political History.* London: Macmillan.

Rasler, Karen, and William Thompson. 1983. "Global Wars, Public Debts, and the Long Cycle." *World Politics* 35:489–516.

Ray, James L. 1974. "Status Inconsistency and War Involvement of European States, 1816–1970." *Peace Science Society (International) Papers* 23:69–80.

———. 1990. "Friends as Foes: International Conflict and War between Formal Allies." In *Prisoners of War,* edited by Charles S. Gochman and Alan Ned Sabrosky. Lexington, Mass.: Lexington Books.

———. 1995. *Democracy and International Conflict.* Columbia: University of South Carolina Press.

Ray, James L., and Bruce M. Russett. 1996. "The Future as Arbiter of Theoretical Controversies: Predictions, Explanations and the End of the Cold War." *British Journal of Political Science* 25:1578.

Reed, William. 1997. "Alliance Duration and Democracy: An Extension and Cross-Validation of 'Democratic States and Commitment in International Relations.' " *American Journal of Political Science* 41:1072–1078.

Reiter, Dani, and Allan Stam. 1996. "Democracy, War Initiation and Victory." *American Political Science Review* 90:377–389.

Richardson, Lewis Fry. 1960. *Arms and Insecurity.* Chicago: Quadrangle.

Riker, William H. 1962. *The Theory of Political Coalitions.* New Haven: Yale University Press.

———. 1996. *The Strategy of Rhetoric: Campaigning for the American Constitution.* New Haven: Yale University Press.

Riker, William H., and Peter C. Ordeshook. 1973. *Introduction to Positive Political Theory.* Englewood Cliffs, N.J.: Prentice-Hall.

Risse-Kappen, Thomas. 1991. "Public Opinion, Domestic Structure, and Foreign Policy in Liberal Democracies." *World Politics* 43:479–512.

Robinson, I. S. 1990. *The Papacy, 1073–1198: Continuity and Innovation.* Cambridge: Cambridge University Press.

Rogowski, Ronald. 1987. "Trade and the Variety of Democratic Institutions." *International Organization* 41:203–224.

———. 1989. *Commerce and Coalitions.* Princeton: Princeton University Press.

Root, Hilton. 1989. "Tying the King's Hands: Credible Commitments and Royal Fiscal Policy During the Old Regime." *Rationality and Society* 1:240–258.

Rosenau, James N. 1963. *National Leadership and Foreign Policy: A Case Study in the Mobilization of Public Support.* Princeton: Princeton University Press.

———, ed. 1969. *Linkage Politics: Essays on the Convergence of National and International Systems.* New York: Free Press.

Rosenberg, Alexander. 1988. *Philosophy of Social Science.* Boulder, Colo.: Westview Press.

Rosenthal, Jean-Laurent. 1998. "The Political Economy of Absolutism Reconsidered." In *Analytic Narratives,* edited by Robert H. Bates et al. Princeton: Princeton University Press.

Ruggie, John G. 1975. "International Responses to Technology: Concepts and Trends." *International Organization* 29:557–584.

———. 1986. "Continuity and Transformation in the World Polity: Toward a Neorealist Synthesis." In *Neorealism and Its Critics,* edited by Robert O. Keohane. New York: Columbia University Press.

———. 1998. *Constructing the World Polity: Essays on International Institutionalization.* New York: Routledge.

Rummel, Rudolph J. 1983. "Libertarianism and International Violence." *Journal of Conflict Resolution* 27:27–71.

Russett, Bruce M. 1972. *No Clear and Present Danger: A Skeptical View of the United States Entry into World War II.* New York: Harper and Row.

———. 1985. "The Mysterious Case of Vanishing Hegemony." *International Organization* 39:207–232.

———. 1993. *Grasping the Democratic Peace.* Princeton: Princeton University Press.

Russett, Bruce M., John R. Oneal, and David R. Davis. 1998. "The Third Leg of the Kantian Tripod for Peace: International Organizations and Militarized Disputes, 1950–1985." *International Organization* 52:441–467.

Sabrosky, Alan. 1980. "Interstate Alliances: Their Reliability and the Expansion of War." In *The Correlates of War II: Testing Some Realpolitik Models,* edited by J. D. Singer. New York: Free Press.

Sagan, Scott D. 1993. *The Limits of Safety.* Princeton: Princeton University Press.

Sample, Susan. 1996. "Arms Races and the Escalation of Disputes to War." Ph.D. dissertation, Vanderbilt University.

———. 1998. "Military Buildups, War, and Realpolitik: A Multivariate Model." *Journal of Conflict Resolution* 42:156–175.

Sandler, Todd. 1992. *Collective Action: Theory and Applications.* Ann Arbor: University of Michigan Press.

Sargent, Thomas J. 1993. *Bounded Rationality in Macroeconomics.* Oxford: Clarendon Press.

Schelling, Thomas. 1960. *Strategy of Conflict.* Cambridge: Harvard University Press.

Schimmelpfennig, Bernhard. 1992. *The Papacy.* New York: Columbia University Press.

Schofield, Norman. 1978. "Instability of Simple Dynamic Games." *Review of Economic Studies* 45:575–594.

Schultz, Kenneth A. 1998. "Domestic Opposition and Signaling in International Crises." *American Political Science Review* 92:829–844.

———. 2001. *Democracy and Coercive Diplomacy.* Cambridge: Cambridge University Press.

Schultz, Kenneth A., and Barry R. Weingast. 1998. "Limited Governments, Powerful States." In *Strategic Politicians, Institutions, and Foreign Policy,* edited by Randolph M. Siverson. Ann Arbor: University of Michigan Press.

Schwartz, Thomas, and Kiron Skinner. 1999. *The Paradox of Power, the Problem of Cooperation, and the End of the Cold War.* Stanford, Calif.: Hoover Institution Working Papers.

Schweller, Randall L. 1994. "Bandwagoning for Profit: Bringing the Revisionist State Back In." *International Security* 19:72–107.

———. 1997. "New Realist Research on Alliances: Refining, Not Refuting, Waltz's Balancing Proposition." *American Political Science Review* 91: 927–930.

Sebenius, James K. 1992. "Challenging Conventional Explanations of International Cooperation: Negotiation Analysis and the Case of Epistemic Communities." *International Organization* 46:323–365.

Senese, Paul D. 1995. "Militarized Interstate Dispute Escalation: The Effects of Geographical Proximity and Issue Salience." Paper presented at the meeting of the Peace Science Society, Ohio State University, Columbus, Ohio, October 13–15.

———. 1997. "Contiguity, Territory, and Their Interaction." Paper presented at the annual meeting of the International Studies Association, Toronto, March 18–22.

Shepsle, Kenneth A., and Barry R. Weingast. 1981. "Structure-Induced Equilibrium and Legislative Choice." *Public Choice* 37:503–519.

Shirk, Susan L. 1993. *The Political Logic of Economic Reform in China.* Berkeley and Los Angeles: University of California Press.

Siegel, Eric. 1997. "I Know What You Know and You Know What I Know: An Information Theory of the Democratic Peace." Paper presented at the annual meeting of the American Political Science Association, Washington, D.C., September.

Signorino, Curtis. 1997. "Information Theory of the Democratic Peace." Paper presented at the annual meeting of the American Political Science Association, Washington, D.C., September.

———. 1999. "Strategic Interaction and the Statistical Analysis of International Conflict." *American Political Science Review* 93:279–298.

Signorino, Curtis, and Jeffrey Ritter. 1999. "Tau B or Not Tau B." *International Studies Quarterly* 43:115–144.

Simmons, Beth A. 1994. *Who Adjusts? Domestic Sources of Foreign Economic Policy during the Interwar Years.* Princeton: Princeton University Press.

Simon, Herbert A. 1957. *Models of Man.* New York: John Wiley.

Singer, J. David, Stuart Bremer, and John Stuckey. 1972. "Capability Distribution, Uncertainty, and Major Power War, 1820–1965." In *Peace, War, and Numbers,* edited by Bruce M. Russett. Beverly Hills, Calif.: Sage.

Singer, J. David, and Thomas Cusack. 1990. "Periodicity, Inexorability, and Steermanship in International War." In *Models, Methods, and Progress in World Politics,* edited by J. David Singer. Boulder, Colo.: Westview Press.

Siverson, Randolph M. 1995. "Democracies and War Participation: In Defense of the Institutional Constraints Argument." *European Journal of International Relations* 1:481–490.

Siverson, Randolph M., and Paul Diehl. 1989. "The Conflict Spiral, Arms Races, and the Outbreak of War." In *The Handbook of War Studies,* edited by Manus Midlarsky. New York: Allen and Hyman.

Siverson, Randolph M., and Joel King. 1980. "Attributes of National Alliance Membership and War Participation." *American Journal of Political Science* 24:1–15.

Siverson, Randolph M., and Charles McCarty. 1978. "War, Implementation Costs, and Minimal Winning Coalitions." *International Interactions* 5:31–42.

Siverson, Randolph M., and Harvey Starr. 1991. *The Diffusion of War.* Ann Arbor: University of Michigan Press.

Siverson, Randolph M., and Michael P. Sullivan. 1983. "The Distribution of Power and the Onset of War." *Journal of Conflict Resolution* 27:473–494.

Skinner, Kiron. 2003. *Linkage and Power: The Demise of Carter's Détente.* Ann Arbor: University of Michigan Press.

Skinner, Kiron, S. Kudelia, Bruce Bueno de Mesquita, and C. Rice. 2002. "Reagan and Yeltsin: Domestic Campaigning and the Beginning of the New World Order." Hoover Institution, Stanford University.

Skocpol, Theda, ed. 1984. *Vision and Method in Historical Sociology.* Cambridge: Cambridge University Press.

Small, Melvin, and J. David Singer. 1976. "The War-Proneness of Democratic Regimes." *Jerusalem Journal of International Relations* 1:46–61.

———. 1982. *Resort to Arms: International and Civil Wars, 1816–1980.* Beverly Hills, Calif.: Sage.

Smith, Alastair. 1995. "Alliance Formation and War." *International Studies Quarterly* 39:405–425.

———. 1996. "The Success and Use of Sanctions." *International Interactions* 21:229–245.

———. 1999. "Testing Theories of Strategic Choice: The Example of Crisis Escalation." *American Journal of Political Science* 43:1254–1283.

Snidal, Duncan. 1991. "Relative Gains and the Pattern of International Cooperation." *American Political Science Review* 85:701–726.

Speer, A. 1971. *Inside the Third Reich.* New York: Macmillan.

Stam, Allan C. 1996. *Win, Lose, or Draw: Domestic Politics and the Crucible of War.* Ann Arbor: University of Michigan Press.

Starr, Harvey. 1978. " 'Opportunity' and 'Willingness' as Ordering Concepts in the Study of War." *International Interactions* 4:363–387.

Stein, Arthur. 1990. *Why Nations Cooperate: Circumstance and Choice in International Relations.* Ithaca: Cornell University Press.

Strange, Susan. 1987. "The Persistent Myth of Lost Hegemony." *International Organization* 41:551–574.

Straussman, Jeffrey D. 1978. *The Limits of Technocratic Politics.* New Brunswick, N.J.: Transaction Books.

Summers, Robert, and Alan Heston. 1988. "A New Set of International Comparisons of Real Product and Price Level Estimates for 130 Countries, 1950–1985." *Review of Income and Wealth* 34:1–25.

———. 1991. "The Penn World Table (Mark 5)." *Quarterly Journal of Economics* 106:327–368.

Tammen, Ronald, Jacek Kugler, Douglas Lemke, Allan Stam III, Carole Alsharabati, Mark Andrew Abdollahian, Brian Efird, and A. F. K. Organski, eds. 2000. *Power Transitions.* Chatham, N.J.: Seven Bridges Press.

Taylor, A. J. P. 1961. *The Origins of the Second World War.* London: Hamish Hamilton.

Taylor, Michael. 1976. *Anarchy and Cooperation.* New York: John Wiley.

———. 1987. *The Possibility of Cooperation.* Cambridge: Cambridge University Press.

Tetlock, Philip, and Aaron Belkin, eds. 1996. *Counterfactual Thought Experiments in World Politics.* Princeton: Princeton University Press.

Thatcher, Margaret. 1993. *The Downing Street Years.* New York: HarperCollins.

Thomas, Daniel C. 2001. *The Helsinki Effect: International Norms, Human Rights, and the Demise of Communism.* Princeton: Princeton University Press.

Thompson, William, Karen Rasler, and Richard Li. 1986. "Polarity, the Long Cycle, and Global Power Warfare." *Journal of Conflict Resolution* 30:587–615.

Thorne, C. 1967. *The Approach of War 1938–1939.* London: Macmillan.

Thucydides. 1959. *History of the Peloponnesian War.* 3 vols. Translated by T. Hobbes. Ann Arbor: University of Michigan Press.

Tsebelis, George. 1990a. "Are Sanctions Effective? A Game Theoretic Analysis." *Journal of Conflict Resolution* 34:3–28.

———. 1990b. *Nested Games: Rational Choice in Comparative Politics.* Berkeley, Calif.: University of California Press.

Tversky, Amos, and Daniel Kahneman. 1986. "Rational Choice and the Framing of Decisions." *Journal of Business* 59:S252–S254.

Van Belle, Douglas A. 1997. "Press Freedom and the Democratic Peace." *Journal of Peace Research* 34:405–414.

Van den Bos, Jan M. M. 1994. "The Policy Issues Analyzed." In *European Community Decision Making,* edited by Bruce Bueno de Mesquita and Frans Stokman. New Haven: Yale University Press.

Vasquez, John A. 1987. "The Steps to War: Toward a Scientific Explanation of Correlates of War Findings." *World Politics* 40:108–145.

———. 1993. *The War Puzzle.* Cambridge: Cambridge University Press.

———. 1995. "Why Do Neighbors Fight? Territoriality, Proximity, or Interactions." *Journal of Peace Research* 32:277–293.

———. 1997. "The Realist Paradigm and Degenerative versus Progressive Research Programs: An Appraisal of Neotraditional Research on Waltz's Balancing Proposition." *American Political Science Review* 91:899–913.

———. 2000. *What Do We Know about War.* Lanham, Md.: Rowman and Littlefield.

Volgy, Thomas, and Alison Bailin. 2003. *International Politics and the Strength of States.* Boulder, Colo.: Lynne Rienner.

Wagner, R. Harrison. 1994. "Peace, War, and the Balance of Power." *American Political Science Review* 88:593–607.

Wallace, Michael. 1973. *War and Rank among Nations.* Lexington, Mass.: Lexington Books.

———. 1979. "Arms Races and Escalation: Some New Evidence." *Journal of Conflict Resolution* 23:3–16.

———. 1982. "Armaments and Escalation: Two Competing Hypotheses." *International Studies Quarterly* 26:37–56.

Walt, Stephen M. 1985. "Alliance Formation and the Balance of Power." *International Security* 9:3–43.

———. 1997. "The Progressive Power of Realism." *American Political Science Review* 91:931–935.

Waltz, Kenneth N. 1959. *Man, the State, and War.* New York: Columbia University Press.

———. 1979. *Theory of International Politics.* Reading, Mass.: Addison-Wesley.

———. 1997. "Evaluating Theories." *American Political Science Review* 91:913–918.

Wandycz, P. 1986. "Poland Between East and West." In *The Origins of the Second World War Reconsidered: The A. J. P. Taylor Debate after Twenty-Five Years,* edited by G. Martel. Boston: Allen and Unwin.

Ward, Michael D., and Kristian S. Gleditsch. 1998. "Democratizing for Peace." *American Political Science Review* 92:51–62.

Watt, Donald Cameron. 1989. *How War Came: The Immediate Origins of the Second World War, 1938–1939.* New York: Pantheon Books.

Wayman, Frank W. 1990. "Alliances and War: A Time Series Analysis." In *Prisoners of War,* edited by Charles Gochman and Alan Sabrosky. New York: Free Press.

Weede, Erich. 1984. "Democracy and War Involvement." *Journal of Conflict Resolution* 28:649–664.

Weingast, Barry R. 1984. "The Congressional-Bureaucratic System: A Principal-Agent Perspective (with applications to the SEC)." In *Carnegie Papers on Political Economy,* edited by Alan Meltzer, Thomas Romer, and Howard Rosenthal. Special supplement to *Public Choice* 44:147–191.

———. 1997. "The Political Foundations of Democracy and the Rule of the Law." *American Political Science Review* 91:245–263.

Weingast, Barry R., Kenneth Shepsle, and Christopher Johnsen. 1981. "The Political Economy of Benefits and Costs: A Neoclassical Approach to Distributive Politics." *Journal of Political Economy* 89:642–669.

Weiss, E. B., and Harold Jacobson, eds. 1998. *Engaging Countries: Strengthening Compliance with International Environmental Accords.* Cambridge: MIT Press.

Wendt, Alexander. 1994. "Collective Identity Formation and the International State." *American Political Science Review* 88:394–398.

———. 1999. *Social Theory of International Politics.* Cambridge: Cambridge University Press.

Werner, Suzanne. 1996. "Absolute and Limited War: The Possibilities of Foreign Imposed Regime Change." *International Interactions* 22:67–88.

Wildavsky, Aaron. 1979. *The Politics of the Budgetary Process.* Boston: Little, Brown.

Williams, John H. P., and Mark J. Webber. 1998. "Evolving Russian Civil-Military Relations: A Rational Actor Analysis." *International Interactions* 24:115–150.

Williamson, Oliver. 1985. *The Economic Institutions of Capitalism.* New York: Free Press.

Winteringham, F. P. W. 1989. *Radioactive Fallout in Soils, Crops, and Food.* FAO Soils Bulletin 61, secs. 2.4.2–2.5.4.

Wintrobe, Ronald. 1990. "The Tinpot and the Totalitarian: An Economic Theory of Dictatorship." *American Political Science Review* 84:849–872.

———. 1998. *The Political Economy of Dictatorship.* Cambridge: Cambridge University Press.

Wohlstetter, Roberta. 1962. *Pearl Harbor: Warning and Decision.* Stanford: Stanford University Press.

Wu, Samuel. 1990. "To Attack or Not to Attack: A Theory and Empirical Assessment of Extended Immediate Deterrence." *Journal of Conflict Resolution* 34:531–552.

Wu, Samuel, and Bruce Bueno de Mesquita. 1994. "Assessing the Dispute in the South China Sea: A Model of China's Security Decision Making." *International Studies Quarterly* 38:379–403.

Yoffie, David B., ed. 1993. *Beyond Free Trade: Firms, Governments, and Global Competition.* Boston: Harvard Business School Press.

Yoffie, David B., and Benjamin Gomes-Casseres. 1994. *International Trade and Competition: Cases and Notes in Strategy and Management.* 2d ed. New York: McGraw-Hill.

Yoffie, David B., John B. Goodman, and Debora Spar. 1996. "Inward Foreign Investment and U.S. Protection." *International Organization* 50:555–591.

Young, Oren, and M. A. Levy. 1999. "The Effectiveness of International Environmental Regimes." In *The Effectiveness of International Environmental Agreements,* edited by O. Young. Cambridge: MIT Press.

Zagare, Frank C. 1987. *The Dynamics of Deterrence.* Chicago: University of Chicago Press.

Zagare, Frank C., and D. Marc Kilgour. 1993. "Asymmetric Deterrence." *International Studies Quarterly* 37:1–27.

# Subject Index

# CITATIONS OF AUTHORS

# PHOTO CREDITS

**Introduction:** 3 AP/Wide World Photos. 9 AP/Wide World Photos. 11 AP/Wide World Photos. 18 AP/Wide World Photos.

**Chapter 1:** 26 Helmolt, H. F., ed. *History of the World.* New York: Dodd, Mead, and Company, 1902. 27 *Codex Mendoza.* The Bodleian Library, University of Oxford, folio 2 recto. 35 Library of Congress. 38 Library of Congress. 46 AP/Wide World Photos. 48 AP/Wide World Photos.

**Chapter 2:** 62 (left) Library of Congress. 62 (right) Copyright Victoria & Albert Museum, London/Art Resource, NY. 74 AP/Wide World Photos. 75 Library of Congress. 79 AP/Wide World Photos.

**Chapter 3:** 83 Library of Congress. 112 Havakuk Levison/Reuters.

**Chapter 4:** 127 (upper right) AP/Wide World Photos. 127 (lower left) AP/Wide World Photos. 136 Reuters. 147 Courtesy of the National Archives.

**Chapter 5:** 157 AP/Wide World Photos. 164 Courtesy of the National Archives.

**Chapter 6:** 207 Reuters. 209 Reuters. 218 Courtesy of the National Archives. 220 Win McNamee/Reuters.

**Chapter 7:** 226 Kirk Anderson. 228 Pool/Reuters. 233 AP/Wide World Photo. 244 Will Burgess/Reuters.

**Chapter 8:** 261 Reuters. 268 Stringer/Iran/Reuters. 276 (left) Courtesy of the National Archives.

276 (right) Courtesy of the National Archives. 280 AP/Wide World Photos.

**Chapter 9:** 290 Courtesy of the National Archives. 306 Corbis/Bettmann. 310 Cecil Stoughton, White House/ John Fitzgerald Kennedy Library.

**Chapter 10:** 326 Osama Silwadi/Reuters. 334 Toshiyuki Aizawa/Reuters.

**Chapter 11:** 356 AP/Wide World Photos. 360 Library of Congress. 363 Reuters. 368 George Bush Library. 371 STR/Reuters.

**Chapter 12:** 383 Howard Burditt/Reuters. 389 STR/Reuters.

**Chapter 13:** 408 STR/Reuters. 411 Anuruddha Lokuhapuarachchi/Reuters. 425 Enrique Marcarian/Reuters. 436 AP/Wide World Photos.

**Chapter 14:** 455 AP/Wide World Photos. 457 AP/Wide World Photos. 460 AP/Wide World Photos. 470 STR/Reuters. 483 Gleb Garanich/Reuters.

**Chapter 15:** 489 Courtesy of the National Archives. 509 AP/Wide World Photos. 516 Jim Hollander/Reuters.

**Chapter 16:** 533 Kimberly White/Reuters. 545 (top) Library of Congress. 545 (bottom) AP/Wide World Photos.

**Chapter 17:** 562 Walt Handelsman/Tribune Media Services. 566 Library of Congress.

**Chapter 18:** 604 AP/Wide World Photos 614 AP/Wide World Photos

**Bruce Bueno de Mesquita** is Silver Professor of Politics and Director of the Center for Conflict Resolution and Multilateral Cooperation at New York University. He is also a senior fellow at the Hoover Institution at Stanford University. An expert on international conflict, foreign policy formation, and the peace process, his many books include *The Logic of Political Survival*, with Alastair Smith, Randolph M. Siverson, and James D. Morrow (MIT Press, 2003); *Predicting Politics* (Ohio State University Press, 2002); *War and Reason*, with David Lalman (Yale University Press, 1992); and *The War Trap* (Yale University Press, 1981), as well as one novel, *The Trial of Ebenezer Scrooge* (Ohio State University Press, 2001). Bueno de Mesquita is on the board of directors of Decision Insights, Inc. In 1985 he won the Karl W. Deutsch Award in International Relations and Peace Research, an award presented biannually to the scholar under the age of forty judged to have made, through a body of publications, the most significant contribution to the study of international relations and peace research. He was elected to the American Academy of Arts and Sciences in 1992, and in 1999 he received an honorary degree from the University of Groningen in the Netherlands. He was president of the International Studies Association in 2001–2002.